Mathematical Thinking in Behavioral Sciences

READINGS FROM
SCIENTIFIC AMERICAN

Mathematical Thinking in Behavioral Sciences

WITH INTRODUCTIONS BY
David M. Messick
UNIVERSITY OF CALIFORNIA, SANTA BARBARA

W. H. Freeman and Company
SAN FRANCISCO AND LONDON

Printed in the United States of America.

Library of Congress Catalog Card Number: 68-25407

PREFACE

Within the past twenty or twenty-five years, those in behavioral and social sciences have found themselves relying more and more heavily on mathematics as a conceptual tool to facilitate an understanding of the phenomena with which they deal. Although many efforts to apply mathematical techniques to behavioral issues have resulted in cul-de-sacs, such failures are far outnumbered by successful applications. Science, however, learns from its mistakes as well as its successes and each new generation of behavioral scientists is a measure more sophisticated and enlightened than the previous generation since it is not likely to make the mistakes of its predecessor. As a result, the rate of fruitful mathematical applications in behavioral sciences is increasing very rapidly.

The rising prevalence of mathematical thinking in behavioral sciences, however, poses a problem to those teaching courses that incorporate mathematical or quantitative ideas to undergraduates—particularly freshmen and sophomores—who have not had time to acquire more than a rudimentary mathematical background. This problem is basically that of communicating interesting (and often sophisticated) mathematical ideas in such a way as to make them comprehensible to such students and to encourage them to acquire the mathematical skill necessary to use and apply the ideas proficiently. It is with this purpose in mind that the articles in this book have been selected.

Of the many mathematical achievements that have been made available to those in the behavioral sciences, two seem to be pre-eminent, in that a familiarity with each is rapidly becoming an indispensable tool to the behavioral scientist. These are the theory of probability and the digital computer. This is not to say that other branches of mathematics have not had important behavioral applications: one need only think of the many important developments in economics, psychology, sociology, and biology that rest on the foundations of linear algebra and the theory of real matrices, for example. It is true, however, that probability theory has attained a much wider and more varied range of applications in behavioral sciences than any other mathematical discipline, and all current indications are that the use of digital computers will soon be equally prevalent. These considerations have been my guidelines in the selection of articles for this reader.

Finally, this book is not intended for the teaching of formal mathematics. Its purpose is rather to supplement the teaching of mathematics or quantitative methods by illustrating the relevance of mathematical thinking to a variety of interesting problems in social and behavioral sciences. But it is my hope that the articles will spark the reader's curiosity or capture his interest to the extent that he will find himself willing to expend the effort required to learn mathematics.

March, 1968 DAVID M. MESSICK

CONTENTS

PART ONE • THE ANALYSIS OF UNCERTAINTY: PROBABILITY

PART TWO • COMMUNICATION AND CONTROL

PART THREE • GAMES AND DECISIONS

PART FOUR • IMITATIONS OF LIFE

PART FIVE • RECENT COMPUTER APPLICATIONS

Note on cross-references: Cross-references within the articles are of three kinds. A reference to an article included in this book is noted by the title of the article and the page on which it begins; a reference to an article that is available as an offprint but is not included here is noted by the article's title and offprint number; a reference to a SCIENTIFIC AMERICAN article that is not available as an offprint is noted by the title of the article and the month and year of its publication.

PART ONE

THE ANALYSIS OF UNCERTAINTY: PROBABILITY

THE ANALYSIS OF UNCERTAINTY: PROBABILITY

INTRODUCTION

There is no doubt that the theory of probability is the single field of mathematics most widely used in the behavioral sciences today. This discipline provides the theoretical foundations for all problems of statistical inference, from survey and sampling problems to problems of experimental design. In addition, we are discovering that probability theory can be used as a language, with its own formal syntax, to describe and explicate many behavioral phenomena. The development of mathematical models in economics, psychology, biology, and sociology is heavily dependent on the mathematical theory of probability.

Strictly speaking, the mathematical theory of probability is a theory of a class of functions, called probability functions, which satisfy three conditions. The first of these is the *non-negativity* condition, which simply states that probabilities may not be negative numbers. The second is a *normalization* condition, which states that the probability of an event which must occur is one. The final condition is the *additivity* condition, which states that if two events are mutually exclusive, so that the occurrence of one precludes the occurrence of the other, then the probability of the occurrence of one *or* the other of the events is the *sum* of the individual probabilities of the two events. From these three conditions, all of the laws of probability theory can be derived.

About the mathematical theory of probability, *per se,* there is little controversy. The theory simply says, "*Given* that numbers have been assigned to events (sets) in such a way that they satisfy the three conditions above, then the following statements (regarding the assignment of numbers to more complex events) must be true." The "following statements" are the theorems of probability theory. There is, in effect, no disagreement about the "meaning" or consistency of the theory itself. It is a mathematical construction, no more and no less.

The theory, however, does not specify the procedures to be used to construct the set of events or to assign numbers to them. Moreover, it does not give any hint of what a probability statement "means" except as it is implied by and implies other such statements. It is at this juncture that one finds disagreement on the nature and meaning of probability statements.

As A. J. Ayer points out in the article "Chance," one can distinguish three broad types of probability statements. The first type, a priori probability, derives from a logical and/or semantic analysis of possible outcomes. Such probabilities frequently rely on notions of symmetry, as in coin-tossing or dice-tossing experiments, in the initial assignment of probabilities.

The second type of probability is statistical probability. Probabilities of this nature are estimated by observing the ratio of the frequency of occurrence of some event to the number of opportunities that were available for the event to occur. When it is said, for example, that the probability of an unborn child being male is .51, this means only that of all recorded births (opportunities for males to be born), 51% of them were male. Such a statement does not rely in any way on a priori considerations—such as the fact that there are only two sexes, and that the occurrence of either is equally likely in the absence of further information. Statistical probability is based on such further information.

The third type is an interpretation of all probability, defining probabilities as opinions that represent degrees of credibility. When one asks "What is the probability that Caesar crossed the Rubicon?" or "What is the probability that California will secede from the United States in the next 50 years?" one is asking for judgments that do not involve either a priori probability or statistical probability. There are no clear physical or logical properties of these events that would permit a priori assignment of probabilities and the events in question are unique: there is no history (nor can there be one) of repetitions that permit statistical probabilities to be estimated.

The papers in this section all deal with some aspect or aspects of probability. Ayer discusses a number of conceptions and misconceptions of chance and focuses on the important distinction between probability as a formal calculus and its applications, and the consequent nuances in the meanings of probability statements. In the second article, "What Is Probability?" Rudolf Carnap not only notes the difference between statistical and "inductive" probability but also stresses the need to develop a logical system employing both types, and suggests what the rudiments of such a system might look like. John Cohen, recognizing the need to understand the nature of subjective or psychological probabilities and their relation to mathematical probabilities, describes in "Subjective Probability" the results of a number of experimental investigations of the development and determinants of psychological probabilities.

The controversy that surrounds the meaning of probability should not be allowed to overshadow the fact that probability theory has had many important applications, some of which are discussed in "Probability" by Mark Kac. Beginning with some elementary principles of combinational analysis, he provides an interesting and informative excursion through selected areas of contemporary probability theory. As probability theory is applied to increasingly complex problems, such as those described by Kac, it becomes correspondingly difficult to find simple analytic solutions. In the last paper of this section, Daniel McCracken describes new techniques, collectively known as Monte Carlo methods, which yield solutions or approximate solutions to many of these problems by actually simulating (or, more frequently, by using a digital computer to simulate symbolically) the processes involved. Such techniques have now become a commonplace tool in the behavioral scientist's workshop.

1

CHANCE

A. J. AYER • October 1965

The word "chance" is commonly used in several different senses. One of the things I hope to accomplish in this article is to disentangle them. In some of these senses, although not in all, "chance" is a synonym for "probability." Thus such statements as that the chance of throwing double-six with a pair of true dice is one in 36, that there is a slightly better than even chance that any given unborn infant will be a boy, and that there is now very little chance that Britain will join the Common Market can all be regarded as expressing judgments of probability.

It is to be noted, however, that each of these examples illustrates a different kind of judgment of probability. The first is an example of what is often called a judgment of a priori probability: it relates to the mathematical calculus of chances. The second is an example of a statistical judgment: it estimates the actual frequency with which some property is distributed among the members of a given class. The third is an example of what, for want of a better expression, I describe as a judgment of credibility: it evaluates the degree of confidence we are entitled to have in the truth of some proposition or in the occurrence of some particular event.

Although any of these judgments of probability can correctly be expressed as an estimate of chances, it is with judgments of the first type that the concept of chance is most closely associated. Thus it is characteristic of what are known as games of chance that their results are substantially in accordance with the a priori probabilities. Our first problem, then, is to try to make clear exactly what this implies.

The Calculus of Chances

In dealing with this problem, the most important point to bear in mind is that the calculus of chances is a branch of pure mathematics. Hence the propositions it sets forth are necessarily true. This point tends to be obscured by the fact that statements such as "The chance of throwing heads with an unbiased penny is a half" are open to more than one interpretation. An unbiased penny (or a true die) could be defined in physical terms as one that was constructed of such and such materials and had its center of gravity in such and such a place. In that case these statements would be statistical; their truth would depend on the actual frequency with which the results in question were obtained with coins or dice that met these physical stipulations.

More commonly, however, what is understood by a true die or an unbiased penny is simply one that yields results matching the a priori probabilities. When our examples are interpreted in this way, they turn into statements of elementary arithmetic. It being presupposed that a penny has two faces, and that when it is tossed it will come down with one or the other of them uppermost, to say that if it is an unbiased penny there is an even chance of its coming up heads is to say no more than that one is the half of two.

Not all our computations of chances are as simple as this, but the principle remains the same. For instance, when it is said that the odds against throwing heads with an unbiased penny three times in succession are seven to one, what is meant is that of all the possible ordered triplets of the numbers 1 and 2—such as 121, 211, 212 and so forth—the sequence 111 is just one out of eight. If we generalize this and say that the odds against throwing heads n times in succession are $2^n - 1$ to 1,

There are no laws of chance in the sense that the laws dictate the pattern of events

what we are saying is that of all the possible ordered n-tuplets of the numbers 1 and 2, the sequence of n 1's is one out of a total of 2^n possibilities.

Now, clearly the value of $1 : 2^n$ diminishes as n increases, and this is what is meant by saying that a long run of consecutive heads or tails or a long run of either red or black at roulette is highly improbable. Whatever the initial fraction representing the chance of a given result for any given turn, the chance of obtaining this result n times in succession will be represented by this fraction raised to the power of n, always provided that the successive turns are independent of each other. This is again a proposition of simple arithmetic. The only empirical assumption being made is that a game like roulette is in fact a game of chance—in other words, that it is possible to construct and operate an object such as a roulette wheel in such a way that the calculus of chances is approximately satisfied by the results.

In applying the calculus to gambling games of this kind the assumption that the turns are independent must be given particular attention. Otherwise one might find oneself committing the celebrated Monte Carlo fallacy, which in this instance can be described as the tendency to think that a run of heads in coin-flipping or of red in roulette increases the likelihood that tails or black will come up on the next turn. As we have just seen, the chances of throwing n successive heads with an unbiased coin or of having a run of n red numbers at roulette are very small if n is at all large; for example, the odds against a series of as few as 10 heads are more than 1,000 to one. Gamblers are tempted to infer from this fact that if n is a large number by these standards and heads have come up $n - 1$ times in succession, the odds against its coming up again the nth time must also be large. Hence a roulette player who has watched red come up nine times in succession will bet heavily on black.

The reasoning, however, is fallacious. The very calculation that makes a long run of red improbable is based on the premise that each spin of the wheel is independent of every other, so that the probability of red—or in the case of the coin the probability of heads—is the same in each instance, no matter what the results of the preceding spins or tosses have been. Even if a million tosses of an unbiased coin had yielded heads on every occasion, the odds against which are astronomical, the chance that it would come up tails on the next toss is still no better than a half.

Many people find this conclusion difficult to accept, because they do not realize that these estimates of chances are no more than the enumeration of abstract possibilities. To say that the odds against a million successive heads are astronomical is merely to say that if we were to list all the possible million-term sequences of heads and tails, the sequence consisting of heads a million times over is just one out of an astronomically large number of alternatives. To say that the odds against heads coming up on the million-and-first occasion are still no more than $1 : 2$ is to say, quite correctly, that one is no less than the half of two.

It will be objected that if we put ourselves in the position of a gambler who has to place his bets, it is not really so clear that the Monte Carlo fallacy is fallacious. If the coin he is tossing is unbiased, it follows by definition that it comes up tails as often as it comes up heads. So if at some stage in the series of tosses a long run of either face of the coin disturbs the balance, the other face will come up more often in order to restore it. Surely, then, the rational course for the gambler to pursue would be to note the relative frequencies with which the two faces have appeared and to support whichever of them has any leeway to make up.

The answer to this assertion is that it would indeed be the right policy if the gambler were justified in making the assumption that there was some finite number of tosses, some number that he could in principle specify, within which equality would be reached. That proposition, however, cannot be derived from the calculus of chances or even from the assumption that the coin is unbiased. If the gambler could know that the coin was unbiased, in the sense here in question, then he would know that any imbalance in the relative frequency of heads and tails would be corrected if the series of tosses were sufficiently continued. As long as no limit is set to the number of further tosses allowed for this end to be reached, however, he can draw no conclusion about the way he ought to bet. All he can say is that if the existing ratio of heads to tails is $m : n$, then the result of the next toss will be to change it either to $m + 1 : n + 1$ or to $m : n + 1$. No matter what numbers m and n may be, and however much one exceeds the other, only these two abstract possibilities exist.

The odds are based on imaginary coins

As far as the calculus of chances goes, there is nothing to choose between them.

An example that may bring this point out more clearly is that of drawing cards from an ordinary pack. Since the number of red and the number of black cards are equal and finite, it is obvious that the greater the preponderance of red cards that have been drawn, the greater is the chance that the next card will be black, provided that when a card is drawn it is not replaced. If, on the other hand, it is replaced, then it is as if the game started afresh with each drawing, so that no matter how large the preponderance of red cards has been, the chance that the next card to be drawn will be black remains even. The Monte Carlo fallacy may then be said to consist in treating the game in which the cards are replaced after being drawn as though it were on a level with the game in which they are not replaced.

It must be remembered, however, that to talk about chance in this way is not in itself to say anything about what is actually likely to happen; it is not to make a judgment of credibility. In actual practice the roulette player who observed that red numbers came up very much more often than black might well conclude that the wheel was biased or that the croupier had discovered some means of spinning it unfairly. Then it would be rational for him to regard the odds on each occasion as being in favor of red.

Whatever view he takes, he has to rely on some empirical assumption, because to suppose that the wheel is true (in the sense that its operations satisfy the calculus of chances) is as much an empirical assumption as to suppose that it is biased. These assumptions are empirical because they are concerned with the way in which some physical object actually behaves. The question is

Deviations from probability may change

whether or not some particular roulette wheel, coin, die pack of cards or whatever it may be is constructed and manipulated in such a way that any one of a number of equally possible alternatives is realized about as often as any other. In the cases where the results have shown themselves to be unequal—in the sense that one side of the coin, one face of the die, some group of numbers or some distribution of the cards has been particularly favored—it is a matter of predicting whether this bias will continue or whether it will be corrected. This is a question not of abstract mathematics but of fact.

It is true that if there is no limit in theory to the duration of the game, the hypothesis that it is fair can never be strictly refuted. No matter how large the deviations have been found to be, it remains conceivable that they will subsequently be corrected—or at least that they would be corrected if the game were sufficiently continued. Although there is never any logical inconsistency in holding to this assumption, there may come a point at which it ceases to be credible.

Applications of the Calculus

It should be clear by now that no conclusions about any matter of fact can be derived solely from the calculus of chances. There are no such things as the laws of chance in the sense in which a law dictates some pattern of events. In themselves the propositions of the calculus are mathematical truisms. What we can learn from them is that if we assume that certain ratios hold with respect to the distribution of some property, then we are committed to the conclusion that certain other ratios hold as well. If each of a pair of dice has six faces, and in each case the faces are respectively numbered one to six, and in each case when the die is thrown any one face comes uppermost as often as any other, then the sum of the numbers that come up when both dice are thrown will be eight on five occasions out of 36. In other words, the chances of making a point of eight with a single throw of two dice are a little worse than seven to one against.

These other words, however, are misleading, because the proposition in question is merely a proposition about numbers. The references to dice, coins, packs of cards or roulette wheels that occur in expositions of the theory of probability are entirely adventitious. These objects are dummies whose only function is to adorn the mathematical theory with concrete illustrations. The proof that they are dummies is that they exercise no control over the propositions they serve to illustrate. The question is whether they measure up to the theory, not whether the theory measures up to them.

Suppose that someone has brought himself to doubt that the odds against making a point of eight with a pair of dice are more than seven to one, and has decided to test the question by experiment. Suppose further that after recording the results of many thousands of throws he finds that the proportion of times in which his pair of dice has yielded a total of eight is as high as one in five. What has he proved? Perhaps no more than that his dice are biased; at most that tossing dice is not an affair of chance in the way that it has been taken to be, but certainly nothing that has any bearing on the theory of probability.

The fact that the propositions of the calculus of chances are not empirically testable does not, of course, entail that they have no factual application. What we require in order to be able to apply them successfully is to discover a set of possible states of affairs that satisfy the following conditions: (1) that they be finite in number, (2) that they be mutually exclusive, (3) that they be logically equal, in a sense that I shall explain, and (4) that they occur with at least approximately equal frequency. When all these conditions are satisfied, the respective states of affairs may be said to be equally probable.

What I mean by saying that the states of affairs in question must be logically equal is that each state has to be treated as a unity on a level with each of the others. This treatment does not preclude their being complex, in the sense of embracing a number of alternatives. If any member of the set is represented as a disjunction of such alternatives, however, we must not allow these disjuncts themselves to rank as members of the set. Otherwise we shall find ourselves falling into contradiction.

For example, it has been held by some writers that in a case where we have no evidence either for or against a given proposition, we are entitled to assume that it is equally likely to be true or false. Suppose, then, that I am playing a game of drawing marbles from a bag and that, relying on this principle, I take it to be an even chance that the first one to be drawn will be blue. This would be a foolish assumption to bet on, but it would not be contradictory as long as I treat not-blue as a single color on a level with blue. If, however, I follow the natural course of breaking down not-blue into a disjunction of other colors—and if, by parity of reasoning, I also take it to be an even chance that the first marble to be drawn will be black, an even chance that it will be red, an even chance that it will be green and so forth—then I am involved in contradiction. If there are more than two possibilities, it is impossible that each of them should have an even chance of being realized. This is again a question of simple arithmetic. One is not the half of any number higher than two.

To avoid contradictions of this sort, we have to decide at the outset what possibilities we are going to regard as logically equal and then adhere consistently to our decision. As Rudolf Carnap of the University of California at Los Angeles has shown in his *Logical Foundations of Probability*, such decisions can be taken on purely semantic grounds. We can construct a language with a limited number of primitive predicates and the power to refer to some finite number of individuals; we can then decide, in a more or less arbitrary fashion, that certain states of affairs, which are describable by these means, are to be counted as equally probable, and we can select our logical operators in such a way that the probability of any possible state of affairs within the selected universe of discourse can be calculated on this basis. This procedure, however, has an unduly narrow application; moreover, there is no reason to suppose that our judgments of equal probability will conform to anything that actually happens.

On the other hand, if we follow a more liberal course by relying on *ad hoc* estimates of what it seems fair to regard as equal possibilities, we shall come on situations in which what appear to be equally reasonable decisions will lead to incompatible results. I borrow a simple example from an article by J. L. Watling of University College London. Suppose "we are following a man along a road and reach a place where the road divides into three, two paths climbing the hillside, one lying in the valley." Knowing nothing but that the man, now out of sight, will take one of the three paths, how are we to estimate the probability that he will take the path lying in the valley? If we follow the classical procedure of assigning equal probability to equal possibilities, and if we regard it as equally possible that the man will take any one of the three paths, we shall have to conclude that the chance of his taking the valley path is one in three. But we might just as well regard it as equally possible that he will go into the valley or into the hills, and in that case it would follow that the chance of his taking the valley path was one in two. These conclusions are mutually incompatible, but in default of further information there is nothing to choose between them.

Watling takes this situation as a proof that "the classical interpretation" of probability is inconsistent. I should prefer to say in cases of this kind that it was inoperative. The calculus of chances is not inconsistent in itself. As long as we have a consistent rule for deciding what states of affairs are to count as equally possible, the calculus can be consistently applied. If its application is to be of any use to us, however—in the way of helping us to win our bets on what will actually happen—we cannot allow the assignment of initial probabilities simply to depend on an arbitrary decision. In the example chosen, if we really knew nothing more than that the man would take one of the three paths, we should have no right to assume either that it was equally likely that he would take any one of the three or that it was equally likely that he would go into the valley or into the hills. Before we could make any such assumptions, we should have to have something further to go on than the mere arithmetical fact that one is the half of two or the third part of three. We should need some factual information such as the man's habits in order to supply the calculus of chances with a foothold in reality. In general, we cannot assume that any two states of affairs are equally probable unless we have reason to believe that they occur with equal frequency. But pure mathematics cannot tell us anything about actual frequencies, and neither can semantics. We must rely on empirical evidence.

The upshot of this argument is that when we come to apply the calculus of chances, our judgments of probability undergo a change of character: they become statistical judgments. To say that there is one chance in eight that a true coin will come up heads on each of three successive tosses may, as we have seen, be just a colorful way of expressing an arithmetical truism, but to say the same applies to the penny that I have in my hand is to make the empirical statement that if it were tossed on a fairly large number of occasions and the results were set out in groups of three, the sequence heads-heads-heads would be found to occur on the average once in eight times. This is, indeed, a consequence of the more general assumption that in a sufficiently long series of tosses with this penny each of the possible sequences of a given length would occur on the average as often as any other.

Here, however, we are faced with the difficulty that unless some limit is set to the length of the sequence within which this equality is to be realized, the empirical evidence in favor of such an assumption is bound to be incomplete. Even if a limit were to be set, so that we could in principle run through all the members of the series to which our judgment of probability refers, it is only as long as we have not done this that a judgment of this kind is of any interest to us. When we already know that a given event has occurred or that it has failed to occur, we do not speculate about its chances. The point of collecting statistics is to extrapolate them.

Samples and Classes

In other words, we normally examine only a sample of the total class of events in which we are interested; if we find that the property about which we are inquiring is distributed in a certain proportion among the members of this sample, we infer that it would be distributed in much the same proportion among the members of a further sample or throughout the class as a whole. Admittedly if we were to toss our penny 50 times, say, and found that heads came up in the ratio of three to two, we should not feel ourselves bound to regard this as a typical sample. In default of physical evidence that the penny was biased, we might rather expect that if the series of tosses were continued, the balance would be re-

What is the probability that the man will take one of three paths?

Confidence that one has beaten the odds may be misplaced

dressed. But the reason for this expectation would be that we were influenced by our knowledge that pennies physically similar to this one had been found to come up heads about as often as they came up tails. In so thinking we should be drawing on a wider range of statistics, but we should still be going beyond our evidence. We should in fact be making a deduction from a general hypothesis about the distribution of heads and tails—a hypothesis that had been derived from our knowledge of their distribution in a reasonably large sample.

The question is how such a procedure can be justified. The usual answer is that inferences from the character of a sample to the character of the total class or population from which the sample is drawn are logically justified (provided that the sample is large enough) by the law of large numbers. I shall not go into the mathematical formulation and proof of this law, which is to be found in the standard textbooks. What it comes to is that if a proportion $m : n$ of the members of some class possess the property P and we select from this class all possible samples of a given size, it must be true of the majority of these samples that the proportion in which P is distributed among their members also lies in the neighborhood of $m : n$. Moreover, as the size of the samples increases, so does the extent of the concentration around $m : n$, with the result that if the samples are made large enough, the frequency with which P occurs in practically all of them will differ only negligibly from the frequency with which it occurs in the parent class.

A common way of expressing this fact is to say that it is very highly probable that the distribution of a property throughout a given class is almost exactly reflected in any large sample drawn from that class; and since if A matches B it must also be true that B matches A, it will follow that if a property is distributed in such and such a proportion among the members of a large sample (A), there is a very high probability that it is distributed in approximately the same proportion among the members of the class (B) from which the sample has been drawn. It is in this way that the law of large numbers is thought to justify this familiar type of inference.

There is, however, a point to be made here that is rather too often overlooked. When one speaks in this context of its being highly probable that what is true of a large sample is also true of the parent class, this judgment of probability belongs to the first of my three types. It is not a judgment of credibility but a judgment that relates merely to the distribution of logical possibilities. What one is saying in fact is that among all possible samples of the size in question the number of those that roughly match the parent class is very much greater than the number of those that do not. It follows that if our sample is seriously deceptive with respect to the incidence of some property in the class from which it is drawn, it is highly untypical. This is all that follows. Even to say that the sample is untypical does not mean that it deviates from most of the samples that are actually drawn but only that it deviates from the vast majority of possible samples. This is the most that can be extracted from the law of large numbers.

But is it really likely that our sampling of nature should be untypical? The trouble with this question is that it smuggles in a judgment of credibility, for which no basis has yet been assigned. If we make suitable assumptions about the constitution of the universe, we can supply ourselves with premises from which to deduce that our sampling is fair. The premises will themselves need to be justified, however, and I do not see how this can be done except by an appeal to our experience. Then, as David Hume saw, we are landed in a circle, because this appeal to our experience makes use of the very assumptions we are attempting to justify. I am strongly inclined to think that this circle is unavoidable, but to develop this argument would lead me into the heart of the problem of induction, which I shall not attempt to penetrate here.

A Valid Application

I have tried to show that although there is nothing wrong with the law of large numbers in itself, the support it gives to arguments from inverse probability—the reasoning that a large sample is unlikely to deviate in character from its parent class—is much more precarious than has commonly been supposed. There is, however, one set of cases in which an argument of this type can be applied with complete safety. These are the cases in which the class that concerns us is finite and the unexamined portion of it is relatively very small. Suppose we know the total number of births within a given area throughout a given period but our statistics on their sex distribution are not quite complete. Then let the fraction of the class for which this information is lacking be comparatively small, say less than 3 percent. In that case, whatever the proportion of male births in our sample may be, we can be sure that the proportion in the whole class does not differ from it much, just because there are not enough unexamined instances to make any substantial difference. By supposing all of the births in the unexamined instances to be male or all of them female, we can establish the fairly narrow limits within which the correct answer for the whole class must lie.

We now find, however, that the very security of this conclusion robs it of any interest. It tells us no more than we know already. The prospective father who wants to know whether his child is more likely to be a boy or a girl learns nothing at all to his purpose from the information that the available statistics are such that the proportion of boys among the children born or about to be born within the relevant period is bound to be more than 50 percent. All he learns is that the figures have now reached a stage where it is not going to make any appreciable difference to the final percentage which his child is. Not only can he deduce nothing about the sex of his own child—since judgments of probability, in the sense of frequency, refer to classes and not to individuals—but also he can deduce nothing about the frequency of male births in the subclass of so-far-unexamined cases to which his child belongs.

In fact, the ratio of male to female births has been found to be fairly constant, so that if the statistics had shown that slightly more female children had been born so far in the course of the year, the prospective father, knowing that there was normally a slight preponderance of males, might be encouraged to expect that his child would be a boy as the result of a belief in what is popularly known as the law of averages. If he did argue in this way, he could easily be disappointed. What is not generally realized is that the law of averages only works deductively. If we already know, with respect to the incidence of some property in a limited series of events, what the final percentage is going to be, and if we also know what the percentage is in the part of the series that has already been traversed, we can calculate what the percentage will be in the instances still to come.

This situation, however, carries the consequence that the law of averages can only be applied with any safety when it is backed by statistical laws that are very well established. We might perhaps rely on the Mendelian laws of heredity for the assurance that if a recessive character had already appeared in a given generation among the members of a certain family of plants or animals, the character of the kind in question that would be displayed in the same generation by the remaining members of the family would be dominant. On the other hand, it would be a foolish man who argued that because the total number of automobile accidents in the current year had already risen to the average of previous years, he could drive as recklessly as he pleased, since the law of averages would keep him safe. The reason he would be foolish is not only that the incidence of automobile accidents is not known to fall under any very constant statistical laws but also that for the most part these accidents, although they may be in some measure due to common causes, are causally independent of one another. The fact that a number of accidents have occurred recently in your neighborhood does not make it any less likely that another one will occur there today—unless, perhaps, the knowledge that the accidents have occurred makes people more careful. Certainly the occurrence of another accident is not made any less likely by the law of averages.

The same reasoning applies to our example of the prospective father, in spite of the greater constancy of the birth statistics. Whatever factors may determine the sex of his child, there is no reason to believe that the sex of other children who are not his kindred but merely happen also to be born in the current year has anything to do with it. Consequently, if there has been an unusual preponderance of female births, the inference he should draw is not that there is any greater likelihood that his child will be a boy but rather that this is a year in which, for a multiplicity of reasons, the usual balance of the sexes has been altered.

Questions about Chance

We have seen that what is required for the application of the calculus of chances is a finite set of logically equal possibilities, which are fulfilled in the long run with equal frequency. It is because we suppose these conditions to be at least roughly satisfied in games played with coins, dice, cards or roulette wheels that we characterize them as games of chance. Conversely, if we play one of these games and find in a particular instance that the different possibilities are not fulfilled with anything like equal frequency, we may decide that the results are not to be ascribed to chance. Then we look for some other explanation.

It is not only in gambling games that this procedure operates. Very often, when a statistical result is said to be significant, what is meant is that it deviates from chance in the sense that it fails to accord with the a priori probabilities. A good illustration of this is to be found in the experiments that are supposed to prove the existence of extrasensory perception. A typical experiment might be conducted with a set of cards numbered one to five and another set of five cards respectively symbolizing a lion, an elephant, a pelican, a zebra and a giraffe. Both packs are shuffled; the experimenter draws a card from the numbered pack, and then he draws from the animal pack the card that corresponds in order to the number he has drawn. This procedure is repeated 100 times, the cards being replaced and the packs reshuffled after each drawing. The subject is required to say on each occasion which animal

A rise in the number of accidents does not imply that there will be a drop to maintain the statistical average

Apparent extrasensory perception in drawing cards may involve other factors

is represented by the card drawn from the animal pack.

It is assumed that if it were merely a matter of guesswork he would be right, on the average, 20 times out of 100. Sometimes, however, a subject fairly consistently gets as many as 28 right. This result is sufficiently improbable to be counted as statistically significant. It is therefore inferred that the subject's achievement cannot be put down to chance, and he is credited with extrasensory perception. (Admittedly, to talk of extrasensory perception is not to give any explanation of the subject's performance but merely to stake the claim that an explanation is called for, but this does not matter for our present purposes. Our only concern is with the meaning and implications of the statement that such things do not occur by chance.)

Let us look into this case a little more closely. Why is it assumed that if the subject had no special power of divination he would pick the right card about 20 times out of 100? The answer is that if we take every possible sequence of 100 drawings from this set of cards and every possible sequence of 100 guesses, then the proportion of cases in which the two selections match is 20 in 100. To say that it is rather improbable that as many as 28 guesses should be right is just to say that out of the total number of possible parallel sequences of 100 drawings and guesses, the proportion in which the two coincide in as many as 28 places is rather small.

It is to be noted that both these calculations are a priori. They relate to the distribution of logical possibilities and are in no way derived from the study of anything that actually happens. Why, then, should we regard it as a matter of no interest—as something only to be expected—that the series of guesses should match the series of drawings in the same proportion as the total of possible matches stands to the total of possible combinations, but think it quite extraordinary that a subject should achieve a number of matchings 8 percent higher than the a priori average? Why should it be more remarkable that the proportion of actual coincidences should deviate from the proportion of possible coincidences than that they should be in conformity with one another? What we must be assuming is that the natural thing in a card-guessing game of this kind is for every possible combination of the members of the two series to appear with equal frequency. What reason could we have for making such an assumption antecedently to any experience? As far as I can see, none whatsoever.

If I am right about this, we are not entitled to assume that it is only a deviation from the a priori frequencies that calls for explanation. Conformity with them may equally have to be accounted for. In fact, there are many cases in which this necessity seems to be recognized. If a coin, a die or a roulette wheel yields "improbable" results, if it favors one side or area at the expense of the others, we do indeed assume that some physical bias is at work: the coin is weighted; its center of gravity has been displaced. Yet equally we think that there is a physical explanation in the case where such objects run true. It is quite an art to make dice and roulette wheels operate in such a way that each number comes up in a reasonably long run about as often as any other. There are physical reasons for this just as much as there are for the fact that one number or set of numbers comes up much more often than the others. In the sense in which chance is contrasted with design, or a chance event is one to which we do not assign a cause, it is not by chance that these operations obey the laws of chance.

Antecedently to experience, then, we have no more reason to expect that the results of tossing coins or throwing dice will conform to the a priori probabilities than that they will deviate from them. The reason we think that results that are highly improbable in this sense call for a special explanation is that they are empirically abnormal. What is significant is not the deviation from the a priori frequencies but the deviation from frequencies that have been empirically established. The special interest we take in the case where a die turns out to be biased stems from the fact that we have found by experience that most dice run true.

I believe that the same applies to the other cases in which we conclude, on purely statistical grounds, that such and such an occurrence cannot be ascribed to chance. Suppose that wherever I go in the course of a day I keep running across the same stranger. I may well conclude that this cannot be a matter of chance: the man must be following me. But my reason for this conclusion is not that our meeting so often is improbable a priori. Of course, I could argue in that way. Starting with the assumption that we are both moving within a certain limited area, I could think of this area as divided into a finite number of equal squares, like a chessboard, and then make the assumption that each of us is as likely at any moment of the day to be in any one of these squares as in any other. My reason for concluding that we were not meeting by chance would then be that out of the total number of possible paths we could severally follow, the number of those that intersected at several places was only a tiny fraction. But not only is this line of argument not necessary for me to arrive at my conclusion; in addition it rests on a premise that is entirely open to question. If the assumption that each of us is as likely to be in any one square as in any other at any given time is merely a way of stating that the squares are equal, then it is true *ex hypothesi* but is not to the purpose. If it implies that over a certain period of time we are actually to be found in any one square as often as in any other, then, in default of empirical evidence, there can be no reason for accepting it. If I nevertheless conclude that these meetings do not occur by chance, my reason will be that experience has shown me that when two people are living independently in a large city with many different venues for business and for recreation, the occasions on which their separate pursuit of their affairs leads them to be in the same place at the same time are relatively few. Here again, what needs to be particularly explained is the deviation not from an a priori frequency but from an empirically established one.

This is also, in my view, the way we should interpret the card-guessing experiments. Antecedently to experience, there is no reason to believe that the degree to which any series of guesses matches any series of drawings will or will not reflect the distribution of the logical possibilities. What is known a priori is that any card drawn will be one of five possibilities, and that any guess will also be one of five possibilities, but from this nothing at all follows about the number of matchings that will actually occur. We have to discover by experiment that certain methods of shuffling and selecting the cards do have the result that any one of them comes up about as often as any other. We have also to discover by experiment that the guesses people make are evenly distributed; or if this is not true, as for psychological reasons it may well not be in many instances, that their tendency to favor certain choices does not result in a number of matchings that is higher than the average. From these empirical premises the standard conclusions about the results that would occur by chance do follow mathematically.

But then if the results show a significant deviation, what is put in doubt is the truth of one or other of the empirical premises. The only thing that is remarkable about the subject who is credited with extrasensory perception is that he is consistently rather better at guessing cards than the ordinary run of people have shown themselves to be. The fact that he also does "better than chance" proves nothing in itself.

The same confusion is commonly found in discussions of the question whether or not the universe exists by chance. It is not, indeed, immediately clear what meaning this question could be given in terms of the a priori calculus of chances. If, however, one can make the assumptions that there is a finite number of ultimate particles in the universe and that the space in which they operate is also finite, then I suppose it could be said that the actual state of the universe is highly improbable, in the sense that the actual distribution of the particles is only one of a fantastically large number of possible distributions. In this sense, of course, any other distribution of the particles would be equally improbable, but it might be argued that their actual distribution was more improbable than some others would be, on the ground that it exhibited a greater deviation from the a priori average.

Alternatively, if we were able by what would have to be a rather arbitrary procedure to draw up a finite list of the simple properties that it was logically possible for anything to have, we might say that the actual state of the universe was improbable in the sense that the number of ways in which these properties were actually found to be com-

Misconceptions of chance are persistent

bined was only a tiny fraction of the total number of possible combinations. In neither case, however, would anything of interest follow unless we had reason to believe that some different constitution of the universe from the one that actually obtains was antecedently more likely. But what reason could there possibly be for such a belief? What meaning can be attached even to this notion of antecedent likelihood?

The most that we can say is that given the number of fundamental particles and the finitude of space, or given the number of primary properties and the range of their possible combinations, the number of possible universes in which the particles are more evenly distributed or the combinations of properties are more various is larger than the number of those in which the particles are not more evenly distributed or the combinations of properties are not more various than they are in our actual universe. But should it be supposed that a more probable universe, in this special sense, is more to be expected than the one in which we actually find ourselves? The answer is that there can be no reason at all for any supposition of this kind. The concept of a priori probability relates only to the counting of logical possibilities. How probable it is that these logical possibilities are realized in a balanced or unbalanced way can be estimated only in the light of our experience. But we can have no experience of a universe other than our own.

It is perhaps worth adding that the fact that our universe can be said to be improbable, in the senses I have just defined, does nothing at all for the traditional argument for a universe arising from design. In order to give any force to this argument, it would have to be shown that we have good reason to believe first that the universe is a teleological, or purposive, system. Secondly, it would have to be shown that it is the kind of teleological system that has been demonstrated by our experience to be usually the result of conscious planning. I take it to be sufficiently obvious that neither of these conditions is actually satisfied.

Chance, Design and Cause

We are now in a position to distinguish with some precision the various senses in which we speak of things as happening by chance. Chief among them are these five:

1. A chance event may be one that is a member of some series that conforms, in the manner we have shown to be required, with the a priori calculus of chances. (It is to be noted that this does not imply that the event is not caused, or even that it is not designed. The results of individual tosses of a coin or throws of a die are commonly not designed, but it is often the fruit of design that the series as a whole conforms to the a priori calculus.) A corollary of this usage is that when the frequency with which a certain type of event has been found to occur conforms to the a priori calculus and we meet with a significant deviation, as in the case of the card-guessing experiments, our inclination is to say that this deviation cannot be attributed to chance.

2. On the other hand, there are cases in which our reason, or one of our reasons, for saying that an event occurs by chance is just that it is a deviation from an established frequency. This is the sense, for example, in which we talk of chance mutations in biology. A similar usage occurs in historical instances where we look on the cause as incommensurate with the effect. "For want of a nail the shoe was lost, for want of a shoe the horse was lost, for want of a horse the rider was lost, for want of the rider the battle was lost, for want of the battle the kingdom was lost, and all for the want of a horseshoe nail." We say it was a mischance that the kingdom was lost because we do not ordinarily expect something so trivial as the loss of a horseshoe nail to have such far-reaching consequences. There is also the point that the loss of a nail at such and such a moment is not easily predictable, although again this is not to say that it lacked a cause.

3. When we are speaking of events brought about by human beings, or by other animals insofar as they can be regarded as purposive agents, to say that an event occurs by chance often means no more than that it was not intended by the agent or, in some cases, by anybody else. This is the sense in which "by chance" is contrasted with "by design." Again there is no implication that such events are not caused, but rather the implication that they are.

4. We talk of chance collocations of events when their concurrence is not designed and when, although we may be able to account for them severally, we have failed to establish any lawlike proposition that binds them together. The ascription of such concurrences to chance is most often made in cases where something of particular interest follows from them or in cases where the concurrence would normally be the fruit of design. Thus if I go away on holiday and in the course of my journey keep running into friends whom I had not arranged to meet, I am struck by the coincidence, although in fact it is no more of a coincidence than my meeting anybody else. As we have seen, however, if such encounters become excessively frequent, I may begin to suspect that they are not occurring by chance. In general, to speak of events as coming together by chance does not imply that they are not connected in a lawlike way or that no law connecting them will ever be discovered, but only that no such laws figure in our accepted system of beliefs.

5. In the case of statistical generalizations it can be said to be a matter of chance which of the individuals that fall under the generalization display the property in question and which do not. Thus in the case of a law of genetics we can be confident that just one out of n individuals in the third generation will display some recessive characteristic, but we regard it as a matter of chance which one of them it will be. In microscopic physics one may accept the generalization that m out of n electrons will move from one orbit to another within a given period but regard it as a matter of chance which individuals move and which remain. This usage of chance is the only one in which it is implied that the individual events themselves, as distinct from their concurrences, have not been found capable of being brought under causal laws.

Actually, might not such events be the outcome of chance in an even stronger sense? Might it not be the case not only that we had been unable to subsume them under causal laws but also that there really were no causal laws that governed them? This is not an easy question to answer, partly because it is not clear what would count as an instance of such a chance event. One difficulty is that if no limit is set to the complexity of our hypotheses, then as long as we are dealing with a closed set of events we shall always be able to find some generalizations the hypotheses satisfy. It might be stipulated, however, that such generalizations were not to be counted as laws unless they applied to events outside the set they were already known to cover, and it might in fact turn out in certain domains that we never succeeded in making any such extrapolations. If this led us to conclude that the phenomena in question were such that attempts of this kind never would succeed, we could reasonably express the conclusion by saying that the phenomena contained an irreducible element of chance.

There are, indeed, those who maintain that this stage has already been reached in quantum physics, but this is still a matter for dispute. The ground for saying that determinism has broken down in this domain is that the determinism that was postulated in classical physics required that it be possible, at least in principle, to ascertain the position and momentum at any given instant of all the particles in the universe. This is a condition that microscopic particles do not satisfy. It can still be argued, however, that this reasoning does not logically preclude their falling into some deterministic pattern. Even so, the fact remains that such a pattern has not yet been found. Until it is found, the view that the fundamental laws of physics are not causal but only statistical would appear to hold the field.

I think there is another important sense in which chance can be held to intrude into the world. Even in a field in which causal laws are well established, there is often a certain looseness in the way they fit the facts. The phenomena that are taken as verifying the laws cover a certain range. If the phenomena are quantitative, the values actually recorded may be scattered around the values the law prescribes. These slight deviations are not held to be significant; they are ascribed to errors of observation.

"Errors of observation," however, is here a term of art. Apart from the existence of the deviations there is usually no reason to suppose that any errors have occurred. Now, I think it possible that this looseness of fit cannot be wholly eliminated; in other words, that there are limits to the precision with which the course of nature can be prospectively charted. If this were so, it might be said that anything that fell outside these limits remained in the hands of chance.

Of course this cannot be proved. Whatever limit is set, there can be no a priori reason for assuming that it will never be overstepped. The person who believes in chance, in this absolute sense, can properly do no more than issue a challenge. He points to certain features of the world and defies anyone to show that they fall entirely in every detail within the grasp of causal laws. But however long he triumphs, there remains, in yet another of the manifold senses of "chance," the chance that his challenge will eventually be met.

2

WHAT IS PROBABILITY?

RUDOLF CARNAP • September 1953

The articles in this book on fundamental questions of science give an illuminating picture of the way scientists work. No one reading these articles can fail to be impressed with the great importance to science of hypotheses—the daring guesses on slender evidence that go into building new theories. The question that I should like to raise in this article is: Can the method of scientific inquiry be made more precise? Can we learn to judge the hypotheses, to weigh the extent to which they are supported by the evidence at hand, as an investigator judges and weighs his data?

The question leads at once into the subject of probability. If you query scientists about the meaning of this term, you will discover a curious situation. Practically everyone will say that probability as used in science has only one meaning, but when you ask what that meaning is, you will get different answers. Most scientists will define it as statistical probability, which means the relative frequency of a given kind of events or phenomena within a class of phenomena, usually called the "population." For instance, when a statistician says the probability that a native of the U. S. has A-type blood is 4/10, he means that four out of 10 people have this type. This meaning of probability has become almost the standard usage in science. But you will also find that there are scientists who define probability in another way. They prefer to use the term in the sense nearer to everyday use, in which it means a measurement, based on the available evidence, of the chances that something is true—as when a jury decides that a defendant is "probably" guilty, or a weather forecaster predicts that it will probably rain tomorrow. This kind of probability amounts to a weighing of the strength of the evidence. Its numerical expression has a meaning quite different from that of statistical probability: if the weather man were to venture to say that the probability of rain tomorrow was 4/10, he would not be describing a statistical fact but would simply mean that, should you bet on it raining tomorrow, you had better ask for odds of 4 to 6.

This concept is called inductive probability. A scientist makes a judgment of the odds consciously or unconsciously, whenever he plans an experiment. Usually the probability ascribed to his hypothesis is stated not in numbers but in comparative terms; that is, the probability is said to be high or low, or one probability is considered higher than another. To some of us it seems that inductive probability could be refined into a more precise tool for science. Given a hypothesis and certain evidence, it is possible to determine, by logical analysis and mathematical calculation, the probability that the hypothesis is correct, or the "degree of confirmation." If we had a system of inductive logic in mathematical form, our inferences about hypotheses in science, business and everyday life, which we usually make by "intuition" or "instinct," might be made more rational and exact. I have made a beginning in the construction of such a system, using the findings of past workers in this field and the exact tools of modern symbolic logic. Before discussing this system, let me review briefly the history of the inductive concept of probability.

The scientific theory of probability began, as a matter of fact, with the inductive concept and not the statistical one. Its study was started in the 16th century by certain mathematicians who were asked by their gambler friends to determine the odds in various games of chance. The first major treatise on probability, written by the Swiss professor Jacob Bernoulli and published posthumously in 1713, was called *Ars Conjectandi*, "The Art of Conjecture"—in other words, the art of judging hypotheses on the basis of evidence. The classical period in the study of probability culminated in the great 1812 work *Théorie analytique des probabilités*, by the French astronomer and mathematician Pierre Laplace. He declared the aim of the theory of probability to be to guide our judgments and to protect us from illusions, and he was concerned primarily not with statistics but with methods for weighing the acceptability of assumptions.

But after the middle of the 19th century the word probability began to acquire a new meaning, and scientists turned more and more to the statistical concept. By the 1920s Robert Aylmer Fisher in England, Richard von Mises and Hans Reichenbach in Germany (both died within a few months of one another) and others began to develop new probability theories based on the statistical interpretation. They were able to use many of the mathematical theorems of classical probability, which hold equally well in statistical probability. But they had to reject some. One of the principles they rejected, called the principle of indifference, sharply points up the distinction between inductive and statistical probability.

Suppose you are shown a die and are told merely that it is a regular cube. With no more information than this, you can only assume that when the die is thrown any one of its six faces is as likely to turn up as any other; in other words, that each face has the same probability, 1/6. This illustrates the principle of indifference, which says that if the evidence does not contain anything that would favor one possible event over another, the events have equal probabilities *relative to this evidence*. Now a second observer may have additional evidence: he

	STATISTICAL DISTRIBUTIONS		INDIVIDUAL DISTRIBUTIONS		METHOD I	METHOD II	
	NUMBER OF BLUE	NUMBER OF WHITE			INITIAL PROBABILITY OF INDIVIDUAL DISTRIBUTIONS	INITIAL PROBABILITY OF: STATISTICAL DISTRIBUTIONS	INDIVIDUAL DISTRIBUTIONS
1.	4	0	1.	● ● ● ●	1/16	1/5	1/5 = 12/60
2.	3	1	2.	● ● ● ○	1/16	1/5	1/20 = 3/60
			3.	● ● ○ ●	1/16		1/20 = 3/60
			4.	● ○ ● ●	1/16		1/20 = 3/60
			5.	○ ● ● ●	1/16		1/20 = 3/60
3.	2	2	6.	● ● ○ ○	1/16	1/5	1/30 = 2/60
			7.	● ○ ● ○	1/16		1/30 = 2/60
			8.	● ○ ○ ●	1/16		1/30 = 2/60
			9.	○ ● ● ○	1/16		1/30 = 2/60
			10.	○ ● ○ ●	1/16		1/30 = 2/60
			11.	○ ○ ● ●	1/16		1/30 = 2/60
4.	1	3	12.	● ○ ○ ○	1/16	1/5	1/20 = 3/60
			13.	○ ● ○ ○	1/16		1/20 = 3/60
			14.	○ ○ ● ○	1/16		1/20 = 3/60
			15.	○ ○ ○ ●	1/16		1/20 = 3/60
5.	0	4	16.	○ ○ ○ ○	1/16	1/5	1/5 = 12/60

INDUCTIVE PROBABILITY METHODS are illustrated in an example which is tabulated above. Four balls are to be drawn in succession from an urn. They are identical in every way except that some are blue and some white. Nothing is known, however, about the proportion of blue to white balls in the urn. First we want to decide on the initial probabilities in the experiment—the probabilities before the first ball is drawn. We list (under "Individual Distributions") all the possible ways in which the drawing can turn out. Now we apply the principle of indifference, which says that if the evidence contains nothing that favors one possibility over another, all possibilities must be considered equally probable. There are two ways to apply the principle to this example. The first is illustrated under "Method I." Since there are 16 possible cases, dividing the probability equally among them gives each a probability of 1/16. But there is another way to look at the table. Instead of taking into account the order in which blue and white turn up, we can concentrate only on the total numbers of blue and white in a drawing—all blue, three blue and one white, and so on. This classifies the table into "Statistical Distributions," which are indicated by the brackets on the left. There are five statistical distributions. If the principle of indifference is applied to them, then each has a probability of 1/5, as shown in the first column of "Method II." Now the individual distributions within each statistical distribution are assigned probabilities that are again determined by the principle of indifference. The first statistical distribution (four blue) has only one member, so it gets the full amount of the probability to be distributed, or 1/5, as shown in the second column of "Method II." The second statistical distribution (three blue, one white) has four members, so the probability must be split four ways, 1/20 to each. Similarly, the remaining three statistical distributions are divided into their individual members. At the extreme right hand of the table, all probabilities are converted to a least common denominator of 60 in order to facilitate comparing and combining them. Method II is superior to Method I because it assigns probabilities to future events on the basis of the frequency of their past occurrence.

may know that the die is loaded in favor of one of the faces, without knowing which face it is. The probabilities are still the same for him, because as far as his information goes, each of the six faces has an equal possibility of being loaded. On the other hand, for a third observer who knows that the load favors the face numbered 1 the probabilities change; on the basis of his evidence the probability of the ace is higher than 1/6.

Thus inductive probability depends on the observer and the evidence in his possession; it is not simply a property of the object itself. In statistical probability, which refers to the actual frequency of an event, the principle of indifference is of course absurd. It would be incautious for an observer who knew only that a die had the accurate dimensions of a cube to assert that the six faces would appear with equal frequency. And if he knew that the die was biased in favor of one side, he would contradict his own knowledge. Inductive probability, on the other hand, does not predict frequencies; rather, it is a tool for evaluating evidence in relation to a hypothesis. Both the statistical and inductive concepts of probability are indispensable to science; each has valuable functions to perform. But it is important to recognize the distinctions between the two concepts and to develop the possibilities of both tools.

In the past 30 years the inductive concept of probability, which had been supplanted by the statistical concept, has been revived by a few workers. The first of these was the great English economist John Maynard Keynes. In his *Treatise on Probability* in 1921 he showed how the inductive concept is implicitly used in all our thinking about unknown events, in science as well as in everyday life. Yet Keynes' attempt to develop this concept was too restricted: he believed it was impossible to calculate numerical probabilities except in well-defined situations such as the throw of dice, the possible distributions of cards, and so on. Moreover, he rejected the statistical concept of probability and argued that all probability statements could be formulated in terms of inductive probability.

I believe that he was mistaken in this point of view. Today an increasing number of those who study both sides of the controversy, which has been going on for 30 years, are coming to the conclusion that here, as often before in the history of scientific thinking, both sides are right in their positive theses, wrong in their polemical remarks. The statistical concept, for which a very elaborate mathematical theory exists, and which has been applied fruitfully in many fields in science and industry, need not be abandoned in order to make room for the inductive concept. Statistical probability characterizes an objective situation, *e.g.*, a state of a physical, biological or social system. On the other hand, inductive probability, as I see it, does not occur in scientific statements but only in judgments *about* such statements. Thus it is applied in the methodology of science—the analysis of concepts, statements and theories.

In 1939 the British geophysicist Harold Jeffreys put forward a much more comprehensive theory of inductive probability than Keynes'. He agreed with the classical view that probability can be expressed numerically in all cases. Furthermore, he wished to apply probability to quantitative hypotheses of science, and he set up an axiom system for probability much stronger than that of Keynes. He revived the principle of indifference in a form which seems to me much too strong: "If there is no reason to believe one hypothesis rather than another, the probabilities are equal." It can easily be shown that this statement leads to contradictions. Suppose, for example, that we have an urn known to be filled with blue, red and yellow balls but do not know the proportion of each color. Let us consider as a starting hypothesis that the first ball we draw from the urn will be blue. According to Jeffreys' (and Laplace's) statement of the principle of indifference, if the question is whether the first ball will be blue or not blue, we must assign equal probabilities to both these hypotheses; that is, each probability is 1/2. If the first ball is not blue, it may be either red or yellow, and again, in the absence of knowledge about the actual proportions in the urn, these two have equal probabilities, so that the probability of each is 1/4. But if we were to start with the hypothesis that the first ball drawn would be, say, red, we would get a probability of 1/2 for red. Thus Jeffreys' system as it stands is inconsistent.

In addition, Jeffreys joined Keynes in rejecting the statistical concept of probability. Nevertheless his book *Theory of Probability* remains valuable for the new light it throws on many statistical problems by discussing them for the first time in terms of inductive probability.

I have drawn upon the work of Keynes and Jeffreys in constructing my mathematical theory of inductive probability, set forth in the book *Logical Foundations of Probability*, which was published in 1950. It is not possible to outline here the mathematical system itself. But I shall explain some of the general problems that had to be solved and some of the basic conceptions underlying the construction.

One of the fundamental questions to be decided is whether to accept a principle of indifference, and if so, in what form. It should be strong enough to allow the derivation of the desired theorems, but at the same time sufficiently restricted to avoid the contradictions resulting from the classical form.

The problem can be made clear by an example illustrating a few elementary concepts of inductive logic. We have an urn filled with blue and white balls in unknown proportions. We are going to draw four balls in succession. Taking the order into account, there are 16 possible drawings (all four blue, the first three blue and the fourth white, the first white and the next three blue, and so on). We list these possibilities in a table (*see table on page 15*).

Now what is the initial probability, before we have drawn at all, that we shall draw any one of these 16 distributions? We might assign any probability to the individual distributions, so long as they all added up to 1. Suppose we apply the principle of indifference and say that all the distributions have equal probabilities; that is, each has a probability of 1/16.

Let us state a specific hypothesis and calculate its probability. The hypothesis is, for example, that among the first three balls we draw, just one will be white. Looking at the table, we can see that six out of the 16 possible drawings will give us this result. The probability of our hypothesis, therefore, is the sum of these initial probabilities, or 6/16.

Suppose now that we are given some evidence, *i.e.*, have drawn some balls, and are asked to calculate the probability of a given hypothesis on the basis of this evidence. For instance, we have drawn first a blue ball, then a white ball, then a blue ball. The hypothesis is that the fourth ball will be blue; what is its probability? Here we run into a question as to how we should apply the principle of indifference. Let us try two different methods.

In Method I we start by assigning equal probabilities to the individual distributions. Referring to the table, we see that two of these distributions (Nos. 4 and 7) will give us the sequence blue, white, blue for the first three balls. Its probability is therefore 2/16. In only one of these distributions is the fourth ball blue; its probability is 1/16. The probability of our hypothesis on the basis of the evidence is obtained by dividing one into the other: *i.e.*, 1/16 divided by 2/16, which equals 1/2. In other words, the chances that our hypothesis is correct are 50-50: the fourth ball is just as likely to be white as blue.

But as a guide to judging a hypothesis, this result contradicts the principle of learning from experience. Other things being equal, we should consider one event more probable than another if it has happened more frequently in the past. We would regard a man as unreasonable if his expectation of a future event were the higher the less often he had seen it before. We must be guided by our knowledge of observed events, and in this example the fact that two out of three balls drawn from an unknown urn were blue should lead us to expect the probabilities to favor the fourth's also being blue. Yet a number of philosophers, including Keynes, have proposed Method I in spite of its logical flaw.

There is a second method which gives us a more reasonable result. We first apply the principle of indifference not to individual distributions but to statistical distributions. That is, we consider only the number of blue balls and of white balls obtained in a drawing, irrespective of order. The table shows that there are five possible statistical distributions (four blue, four white, three blue and one white, three white and one blue, two blue and two white). By the principle of indifference we assign equal probabilities to these, so that the probability of each is 1/5. We distribute this value (expressed for arithmetical convenience as 12/60) in equal parts among the corresponding individual distributions (*see last column of table*). Now the probabilities of distributions No. 4 and No. 7 are 3/60 and 2/60, respectively, and the probability of the hypothesis on the basis of the evidence is 3/60 divided by 5/60, or 3/5. In short, the chances that the fourth ball will be blue are not even but 3 to 2, which is more consistent with what experience, meaning the evidence we have acquired, should lead us to expect.

Method II, as well as Method I, leads to contradictions if it is applied in an unrestricted way. If it is used in cases characterized by more than one property difference (such as the difference between blue and white balls in our example) then all the relevant differences must be specified. Thus restricted, this system, which I proposed in 1945, is the first consistent inductive method, so far as I am aware, that succeeded in satisfying the principle of learning from experience. Since then I have found that there are many others. None of them seems as simple to define as Method II, but some of them have other advantages.

Having found a consistent and suitable inductive method, we can proceed to develop a general procedure for calculating, on the basis of given evidence, an estimate of an unknown value of any quantity. Suppose that the evidence indicates a certain number of possible values for a quantity at a given time, *e.g.*, the amount of rain tomorrow, the number of persons coming to a meeting, the price of wheat after the next harvest. Let the possible values be x_1, x_2, x_3, etc., and their inductive probabilities be p_1, p_2, p_3, etc. Then p_1x_1 is the "expectation value" of the first case at the present moment, p_2x_2 of the second case, and so on. The total expectation value of the quantity on the given evidence is the sum of the expectation values for all the possible cases. To take a specific example, suppose there are four prizes in a lottery, a first prize of $200 and three prizes of $50 each. It is known that the probability of a ticket winning the first prize is 1/100, and of a second prize, 3/100; the probability that the ticket will win nothing is therefore 96/100. Applying the method I have described above, a ticket holder can estimate that the ticket is worth to him 1/100 times $200 plus 3/100 times $50 plus 96/100 times 0, or $3.50. It would be irrational to pay more for it.

The same method may be used to make a rational decision in a situation where one among various possible actions is to be chosen. For example, a man considers several possible ways of investing a certain amount of money. He can—in principle, at least—calculate the estimate of his gain for each possible way. To act rationally, he should then choose that way for which the estimated gain is highest.

Bernoulli, Laplace and their followers envisaged a theory of inductive probability which, when fully developed, would supply the means for evaluating the acceptability of hypothetical assumptions in any field of theoretical research and for making rational decisions in the affairs of practical life. They were a great deal farther from this audacious objective than they realized. In the more sober cultural atmosphere of the late 19th and early 20th centuries their idea was dismissed as Utopian. But today a few men dare to think that these pioneers were not mere dreamers.

3

SUBJECTIVE PROBABILITY

JOHN COHEN • November 1957

Only on things uncertain I rely
I have no doubt except in certainty
And from blind chance for knowledge I inquire

So wrote François Villon, the 20th-century French poet who happened to live in the 15th. He spoke for all of us, for whenever we choose, judge or decide, whether we interpret the past or foretell what is to come, we do so with incomplete or unsure knowledge. Uncertainty dogs our every step. Since we must act on incomplete information, risk attends our daily decisions and undertakings—in driving a car and crossing a road, on the field of sport and in the marriage bed, in picking a winner on the stock exchange or in a political election.

How do we measure the probabilities of success or failure? An inquiry into this subject of course falls in the domain of psychology. Our actions are based upon our private assessment of our chances, which in turn depends upon our experiences and maturity in reasoning. We develop subjective concepts of probability which permeate and guide our thoughts and actions. In the department of psychology of the University of Manchester we have been exploring the elusive processes of subjective probability for some time by experiments. One of our aims has been to determine whether subjective probability has anything in common with mathematical probability, and to what extent subjective probability obeys distinctive psychological rules of its own. We have endeavored to trace the development of ideas about probability, especially in youngsters of school age.

To start with, take a simple experiment testing the notion of statistical distribution. We show children aged 10 to 16 a bowl containing blue and yellow beads and inform them that there are equal numbers of blue and yellow beads in the bowl. The experimenter then draws beads from it at random, four at a time, and puts four beads in each of 16 cups. The children are asked to tell how many of the cups will contain respectively: (1) four blue beads, (2) three blue and one yellow, (3) two blue and two yellow, (4) one blue and three yellow, (5) four yellow.

On the basis of such experiments we have found that children apparently progress through four stages. The younger children (around 10) merely guess vaguely that the five possible combinations are not equally likely. Those a little more mature realize that the most frequent (or most probable) content of the cups will be two blue and two yellow beads. At the third stage youngsters advance to the conclusions that one blue and three yellow beads will occur as often as one yellow and three blue, and that four blue and four yellow also have equal probabilities. Finally the older children conclude that the combination of one and three is more likely than all four of the same color. These experiments thus show how, with increasing age and experience, uncertain situations are structured in closer and closer accord with the objectivity of mathematical expectation.

The idea of sampling is an essential element for making sensible decisions; indeed, it may be the basis of thought itself. We send out mental antennas to feel or taste the universe, and from these samples, which give us only partial information, we learn to form sound judgments about the total "populations" they are supposed to represent. Sometimes the populations vary continuously; in such cases the fluctuations in successive samples themselves may lead to discovery of a law of nature.

Let us now consider whether estimates of the probability of success in a given task obey rules similar to those of mathematical probability or are subject to different, psychological rules. One rule of mathematical probability convenient for such a test is the additive theorem: namely, that small, independent probabilities of a particular event add up to a larger probability. Thus if you are drawing for a lucky ticket in a pool, your chances of success will increase in proportion to the number of tickets you take. In one of our experiments we confronted our subjects with a choice between taking a single large probability or a set of smaller probabilities: *e.g.*, they were allowed to draw either one ticket from a box of 10 or 10 tickets from 100, in the latter case putting back the ticket drawn each time before making the next draw. Mathematically, of course, the chance of drawing the prize ticket was exactly the same in both cases. But most of the subjects proved to be guided mainly by psychological rather than mathematical considerations.

If the 10 draws had to be made from 100 tickets in one box, about four fifths of the subjects preferred to make a single draw from a box of 10. Indeed, this preference held even when they were allowed to make 50 draws from the box of 100. Apparently the subjects feared that they might repeatedly draw the same ticket that they had put back. On the other hand, when they were allowed to draw the 10 tickets (or even fewer) from 10 separate boxes of 100 each, then a majority of the subjects swung to a preference for the plural chance over the single draw from a box of 10. That is to

A bus is driven between two posts in an experiment by the author and his colleagues at the University of Manchester

say, they swung from underestimating the plural chance to overestimating it. There is a type of mentality, in fact, which regards two draws as better than one under any circumstances. Some of the subjects preferred drawing two tickets from a box of 100 to drawing one from a box of 10.

Everyday life presents many situations of this kind, where we must choose between a large chance and a combination of smaller ones. For example, a jury (or a scientist) sometimes has to weigh one large item of evidence against the sum of several small items. Now there is also another type of situation which resembles the foregoing but in which the chances are not actually additive. For instance, a general may have to decide whether to stake success on a single big battle or a succession of smaller ones. Assume that he must win each of the smaller battles in order to undertake the next in the series. Then the chances are not additive but multiplicative: that is, if the chance of success in each battle is 1/2 (50 per cent), the over-all chance for the series is $1/2 \times 1/2 \times 1/2$. . . . The more battles he has to win on this basis, the smaller is his chance of final success. We have tested the responses of subjects to such a situation, offering them a choice between a single chance (ranging from certainty of success down to one chance in 1,000) and a set of chances amounting to, say, $1/3 \times 1/3 \times 1/3$. Even highly intelligent adults often choose the multiple chance although it is mathematically smaller than the single chance. They tend to interpret the successive chances as additive, and the more stages there are, the bigger is their overestimation of the probability of success.

We have studied people's estimates of the chance of success, or the risk of failure, both in tasks that involve no danger (*e.g.*, throwing a ball at a target) and in others that do involve danger (*e.g.*, driving a bus between two posts). In the latter experiment the posts were set at various distances, ranging from gaps which the bus could clear very easily to openings narrower than the bus. We compared the risk-taking of a group of beginners just starting training as bus drivers with that of trained drivers and of an experienced instructor.

We found that the experienced drivers not only performed more successfully than the inexperienced but also took less risk. That is, while the beginners attempted the task even when they were far from sure that they would succeed, and sometimes tried to drive the bus through an impossibly narrow gap, the trained drivers seldom did; the instructor never. He was able to judge accurately whether he could or could not drive his bus through a given gap. His maximum risk-taking level (the smallest gap through which he would attempt to take the bus) was one at which he thought he would always succeed and did in fact always succeed.

Plainly this kind of investigation could be useful in improving safety, not only in automobile driving but also in many other activities involving a human operator. We are at present studying how risk-taking by drivers is affected by imbibing various quantities of alcohol.

Uncertainty pervades our lives so thoroughly that it dominates our language. Our everyday speech is made up in large part of words like "probably," "many," "soon," "great," "little." What do these words mean? "Atomic war," declared a recent editorial in the London *Times*, "is likely to ruin forever the nation that even victoriously wages it." How exactly are we to understand the word "likely"? Lacking any standard for estimating the odds, we are left with the private probability of the editorial writer.

Such verbal imprecision is not necessarily to be condemned. Indeed, it has a value just because it allows us to express judgments when a precise quantitative statement is out of the question. All the same, we should not and need not hide behind a screen of complete indefinite-

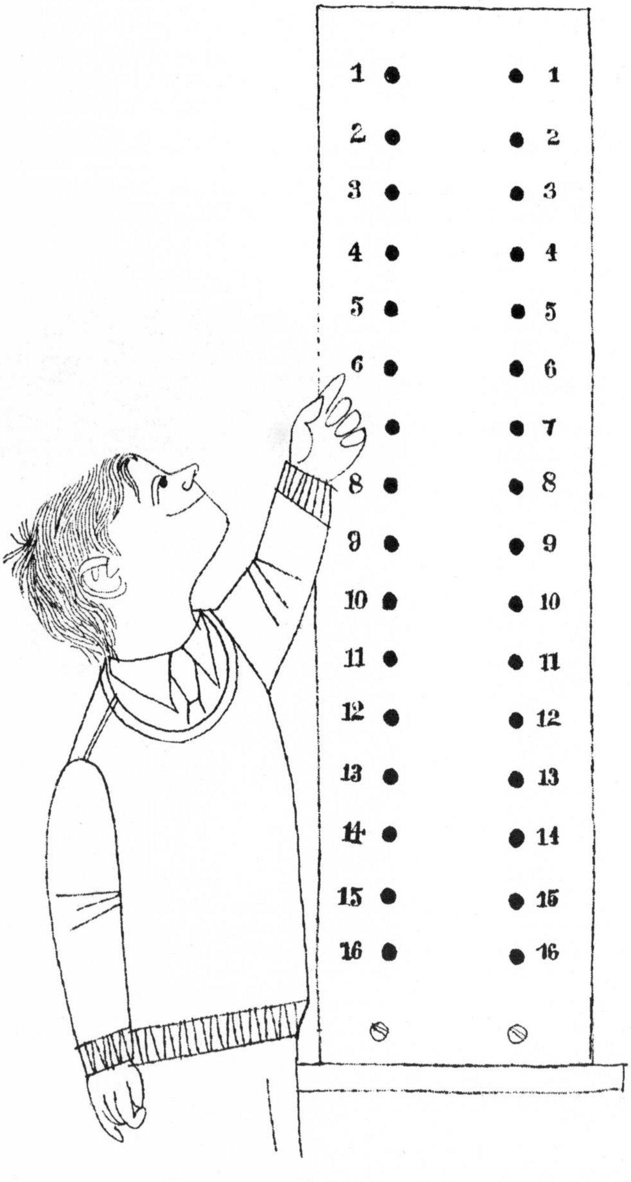

Children were asked to guess in which of two columns a light would flash

ness. Often it is possible to indicate the bounds or limits of the quantitative value we have in mind.

The language of uncertainty has three main categories: (1) words such as "probably," "possibly," "surely," which denote a subjective probability and are potentially quantifiable; (2) words like "many," "often," "soon," which are also quantifiable but denote not so much a condition of uncertainty as a quantity imprecisely known; (3) words like "fat," "rich," "drunk," which are not reducible to any accepted number because they are given various values by different people.

We have been trying to pin down, by experimental studies, what people mean by these expressions in specific contexts, and how the meanings change with age. For instance, a subject is told "There are many trees in the park" and is asked to say what number the word "many" means to him. Or a child is invited to take "some" sweets from a bowl and we then count how many he has taken. We compare the number he takes when alone with the number when one or more other children are present and are to take some sweets after him, or with the number he takes when instructed to give "some" sweets to another child.

First, we find that the number depends, of course, on the items involved. To most people "some friends" means about five, while "some trees" means about 20. However, unrelated areas sometimes show parallel values. For instance, the language of probability seems to mean about the same thing in predictions about the weather and about politics: the expression "is certain to [rain, or be elected]" signifies to the average person about a 70 per cent chance; "is likely to," about a 60 per cent chance; "probably will," about 55 per cent.

Secondly, the size of the population of items influences the value assigned to an expression. Thus, if we tell a subject to take "a few" or "a lot of" beads from a tray, he will take more if the tray contains a large number of beads than if it has a small number. But not proportionately more: if we increase the number of beads eightfold, the subject takes only half as large a percentage of the total.

Thirdly, there is a marked change with age. Among children between six and 14 years old, the older the child, the fewer beads he will take. But the difference between "a lot" and "a few" widens with age. This age effect is so consistent that it might be used as a test of intelligence. In place of a long test we could merely ask the subject to give numerical values to expressions such as "nearly always" and "very rarely" in a given context, and then measure his intelligence by the ratio of the number for "nearly always" to the one for "very rarely." We have found that this ratio increases systematically from about 2 to 1 for a child of seven to about 20 to 1 for a person 25 years old.

Nowhere are the processes of subjective probability more beautifully exhibited than in gambling. This is, of course, an ancient and universal practice of mankind. It seems to be linked, like ideas of destiny, primitive justice and divination, with the human awe of unpredictable events. The gods of folklore, in Indian, Greek and Nordic mythology, shaped human destiny by lots or dice. Primitive justice was, therefore, like a game of chance, a way of discovering the decision of the gods. The lawsuit was probably at first a contest which took the form of judgment by ordeal: victory was taken as supernatural proof of the justice of one's cause. No single feature of our lives is more charged with anxiety or passionate beliefs than a gamble such as the toss of a coin to decide an issue. No wonder that gamblers get worked up into violent frenzies (sometimes eating the cards or smashing the dice) and are ready to stake anything: wives, families, fingers, teeth, eyebrows, even personal freedom. Perhaps, as Sigmund Freud suggested, there is a sexual element in gambling; indeed, it often produces the same sequence of pleasure, guilt and remorse as the practice of masturbation.

In our studies of the manifestations of subjective probability in gambling we have given particular attention to the Monte Carlo fallacy: the well-nigh unanimous belief that after a run of successes a failure is inevitable, and *vice versa.* We tested young children with a display board containing two vertical columns of lights [*see drawing on page 20*]. The lights were lit in succession, on one side or the other, up to a certain

For elections and rain the prediction "is certain to" means about a 70 per cent chance

One big battle, or several small ones?

point, and the child then had to guess whether the next light would be in the right-hand or left-hand column.

Children from the age of six to 11 underwent this test. The youngest tended to alternate their guesses from one column to the other: that is, they might guess that the light would appear on the left side; if that guess failed, they would switch to the right side the next time, and so on. Older children followed the pattern of what had happened on the board: if more lights were lit on the left side, they would predict that the next light would appear on the right, regardless of their preceding guess.

Not until about the age of 12 do children begin to sense that each event may be independent of those that have gone before. At this age, as we found in coin-tossing experiments, youngsters start to predict that any given toss may be either heads or tails. As a 12-year-old girl expressed it: "When you toss a penny, nobody, *nobody* can tell you, even the cleverest of people, which it is going to be, because it might be either." Nevertheless, even with this appreciation, youngsters do not fully grasp the idea of a statistically independent outcome. Very few, it appears, realize that the guesses must be made in a purely random manner. From the youngster of six to the very bright adolescent of 16, predictions follow a complex system of pattern-seeking, associated with preferences for esthetic symmetry, fairness or magic.

These experiments give us a glimpse into the mind of the gambler. He seems unable to detach his prediction of an event from outcomes of similar events in the past, although in a sense he may "know" that the new event is entirely independent of those previous outcomes. Like many children, he is apt to treat luck and ill luck as stores which can be used up, and to think that success in guessing is due to the possession of some uncanny shrewdness or occult power which acts like a divining rod.

The further study of subjective probability promises to be of considerable theoretical interest as well as practical importance. It offers a novel method of investigating the growth of our mental powers from infancy onward, providing a single conceptual scheme for the study of how we perceive, think, learn, decide and act. It suggests new possibilities for comparative researches into abnormalities of thought and behavior, such as in schizophrenia, obsessional disorders and brain injuries.

There may also be a moral for teachers. Our system of education tends to give children the impression that every question has a single, definite answer. This is unfortunate, because the problems they will encounter in later life will generally have an indefinite character. It seems important that during their years of schooling children should be trained to recognize degrees of uncertainty, to compare their private guesses and extrapolations with what actually takes place—in short, to interpret and become masters of their own uncertainties.

How many are "some" sweets?

Sigmund Freud reflects on gambling

Subjective probability also has its place in the study of crime. Certain classes of criminals may differ from their law-abiding neighbors only in being more sure that they will escape detection. Or they may differ only in their level of maximum risk-taking, that is, in being ready to act at a level of uncertainty of success where their neighbors would hold back. Further, we have started some studies which may form a bridge between psychology and economics. For example, we are studying people's behavior at auctions in an attempt to relate subjective expectations of gain or loss to the actual risks of an economic enterprise. Finally, the study of subjective probability makes possible an experimental attack on all sorts of problems involving uncertain situations. In particular, it offers a new perspective for the study of accidents—in transport, in industry and, not least, in the home.

4

PROBABILITY

MARK KAC • September 1964

A secretary has typed 10 letters and addressed 10 envelopes. If she now puts the letters in the envelopes entirely at random (without looking at the addresses), what is the probability that not a single letter will wind up in its correct envelope? It may surprise the reader to learn that the probability is better than one chance in three: more specifically, it is almost 1/2.71828.... (This famous number 2.71828..., or *e*, the base of the natural logarithms, turns out to be an important one in the theory of probability and comes up again and again, as we shall see.)

The method used to solve the problem is called combinatorial analysis. An older and more familiar example of problems in combinatorial analysis is: What is the probability of drawing a flush in a single deal of five cards from a deck of 52? Combinatorial analysis has more profound and more practical applications, of course, than estimating the chances of poker hands or answering amusing questions about the hypothetical behavior of absentminded secretaries. It has become an extremely useful branch of mathematics. But its principles are best illustrated by simple examples. Let us work out the poker problem in detail so that we can perceive some of its probabilistic implications.

Pierre Simon de Laplace (1749–1827) based an entire theory of probability on combinatorial analysis by defining probability as $p = n/N$. This expression states that the probability of an event is the ratio of the number of ways in which the event can be realized (n) to the total number of possible events (N), provided that all the possible events are equally likely—an important proviso. The probability of a poker flush therefore is the ratio of the number of possible flushes to the total number of possible poker hands. The problem of combinatorial analysis is to calculate both numbers.

Let us start with a simpler case involving more manageable numbers. Given a set of four objects, *A*, *B*, *C*, *D*, how many subsets, or combinations, of two objects can be made from them? It is easy to answer by simple pairing and counting: there are six possible combinations of size 2, *AB*, *AC*, *AD*, *BC*, *BD*, *CD*. As we go on to larger numbers of objects, however, this process soon becomes all but impossible. We must find shortcuts—ways to make the calculations without actually counting. (Combinatorial analysis is sometimes called "counting without counting.")

Suppose we add a fifth object and consider how many pairs can be formed from the five. It is apparent that the new object, *E*, adds just four to the total of possible pairs, because it can combine with each of the other four. So the total is $6 + 4$, or 10, possible pairs. To put it in the conventional symbols of combinatorial analysis, we have $C(5,2) = C(4,2) + C(4,1)$. C represents the number of combinations, and the numbers in parentheses stand respectively for the total number of objects and the number in each subset: for instance, $C(5,2)$ means the combinations of five objects taken two at a time. To calculate on the same principle the number of combinations of four objects that could be made out of a total of 10 objects, we could write $C(10,4) = C(9,4) + C(9,3)$ and then continue the reduction to smaller and smaller numbers until we finally computed the answer by simple addition of all the numbers. In practice what we actually do in such a case is to build the C's from the ground up (the bookkeeping is easier).

The whole scheme is conveniently summarized in a handy table known as Pascal's triangle after Blaise Pascal (1623–1662), one of the founders of the theory of probability. The triangle is made up of the coefficients of the binomial expansion, each successive row representing the next higher power [*see top illustration on page 25*]. Each number in the table is the sum of the two numbers to the right and the left of it in the row above. The number of combinations for any set of objects can be read from left to right across a row. For example, the fourth row describes the possible combinations when the total number of objects is four: reading from the left, we have first the number 1, for the "empty set" (containing no objects); then 4, the number of subsets containing one object; then 6, the number of possible combinations of two objects; then 4, the number of three-object combinations, and finally 1 for the "full set" of four objects. With this table, to find the number of quadruplets that can be formed from a total of 10 objects one goes to the 10th row, reads across five steps to the right and finds the answer: 210.

Even the Pascal triangle becomes inconvenient when it has to be extended to large numbers such as are involved in our poker problem. Fortunately the pioneers of the theory of probability were able to work out and prove a simple general formula. This now familiar formula, in which (n,r) means n objects taken r at a time and "!" is the symbol meaning "factorial," is

$$C(n,r) = \frac{n!}{r!(n-r)!}\,.$$

In the case of $C(10,4)$ the formula—simplified by dividing both numerator

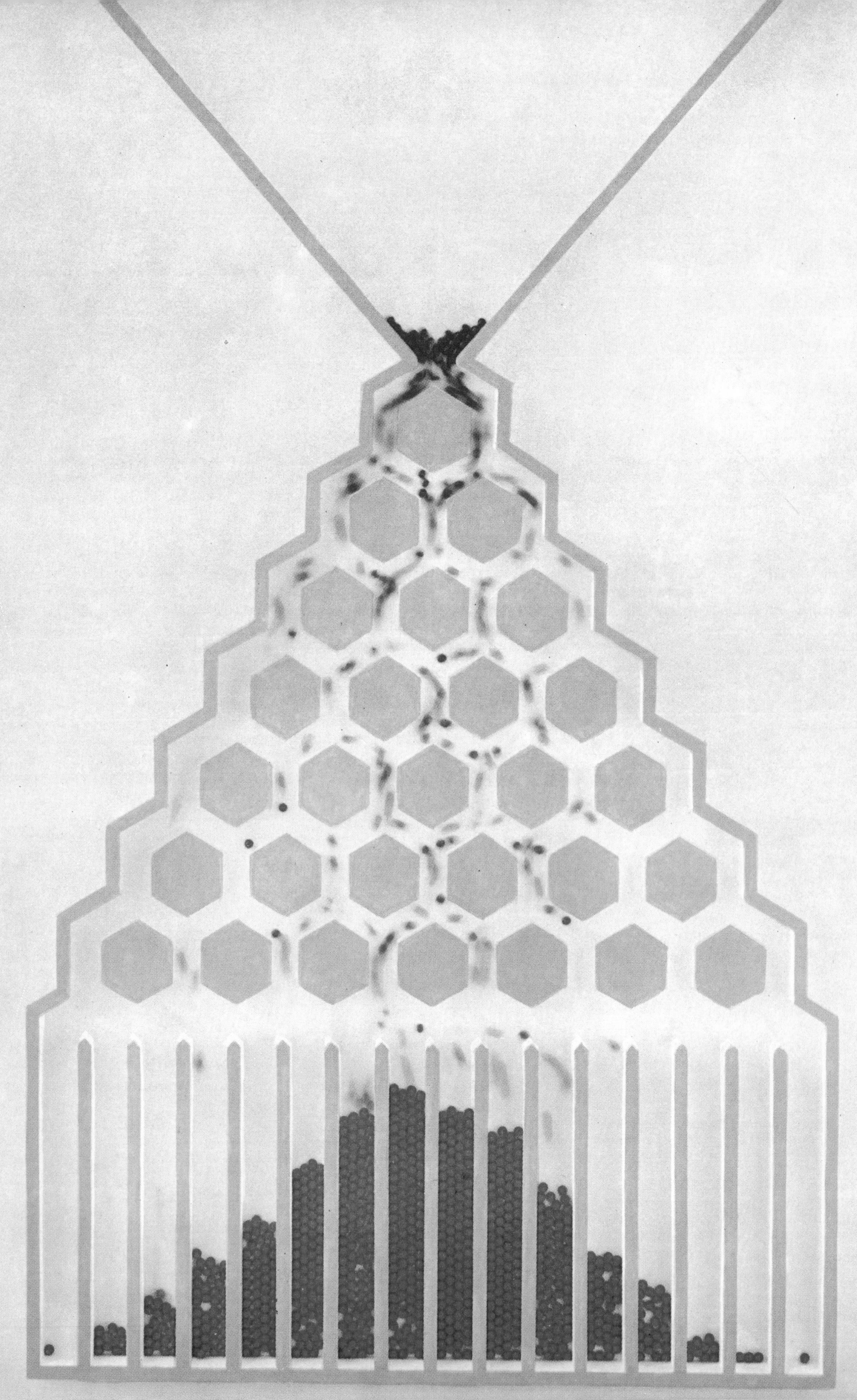

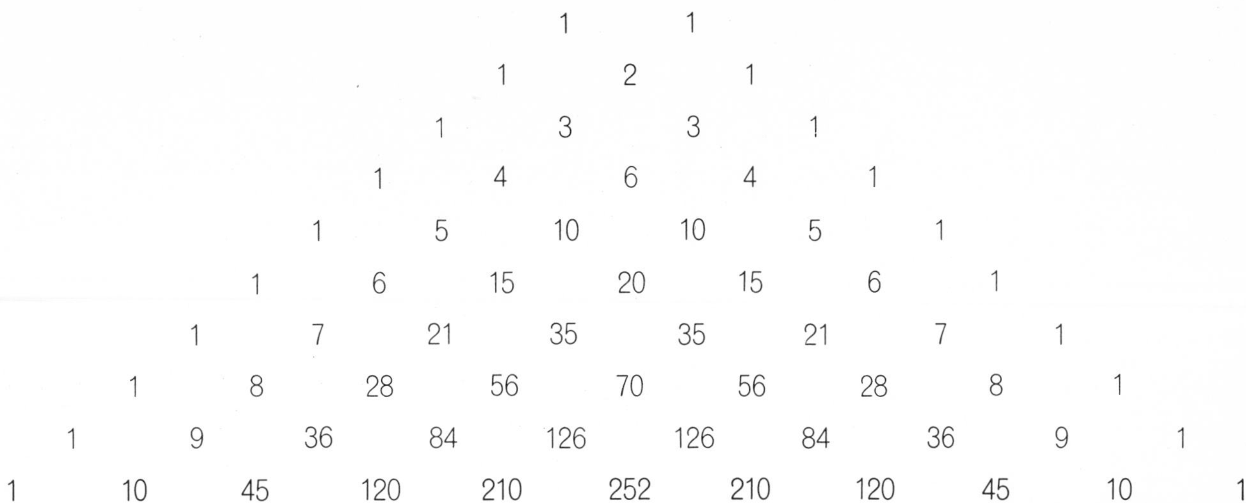

PASCAL'S TRIANGLE, an aid to calculating probabilities, is made up of the coefficients of the binomial expansion. Each number is the sum of the two numbers immediately above it. Some of its characteristics and applications are discussed in the text.

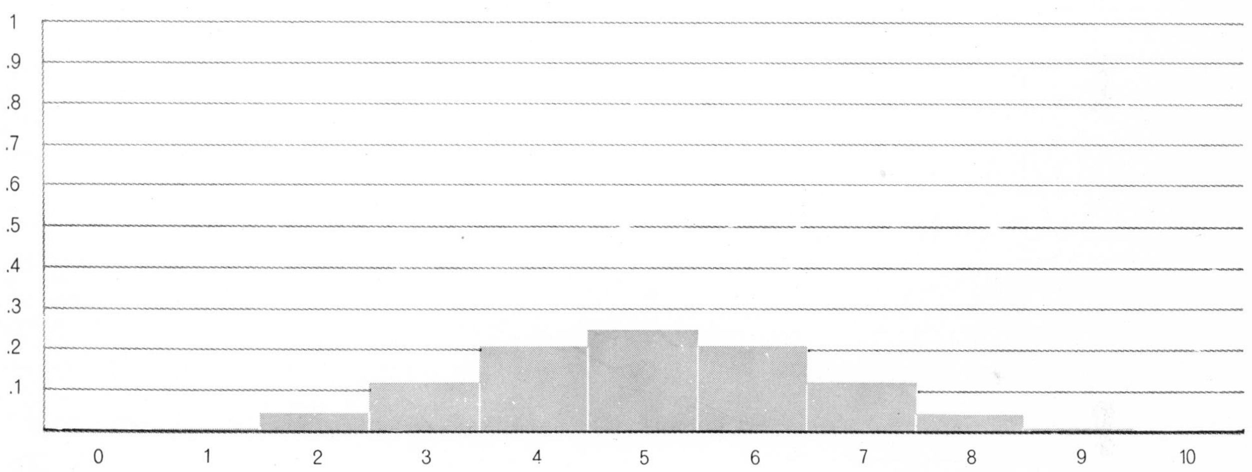

PROBABILITY OF HEADS in 10 tosses of a coin produces a histogram that is reminiscent of the normal distribution. As the 10th row of Pascal's triangle shows, there are 210 possible sequences containing exactly four heads out of a total of 1,024 possible sequences of heads in 10 tosses. Thus the chance of four heads is about 21 percent. Roughly the chances of zero, one, two, three, four and five heads in 10 tosses (*horizontal scale*) are respectively .001, .01, .045, .12, .21 and .25 (*vertical scale*). The probabilities and the bars representing them occur in descending order for six through 10 heads in 10 tosses. On the same scale a histogram for 10,000 tosses would be much wider and lower, and would have to be rescaled to bring out its relation to the normal curve.

and denominator by $(n - r)!$—becomes

$$C(10,4) = \frac{10 \cdot 9 \cdot 8 \cdot 7}{1 \cdot 2 \cdot 3 \cdot 4} = 210.$$

Now it is not difficult to compute the probability of a poker flush. There are $C(13,5)$ possible flushes in each suit, a total of $4C(13,5)$ in the four suits. The total number of possible poker hands is $C(52,5)$. Hence the probability of getting a flush out of all the hands that might be dealt is

$$\frac{4C(13,5)}{C(52,5)} = \frac{4\frac{13 \cdot 12 \cdot 11 \cdot 10 \cdot 9}{1 \cdot 2 \cdot 3 \cdot 4 \cdot 5}}{\frac{52 \cdot 51 \cdot 50 \cdot 49 \cdot 48}{1 \cdot 2 \cdot 3 \cdot 4 \cdot 5}} = \frac{33}{16{,}600}.$$

This comes out to about two chances in 1,000 of drawing a flush of any kind in a five-card deal from a full deck.

Let us proceed to investigate probability further by the classic device of coin-tossing. Suppose I toss a coin 10 times; what is the probability that in the 10 throws I shall get exactly four

PROBABILITY DEMONSTRATOR shown on the opposite page mechanically produces an approximation to the bell-shaped "normal," or Gaussian, distribution. The little brown balls rolling from the reservoir at the top pass an array of hexagonal obstacles and collect in receptacles at the bottom. At each obstacle the probability ought in theory to be one-half that a ball will go to the right and one-half that it will go to the left. Thus the balls tend to distribute themselves according to the proportions of Pascal's triangle, shown in the top illustration above. In the photograph the balls falling through the array of obstacles are blurred because of their motion. The balls have not produced the full distribution curve because some are still moving through the channels. The apparatus is known as a Galton Board after Sir Francis Galton, who constructed the first one. The version shown here is based on a design by the Science Materials Center, patented under the name "Hexstat."

heads? Looking at the 10th row of the Pascal triangle, we see that the possible sequences of heads and/or tails for 10 tosses add up to a total of 1,024. In this total there are 210 sequences containing exactly four heads. Therefore, if the coin-tossing is "honest," in the sense that all the 1,024 possible outcomes are equally likely, the probability of just four heads in 10 throws is 210/1,024, or roughly 21 percent.

The sum of all the entries in any given row (numbered n) of the Pascal triangle is equal to 2 to the nth power (for example, $1,024 = 2^{10}$). Thus in general the probability of tossing exactly k heads in a sequence of n throws is $C(n,k)/2^n$. Suppose we plot the various probabilities of tossing exactly 0, 1, 2, 3 and so on up to 10 heads in 10 throws in the form of a series of rectangles, with the height of each rectangle representing the probability [*see **bottom illustration on preceding page***]. The graph peaks at the center (a probability of 252/1,024 for five heads) and tapers off gradually to both sides (down to probabilities of 1/1,024 for no heads and for 10 heads). If we plot the same kind of graph for 10,000 tosses, it becomes much wider and lower: the high point (for 5,000 heads) is not in the neighborhood of 25 percent but only $1/100\sqrt{\pi}$, or approximately .56 percent. (It may seem odd that in increasing the number of tosses we greatly reduce the chances of heads coming up exactly half the time, but the oddity disappears as soon as one realizes that a strict 50–50 division between heads and tails is still only one of the possible outcomes, and with each toss we have increased the total number of possible results.)

Drawn on the basis I have just described, the probability graph for a large number of tosses is so flat that it is hardly distinguishable from a straight line. But by increasing the heights of all the rectangles by a certain factor ($\sqrt{n/2}$) and shrinking the width of the base by the same factor, one can see that the tops of the rectangles trace out a symmetrical curve with the peak in the middle. The larger the number of tosses, the closer this profile comes to a smooth, continuous curve, which is described by the equation

$$y = \frac{1}{\sqrt{2\pi}} e^{-x^2/2}.$$

The e is our celebrated number 2.71828..., the base of the natural logarithms. (If a bank were foolish enough to offer interest at the annual rate of 100 percent and were to compound this interest continuously—not just daily, hourly or even every second but every instant—one dollar would grow to \$2.71828... at the end of a year.)

The close approach of the probability diagram to a continuous curve with many tosses of a coin illustrates what is called a law of large numbers. If an "honest" coin is tossed hundreds of thousands or millions of times, the distribution of heads in the series of trials, when properly centered and scaled on a graph, will follow almost exactly the curve whose formula I have just given. This curve has become one of the most celebrated in science. Known as the "normal" or "Gaussian" curve, it has been used (with varying degrees of justification) to describe the distribution of heights of men and of women, the sizes of peas, the weights of newborn babies, the velocities of particles in a gas and numerous other properties of the physical and biological worlds.

The remarkable connection between coin-tossing and the normal curve was both gratifying and suggestive. It provided one of the main stimuli for the further development of probability theory. It also formed the basis for the "random walk" model of tracing the paths of particles. This in turn solved the mystery of Brownian motion, thus establishing the foundations of modern atomic theory.

Probability today is a cornerstone of all the sciences, and its daughter, the science of statistics, enters into all human activities. How prophetic, in retrospect, are the words of Laplace in his pioneering work *Théorie analytique des probabilités*, published in 1812: "It is remarkable that a science which began with the consideration of games of chance should have become the most important object of human knowledge. ... The most important questions of life are, for the most part, really only problems of probability."

It seems to be a characteristic of "the most important objects of human knowledge" that they generally take a long time to become established as such. After Laplace interest in probability theory declined, and through the rest of the 19th century and the first two decades of the 20th it all but disappeared as a mathematical discipline. Only a few mathematicians went on with the work; among these were the brilliant and original Russian mathematicians P. L. Chebyshëv and his pupil A. A. Markov (which accounts for the strong development of probability theory in the U.S.S.R. today). There were spectacular applications of probability theory to physics, not only by Albert Einstein and Marian Smoluchowski in their solution of the problem of Brownian motion but also by James Clerk Maxwell, Ludwig Boltzmann and Josiah Willard Gibbs in the kinetic theory of gases. At the turn of the century Henri Poincaré and David Hilbert,

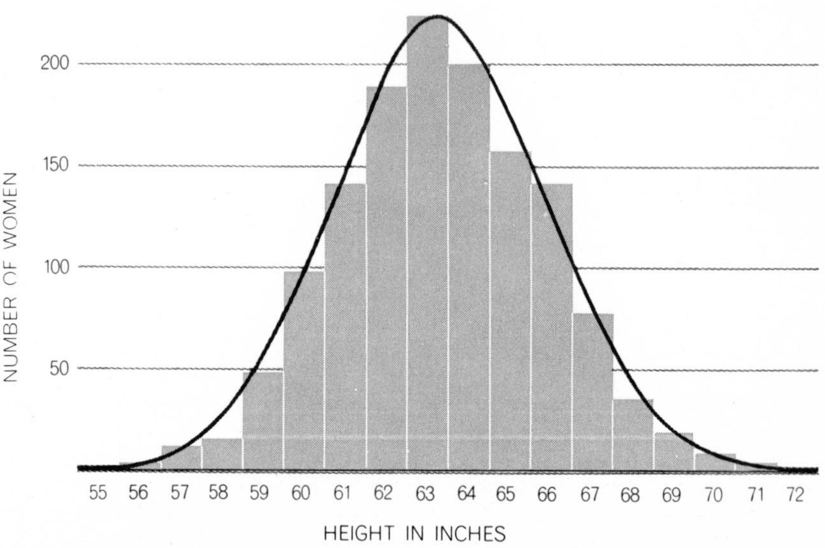

HEIGHTS OF WOMEN produce a histogram to which the normal-distribution curve can be fitted. There were 1,375 women in this sample population. The bell-shaped curve conforms to many other empirical distributions found in the physical and biological worlds.

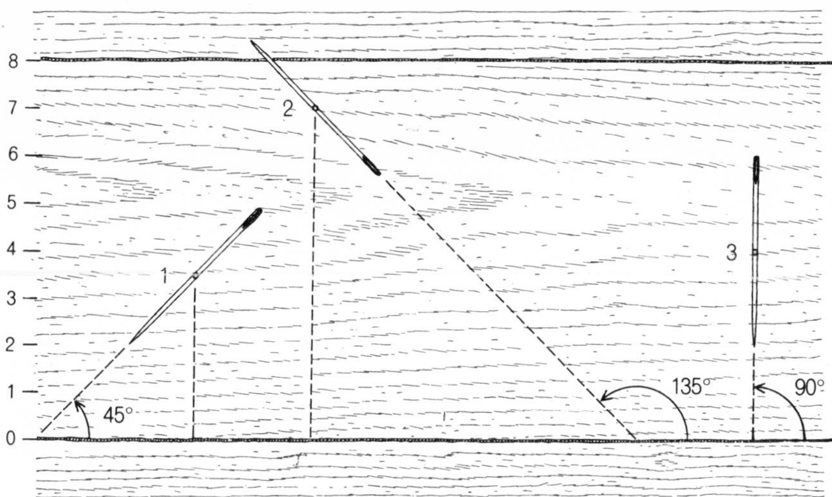

BUFFON NEEDLE PROBLEM involves the probability that a needle shorter than the width of a plank will fall across the crack between two planks. Here each needle is half as long as the plank is wide. The eight units used to measure the plank represent inches.

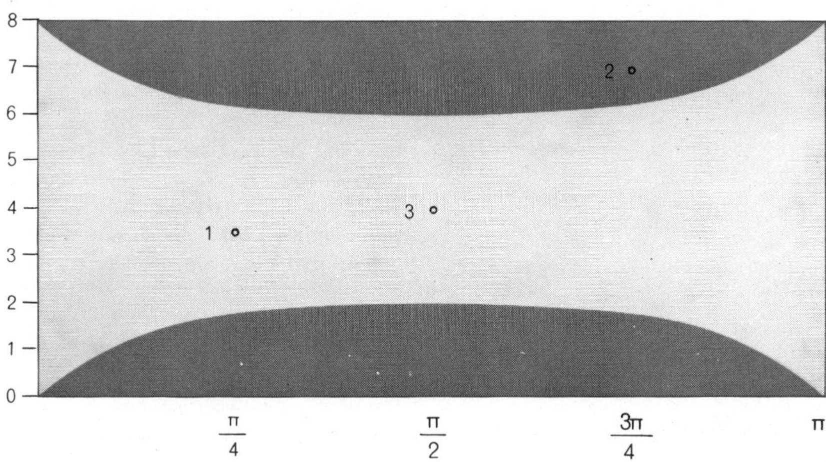

ABSTRACT DIAGRAM also shows positions of the three needles. The horizontal scale represents the angle of each needle with respect to the bottom edge of the plank. The angle is given in terms of π, which is defined as 180 degrees. The vertical scale is the width of the plank in inches. The three dots are the center points of the needles. Called the "sample space," the rectangle represents all the possible positions in which a needle can fall. The dark colored areas cover all the positions in which a needle lies across a crack.

the two greatest mathematicians of the day, tried to revive interest in probability theory, but in spite of their original and provocative contributions there was remarkably little response.

Why this apathy toward the subject among professional mathematicians? There were various reasons. The main one was the feeling that the entire theory seemed to be built on loose and nonrigorous foundations. Laplace's definition of probability, for instance, is based on the assumption that all the possible outcomes in question are equally likely; since this notion itself is a statement of probability, the definition appears to be a circular one. And that was not the worst objection. The field was plagued with apparent paradoxes and other difficulties. The rising standards of rigor in all branches of mathematics made probability seem an unprofitable subject to cultivate.

In the 1930's, however, it was restored to high standing among mathematicians by a significant clarification of its basic concepts and by its relation to measure theory, a branch of mathematics that goes back to Euclid and that early in this century was greatly extended and generalized by the French mathematicians Émile Borel and Henri Lebesgue. To understand and appreciate this development let us start with a celebrated problem in geometrical probability known as the Buffon needle problem. If a needle of a certain length (say four inches) is thrown at random on a floor made of planks wider than that length (say eight inches wide), what is the probability that the needle will fall across a crack between two planks? We can define the position of the needle at each throw by noting the location of the midpoint of the needle on a plank and the angle between the needle and a given crack [*see upper illustration at left*]. Now, we can also show the various possible positions of the needle by means of an abstract diagram in the form of a rectangle [*see lower illustration at left*], in which the height represents the width of the plank and the base represents the angle (in terms of π, with π equal to 180 degrees, $\pi/2$ equal to 90 degrees and so on).

This rectangle as a whole, whose area is πd, represents all the possible positions in which the needle can fall. Technically it is called the "sample space," a general term used to denote all the possible outcomes in any probability experiment. (In tossing 10 coins the sample space is the set of all the 1,024 possible 10-item sequences of heads and/or tails.) In the needle experiment what part of the area of the rectangle corresponds to those positions of the needle in which it crosses a crack? This can be calculated by simple trigonometry, and it is represented by two sections within the rectangle with curved boundaries. Their combined area, which can be calculated by elementary calculus, turns out to be 2 times l, the length of the needle.

Now, if all the possible positions of the needle are equally likely, then the probability of the needle falling on a crack is the ratio of the dark colored areas in the illustration to the total area of the rectangle, or $2l/\pi d$. This is where the theory stumbles over its own arbitrary assumption. There is really no compelling reason to treat all the points in this abstract rectangle as equally likely, but the assumption is so natural as to appear inevitable. The degree of arbitrariness was dramatized by the French mathematician J. L. F. Bertrand, who devised examples (known as Bertrand paradoxes) in which, from assumptions that seemed equally natural, he could obtain quite different answers to a probability problem.

This was an unhappy situation, and a deeper understanding of the role and of the nature of probabilistic assumptions

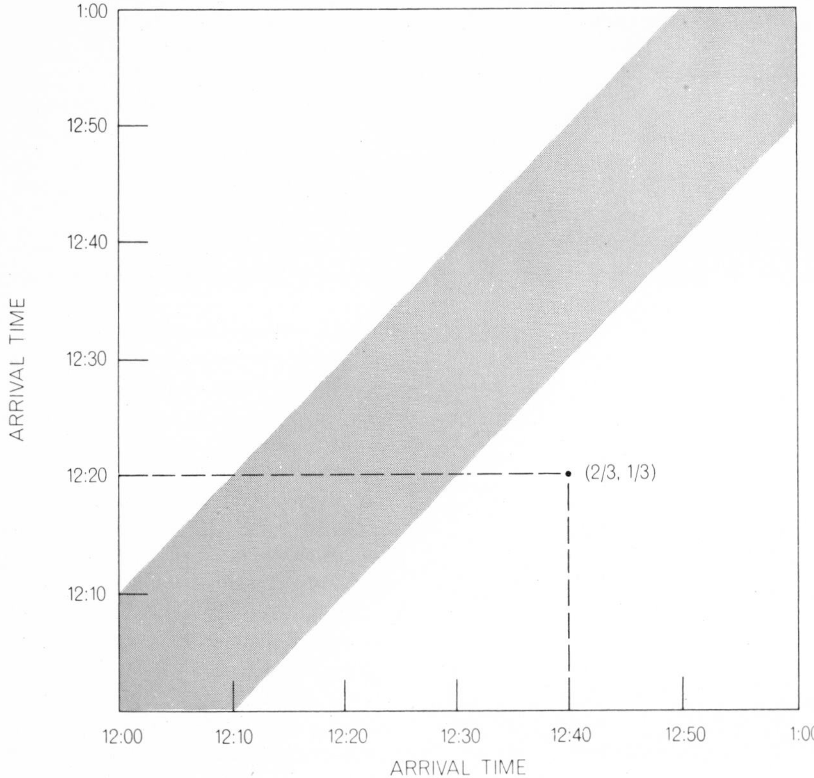

POSSIBLE ARRIVAL TIMES of two suburbanites planning to meet at a library between 12:00 noon and 1:00 P.M. can be plotted. Arrival times for one person are on the vertical scale, for the other on the horizontal scale. Colored area covers region corresponding to a meeting. In order to meet they must arrive at library within 10 minutes of each other. As can be seen, if one arrives at 12:20 (a third of the way up) and the other at 12:40 (two-thirds of the way across), they will not meet. The (1/3, 2/3) point falls outside the shaded region.

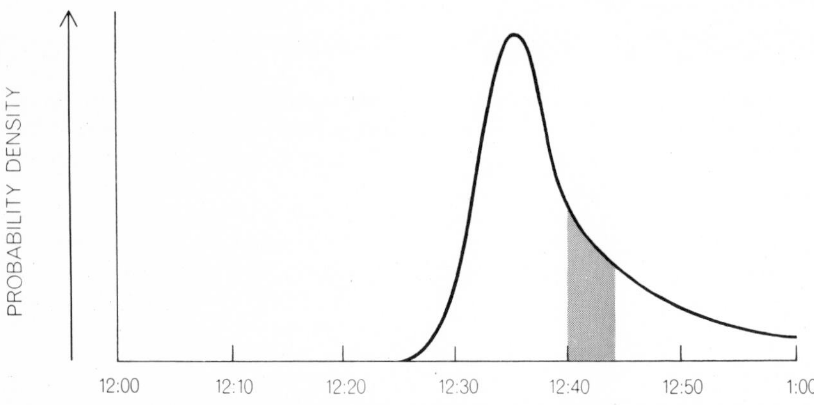

PROBABILITY-DENSITY CURVE illustrates degree of unpredictability of arrival time if there is only one train, coming in at 12:20. Most likely meeting time at library is 12:35. Area of shaded portion represents probability of arrival between 12:40 and 12:44 P.M.

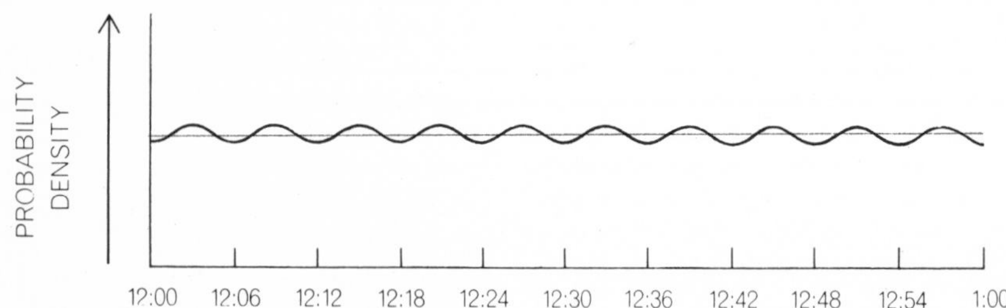

TRAINS ARRIVING EVERY SIX MINUTES give density curve shown by black line. The colored straight line is the "curve" in case all the arrival times are equally likely.

was called for. I can best explain the modern view of these matters by means of another example.

Suppose two friends living in different suburbs of New York City want to meet in front of the Forty-second Street Public Library at noontime. Railroad schedules (and performance) being what they are, the friends can only count on arriving sometime between 12:00 noon and 1:00 P.M. They agree to show up at the library somewhere in that interval, with the stipulation that, in order not to waste too much time waiting, each will wait only 10 minutes after arriving and then leave if the other has not shown up. What is the probability of their actually meeting?

I should mention that, although this case is admittedly artificial, it is by no means a trivial problem. Extended to many members instead of just two, it is analogous to (but far simpler than) an important unsolved problem in statistical mechanics whose solution would shed much light on the theory of changes of states of matter—for instance, from solid to liquid.

If we assume that each of the two friends may arrive anytime between 12:00 and 1:00, we can plot a geometrical "sample space" as in the Buffon needle problem. One person's possible times of arrival are denoted on the x axis, the other's on the y axis [*see top illustration on this page*]. We can then designate every possible pair of arrival times by a point in the square graph. Those points that lie within the part of the square that represents arrival times no more than 10 minutes apart will signify a meeting; all the other points will mean "no meeting." Taking the ratio of the two areas as the probability, as in the needle problem, we can calculate that the probability of the two friends meeting is 11/36—not quite one chance in three.

This case makes clear that we have made two different assumptions. Let us analyze them in a more general context.

In very general terms probability theory, as a mathematical discipline, is concerned with the problem of calculating the probabilities of complex events consisting of collections of "elementary" events whose probabilities are known or postulated. For example, in rolling two dice the appearance of a 10 is a "complex" event that consists of three elementary events: (1) the first die shows a 4 and the second a 6, (2) the first die shows a 5 and the second a 5 and

(3) the first die shows a 6 and the second a 4. The meeting of our two friends is also a complex event; an example of an elementary event would be the arrival of one of the friends in the interval between 12:20 and 12:25.

In our calculation of the probability of the two friends meeting, the first assumption we made was that each of the two individuals may arrive anytime between 12:00 and 1:00, all times of arrival being "equally likely." (The corresponding assumption about the dice is that any one of the six faces of each die may come up with equal probability.) But if each person is limited to only one train scheduled to arrive at Grand Central during the hour (say at 12:20 or later), this assumption is completely unrealistic: he will certainly not arrive in the early part of the hour. The situation corresponds to the two dice being loaded. On the other hand, if there are six scheduled trains, due to arrive at 10-minute intervals from 12:00 on, and if they tend to be haphazardly off schedule, the assumption becomes more reasonable, although it may still not be strictly correct to say that all the times of arrival are equally probable.

The second assumption we made was that the arrival times of the two friends are completely independent of each other. This assumption, like the first, is of crucial importance. In mathematical terms it is reflected in the rule of the multiplication of probabilities. This rule states that when individual events are independent of each other, the probability of the complex event that *all* of them will occur is the product of individual probabilities. (Actually from a strictly logical point of view the rule of the multiplication of probabilities constitutes a *definition* of independence.) Independence is assumed in the throw of two dice (which presumably are not linked in any way) as well as in the case of the two suburbanites coming into New York (provided that they have not "coupled" their arrival times by an understanding about the selection of particular trains).

It should be noted that there is an important difference between the dice-throwing and suburbanite-meeting problems. In the first case the number of possible outcomes is finite (just 36), whereas in the second it is infinite, in the sense that the arrival times may occur at any instant within the hour; that is to say, the sample space is a continuum with an infinite number of "points."

To enable one to go on with calculations of probabilities two very general rules, or axioms, are introduced. The first concerns mutually exclusive events: events such that the occurrence of one precludes the occurrence of any other. For such events the probability that at least one will occur is the *sum* of individual probabilities (the axiom of additivity). The second concerns pairs of events such that one *implies* the other. In this case the probability that one will occur but not the other is obtained by subtracting the smaller probability from the larger.

Now, these rules for calculating probabilities of complex events are identical with those used for calculating areas and volumes in geometry. We can substitute the word "set" for "event" and "area" or "volume" for "probability." The problem then is to assign

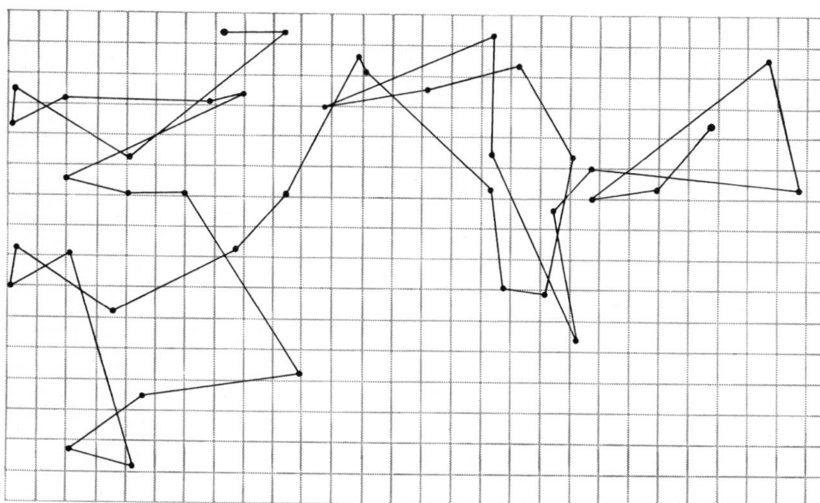

BROWNIAN PATH is taken by a particle being "kicked around" by molecules of a surrounding liquid or gas. A stochastic process (it varies continuously with time), Brownian motion can be analyzed and modeled (*illustration below*) by probabilistic techniques.

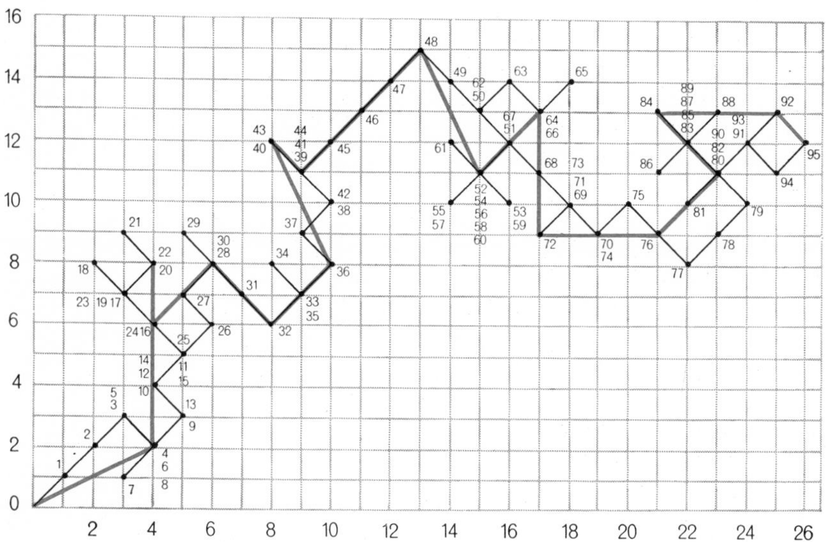

BROWNIAN MODEL can be constructed from records of coin tosses. Two series of 90-odd tosses of a coin were used, one plotted on the horizontal scale, the other on the vertical scale. The cumulative total of tails at each toss was subtracted from the cumulative total of heads. The first three tosses in both series were heads and the fourth toss in the horizontal series was heads, but the fourth toss in the vertical series was tails. Numbers on the dots are the toss numbers. Colored line traces "position" at every fourth toss, just as the track of a Brownian particle recorded by a camera shows only a small fraction of the staggering number of "kicks" such a particle receives from molecules around it.

appropriate areas to sets, and this is the province of measure theory, which has been given that name because the word "measure" is now used to refer to areas of very complex sets.

If we go back to the problem of the two suburbanite friends, we note that the set that corresponds to their meeting is quite simple. Its area, or probability, is well within Euclid's framework, and its calculation can be based on the manipulation of only a finite number of nonoverlapping rectangles. In the Buffon needle problem, since the region of interest is bounded by curves, one must allow an infinite number of rectangles, but the calculation of the area is still relatively simple and requires nothing more than elementary calculus. What was surprising and exciting about measure theory as it was de-

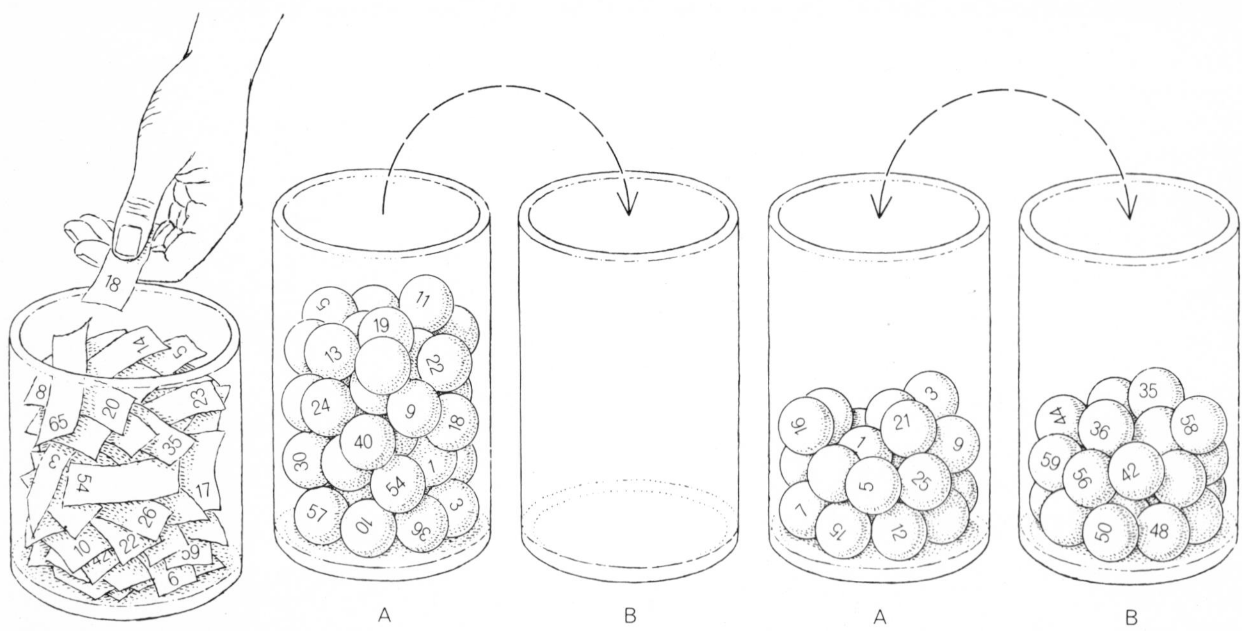

EHRENFEST MODEL for illustrating a Markov chain involves a game in which balls are moved from one container to another according to numbers drawn at random from a third container (*left*). As long as there are many more balls in container *A* than in container *B*, the flow of balls will be strongly from *A* to *B*. The probability of finding in *A* the ball with the drawn number changes in a way that depends on past drawings. This form of dependence of probability on past events is called a Markov chain.

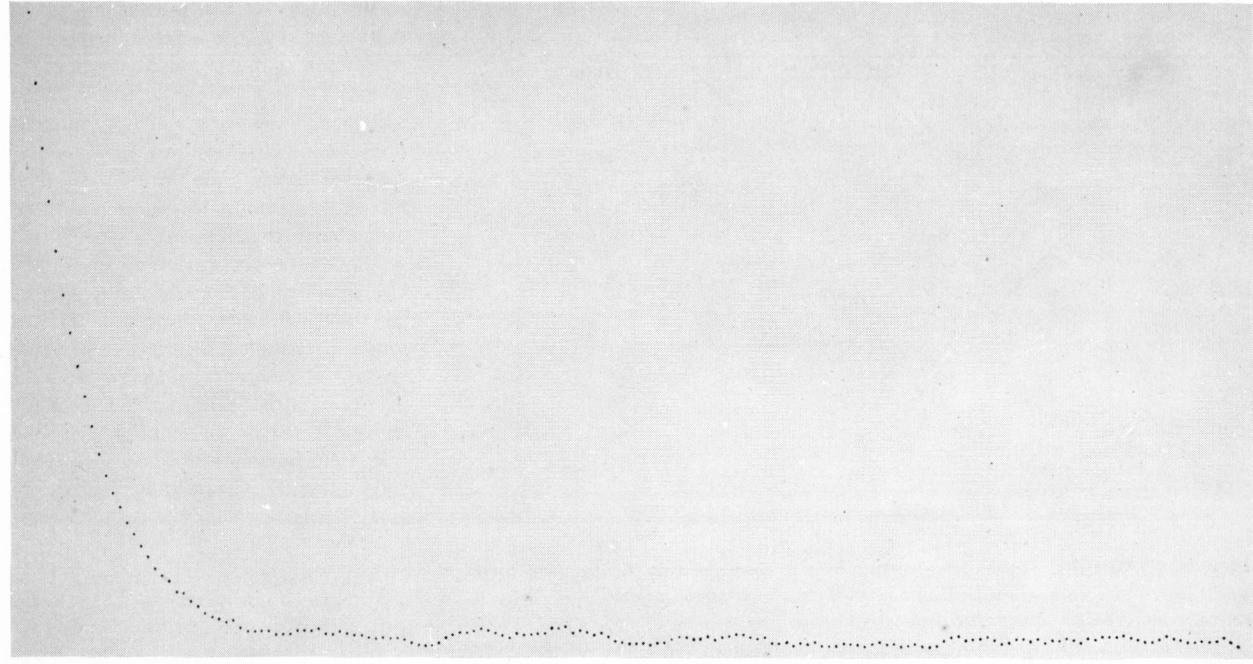

PLAYED ON A COMPUTER, an Ehrenfest game with 16,384 hypothetical balls and 200,000 drawings took just two minutes. Starting with all the balls in container *A*, the number of balls in *A* was recorded with a dot every 1,000 drawings. It declined exponentially until equilibrium was reached with 8,192 balls (half of them) in each container. After that fluctuations were not great.

veloped by Borel and Lebesgue was that, by merely postulating that the measure of an *infinite* collection of unconnected sets should be the *sum* of the measures of the individual ones (corresponding to requiring that the probability that at least one out of *infinitely many* mutually exclusive events will occur should be the sum of individual probabilities), it was possible to assign measures to extremely complex sets.

Because of this, measure theory opened the way to the posing and solving of problems in probability that would have been unthinkable in Laplace's time. Here, for instance, is one of the problems that received much attention in the 1920's and 1930's and contributed greatly to bringing probability theory into the mainstream of mathematics.

Consider the infinite series

$$\frac{1}{1}+\frac{1}{2}+\frac{1}{3}+\frac{1}{4}+\frac{1}{5}+\frac{1}{6}+\frac{1}{7}+\frac{1}{8}+\cdots$$

This is known as a diverging series; that is, by adding more and more terms one could exceed any given number.

Suppose the signs between the terms, instead of being all pluses, were made plus or minus at random by means of independent tosses of an honest coin. What is the probability that the resulting series would converge? That is to say, what is the probability that by extending the series to more and more terms one would come closer and closer to some terminating number?

To answer the question one must consider all the possible infinite sequences of heads and tails as the sample space. One sequence might begin: *H H T T T H T H*.... If we let *H* represent plus and *T* represent minus, the number series above becomes

$$+\frac{1}{1}+\frac{1}{2}-\frac{1}{3}-\frac{1}{4}-\frac{1}{5}+\frac{1}{6}-\frac{1}{7}+\frac{1}{8}\cdots$$

With each such sequence we can associate a real number, t, between 0 and 1, and each t can be represented by a binary number in which the digit 1 denotes *H* and the digit 0 stands for *T*. The sequence cited above is then written as $t = .11000101\ldots$. The binary digits form a model of independent tosses of a coin. Now those t's that will yield convergent series form a set, and the probability that t falls into this set is the "measure" of the set. It turns out that the set of hypothetical t's that do *not* yield convergent series is so sparse that its measure, or probability, is zero (although the set has a very complex structure and is far from being empty). Hence the answer to the problem is that, when the series above is given random signs, the probability that it will converge is 1.

The foregoing is an example of problems in "denumerable probabilities," that is, those involving events described in discrete terms. During the past two decades mathematicians have pursued an even more productive investigation of the theory of "stochastic processes": the probabilistic analysis of phenomena that vary continuously in time. Stochastic processes arise in physics, astronomy, economics, genetics, ecology and many other fields of science. The simplest and most celebrated example of a stochastic process is the Brownian motion of a particle.

The late Norbert Wiener conceived the idea of basing the theory of Brownian motion on a theory of measure in a set of all continuous paths. This idea proved enormously fruitful for probability theory. It breathed new life into old problems such as that of determining the electrostatic potential of a conductor of "arbitrary" shape, a problem that occupied the minds of illustrious mathematicians for more than a century. More than that, it opened up entire new areas of research and led to fascinating connections between probability theory and other branches of mathematics.

A single article can only touch on a few of the main developments and sample problems in probability theory. The subject today embraces vast new fields such as information theory, the theory of queues, diffusion theory and mathematical statistics. One can sum up the position of probability in general by observing that it has become both an indispensable tool of the engineer and a thriving branch of pure mathematics now raised to a high level of formalism and rigor.

I want to close with a brief comment on the philosophical aspect of probability theory (in itself a vast subject on which many volumes have been written). The philosophical implications can be best illustrated by a specific case, and the one I shall discuss has to do with a conflict between the thermodynamic and the mechanical views of the behavior of matter.

Consider two containers, one containing gas, the other a vacuum. If the two containers are connected by a tube and a valve in the tube is suddenly opened, what happens? According to the second law of thermodynamics, gas rushes from container *A* into container *B* at an exponential rate until the pressure in the two containers is the same. This is an expression of the law of increasing entropy, which in its most pessimistic form predicts that ultimately all matter and energy in the universe will even out and settle down to what Rudolf Clausius, one of the fathers of the second law, called *Wärmetod* (heat death).

Now, the mechanical, or kinetic, view of matter pictures the situation in an entirely different way. True, the molecules of gas will tend to move from the region of higher pressure into the one of lower pressure, but the movement is not merely one-way. Bouncing against the walls and against one another, the molecules will take off in random directions, and those that travel into container *B* will be as likely to wander back to container *A* as to remain where they are. As a matter of fact, Poincaré showed in a mathematical theorem that a dynamical system such as this one would eventually return arbitrarily close to its original state, with all or virtually all the gas molecules back in container *A*.

In 1907 Paul and Tatiana Ehrenfest illustrated this idea with a simple and beautiful probabilistic model. Consider two containers, *A* and *B*, with a large number of numbered balls in *A* and none in *B*. From a container filled with numbered slips of paper pick a numeral at random (say 6) and then transfer the ball marked with that number from container *A* to container *B*. Put the slip of paper back and go on playing the game this way, each time drawing at random a number between 1 and *N* (the total number of balls originally in container *A*) and moving the ball of that number from the container where it happens to be to the other container [*see upper illustration on page 30*].

It is intuitively clear that as long as there are many more balls in *A* than there are in *B* the probability of drawing a number that corresponds to a ball in *A* will be considerably higher than vice versa. Thus the flow of balls at first will certainly be strongly from *A* to *B*. As the drawings continue, the probability of finding the drawn number in *A* will change in a way that depends on the past drawings. This form of dependence of probability on past events is called a Markov chain, and in the game we are considering, all pertinent facts can be explicitly and rigorously deduced. It turns out that, on an averaging basis, the number of balls in container *A* will indeed decrease at an exponential rate, as the thermodynamic theory predicts, until about half of the balls are in container *B*. But the calculation also shows that if the game is played long enough, then, with probability equal to 1, all the balls will eventually wind up back in container *A*, as Poincaré's theorem says!

How long, on the average, would it take to return to the initial state? The answer is 2^N drawings, which is a staggeringly large number even if the total number of balls (N) is as small as 100. This explains why behavior in nature, as we observe it, moves only in one direction instead of oscillating back and forth. The entire history of man is pitifully short compared with the time it would take for nature to reverse itself.

To test the theoretical calculations experimentally, the Ehrenfest game was played on a high-speed computer. It began with 16,384 "balls" in container *A*, and each run consisted of 200,000 drawings (which took less than two minutes on the computer). A curve was drawn showing the number of balls in *A* on the basis of the number recorded after every 1,000 drawings [*see lower illustration on page 30*]. As was to be expected, the curve of decline in the number of balls in *A* was almost perfectly exponential. After the number nearly reached the equilibrium level (that is, 8,192, or half the original number) the curve became wiggly, moving randomly up and down around that number. The wiggles were somewhat exaggerated by the vagaries of the machine itself, but they represented actual fluctuations that were bound to occur in the number of balls in *A*.

Those small, capricious fluctuations are models of the variability in nature and are all that stands between us and the heat death to which we are seemingly condemned by the second law of thermodynamics! Probability theory has reconciled the apparent conflict between the thermodynamic and the kinetic views of nature by showing that there is no real contradiction between them if the second law is interpreted flexibly. In fact, the development of the theory of probability in the 20th century has changed our attitudes to such an extent that we no longer expect the laws of nature to be construed rigidly or dogmatically.

5

THE MONTE CARLO METHOD

DANIEL D. McCRACKEN • May 1955

During World War II physicists at the Los Alamos Scientific Laboratory came to a knotty problem on the behavior of neutrons. How far would neutrons travel through various materials? The question had a vital bearing on shielding and other practical considerations. But it was an extremely complicated one to answer. To explore it by experimental trial and error would have been expensive, time-consuming and hazardous. On the other hand, the problem seemed beyond the reach of theoretical calculations. The physicists had most of the necessary basic data: they knew the average distance a neutron of a given speed would travel in a given substance before it collided with an atomic nucleus, what the probabilities were that the neutron would bounce off instead of being absorbed by the nucleus, how much energy the neutron was likely to lose after a given collision, and so on. However, to sum all this up in a practicable formula for predicting the outcome of a whole sequence of such events was impossible.

At this crisis the mathematicians John von Neumann and Stanislas Ulam cut the Gordian knot with a remarkably simple stroke. They suggested a solution which in effect amounts to submitting the problem to a roulette wheel. Step by step the probabilities of the separate events are merged into a composite picture which gives an approximate but workable answer to the problem.

The mathematical technique von Neumann and Ulam applied had been known for many years. When it was revived for the secret work at Los Alamos, von Neumann gave it the code name "Monte Carlo." The Monte Carlo method was so successful on neutron diffusion problems that its popularity later spread. It is now being used in various fields, notably in operations research.

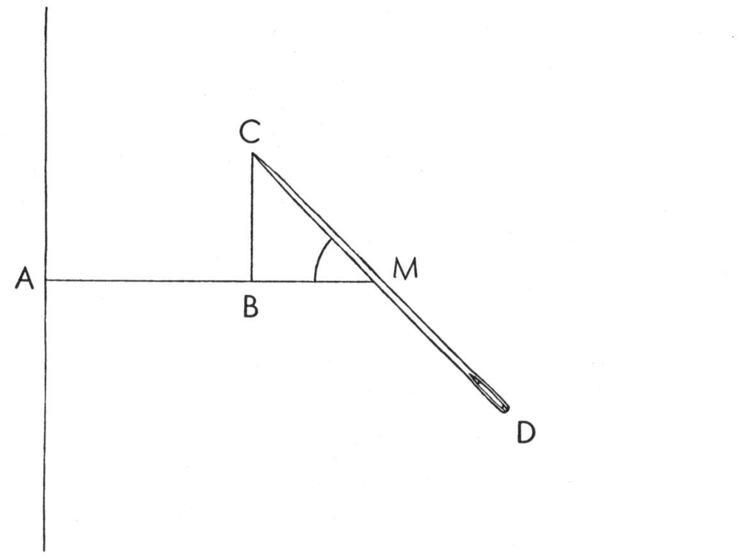

NEEDLE PROBLEM is illustrated by a needle lying on a piece of paper ruled with parallel lines. The length of the needle is two inches; the distance between the lines, four inches. If the needle is thrown on the paper at random, how often will it land on one of the lines?

To illustrate the method let us start with the simple, classic Buffon needle problem. You get a short needle, draw on a sheet of paper several parallel lines spaced precisely twice the length of the needle apart, and then toss the needle onto the paper again and again in a random fashion. How often will the needle land on a line? The mathematicians say that the ratio of hits to trials should be 1 to 3.1416. That is, dividing the number of hits into the number of throws, you should come out with the number 3.1416 (pi) if you continue the trials long enough (and throw the needle truly at random, without trying either to hit or to miss the lines).

I tried the experiment, with the following results. In the first 10 throws, the needle landed on a line four times. In the language of the statistician, there were four "successes" in 10 trials. The quotient is 2.5, which one must admit is not very close to 3.1416. In 100 trials there were 28 hits for an estimate of 3.57, also not good, but better. After 1,000 trials there were 333 hits for an estimate of 3, and my arm was tired.

This was hardly good enough to quit on, but the improvement with increasing numbers was not rapid, so it did not seem practicable to go on by hand. The fact is that the accuracy of a Monte Carlo approximation improves only as the square of the number of trials: to double the expected accuracy of the answer, you must quadruple the number of trials. I decided to make a calculating machine do the work, and I translated the problem to a medium-sized electronic calculator.

It is no difficult matter to make a calculating machine carry out operations which simulate the results of dropping a needle on ruled paper. Consider the diagram on the preceding page. To describe the situation to the machine we must decide on a way of specifying the position of the needle relative to the nearest line. It does not matter on which side of this line the needle lies; nothing is changed if we turn the paper around. We can see that the distance from the midpoint of the needle to the nearest line (MA) is specified by a number between zero and two inches. The only other information needed to specify the position of the needle completely is the angle it makes with the perpendicular (MA) to the line. The angle is somewhere between zero and 90 degrees (not 180 degrees, because we are concerned only with the closer end of the needle). Given these two quantities, the machine can easily decide whether the needle touches a line; all it needs to do is to compute the distance MB (the cosine of the angle) and note whether it is less or greater than the distance MA—in the machine's terms, whether the difference is positive or negative.

Now to find out by experiment in what proportion of the trials a needle dropped at random would touch the line, we would like to test all possible positions in which the needle might land. To do this we would have to consider all possible combinations of distances and angles—essentially the method of the integral calculus. Obviously we are not going to tackle this infinite task. But in place of attempting a systematic exploration of all positions, we can take a random sample of them, and this should give us a reasonably accurate approximation of the correct answer, as a sampling poll may do.

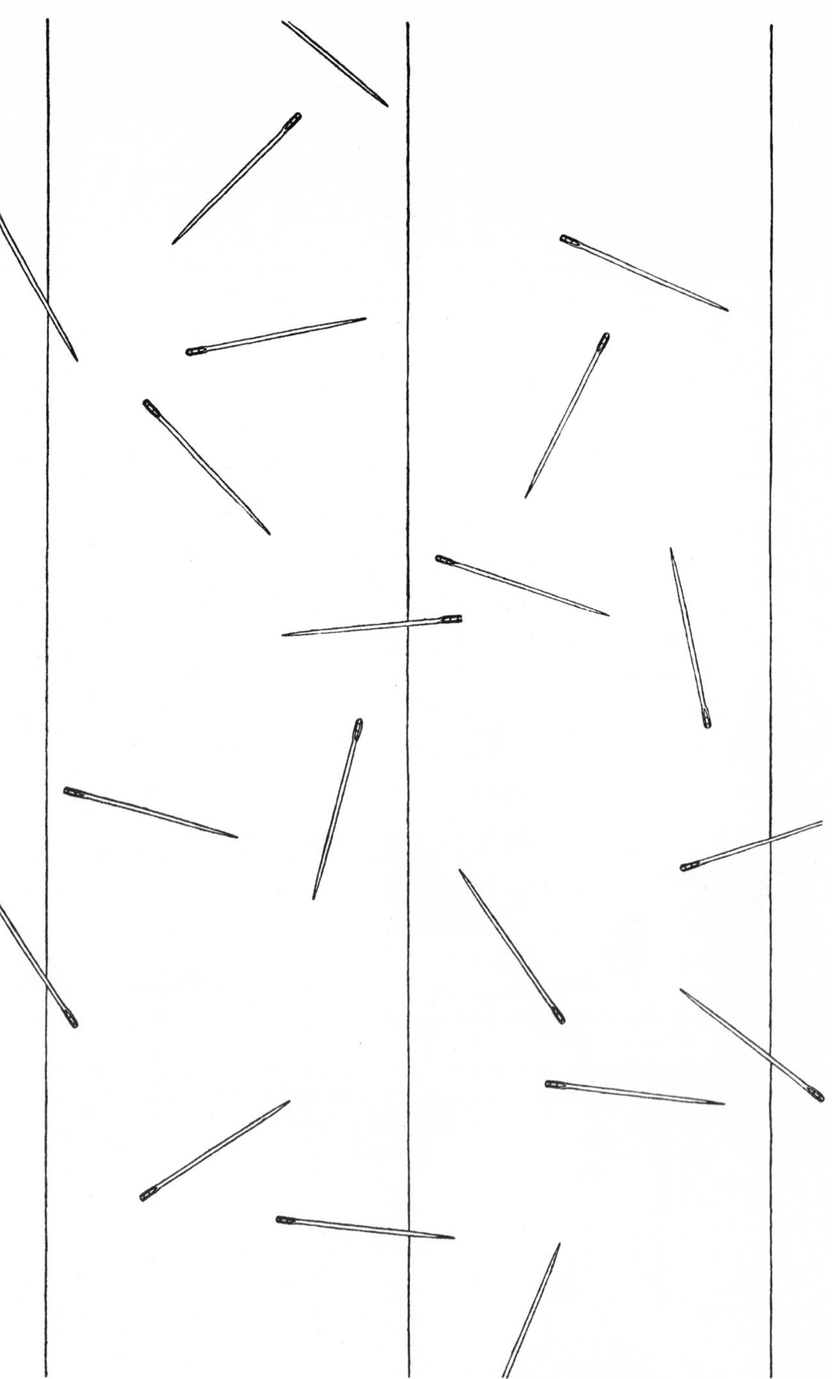

ACTUAL EXPERIMENT on the needle problem was tried by artist Eric Mose. Each needle represents a toss and shows the position in which the needle landed with respect to the lines. In a sufficiently large number of trials, the ratio of hits to trials will be 1 to 3.1416 or pi.

How shall we select the random sample? This is where the Monte Carlo method comes in. Suppose we built a roulette wheel with 20 compartments, representing 20 different distances from the line (up to two inches) for the needle midpoint. A spin of the wheel would select the distance for us in a random manner, and over many trials each of the 20 distances would be selected about the same number of times. With a similar wheel we would pick the angle each time in the same random fashion. Then a series of spins of the two wheels would give us a random set of positions, just as if we had actually dropped a needle at random on ruled paper.

Of course the wheel-spinning method would be more cumbersome than dropping the needle, but there are ways of doing about the same thing with numbers and a calculating machine. First we get up two lists of numbers: one for distances in the range between zero and two inches, the other for angles in the range between zero and 90 degrees. The numbers are chosen at random to cover the whole range in each case without favoring any part of the range; we can take them from some list of numbers already checked for randomness or we can make our own list from, say, a table of logarithms, taking the numbers' last three digits. Then we put the calculator to work computing whether various combinations of the distance and angle numbers place the needle on a line or not (*i.e.*, whether the difference between MB and MA is positive or negative). Repeating the operation many, many times, we can get as close to precision as we like; statistical principles tell us the degree of precision we can expect from a given number of trials.

The moderately fast computer I had available when I made the experiment was able to perform 100 "trials" per minute. In about an hour the machine ran through 6,000 trials, and there were 1,925 "hits." In other words, the estimate of pi was 3.12, which is as good as can be expected for 6,000 trials.

Even this simple case required a rapid computer. Most applications of the Monte Carlo method of course are much more complex. However, the present high-speed computers make them feasible: there are machines which can perform 5,000 trials per minute on the Buffon needle problem.

Let us see now how the method works on a simple problem in neutron diffusion. Suppose we want to know what percentage of the neutrons in a given beam would get through a tank of water of a given size without being absorbed or losing most of their speed. No formula could describe precisely the fate of all the neutrons. The Monte Carlo approach consists in pretending to trace the "life histories" of a large sample of neutrons in the beam. We imagine the neutrons wandering about in the water and colliding occasionally with a hydrogen or oxygen nucleus—remember that to a neutron water looks like vast open spaces dotted here and there with tiny nuclei. We shall follow our neutrons one by one through their adventures.

We know how far a neutron travels, on the average, before it encounters a nucleus, the relative probability that this encounter will be with oxygen or with hydrogen, the relative chances that the neutron will be absorbed by the nucleus or bounce off, and certain other necessary information. Let us, then, take a specific neutron and follow its life history. It is a slow-moving neutron, and its first incident is a collision with a hydrogen nucleus. We know (from experiments) that the chances are 100 to one the neutron will bounce off from such a collision. To decide what it will do in this instance, we figuratively spin a roulette wheel with 100 equal compartments marked "bounced off" and one marked "absorbed." If the wheel says "absorbed," that is the end of the neutron's history. If it says "bounced off," we perhaps spin another appropriately marked wheel to decide what the neutron's new direction is and how much energy it lost. Then we must spin another wheel to decide how far it travels to the next collision and whether that collision is with oxygen or hydrogen. Thus we follow the neutron until it is absorbed, loses so much energy that it is no longer of interest or gets out of the tank. We go on to accumulate a large number of such histories and obtain a more or less precise figure for the percentage of neutrons that would escape from the tank. The degree of precision depends on the number of trials.

In practice, of course, we do not use roulette wheels but random numbers, as in the previous example. I have omitted much of the detail of the calculation for the sake of simplicity and clarity. In one very simple problem on which I assisted, an electronic calculator labored for three hours to trace the life histories of 10,000 neutrons through 1.5 million collisions. I would have had to sit at a desk calculator for some years to accomplish the same results.

As a third illustration of the Monte Carlo method, let us take a simple problem in operations research. Imagine a woodworking shop consisting of a lathe, a drill press and a saw, with three men to operate the machines. The shop makes one model of chair and one model of table. The question is: How should the work of the shop be scheduled to yield the greatest production, considering a number of variable conditions affecting output?

Certain basic information must be gathered before any calculation can begin. How long does it take on each machine to do the necessary work on each piece of wood? How much does the time needed for each job fluctuate because of fatigue, boredom or other personal factors? How frequently do the machines break down? After the data are gathered, a way is devised to make the computer simulate the operation of the shop under specified conditions of scheduling. We will not go into the details here; perhaps enough has been presented in the other examples to give an indication of what has to be done. The computation is properly classified as Monte Carlo

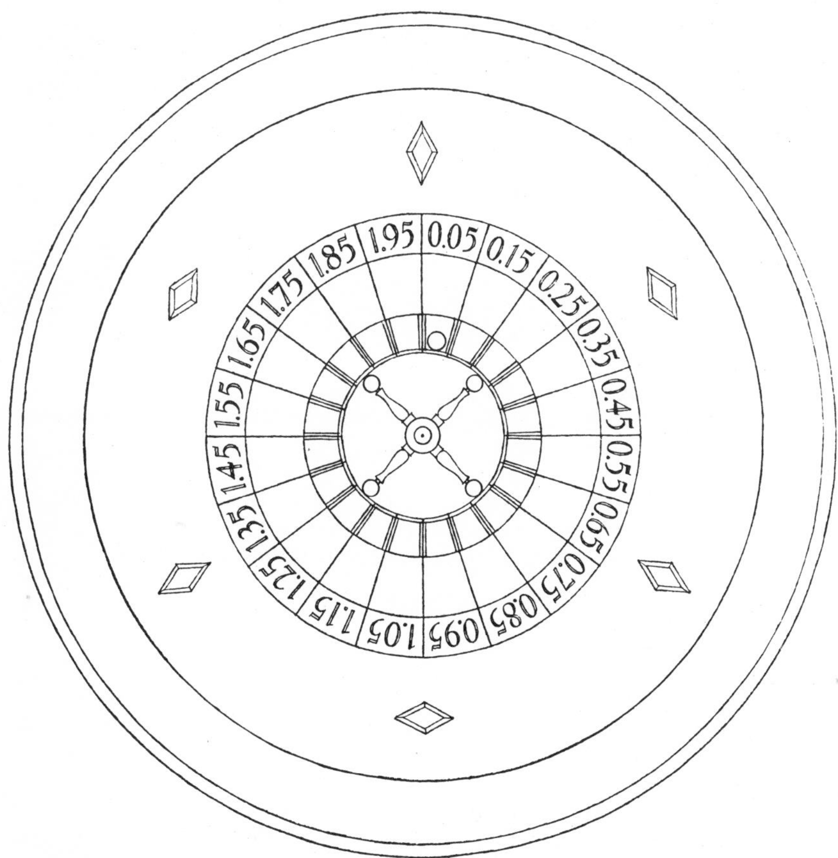

ROULETTE WHEEL especially designed for the needle problem depicted on the preceding two pages illustrates a basic feature of the Monte Carlo method. Each compartment of the wheel represents one of 20 distances between zero and two inches, the length of the needle.

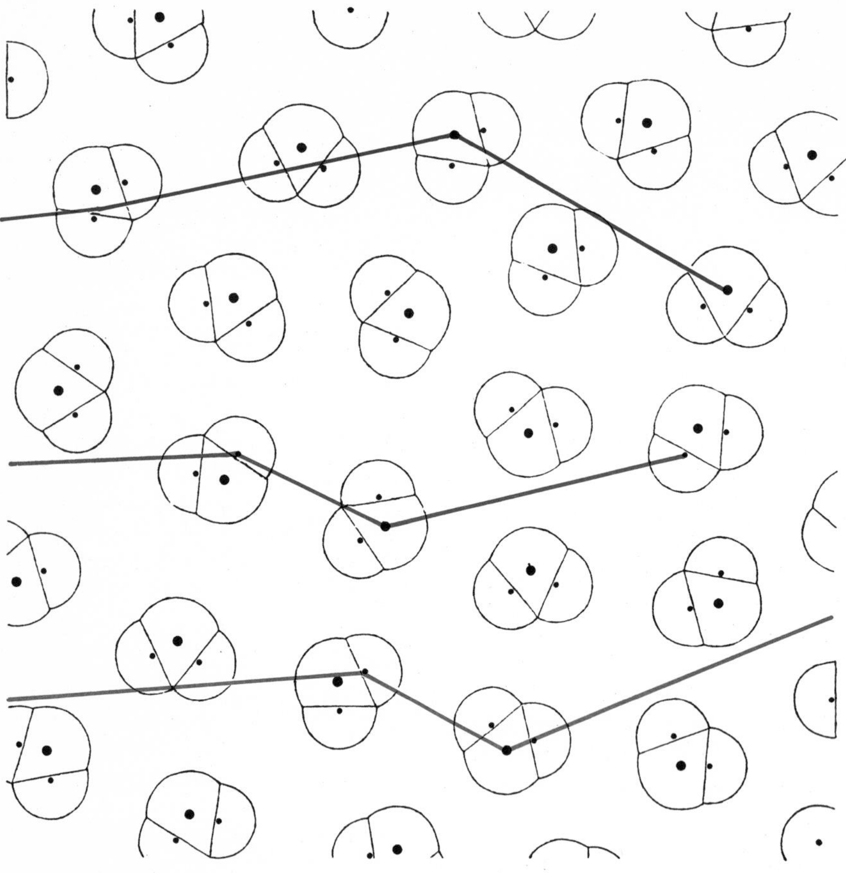

NEUTRONS wander through water in a series of events, each with a known probability. Here the microscopic structure of water is depicted in highly idealized form as consisting of simple molecules of H_2O. The larger sphere in each molecule is oxygen; the two smaller spheres are hydrogen. The neutrons (*colored lines*) may be absorbed by either an oxygen or a hydrogen nucleus or may bounce off from the collision. Some may escape from the water.

because it is necessary to spin a roulette wheel, or the equivalent, to pick samples from the known distributions. For example, we may know that a certain job may take anywhere from 12 to 16 minutes, and we have noted the percentages of the cases in which it is performed in 12, 13, 14, 15 and 16 minutes respectively. Which time shall we use for a particular case as we follow the course of a day's work in the shop? The question must be decided by random sampling of the type I have described.

With the Monte Carlo method high-speed computers can answer such questions as these: How should the schedule be changed to accommodate a market change demanding twice as many chairs as tables? How much could the shop produce, and at what cost, if one man should be absent for two days? How much would the total output be increased if one man should increase his work rate 20 per cent? Under a given schedule of work flow, what percentage of the time are the men idle because the work is piled up behind a bottleneck machine? If money values can be assigned to idle time, loss of orders due to low production and so on, dollars-and-cents answers can be given to problems of this kind in business operation.

The Monte Carlo method, in general, is used to solve problems which depend in some important way upon probability—problems where physical experimentation is impracticable and the creation of an exact formula is impossible. Often the process we wish to study consists of a long sequence of steps, each of which involves probability, as for instance the travels of the neutron through matter. We can write mathematical formulas for the probabilities at each collision, but we are often not able to write anything useful for the probabilities for the entire sequence.

Essentially the Monte Carlo method goes back to probability theory, which was developed from studies of gambling games. But it takes the opposite approach. The mathematicians who originated the probability theory derived their equations from theoretical questions based on the phenomenon of chance; the Monte Carlo method tries to use probability to find an answer to a physical question often having no relation to probability.

In the neutron problem, for example, the investigator's thinking might have been along these lines: "I have a physical situation which I wish to study. I don't think I'll even try to find an equation representing the entire problem. Even if I could find one, which is very doubtful, I probably wouldn't be able to get much useful information out of it. I'll just see if I can't find a game of chance which will give an answer to my questions, without ever going through the step of deriving an equation." In some other situations the investigator would reason: "The physical situation I am interested in has resulted in an equation which is very difficult to solve. I cannot possibly solve it in any reasonable length of time by usual methods. I wonder if I could devise some statistical method which would approximate the answer to my problem."

Much work remains to be done on the method. One is always faced with the unhappy choice of either inaccurate results or very large amounts of calculation. A problem which demands 100 million trials of some "experiment" is still impracticable, even on the fastest present computers. Another difficulty is that it is seldom possible to extend the results of a Monte Carlo calculation to another set of conditions. For instance, after we have solved the problem of the passage of neutrons through ordinary water, we have to start all over again to find out how they will behave in heavy water. Nevertheless, in spite of its various limitations the Monte Carlo method is able to give at least approximate answers to many questions where other mathematical techniques fail.

Many mathematicians are working to improve the method, especially to reduce the computation required and to determine exactly how much reliability can be attributed to its results in various types of problems. Up to now the technique has been used mainly on problems of nuclear physics, such as the diffusion of neutrons, the absorption of gamma rays, atomic pile shielding and the like. In the author's opinion, one of the most promising applications of the method is in operations research. It could be useful not only on production problems such as the one described here but also in telephone operation, traffic control, department-store inventory control and so on. Some of these possibilities are already being investigated. It is safe to say that we shall hear more from Monte Carlo in the next few years.

PART TWO

COMMUNICATION AND CONTROL

COMMUNICATION AND CONTROL

INTRODUCTION

The word "cybernetics" was invented by Norbert Wiener, the author of the first article in this section, about thirty years ago, to describe a new branch of science concerned with problems of communication and control. The preceding emphasis on "hard" science, which dealt with such concepts as energy, force, and power, had produced a technology whose achievements ranged from the internal combustion engine to the nuclear power plant. The field of cybernetics, which is only now emerging from adolescence, is the study of concepts such as information, communication, reliability, and feedback. At the heart of the attendant technology is the digital computer, which may well prove to be man's most important scientific creation of this century.

The key concepts of the cybernetic movement—communication and control—are closely allied, with interconnections and interdependencies at many levels, but it is helpful to view each of the two problems separately. The general topic of communication refers to the emission, transmission, reception, and storage of information. The engineering problem is how to do these things as efficiently as possible. The study of control is that of the effects of interdependence between behaving systems, with particular emphasis on the use of interdependence to establish and maintain stability in the behavior of one or more of the systems involved. One of the most fundamental concepts in control theory is that of feedback, the use of a fraction of the output of a system to activate a second system which then adjusts, in some way, the output of the first.

That the individuals who originated and have developed the field of cybernetics did not see their task as one of innovation in engineering is amply clear in the articles in this section. Indeed, these authors are convinced that the principles they are working with have universal pertinence in the understanding of behavioral processes. Moreover, they have not hesitated to say so.

As a result, the ideas that were developed by mathematicians and engineers to deal with the engineering problems were not overlooked by scientists studying physiological, behavioral, societal, and economic systems. These fresh conceptions, which were proving their usefulness in solving engineering problems, producing one astounding success after another, offered new insights, approaches, and conceptual tools to those studying the behavior of living organisms and groups of living organisms. New views emerged about the organization and function of the nervous system, both as a communication system in which "messages" are encoded and transmitted and as a control system regulating voluntary and involuntary muscular activity. Solutions to the problem of detecting a signal in a noisy channel have proven exceptionally helpful in the study of sensory and perceptual processes and are now being applied in the investigation of human memory, an area in which the principles of encoding and organization have already produced new understanding. Studies of communication networks led to important advances in the analysis of influence and friendship patterns in social groups, and economists have found many concepts in control theory ideally suited to the study of economic decision making and planning.

The examples of behavioral applications mentioned above are merely illustrative of the profound influence cybernetics has had on behavioral sciences. Indeed, in a very broad sense, all of the remaining papers in this book are indebted in some way to this general movement.

Of the six papers in this section, three are more than fifteen years old. These three "mature" articles are included, first because they provide nontechnical introductions to their respective concepts that are as eloquent and comprehensible as any available. Warren Weaver, for example, in "The Mathematics of Communication" is able to describe the crux of information theory without even mentioning the now famous equation $H=-k\Sigma p_i \log p_i$. Second, the articles express the aspirations these scientists had and the scope of scientific and technological advancements they hoped their ideas would implement. Finally, the inclusion of these papers will enable the reader to gain some understanding of the historical growth and maturation that has been occurring in this field. The articles "Error Correcting Codes" by W. Wesley Peterson and "Redundancy in Computers" by William H. Pierce focus on the fundamental communication problem of the reliable transmission of information but they do so from different points of view. Both are historical descendants of the ideas presented by Weaver. Likewise, Richard Bellman's article "Control Theory" can be viewed as a modern offspring of the basic principles of feedback discussed by Arnold Tustin.

6

CYBERNETICS

NORBERT WIENER • November 1948

Cybernetics is a word invented to define a new field in science. It combines under one heading the study of what in a human context is sometimes loosely described as thinking and in engineering is known as control and communication. In other words, cybernetics attempts to find the common elements in the functioning of automatic machines and of the human nervous system, and to develop a theory which will cover the entire field of control and communication in machines and in living organisms.

It is well known that between the most complex activities of the human brain and the operations of a simple adding machine there is a wide area where brain and machine overlap. In their more elaborate forms, modern computing machines are capable of memory, association, choice and many other brain functions. Indeed, the experts have gone so far in the elaboration of such machines that we can say the human brain behaves very much like the machines. The construction of more and more complex mechanisms actually is bringing us closer to an understanding of how the brain itself operates.

The word cybernetics is taken from the Greek *kybernetes,* meaning steersman. From the same Greek word, through the Latin corruption *gubernator,* came the term governor, which has been used for a long time to designate a certain type of control mechanism, and was the title of a brilliant study written by the Scottish physicist James Clerk Maxwell 80 years ago. The basic concept which both Maxwell and the investigators of cybernetics mean to describe by the choice of this term is that of a feedback mechanism, which is especially well represented by the steering engine of a ship. Its meaning is made clear by the following example.

Suppose that I pick up a pencil. To do this I have to move certain muscles. Only an expert anatomist knows what all these muscles are, and even an anatomist could hardly perform the act by a conscious exertion of the will to contract each muscle concerned in succession. Actually what we will is not to move individual muscles but to pick up the pencil. Once we have determined on this, the motion of the arm and hand proceeds in such a way that we may say that the amount by which the pencil is not yet picked up is decreased at each stage. This part of the action is not in full consciousness.

To perform an action in such a manner, there must be a report to the nervous system, conscious or unconscious, of the amount by which we have failed to pick up the pencil at each instant. The report may be visual, at least in part, but it is more generally kinesthetic, or to use a term now in vogue, proprioceptive. If the proprioceptive sensations are wanting, and we do not replace them by a visual or other substitute, we are unable to perform the act of picking up the pencil, and find ourselves in a state known as ataxia. On the other hand, an excessive feedback is likely to be just as serious a handicap. In the latter case the muscles overshoot the mark and go into an uncontrollable oscillation. This condition, often associated with injury to the cerebellum, is known as purpose tremor.

Here, then, is a significant parallel between the workings of the nervous system and of certain machines. The feedback principle introduces an important new idea in nerve physiology. The central nervous system no longer appears to be a self-contained organ receiving signals from the senses and discharging into the muscles. On the contrary, some of its most characteristic activities are explainable only as circular processes, traveling from the nervous system into the muscles and re-entering the nervous system through the sense organs. This finding seems to mark a step forward in the study of the nervous system as an integrated whole.

The new approach represented by cybernetics—an integration of studies which is not strictly biological or strictly physical, but a combination of the two—has already given evidence that it may help to solve many problems in engineering, in physiology and very likely in psychiatry.

This work represents the outcome of a program undertaken jointly several years ago by the writer and Arturo Rosenblueth, then of the Harvard Medical School and now of the National Institute of Cardiology of Mexico. Dr. Rosenblueth is a physiologist; I am a mathematician. For many years Dr. Rosenblueth and I had shared the conviction that the most fruitful areas for the growth of the sciences were those which had been neglected as no-man's lands between the various established fields. Dr. Rosenblueth always insisted that a proper exploration of these blank spaces on the map of science could be made only by a team of scientists, each a specialist but each possessing a thoroughly sound acquaintance with the fields of his fellows.

Our collaboration began as the result of a wartime project. I had been assigned, with a partner, Julian H. Bigelow, to the problem of working out a fire-control apparatus for anti-aircraft artillery which would be capable of tracking the curving course of a plane and predicting its future position. We soon came to the conclusion that any solution of the problem must depend heavily on the feedback principle, as it operated not only in the apparatus but in the human operators of the gun and of the plane. We approached

Dr. Rosenblueth with a specific question concerning oscillations in the nervous system, and his reply, which cited the phenomenon of purpose tremor, confirmed our hypothesis about the importance of feedback in voluntary activity.

The ideas suggested by this discussion led to several joint experiments, one of which was a study of feedback in the muscles of cats. The scope of our investigations steadily widened, and as it did so scientists from widely diverse fields joined our group. Among them were the mathematicians John von Neumann of the Institute for Advanced Study and Walter Pitts of Massachusetts Institute of Technology; the physiologists Warren McCulloch of the University of Pennsylvania and Lorente de No of the Rockefeller Institute; the late Kurt Lewin, psychologist, of M.I.T.; the anthropologists Gregory Bateson and Margaret Mead; the economist Oskar Morgenstern of the Institute for Advanced Study; and others in psychology, sociology, engineering, anatomy, neurophysiology, physics, and so on.

The study of cybernetics is likely to have fruitful applications in many fields, from the design of control mechanisms for artificial limbs to the almost complete mechanization of industry. But in our view it encompasses much wider horizons. If the 17th and early 18th centuries were the age of clocks, and the latter 18th and 19th centuries the age of steam engines, the present time is the age of communication and control. There is in electrical engineering a division which is known as the split between the technique of strong currents and the technique of weak currents; it is this split which separates the age just passed from that in which we are living. What distinguishes communication engineering from power engineering is that the main interest of the former is not the economy of energy but the accurate reproduction of a signal.

At every stage of technique since Daedalus, the ability of the artificer to produce a working simulacrum of a living organism has always intrigued people. In the days of magic, there was the bizarre and sinister concept of the Golem, that figure of clay into which the rabbi of Prague breathed life. In Isaac Newton's time the automaton became the clockwork music box. In the 19th century, the automaton was a glorified heat engine, burning a combustible fuel instead of the glycogen of human muscles. The automaton of our day opens doors by means of photocells, or points guns to the place at which a radar beam picks up a hostile airplane, or computes the solution of a differential equation.

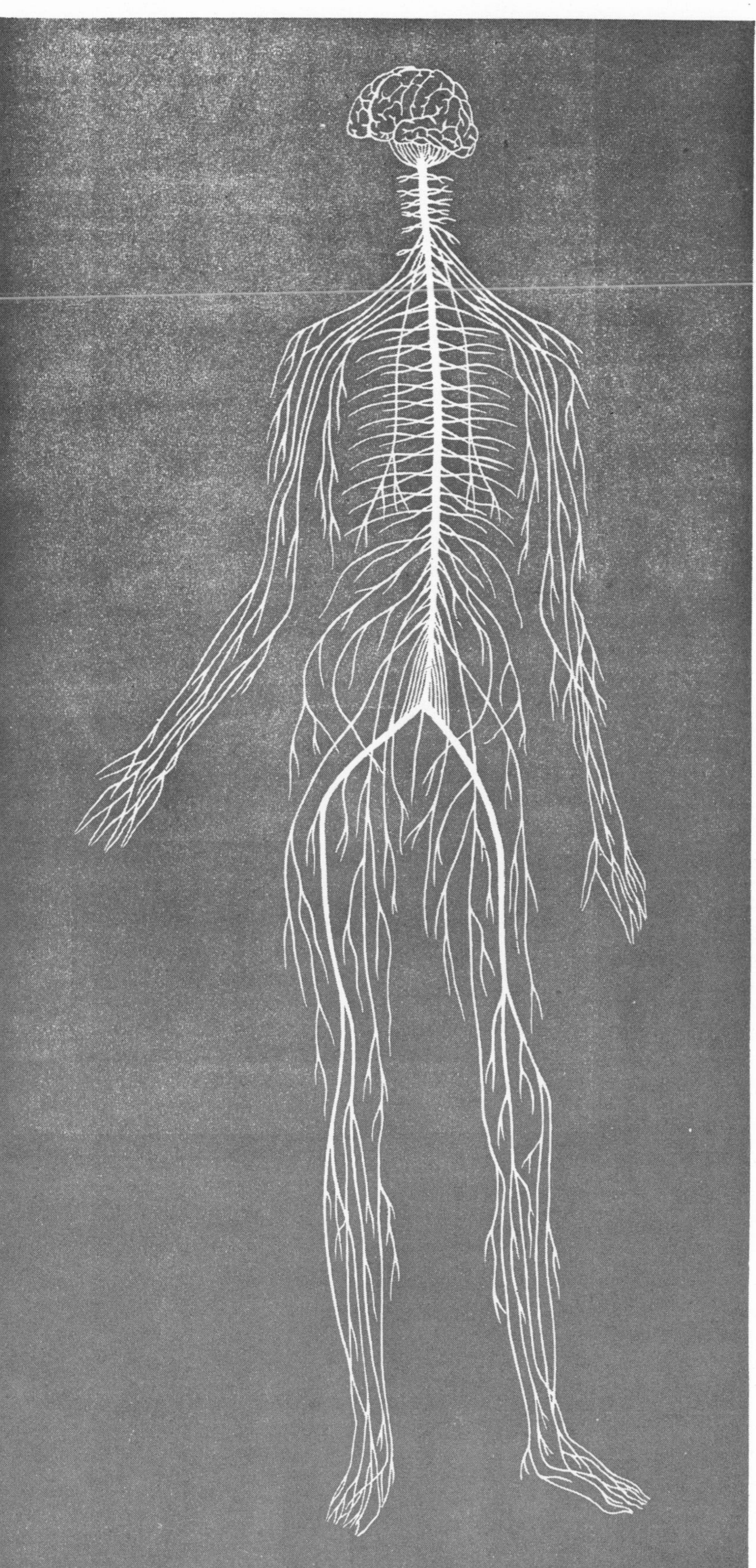

THE NERVOUS SYSTEM, in the cybernetic view, is more than a self-contained apparatus for receiving and transmitting signals. It is a circuit in which a feedback principle operates as certain impulses enter muscles and re-enter the nervous system through the sense organs.

Under the influence of the prevailing view in the science of the 19th century, the engineering of the body was naturally considered to be a branch of power engineering. Even today this is the predominant point of view among classically minded, conservative physiologists. But we are now coming to realize that the body is very far from a conservative system, and that the power available to it is much less limited than was formerly believed. We are beginning to see that such important elements as the neurones—the units of the nervous complex of our bodies—do their work under much the same conditions as vacuum tubes, their relatively small power being supplied from outside by the body's circulation, and that the bookkeeping which is most essential to describe their function is not one of energy.

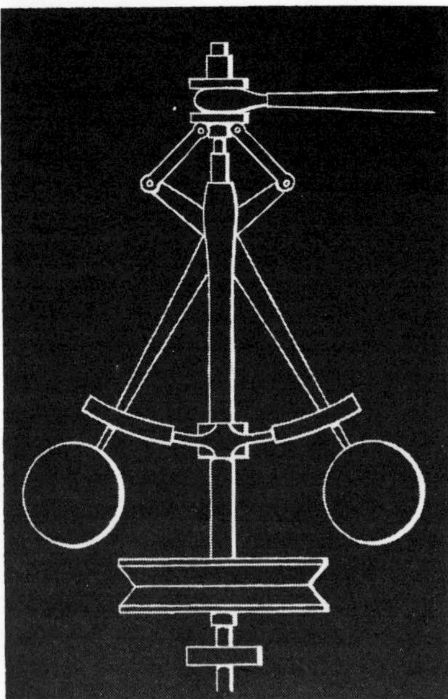

GOVERNOR of a steam engine is an example of feedback, one of the most important fundamental concepts in cybernetics.

In short, the newer study of automata, whether in the metal or in the flesh, is a branch of communications engineering, and its cardinal ideas are those of the message, of the amount of disturbance or "noise" (a term taken from the telephone engineer), of the quantity of information to be transmitted, of coding technique, and so on.

This view obviously has implications which affect many branches of science. Let us consider here the application of cybernetics to the problem of mental disorders. The realization that the brain and computing machines have much in common may suggest new and valid approaches to psychopathology, and even to psychiatry.

These begin with perhaps the simplest question of all: how the brain avoids gross blunders or gross miscarriages of activity due to the malfunction of individual parts. Similar questions referring to the computing machine are of great practical importance, for here a chain of operations, each of which covers only a fraction of a millionth of a second, may last a matter of hours or days. It is quite possible for a chain of computational operations to involve a billion separate steps. Under these circumstances, the chance that at least one operation will go amiss is far from negligible, even though the reliability of modern electronic apparatus has exceeded the most sanguine expectations.

In ordinary computational practice by hand or by desk machines, it is the custom to check every step of the computation and, when an error is found, to localize it by a backward process starting from the first point where the error is noted. To do this with a high-speed machine, the check must proceed at the pace of the original machine, or the whole effective order of speed of the machine will conform to that of the slower process of checking.

A much better method of checking, and in fact the one generally used in practice, is to refer every operation simultaneously to two or three separate mechanisms. When two such mechanisms are used, their answers are automatically collated against each other; and if there is a discrepancy, all data are transferred to permanent storage, the machine stops and a signal is sent to the operator that something is wrong. The operator then compares the results, and is guided by them in his search for the malfunctioning part, perhaps a tube which has burned out and needs replacement. If three separate mechanisms are used for each stage, there will practically always be agreement between two of the three mechanisms, and this agreement will give the required result. In this case the collation mechanism accepts the majority report, and the machine need not stop. There is a signal, however, indicating where and how the minority report differs from the majority report. If this occurs at the first moment of discrepancy, the indication of the position of the error may be very precise.

It is conceivable, and not implausible, that at least two of the elements of this process are also represented in the nervous system. It is hardly to be expected that any important message is entrusted for transmission to a single neurone, or that an important operation is entrusted to a single neuronal mechanism. Like the computing machine, the brain probably works on a variant of the famous principle expounded by Lewis Carroll in *The Hunting of the Snark:* "What I tell you three times is true."

It is also improbable that the various channels available for the transfer of information generally go from one end of their course to the other without connecting with one another. It is much more probable that when a message reaches a certain level of the nervous system, it may leave that point and proceed to the next by one or more alternative routes. There may be parts of the nervous system, especially in the cortex, where this interchangeability is much limited or abolished. Still, the principle holds, and it probably holds most clearly for the relatively unspecialized cortical areas which serve the purpose of association and of what we call the higher mental functions.

So far we have been considering errors in performance that are normal, and pathological only in an extended sense. Let us now turn to those that are much more clearly pathological. Psychopathology has been rather a disappointment to the instinctive materialism of the doctors, who have taken the view that every disorder must be accompanied by actual lesions of some specific tissue involved. It is true that specific brain lesions, such as injuries, tumors, clots and the like, may be accompanied by psychic symptoms, and that certain mental diseases, such as paresis, are the sequelae of general bodily disease and show a pathological condition of the brain tissue. But there is no way of identifying the brain of a schizophrenic of one of the strict Kraepelin types, nor of a manic-depressive patient, nor of a para-

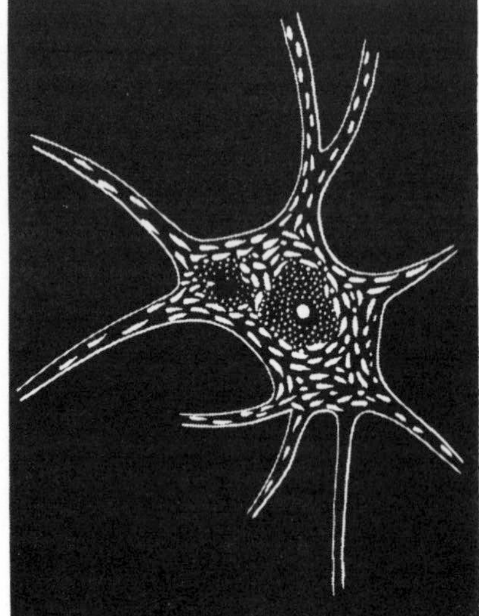

NERVE CELL performs its functions under much the same conditions as a vacuum tube, obtaining its power from outside.

noiac. These we call functional disorders.

This distinction between functional and organic disorders is illuminated by the consideration of the computing machine. It is not the empty physical structure of the computing machine that corresponds to the brain—to the adult brain, at least—but the combination of this structure with the instructions given it at the beginning of a chain of operations and with all the additional information stored and gained from outside in the course of its operation.

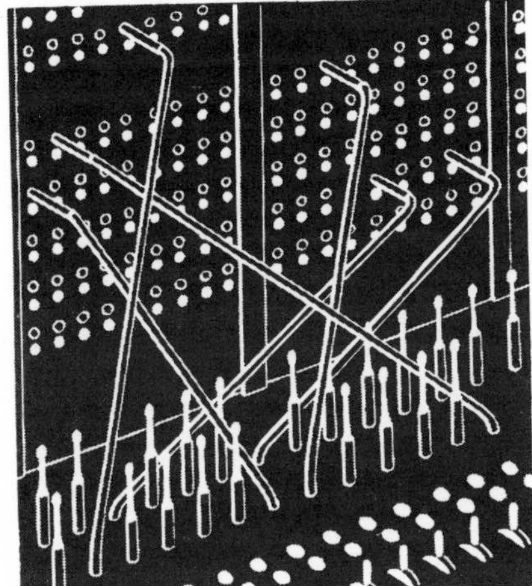

TELEPHONE EXCHANGE, when it is overloaded, has breakdowns rather similar to the kind that occur in human beings.

This information is stored in some physical form — in the form of memory. But part of it is in the form of circulating memories, with a physical basis that vanishes when the machine is shut down or the brain dies, and part is in the form of long-time memories, which are stored in a way at which we can only guess, but probably also in a form with a physical basis that vanishes at death.

There is therefore nothing surprising in considering the functional mental disorders fundamentally as diseases of memory, of the circulating information kept by the brain in active state and of the long-time permeability of synapses. Even the grosser disorders such as paresis may produce a large part of their effects not so much by the destruction of tissue which they involve and the alteration of synaptic thresholds as by the secondary disturbances of traffic, the overload of what remains of the nervous system and the rerouting of messages which must follow such primary injuries.

In a system containing a large number of neurones, circular processes can hardly be stable for long periods of time. Either they run their course, dissipate themselves and die out, as in the case of memories belonging to the specious present, or they embrace more and more neurones in their system, until they occupy an inordinate part of the neurone pool. This is what we should expect to be the case in the malignant worry that accompanies anxiety neuroses. In such a case, it is possible that the patient simply does not have the room —*i.e.*, a sufficient number of neurones—to carry out his normal processes of thought. Under such conditions, there may be less going on in the brain to occupy the neurones not yet affected, so that they are all the more readily involved in the expanding process. Furthermore, the permanent memory becomes more and more deeply involved, and the pathological process which began at the level of the circulating memories may repeat itself in a more intractable form at the level of the permanent memories. Thus what started as a relatively trivial and accidental disturbance of stability may build itself up into a process totally destructive to the normal mental life.

Pathological processes of a somewhat similar nature are not unknown in the case of mechanical or electrical computing machines. A tooth of a wheel may slip under such conditions that no tooth with which it engages can pull it back into its normal relations, or a high-speed electrical computing machine may go into a circular process that seems impossible to stop.

How do we deal with these accidents in the case of the machine? We first try to clear the machine of all information, in the hope that when it starts again with different data the difficulty will not recur. If this fails and the difficulty is inaccessible to the clearing mechanism, we shake the machine or, if it is electrical, subject it to an abnormally large electrical impulse in the hope that we may jolt the inaccessible part into a position where the false cycle of its activities will be interrupted. If even this fails, we may disconnect an erring part of the apparatus, for it is possible that what remains may be adequate for our purpose.

In the case of the brain, there is no normal process, except death, that can clear it of all past impressions. Of the normal non-fatal processes, sleep comes closest to clearing the brain. How often we find that the best way to handle a complicated worry or an intellectual muddle is to sleep on it! Sleep, however, does not clear away the deeper memories, nor indeed is a malignant state of worry compatible with adequate sleep.

Thus we are often forced to resort to more violent types of intervention in the memory cycle. The most violent of these involve surgery on the brain, leaving behind permanent damage, mutilation and the abridgement of the powers of the victim, for the mammalian central nervous system seems to possess no power of regeneration. The principal type of surgical intervention that has been practiced is known as prefrontal lobotomy, or leucotomy. It consists in the removal or isolation of a portion of the prefrontal lobe of the cortex. It is currently having a certain vogue, probably not unconnected with the fact that it makes the custodial care of many patients easier. (Let me remark in passing that killing them makes their custodial care still easier.) Prefrontal lobotomy does seem to have a genuine effect on malignant worry, not by bringing the patient nearer to a solution of his problem, but by damaging or destroying the capacity for maintained worry, known in the terminology of another profession as the conscience. It appears to impair the circulating memory, *i.e.*, the ability to keep in mind a situation not actually presented.

AUTOMATON of the 15th century was one of a long series of attempts to produce a working simulacrum of a living organism.

The various forms of shock treatment—electric, insulin, metrazol — are less drastic methods of doing a very similar thing. They do not destroy brain tissue, or at least are not intended to destroy it, but they do have a decidedly damaging effect on the memory. In so far as the shock treatment affects recent disordered memories, which are probably scarcely worth preserving anyhow, it has something to recommend it as against lobotomy, but it is sometimes followed by deleterious effects on the permanent memory and the personality. As it is used at present, it is another violent, imperfectly understood, imperfectly controlled method to interrupt a mental vicious circle.

In long-established cases of mental disorder, the permanent memory is as badly deranged as the circulating memory. We do not seem to possess any purely pharmaceutical or surgical weapon for intervening selectively in the permanent memory. This is where psychoanalysis and the other psychotherapeutic measures come in.

Whether psychoanalysis is taken in the orthodox Freudian sense or in the modified senses of Jung and of Adler, or whether the psychotherapy is not strictly psychoanalytic at all, the treatment is clearly based on the concept that the stored information of the mind lies on many levels of accessibility. The effect and accessibility of this stored information are vitally conditioned by affective experiences that we cannot always uncover by introspection. The technique of the psychoanalyst consists in a series of means to discover and interpret these hidden memories, to make the patient accept them for what they are, and thus to modify, if not their content, at least the affective tone they carry, and make them less harmful.

All this is perfectly consistent with the cybernetic point of view. Our theory perhaps explains, too, why there are circumstances in which a joint use of shock treatment and psychotherapy is indicated, combining a physical or pharmacological therapy for the malignant reverberations in the nervous system and a psychological therapy for the damaging long-time memories which might re-establish the vicious circle broken up by the shock treatments.

We have already mentioned the traffic problem of the nervous system. It has been noted by many writers that each form of organization has an upper limit of size beyond which it will not function. Thus insect organization is limited by the length of tubing over which the spiracle method of bringing air by diffusion directly to the breathing tissues will function; a land animal cannot be so big that the legs or other portions in contact with the ground will be crushed by its weight, and so on. The same sort of thing is observed in engineering structures. Skyscrapers are limited in size by the fact that when they exceed a certain height, the elevator space needed for the upper stories consumes an excessive part of the cross section of the lower floors. Beyond a certain span, the best possible suspension bridge will collapse under its own weight. Similarly, the size of a single telephone exchange is limited.

In a telephone system, the important limiting factor is the fraction of the time during which a subscriber will find it impossible to put a call through. A 90 per cent chance of completing calls is probably good enough to permit business to be carried on with reasonable facility. A success of 75 per cent is annoying but will permit business to be carried on after a fashion; if half the calls are not completed, subscribers will begin to ask to have their telephones taken out. Now, these represent all-over figures. If the calls go through a number of distinct stages of switching, and the probability of failure is independent and equal for each stage, in order to get a high probability of final success the probability of success at each stage must be higher than the final one. Thus to obtain a 75 per cent chance for the completion of the call after five stages, we must have about 95 per cent chance of success at each stage. The more stages there are, the more rapidly the service becomes extremely bad when a critical level of failure for the individual call is exceeded, and extremely good when this critical level of failure is not quite reached. Thus a switching service involving many stages and designed for a certain level of failure shows no obvious signs of failure until the traffic comes up to the edge of the critical point, when it goes completely to pieces and we have a catastrophic traffic jam.

So man, with the best developed nervous system of all the animals, probably involving the longest chains of effectively operated neurones, is likely to perform a complicated type of behavior efficiently very close to the edge of an overload, when he will give way in a serious and catastrophic manner. This overload may take place in several ways: by an excess in the amount of traffic to be carried; by a physical removal of channels for the carrying of traffic; or by the excessive occupation of such channels by undesirable systems of traffic, such as circulating memories that have accumulated to the extent of becoming pathological worries. In all these cases, a point is reached—quite suddenly—when the normal traffic does not have space enough allotted to it, and we have a form of mental breakdown, very possibly amounting to insanity.

This will first affect the faculties or operations involving the longest chains of neurones. There is appreciable evidence, of various kinds, that these are precisely the processes recognized as the highest in our ordinary scale of valuation.

If we compare the human brain with that of a lower mammal, we find that it is much more convoluted. The relative thickness of the gray matter is much the same, but it is spread over a far more involved system of grooves and ridges. The effect of this is to increase the amount of gray matter at the expense of the amount of white matter. Within a ridge, this decrease of the white matter is largely a decrease in length rather than in number of fibers, as the opposing folds are nearer together than the same areas would be on a smooth-surfaced brain of the same size. On the other hand, when it comes to the connectors between different ridges, the distance they have to run is increased by the convolution of the brain.

Thus the human brain would seem to be fairly efficient in the matter of the short-distance connectors, but defective in the matter of long-distance trunk lines. This means that in the case of a traffic jam, the processes involving parts of the brain quite remote from one another should suffer first. That is, processes involving several centers, a number of different motor processes and a considerable number of association areas should be among the least stable in cases of insanity. These are precisely the processes which we should normally class as higher, thereby confirming our theory, as experience does also, that the higher processes deteriorate first in insanity.

The phenomena of handedness and of hemispheric dominance suggest other interesting speculations. Right-handedness, as is well known, is generally associated with left-brainedness, and left-handedness with right-brainedness. The dominant hemisphere has the lion's share of the higher cerebral functions. In the adult, the effect of an extensive injury in the secondary hemisphere is far less serious than the effect of a similar injury in the dominant hemisphere. At a relatively early stage in his career, Louis Pasteur suffered a cerebral hemorrhage on the right side which left him with a moderate degree of one-sided paralysis. When he died, his brain was examined and the damage to its right side was found to be so extensive that it has been said that after his injury "he had only half a brain." Nevertheless, after his injury he did some of his best work. A similar injury to the left side of the brain in a right-handed adult would almost certainly have been fatal; at the least it would have reduced the patient to an animal condition.

In the first six months of life, an extensive injury to the dominant hemisphere may compel the normally secondary hemi-

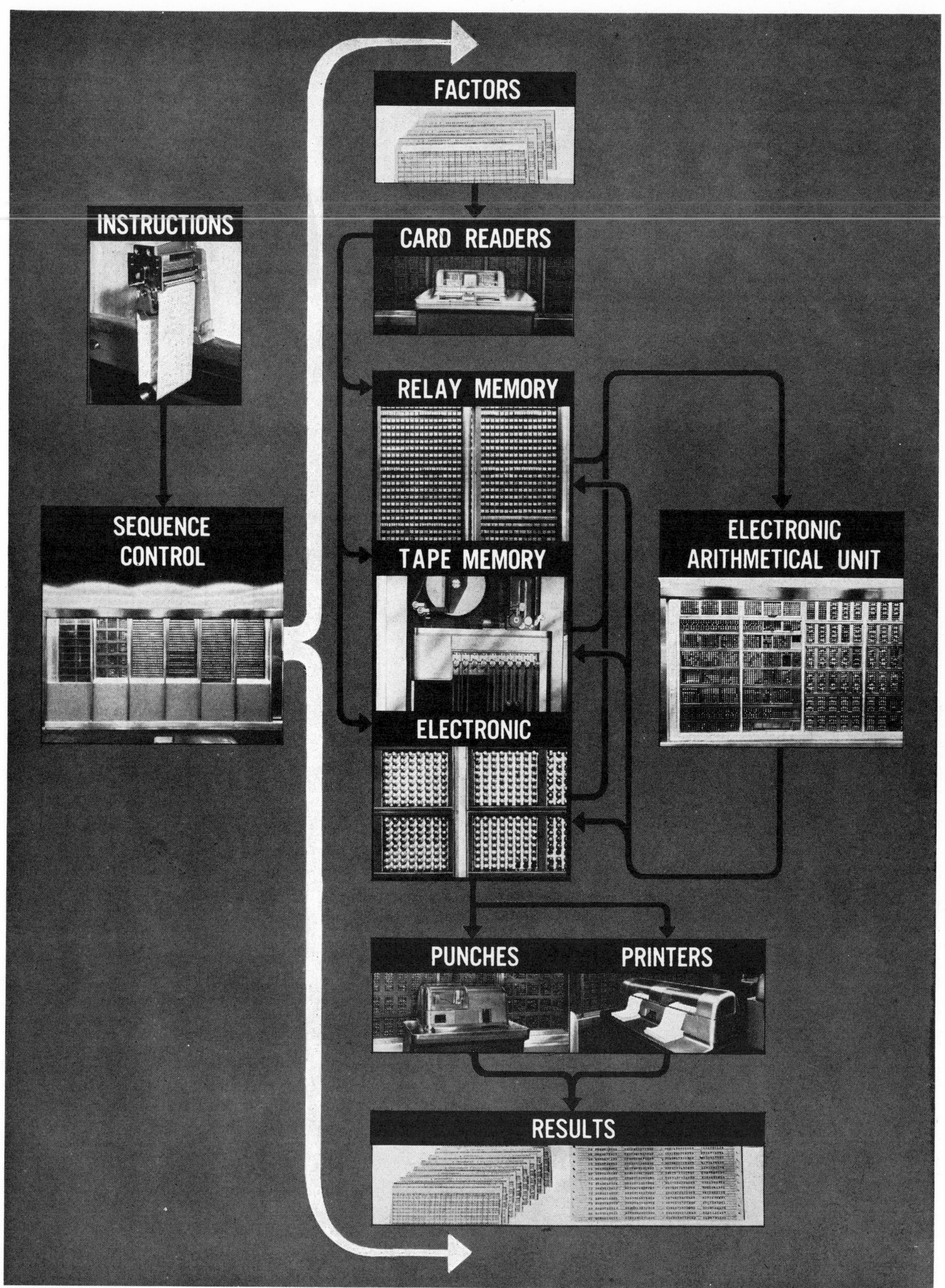

DIAGRAM of the Selective Sequence Electronic Calculator built by the International Business Machines Corporation, provides another cybernetic comparison. Physical structure of the machine is not analogous to the brain, The structure plus instructions and stored memories is analogous. The machine has electronic and relay circuits for temporary memory, punched cards for permanent memory.

sphere to take its place, so that the patient appears far more nearly normal than he would have been had the injury occurred at a later stage. This is quite in accordance with the great flexibility shown by the nervous system in the early weeks of life. It is possible that, short of very serious injuries, handedness is reasonably flexible in the very young child. Long before the child is of school age, however, the natural handedness and cerebral dominance are established for life. Many people have changed the handedness of their children by education, though of course they could not change its physiological basis in hemispheric dominance. These hemispheric changelings often become stutterers and develop other defects of speech, reading and writing.

We now see at least one possible explanation for this phenomenon. With the education of the secondary hand, there has been a partial education of that part of the secondary hemisphere which deals with skilled motions such as writing. Since these motions are carried out in the closest possible association with reading, and with speech and other activities which are inseparably connected with the dominant hemisphere, the neurone chains involved in these processes must cross over from hemisphere to hemisphere, and in any complex activity they must do this again and again. But the direct connectors between the hemispheres in a brain as large as that of man are so few in number that they are of very little help. Consequently the interhemispheric traffic must go by roundabout routes through the brain stem. We know little about these routes, but they are certainly long, scanty and subject to interruption. As a consequence, the processes associated with speech and writing are very likely to be involved in a traffic jam, and stuttering is the most natural thing in the world.

The human brain is probably too large already to use in an efficient manner all the facilities which seem to be present. In a cat, the destruction of the dominant hemisphere seems to produce relatively less damage than in man, while the destruction of the secondary hemisphere probably produces more damage. At any rate, the apportionment of function in the two hemispheres is more nearly equal. In man, the gain achieved by the increase in the size and complexity of the brain is partly nullified by the fact that less of the organ can be used effectively at one time.

It is interesting to reflect that we may be facing one of those limitations of nature in which highly specialized organs reach a level of declining efficiency and ultimately lead to the extinction of the species. The human brain may be as far along on its road to destructive specialization as the great nose horns of the last of the titanotheres.

7

THE MATHEMATICS OF COMMUNICATION

WARREN WEAVER • July 1949

HOW do men communicate, one with another? The spoken word, either direct or by telephone or radio; the written or printed word, transmitted by hand, by post, by telegraph, or in any other way—these are obvious and common forms of communication. But there are many others. A nod or a wink, a drumbeat in the jungle, a gesture pictured on a television screen, the blinking of a signal light, a bit of music that reminds one of an event in the past, puffs of smoke in the desert air, the movements and posturing in a ballet—all of these are means men use to convey ideas.

The word communication, in fact, will be used here in a very broad sense to include all of the procedures by which one mind can affect another. Although the language used will often refer specifically to the communication of speech, practically everything said applies equally to music, to pictures, to a variety of other methods of conveying information.

In communication there seem to be problems at three levels: 1) technical, 2) semantic, and 3) influential.

The technical problems are concerned with the accuracy of transference of information from sender to receiver. They are inherent in all forms of communication, whether by sets of discrete symbols (written speech), or by a varying signal (telephonic or radio transmission of voice or music), or by a varying two-dimensional pattern (television).

The semantic problems are concerned with the interpretation of meaning by the receiver, as compared with the intended meaning of the sender. This is a very deep and involved situation, even when one deals only with the relatively simple problems of communicating through speech. For example, if Mr. X is suspected not to understand what Mr. Y says, then it is not possible, by having Mr. Y do nothing but talk further with Mr. X, completely to clarify this situation in any finite time. If Mr. Y says "Do you now understand me?" and Mr. X says "Certainly I do," this is not necessarily a certification that understanding has been achieved. It may just be that Mr. X did not understand the question. If this sounds silly, try it again as "Czy pan mnie rozumie?" with the answer "Hai wakkate imasu." In the restricted field of speech communication, the difficulty may be reduced to a tolerable size, but never completely eliminated, by "explanations." They are presumably never more than approximations to the ideas being explained, but are understandable when phrased in language that has previously been made reasonably clear by usage. For example, it does not take long to make the symbol for "yes" in any language understandable.

The problems of influence or effectiveness are concerned with the success with which the meaning conveyed to the receiver leads to the desired conduct on his part. It may seem at first glance undesirably narrow to imply that the purpose of all communication is to influence the conduct of the receiver. But with any reasonably broad definition of conduct, it is clear that communication either affects conduct or is without any discernible and provable effect at all.

One might be inclined to think that the technical problems involve only the engineering details of good design of a communication system, while the semantic and the effectiveness problems contain most if not all of the philosophical content of the general problem of communication. To see that this is not the case, we must now examine some important recent work in the mathematical theory of communication.

THIS is by no means a wholly new theory. As the mathematician John von Neumann has pointed out, the 19th-century Austrian physicist Ludwig Boltzmann suggested that some concepts of statistical mechanics were applicable to the concept of information. Other scientists, notably the late Norbert Wiener of the Massachusetts Institute of Technology, have made profound contributions. The work which will be here reported is that of Claude Shannon of the Bell Telephone Laboratories, which was preceded by that of H. Nyquist and R. V. L. Hartley in the same organization. This work applies in the first instance only to the technical problem, but the theory has broader significance. To begin with, meaning and effectiveness are inevitably restricted by the theoretical limits of accuracy in symbol transmission. Even more significant, a theoretical analysis of the technical problem reveals that it overlaps the semantic and the effectiveness problems more than one might suspect.

A communication system is symbolically represented in the drawing on pages 48 and 49. The information source selects a desired message out of a set of possible messages. (As will be shown, this is a particularly important function.) The transmitter changes this message into a signal which is sent over the communication channel to the receiver.

The receiver is a sort of inverse transmitter, changing the transmitted signal back into a message, and handing this message on to the destination. When I talk to you, my brain is the information source, yours the destination; my vocal system is the transmitter, and your ear with the eighth nerve is the receiver.

In the process of transmitting the signal, it is unfortunately characteristic that certain things not intended by the information source are added to the signal. These unwanted additions may be distortions of sound (in telephony, for example), or static (in radio), or distortions in the shape or shading of a picture (television), or errors in transmission (telegraphy or facsimile). All these changes in the signal may be called noise.

The questions to be studied in a communication system have to do with the amount of information, the capacity of the communication channel, the coding process that may be used to change a message into a signal and the effects of noise.

First off, we have to be clear about

the rather strange way in which, in this theory, the word "information" is used; for it has a special sense which, among other things, must not be confused at all with meaning. It is surprising but true that, from the present viewpoint, two messages, one heavily loaded with meaning and the other pure nonsense, can be equivalent as regards information.

In fact, in this new theory the word information relates not so much to what you *do* say, as to what you *could* say. That is, information is a measure of your freedom of choice when you select a message. If you are confronted with a very elementary situation where you have to choose one of two alternative messages, then it is arbitrarily said that the information associated with this situation is unity. The concept of information applies not to the individual messages, as the concept of meaning would, but rather to the situation as a whole, the unit information indicating that in this situation one has an amount of freedom of choice, in selecting a message, which it is convenient to regard as a standard or unit amount. The two messages between which one must choose in such a selection can be anything one likes. One might be the King James version of the Bible, and the other might be "Yes."

THE remarks thus far relate to artificially simple situations where the information source is free to choose only among several definite messages—like a man picking out one of a set of standard birthday-greeting telegrams. A more natural and more important situation is that in which the information source makes a sequence of choices from some set of elementary symbols, the selected sequence then forming the message. Thus a man may pick out one word after another, these individually selected words then adding up to the message.

Obviously probability plays a major role in the generation of the message, and the choices of the successive symbols depend upon the preceding choices. Thus, if we are concerned with English speech, and if the last symbol chosen is "the," then the probability that the next word will be an article, or a verb form other than a verbal, is very small. After the three words "in the event," the probability for "that" as the next word is fairly high, and for "elephant" as the next word is very low. Similarly, the probability is low for such a sequence of words as "Constantinople fishing nasty pink." Incidentally, it is low, but not zero, for it is perfectly possible to think of a passage in which one sentence closes with "Constantinople fishing," and the next begins with "Nasty pink." (We might observe in passing that the sequence under discussion *has* occurred in a single good English sentence, namely the one second preceding.)

As a matter of fact, Shannon has shown that when letters or words chosen at random are set down in sequences dictated by probability considerations alone, they tend to arrange themselves in meaningful words and phrases (*see illustration on page 50*).

Now let us return to the idea of information. The quantity which uniquely meets the natural requirements that one sets up for a measure of information turns out to be exactly that which is known in thermodynamics as entropy, or the degree of randomness, or of "shuffledness" if you will, in a situation. It is expressed in terms of the various probabilities involved.

To those who have studied the physical sciences, it is most significant that an entropy-like expression appears in communication theory as a measure of information. The concept of entropy, introduced by the German physicist Rudolf Clausius nearly 100 years ago, closely associated with the name of Boltzmann, and given deep meaning by Willard Gibbs of Yale in his classic work on statistical mechanics, has become so basic and pervasive a concept that Sir Arthur Eddington remarked: "The law that entropy always increases—the second law of thermodynamics—holds, I think, the supreme position among the laws of Nature."

Thus when one meets the concept of entropy in communication theory, he has a right to be rather excited. That information should be measured by entropy is, after all, natural when we remember that information is associated with the amount of freedom of choice we have in constructing messages. Thus one can say of a communication source, just as he would also say of a thermodynamic ensemble: "This situation is highly organized; it is not characterized by a large degree of randomness or of choice—that is to say, the information, or the entropy, is low."

We must keep in mind that in the mathematical theory of communication we are concerned not with the meaning of individual messages but with the whole statistical nature of the information source. Thus one is not surprised that the capacity of a channel of communication is to be described in terms of the amount of information it can transmit, or better, in terms of its ability to transmit what is produced out of a source of a given information.

The transmitter may take a written message and use some code to encipher this message into, say, a sequence of numbers, these numbers then being sent over the channel as the signal. Thus one says, in general, that the function of the transmitter is to encode, and that of the receiver to decode, the message. The theory provides for very sophisticated transmitters and receivers—such, for example, as possess "memories," so that the way they encode a certain symbol of the message depends not only upon this one symbol but also upon previous symbols of the message and the way they have been encoded.

We are now in a position to state the fundamental theorem for a noiseless channel transmitting discrete symbols. This theorem relates to a communication channel which has a capacity of C units per second, accepting signals from an information source of H units per second. The theorem states that by devising proper coding procedures for the transmitter it is possible to transmit symbols over the channel at an average rate

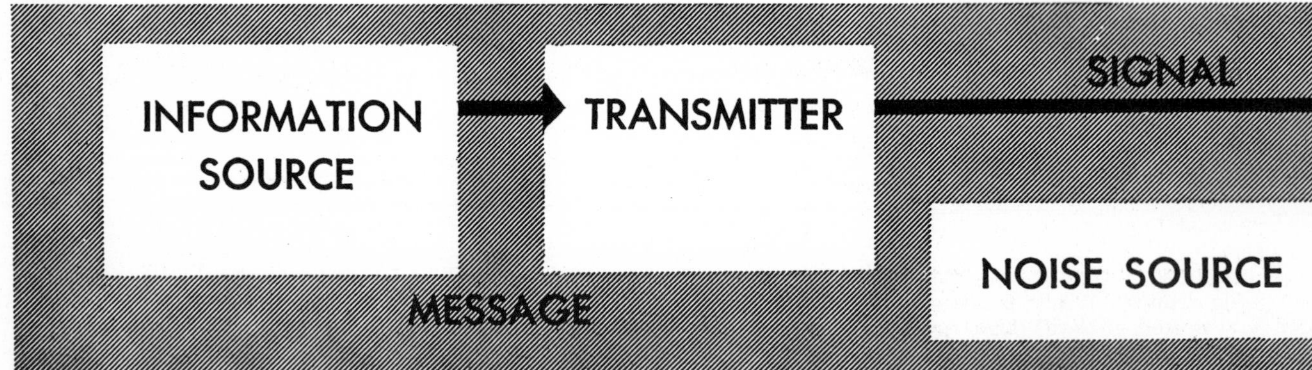

A COMMUNICATION SYSTEM may be reduced to these fundamental elements. In telephony the signal is a varying electric current, and the channel is a wire. In speech the signal is varying sound pressure, and the

which is nearly C/H, but which, no matter how clever the coding, can never be made to exceed C/H.

VIEWED superficially, say in rough analogy to the use of transformers to match impedances in electrical circuits, it seems very natural, although certainly pretty neat, to have this theorem which says that efficient coding is that which matches the statistical characteristics of information source and channel. But when it is examined in detail for any one of the vast array of situations to which this result applies, one realizes how deep and powerful this theory is.

How does noise affect information? Information, we must steadily remember, is a measure of one's freedom of choice in selecting a message. The greater this freedom of choice, the greater is the uncertainty that the message actually selected is some particular one. Thus greater freedom of choice, greater uncertainty and greater information all go hand in hand.

If noise is introduced, then the received message contains certain distortions, certain errors, certain extraneous material, that would certainly lead to increased uncertainty. But if the uncertainty is increased, the information is increased, and this sounds as though the noise were beneficial!

It is true that when there is noise, the received signal is selected out of a more varied set of signals than was intended by the sender. This situation beautifully illustrates the semantic trap into which one can fall if he does not remember that "information" is used here with a special meaning that measures freedom of choice and hence uncertainty as to what choice has been made. Uncertainty that arises by virtue of freedom of choice on the part of the sender is desirable uncertainty. Uncertainty that arises because of errors or because of the influence of noise is undesirable uncertainty. To get the useful information in the received signal we must subtract the spurious portion. This is accomplished, in the theory, by establishing a quantity known as the "equivocation," meaning the amount of ambiguity introduced by noise. One then refines or extends the previous definition of the capacity of a noiseless channel, and states that the capacity of a noisy channel is defined to be equal to the maximum rate at which useful information (*i.e.*, total uncertainty minus noise uncertainty) can be transmitted over the channel.

Now, finally, we can state the great central theorem of this whole communication theory. Suppose a noisy channel of capacity C is accepting information from a source of entropy H, entropy corresponding to the number of possible messages from the source. If the channel capacity C is equal to or larger than H, then by devising appropriate coding systems the output of the source can be transmitted over the channel with as little error as one pleases. But if the channel capacity C is less than H, the entropy of the source, then it is impossible to devise codes which reduce the error frequency as low as one may please.

However clever one is with the coding process, it will always be true that after the signal is received there remains some undesirable uncertainty about what the message was; and this undesirable uncertainty—this noise or equivocation—will always be equal to or greater than H minus C. But there is always at least one code capable of reducing this undesirable uncertainty down to a value that exceeds H minus C by a small amount.

This powerful theorem gives a precise and almost startlingly simple description of the utmost dependability one can ever obtain from a communication channel which operates in the presence of noise. One must think a long time, and consider many applications, before he fully realizes how powerful and general this amazingly compact theorem really is. One single application can be indicated here, but in order to do so, we must go back for a moment to the idea of the information of a source.

Having calculated the entropy (or the information, or the freedom of choice) of a certain information source, one can compare it to the maximum value this entropy could have, subject only to the condition that the source continue to employ the same symbols. The ratio of the actual to the maximum entropy is called the relative entropy of the source. If the relative entropy of a certain source is, say, eight-tenths, this means roughly that this source is, in its choice of symbols to form a message, about 80 per cent as free as it could possibly be with these same symbols. One minus the relative entropy is called the "redundancy." That is to say, this fraction of the message is unnecessary in the sense that if it were missing the message would still be essentially complete, or at least could be completed.

It is most interesting to note that the redundancy of English is just about 50 per cent. In other words, about half of the letters or words we choose in writing or speaking are under our free choice, and about half are really controlled by the statistical structure of the language, although we are not ordinarily aware of it. Incidentally, this is just about the minimum of freedom (or relative entropy) in the choice of letters that one must have to be able to construct satisfactory crossword puzzles. In a language that had only 20 per cent of freedom, or 80 per cent redundancy, it would be impossible to construct crossword puzzles in sufficient complexity and number to make the game popular.

Now since English is about 50 per cent redundant, it would be possible to save about one-half the time of ordinary telegraphy by a proper encoding process, provided one transmitted over a noiseless channel. When there is noise on a channel, however, there is some real advantage in not using a coding process that eliminates all of the redundancy. For the remaining redundancy helps combat the noise. It is the high redundancy of English, for example, that makes it easy to correct errors in spelling that have arisen during transmission.

THE communication systems dealt with so far involve the use of a dis-

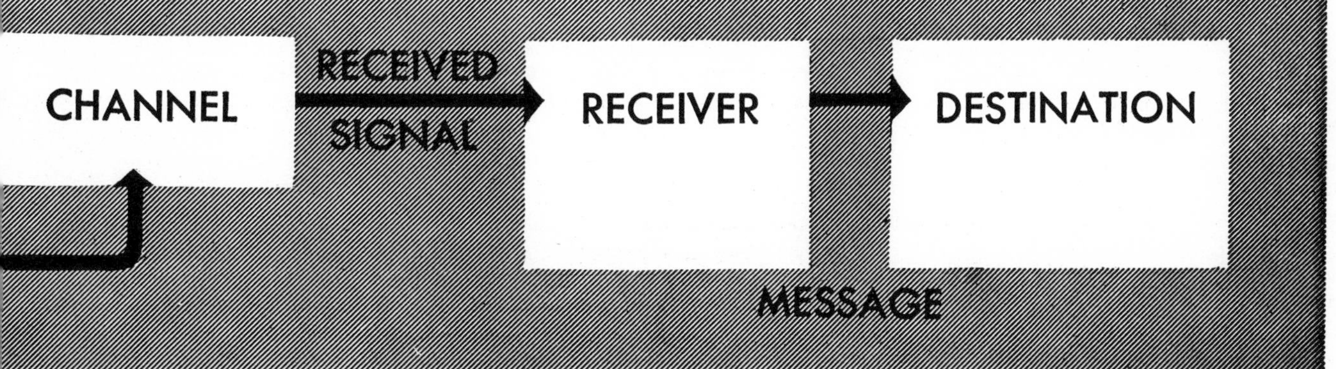

channel the air. Frequently things not intended by the information source are impressed on the signal. The static of radio is one example; distortion in telephony is another. All these additions may be called noise.

crete set of symbols—say letters—only moderately numerous. One might well expect that the theory would become almost indefinitely more complicated when it seeks to deal with continuous messages such as those of the speaking voice, with its continuous variation of pitch and energy. As is often the case, however, a very interesting mathematical theorem comes to the rescue. As a practical matter, one is always interested in a continuous signal which is built up of simple harmonic constituents, not of all frequencies but only of those that lie wholly within a band from zero to, say, W cycles per second. Thus very satisfactory communication can be achieved over a telephone channel that handles frequencies up to about 4,000, although the human voice does contain higher frequencies. With frequencies up to 10,000 or 12,000, high-fidelity radio transmission of symphonic music is possible.

The theorem that helps us is one which states that a continuous signal, T seconds in duration and band-limited in frequency to the range from zero to W, can be completely specified by stating 2TW numbers. This is really a remarkable theorem. Ordinarily a continuous curve can be defined only approximately by a finite number of points. But if the curve is built up out of simple harmonic constituents of a limited number of frequencies, as a complex sound is built up out of a limited number of pure tones, then a finite number of quantities is all that is necessary to define the curve completely.

Thanks partly to this theorem, and partly to the essential nature of the situation, it turns out that the extended theory of continuous communication is somewhat more difficult and complicated mathematically, but not essentially different from the theory for discrete symbols. Many of the statements for the discrete case require no modification for the continuous case, and others require only minor change.

The mathematical theory of communication is so general that one does not need to say what kinds of symbols are being considered—whether written letters or words, or musical notes, or spoken words, or symphonic music, or pictures. The relationships it reveals apply to all these and to other forms of communication. The theory is so imaginatively motivated that it deals with the real inner core of the communication problem.

One evidence of its generality is that the theory contributes importantly to, and in fact is really the basic theory of, cryptography, which is of course a form of coding. In a similar way, the theory contributes to the problem of translation from one language to another, although the complete story here clearly requires consideration of meaning, as well as of information. Similarly, the ideas developed in this work connect

1. Zero-order approximation
XFOML RXKHRJFFJUJ ZLPWCFWKCYJ FFJEYVKCQSGXYD QPAAMKBZAACIBZLHJQD

2. First-order approximation
OCRO HLI RGWR NMIELWIS EU LL NBNESEBYA TH EEI ALHENHTTPA OOBTTVA NAH BRL

3. Second-order approximation
ON IE ANTSOUTINYS ARE T INCTORE ST BE S DEAMY ACHIN D ILONASIVE TUCOOWE AT TEASONARE FUSO TIZIN ANDY TOBE SEACE CTISBE

4. Third-order approximation
IN NO IST LAT WHEY CRATICT FROURE BIRS GROCID PONDENOME OF DEMONSTURES OF THE REPTAGIN IS REGOACTIONA OF CRE

5. First-Order Word Approximation
REPRESENTING AND SPEEDILY IS AN GOOD APT OR COME CAN DIFFERENT NATURAL HERE HE THE A IN CAME THE TO OF TO EXPERT GRAY COME TO FURNISHES THE LINE MESSAGE HAD BE THESE.

6. Second-Order Word Approximation
THE HEAD AND IN FRONTAL ATTACK ON AN ENGLISH WRITER THAT THE CHARACTER OF THIS POINT IS THEREFORE ANOTHER METHOD FOR THE LETTERS THAT THE TIME OF WHO EVER TOLD THE PROBLEM FOR AN UNEXPECTED

ARTIFICIAL LANGUAGE results when letters or words are set down statistically. 1. Twenty-six letters and one space are chosen at random. 2. Letters are chosen according to their frequency in English. 3. Letters are chosen according to the frequency with which they follow other letters. 4. Letters are chosen according to frequency with which they follow two other letters. Remaining examples do the same with words instead of letters.

so closely with the problem of the logical design of computing machines that it is no surprise that Shannon has written a paper on the design of a computer that would be capable of playing a skillful game of chess. And it is of further pertinence to the present contention that his paper closes with the remark that either one must say that such a computer "thinks," or one must substantially modify the conventional implication of the verb "to think."

The theory goes further. Though ostensibly applicable only to problems at the technical level, it is helpful and suggestive at the levels of semantics and effectiveness as well. The formal diagram of a communication system on pages 48 and 49 can, in all likelihood, be extended to include the central issues of meaning and effectiveness.

Thus when one moves to those levels it may prove to be essential to take account of the statistical characteristics of the destination. One can imagine, as an addition to the diagram, another box labeled "Semantic Receiver" interposed between the engineering receiver (which changes signals to messages) and the destination. This semantic receiver subjects the message to a second decoding, the demand on this one being that it must match the statistical semantic characteristics of the message to the statistical semantic capacities of the totality of receivers, or of that subset of receivers which constitutes the audience one wishes to affect.

Similarly one can imagine another box in the diagram which, inserted between the information source and the transmitter, would b~ labeled "Semantic Noise" (not to be confused with "engineering noise"). This would represent distortions of meaning introduced by the information source, such as a speaker, which are not intentional but nevertheless affect the destination, or listener. And the problem of semantic decoding must take this semantic noise into account. It is also possible to think of a treatment or adjustment of the original message that would make the sum of message meaning plus semantic noise equal to the desired total message meaning at the destination.

ANOTHER way in which the theory can be helpful in improving communication is suggested by the fact that error and confusion arise and fidelity decreases when, no matter how good the coding, one tries to crowd too much over a channel. A general theory at all levels will surely have to take into account not only the capacity of the channel but also (even the words are right!) the capacity of the audience. If you overcrowd the capacity of the audience, it is probably true, by direct analogy, that you do not fill the audience up and then waste only the remainder by spilling. More likely, and again by direct analogy, you force a general error and confusion.

The concept of information developed in this theory at first seems disappointing and bizarre—disappointing because it has nothing to do with meaning, and bizarre because it deals not with a single message but rather with the statistical character of a whole ensemble of messages, bizarre also because in these statistical terms the words information and uncertainty find themselves partners.

But we have seen upon further examination of the theory that this analysis has so penetratingly cleared the air that one is now perhaps for the first time ready for a real theory of meaning. An engineering communication theory is just like a very proper and discreet girl at the telegraph office accepting your telegram. She pays no attention to the meaning, whether it be sad or joyous or embarrassing. But she must be prepared to deal intelligently with all messages that come to her desk. This idea that a communication system ought to try to deal with all possible messages, and that the intelligent way to try is to base design on the statistical character of the source, is surely not without significance for communication in general. Language must be designed, or developed, with a view to the totality of things that man may wish to say; but not being able to accomplish everything, it should do as well as possible as often as possible. That is to say, it too should deal with its task statistically.

This study reveals facts about the statistical structure of the English language, as an example, which must seem significant to students of every phase of language and communication. It suggests, as a particularly promising lead, the application of probability theory to semantic studies. Especially pertinent is the powerful body of probability theory dealing with what mathematicians call the Markoff processes, whereby past events influence present probabilities, since this theory is specifically adapted to handle one of the most significant but difficult aspects of meaning, namely the influence of context. One has the vague feeling that information and meaning may prove to be something like a pair of canonically conjugate variables in quantum theory, that is, that information and meaning may be subject to some joint restriction that compels the sacrifice of one if you insist on having much of the other.

Or perhaps meaning may be shown to be analogous to one of the quantities on which the entropy of a thermodynamic ensemble depends. Here Eddington has another apt comment:

"Suppose that we were asked to arrange the following in two categories—*distance, mass, electric force, entropy, beauty, melody*.

"I think there are the strongest grounds for placing entropy alongside beauty and melody, and not with the first three. Entropy is only found when the parts are viewed in association, and it is by viewing or hearing the parts in association that beauty and melody are discerned. All three are features of arrangement. It is a pregnant thought that one of these three associates should be able to figure as a commonplace quantity of science. The reason why this stranger can pass itself off among the aborigines of the physical world is that it is able to speak their language, *viz.*, the language of arithmetic."

One feels sure that Eddington would have been willing to include the word meaning along with beauty and melody; and one suspects he would have been thrilled to see, in this theory, that entropy not only speaks the language of arithmetic; it also speaks the language of language.

8

ERROR-CORRECTING CODES

W. WESLEY PETERSON • February 1962

Error-free performance is the goal of every good communication system. It was apparent from the earliest days of telegraphy and radio that the signals emanating at the receiving end of a system were never quite the same as those fed in at the transmitter. Over the years the term "noise" came to be applied to the various electrical and electromagnetic disturbances that degrade the quality of transmitted signals. At times the signals are not just degraded but are totally unintelligible. Until quite recently the engineer who wanted to improve the quality of a communication channel concentrated his attention on reducing noise, or, to be more precise, on increasing the signal-to-noise ratio. The most direct way to achieve this is to increase the power of the signal. Beyond that the engineer can try to improve the circuit and its components or enlarge the capacity of the communication channel with respect to the amount of information transmitted. Frequency-modulation (FM) radio is an example of the second approach; noise is reduced by the use of a channel many times broader than that used in amplitude-modulation (AM) radio.

Within the past 15 years a host of new signal-processing devices—notably the electronic computer—have stimulat-

TRANSMISSION ERRORS afflict all communication systems. When errors are made in ordinary speech or writing, however, it is usually possible to tell from a knowledge of spelling and language structure that an error has occurred. The redundancy of

ed a different approach for transmitting signals with a minimum of error: the use of error-detecting codes. The principle underlying such codes has a long history. What is new is (1) a body of theory that tells the engineer how close the codes come to ideal performance and (2) techniques for constructing codes.

The classic first papers on information theory, written in 1948 by Claude E. Shannon at the Bell Telephone Laboratories, included an important theorem on transmission of information over a noisy channel. The theorem states that such a channel has a definite capacity for transmitting information, measured in "bits" per second. A bit is defined as the amount of information required to specify one of two alternatives, such as yes or no, or, as is more common in computer systems, 1 or 0. The theorem states in addition that it is possible to encode information, transmit it over the noisy channel and decode it at any specified transmission rate less than the channel capacity in such a way that the probability of error is as near zero as one wishes.

This was a surprising idea. The obvious way to achieve more reliable communication is to repeat the message as many times as may seem necessary to ensure its being received correctly. The more times the message is repeated, the smaller will be the total amount of new information received. But Shannon's theorem shows that there is an alternative. With error-correcting codes it is possible to reduce the probability of error to the degree one wishes and to transmit much more information than could be sent if the message were simply repeated. Shannon's theorem gave no indication of how this coding for correction of errors could be accomplished, but it did show that it was possible.

Since that time many people have worked on the problem of devising error-correcting codes. A number of coding methods have been found, some simple and others complicated and difficult to understand. The basic principles are the same for all these codes, and I shall attempt to explain them by using several of the simpler codes as examples.

A familiar error-detection scheme is the one often found in business expense accounts [*see illustration on next page*]. The expenses for each day, suitably itemized, run across the sheet and are totaled in a column at the far right. This column of daily totals is then added to provide a grand total for, say, a week. As a check on this figure, the column of expenditures under each item (meals, hotel and so on) is totaled separately. These separate totals, when added, should match the sum of the daily totals.

If the expense account were transmitted over some communication system—or if it were retyped—and an error occurred in any single number, it would be possible to determine which number is wrong and to correct it. It is the extra, or redundant, information that makes error correction possible. The expense account illustrated on the next page contains 30 numbers, of which 10 are redundant. In general, any system for introducing redundancy into messages in a way that makes it possible to detect or correct errors is an error-detecting or error-correcting code.

Ordinary speech is redundant and can

language provides a sort of error-correcting code. When the redundancy is reduced, as in a telegram, the difficulty of detecting a transmission error increases. In the example illustrated, "noise" in the telegraph line has caused the letter *B* to be received as *T*.

be regarded as an error-correcting code. We have all had the experience of listening to another person in a noisy room and being able to understand what was said even though many syllables and even whole words were drowned out. Redundancy also appears in written language. If, for example, you received the following telegram, you would have no difficulty understanding the message: TWINS ARZIVED LAST NIGET EVERYON IS6FINE.

More serious errors could obliterate a word completely, but the chances are that it could be guessed from the context. Shannon has estimated that ordinary written English is 75 to 80 per cent redundant. Languages have very likely developed in this way because of man's need for reliable communication; that is, for communication with a certain amount of error detection and error correction built into it. In most situations they work quite well.

When we turn from language to information expressed numerically, we find that there is usually too little natural redundancy to be useful for error detection or correction. In any given sequence of numbers each digit is independent enough so that it cannot be guessed from context. It is, in fact, the increased processing of numerical data in business and industry, and the necessity for handling such data speedily and accurately, that has inspired much of the search for error-correcting codes.

It is not surprising that the first error-correcting systems were devised by men who dealt with numbers. Their chief concern was the detection of errors in computation rather than in transmission. These, however, are related problems. One method used for checking arithmetic operations is to repeat them. Another is to use the inverse operation: to check addition by subtraction, and multiplication by division. Both of these methods are analogous to repeating data in transmission.

Still another method, known as casting out 9's, is a much shorter but less thorough check for errors in arithmetic. It seems to have originated among the Arabs about A.D. 800, and has been widely used since about 1100, although it has not been commonly taught in this country since the 18th century.

In the casting-out-9's method one calculates for each number a "residue" that is obtained by throwing away as large as possible a multiple of 9. In other words, one divides by 9 and calls the remainder the residue. Thus the residue of 1,273 is 4 because 1,273 ÷ 9 = 141 with 4 left over. The residue of the sum of two numbers equals the sum of the residues. (It may be necessary to cast out a 9 in the sum of the residues.) Similarly, the residue for the product of two numbers is the product of the residues. If the residues do not check, there is an error. Three examples follow:

391 + 731 = 1,122

(RESIDUES) 4 + 2 = 6

391 × 731 = 285,821

4 × 2 = 8

66 × 77 = 5,082

3 × 5 = 15

(RESIDUE OF 5,082 = 6, RESIDUE OF 15 = 6)

Checking can be accomplished by casting out other numbers, for example by casting out 7's or 11's. Casting out 9's has been the most popular, however, because there is a simple short cut for calculating the residue. The sum of the digits in a number has the same residue as the number. Thus the residue of 285,821 is the same as the residue of 2+8+5+8+2+1=26, which is the same as the residue of 2+6=8.

Error-detecting and error-correcting codes for data transmission usually make use of the idea of casting out *n*'s, *n*, of course, being a given number. If decimal numbers are to be transmitted, the residue after casting out 10's of the sum of the digits could be transmitted as a "check." This permits detection (but not correction) of any single error. For the number 179,287,624, the sum of the digits is 46. Four 10's would be cast out, leaving 6 to be sent as the check digit. If any one digit is altered in transmission,

a

	MEALS	HOTEL	TRANS.	MISC.	TOTAL
MONDAY	4.75	7.00	84.79	2.79	99.33
TUESDAY	5.25	7.00	2.60	1.80	16.65
WEDNESDAY	6.50	7.00	5.98	3.11	22.59
THURSDAY	4.80	7.00	111.29	1.29	124.38
FRIDAY	7.25	.00	12.40	5.17	24.82
TOTAL	$28.55	$28.00	$217.06	$14.16	$287.77

b

	MEALS	HOTEL	TRANS.	MISC.	TOTAL
MONDAY	4.75	7.00	84.79	2.79	99.33
TUESDAY	5.25	7.00	2.60	4.80	16.65
WEDNESDAY	6.50	7.00	5.98	3.11	22.59
THURSDAY	4.80	7.00	111.29	1.29	124.38
FRIDAY	7.25	.00	12.40	5.17	24.82
TOTAL	$28.55	$28.00	$217.06	$14.16	$287.77

c

	MEALS	HOTEL	TRANS.	MISC.	TOTAL
MONDAY	9.00	11.00	23.00	1.00	53.00
TUESDAY	5.00	11.00	12.00	2.00	30.00
WEDNESDAY	6.00	7.00	13.00	1.00	27.00
THURSDAY	6.00	7.00	5.00	3.00	21.00
FRIDAY	7.00	12.00	79.00	2.00	100.00
TOTAL	$33.00	$48.00	$141.00	$9.00	$231.00

SIMPLE ERROR-CHECKING SYSTEM is that often found in expense accounts. Daily totals form a column at the far right and item totals form a row across the bottom. The two sets of totals must add up to produce the same grand total. If, in transcription or transmission, an error were to occur in any single number, it could be detected and corrected. Such an error is shown in *b*, where the totals for "Tuesday" and "Misc." are $3 less than the separate row and column entries indicate. Evidently the Tuesday entry for miscellaneous must be $3 too large. A similar error appears in *c*; the reader is invited to find it.

the sum of the digits will not check against the check digit.

To produce an error-correcting code for decimal digits one can adopt the principle discussed earlier for the expense account. The information digits are arranged in a rectangle. A casting-out-10's sum check is given in each row and each column, as shown in the first example, at the left below.

72965	9
90271	9
71107	6
20366	7
53599	1

72965	9
90271	9
77107	6
20366	7
53599	1

1402	1
7209	8
6661	9
1231	7
5893	5

Note that the digit 1 in the lower right-hand corner can be obtained as the casting-out-10's sum of either the last row or the last column. It is the casting-out-10's grand total for the array. One digit is wrong in the array shown in the middle example. It can be found by recalculating the row and column checks and seeing which fail. The third row fails: the sum is 22, so the check digit would be 2 if there were no error in that row. The second column fails: it adds up to 9, which would be the check digit if there were no error. The single error must be at the intersection of the third row and second column. That it should be 1 instead of 7 can be seen either from the fact that the column sum is 6 too large or from the fact that the row sum is 4 too small. The third array shown at the right also contains one error; the reader may wish to find it for himself.

Most computers and most data transmission systems handle information coded in binary digits. This means that everything is expressed as a combination of 1's and 0's. The illustration on the opposite page shows the most common way of representing the numbers 0 to 15 in the binary system.

In processing binary data the usual error-detection systems are based on casting out 2's. For example, the sum of the digits in the binary sequence 111001010 is 5. Since this is an odd number, the residue after casting out 2's is 1, which constitutes the check symbol. The number would therefore be transmitted as 1110010101 (the original number with its residue added at the right). The number 110101101 would be transmitted as 1101011010, since it has an even number of 1's. It is readily observed that the residue or check digit always makes the total number of 1's even. For this reason the method is often called a parity check. If a single error occurs in transmission, the total number of 1's is odd and the error can be readily detected.

To go a step further and obtain an error-correcting code one simply arranges the binary information in the form of a rectangular array. Three typical arrays are shown below.

1110	1
1010	0
0111	1
0101	0
1011	1
1101	1

1110	1
1110	0
0111	1
0101	0
1011	1
1101	1

11111	1
10101	1
11100	0
10110	1
11001	1
11000	0

A casting-out-2's check digit is placed at the end of each row and each column, and a casting-out-2's grand total appears in the bottom right-hand corner. This digit can be obtained either from the row sums or from the column sums. Note also that each row now has an even number of 1's and each column also has an even number of 1's. There is one error in the middle array. All row and column sums check except the second row and the second column, both of which have an odd number of 1's. Therefore the error must be at the intersection of the second row and second column. Changing this digit from 1 to 0 effects the correction. There is also an error in the array at the right.

This type of rectangular-array code provides the error check for most of the magnetic-tape storage systems found in today's large computers. Although the code could be used to correct errors, it is commonly employed only to detect them. The minimum undetectable error pattern consists of four errors so placed as to define a rectangle anywhere within the large array. In this case every row and every column would still exhibit even parity in spite of the errors.

Although simple, the rectangular-array codes are not particularly efficient. For example, if nine information digits are arranged in a three-by-three array, seven check digits would be required, making a total of 16 digits. In 1950 Richard W. Hamming of the Bell Telephone Laboratories described a class of single-error-correcting codes that require a minimum number of check symbols. One of these codes has 11 information digits and only four check digits, or a redundancy of 37 per cent. The next code in the series has 26 information digits and five check digits, for a redundancy of only 16 per cent. As the codes increase in length, the redundancy decreases still further. The Hamming code takes many forms. I shall describe what is called the cyclic form.

Let $X_1, X_2, X_3, \ldots, X_{11}$ be the information symbols and X_{12}, X_{13}, X_{14} and X_{15} the check symbols. The formulas for computing the check symbols appear at the top of the next page. These are not ordinary equations but mean rather that the quantity on the left of the equal sign is the residue after casting out 2's of the sum on the right of the equal sign.

The illustration at the bottom of the next page shows in chart form which symbols appear in each check equation. For example, X_{10} is involved in the equation for calculating X_{14}, and thus in the row that has X_{14} at the left there is a "yes" in the column headed X_{10}. Each column in this chart is a different arrangement of yeses and noes. In fact, the 15 columns contain all the combinations possible with just four yeses or noes—except for all noes—and represent, in effect, another way to count to 15 in binary

DECIMAL	BINARY
00	0000
01	0001
02	0010
03	0011
04	0100
05	0101
06	0110
07	0111
08	1000
09	1001
10	1010
11	1011
12	1100
13	1101
14	1110
15	1111

BINARY SYSTEM employs only two symbols, 0 and 1, and therefore requires writing down more symbols than in the decimal system to express any number greater than one. In decimal notation a 1 increases in value by multiples of 10 for each place that it moves to the left. Thus the decimal number 1,000 is 10 × 10 × 10. In binary notation a 1 increases by multiples of 2 as it moves to left. Thus in binary, 1000 is 2 × 2 × 2, or 8.

$$X_{12} = X_9 + X_8 + X_6 + X_4 + X_3 + X_2 + X_1$$

$$X_{13} = X_{10} + X_9 + X_7 + X_5 + X_4 + X_3 + X_2$$

$$X_{14} = X_{11} + X_{10} + X_8 + X_6 + X_5 + X_4 + X_3$$

$$X_{15} = X_{12} + X_{11} + X_9 + X_7 + X_6 + X_5 + X_4$$

ERROR-CORRECTING CODE devised in 1950 by Richard W. Hamming of the Bell Telephone Laboratories uses four check symbols to protect 11 information symbols (and the check symbols themselves) from single errors. X_1, X_2, ..., X_{11} represent the information symbols; X_{12}, X_{13}, X_{14}, X_{15} represent the check symbols. The symbols are either 0 or 1. These four equations employ the casting-out-2's method to yield the binary check symbols. The check symbol is 0 if the sum of the symbols at the right is 0 or even, 1 if the sum is odd.

notation. Each symbol, including the check symbols, is used in a different set of check equations. If a particular symbol is wrong, each equation involving it will fail. From the pattern of failures one can determine where the error lies.

Let us take an example. Suppose the information symbols X_1 through X_{11} are 11010010111, in that order. Then on the basis of the check equations X_{12} is the residue of 4 after casting out 2's, which is 0. Symbol X_{13} is the residue of 5, or 1, X_{14} is the residue of 3, or 1, and X_{15} is the residue of 4, or 0. Therefore the 15 digits that would be transmitted are 110100101110110, of which the last four at the right are checking digits. Suppose 110101101110110 is received. In order to locate the error the following questions must be posed and answered:

Does the X_{12} equation fail? Yes.
Does the X_{13} equation fail? No.
Does the X_{14} equation fail? Yes.
Does the X_{15} equation fail? Yes.

This combination of yeses and noes appears under X_6 in the illustration below. Therefore X_6 must be the incorrect symbol, for only this particular single error would cause the first, third and fourth equations to fail. Even an error in a check symbol can be corrected.

The "memories" of the International Business Machines giant Stretch computer and the Bell System experimental electronic switching system at Morris, Ill., use Hamming codes to protect against single errors. These computers can detect and correct such errors automatically.

Cyclic codes have some remarkable algebraic properties, and for some cyclic codes these involve rather deep algebraic theory. One interesting and useful property is that the successive check equations are formed by shifting the last previous sequence of yeses and noes one space to the right. The resulting pattern can be seen in the illustration below. Moreover, if a correctly coded message is shifted cyclicly—that is, X_1 into X_2, X_2 into X_3, ..., X_{14} into X_{15}, and X_{15} into X_1—the resulting message will also satisfy the check equations.

The most important consequence of the cyclic structure is that it can be exploited in designing a simple electronic encoder and error corrector, which requires only a modest number of electronic components, such as transistors. The device for calculating parity checks takes the form of a "shift register," a type of electronic circuit commonly used in computers. A diagram of the shift register for the cyclic Hamming code appears at the top of page 57. As the 0's and 1's of the code are fed into the register, one at a time, the register carries out a simple adding and shifting operation. After each step a 0 or 1 appears in a series of four storage units, which are designated *a*, *b*, *c* and *d*. In connection with the Hamming code this device has three uses. In each case the shift register is assumed to contain all 0's initially.

1. To calculate the check digits, the information symbols are entered in sequence, with a shift taking place after each entry. After the 11th symbol has been entered, the check symbols appear in the storage units: X_{12} appears in *a*, X_{13} in *b*, X_{14} in *c* and X_{15} in *d*.

2. To check for errors in a received message all 15 received symbols are entered in the register, which again shifts after each entry. If, and only if, the received message satisfies the check equations, the four storage units will contain all 0's after the 15th message symbol enters.

3. If the checking operation indicates that an error has occurred, and if it is a single error, the symbol in error can be determined as follows. After the operation described in the second step is completed, the shift register is shifted with 0's as input until 1000 appears in the four storage units. The number of the erroneous symbol is one greater than the number of shifts required to obtain this sequence of digits [*see illustration on page 58*].

Some remarkable cyclic codes have been discovered in the past few years. One class, discovered independently by A. Hocquenghem of the Conservatoire National des Arts et Métiers in Paris and by Raj Chandra Bose and D. K. Ray-Chaudhuri at the University of North Carolina, corrects multiple errors in any arrangement, the maximum number of errors correctable depending on the number of check symbols. Other

SYMBOL

	X_1	X_2	X_3	X_4	X_5	X_6	X_7	X_8	X_9	X_{10}	X_{11}	X_{12}	X_{13}	X_{14}	X_{15}
EQUATION X_{12}	YES	YES	YES	YES	NO	YES	NO	YES	YES	NO	NO	YES	NO	NO	NO
EQUATION X_{13}	NO	YES	YES	YES	YES	NO	YES	NO	YES	YES	NO	NO	YES	NO	NO
EQUATION X_{14}	NO	NO	YES	YES	YES	YES	NO	YES	NO	YES	YES	NO	NO	YES	NO
EQUATION X_{15}	NO	NO	NO	YES	YES	YES	YES	NO	YES	NO	YES	YES	NO	NO	YES

CHECKING SCHEME for the Hamming cyclic code is based on this array showing which symbols appear in each check equation. Each pattern of yeses and noes in the 15 columns is different. How the array is used to correct single errors is described in the text.

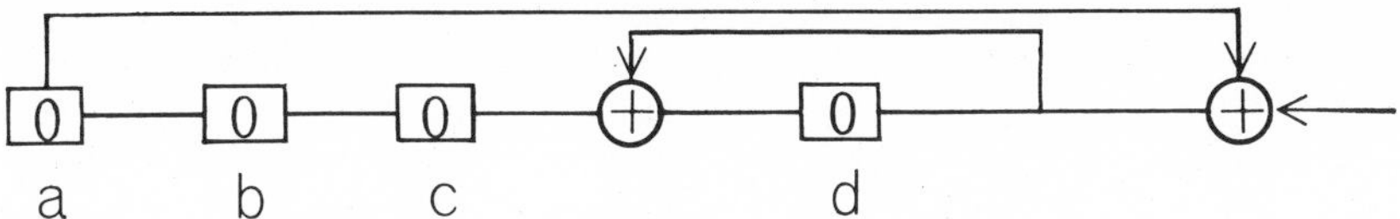

SHIFT REGISTER is a simple electronic device for putting binary messages into a Hamming code and for checking the accuracy of the received message. The input is either a 0 or 1 of the primary message. The circles containing a plus sign represent "adders." The signal coming out of them is a 0 if the sum of the input signals is 0 or 2 and 1 if the sum is 1. The square blocks (*a, b, c, d*) are shifting storage devices; they store either 0 or 1. When a shift signal is given, the stored symbols appear as signals on the output lines (*extending to left*), and the storage devices store the new symbols carried by signals entering from the right.

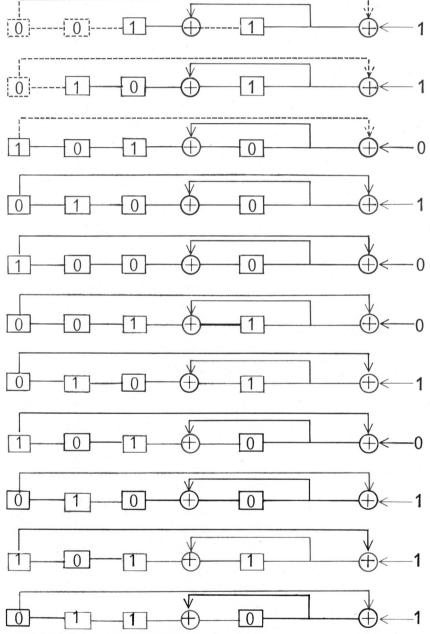

DERIVATION OF CHECK SYMBOLS is shown for the 11-symbol message 11010010111. At the start the four storage devices contain 0's, as shown at the top of page. Entry of the first symbol, 1 (*reading the message from the left*), makes each adder put out a signal for 1 (*color*), leading to the storage of 1's in *c* and *d*. Entry of the second symbol, also 1, makes the first adder put out a 1, but the second adder, having received two 1's as an input, puts out a 0, which is stored in *c*. The 1 previously stored in *c* passes to *b*. (Broken lines indicate parts of register not yet activated.) The register continues to shift in this fashion until all 11 symbols have been entered. The symbols remaining in the four storage devices, 0110, are the four check symbols that must be added to the message, which becomes 110100101110110.

codes protect against errors clustered in widely spaced groups or bursts.

Because of their cyclic structure these codes are also relatively easy to use. A prototype decoder for a 127-symbol, five-error-correcting Bose-Chaudhuri code is being built by Thomas C. Bartee at the Lincoln Laboratory of the Massachusetts Institute of Technology. Employing transistors, the decoder will occupy no more space than an ordinary file drawer. Prototype decoders for burst-error-correcting codes have been built by IBM and by the Bell Telephone Laboratories.

When cyclic codes are used only for error detection rather than for error correction, the equipment can be simpler still. For example, at the Lincoln Laboratory an experimental system embodying error detection is being built for high-speed, two-way data transmission over a telephone line. When an error is detected, a request for a repeat transmission is automatically made over the return channel. The code used in this system is a Bose-Chaudhuri code with 255 symbols, of which only 24 are check symbols. The encoder and error detector use a 24-stage shift register of the type shown at the top left. It is estimated that the code will fail to detect an error on the average of once every 300 years. This, of course, is much longer than the terminal equipment can be expected to operate without failure.

For a specified number of information symbols and a specified number of check symbols, there are many ways in which to set up equations for calculating check symbols. Depending on the transmission characteristics of a given channel, some are good and some are poor choices. For each choice there is an optimum procedure for correcting errors and a certain probability that an uncorrectable pattern of errors will occur. For codes of appreciable length it is difficult to calculate the probability of an uncorrectable error. For a binary code of 50 symbols, of which half are check symbols, many hours of computer time are required to calculate the error probability. It is possible, however, by a mathematical stratagem to calculate the *average* error probability for *all* codes with a given total number of symbols. The stratagem is actually the basis for Shannon's original proof of his fundamental theorem on error-correcting codes.

As an example, consider a channel that transmits binary symbols and in which the probability of error is .01; that is, on the average, 99 times out of 100, transmitted symbols are received correctly, but once in 100 symbols a

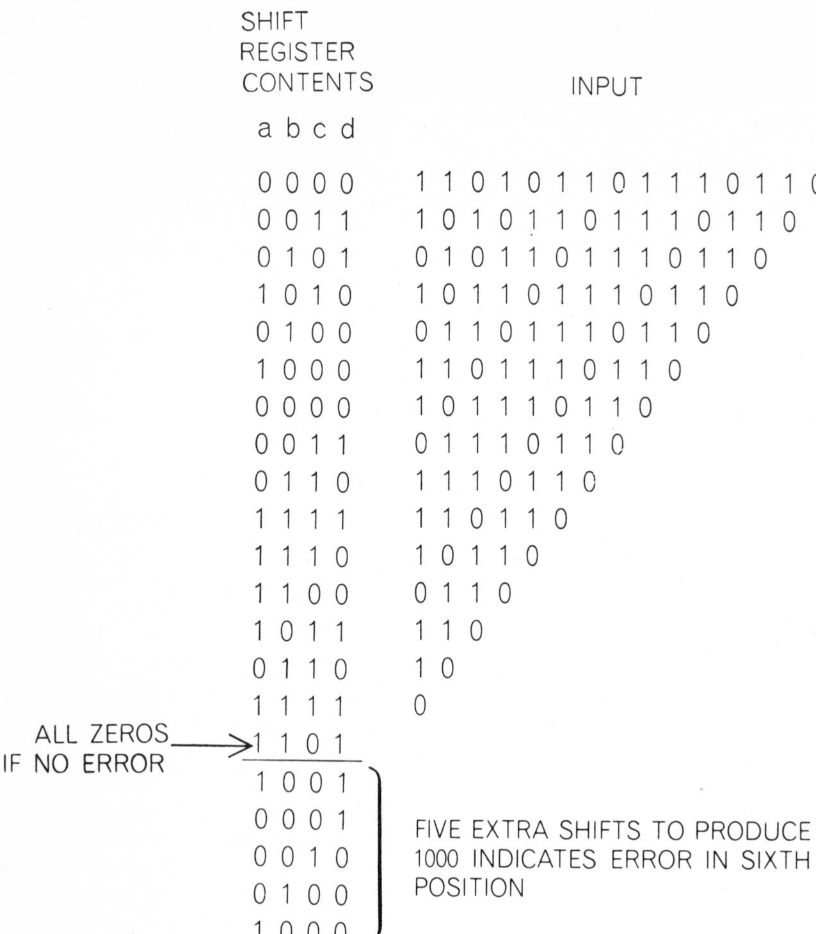

ERROR CHECKING is accomplished with the same shift register used for calculating the check symbols, illustrated on page 57. There it was seen that the 11-symbol message 11010010111 requires 4 checking symbols, 0110, so that the total message transmitted is 110100101110110. This illustration shows the successive storage contents of the shift register if the message as received contains one error: 110101101110110. When all 15 symbols have been entered into the register, the reading of 1101 indicates that an error has occurred. The register is then shifted (with 0's as input) until it reads 1000. The number of the erroneous symbol is one greater than the number of shifts required: it is the sixth symbol from left.

0 is received as a 1, or vice versa. Then the probability of an uncorrectable error, *averaged over all possible codes* of 511 symbols, of which 171 are check symbols, is approximately .00000000000000035; that is, for an average code it can be shown mathematically that only one in approximately three million billion code blocks of 511 symbols would contain uncorrectable errors. Now, if we write out a set of parity-check equations for a code of this size, there is about a 50–50 chance that it will be as good as the mathematical average. Certainly many of the codes must be better than this. Yet we do not know how to write check equations for any code that we can prove is as good as the average.

The Bose-Chaudhuri codes are by far the best codes for which the check symbol calculation and the error-correction procedure are explicitly known. For the Bose-Chaudhuri code of length 511 with 171 check symbols, and with the same assumptions as in the preceding paragraph, the probability of an error pattern uncorrectable by the known correction procedure is .00000009. It can be shown that this is not the best mathematical correction procedure, but we know of no better practical procedure; and we do not know what the probability of error would be for this code with the best error-correction procedure. Although this is the best-understood code, we have not yet been able to prove that it is as good as average!

This state of affairs has presented a challenge and a source of some frustration to specialists in the field. Surely it must be possible to construct a better-than-average code. Yet it seems that when we construct a code by regular rules, its very structure makes it poor for combating random errors.

Some information theorists, notably Robert M. Fano, John McReynolds Wozencraft and Patrick Ximenes Gallagher of the Massachusetts Institute of Technology, believe that the best solution is to pick a code at random or construct the check-symbol equations at random. Some fairly effective systems based on randomly chosen codes have been devised. An experimental model of one such system is being built at the Lincoln Laboratory, and there will be great interest in the outcome of this experiment. It is quite possible that such systems will be increasingly important in the future.

It has been only in the past two or three years that the theory of error-correcting codes has advanced sufficiently to provide the basis for practical systems. Computer technology also has continued to advance, decreasing the cost and increasing the speed of equipment used to implement error correction. At the same time, there is a growing need for communication channels of extreme reliability for computers and automatic control systems. As the need grows and as coding theory and computer technology continue to develop, error detection and error correction will play an essential role in the success of complex systems.

ARAB MATHEMATICIANS of about A.D. 800 are credited with inventing one of the earliest error-detecting schemes, known as casting out 9's. This technique, seldom taught any more, would be useful to school children. How it works is explained in text.

9

REDUNDANCY IN COMPUTERS

WILLIAM H. PIERCE • February 1964

One of the difficult problems facing the engineer in an imperfect world is how to get reliable performance from complex electrical systems such as computers, in which any of perhaps a million things can go wrong. The traditional way to make a system more reliable is to improve the reliability of each of its parts, but in many cases component reliability has been pushed so close to its limits that further improvement may be uneconomical or even impossible. An alternative is available: to design a system so that it functions properly even when some of its parts fail. To accomplish this one must provide redundant, or extra, parts that are required to overcome errors but that would be quite unnecessary if no errors ever occurred. Techniques for inserting such redundancy have been developed in the past 10 years. This article will discuss some of these techniques and some recently discovered mathematical laws describing their effectiveness.

The most compelling reason for the current interest in redundancy theory and techniques is that modern technology is increasingly dependent on the reliability of complex electrical equipment, much of it involving digital computing machinery; the survival of an orbiting astronaut, for example, depends on the rapid and accurate calculation of arithmetical problems on digital computers. Moreover, the development of redundancy techniques for engineering man-made systems seems likely to lead to new insights into the arrangements evolved by nature to control errors in biological nervous systems. Redundancy theory, finally, presents an intellectual challenge rather closely related to that of its sister field, information theory.

Parts fail at random and in unpredictable combinations, but these failures are subject to mathematical analysis on a statistical basis. The great power of the statistical treatment of engineering problems was first realized during World War II, when it was applied to such tasks as discriminating electrical signals from noise, and led to improvements in radar and similar systems. Soon it was seen that statistics could be applied to the analysis of engineering possibilities. In a classic paper published in 1948, Claude E. Shannon, then of the Bell Telephone Laboratories, showed that statistical techniques could even be used to study a piece of hardware that had not yet been invented and to predict both its potentialities and its limitations. He did this by defining mathematically the concept of "information" and finding theorems stating how much information can ever be extracted from data of given reliability. One might say that whereas information theory deals with

DEMONSTRATION MODEL built at the Westinghouse Defense and Space Center in Baltimore illustrates the effectiveness of redundancy. A visitor is invited to snip a substantial number of wires at random; the demonstrator continues to function reliably. This photograph shows four of the six banks of circuit cards that make up the demonstrator. There are two different types of cards. One type (*exemplified by card at top left corner*) carries the components of the "vote-taker" restoring organs that suppress error. Most of the components that perform the logical operations are on the other cards (*such as the one second from right in top row*).

the manipulation of unreliable information with circuits assumed to be reliable, redundancy theory faces up to the handling of unreliable information with unreliable circuits.

Redundancy techniques are particularly well adapted to computer circuits in which the signals are binary, as they are in all commercial digital computers. A binary signal is one that has two possible physical conditions: either zero volts or one volt, typically (and in all examples given in this article). Circuits manipulating these binary voltages to produce other binary voltages can perform any arithmetical operation. One of the simplest binary devices is the relay, in which the two conditions are closed or open, "on" or "off." Relays have been basic components of telephone switching systems for years, and in the late 1930's it was relay computers that demonstrated the feasibility of automatic electrical computation. When the first modern electronic computers were built in the late 1940's, they were put together, with tubes and other radio parts dating from the 1920's, by people thinking in terms of relays.

It is easy to add redundancy to a relay circuit. Consider, by way of analogy, a water-flow system with four unreliable valves that are all opened or closed together [*see top illustration at right*]. One valve can be faulty in that it does not open or close when it should, and still the water will flow when it should and will not flow when it should not. The same thing happens with electrical current in a redundant relay system such as the one illustrated at the bottom of this page, which will function properly even if one relay fails. Although this system illustrates the principle of redundancy, and although some redundancy techniques are extensive generalizations of just such simple arrangements, for the most part what works for relays is not appropriate for electronic tubes and transistors. Before considering the techniques that are applicable to computers, let us consider the mathematical reasoning that shows just how effective redundancy can be against the unrelated, random failures that are so hard to eliminate from large electrical machines.

The effectiveness of redundancy when failures are unrelated derives from an important property of "statistically independent," or unrelated, events: The probability that several statistically independent events will all occur is the product of the probabilities that each of the events will occur. For example, if the probability that it will rain while you

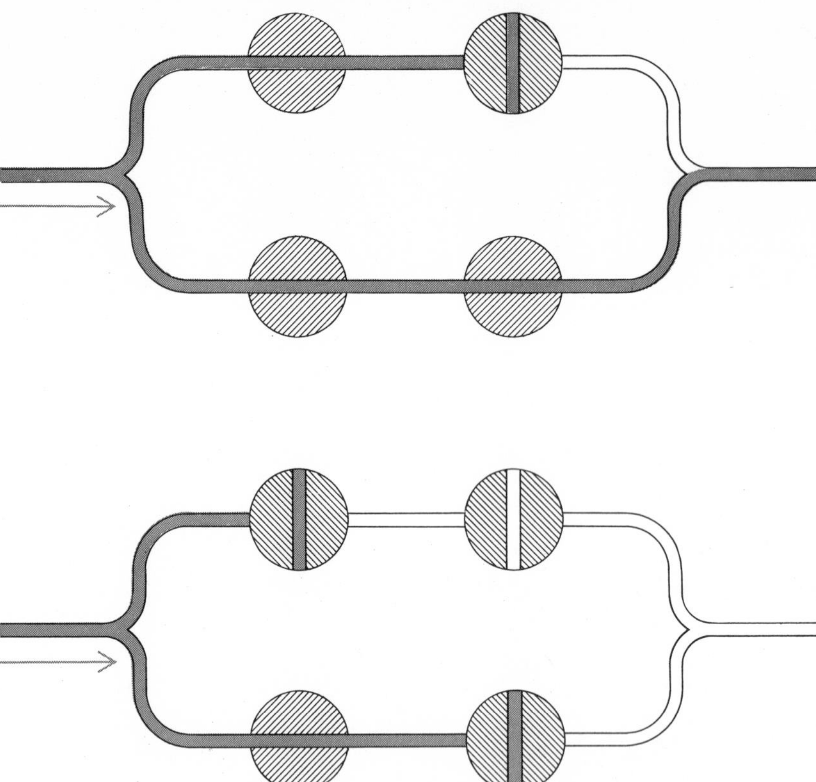

WATER SYSTEM illustrates the principle of redundancy. If four petcocks take the place of one, any single error is nullified. In the top drawing water flows from left to right in spite of the fact that the valve at upper right is stuck closed; in the bottom drawing water does not flow when it should not, even though the valve at lower left is improperly open.

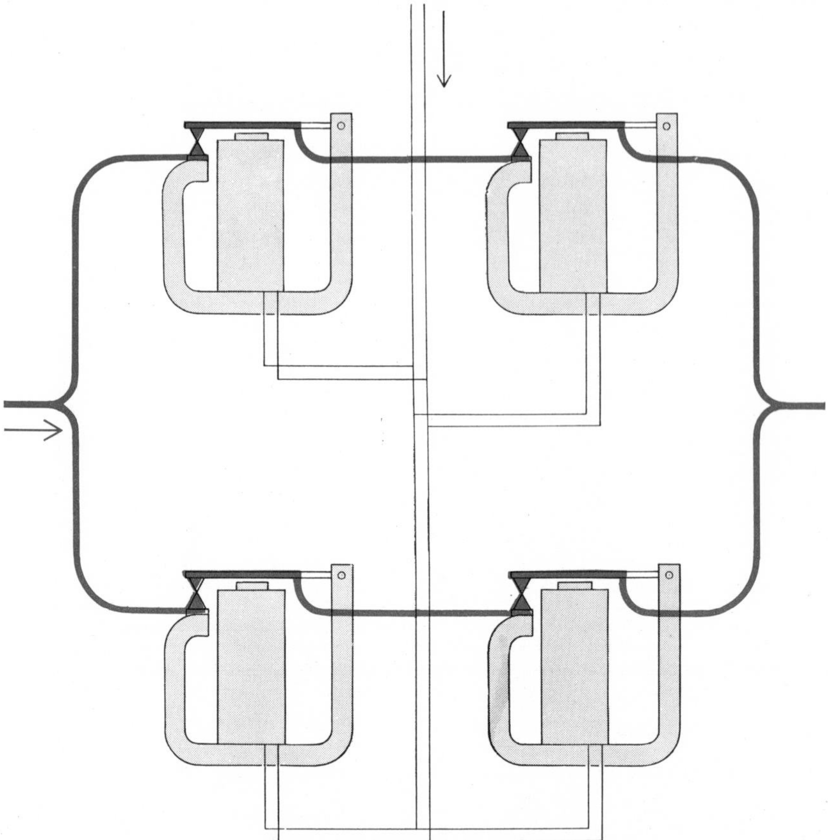

RELAY SYSTEM is directly analogous with the water system at the top of the page. When the electromagnets are energized, the four pairs of contact points close and electricity flows. With four relays, one can be improperly open or closed; the system will still work properly.

drive home from work is one in 10 (10^{-1}), the probability of having a flat tire on the way is one in 100 (10^{-2}) and the probability that you will get a toothache during the trip is one in 1,000 (10^{-3}), then the probability that all these events will occur is $10^{-1} \times 10^{-2} \times 10^{-3}$, or 10^{-6} (one in a million). In other words, it would be an extremely rare bit of bad luck.

In many redundancy techniques the number of extra circuits can be increased indefinitely to make the probability of failure as small as one wants—or as small as the customer is willing to pay for. The laws governing the relation between the number of extra circuits and a computer's failure probability depend essentially on the product rule of probabilities for independent events. The exact formulas for the relevant probabilities are complicated, as are similar formulas for the probabilities that arise in information theory. In both cases, however, the complicated expressions can often be accurately approximated by simple functions that are "asymptotic" to them. By way of illustration, consider the factorial function $n!$, or $1 \times 2 \times 3 \ldots \times n$. Its logarithm is well approximated, when n is at least 100, by the simple formula $n(-.435 + \log n)$. The approximation becomes better—its ratio to the exact expression comes closer to 1—as n becomes larger. Any such approximation is called an asymptote.

In the complicated probability calculations of redundancy theory one often deals with probabilities that are the sums of individual products of probabilities. For example, the probability that a coin flipped $3n$ times will come up heads on two-thirds or more of these occasions is the probability that the number of heads will be $2n$ plus the probability that it will be $2n + 1$ and so on up to $3n$. Each term in this sum contains a product of probabilities, and the sum of these probabilities has, for a large n, an asymptote that also contains a product of probabilities. Workers interested in both information theory and the newer field of redundancy theory have discovered asymptotes for probabilities that are sums of other probabilities, and with them they have established a number of fundamental theorems.

One such theorem, which has been discovered only recently, predicts that the probability of failure in a redundant system can decrease exponentially as the redundancy is increased. The theorem applies to a system that will fail only if at least a fraction B of its redundant parts should fail. If each part fails independently with some probability less than B, the failure probability of the system as a whole can be divided by two if one adds a specific number of redundant parts. The number depends on the failure probability of the individual parts and on the fraction B. And its dependence on B, interestingly enough, is the same kind of mathematical expression as the term for "information" in information theory. The important implication of this theorem is that the redundancy—and the cost—will go up only arithmetically, whereas the failure probability goes down geometrically.

A second theorem states that in a system with many different functions performed by parts of varying cost and reliability, it is generally better to add redundancy in order to give each function the same probability of failure, regardless of the relative cost of the parts. In other words, it is generally best to allocate costs in order to improve the strength of the weakest link in the chain, even when it costs more to strengthen some links than others. Finally, the product rule for independent probabilities indicates that as larger and larger computers are built, relatively little of the additional expense will be required to maintain reliability through redundancy.

These, at least, are the theoretical predictions. A number of practical problems can prevent their fulfillment, notably the difficulty of seeing to it that the failures are indeed random and independent of one another. Redundancy does no good, and can even do harm, if the various parts of a circuit are not isolated so that a local failure cannot cause damage to nearby parts. In devising redundancy techniques an engineer must therefore understand and keep in mind the physical implications of his mathematical models and his theorems.

One of the first systematic redundancy techniques to be discovered is based on the replacement of an individual wire by a bundle of wires, each of which, in the absence of error, carries the same signal. It is as though there were a nation in which no citizen could be trusted, and accordingly several citizens were required to act together in making decisions, executing orders or delivering messages. As a simple example of the bundle idea consider a part of a nonredundant computer that is required to have a binary output (c) of one volt if one input (a) is one volt and the other (b) is zero. A two-input, one-output logic gate, or electrical circuit, can be made with this property [*see illustration at left*]. In a redundant version of this circuit each wire is replaced by a bundle of wires and the logic gate is replaced by several independent but identical gates. (The number of wires in each bundle and the number of gates is three in the illustration, but it could be any odd number.) Such a redundant scheme is incomplete, however, because the information on the redundant wires of the output bundle has not been made to interact. The circuit still requires some modification that will interconnect the components and suppress errors.

The device that does this is a "restoring organ," which receives as inputs the several wires of a bundle, allows their redundant information to interact and thereby produces an output bundle that contains a more reliable version of

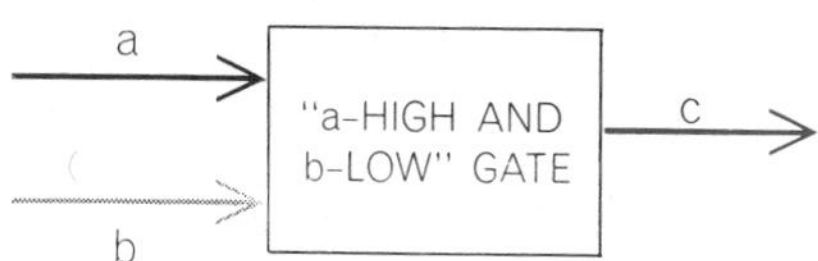

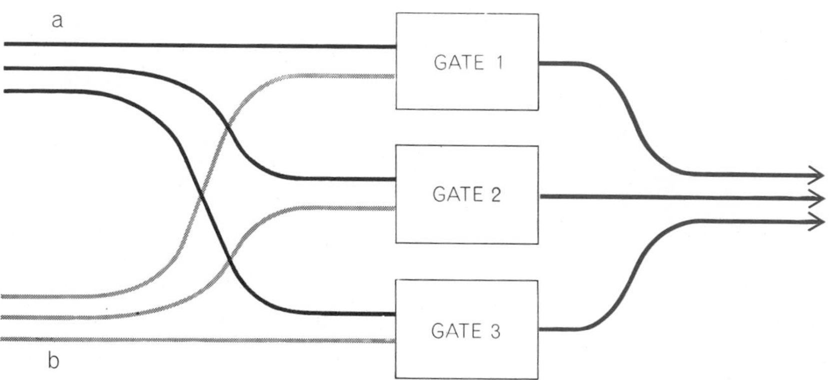

BUNDLE CONCEPT is basic in redundancy. Assume that the simple circuit shown at the top is to be made redundant; it is a circuit that puts out a one-volt signal if input *a* is one volt and input *b* is zero. In the redundant version below, each input and output wire is replaced by a bundle of three wires and there are three logic gates rather than one.

the input signal. In one type of restoring organ [*see illustration at right*] the signal on each output line is obtained by a "vote-taker," a logic circuit that can take a majority vote of its inputs. If two or three of its inputs are one-volt signals, the output will be one volt; otherwise it will be zero. A restoring organ of this type can correct any single error. If perfectly reliable vote-takers were available, only one of them would be needed in a restoring organ. Because they are fallible, however, a separate one is used for each output. A mistake by one vote-taker is no more harmful than an error in the unreliable circuit carrying that vote-taker's output.

Clearly vote-taking could be a great deal more effective if the various inputs had an influence proportional to their degree of reliability—an aristocratic rather than a democratic suffrage, as it were. This can be accomplished by giving the inputs unequal weights; the output is the signal "voted for" by the greater sum of weights rather than simply by the larger number of inputs. The beauty of such a vote-taker is that it can compute the correct output from a single reliable input, even in the face of a large number of contradictory, unreliable inputs.

In order to weight the votes properly, self-adjusting, or "adaptive," circuits are added to the vote-taker to adjust each input's vote-weight in accordance with its reliability. The error probability of each input can be estimated from the number of times the input disagrees with a special "training" answer supplied during a check program run from time to time for this purpose. Alternatively, the reliability of each input can be found by continually counting the disagreements between that input and the output of the vote-taker itself. In this way, by a kind of feedback of information, each input's weight is continually adjusted in accordance with its recent reliability.

Restoring organs can be constructed in a number of ways. Circuit constraints, for instance, might make it necessary to limit the number of inputs to a vote-taker to three when reliability considerations dictate a redundancy of five. The restoring organ will be composed of five three-input vote-takers. Each vote-taker cannot receive all input lines, and the problem arises of deciding which inputs to assign to which vote-taker. One solution is simply to avoid the decision: to allow a "random maze" to establish the connections. At first thought the idea of placing a

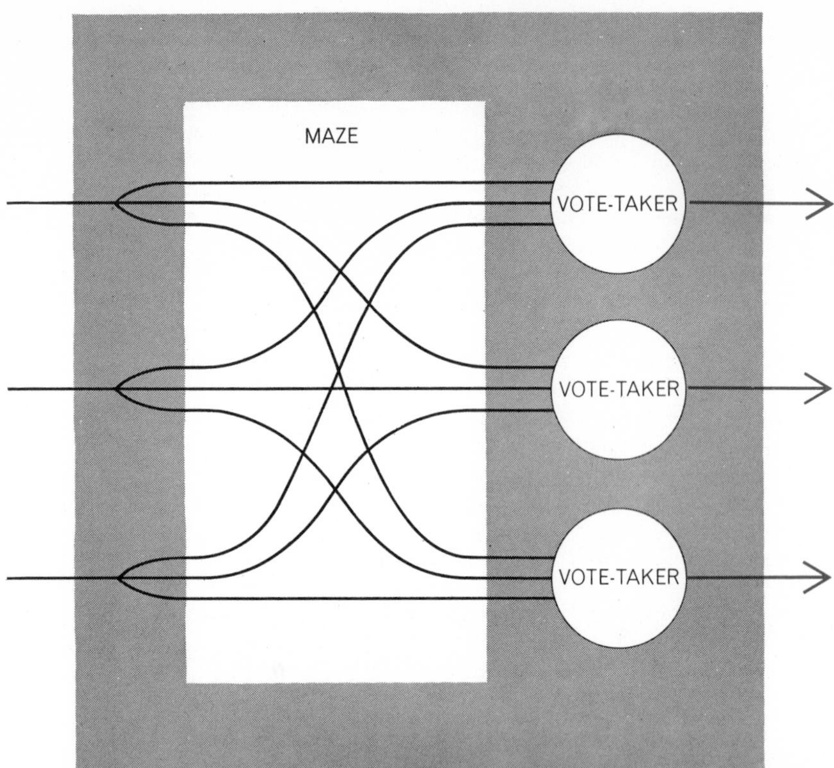

RESTORING ORGAN causes the several wires of a bundle to interact and so to produce a more reliable bundle. This type depends on "vote-takers" to create the output bundle (*color*). In this example each vote-taker receives an input from each wire of the bundle. A "majority vote" (two out of three here) determines the output, correcting any single error.

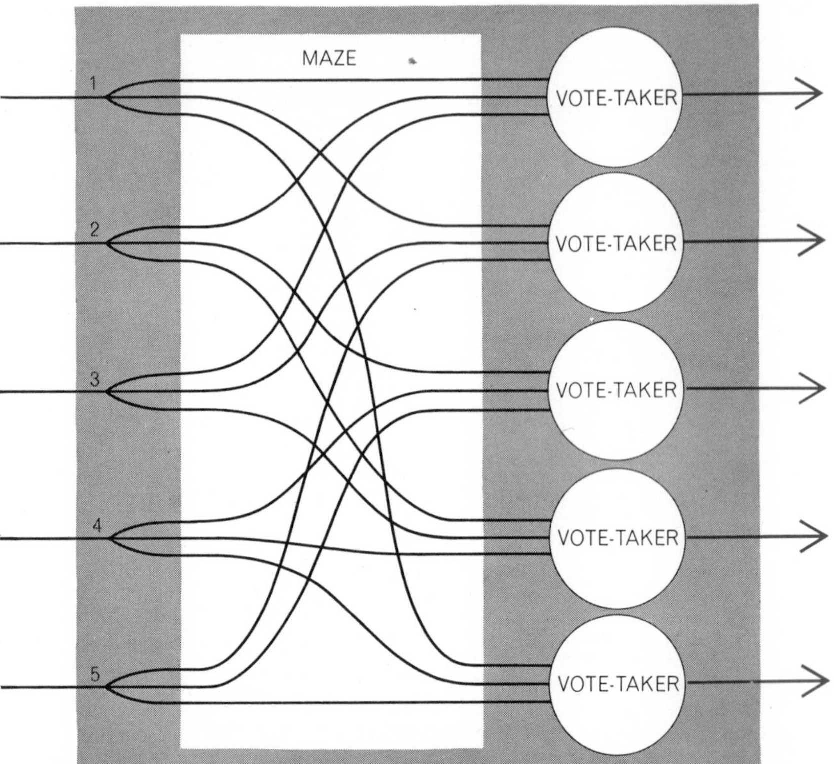

MAZE becomes important if the inputs to each vote-taker must be fewer than the number of vote-takers. In this restoring organ each vote-taker receives a signal from only three of the five input wires. The inputs could simply be connected haphazardly in a "random maze." Or, as in this example, the connections can be worked out in a "deterministic maze" designed to reduce the number of double errors that can get through the restoring organ.

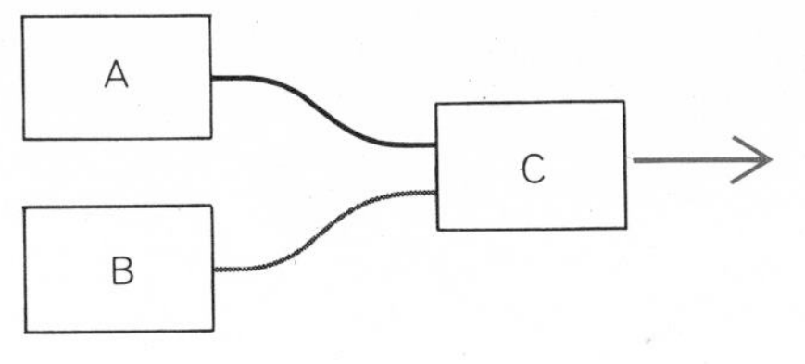

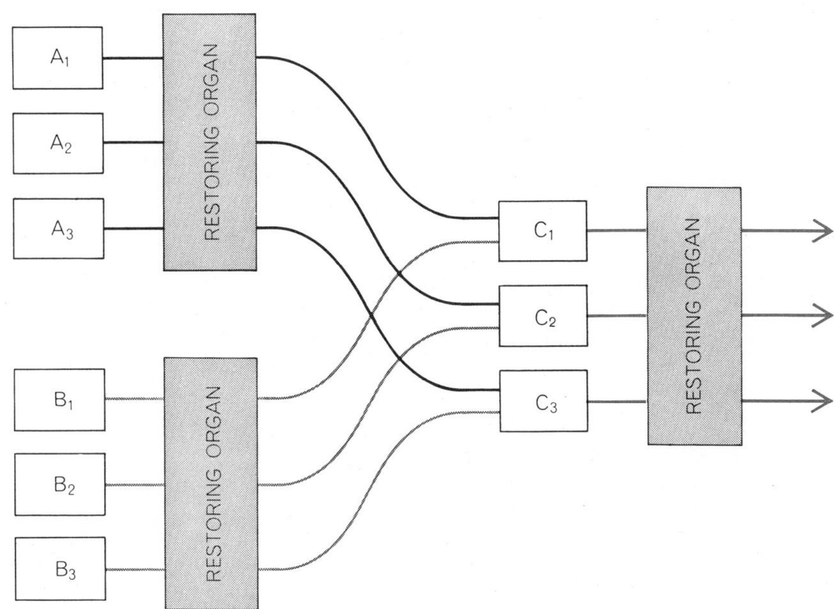

REDUNDANT CIRCUIT is constructed by combining logic elements and restoring organs. A nonredundant circuit (*top*) includes logic gates *A* and *B*, which feed their output to gate *C* for processing. In the redundant version (*bottom*) each gate becomes three gates, each wire a bundle of three, and restoring organs are inserted after each logical operation.

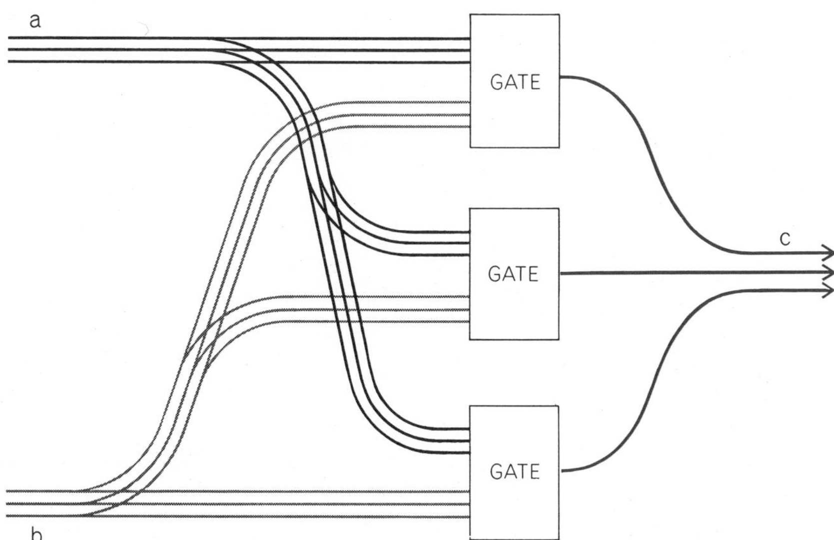

THRESHOLD GATE can perform digital logic and error-correction simultaneously. If each wire in the *c* bundle is to carry one volt when the signals on the *a* or the *b* bundle are one volt, the *c* signal can be synthesized by threshold gates as illustrated. Each threshold gate has six excitatory inputs and has an output of one volt only when at least two of its inputs are one volt; that is, it has a threshold of two. Additional restoring organs are unnecessary.

randomly wired circuit in an intricate computer may seem about as sensible as expecting a blindfolded pigeon to write a poem by pecking at typewriter keys, but on statistical analysis it makes sense. The reasoning goes like this: Even without knowing which is the best maze to use, one can at least analyze the properties of a random maze and see how reliable it is. If the average random maze performs successfully, use it. Or, knowing how reliable a random maze is, try to design a systematic one that is better than average.

Recently a few systematic mazes have been worked out that are definitely better than random mazes. In a restoring organ with one of these deterministic mazes any single error will, as in simpler restoring organs, be corrected by all the vote-takers it enters [*see bottom illustration on page 62*]. As a result of the particular pattern of connections, some double errors, such as an error on both line 1 and line 2, will be reduced to single errors, which can be corrected by the next restoring organ. Other double errors, however—on lines 1 and 3, for instance—will still be double errors when they emerge from this restoring organ. This does not mean that there is no hope of correcting all double errors. It turns out that of the 10 possible double errors that can enter this organ, only five will produce double output errors. It is possible to arrange the connections in such a way that the five double errors emerge in exactly those positions that will be reduced to single errors in the next restoring organ. By using similar restoring organs throughout a computer one can therefore eliminate all double errors.

A redundancy theory based on restoring organs is elegant and satisfying, but it does have some weaknesses. For one thing, a redundancy theory truly applicable to biological nervous systems ought to have more homogeneity in its circuits, namely fewer different kinds of components. Moreover, if the theory is to be optimum in an engineering sense, the restoring organ should be made to do more useful computation. In brief, one would like a more generalized theory that offers homogeneity to the biologist and efficiency to the engineer.

Both of these objectives are served by a theory in which error correction and the execution of digital logic are combined in a single logic gate. One type of circuit with which this can be accomplished is a "threshold gate." This is a gate that is "excited," or has an output other than zero, only if the number of excitatory inputs minus the number of inhibitory inputs equals or exceeds a threshold level. Suppose, for example, that an output of one is desired if either input *a* or input *b* or both is one. This can be done by a threshold-gate circuit in which *a* and *b* are excitatory and the threshold is one. The operation can be made redundant if three six-input threshold gates are substituted. Three of the six inputs to each are independent versions of *a* and three are versions of *b*, and the threshold is set at two [*see bottom illustration on preceding page*]. Threshold gates and several other types of gate can be arranged in a network in which redundant signals are interwoven much as they are in the input mazes of restoring organs.

The nervous systems of higher animals, including man, can sustain local injuries without showing any detectable sign of damage. This fact and the observation that most neurons, or nerve cells, receive inputs from more than one other neuron suggest that biological nervous systems must have considerable redundancy. The general theory of interwoven, redundant logic has developed to the point where it is possible to speculate on how redundant neurons work.

If two sets of three-input vote-takers are placed end to end, a single input wire or vote-taker can fail and the output bundle will still have a correct majority. A majority-rule vote-taker can be thought of as a threshold gate in which the threshold is equal to half the number of inputs. Biological neurons behave as just such gates, firing when the number of excitatory inputs minus the number of inhibitory inputs equals or exceeds the neuron's threshold. When the neuron fires, a nerve impulse—a traveling discharge of electrical energy—propagates down the long, slender axon and affects another neuron, apparently by injecting into it a chemical substance that either stimulates it to fire (excitatory input) or prevents it from firing (inhibitory input). A simple network that would be the biological version of a chain of two restoring organs might be arranged as in the bottom illustration at right. One neuron could fail, or the signal in one axon could be delayed, and the "bundle" of axons would still carry the correct signals.

Actual neuron networks are, to be sure, a great deal more complicated, but the basic principles of redundancy seem applicable still. The top illustration at right, for example, shows a neuron model that might explain a person's ability to

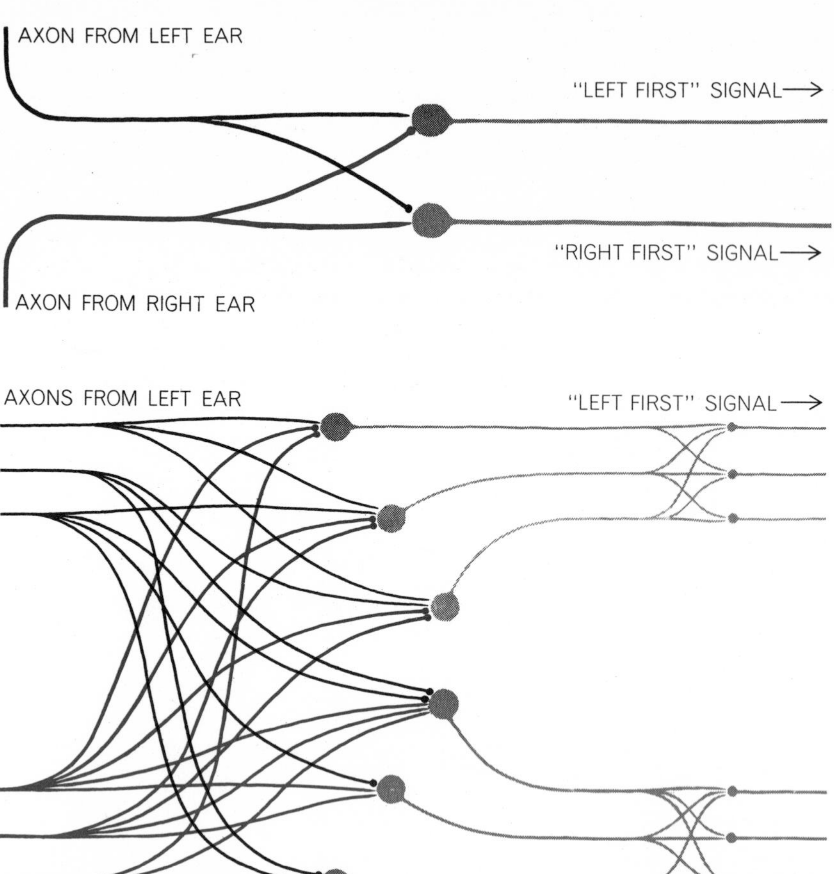

NERVOUS SYSTEMS apparently are richly redundant. This example shows a hypothetical arrangement of nerve cells for localizing sound (*top*). In it signals from each ear are assumed to be excitatory (*pointed*) for one kind of neuron and inhibitory (*rounded*) for another. In a redundant version of this model (*bottom*) three axons from each ear branch at random to the neurons that make the "right first" or "left first" decision. Notice that a "restoring organ" of three other neurons follows the "logic" neurons and tends to suppress errors.

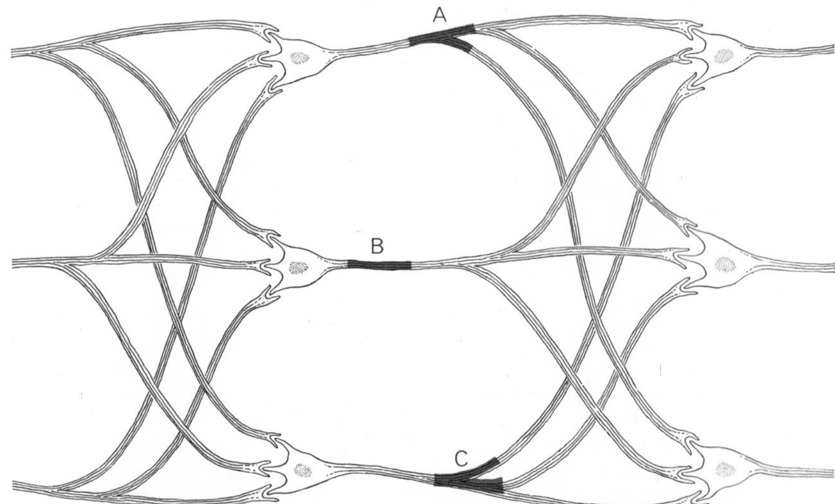

BIOLOGICAL NEURONS are like vote-takers that fire if the number of excitatory inputs minus the inhibitory ones exceeds a threshold. In this simplified biological network, neurons with a threshold of two replace vote-takers and axons replace wires. Nerve impulse *B* is delayed but *A* and *C* will reach all three neurons at the right on time and trigger them.

localize sound by distinguishing which ear receives a sound wave first. It seems likely that there are two kinds of neuron involved. One kind is stimulated by a signal from the right ear and inhibited by a signal from the left; the other is stimulated by a signal from the left ear and inhibited by one from the right. The thresholds are such that the neurons fire only if the stimulating impulse arrives first. One neuron is therefore a "left first" receptor and the other a "right first" receptor. In a redundant version of such a system each signal is carried by several axons, so that none is indispensable. The neurons have somewhat random connections, some of them receiving more axons than others, but each has the appropriate excitatory or inhibitory connections. A "restoring organ" of neurons follows each set of three neurons that makes the decisions as to which ear received the sound first. This restoring organ tends to emphasize the decision of the majority and suppress the decision of the minority.

The richly redundant networks of biological nervous systems must have capabilities beyond anything our theories can yet explain. For example, there is probably a considerable degree of flexibility in biological networks that allows redundant circuits to improve reliability when errors are common and leaves them free to improve the organism's over-all nervous capability when errors are infrequent. No one, however, has yet suggested a plausible scheme for such self-organization.

10

FEEDBACK

ARNOLD TUSTIN • September 1952

FOR hundreds of years a few examples of true automatic control systems have been known. A very early one was the arrangement on windmills of a device to keep their sails always facing into the wind. It consisted simply of a miniature windmill which could rotate the whole mill to face in any direction. The small mill's sails were at right angles to the main ones, and whenever the latter faced in the wrong direction, the wind caught the small sails and rotated the mill to the correct position. With steam power came other automatic mechanisms: the engine-governor, and then the steering servo-engine on ships, which operated the rudder in correspondence with movements of the helm. These devices, and a few others such as simple voltage regulators, constituted man's achievement in automatic control up to about 20 years ago.

In the past two decades necessity, in the form of increasingly acute problems arising in our ever more complex technology, has given birth to new families of such devices. Chemical plants needed regulators of temperature and flow; air warfare called for rapid and precise control of searchlights and anti-aircraft guns; radio required circuits which would give accurate amplification of signals.

Thus the modern science of automatic control has been fed by streams from many sources. At first, it now seems surprising to recall, no connection between these various developments was recognized. Yet all control and regulating systems depend on common principles. As soon as this was realized, progress became much more rapid. Today the design of controls for a modern boiler or a guided missile, for example, is based largely on principles first developed in the design of radio amplifiers.

Indeed, studies of the behavior of automatic control systems give us new insight into a wide variety of happenings in nature and in human affairs. The notions that engineers have evolved from these studies are useful aids in understanding how a man stands upright without toppling over, how the human heart beats, why our economic system suffers from slumps and booms, why the rabbit population in parts of Canada regularly fluctuates between scarcity and abundance.

The chief purpose of this article is to make clear the common pattern that underlies all these and many other varied phenomena. This common pattern is the existence of feedback, or—to express the same thing rather more generally—interdependence.

We should not be able to live at all, still less to design complex control systems, if we did not recognize that there are regularities in the relationship between events—what we call "cause and effect." When the room is warmer, the thermometer on the wall reads higher. We do not expect to make the room warmer by pushing up the mercury in the thermometer. But now consider the case when the instrument on the wall is not a simple thermometer but a thermostat, contrived so that as its reading goes above a chosen setting, the fuel supply to the furnace is progressively reduced, and, conversely, as its reading falls below that setting, the fuel flow is increased. This is an example of a familiar control system. Not only does the reading of the thermometer depend on the warmth of the room, but the warmth of the room also depends on the reading of the thermometer. The two quantities are interdependent. Each is a cause, and each an effect, of the other. In such cases we have a closed chain or sequence—what engineers call a "closed loop" (*see diagram on the opposite page*).

In analyzing engineering and scientific problems it is very illuminating to sketch out first the scheme of dependence and see how the various quantities involved in the problem are determined by one another and by disturbances from outside the system. Such a diagram enables one to tell at a glance whether a system is an open or a closed one. This is an important distinction, because a closed system possesses several significant properties. Not only can it act as a regulator, but it is capable of

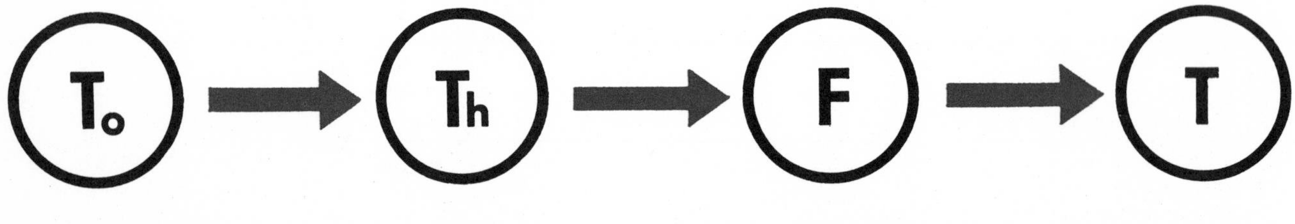

T_o → Th → F → T

OPEN SEQUENCE of control is illustrated by a system for regulating the temperature of a room. T_o is a variation in the temperature outdoors. Th is the variation of a thermometer. F is the fuel control of a furnace. T is the variation of the temperature in the room. In such a system of control there is no feedback.

various "self-excitatory" types of behavior—like a kitten chasing its own tail.

The now-popular name for this process is "feedback." In the case of the thermostat, the thermometer's information about the room temperature is fed back to open or close the valve, which in turn controls the temperature. Not all automatic control systems are of the closed-loop type. For example, one might put the thermometer outside in the open air, and connect it to work the fuel valve through a specially shaped cam, so that the outside temperature regulates the fuel flow. In this open-sequence system the room temperature has no effect; there is no feedback. The control compensates only that disturbance of room temperature caused by variation of the outdoor temperature. Such a system is not necessarily a bad or useless system; it might work very well under some circumstances. But it has two obvious shortcomings. Firstly, it is a "calibrated" system; that is to say, its correct working would require careful preliminary testing and special shaping of the cam to suit each particular application. Secondly, it could not deal with any but standard conditions. A day that was windy as well as cold would not get more fuel on that account.

The feedback type of control avoids these shortcomings. It goes directly to the quantity to be controlled, and it corrects indiscriminately for all kinds of disturbance. Nor does it require calibration for each special condition.

Feedback control, unlike open-sequence control, can never work without *some* error, for the error is depended upon to bring about the correction. The objective is to make the error as small as possible. This is subject to certain limitations, which we must now consider.

The principle of control by feedback is quite general. The quantities that it may control are of the most varied kinds, ranging from the frequency of a national electric-power grid to the degree of anesthesia of a patient under surgical operation. Control is exercised by negative feedback, which is to say that the information fed back is the amount of departure from the desired condition.

ANY QUANTITY may be subjected to control if three conditions are met. First, the required changes must be controllable by some physical means, a regulating organ. Second, the controlled quantity must be measurable, or at least comparable with some standard; in other words, there must be a measuring device. Third, both regulation and measurement must be rapid enough for the job in hand.

As an example, take one of the simplest and commonest of industrial requirements: to control the rate of flow of liquid along a pipe. As the regulating organ we can use a throttle valve, and as the measuring device, some form of flowmeter. A signal from the flowmeter, telling the actual rate of flow through the pipe, goes to the "controller"; there it is compared with a setting giving the required rate of flow. The amount and direction of "error," *i.e.*, deviation from this setting, is then transmitted to the throttle valve as an operating signal to bring about adjustment in the required direction (*see diagram at the top of page 71.*)

In flow-control systems the signals are usually in the form of variations in air pressure, by which the flowmeter measures the rate of flow of the liquid. The pressure is transmitted through a small-bore pipe to the controller, which is essentially a balance piston. The difference between this received pressure and the setting regulates the air pressure in another pipeline that goes to the regulating valve.

Signals of this kind are slow, and difficulties arise as the system becomes complex. When many controls are concentrated at a central point, as is often the case, the air-pipes that transmit the signals may have to be hundreds of feet long, and pressure changes at one end reach the other only after delays of some seconds. Meanwhile the error may have become large. The time-delay often creates another problem: overcorrection of the error, which causes the system to oscillate about the required value instead of settling down.

For further light on the principles involved in control systems let us consider the example of the automatic gun-director. In this problem a massive gun must be turned with great precision to angles indicated by a fly-power pointer on a clock-dial some hundreds of feet away. When the pointer moves, the gun must turn correspondingly. The quantity to be controlled is the angle of the gun. The reference quantity is the angle of the clock-dial pointer. What is needed is a feedback loop which constantly compares the gun angle with the pointer angle and arranges matters so that if the gun angle is too small, the gun is driven forward, and if it is too large, the gun is driven back.

The key element in this case is some device which will detect the error of angular alignment between two shafts remote from each other, and which does not require more force than is available at the fly-power transmitter shaft. There are several kinds of electrical elements that will serve such a purpose. The one usually selected is a pair of the miniature alternating-current machines known as selsyns. The two selsyns, connected respectively to the transmitter shaft and the gun, provide an electrical signal proportional to the error of alignment. The signal is amplified and fed to a generator which in turn feeds a motor that

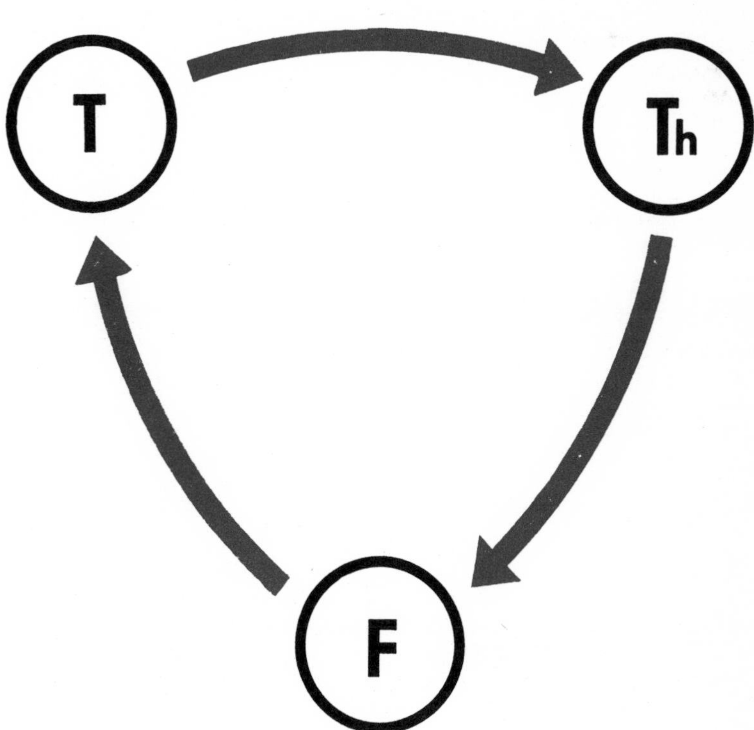

CLOSED SEQUENCE of control is illustrated by a system for regulating the temperature of a room by means of a thermostat. Here Th is a thermostat rather than a thermometer. In such a system there is feedback.

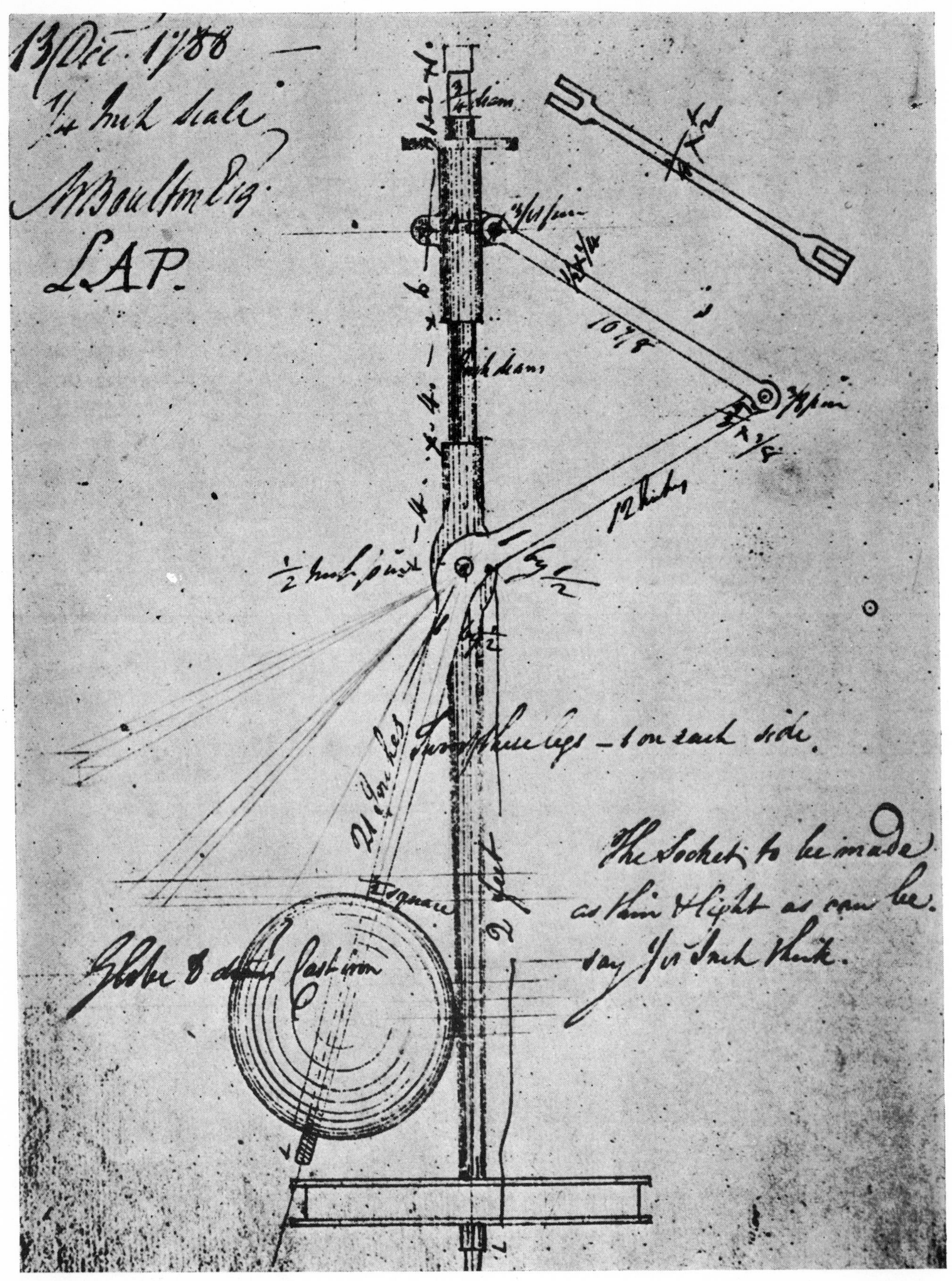

EARLIEST KNOWN DRAWING of the flyball-governor was made in 1788. The governor was invented by James Watt. At the upper left appear the date and the name of Watt's associate Matthew Boulton. Only half of a governor is shown in the drawing, but below the center are the words: "Two of these legs—1 on each side." Later Watt attempted to prevent the oscillation of the governor by fitting it with stops for the balls, one to keep them from coming too close together and the other to prevent them from "opening too wide asunder."

drives the gun (*see diagram on the next page*).

THIS GIVES the main lines of a practicable scheme, but if a system were built as just described, it would fail. The gun's inertia would carry it past the position of correct alignment; the new error would then cause the controller to swing it back, and the gun would hunt back and forth without ever settling down.

This oscillatory behavior, maintained by "self-excitation," is one of the principal limitations of feedback control. It is the chief enemy of the control-system designer, and the key to progress has been the finding of various simple means to prevent oscillation. Since oscillation is a very general phenomenon, it is worth while to look at the mechanism in detail, for what we learn about oscillation in man-made control systems may suggest means of inhibiting oscillations of other kinds—such as economic booms and slumps, or periodic swarms of locusts.

Consider any case in which a quantity that we shall call the output depends on another quantity we shall call the input. If the input quantity oscillates in value, then the output quantity also will oscillate, not simultaneously or necessarily in the same way, but with the same frequency. Usually in physical systems the output oscillation lags behind the input. For example, if one is boiling water and turns the gas slowly up and down, the amount of steam increases and decreases the same number of times per minute, but the maximum amount of steam in each cycle must come rather later than the maximum application of heat, because of the time required for heating. If the first output quantity in turn affects some further quantity, the variation of this second quantity in the sequence will usually lag still more, and so on. The lag (as a proportion of one oscillation) also usually increases with frequency—the faster the input is varied, the farther behind the output falls.

Now suppose that in a feedback system some quantity in the closed loop is oscillating. This causes the successive quantities around the loop to oscillate also. But the loop comes around to the original quantity, and we have here the mechanism by which an oscillation may maintain itself. To see how this can happen, we must remember that with the feedback negative, the motion it causes would be opposite to the original motion, if it were not for the lags. It is only when the lags add up to just half a cycle that the feedback maintains the assumed motion. Thus any system with negative feedback will maintain a continuous oscillation when disturbed if (a) the time-delays in response at some frequency add up to half a period of oscillation, and (b) the feedback ef-

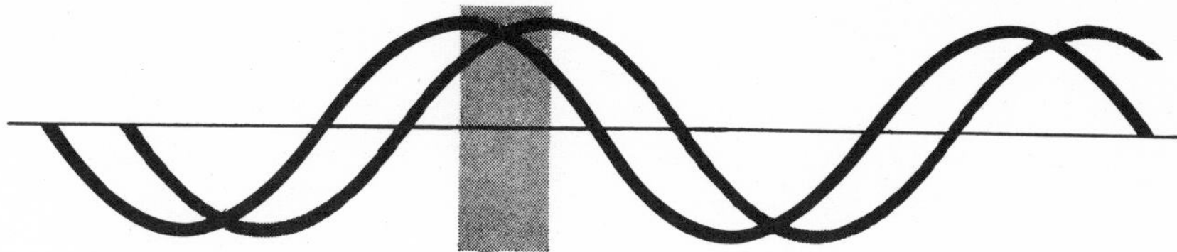

REGULAR OSCILLATORY VARIATION of a quantity put into a feedback system (*black curve*) is followed by a similar variation in the output quantity (*gray curve*). The gray rectangle indicates the time-delay.

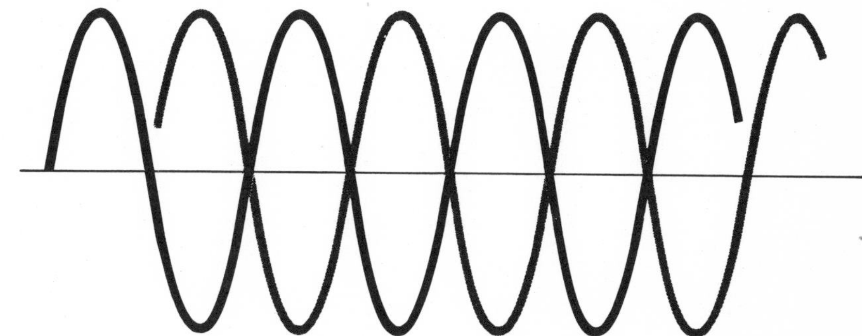

ONE TYPE OF OSCILLATION occurs when the feedback (*gray curve*) of a system is equal and opposed to its error (*black curve*). Here the term error is used to mean any departure of the system from its desired state.

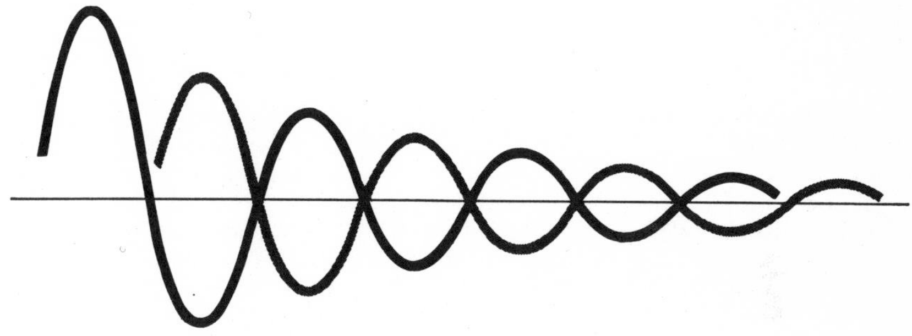

SECOND TYPE OF OSCILLATION occurs when the feedback (*black curve*) of a system is less than and opposed to the error (*gray curve*). This set of conditions tends to damp the disturbance in the system.

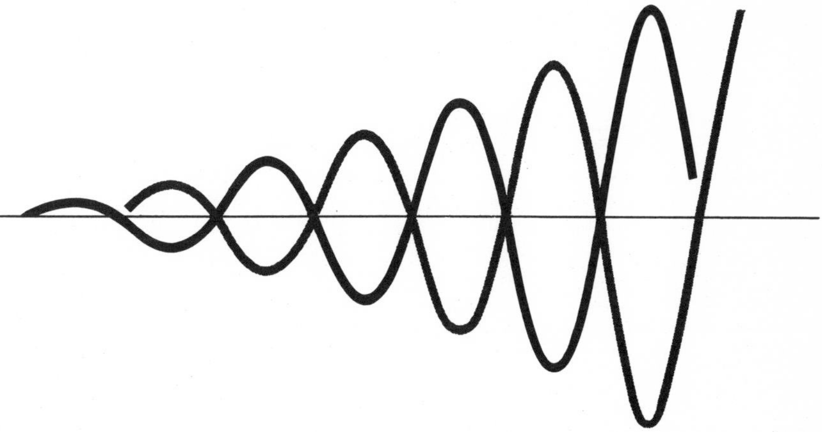

THIRD TYPE OF OSCILLATION occurs when the feedback (*gray curve*) of a system is greater than and opposed to the error (*black curve*). This set of conditions tends to amplify the disturbance in the system

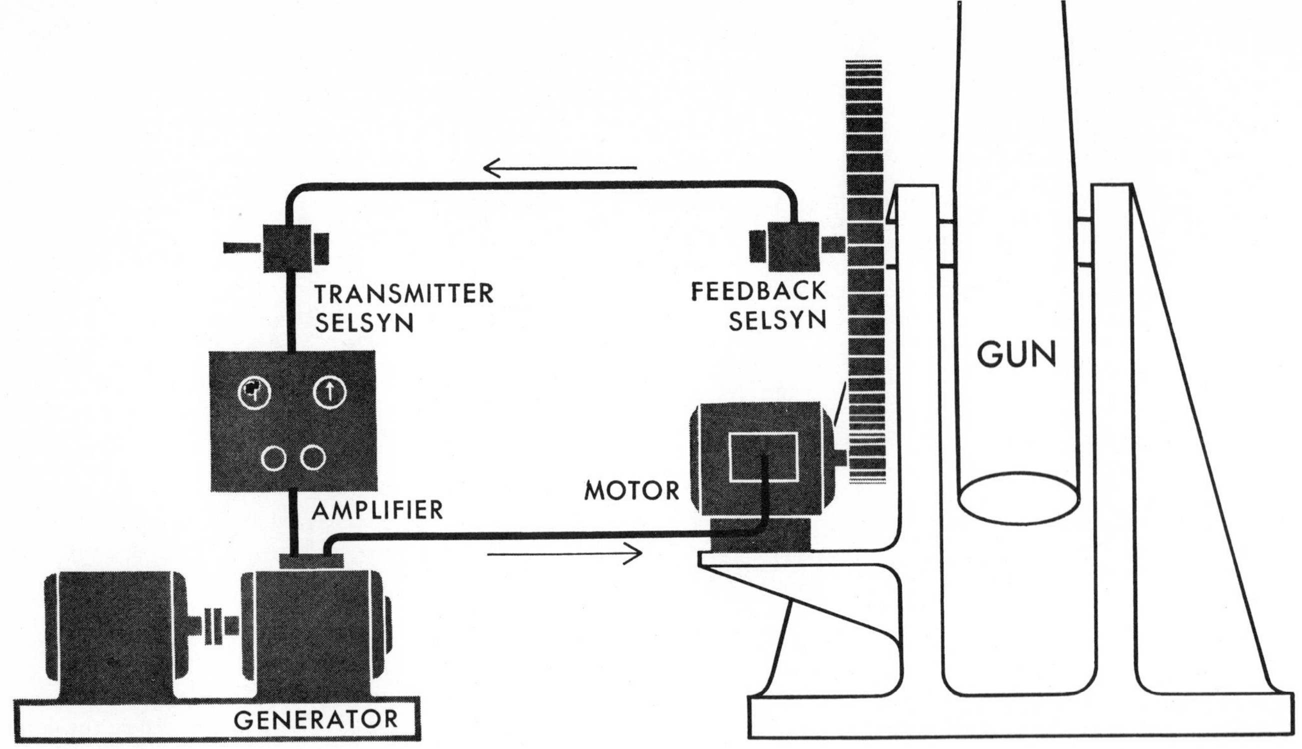

ELEVATION OF A GUN is controlled by an electrical feedback system. The closed sequence, or closed loop, runs from the position of the gun through the feedback selsyn, the transmitter selsyn, the amplifier and the generator to the motor. The selsyn is an electrical device which transmits position or speed of rotation.

fect is sufficiently large at this frequency.

In a linear system, that is, roughly speaking, a system in which effects are directly proportional to causes, there are three possible results. If the feedback, at the frequency for which the lag is half a period, is equal in strength to the original oscillation, there will be a continuous steady oscillation which just sustains itself. If the feedback is greater than the oscillation at that frequency, the oscillation builds up; if it is smaller, the oscillation will die away.

This situation is of critical importance for the designer of control systems. On the one hand, to make the control accurate, one must increase the feedback; on the other, such an increase may accentuate any small oscillation. The control breaks into an increasing oscillation and becomes useless.

TO ESCAPE from the dilemma the designer can do several things. Firstly, he may minimize the time-lag by using electronic tubes or, at higher power levels, the new varieties of quick-response direct-current machines. By dividing the power amplification among a multiplicity of stages, these special generators have a smaller lag than conventional generators. The lag is by no means negligible, however.

Secondly, and this was a major advance in the development of control systems, the designer can use special elements that introduce a time-lead, anticipating the time-lag. Such devices, called phase-advancers, are often based on the properties of electric capacitors, because alternating current in a capacitor circuit leads the voltage applied to it.

Thirdly, the designer can introduce other feedbacks besides the main one, so designed as to reduce time-lag. Modern achievements in automatic control are based on the use of combinations of such devices to obtain both accuracy and stability.

So far we have been treating these systems as if they were entirely linear. A system is said to be linear when all effects are strictly proportional to causes. For example, the current through a resistor is proportional to the voltage applied to it; the resistor is therefore a linear element. The same does not apply to a rectifier or electronic tube. These are non-linear elements.

None of the elements used in control systems gives proportional or linear dependence over all ranges. Even a resistor will burn out if the current is too high. Many elements, however, are linear over the range in which they are required to work. And when the range of variation is small enough, most elements will behave in an approximately linear fashion, simply because a very small bit of a curved graph does not differ significantly from a straight line.

We have seen that linear closed-sequence systems are delightfully simple to understand and—even more important—very easy to handle in exact mathematical terms. Because of this, most introductory accounts of control systems either brazenly or furtively assume that all such systems are linear. This gives the rather wrong impression that the principles so deduced may have little application to real, non-linear, systems. In practice, however, most of the characteristic behavior of control systems is affected only in detail by the non-linear nature of the dependences. It is essential to be clear that non-linear systems are not excluded from feedback control. Unless the departures from linearity are large or of special kinds, most of what has been said applies with minor changes to non-linear systems.

LONG BEFORE man existed, evolution hit upon the need for anti-oscillating features in feedback control and incorporated them in the body mechanisms of the animal world. Signals in the animal body are transmitted by trains of pulses along nerve fibers. When a sensory organ is stimulated, the stimulus will produce pulses at a greater rate if it is increasing than if it is decreasing. The pattern of nerve response to an oscillatory stimulus is shown in the diagram on page 73. The maximum response, or output signal, occurs before the maximum of the stimulus. This is just the anticipatory type of effect (the time-lead) that is required for high-

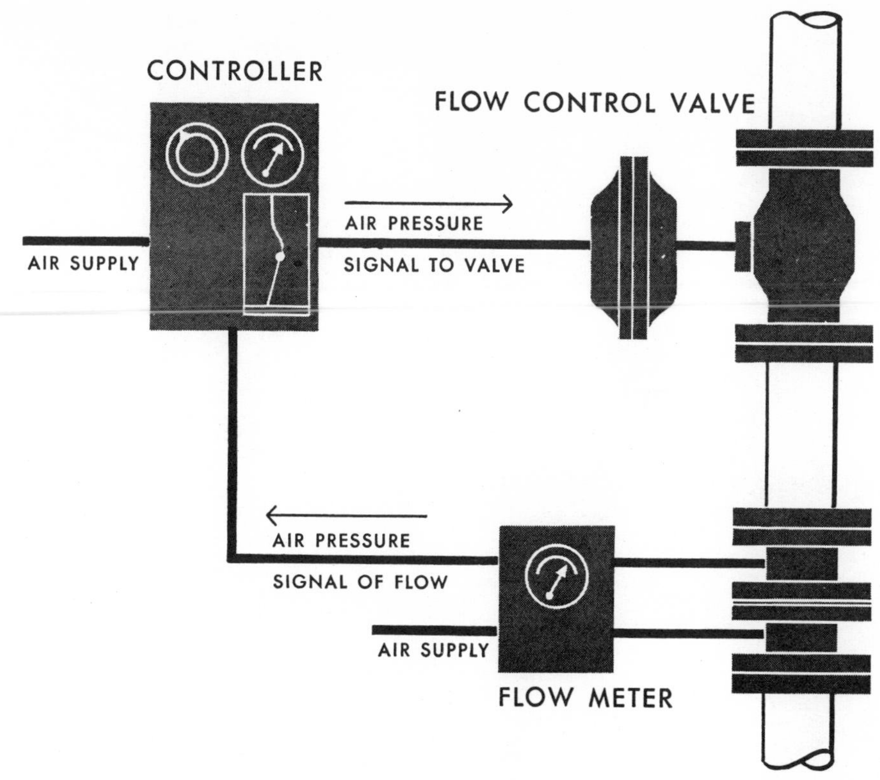

RATE OF FLOW IN A PIPE is controlled by a pneumatic feedback system. Here the closed loop runs from the flow of fluid in the pipe through the flow meter and the recording controller to the flow-control valve.

accuracy control. Physiologists now believe that the anticipatory response has evolved in the nervous system for, at least in part, the same reason that man wants it in his control mechanisms—to avoid overshooting and oscillation. Precisely what feature of the structure of the nerve mechanism gives this remarkable property is not yet fully understood.

Fascinating examples of the consequences of interdependence arise in the fluctuations of animal populations in a given territory. These interactions are sometimes extremely complicated. Charles Darwin invoked such a scheme to explain why there are more bumblebees near towns. His explanation was that near towns there are more cats; this means fewer field mice, and field mice are the chief ravagers of bees' nests. Hence near towns bees enjoy more safety.

The interdependence of animal species sometimes produces a periodic oscillation. Just to show how this can happen, and leaving out complications that are always present in an actual situation, consider a territory inhabited by rabbits and lynxes, the rabbits being the chief food of the lynxes. When rabbits are abundant, the lynx population will increase. But as the lynxes become abundant, the rabbit population falls, because more rabbits are caught. Then as the rabbits diminish, the lynxes go hungry and decline. The result is a self-maintaining oscillation, sustained by negative feedback with a time-delay (*see diagram below*).

Curves of variation such that when R is large L is rising, but when L becomes large R is falling must have the periodic oscillatory character indicated. This is not, of course, the complete picture of such phenomena as the well-known "fur cycle" of Canada, but it illustrates an important element in the mechanisms that cause it.

THE PERIODIC booms and slumps in economic activity stand out as a major example of oscillatory behavior due to feedback. In 1935 the economist John Maynard Keynes gave the first adequate and satisfying account of the essential mechanisms on which the general level of economic activity depends. Although Keynes did not use the terminology of control-system theory, his account fits precisely the same now-familiar pattern.

Keynes' starting point was the simple notion that the level of economic activity depends on the rate at which goods are bought. He took the essential further step of distinguishing two kinds of buying—of consumption goods and of capital goods. The latter is the same thing as the rate of investment. The money available to buy all these goods is not automatically provided by the wages and profits disbursed in making them, because normally some of this money is saved. The system would therefore run down and stop if it were not for the constant injection of extra demand in the form of new investment. Therefore the level of economic activity and employment depends on the rate of invest-

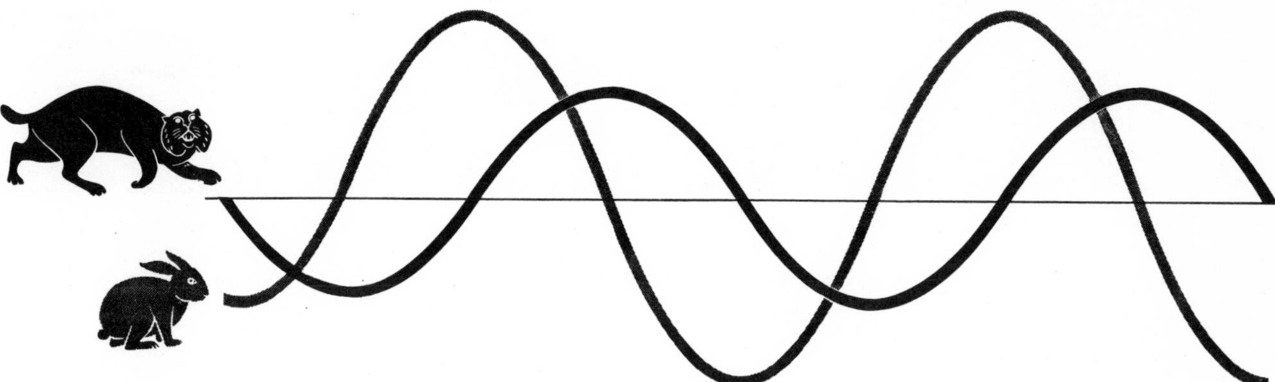

RABBIT AND LYNX population cycles are an example of a feedback system in nature. Here a fall in the relatively small population of lynxes (*black curve*) is followed by a rise in the large population of rabbits (*gray curve*). This is followed by a rise in the lynx population, a fall in the rabbit population and so on.

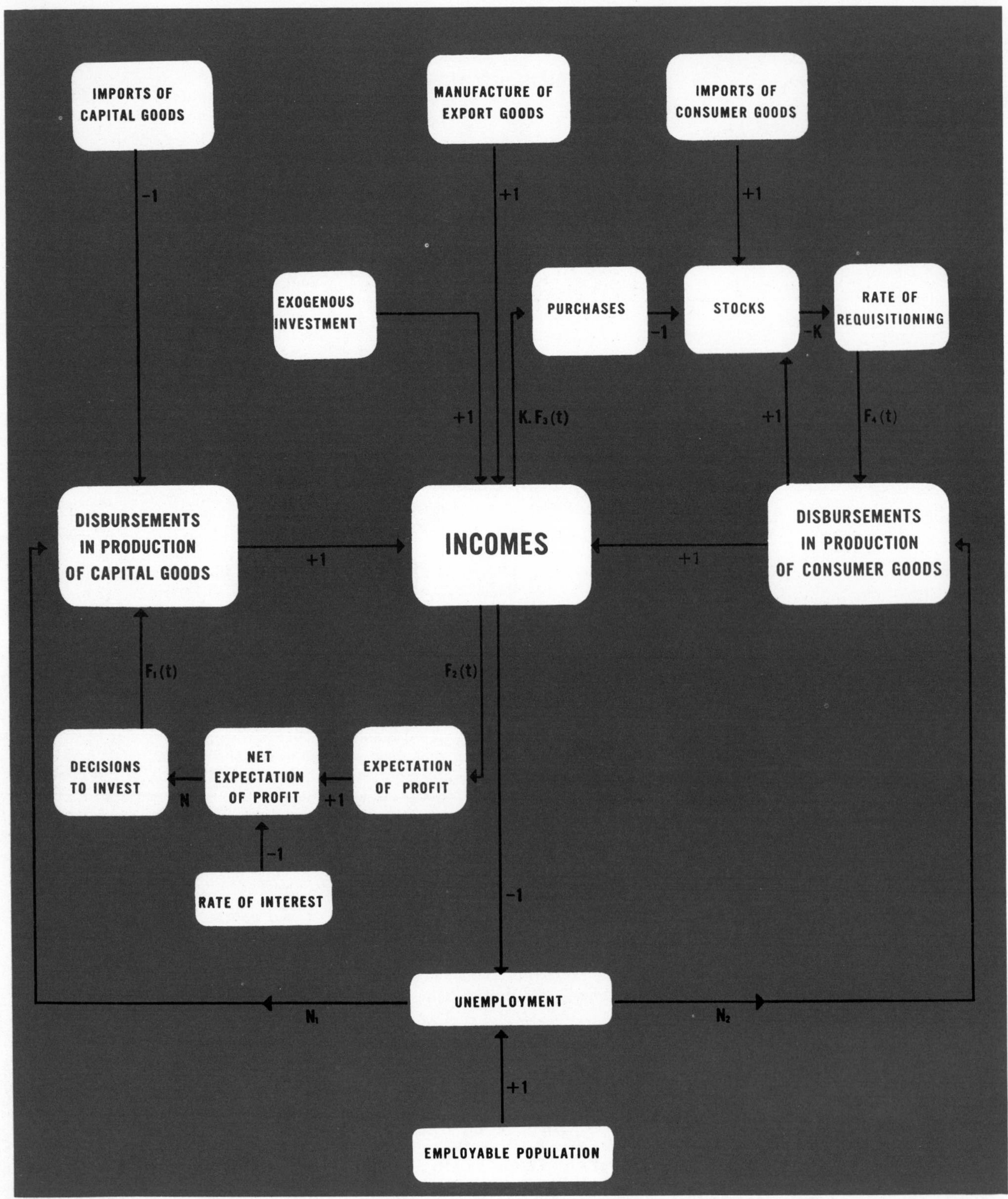

FEEDBACK IN AN ECONOMIC SYSTEM is blocked out in this diagram by the author. The scheme of dependence is based upon the ideas advanced by the late J. M. Keynes. Total incomes arise from disbursements for consumer goods on the one hand and capital goods on the other. But each of these is dependent in turn, *via* its subsidiary closed loop, upon total incomes. Keynes was especially concerned with the factors which determine the relationship between the two loops and the relative flow of money into them from total incomes. He showed this to be a highly sensitive relationship, since a comparatively small increase in the flow of money around the capital-goods loop is amplified *via* the consumer-goods loop into a much larger change in total incomes. This is precisely analogous to the behavior of similarly coupled electrical feedback circuits. Pursuing the analogy, the author has entered on the diagram some symbols for values that would have to be defined to design a complete electrical analogue for the economic system. K, for example, is Keynes' "propensity to consume"; F_1 (t) represents the time-lag between the decision to invest and the purchase of capital goods; N_1 and N_2 stand for non-linear functions which curtail increase in production as unemployment approaches zero.

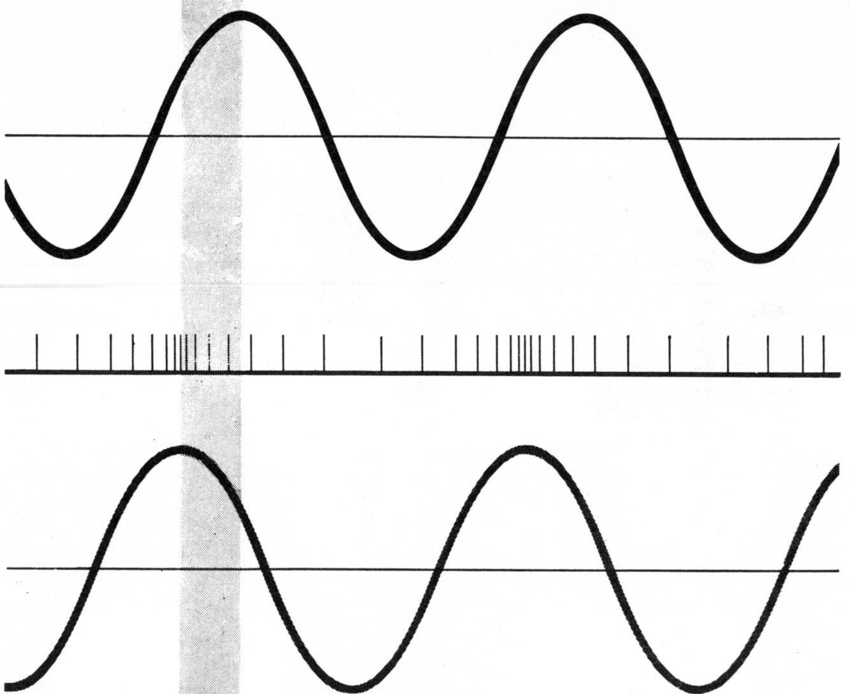

FEEDBACK IN THE NERVOUS SYSTEM has a sophisticated feature: the anticipation of the input signal by the output. The black curve at the top of this diagram represents the input signal. The row of vertical lines in the middle indicates the number of nerve pulses in a given time. The gray curve at the bottom translates these pulses into an output signal. The gray rectangle indicates how much the output signal leads the input.

ment. This is the first dependence. The rate of investment itself, however, depends on the expectation of profit, and this in turn depends on the trend, present and expected, of economic activity. Thus not only does economic activity depend on the rate of investment, but the rate of investment depends on economic activity.

Modern theories of the business cycle aim to explain in detail the nature of these dependences and their characteristic non-linearities. This clarification of the mechanisms at work immediately suggests many ways in which, by proper timing of investment expenditure, by more rational business forecasting, and so on, a stable level of optimal economic activity may be achieved in the near future. The day when it can unequivocally be said that slumps belong to the past will certainly be the beginning of a brighter chapter in human history.

THE EXAMPLES of feedback given here are merely a few selected to illustrate general principles. Many more will be described in other articles in this issue. In this article on "theory" I should like to touch on a further point: some ways in which the properties of automatic control systems or other complex feedback systems may be investigated in detail, and their performance perfected.

Purely mathematical methods are remarkably powerful when the system happens to be linear. Sets of linear differential equations are the happy hunting ground of mathematicians. They can turn the equations into a variety of equivalent forms, and generally play tunes on them. For the more general class of non-linear systems, the situation is quite different. There exact determination of the types of motion implied by a set of dependences is usually very laborious or practically impossible.

To determine the behavior of such complex systems two principal kinds of machines are being used. The first is the "analogue" computer. The forms of this type of computer are varied, but they all share a common principle: some system of physical elements is set up with relationships analogous to those existing in the system to be investigated, and the interdependence among them is then worked out in proportional terms. The second kind of aid is the new high-speed digital computer. In this type of machine the quantities are represented by numbers rather than by physical equivalents. The implications of the equations involved are explored by means of arithmetical operations on these numbers. The great speed of operation of these modern machines makes possible calculations that could not be attempted by human computers because of the time required.

The theory of control systems is now so well understood that, with such modern aids, the behavior of even extremely complex systems can be largely predicted in advance. Although this is a new branch of science, it is already in a state that ensures rapid further progress.

AT THE commencement of this account of control systems it was necessary to assume that the human mind can distinguish "cause" and "effect" and describe the regularities of nature in these terms. It may be fitting to conclude by suggesting that the concepts reviewed are not without relevance to the grandest of all problems of science and philosophy: the nature of the human mind and the significance of our forms of perception of what we call reality.

In much of the animal world, behavior is controlled by reflexes and instinct-mechanisms in direct response to the stimulus of the immediate situation. In man and the higher animals the operation of what we are subjectively aware of as the "mind" provides a more flexible and effective control of behavior. It is not at present known whether these conscious phenomena involve potentialities of matter other than those we study in physics. They may well do so, and we must not beg this question in the absence of evidence.

Whatever the nature of the means or medium involved, the function of the central nervous system in the higher animals is clear. It is to provide a biologically more effective control of behavior under a combination of inner and environmental stimuli. An inner analogue or simulation of relevant aspects of the external world, which we are aware of as our idea of the environment, controls our responses, superseding mere instinct or reflex reaction. The world is still with us when we shut our eyes, and we use the "play of ideas" to predict the consequences of action. Thus our activity is adjusted more elaborately and advantageously to the circumstances in which we find ourselves.

This situation is strikingly similar in principle (though immensely more complex) to the introduction of a predictor in the control of a gun, for all predictors are essentially analogues of the external situation. The function of mind is to predict, and to adjust behavior accordingly. It operates like an analogue computer fed by sensory clues.

It is not surprising, therefore, that man sees the external world in terms of cause and effect. The distinction is largely subjective. "Cause" is what might conceivably be manipulated. "Effect" is what might conceivably be purposed.

Man is far from understanding himself, but it may turn out that his understanding of automatic control is one small further step toward that end.

11

CONTROL THEORY

RICHARD BELLMAN • September 1964

Control theory, like many other broad theories, is more a state of mind than any specific amalgam of mathematical, scientific or technological methods. The term can be defined to include any rational approach used by men to overcome the perversities of either their natural or their technological environment. The broad objective of a control theory is to make a system—any kind of system—operate in a more desirable way: to make it more reliable, more convenient or more economical. If the system is a biological one, the goal may be to understand how the system works and to reduce pain and distress.

In this article I shall mainly discuss control theories that have some explicit mathematical content, but it is clear that some of the most interesting control problems arise in fields such as economics, biology and psychology, where understanding is still notably limited. To prove that he understands, the scientist must be able to predict, and to predict he requires quantitative measurements. To make predictions that are merely qualitative, such as the prediction that an earthquake, a hurricane or a depression will occur in the near future, is not nearly so satisfying as a similar prediction associated with a specific time and place.

The ability to make a quantitative prediction is normally a prerequisite for the development of a control theory. In order to make quantitative predictions one must have a mechanism for producing numbers, and this requires a mathematical model. It might seem that the more realistic the mathematical model is, the more accurate the prediction will be and the more effective the control. Unfortunately, diminishing returns set in rapidly. The real world is so rich in detail that if one attempts to make a mathematical model too realistic, one is soon engulfed by complicated equations containing unknown quantities and unknown functions. The determination of these functions leads to even more complicated equations with even more quantities and functions—a tale without end.

The richness of the problems presented by modern civilization have led to the study of control theory on a broad front and to the development of a large variety of control systems. Although this development began long before the invention of electronic computers, the explosive growth of control theory dates from the appearance of these devices soon after World War II. For the past 20 years control theory and computers have grown side by side in an almost symbiotic relation. Without the computer most of the advanced control systems used in the military domain, in space technology and in many branches of industry could not have been developed, and without the computer they certainly could not be effectuated.

In industry, control theory, implemented by the computer, is now widely used to regulate inventories, to schedule production lines and to improve the performance of power stations, steel mills, oil refineries and chemical plants. It is estimated that about 500 computers specially designed for process control are now installed or on order. Five years ago scarcely a dozen such machines were in service.

A majority of process-control computers still operate in "open loop" fashion, which means that they monitor the process variables, analyze them in a search for possible improvements and present their recommendations to a human operator for action. In a growing number of plants, however, the loop has been closed. The decisions of the computer are directly linked to the process controls so that adjustments are made automatically.

In Rotherham, England, to select one remarkable example, a new steel plant built by Tube Investments Ltd. has been provided with three large digital computers arranged in a chain of command. The computer at the top is "off line" and is used for production planning. It receives customers' orders and classifies them according to the composition of the steel and the form of the finished product. It then calculates an efficient three-week program for the steel furnaces and rolling mills and keeps track of the program's progress. The second computer takes over when a billet has been produced by one of the furnaces and produces a full set of instructions for its subsequent treatment. This computer is "on line" and actually supervises the rolling mill. The third computer has the single task of receiving measurements of billet size and computing how they should be cut to minimize waste. This kind of integrated operation from receipt of the customer's order to final billing has become the goal of many manufacturing firms.

The industrial, military and space-flight control problems that have been presented to mathematicians for solution in the past 25 years have brought about

CLOSED-LOOP CONTROL is implemented by a computer (*console in foreground in photograph on opposite page*) in the operation of a 650-million-watt, coal-fired power plant at the Paradise Station of the Tennessee Valley Authority near Drakesboro, Ky. One of the largest power plants in the world, the station has two such computer-controlled units. In a closed-loop system the computer directly adjusts the process variables.

UNIT 1
PANEL A
MEGAWATTS

the revitalization of a number of moribund mathematical disciplines and have led to the creation of new theories of considerable intrinsic interest. Since control and stability are intimately related, mathematical theories devised in the 18th and 19th centuries to study such matters as the stability of the solar system have been dusted off, refurbished and applied to many problems of more current interest. These theories have included highly abstruse conceptions of the great French mathematician Henri Poincaré and the Russian mathematician A. M. Liapunov, which are now routinely employed in control studies.

The most challenging control problems encountered in science, technology, economics, medicine and even politics can be described as multistage decision processes. Traditionally they have been treated on the basis of experience, by rule of thumb and by prayerful guesses. The basic task is to determine feasible and reasonable courses of action based on partial understanding and partial information. As more information is obtained one can expect to do better, but the crux of the problem is to do something sensible *now*.

A familiar problem characterized by partial understanding is that of maintaining a healthy national economy—of avoiding a depression on the one hand and inflation on the other. A variety of regulatory devices are available for achieving the desired control. One device is to regulate the interest rate on loans. If inflationary trends develop, the interest rate is raised and money gets tighter; if a depression impends, interest rates are decreased, the investment rate rises in response and more money enters circulation.

The policy that should be pursued depends critically on what is occurring in the system at the moment. For one to know what is going on requires a feedback of information. The concept of feedback control is now familiar to almost everyone. It means an automatic regulating linkage between some variable and the force producing it. One of the earliest applications of feedback control in technology is the governor used by James Watt on his steam engine. Even earlier Christian Huygens had devised what might be called a static feedback system to regulate the period of a clock pendulum [*see top illustration on next page*].

Usually it is a combination of complexity and ignorance (in polite circles referred to as "uncertainty") that forces one to employ feedback control. If, for example, the workings of the economy were as fully understood, let us say, as the movements of the planets, one could predict well in advance the behavior of producers and consumers; one could predict such things as the effects of population growth and the consequences of introducing new goods and

CHEMICAL PROCESS CONTROL SYSTEM in which a digital computer (*foreground*) exercises closed-loop control is shown in the Bishop, Tex., plant of the Celanese Chemical Company. The plant converts petroleum gases to acetic acid, acetaldehyde and other chemicals that are used in paints, plastics, fibers, drugs, cosmetics, fuels and lubricants. This computer and those at Paradise Station of TVA were built by Bunker-Ramo Corporation. Closed-loop computer systems are also installed in steel-rolling mills.

services. On the basis of this knowledge one could compute and announce the desired interest rate for years ahead. It should be observed that one would then have to reckon with the consequences of publishing the rates in advance, because producers and consumers would include the *future* rates in their *current* economic decisions.

In actuality one must adopt a wait-and-see policy. One observes the economic scene for a period of time and draws conclusions about current trends. On the basis of these conclusions the interest rate, or some other control lever, is changed. One hopes that the action is well timed, or in phase. The matter of the timing of external influences is of crucial importance in control theory. Anyone who has pushed a swing is familiar with the consequences of applying the impulse a fraction of a second too soon or too late.

Since complexity and uncertainty abound in modern control problems, the use of feedback has become routine. In fact, it is sometimes forgotten that control problems are still solved without direct, or active, feedback. This is the case, for example, when an automatic machine tool is set up to turn out a number of identical parts. It is assumed that the control problem is completely solved in advance. In practice, of course, the parts vary slightly and finally exceed the prescribed tolerance, whereupon the machine is readjusted. This is feedback control after the fact.

In the newest machine tools the dimensions of the workpiece are monitored continuously, and feedback control is employed to regulate precisely the amount of metal removed. In this way it is possible to turn out parts that are as nearly identical as one might wish. For such jobs digital computers can be used, but they are not essential.

The computer is essential when complex decisions must be made at high speed, as in the launching of a space vehicle. This is a multistage decision process whose solution is contingent on information acquired and fed back to the control system as the process unfolds. A computer, either aboard the rocket or on the ground, is essential for making a succession of decisions as rapidly as may be necessary. Such a computer is said to be operating in "real" time, because it must keep pace with the problem being solved.

A process-control computer installed in a refinery must also operate in real time, but the time available for making a decision may be 10 or 100 times longer than that available for rocket

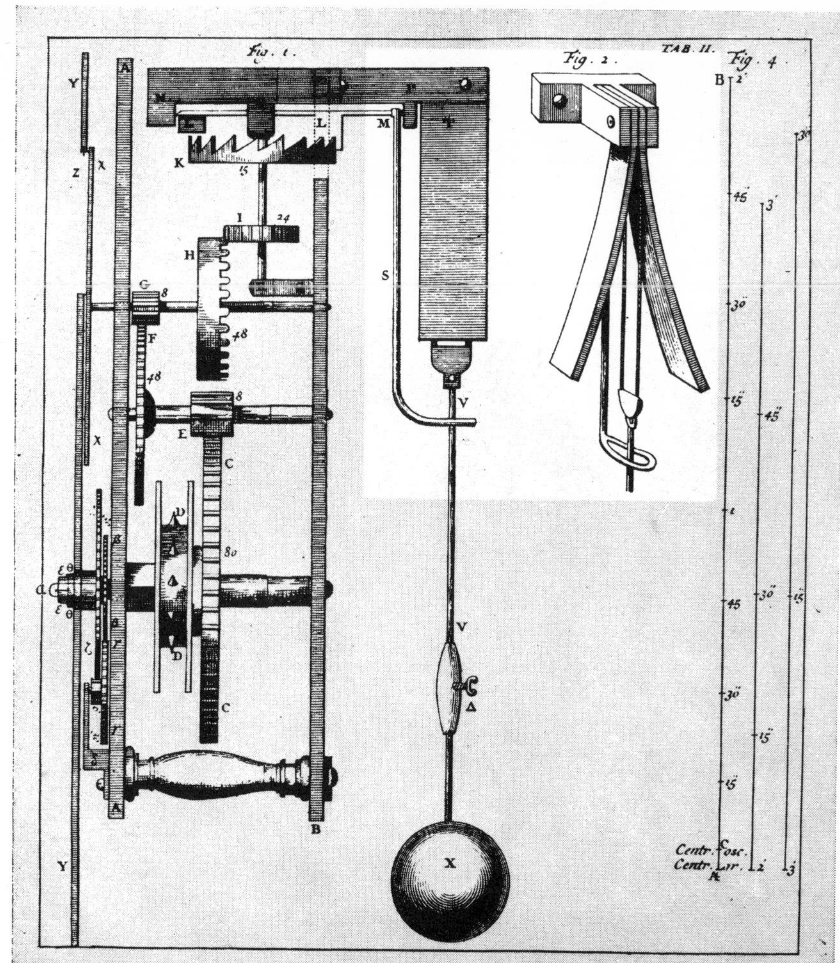

FEEDBACK CONTROL for a clock pendulum was invented in 1673 by the Dutch mathematician Christian Huygens. The curved metal strips on each side of the pendulum cords (*seen in perspective at right and labeled "T" in the side elevation of the clockwork at left*) were designed to make the period of the pendulum constant regardless of the length of its arc. The rod *S* moved with the pendulum, transmitting its motion to the clock.

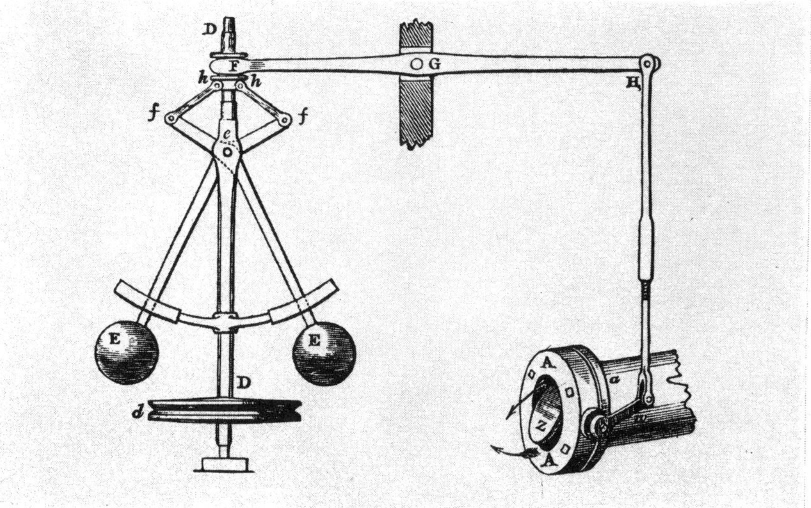

FLYBALL GOVERNOR (*left*), one of the earliest automatic control devices, was invented by James Watt to govern the speed of the steam engine. As the engine speeds up, the rod (*D*) on which the balls (*E*) are mounted spins faster, causing the balls to fly outward. This in turn closes the butterfly valve (*Z*), decreasing the supply of steam to the engine (*not shown*) and slowing it. A fraction of the output of the engine goes into the rotation of the flyballs; a fraction of this fraction is fed back to govern the speed of the engine.

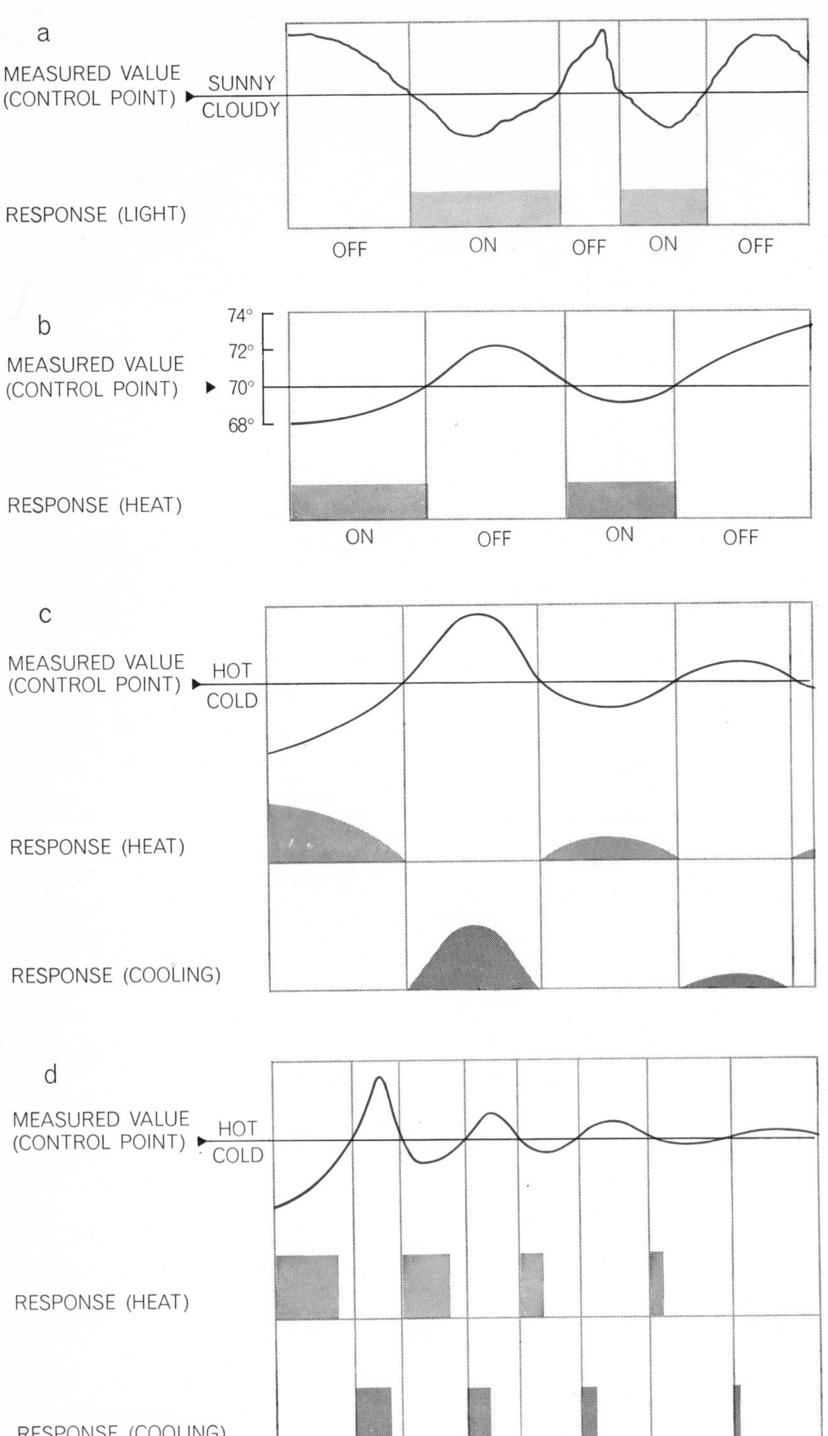

FOUR CONTROL SYSTEMS show how a measured variable can be brought under increasing refinement of control. Diagram *a* depicts a simple on-off response to a measured value, such as turning on the lights in a room when the sun goes behind a cloud. The measured value is not regulated and feedback is not employed. In *b*, which represents a typical home-heating system, on-off response is combined with feedback. When the temperature falls below the desired value, the furnace goes on, but since no cooling system is provided the room temperature may climb higher than desired on a sunny afternoon. The system in *c*, which could represent the heating of a chemical reaction vessel, provides both heating and cooling. The response is graduated so that as the control point is approached the rate of heating or cooling is reduced. The control problem in *d* is the same as in *c* but two modifications have been introduced to improve the speed and accuracy of control. Heating and cooling are not graduated but operate at a constant high rate when called for. This is known as "bang-bang" response. In addition a computer in the control system measures the rate of change in the controlled variable, takes account of the time lag in the temperature-recording mechanism and shuts off the heating or cooling before the control point is reached. Thus oscillation, or "hunting," of the system is damped out quickly.

guidance. On the other hand, a process-control computer may have to deal with 10 or 100 more variables than the rocket computer. And it may have to review a lengthier sequence of logical alternatives before making a decision.

What tools does the mathematician have for trying to control a multistage decision process? The conventional approach can be labeled "enumerative." Each decision can be regarded as a choice among a certain number of variables that determine the state of the process in the next stage; each sequence of choices defines a larger set of variables. By lumping all these choices together the mathematician can "reduce" the problem to a Newtonian one of determining the maximum of a given function.

It would seem simple enough to maximize a reasonably well-behaved function; using the familiar technique of calculus, the mathematician takes partial derivatives and solves the resulting system of equations for the maximizing point. Unfortunately the effective analytic or numerical solution of many equations, even apparently uncomplicated linear ones, is a difficult matter. By itself this is nothing more than the "curse of dimensionality," with which physicists have had to live for many years; significant results can be obtained in spite of it.

There are, however, more serious difficulties. In many cases the solution is a boundary point of the region of variation. This corresponds to the constraints, or restrictions, of real physical and engineering systems. When this is so, calculus is often inadequate for discovering maximum and minimum points and must be supplemented by tedious (and usually impossible) hunt-and-search techniques. Finally there is the frequent complexity that the outcome of a decision is not explicitly determined but is itself a random variable. The process is then said to be stochastic. Here to an even greater extent any simple enumerative technique is doomed by the vast proliferation of possible outcomes at every stage in the process. One cannot enumerate "all" possibilities and choose the best—not when there are 10^{50} or 10^{100} possibilities.

Has the mathematician now reached the end of his resources? Not if he will step back and ask himself if he has understood the nature of the solution he is seeking. How, he must ask himself, is the form of the solution influenced by the physical properties of the system? In other words, the mathematician cannot consider his problem solved until he has understood the structure of the optimal policy. Let me explain.

We have seen that in the conventional approach the entire multistage decision process is regarded as if it were a one-stage process. Thus if the process has N stages and there are M decisions to be made at each stage, the conventional approach envisages a single-stage process in MN dimensions. What one would like is to avoid this multiplication of dimensions, which stifles analysis, fogs the imagination and inevitably impedes computation.

The alternative approach—the policy approach—places emphasis on the characteristics of the system that determine the decision to be made at *any* stage of the process. In other words, instead of determining the optimal sequence of decisions from some *fixed* state of the system we wish to determine the optimal decision to be made at *any* state of the system. Only if we know the latter state do we understand the intrinsic structure of the solution.

The mathematical virtue of this approach lies first of all in the fact that it reduces the dimension of the problem to its proper level, which is the dimension of the decision that confronts one at any given stage. This makes the problem analytically more tractable and computationally much simpler. In addition this approach provides a type of approximation ("approximation in policy space") that has a unique mathematical property ("monotocity of convergence"). This means that each successive approximation improves performance [*see illustration on page 80*].

The name I proposed some years ago for this policy approach to multistage decision processes is dynamic programming. One of its goals is the determination of optimal feedback control. The adjective "dynamic" indicates that time plays a significant role in the process and that the order of operations may be crucial. The approach is equally applicable, however, to static processes by the simple expedient of reinterpreting them as dynamic processes in which time is artificially introduced.

Dynamic programming has given rise, in turn, to subsidiary and auxiliary control theories that go by a variety of names: theories of stochastic and adaptive variational processes, theories of Markovian decision processes, theories of quasi-linearization and invariant embedding. They cannot be explained in a few words; I mention them merely to indicate how control theory has branched and developed in recent years.

Let me now illustrate how the adoption of a policy can simplify a problem that otherwise would be hard to handle on a computer. (Complex versions of the problem cannot be handled without a computer.) Consider the problem of a hotel manager who wants to provide chairs for a group of people in a room. He has a helper who carries chairs with ease but who cannot count. What does the manager do?

He employs the primitive and powerful concept of equivalence, together with feedback control. He tells the helper to keep bringing chairs until everyone in the room has a chair. This sequential procedure guarantees that each person will have a chair, without ever determining how many people or chairs there are. Furthermore, if some chairs are defective, a simple modification guarantees that everyone will eventually have a sound chair.

Consider next the case of an elderly woman whose memory is failing. It irritates her to have to hunt through her wardrobe for various items of clothing when she dresses in the morning. She could create a filing system, complete with a written index, but this would be a lot of trouble. Instead she solves her problem by putting a complete outfit in every available drawer.

In both cases the solution is quite "simple," but it is not necessarily obvious. Both ideas are currently used in programming computers to solve complex problems. The first is used in certain simulation processes and in Monte Carlo calculations. The second is used for retrieving key items of information from a very large computer memory. Since the items are needed frequently they are stored in several places, thus considerably reducing retrieval time.

I might add that many mathematicians have the nagging suspicion that the universe is much simpler than it appears in their complex mathematical models. It is not easy, however, to capture the fresh view required for the simple approach. In the use of computers, changes in viewpoint such as the two just mentioned have time and again changed an impossible problem into a possible one, a merely difficult one into a routine exercise.

The next example is chosen to show how the concept of policy can not only simplify a multistage decision problem

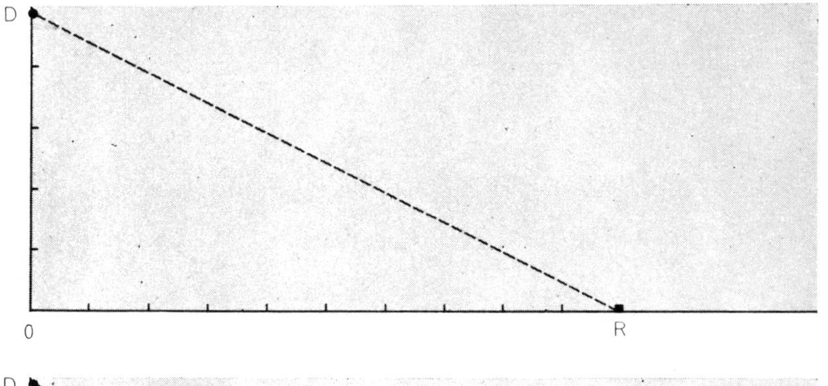

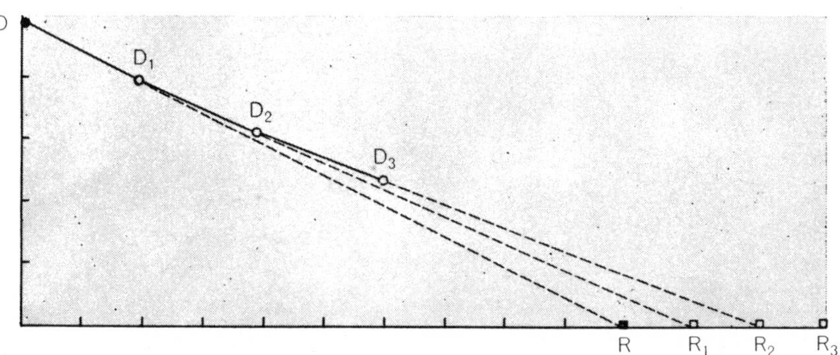

PURSUIT PROBLEM can be solved by adoption of a simple policy that lends itself to computer implementation. The problem is to find the path traced by a dog (D) chasing a rabbit (R). At the outset (*top*) the rabbit is 100 feet from 0 and the dog is 50 feet from 0. The dog runs at 22 feet per second, the rabbit at 11 feet per second. The dog always continues in a particular direction for one second. After the first second the dog has reached D_1 and the rabbit R_1 (*bottom*). To determine the point D_1 a straight line is drawn between D and R and 22 units are measured along it. Similarly, D_2 is determined by connecting D_1 and R_1, and so on. The resulting path approximates the one taken by the dog and can be refined by changing the direction of the path at shorter and shorter intervals.

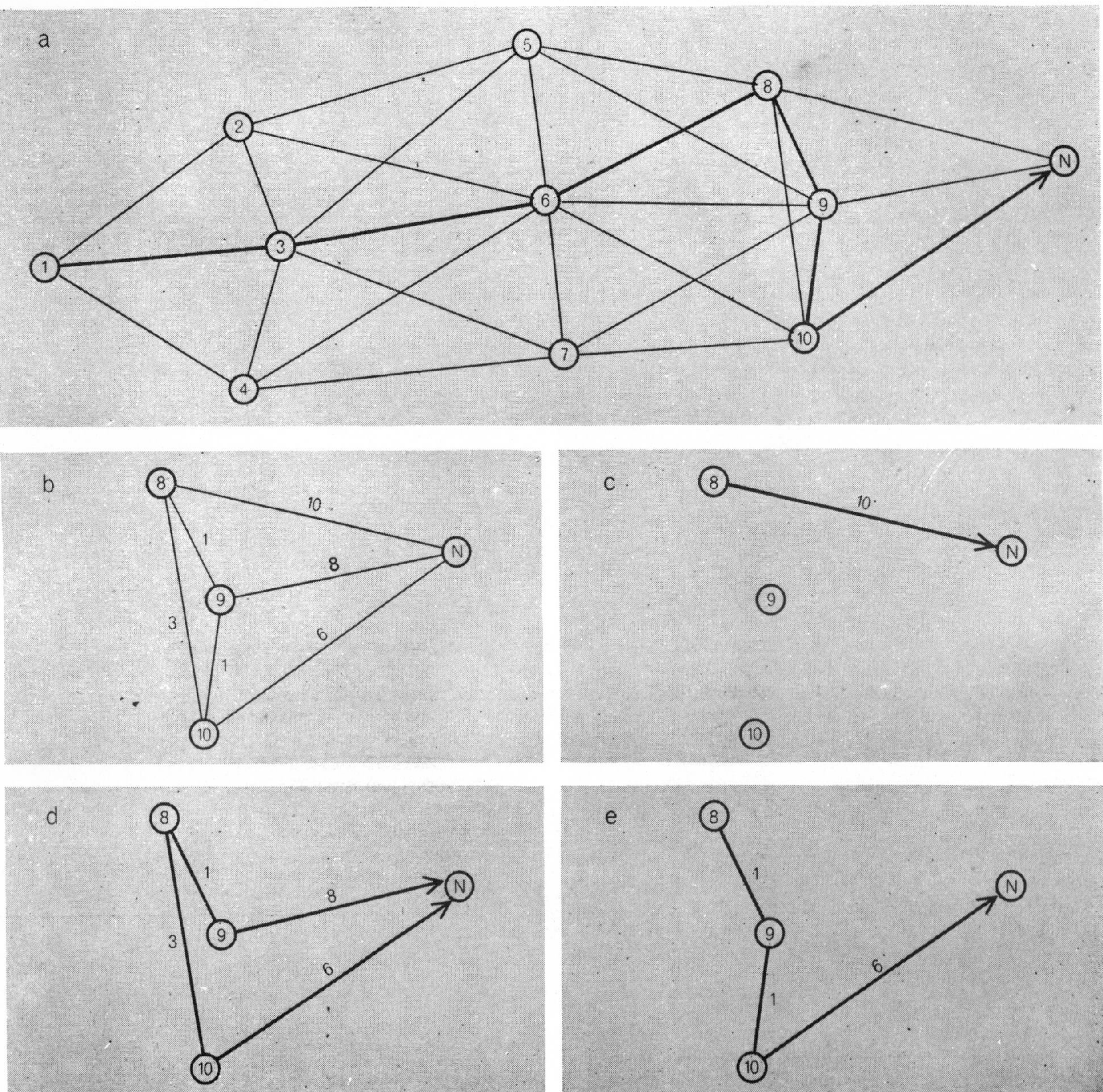

ROUTING PROBLEM is commonly met in control theory and was generally difficult to solve before computers and special programming methods were developed. The problem shown here is to find the path from *1* to *N* that requires the minimum time. The circles represent towns that are connected by a network of roads and the travel time between all pairs of towns is known. The traditional approach to such a problem was simply to enumerate all possibilities. This quickly leads to a "race against *N*." In the example as drawn, in which *N* is only 11, the number of different routes from *1* to *N* (with no backtracking) is more than 10,000. If *N* were 30, a high-speed computer would need more than 100 hours just to enumerate all the possible routes. One way to make such problems tractable is to use "dynamic programming," which depends on a selection of "policies." The virtue of such policies is that they can be applied from any point *i* in the network and thus satisfy the injunction: Do the best you can from where you are. The four smaller diagrams show how policies are selected assuming that *i* is point *8*. The travel times, in hours, for the various routes from *8* to *N* are shown in *b*. The initial policy (*c*) is to go directly from *8* to *N*, which takes 10 hours. The second policy (*d*) is to make one stop, which provides two alternative routes of nine hours each. The third policy (*e*) is to make two stops, which provides the minimum-time route. If point *1* were selected as the initial point *i*, the same procedure would be followed, but since this particular network does not provide a direct path from *1* to *N*, the first policy that could be examined would be one with the least number of stops, in this case three. There are, of course, ways of formulating this policy approach in terms of a computer program. The equation for solving the problem is

$$f_i = \min_{j \neq i} [t_{ij} + f_j],$$

in which f_i is the minimum time from any point i to N; t_{ij} is the time required to go from i to any other point j, which may be N itself, and f_j is the minimum time to go from j to N. This dynamic programming equation is solved by successive approximations—"approximations in policy space"—in which each successive approximation improves the result. The equation can be solved numerically for networks of several hundred points by hand in a few hours and by electronic computer in a few seconds. The equation determines both the optimal policy ("Where does one go next?") and the minimum time. Moreover, the equation embodies all the mathematical power of the classical calculus of variations.

but also yield numerical answers. To follow this example the reader must refer to the illustration on page 79, which shows the path of a dog chasing a rabbit. The dog is initially at D; the rabbit is at R and is running to the right along the x axis. If the dog always heads straight toward the rabbit, what curve does the dog follow?

This is a standard problem in the theory of differential equations, but the nonmathematical reader would hardly be edified if he were given the explicit form of the solution. To understand it requires a certain amount of mathematical training. This is strange when one thinks about it; the dog solves the problem without hesitation, although of course he does not get numerical answers.

It is easy to obtain a good approximation of the shape of the curve in the following way. Let us assume that the dog can run 15 miles per hour, or 22 feet per second, and that the rabbit can run just half as fast, or 11 feet per second. The rabbit is originally 100 feet from 0 and the dog is 50 feet from 0 at a point perpendicular to the x axis. Assume now that the dog continues in any particular direction for one second at a time. At the end of one second the dog has reached D_1 and the rabbit R_1. Another second later the dog has reached D_2, the rabbit R_2 and so on.

The point D_1 is determined by connecting D and R with a ruler and measuring 22 units along it. Similarly, D_2 is determined by connecting D_1 and R_1 and repeating the same measurement. The process is continued until the distance between dog and rabbit is closed. (We will ignore the fact that the closing stages are made a little messy by this method.) The broken-line path is a simple approximation of the actual path traversed by the dog. It is evident that the approximation can be made as close as desired by carrying out the change in the dog's direction at shorter and shorter time intervals, say every hundredth or every millionth of a second. By hand computation this would be increasingly tedious, but an electronic computer can do the job easily in a matter of seconds.

More sophisticated versions of this problem occur in the determination of optimal trajectories for space vehicles. In some of these cases the "rabbit" is imaginary and the problem is to determine where to point to achieve a desired course; in other cases the "rabbit" is real enough—another craft or a planet, perhaps—and establishing exactly where it is provides a further significant complication.

The point I wish to emphasize is that one can obtain a solution to the original problem by concentrating on the original process. One merely follows the instructions for what to do at every point in time and space. In mathematical terms, one carries out a policy.

The importance of this from the standpoint of control theory is manifold. In the first place, it is easy to use computers to implement policies. In the second place, the mathematical level is more fundamental, deeper and yet relatively uncomplicated by symbol manipulation. Policies are invariably simpler than time histories. Much more emphasis is now placed on the formulation of the problem. The idea is to take full advantage of the structure of the process in order to describe it in a most convenient analytical fashion and in order to make clear the structure of the optimal policy. One tries to avoid any routine description in terms of complicated equations that do not easily yield to numerical approach. One does not try to fit every new type of decision process into the rigid mold of 18th-century mathematics. This is the policy concept behind dynamic programming.

With this concept, which recognizes the resources of the digital computer and accepts it as an ally, one can easily and quickly obtain the numerical solution of control problems in many different fields that defied even the most resourceful mathematicians 20 years ago. The new approach has made it possible to solve formidable problems in trajectory analysis, process control, equipment replacement and inspection procedures, communication theory, the allocation of water resources and hydroelectric power, the use of forest resources and investment planning—to mention only a few important areas.

Beyond this, the concept of policy can readily be applied to study the more difficult and realistic classes of decision processes involving uncertainty and learning. I have already referred to the former as stochastic processes; the latter are known as adaptive control processes.

The dog-rabbit pursuit process was an example of a deterministic process in which the basic mechanisms are fully understood and it is "merely" a matter of devising a suitable procedure for solving it. Thus we assumed that the positions of both the dog and the rabbit can be precisely observed and determined at each instant, that the speeds remain constant, that nothing distracts the animals and so forth.

Even this idealized situation leads to difficult enough mathematics and a plethora of unsolved problems, as the study of classical celestial mechanics has demonstrated. After centuries of observation and computing, the positions of the planets next year or 10 years from now cannot be predicted with the accuracy desired. There will be a significant discrepancy between their predicted positions and those actually observed. A more upsetting problem for long-term planners is that no one knows if the solar system is completely stable.

It is obvious that if the idealized situation of perfect information and prediction cannot be found in the planetary motions, it can hardly be found in problems of trajectory optimization, satellite control and space rendezvous, much less in chemical process control, economic planning and medical diagnosis. In practice we are constantly using fallible devices for sensing and measuring, for processing, storing and retrieving information and for carrying out control decisions. Thus at every step we introduce error: error in observation, in calculation, in decision, in operation and even in the evaluation of outcomes.

The concept of a policy involving feedback control is ideally designed to handle the certain uncertainties of the actual world. By means of dynamic programming the injunction "Do the best you can in terms of where you are" (which is eminently sound common sense) can be readily translated into algorithms, or sets of rules, for the rigorous formulation and numerical solution of stochastic control problems.

When we turn to adaptive control processes we find a still higher order of uncertainty. In the stochastic case it is tacitly assumed that we know the detailed structure of the system we are studying, that we know various causes and various effects and, perhaps most essential of all, that we know what we want to do. In the case of an adaptive control process none of these assumptions may be valid.

Virtually all the unsolved major health problems can be regarded as adaptive control problems. Since no one knows the causes of cancer, coronary disease or mental illness, therapies aimed at control are necessarily based on a wide variety of hypotheses. This explains, of course, why so much caution must be exercised in treating patients. In the study of our national economy no one knows exactly what will happen if taxes are cut or if military spending is reduced. Furthermore, there is a continuing controversy even about what constitutes a desirable economic condition.

When faced with an adaptive control problem, one expects to learn more about the system as time goes on and to modify one's policies accordingly. All major decision processes in life are adaptive control processes. It should not be surprising, therefore, that biological evolution has equipped animals to deal more or less successfully with adaptive control problems. Deterministic and, to a degree, stochastic control problems can be handled by animals on the basis of instinct. Instinct can be described as feedback control of a deterministic type. The same stimulus produces the same reaction, regardless of what else has changed in the environment.

To handle adaptive control problems the higher animals are equipped with something we identify as "intelligence." In fact, intelligence can be defined as the capacity to solve, in some degree, an adaptive control problem. Intelligence manifests itself by adaptation, by flexible policies. It is difficult, of course, to draw a sharp dividing line between instinct and intelligence. It is probably better, then, to call every type of feedback behavior "intelligence" and subsequently distinguish between levels of intelligence.

Norbert Wiener, the eminent mathematician who died last winter, formulated the provocative idea that it should be possible to develop a unified theory of feedback control applicable both to living organisms and to machines. To express this idea he coined the term "cybernetics." It was his hope, shared by others, that techniques used so successfully in control engineering could be applied to biomedical problems (for example the design of artificial human organs) and also that research into neurophysiology might provide valuable clues in the design and study of communication systems, computers and more general control systems of all kinds. But as mathematicians, physiologists and engineers explore the subtle difficulties of dealing with large-scale systems—living and nonliving—of different degrees of complexity, it seems less and less likely that any single "cybernetic" theory will serve all purposes. Nonetheless, for those who want to understand both modern science and modern society, there is no better place to start than control theory.

PART THREE

GAMES AND DECISIONS

GAMES AND DECISIONS

INTRODUCTION

A major thread that is inextricably woven through the fabric of cybernetics and related disciplines is the principle of optimization. The principle of optimization refers to the comparison of the actual performance of a system to an "ideal" level of performance, with the aim of making the two coincide. An ideal control system, for example, is one that keeps the process exactly on "target" at all times. This task, as we have seen in the preceding section, is not trivial. In communication systems, it is desirable to maximize the rate of information transmission while, at the same time, minimizing the possibilities for error. However, these two goals are often in conflict since redundancy, which is used to detect and correct errors, reduces the rate of transmission. The routing problem described by Bellman in the last article of the preceding section is a straightforward optimization problem: "What is the shortest path through this network?" In this case, the problem is to discover the "ideal," the shortest path.

Decision theory and game theory deal explicitly with problems of optimization. Both are used to formulate principles that will lead to the "best" course of action when followed in appropriate decision contexts. They are not, in general, focused on the solution of any one problem but, instead, on techniques for finding solutions to all problems of a given sort. Rather than asking, for example, "What is the shortest route through this network of paths?" decision theory asks, "What techniques can we develop that will allow one to find the shortest route through *any* network?" An answer to the first question will provide little help in answering the second; but an answer to the second, more general question will tell us *how* to find an answer to the first.

Game theory, as a subdiscipline of decision theory, is concerned with the rational choice of acts or strategies in social contexts characterized, at least in part, by the existence of a conflict of interest between two or more intelligent decision makers. In such situations, classical decision theory is useless since it does not incorporate techniques or procedures that make allowances for intelligent and frequently hostile influences which are not directly controllable by the decision maker. Because it makes provisions for such factors, game theory is an important extension of decision theory.

Perhaps the key principle in game theory is that the optimal "solution" of a conflict is the establishment of an *equilibrium* among the concerned parties. This is quite different from the "maximization" principle encountered in simpler contexts, as Hurwicz notes in the second article in this section. The equilibrium concept, as it applies to strictly competitive two-person situations, advises the participants to focus on that strategy for which the worst possible outcome is the least undesirable. If this "minimax" outcome (which minimizes the maximum harm) is the same for both individuals, then both individuals should use the strategy that leads to this outcome since the use of any other strategy can only improve the other's outcome and reduce one's own. This "minimax" outcome is called a "saddle-point." The famous minimax theorem of John von Neumann proves that such an equilibrium exists in all of these conflicts if one considers probability mixtures of pure strategies as strategies themselves. (A "probability mixture of pure strategies" means simply that some random device is used to make the actual choice. "Heads, I go to the movies; tails, I continue to read" is precisely such a mixture.)

From a historical perspective, game theory has been a major advance in the use of formal mathematics to analyze an important class of social phenomena. Because it has clearly demonstrated the feasibility of such a mathematical application, it has had a profound impact in all sciences that deal with the nature and resolution of conflict. It has influenced the thinking of social psychologists who study human interaction. It has suggested techniques for the measurement of political power and has provided a conceptual framework within which the processes of coalition formation, bargaining, and negotiation may be interpreted. In the avoidance and resolution of conflict, game theory has helped to clarify the role of communication (and deception) by the analysis of the situations in which the establishment of honest communication of intentions and values can improve the outcomes for all parties involved. One of the key assumptions of the theory, namely, that it is possible to measure "satisfaction" on a numerical scale, has generated numerous investigations by both economists and psychologists, to whom this issue is of singular importance.

The first of the four articles in this section is "The Theory of Games" by Oskar Morgenstern, coauthor of the now classic book *Theory of Games and Economic Behavior.* In this paper, Morgenstern describes some of the principal concepts and results of game theory, from simple two-party games with a saddle-point to the properties of solutions to *n*-person games. In "Game Theory and Decisions," Leonid Hurwicz illustrates some of the similarities and differences between game theory and decision theory. In addition, he introduces the important idea that the critical variable in decision making is not money per se, but rather the psychological satisfaction or dissatisfaction accruing to money. This psychological variable is known as the *utility* of money. It can be measured by techniques similar to those described by Hurwicz. Anatol Rapoport, in "The Use and Misuse of Game Theory," issues a warning against the unbridled use of game theory as a decision-making technique. After viewing a number of problems that tend to restrict the generality of the theory, Rapoport suggests that the lasting value of the theory derives from its success at exposing the logical foundations of conflicts of various types. Linear programming, the topic of the final paper in this section, is an optimization technique that has many important applications, particularly in industrial settings. In terms of its formal mathematical structure, it shares many significant features with game theory. Consequently, in their paper, William W. Cooper and Abraham Charnes not only describe the types of problems that can be solved by linear programming, but also provide a glimpse of mathematical structure underlying the theory of games.

12

THE THEORY OF GAMES

OSKAR MORGENSTERN • May 1949

THE analogy between games of strategy and economic and social behavior is so obvious that it finds wide expression in the thinking and even the language of business and politics. Phrases such as "a political deal" and "playing the stock market" are familiar reflections of this. The connection between games and these other activities is more than superficial. When they are examined by the methods of modern mathematics, it becomes evident that many of the forms of economic and social behavior are strictly identical with—not merely analogous to—games of strategy. Thus the mathematical study of games offers the possibility of new insights and precision in the study of economics.

The theory of probability arose from a study of lowly games of chance and from the desire of professional gamblers to find ways of taking advantage of the odds. Far more difficult problems are presented by games of strategy such as poker, bridge and chess. In these games, where the outcome no longer depends on chance alone but also on the acts of other players and on their expectations of one's own present and future acts, a player must choose among relatively complex strategies. Mathematically, these problems remained not only unsolved, but even untouched.

Gottfried Wilhelm Leibnitz, the German philosopher and mathematician, seems to have recognized that a study of games of strategy would form the basis of a theory of society. On the other hand, many efforts along quite different lines were made by philosophers and economists to provide a theory for "rational behavior" for individuals, business corporations, or even for entire communities.

Such a theory must be quantitative, which means that it must ultimately assume a mathematical character. A theory of games fulfilling these requirements would take into account that participants in a game vary in information and intelligence, that they have various expectations about the other players' behavior, and that different paths of reaching their goal may be open to them. The theory must also allow for the fact that the position of a player (or, equivalently, of an economic individual or a firm) is often adversely affected if his opponent finds out his intentions. The player has to take steps to protect himself against this contingency, and the theory must indicate how he should proceed most efficiently—and what his countermeasures would mean to the other players.

Why should such a theory be of interest to the sociologist and, in particular, to the economist? Does not the economics of today have an adequate model in mechanics, with its notions of forces, of equilibrium and stability? Physics is, indeed, at the bottom of current efforts to provide a statement of rational economic behavior, whether it is mathematically formulated or not. But many important situations that arise at all levels in economics find no counterpart whatever in physics.

A typical example is the fixing of wage rates between workers and employers when both groups have found it to their advantage to combine into unions and associations. Current economics cannot tell us, except in a general manner, under what circumstances such combinations will arise, who will profit, and by how much. The two groups have opposing interests, but do not have separate means to pursue their contrary aims. They must finally come to some agreement, which may turn out to be more advantageous to one side than to the other. In settling their differences they will feint, bluff, use persuasion; they will try to discover each other's strategies and prevent discovery of their own. Under such circumstances a theory of rational behavior will have to tell a participant how much a given effort will be worth in view of the obstacles encountered, the obstacles being the behavior of his opponents and the influence of the chance factor.

Monopoly and monopolistic market forms—that is, trading among only a few individuals or firms on one side of the market at least—are characteristic of all social economies. They involve serious feuds and fights, a very different picture from the general, "free" competition with which classical economic theory usually deals. On the orthodox theory, the individual is supposed to face prices and other conditions that are fixed, and is supposed to be in a position to control all the variables, so that his profit or utility depends only on his own actions. Actually, however, when there are only a few individuals, or many individuals organized into a few combinations, the outcome never depends on the actions of the individual alone. No single person has control of all the variables, but only of a few.

The case of an individual acting in strict isolation can be described mathematically as a simple maximum problem—that is, finding the behavior formula that will yield the maximum value or return. The cases involving combinations are of an entirely different mathematical and logical structure. Indeed, they present a peculiar mixture of maximum problems, creating a profound mathematical question for which there is no parallel in physical science or even in classical mathematics.

Yet this is the level at which the problem of economic behavior needs to be attacked. Clearly it is far more realistic to investigate from the outset the nature of the all-pervading struggles and fights in economic and social life, rather than to deal with an essentially artificial, atomistic, "free" competition where men are supposed to act like automatons confronted by rigidly given conditions.

THE theory of games defines the solution of each game of strategy as the distribution or distributions of payments to be made by every player as a function of all other individuals' behavior. The solution thus has to tell each player, striving for his maximum advantage, how to behave in all conceivable circumstances, allowing for all and any behavior of all the other players. Obviously this concept of a solution is very comprehensive, and finding such a solution for each type of game, as well as computing it numerically for each particular instance, poses enormous mathematical difficulties. The theory makes important use of mathematical logic, as well as combinatorics (the study of possible ways of combining and ordering objects) and set theory (the techniques for dealing with any collection of objects which have one or more exactly specified properties in common). This domain of modern mathematics is one of exceptional rigor. But it is believed that great mathematical discoveries are required to make a break-through into the field of social phenomena.

A single individual, playing alone, faces the simplest maximum problem; his best strategy is the one that brings him the predetermined maximum gain. Consider a two-person game: Each player wishes to win a maximum, but he can do this only at the expense of the other. This situation results in a zero-sum game, since the sum of one player's gains and the other's losses (a negative number) is zero. One player has to design a strategy that will assure him of the maximum advantage. But the same is true of the other, who naturally wishes to minimize the first player's gain, thereby maximizing his own. This clear-cut opposition of interest introduces an entirely new concept, the so-called "minimax" problem.

SOME games have an optimal "pure" strategy. In other words, there is a sequence of moves such that the player using it will have the safest strategy possible, whatever his opponent does. His position will not deteriorate even if his strategy is found out. In such "strictly determined" games, every move—and hence every position resulting from a series of moves— is out in the open. Both players have complete information. The mathematical expression of this condition is that the function describing the outcome of a game has a "saddle point." This mathematical term is based on an analogy with the shape of a saddle, which can be regarded as the intersection of two curves at a single point. One curve in a saddle is the one in which the rider sits; the other is the one that fits over the horse's back and slopes down over its sides. The seat of the saddle represents the "maximum" curve, and its low point is the "maximin." The curve that straddles the horse's back is the "minimum" curve, and its high point is the "minimax." The point at which the two curves meet at the center of the saddle is the "saddle point." In the theory of games, the somewhat more special saddle point is the intersection of two particular strategies.

The mathematical values of the strategies involved in a hypothetical game of this kind are represented in the diagram on this page. This shows a simple game between two players, A and B, each of whom has available three possible strategies. There are nine possible combinations of moves by A and B. The numbers in the boxes represent A's gains or losses for all combined strategies and, since this is a zero-sum game, their negatives represent B's losses or gains. A's minimax strategy is A-2, because if he follows that sequence of moves, he is sure to win at least two units no matter what B does. Similarly, B's minimax strategy is B-1, because then he cannot possibly lose more than two units whatever A's plan of action. If a spy informed A that B was planning to use B-1, A could make no profit from that information. The point where the A-2 row intersects the B-1 column is the saddle point for this game.

It may seem that B has no business playing such a game, since he must lose two units even with his best strategy, and any other strategy exposes him to even heavier loss. At best he can win only a single unit, and then only if A makes a mistake. Yet all strictly determined games are of this nature. A simple example is ticktacktoe. In perfectly played ticktacktoe every game would result in a tie. A more complex example is chess, which has a saddle point and a pure strategy. Chess is exciting because the number of possible moves and positions is so great that the finding of that strategy is beyond the powers of even the best calculating machines.

A \ B	B-1	B-2	B-3
A-1	2	1	4
A-2	2	3	2
A-3	2	-1	1

GAME OF STRATEGY between two players, each with three possible strategies, has nine possible results. Numbers in boxes represent A's gains or losses for each combination of plays by both players.

Other two-person, zero-sum games, however, have no single best possible strategy. This group includes games ranging from matching pennies to bridge and poker—and most military situations. These games, in which it would be disastrous if a player's strategy were discovered by his opponent, are not strictly determined. The player's principal concern is to protect his strategy from discovery. Do safe and good strategies exist for "not strictly determined" games, so that their choice would make the games again strictly determined? Can a player in such a game find strategies other than "pure" strategies which would make his behavior completely "rational"? Mathematically speaking, does a saddle point always exist?

It does, and the proof was originally established in 1927 by the mathematician John von Neumann, the originator of the theory of games, now at the Institute for Advanced Study in Princeton. He used various basic tools of modern mathematics, including the so-called fixed-point theorem of the Dutch mathematician L. E. J. Brouwer. Von Neumann proved, by a complex but rigorous application of this theorem to the theory of games, that there is a single "stable" or rational course of action that represents the best strategy or saddle point even in not strictly determined games.

This principle can also be demonstrated in practical terms. Observation shows that in games where the discovery of a player's plan of action would have dangerous consequences, he can protect himself by avoiding the consistent use of a pure strategy and choosing it with a certain probability only. This substitution of a statistical strategy makes discovery by the opponent impossible. Since the player's chief aim must be to prevent any leakage of information from himself to the other player, the best way to accomplish this is not to have the information oneself. Thus, instead of choosing a precise course of action, the various possible alternatives are considered with different probabilities.

It is in the nature of probability that individual events cannot be predicted, so that the strategy actually used will remain a secret up to the decisive moment, even to the player himself, and necessarily to his opponent as well. This type of indecision is a well-known empirical fact. Wherever there is an advantage in not having one's intentions found out—obviously a very common occurrence—people will be evasive, try to create uncertainty in the minds of others, produce doubts, and at the same time try to pierce the veil of secrecy thrown over their opponents' operations.

The example *par excellence* is poker. In a much simpler form, this type of behavior is illustrated in the game of matching pennies. Here the best strategy is to show heads or tails at random, taking care only to play each half the time. Since the same strategy is available to the opponent, both players will break even if they play long enough and both know this principle. The calculation of the best strategy grows in difficulty as the number of possible moves increases: *e.g.*, in the Italian game called morra, in which each player shows one, two or three fingers and simultaneously calls out his guess as to the sum of fingers shown by himself and his opponent, a player has nine possible strategies. His safest course is to guess a total of four fingers every time, and to vary his own moves so that out of every 12 games he shows one finger five times, two fingers four times and three fingers three times. If he plays according to this mixture of strategies, he will at least break even, no matter what his opponent does.

LET us apply these principles to a simple economic problem. Suppose that two manufacturers are competing for a given consumer market, and that each is considering three different sales strategies. The matrix on this page specifies the possible values of the respective strategies to manufacturer A: This situation does not have a single best strategy. If A chooses strategy A-1, B can limit his profit to one unit by using strategy B-2 or B-3; if A chooses strategy A-2 or A-3, B can deprive him of any profit by choosing strategy B-1. Thus each manufacturer stands to lose if he concentrates on a single sales technique and his rival discovers his plan. Analysis shows that A will lose unless he uses a combination of A-1, A-2 and A-3, each a third of the time. On the other hand, if manufacturer B fails to employ his best mixed strategy—B-1 a ninth of the time, B-2 two ninths of the time, and B-3 two thirds of the time—his competitor will gain. These mixed strategies are the safest strategies. They should be used whenever each manufacturer does not know what the other will do.

An example which illustrates in statistical terms many of the conflicts of choices involved in everyday life is the famous story of Sherlock Holmes' pursuit by his archenemy, Professor Moriarty, in Conan Doyle's story, "The Final Problem." Holmes has planned to take a train from London to Dover and thence make his escape to the Continent. Just as the Dover train is pulling out of Victoria Station, Moriarty rushes on the platform and the two men see each other. Moriarty is left at the station. He charters a special train to continue the chase. The detective is faced with the problem of outguessing his pursuer. Should he get off at Canterbury—the only intermediate stop—or go all the way to Dover? And what should Moriarty do? In effect, this situation can be treated as a rather unusual version of matching pennies—a "match" occurring if the two men decide to go to the same place and meet there. It is assumed that such a meeting would mean the death of Sherlock Holmes; therefore it has an arbitrarily assigned value of 100 to Moriarty. If Holmes goes to Dover and makes his way to the Continent, it is obviously a defeat for the professor, but—also obviously—not as great a defeat as death would be for the detective. Hence, a value of minus 50 to Moriarty is given to this eventuality. Finally, if Holmes leaves the train at Canterbury and Moriarty goes on to Dover, the chase is not over and the temporary outcome can be considered a draw. According to the theory of games, the odds are 60 to 40 in favor of the professor.

In the story, of course, this game is played only once: Sherlock Holmes, deducing that Moriarty will go to Dover, gets off at Canterbury and watches triumphantly as the professor's pursuing train speeds past the intermediate station. If the game were continued, however, Holmes' look of triumph would hardly be justified. On the assumption that Moriarty persisted in the chase, calculations indicate that the great detective was actually as good as 40 per cent dead when his train left Victoria Station!

The theory of games has already been applied to a number of practical problems. Situations similar to that of Holmes are being analyzed in that branch of operational research which deals with military tactics, the possible courses of action being various dispositions of troops or combinations of measures and countermeasures. The handling of the more complex situations that exist in economics is expected to require the aid of calculating machines. For example, two competing automobile manufacturers may each have a large number of strategies involving the choice of various body designs, the addition of new accessories, the best times to announce new models and price changes, and so on. It has been estimated that the calculations for a game in which one manufacturer had 100 possible strategies and his competitor had 200 (a not uncommon situation) would take about a year on an electronic computer.

A \ B	B-1	B-2	B-3
A-1	4	1	1
A-2	0	3	1
A-3	0	0	2

BUSINESS RIVALRY between two firms with three strategies each again diagrams A's possible gains. No single strategy is best if the opponent discovers it; hence the rivals must use a mixture of all three.

If we now make the transition to games involving three or more persons, a fundamentally new phenomenon emerges—namely, the tendency among some players to combine against others, or equivalently in markets to form trade unions, cartels and trusts. Such coalitions will be successful only if they offer the individual members more than they could get acting separately. Games where that is the case are called essential. Coalitions will then oppose each other in the manner of individual players in a two-person game. A coalition will have a value for the players who form it, and they may therefore require payments or "compensations" from newcomers who want to enter the coalition and share in its proceeds. As a rule a great deal of bargaining will precede the determination of the system of distribution of gains or profits among the members of the coalition.

Basically, the formation of a coalition expresses the fundamental tendency toward monopoly, which is thus found to be deeply characteristic of social and economic life. Indeed, Adam Smith already had noted the tendency of businessmen to "conspire" against the common welfare, as he stated it, by getting together into groups for better exploitation. Important chapters of American economic history deal with the efforts of government to break conspiracies of various kinds in order to limit the power of trusts and other amalgamations. When these are broken—if at all—they tend to arise again, so a continuous watchfulness is necessary.

The powerful forces working toward monopoly ought therefore to be at the very center of economic studies. They should replace the preoccupation with a nonexistent pure or free competition where nobody has any perceptible influence on anything, and where all data are assumed to be immutably given. Since this is the imaginary setup from which current economic theory starts, it encounters insuperable difficulties when it enters the realm of monopolistic competition. It is not surprising, therefore, that classical economics has failed to yield a general theory that embraces all economic situations.

THE approach to the coalition problem in the theory of games can be shown by a three-person situation in which it is assumed that a player can achieve a gain in any given play only if he joins with one other player. The gains and losses that would result for the individual players in the case of each possible coalition are shown in the diagram on page 89. Thus if A and B form a coalition, each gains a half unit and C loses one unit. What keeps the players in the game is that they all stand a chance of profit; each player's problem is to succeed in forming a coalition with one of the other two on any given deal. This simplified situation illustrates in essence much of the conflict that occurs in modern economic life.

Now the important characteristic of this type of game is that there is no single "best" solution for any individual player. A, for example, can gain as much by forming a coalition with C as with B. Therefore all three of the possible distributions of payments, taken together, must be viewed as the solution of this three-person game.

There are, of course, many other distribution schemes that might be considered by the players. For example, one of the partners in a coalition could make a deal with the third player whereby both improved their positions (the third player reducing his losses) at the expense of the other partner. What is to prevent the participants in the game from considering all these other possibilities?

The question can be answered by introducing the concept of "domination." In mathematical terminology the various possible schemes for distribution of payments are called "imputations." One imputation is said to dominate another if it is clearly more advantageous to all the players in a given coalition. It is found, as shown in the three-person game described above, that the imputations belonging to a solution do not dominate each other: in this case all three imputations have an equal chance of being chosen; none is most advantageous to the players in each coalition. While it is extremely difficult to prove mathematically that such a solution would exist for every game with arbitrarily many players, the principle can be expected to hold true.

Now it is also found that while the imputations belonging to the solution do not dominate each other, individually they are not free from domination by imputations outside the solution. In other words, there are always outside schemes from which some of the players could profit. But any and every imputation outside the solution is dominated by one belonging to the solution, so that it will be rejected as too risky. It will be considered unsafe not to conform to the accepted standard of behavior, and only one of the imputations which are part of the solution will materialize.

These examples give an idea of the great complexity of social and economic organization. In this realm "stability" is far more involved than it is in the physical sciences, where a solution is usually given by a number or a set of numbers. In essential games, in economics and in warfare, there is instead a set of alternatives, none of which is clearly better than another or all others. One imputation in a set is not more stable than any other, because every one may be threatened by one outside the solution. But each has a certain stability because it is protected by other potential imputations in the solution against upsets from outside. Collectively they eliminate the danger of revolutions. The balance is most delicate, however, and it becomes more sensitive as the number of players increases. These higher-order games may have many solutions instead of a single one, and while there is no conflict within an individual solution, the various solutions or standards of behavior may well conflict with one another.

This multiplicity of solutions may be interpreted as a mathematical formulation of the undisputed fact that on the same physical background of economic and social culture utterly different types of society can be established. Within each society, in turn, there is possible considerable variation in the distribution of income, privileges and other advantages—which corresponds to the multiplicity of imputations or distribution schemes in a single solution in a game.

The theory also yields insight into even more delicate social phenomena. Although it assumes that every player has full information, discrimination may exist: two players may make a third player "tabu," assigning him a fixed payment and excluding him from all negotiations and coalitions. Yet this arrangement need not lead to complete exploitation of the third player. In practical economic life, for example, cartels do not annihilate all outside firms, although it would not be a technically difficult operation. Rather, in deference to socially accepted standards of behavior they allow certain outsiders a share in the industry, so as not to attract undue attention—and to be able to point out to the government and the public that "competition" exists in the particular industry.

INDIVIDUAL PLAYERS / COALITIONS	A	B	C
A,B	1/2	1/2	-1
A,C	1/2	-1	1/2
B,C	-1	1/2	1/2

COALITION GAME with three players produces still another matrix. Here gains or losses to players resulting from various possible coalitions are shown in vertical columns. Player must form partnership to win.

It is surprising and extremely significant that, although the theory of games was developed without any specific consideration of such situations, the fact that they exist was derived from general theorems by purely mathematical methods. Furthermore, the theory shows—again purely mathematically—that certain privileges, even if anchored in the rules of a game (or of a society), cannot always be maintained by the privileged if they come into conflict with the accepted standard of behavior. A privileged person or group may have to give up his entire "bonus" in order to survive economically.

These and many other implications can be derived from the study of simple three-person games. Games of more than three players provide further interesting insights—but at the price of great and, in many cases, still insuperable mathematical difficulties. The almost unimaginable complexity involved may be illustrated by poker, the game which, above all others, furnishes a model for economic and social situations. The subtleties of poker and the countless number of available strategies—*e.g.*, the technique of purposely being caught bluffing now and then so that future bluffs may be successful—prevent the thorough analysis that would be necessary to throw light on corresponding problems in practical everyday affairs. The matrix of possible strategies for poker is so large that it has not even been calculated, much less drawn. Consider a radically simplified version of the game which assumes a deck of only three cards, a one-card, no-draw hand, only two players, three bids between them (the first player gets two, the second one), and no overbetting. Even this watered-down version of poker involves a matrix of 1,728 boxes, and computing a single best possible strategy for each player to an accuracy of about 10 per cent might require almost two billion multiplications and additions.

BUT even with its present limitations the theory of games has made it possible to analyze problems beyond the scope of previous economic theory. Besides those already indicated, the problems now being explored include the application of the mathematics for a game involving seven persons to the best location of plants in a particular industry, the relation between labor unions and management, the nature of monopoly.

The initial problem in the theory of games was to give precision to the notion of "rational behavior." Qualitative or philosophical arguments have led nowhere; the new quantitative approach may point in the right direction. Applications are still limited, but the approach is in the scientific tradition of proceeding step by step, instead of attempting to include all phenomena in a great general solution. We all hope eventually to discover truly scientific theories that will tell us exactly how to stabilize employment, increase national income and distribute it adequately. But we must first obtain precision and mastery in a limited field, and then proceed to increasingly greater problems. There are no short cuts in economics.

13

GAME THEORY AND DECISIONS

LEONID HURWICZ • February 1955

We are often forced to make decisions without complete information as to the consequences of the possible alternative actions. Such is the case, for instance, when an individual must decide in May whether to take his vacation in July or in August, when a nation must decide on the size of its defense program though uncertain about other nations' intentions, when a scientist must decide on a plan for an experiment. Uncertainty is present in many decision problems, big and little, routine and unusual.

Some problems involving uncertainty can be treated scientifically by means of the mathematics of probability. The modern sciences of genetics and physics are largely based on probability theory. But what of the innumerable kinds of situations in which the probabilities cannot be computed? Think, for instance, of Columbus' problem when his crew demanded that he turn back. Could he have evaluated the probability of finding land to the west before food and water gave out?

Within the last few years mathematicians have begun to develop a systematic theory of "rational" decision-making in problems involving such uncertainties. Like the probability theory, originally developed in the 17th century from studies of simple games of chance (*e.g.*, dice), the new theory has grown out of studies of a "laboratory model"—in this case certain simple games of strategy against a thinking opponent (*e.g.*, chess and poker).

John von Neumann constructed the theory of games in the 1920s (earlier the mathematician Emile Borel had also had some ideas on the subject), but the subject did not achieve prominence until the publication in 1944 of the now classic *Theory of Games and Economic Behavior* by von Neumann and the economist Oskar Morgenstern. The theory then "caught on," and there has been a multitude of studies and papers developing it in a great many directions.

The theory of games and the theory of decision-making met on the territory of statistical inference. It had occurred to Abraham Wald, one of the founders of modern statistics, that statistical inference could be thought of as a game played against nature by the statistician attempting to uncover its secrets. Wald's principle of "minimizing the maximum risk," indeed, turned out to be equivalent to a principle of choosing a strategy in a game.

Game theory is so complex and heavily mathematical that it cannot be presented in a comprehensive fashion in one article. But many of us are not so much interested in the details of the theory as in its underlying logic, and of that one can get a rough idea from some simplified examples.

Among games of strategy it is convenient to distinguish between games of pure chance and what we shall call games with strategic uncertainty. In a game of pure chance (*e.g.*, dice) wheth-

Could Columbus have used the theory of games?

er a player wins or loses, and how much, depends only on his own choices and on luck. In a game with strategic uncertainty (*e.g.*, poker) he must think about an additional factor: What will the other fellow do? Our main interest is in games involving strategic uncertainty, but we shall find them easier to understand if we first devote some attention to how one might apply general principles of "rational" conduct to games of pure chance.

Suppose that I am invited to place a bet on the outcome of a simultaneous throw of two dice: I will be paid $10 if two aces (single dots) show, otherwise I shall have to pay $1. Should I accept the bet? To answer, we start by doing a little computing. On the average a double ace will appear once in 36 throws. Hence I can expect that in 36 throws I shall win $10 once and lose $1 35 times. The "mathematical expectation" would be a loss of $25, about 69 cents per throw. If all I cared about was the mathematical odds, I would obviously refuse to bet on such terms, since my expectation when not playing is zero—which is better than minus 69 cents! In fact, if I cared only about the mathematical expectation, I would insist that if I am to pay $1 whenever I lose, I ought to be paid at least $35 when the two aces come up; for only then would I be, in terms of my expectation, no worse off than if I refrained from betting.

But we know that people do make bets on a roulette wheel or in a lottery where their expectation is negative, *i.e.*, where, on the average, they must expect to lose. Of course, one could say that this only shows how irrational they are. Yet simple examples will show that a reasonable person will sometimes refuse a bet with a positive expectation and accept one with a negative expectation.

Imagine, for instance, a rich man who has walked far from his house, is tired and plans to take a bus home. The bus fare is 20 cents and it so happens he has only 20 cents in his pocket. At this point someone offers him the following bet: A coin will be tossed; if heads come up, he will be paid $1, if tails come up, he will have to pay 20 cents. In other words, he is offered five to one on what should be an even money bet. Yet we can be pretty sure that the rich man would not be lured into the game, for winning a dollar would mean very little to him, but having to walk home would be a darned nuisance.

Thus the amount of money one can expect to win or lose per throw is not all that matters. What does matter is the amount of satisfaction (or discomfort) associated with the possible outcome of a gamble. If one is willing to measure satisfaction in numerical units, there is a way to explain the rich man's decision in mathematical terms. Suppose that walking home would mean to him a loss of five units of satisfaction while winning a dollar would mean a gain of only three units of satisfaction. In units of satisfaction rather than in dollars his expectation on each toss of the coin would be negative.

On the other hand, the expectation in terms of satisfaction units may be positive when that in terms of dollars is negative. Imagine that it costs $2 to buy a ticket in a lottery where there is one chance in a million of winning a million dollars. Since one would have to bet $2 a million times in order to win a million dollars once, on the average, the expectation here is minus one million dollars, or minus $1 per drawing. But to a person with drab prospects in life the gain of one million dollars might mean, say, 10 million units of satisfaction as against only four units being lost when $2 is paid out. For such an individual the outcome in a million drawings, *in satisfaction units,* would be 10 million minus four times one million, which amounts to an expectation of gain of one and a half units per drawing.

Is it meaningful to speak of satisfac-

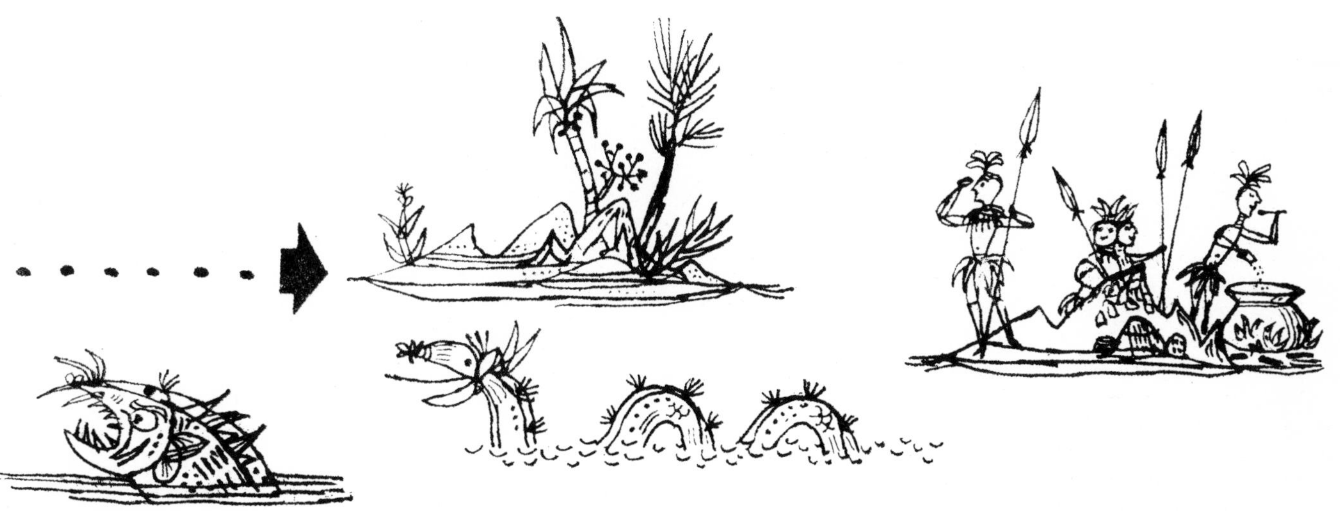

cide whether it was really worth while to sail on?

Rabelais's Judge Bridlegoose couldn't see the dice

tion units? Isn't satisfaction an inner psychological phenomenon that defies numerical measurement? It turns out that such measurement is possible if one is willing to postulate that the individual will always try to make his decision so as to maximize the expectation. Of course we have to construct a satisfaction scale, but, as in measuring temperature, we are free to select the zero point and the unit arbitrarily. Suppose, for instance, that I locate the zero of my scale at my present money holdings and decide that a $10 gain would mean one positive satisfaction unit. Imagine, further, that I am offered $10 for a correct call on the toss of a coin at various odds and that I am unwilling to bet $8, eager to bet $4 and more or less indifferent as to betting $7 against the $10. Assuming that my behavior is consistent with choosing the course of action leading to highest expectations, it must be that to me a loss of $8 means losing more than one unit of satisfaction, a loss of $4 means losing less than one unit of satisfaction and a loss of $7 is just about equivalent to one unit of satisfaction. Thus my satisfaction scale can be constructed by experimental methods.

In what follows the numbers in our examples can be interpreted as units of satisfaction. But readers who feel some reluctance to indulge in satisfaction measurement may prefer to think of the units as dollars.

The idea of computing expectations in terms of satisfaction units dates back at least to Daniel Bernoulli, who in the first half of the 18th century formulated a concept which he called the "moral expectation." Now the computation, with the new approach via maximizing expectations, has been put on a rigorous theoretical basis by the recent work of von Neumann and Morgenstern, Jacob Marschak, Milton Friedman, L. J. Savage and others, while Frederick Mosteller and others have done some interesting experiments.

Let us proceed to games possessing strategic uncertainty. If you knew the chances of the other fellow's playing one way or another in a poker game, you could determine the best strategy simply by computing expectations as in a game of chance. But in most social games peeking is frowned upon. It is precisely this lack of knowledge as to the opponent's probable strategy that gives poker its additional element of uncertainty and makes it so exciting.

In order to get a better picture of the problem, we shall consider an artificially simple game. Jones plays against Smith. Jones is to choose one of the three letters A, B or C; Smith, one of the four Roman numerals I, II, III or IV. Each writes his choice on a slip of paper and then the choices are compared. A payment is made according to the upper table on the opposite page. The figure zero means that neither pays; a positive number means that Smith pays that amount to Jones; a negative number, that Jones pays Smith. Thus if Jones chooses A and Smith chooses II, for example, Smith pays Jones $100.

Let us put ourselves in Jones's shoes and see how he might make his choice. If he peeked and knew what Smith had chosen, the answer would be simple; for instance, if he knew Smith had selected II, he would choose A, because C would get him only $2 and if he chose B he would have to pay Smith $1,000. Suppose that Jones happens to know only that Smith has eliminated III and IV and the chances are even as between I and II. If he played A, his expectation would then be minus 50 (dividing minus 200 plus 100 by 2); if he played B, it would be minus 500 (0 minus 1,000 divided by 2); if he played C, the expectation would be $1\frac{1}{2}$ (1 plus 2 divided by 2). Thus in terms of the expectation C is the best choice.

But ordinarily Jones will have no such information. Nonetheless there are principles which can guide his play; we shall present a few of them. The first is "the principle of insufficient reason," associated with the names of the mathematicians Thomas Bayes and Pierre-Simon de Laplace. This principle would require that Jones behave as if Smith were equally likely to make any of his four choices. He would compute his expectations on that basis, and would find that if he chose A his expectation would be 49.5, for B it would be 0 and for C it would be 2.5. Thus A would be the best choice.

If Jones is an optimist, he might make his choice on the basis of another principle we shall call "visualize the best." In that case he would choose B, because it offers the opportunity for the largest pay-off ($1,000).

On the other hand, Jones may be a conservative man, even a pessimist. It would then be natural for him to follow the "visualize the worst" principle, named by mathematicians "minimax," because it amounts to minimizing the maximum possible loss—the principle suggested, as we have seen, by Wald.

Pascal applied mathematics to gambling

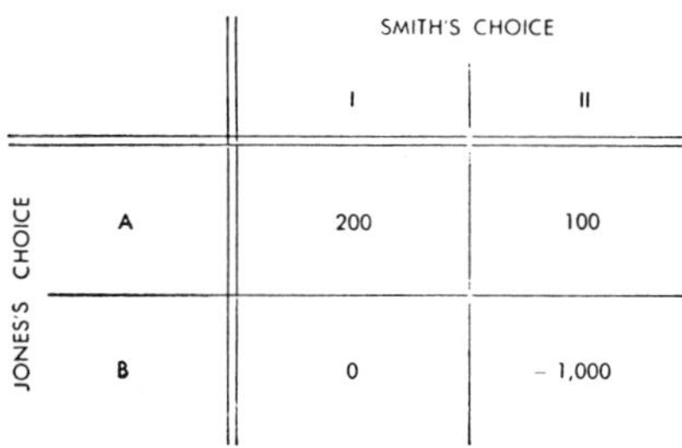

JONES'S CHOICE	SMITH'S CHOICE I	II	III	IV
A	−200	100	300	−2
B	0	−1,000	1,000	0
C	1	2	3	4

JONES'S CHOICE	SMITH'S CHOICE I	II
A	200	100
B	0	−1,000

Smith v. Jones

Jones would then choose C, for while it affords no possibility of a large gain, its "worst" is a gain of 1.

Similar computations on Smith's behalf would show that the principle of insufficient reason and the "visualize the best" principle lead to the choice of II, while "visualize the worst" favors I. We should note that under no principle would it make sense for Smith to choose IV, because I is superior to IV if Jones chooses A or C and just as good as IV if Jones's choice is B. In the jargon of the decision theory, IV is "inadmissible." Similar comparison shows that III also is inadmissible. Thus the principle of insufficient reason, postulating that all four of Smith's choices are equally likely, is actually ruled out for Jones; he knows that Smith will never play III or IV.

Suppose that Smith knows Jones to be of the "visualize the best" school. He can collect $1,000 from Jones by playing II, anticipating that Jones will play B according to the optimistic principle. On the other hand, if Jones gets wind of this reasoning by Smith, he may switch to A and win $100. Thus a stable pattern of behavior is not likely to be established.

But things are strikingly different when both players visualize the worst, so that Jones plays C and Smith plays I. In this case it makes no difference whether the two players know each other's strategy; they can still do no better than play C and I, respectively. In other words, the "visualize the worst" principle apparently is spyproof—if either player had hired a spy to find out the other's strategy, he would have wasted his money.

Now it is easy to construct a game in which this principle seemingly is not spyproof. For instance, suppose we give each player only two choices—the first two choices of the preceding game, with the same pay-off schedule [*see lower table at left*]. In the new game if both players visualize the worst Jones will choose A and Smith I. But now if Jones knows that Smith is operating on this principle, he will switch to B, because he would lose $200 by playing A and break even by playing B. Certainly Smith has good reason to guard against espionage.

So it seems that the "visualize the worst" policy is not always spyproof after all. But at this point one of the most ingenious ideas of the theory of games enters the stage. The idea is to let chance play a role in the choice of strategy, that is, to use a randomized or "mixed" strategy.

Suppose that Jones marks A on 10 slips of paper and B on three slips, then mixes them up very thoroughly and proceeds to draw blindly to determine his play. What is his expectation? On the average he will play A 10 times and B three times in 13 games. If Smith were to play I all the time, Jones would lose 200 units 10 times and break even three times, thus losing 2,000. If Smith were to play II all the time, in 13 games Jones would, on the average, gain 100 units 10 times and lose 1,000 units three times; the total net loss again would be 2,000. Were Smith to alternate between I and II, whether according to a system or at random, Jones's expectation would still be minus 2,000 for 13 games. Thus his randomized strategy would yield the same result no matter what Smith did—and the result would be better than the worst he could expect (a loss of 200 per game) if he played A all the time, which, on the "visualize the worst" principle, is the best of the "pure" (nonrandomized) strategies.

This example shows that a mixed strategy may be better than the best pure strategy. It does not, of course, imply that any strategy using random choices has this property. The fact that the slips were marked A and B in the ratio 10 to 3 was of crucial importance. Had there been five As and five Bs to draw from, for instance, the outcome would have been inferior to playing "pure" A. It can be shown by algebraic computation that the 10-to-3 ratio yields the optimal strategy for Jones.

Let us now recall that what started us on the investigation of the mixed strategies was the fact that Smith's best "pure" strategy, namely I, was not spyproof. With mixed strategies in the picture, has the situation changed? To answer the question we must first find Smith's optimal strategy, which turns out, like Jones's, to be of the mixed variety; in his case he must play I and II in the ratio 11 to 2. On the assumption that Jones plays A, this mixture gives Smith the expectation of a gain of 2,000 units in 13 games (11 times 200 plus 2 times minus 100). And his expectation is exactly the same if he assumes that Jones will play B; Smith then wins 1,000 twice and breaks even 11 times for a total gain of 2,000 in 13 games. Indeed, it would make no difference if Jones were to alternate, in any manner whatsoever, between A and B. Thus Smith's strategy is spyproof in the sense that it would not help Jones to know that Smith was playing I and II in the ratio 11 to 2; Jones could still do no better than play 10 As to three Bs.

The preceding example illustrates a general phenomenon discovered and proved by von Neumann: in "zero-sum" two-person games (*i.e.*, in games where the amount lost by one player equals the amount gained by the other) the "visualize the worst" principle is spyproof provided mixed strategies are not disregarded.

Let us go back to Columbus and see whether the theory of games would have helped him in his dilemma, or at least how it might have formulated the problem for him. We start by setting up in table form Columbus' two possible choices (to turn back or keep going), the uncertain factual alternatives (that land was near or not near) and the probable consequences of Columbus' decisions in either case [*see top table on page 94*]. Now as an experimental approach suppose we assign very hypothetical and preliminary values in satisfaction units to the various consequences [*middle table on page 94*]. That is to say, let us assume that Columbus, attempting to envisage how disappointed he would feel if he later learned that he had turned back on the verge of discovering land, appraises this disappointment as a loss of 50 satisfaction units; that he values the saving of life by turning back from a hopeless quest as a gain of 20 satisfaction units, and so on. Let us also make one further assumption: that Columbus feels he can make some kind of estimate as to the probability of land being near.

If he supposed that the chances of land being near were 3 to 1, he would compute the expectation of "satisfaction" (actually dissatisfaction!) from turning back as follows: 3 times minus 50 added to 1 times 20 and the sum divided by 4—*i.e.*, minus 32.5. In other words, if he turns back, the net expectation is a loss of 32.5 satisfaction units. On the other hand, if he keeps going, the expectation is a loss of 175 satisfaction units (3 times 100 added to 1 times minus 1,000 and the sum divided by 4). Since the expectation of loss in going on is so much greater than that in turning back, Columbus' decision would be: better turn back. On the basis of the satisfaction values we have postulated, it would have taken a probability of 9 to 1 that land was near to induce Columbus to keep going.

Would he actually have insisted on such high odds in favor of success? If not, it must be that the satisfaction units we have assigned to the various possible consequences are unrealistic; perhaps we have overvalued Columbus' fear of death and undervalued his eagerness for the prize of discovery. We may therefore construct another table of values which might be considered more realistic [*see the lowest table on this page*]. On this new basis a probability of 3 to 1 that land was near would have been sufficient to make Columbus decide to keep going.

But what if he had no idea as to the chances of land being near? The theory of games and decision-making would still have offered him several means of calculating his expectations. He might have followed the principle of insufficient reason, the strategy of "visualize the best" or the strategy of "visualize the worst." On the basis of the satisfaction figures in our last table Columbus would have found it worth while to keep going no matter which of these principles he applied. But on the basis of the first figures [*middle table*] he would have turned back unless he belonged to the "visualize the best" school—which may not be too unrealistic an assumption.

It may seem strange that principles for making decisions should be served cafeteria style—take your choice. Is there not some way of proving that only one of these principles is truly rational? A great deal of thought has been devoted to this problem, mainly via attempts to find logical flaws or paradoxes which would eliminate one or another of the principles from consideration. For instance, it has been argued that nature, being presumably nonmalicious and not out to inflict maximum loss on its "opponents" (investigators), might well use an "inadmissible" strategy though a smart player would not. Also, some argue that there is no need for spyproofing against nature, and this raises doubts as to whether a principle leading to the use of randomized strategies is reasonable. In defense of the rationality of randomized decision-making, one is tempted to recall Rabelais's Judge Bridlegoose, who decided lawsuits by the throw of dice and was known for his wisdom and fairness until his failing eyesight made him commit errors in reading the spots. (Less facetious arguments in favor of randomized decision-making also are available!)

The development of methods for rational decision-making where uncertainties exist certainly has a long way to go. The field is still rife with differences of opinion. Nevertheless, it is highly instructive to study the tools we have, and particularly to notice how often the various principles, despite the difference of their underlying assumptions, all lead to very similar if not identical conclusions as to the best decision to take in a given situation.

COLUMBUS' DECISION	ACTUAL LOCATION OF LAND: LAND NEAR	ACTUAL LOCATION OF LAND: NO LAND NEAR
TURN BACK	PROBABLE LATER DISAPPOINTMENT	LIFE SAVED
KEEP GOING	PROSPECT OF GLORY	PROSPECT OF DEATH

COLUMBUS' DECISION	ACTUAL LOCATION OF LAND: LAND NEAR	ACTUAL LOCATION OF LAND: NO LAND NEAR
TURN BACK	−50	20
KEEP GOING	100	−1,000

COLUMBUS' DECISION	ACTUAL LOCATION OF LAND: LAND NEAR	ACTUAL LOCATION OF LAND: NO LAND NEAR
TURN BACK	−1,000	20
KEEP GOING	500	−500

Columbus v. nature

14

THE USE AND MISUSE OF GAME THEORY

ANATOL RAPOPORT • December 1962

We live in an age of belief—belief in the omnipotence of science. This belief is bolstered by the fact that the problems scientists are called on to solve are for the most part selected by the scientists themselves. For example, our Department of Defense did not one day decide that it wanted an atomic bomb and then order the scientists to make one. On the contrary, it was Albert Einstein, a scientist, who told Franklin D. Roosevelt, a decision maker, that such a bomb was possible. Today, in greater measure than ever before, scientists sit at the decision makers' elbows and guide the formulation of problems in such a way that scientific solutions are feasible. Problems that do not promise scientific solutions generally tend to go unformulated. Hence the faith in the omnipotence of science.

The self-amplifying prestige of science among decision makers has been further amplified in this period by the popularization of a scientific aid to the task of decision making itself. This is game theory—a mathematical technique for the analysis of conflict first propounded by the late John Von Neumann in 1927 and brought to wide notice by Von Neumann and Oskar Morgenstern in 1944 in a book entitled *Theory of Games and Economic Behavior*. Now, game theory is an intellectual achievement of superlative originality and has opened a large new field of research. Unfortunately this is not the way game theory has been embraced in certain quarters where Francis Bacon's dictum "Knowledge is power" is interpreted in its primitive, brutal sense. The decision makers in our society are overwhelmingly preoccupied with power conflict, be it in business, in politics or in the military. Game theory is a "science of conflict." What could this new science be but a reservoir of power for those who get there fastest with the mostest?

A thorough understanding of game theory should dim these greedy hopes. Knowledge of game theory does not make any one a better card player, businessman or military strategist, because game theory is not primarily concerned with disclosing the optimum strategy for any particular conflict situation. It is concerned with the logic of conflict, that is, with the theory of strategy. In this lies both the strength and the limitation of the technique. Its strength derives from the powerful and intricate mathematical apparatus that it can bring to bear on the strategic analysis of certain conflict situations. The limitations are those inherent in the range of conflicts to which this analysis can be successfully applied.

No one will doubt that the logic of strategy does not apply to certain conflicts. For example, there are no strategic considerations in a dogfight. Such a conflict is better thought of as being a sequence of events, each of which triggers the next. A growl is a stimulus for a countergrowl, which in turn stimulates the baring of teeth, sudden thrusts and so on. Signals stimulate postures; postures stimulate actions. Human quarrels, where symbolic rather than physical injuries are mutually stimulated, are frequently also of this sort. Conflicts of this kind can be called fights. The motivation in a fight is hostility. The goal is to eliminate the opponent, who appears as a noxious stimulus, not as another ego, whose goals and strategies, even though hostile, must be taken into account. Intellect, in the sense of calculating capacity, foresight and comparison of alternative courses of action, need not and usually does not play any part in a fight.

Game theory applies to a very different type of conflict, now technically called a game. The well-known games such as poker, chess, ticktacktoe and so forth are games in the strict technical sense. But what makes parlor games games is not their entertainment value or detachment from real life. They are games because they are instances of formalized conflict: there is conflict of interest between two or more parties; each party has at certain specified times a range of choices of what to do prescribed by the rules; and the outcome representing the sum total of choices made by all parties, and in each case involving consideration of the choice made by or open to the other parties, determines an assignment of pay-offs to each party. By extension, any conflict so conducted falls into the category of games, as defined in game theory. Nor does it matter whether the rules are results of common agreement, as in parlor games, or simply of restraints imposed by the situation. Even if no rules of warfare are recognized, a military situation can still be considered as a game if the range of choices open to each opponent at any given stage can be exactly specified.

Let us see how chess and poker each fulfill these requirements. In chess the conflict of interest is, of course, implied

The omnipotent scientist

in each player's desire to win. The range of choices consists for each player of all the legal moves open to him when it is his turn to move. The outcome is determined by all the choices of both players. The pay-offs are usually in psychological satisfaction or dissatisfaction. In poker the situation is much, but not entirely, the same. The choices are (at specified times) whether or not to stay in; which cards, if any, to throw off; whether or not to raise and by how much and so on. The outcome of each round is the designation of one of the players as the winner. Pay-offs are usually in money.

Poker differs from chess in one important respect. In a poker game there is an extra (invisible) player, who makes just one choice at the beginning of each round. This choice is important in determining the outcome, but the player who makes it has no interest in the game and does not get any pay-off. The player's name is Chance, and his choice is among the nearly 100 million trillion trillion trillion trillion trillion (10^{68}) arrangements of the deck at the beginning of each round. Chance makes no further choices during the round; the rest is up to the players. One can argue that Chance continues to interfere, for example by causing lapses of memory, directing or misdirecting the attention of the players and so forth. But game theory is concerned only with what perfect players would do.

Although Chance may thus play a part, the game as defined by game theory is clearly distinguished from gambling as treated by the much older and better-known mathematics of gambling. The latter has considerable historical importance, since it is in the context of gambling theory that the mathematical theory of probability was first developed some 300 years ago. This theory has since been incorporated into all branches of science where laws of chance must be taken into account, as in the physics of small particles, genetics, actuarial science, economics, experimental psychology and the psychology of mass behavior. For the gambler the mathematical theory of probability makes possible a precise calculation of the odds. This often calls for considerable mathematical sophistication. It is irrelevant, however, to the playing of the game; it is relevant only in deciding whether or not to play. The gambling problem is solved when the odds of the possible outcomes have been calculated. If there are several such outcomes, the gains or losses associated with each are multiplied by the corresponding probabilities and the products are added (with proper signs attached). The resulting number is the expected gain; that is, what can be reasonably expected over a long series of bets when the bets are placed according to the odds offered. A rational gambler is one who accepts or offers the gambles in such a way as to maximize his expected gain. All gambling houses are rational gamblers. That is why they stay in business.

Bark and counterbark

The inadequacy of gambling theory as a guide in a true game is shown clearly in the well-known fact that the rational gambler is likely to meet with disaster in a poker game. The rational gambler will make his decisions strictly in accordance with the odds. He will never bluff, and he will bet in proportion to the strength of his hand. As a result he will betray his hand to his opponents, and they will use the information to his disadvantage.

Gambling theory is of even less use to the ticktacktoe player. Ticktacktoe is a game in which there is a best move in every conceivable situation. Chance, we know, is not involved at all in some games. To be sure, chance is involved in all card games but, as the example of poker shows, something else is involved, namely a strategic skill that is not part of gambling theory at all.

Consider what goes on in the mind of a chess player: If I play Knight to Queen's Bishop's 4, thus threatening his rook, he can reply Rook to King's 2, check. In that case I have the choice of either interposing the Bishop or King to Queen's 1. On the other hand, he can ignore the threat to the rook and reply with a counterthreat by Bishop to Knight's 5, in which case I have the following choices . . .

The stronger the player, the longer this chain of reasoning is likely to be. But because of the limitations on how much we can hold in our minds at one time, the chain of reasoning must stop somewhere. For the chess player it stops a few moves ahead of the situation at hand, at a set of possible new situations among which he must choose. The one situation that will actually occur depends partly on his own choices and partly on the choices available to the opponent (over whom the first player has no control). Two decisions are involved in the choice of action: first, which situations may actually occur? Second, which of all those situations is to be preferred?

Now, these questions can be answered without ambiguity if the game is thought out to the end. In a game such as chess, however, it is out of the question to foresee all the alternatives to the end (except where checkmates or clear wins are foreseen as forced). The good chess player then does the next best thing: he calculates the relative values of the various possible future positions according to his experience in evaluating such positions. How then does he know which position will be actually arrived at, seeing that he controls only his own moves, not those of the opponent? Chess players recognize two chess philosophies.

Bite and counterbite

Escalated conflict

Playing the stock market or a slot machine involves no game theory

One is "playing the board," the other is "playing the opponent."

Playing the opponent makes chess akin to psychological warfare. The great chess master José Capablanca tells in his memoirs of an incident that illustrates the drama of such conflicts. In a tournament in 1918 he was matched with Frank J. Marshall, the U.S. champion. Marshall offered an unexpected response to Capablanca's accustomed opening attack, and the play proceeded not at all in line with the usual variations of this opening. Capablanca suspected that Marshall had discovered a new variation in the attack and had kept this knowledge as a secret weapon, to be used only at the most propitious time, namely in an international tournament with the eyes of the chess world on his play against a truly formidable opponent. Capablanca had been picked as the victim of the new strategy.

"The lust of battle, however," Capablanca continues, "had been aroused within me. I felt that my judgment and skill were being challenged by a player who had every reason to fear both (as shown by the records of our previous encounters), but who wanted to take advantage of the element of surprise and of the fact of my being unfamiliar with a thing to which he had devoted many nights of toil.... I considered the position then and decided that I was in honor bound ... to accept the challenge."

Psychological warfare in chess

Advanced psychological warfare in chess

He did and went on to win the game. Capablanca's decision was based on taking into account his opponent's thought processes, not only those pertaining to the game but also Marshall's ambitions, his opinion of Capablanca's prowess, his single-mindedness and so on. Capablanca was playing the opponent.

Although the drama of games of strategy is strongly linked with the psychological aspects of the conflict, game theory is not concerned with these aspects. Game theory, so to speak, plays the board. It is concerned only with the logical aspects of strategy. It prescribes the same line of play against a master as it does against a beginner. When a stragetic game is completely analyzed by game-theory methods, nothing is left of the game. Ticktacktoe is a good example. This game is not played by adults because it has been completely analyzed. Analysis shows that every game of ticktacktoe must end in a draw. Checkers is in almost the same state, although only exceptionally good players know all the relevant strategies. A generation ago it was thought that chess too was approaching the "draw death." But new discoveries and particularly the introduction of psychological warfare into chess, notably by the Russian masters, has given the game a reprieve. Nevertheless H. A. Simon and Allen Newell of the Carnegie Institute of Technology have seriously predicted that within 10 years the world's chess champion will be an electronic computer. The prediction was made more than three years ago. There is still a good chance that it will come true.

Is the aim of game theory, then, to reveal the logic of every formalized game so that each player's best strategy is discovered and the game as a whole is killed because its outcome in every instance will be known in advance? This is by no means the case. The class of games for which such an analysis can be carried through even in principle, let alone the prodigious difficulty of doing it in practice, is only a very small class.

Games of this class are known as games of perfect information. They are games in which it is impossible to have military secrets. Chess is such a game. Whatever the surprise Marshall thought he had prepared for Capablanca, he was not hiding something that could not be discovered by any chess player. He only hoped that it would be overlooked because of human limitations.

Not all games are games of perfect information. Poker is definitely not such a game. The essence of poker is in the circumstance that no player knows the entire situation and must be guided by guesses of what the situation is and what the others will do. Both chess and poker are "zero-sum" games in the sense that what one player wins the other or others necessarily lose. Not all games are of this sort either.

To understand the differences among these various classes of games, let us look at some examples from each class. The essential idea to be demonstrated is that each type of situation requires a different type of reasoning.

An improbably elementary situation in business competition will serve to illustrate the class of games of perfect information. The situation is otherwise a two-person zero-sum game. The Castor Company, an old, established firm, is being squeezed by Pollux, Incorporated, an aggressive newcomer. The Castor people guide their policies by the balance sheet, which is projected one year ahead. The Pollux people also guide their policies by a balance sheet, not their own but the Castor Company's. Their aim is to put Castor out of business, so they consider Castor's losses their gains and vice versa, regardless of what their own balance shows. Both are faced with a decision, namely whether or not to undertake an extensive advertising campaign. The outcome depends on what both firms do, each having control over only its own decision. Assume, however, that both firms have enough information to know what the outcomes will be, given both decisions [*see matrix at left in bottom illustration on page 99*].

From Castor's point of view, a better or a worse outcome corresponds to each of its decisions, depending on what Pollux does. Of the two worse outcomes associated with Castor's two possible decisions, \$3 million in the red and \$1 million in the red (both occurring if Pollux advertises), clearly the second is preferred. Castor's manager now puts himself into the shoes of Pollux' manager and asks what Pollux would do if Castor chose the lesser of the two evils. Clearly Pollux would choose to advertise to prevent the outcome that would be better for Castor ($1 million in the black). Getting back into his own shoes, Castor's manager now asks what he would do knowing that this was Pollux' decision. Again the answer is advertise. Exactly similar reasoning leads Pollux to its decision, which is advertise. Each has chosen the better of the two worse alternatives. In the language of game theory this is called the minimax (the maximum of the minima). This solution is always prescribed no matter how many alternatives there are, provided that the gains of one are the losses of the other and provided that what is the "best of the worst" for one is also the "best of the worst" for the other. In this case the game has a saddle point (named after the position on the saddle that is lowest with respect to front and back and highest with respect to right and left). Game theory shows that whenever a saddle point exists, neither party can improve the outcome for itself (or worsen it for the other). The outcome is forced, as it is in ticktacktoe.

The next situation is quite different. It is a two-person zero-sum game, again involving the choice of two strategies on each side. In this case, however, the choices must be made in the absence of the information that guides the opponent's decision. Appropriately this is a military situation enveloped in the fog of battle.

A commander of a division must decide which of two sectors to attack. A breakthrough would be more valuable in one than in the other, but the more valuable sector is also likely to be more strongly defended. The defending commander also has a problem: which sector to reinforce. It would seem obvious that the more critical sector should be reinforced at the expense of the secondary one. But it is clear to the defending commander that the problem is more complicated. Secrecy is of the essence. If he does exactly what the enemy expects him to do, which is to reinforce the critical sector, will this not be to the enemy's advantage? Will not the attacker, knowing that the important sector is more strongly defended, attack the weaker one, where a breakthrough, even though less valuable, is more certain? Should the defender therefore not do the opposite of what the enemy expects and reinforce the secondary sector, since that is where the enemy, wishing to avoid the stronger sector, will probably attack? But then is not the enemy smart enough to figure this out and so attack the primary center and achieve a breakthrough where it counts?

The attacking commander is going through the same tortuous calculations. Should he attack the secondary sector because the primary one is more likely to be strongly defended or should he attack the primary one because the enemy expects him to avoid it?

In despair the attacking commander calls in a game theorist for consultation. If the game theorist is to help him, the general must assign numerical values to each of the four outcomes; that is, he must estimate (in relative units) how much each outcome is "worth" to him. He assigns the values shown in the top illustration on the next page. Working with these figures, the game theorist will advise the general as follows: "Roll a die. If ace or six comes up, attack sector 1, otherwise attack sector 2."

If the defending commander assigns the same values (but with opposite signs, since he is the enemy) to the four outcomes, his game theorist will advise him to throw two pennies and reinforce sector 1 if they both come up heads,

Game theory in "Tosca": Tosca double-crosses Scarpia

Scarpia derives satisfaction from the thought of what is going to happen

Tosca and Cavaradossi discover the double double cross

ATTACKER'S PAY-OFF

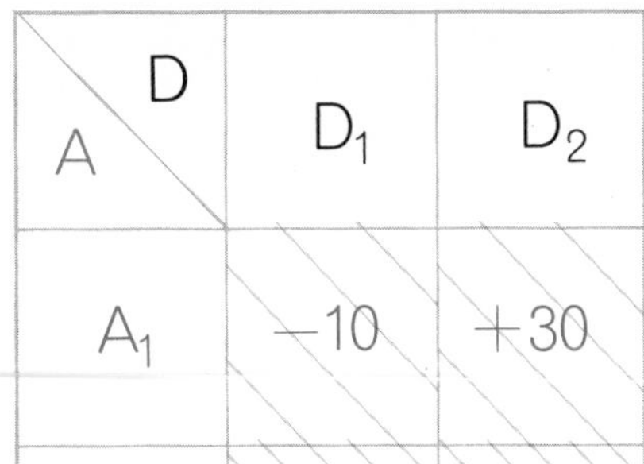

A \ D	D_1	D_2
A_1	−10	+30
A_2	+5	−15

DEFENDER'S PAY-OFF

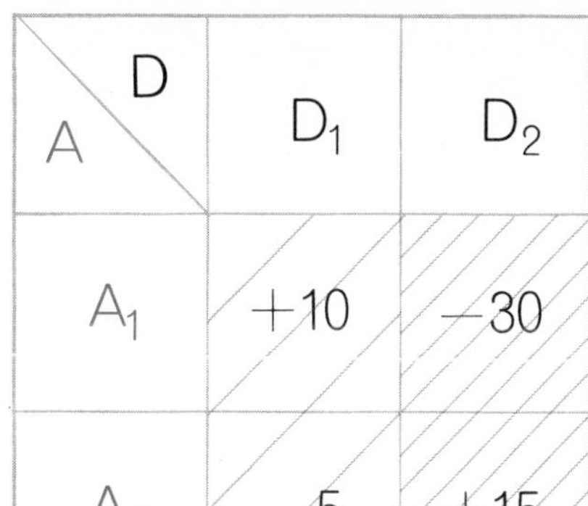

A \ D	D_1	D_2
A_1	+10	−30
A_2	−5	+15

MINIMAX SOLUTION

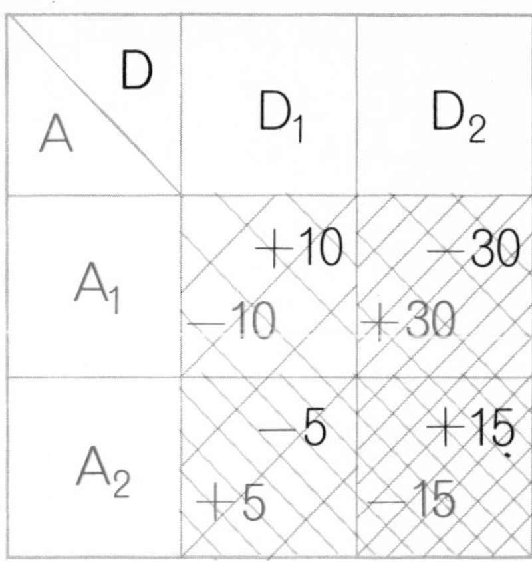

A \ D	D_1	D_2
A_1	+10 / −10	−30 / +30
A_2	−5 / +5	+15 / −15

TWO-PERSON ZERO-SUM GAME of an attacking (A) and a defending commander (D), in which neither possesses the information that guides his opponent's decisions, is summarized in these three matrices. The first commander has the choice of attacking a primary sector (A_1) or a secondary sector (A_2). The matrix at left shows the values he assigns to the four possibilities. The second commander has the choice of defending either sector. The matrix at center shows his assigned values. As the number of diagonal lines in each matrix square indicates, the first commander should decide by chance, using two-to-one odds in favor of the secondary sector; likewise for the defending commander, except that the odds are three to one. These results are combined in the matrix at right.

otherwise he should reinforce sector 2.

The solutions seem bizarre, because we think of tossing coins to make decisions only in matters of complete indifference. To be sure, a tossed-coin decision is sometimes used to settle an argument, but we do not think of such decisions as being rational and do not hire experts to figure them out. Nevertheless, the game theorists' decisions are offered not only as rational decisions but also as the best possible ones under the circumstances.

To see why this is so, imagine playing the game of button-button. You hide a button in one hand and your opponent tries to guess which. He wins a penny if he guesses right and loses a penny if he guesses wrong. What is your best pattern of choices of where to hide the button in a series of successive plays? You will certainly not choose the same hand every time; your opponent will quickly find this out. Nor will you alternate between the two hands; he will find this out too. It is reasonable to conclude (and it can be proved mathematically) that the best pattern is no pattern. The best way to ensure this is to abdicate your role as decision maker and let chance decide for you. Coin tossing as a guide to strategy is in this case not an act of desperation but a rational policy.

In the button-button game the pay-offs are exactly symmetrical. This is why decisions should be made by a toss of a fair coin. If the pay-offs were not symmetrical—for example, if there were more advantage in guessing when the coin was in the right hand—this bias would have to be taken into account. It would be reflected in letting some biased chance device make the decision. Game theory provides the method of computing the bias that maximizes the long-run expected gain.

CASTOR AND POLLUX

C \ P	PY	PN
CY	−1	+1
CN	−3	+2

TOSCA'S PAY-OFF

T \ S	SK	SD
TK	+5	−10
TD	+10	−5

SCARPIA'S PAY-OFF

T \ S	SK	SD
TK	+5	+10
TD	−10	−5

ZERO-SUM AND NONZERO-SUM GAMES are represented in these three game-theory matrices. The matrix at left is that of the two-person zero-sum game of perfect information discussed in the text. The matrix tabulates the results for Castor Company (in millions of dollars) of any combination of decisions; e.g., if Castor and Pollux, Incorporated, both advertise (*Cy and Py*), Castor loses $1 million. For Pollux, which will decide on the basis of the effect on Castor, this is a positive pay-off. Tosca and Scarpia are involved in a nonzero-sum game (also discussed in the text), that is, a gain for one does not imply a loss for the other. Tosca's line of reasoning can be determined from the matrix at center: if she keeps her bargain with Scarpia (*Tk*), then she loses everything if he double-crosses her (*Sd*); her gain is greatest and her loss least if she double-crosses him (*Td*). Scarpia, as the matrix at right indicates, reasons along the same line, in reverse. They both lose equally; if they had trusted each other, they would have gained equally.

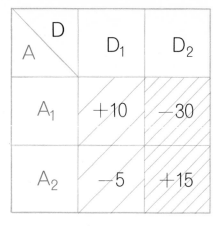

The attacker's game theorist, then, has figured out that the attacker stands the best chance if he allows chance to decide, using two-to-one odds in favor of sector 2. This is the meaning of rolling a die and allowing four sides out of six to determine the second sector. This is the best the attacker can do against the best the defender can do. The defender's best is to let chance decide, using three-to-one odds in favor of sector 2. Game theory here prescribes not the one best strategy for the specific occasion but the best mixture of strategies for this kind of occasion. If the two commanders were confronted with the same situation many times, these decisions would give each of them the maximum pay-offs they can get in these circumstances if both play rationally.

At this point one may protest that it is difficult, if not impossible, to assign numerical values to the outcome of real situations. Moreover, identical situations do not recur, and so the long-run expected gain has no meaning. There is much force in these objections. We can only say that game theory has gone just so far in baring the essentials of strategic conflict. What it has left undone should not be charged against it. In what follows some further inadequacies of game theory will become apparent. Paradoxically, in these inadequacies lies most of the value of the theory. The shortcomings show clearly how far strategic thinking can go.

In the next class of games to be illustrated there are choices open to the two parties where the gain of one does not imply loss for the other and vice versa. Our "nonzero-sum" game is a tale of lust and betrayal. In Puccini's opera *Tosca* the chief of police Scarpia has condemned Tosca's lover Cavaradossi to death but offers to save him in exchange for Tosca's favors. Tosca consents, the agreement being that Cavaradossi will go through a pretended execution. Scarpia and Tosca double-cross each other. She stabs him as he is about to embrace her, and he has not given the order to the firing squad to use blank cartridges.

The problem is to decide whether or not it was to the best advantage of each party to double-cross the other. Again we must assign numerical values to the outcome, taking into account what each outcome is worth both to Tosca and to Scarpia [*see two matrices at right in bottom illustration on preceding page*].

The values, although arbitrary, present the situation reasonably. If the bargain is kept, Tosca's satisfaction of getting her lover back is marred by her surrender to the chief of police. Scarpia's satisfaction in possessing Tosca will be marred by having had to reprieve a hated rival. If Tosca double-crosses Scarpia and gets away with it, she will win most (+ 10) and he will lose most (− 10), and vice versa. When both double-cross each other, both lose, but not so much as each would have lost had he or she been the sucker. For example, the dying Scarpia (we assume) derives some satisfaction from the thought of what is going to happen just before the final curtain, when Tosca rushes to her fallen lover and finds him riddled with bullets.

Let us now arrive at a decision from Tosca's point of view: whether to keep the bargain or to kill Scarpia. Tosca has no illusions about Scarpia's integrity. But she is not sure of what he will do, so she considers both possibilities: If he keeps the bargain, I am better off double-crossing him, since I will get Cavaradossi without Scarpia if I do and Cavaradossi with Scarpia if I don't. If he double-crosses me, I am certainly better off double-crossing him. It stands to reason that I should kill him whatever he does.

Scarpia reasons in exactly the same way: If she keeps the bargain, I am better off double-crossing her, since I will get rid of Cavaradossi if I do and have to put up with him if I don't. If she double-crosses me, I certainly should see to it that I am avenged. The execution, therefore, must go on.

The result is the denouement we know. Tosca and Scarpia both get − 5. If they had trusted each other and had kept the trust, each would have got + 5.

The shortcoming of strategic thinking becomes obvious in this example. Evidently more is required than the calculation of one's own pay-offs if the best decisions are to be made in conflict situations. Game theory can still treat the foregoing case satisfactorily by introducing the notion of a coalition. If Tosca and Scarpia realize that the interests of both will be best served if both keep the bargain, they need not both be losers. Coalitions, however, bring headaches of their own, as will be seen in the next example.

Abe, Bob and Charlie are to divide a dollar. The decision as to how to divide it is to be by majority vote. Abe and Bob form a coalition and agree to split the dollar evenly between them and so freeze Charlie out. The rules of the game allow bargaining. Charlie approaches Bob

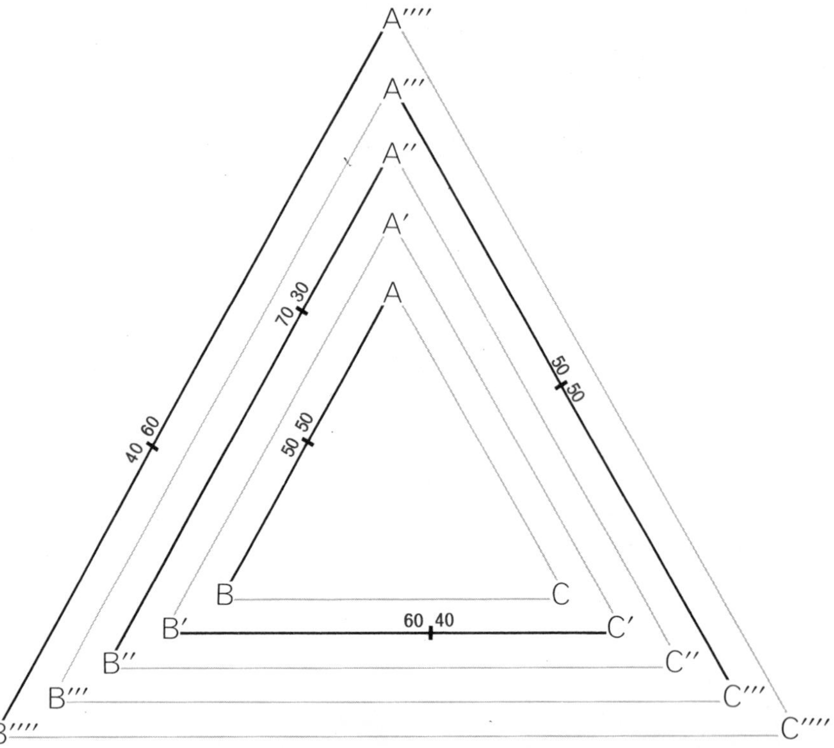

COALITION GAME involves splitting a dollar among three individuals; the split is decided by majority vote. Abe and Bob (*A and B*) form a coalition that excludes Charlie (*C*). Charlie then (*C′*) offers Bob (*B′*) 60 cents of the dollar, and so on. Any division is inherently unstable because two can always do better for themselves than can three, and two can enforce any division. No game-theory strategy will guarantee a division satisfactory to all.

Maximum in the military application of game theory

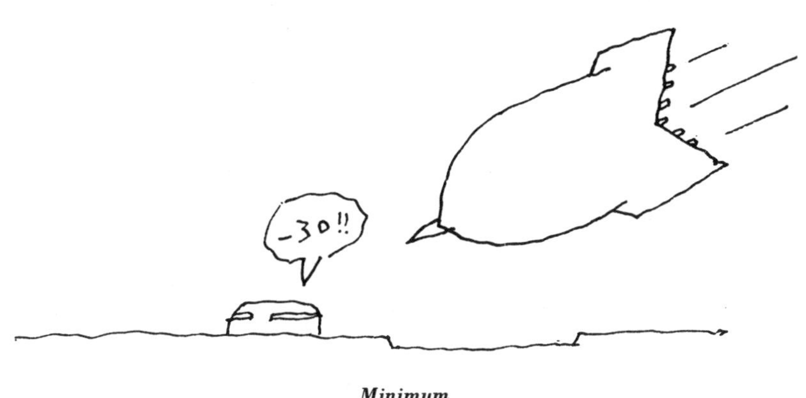

Minimum

with a proposition. He offers Bob 60 cents of the dollar if Bob will shift his vote to freeze Abe out. Abe does not like this arrangement, so he offers Bob 70 cents to shift his vote again to freeze Charlie out. Bob is about to rejoice in his good fortune, which he attributes to his bargaining shrewdness, when he notices that Abe and Charlie are off in a corner. Bob is shrewd enough to guess what they are discussing, and he is right. They are discussing the folly of respectively getting 30 cents and nothing when they have the power to freeze Bob out and split the dollar between them. In fact, they do this. Bob now approaches Abe hat in hand and offers him 60 cents if he will come back. The question is: Should Abe accept the offer?

The game-theory solutions to problems of this sort are extremely involved and need not be pursued here. Instead let us try to summarize in general terms the values and limitations of the game-theory approach to human conflict.

The value of game theory is not in the specific solutions it offers in highly simplified and idealized situations, which may occur in formalized games but hardly ever do in real life. Rather, the prime value of the theory is that it lays bare the different kinds of reasoning that apply in different kinds of conflict.

Let us go back to our examples and compare them. The decisions made by Castor and Pollux were clear-cut, and they were the best decisions on the basis of the knowledge at hand. As we have seen, both firms were guided by the principle of the minimax, choosing the best of the worst outcomes. When both choose the minimax, neither firm can improve its position. Had one of the generals used such a decision, he would have been clearly at a disadvantage. Military secrecy introduces an element of randomness to confound the enemy and brings in a different kind of reasoning. Such reasoning would have been useless in the Castor and Pollux example, because in their case each knew what the other's best decision had to be, and this knowledge made no difference to either. The difference between the two situations is immediately apparent to the game theorist. In the first case the minimax choice of one player is also the minimax choice of the other, in the second case it is not.

Consider the Tosca-Scarpia game. Here both parties have the same minimax choice, which, in fact, they choose. The outcome is bad for both. Why is this? Again the answer is clear to the game theorist. Tosca and Scarpia were playing the game as if it were a zero-sum game, a game in which what one party wins the other necessarily loses. If we examine the pay-offs, we find that this is not the case. Both parties could have improved their pay-offs by moving from the minimax solution to the coalition solution (keeping the bargain and getting + 5 each). Life would be simple if advantage in conflicts could always be obtained by forming and keeping proper coalitions. But the dilemma plaguing Abe, Bob and Charlie deprives us of that hope also. Moreover, both the Tosca-Scarpia game and the divide-the-dollar game reveal that decisions based on calculated self-interest can lead to disaster.

Whether game theory leads to clear-cut solutions, to vague solutions or to impasses, it does achieve one thing. In bringing techniques of logical and mathematical analysis to bear on problems involving conflicts of interest, game theory gives men an opportunity to bring conflicts up from the level of fights, where the intellect is beclouded by passions, to the level of games, where the intellect has a chance to operate. This is in itself no mean achievement, but it is not the most important one. The most important achievement of game theory, in my opinion, is that game-theory analysis reveals its own limitations. Because this negative aspect is far less understood than the positive aspect, it will be useful to delve somewhat deeper into the matter.

The importance of game theory for decision making and for social science can be best understood in the light of the history of science. Scientists have been able to avoid much futile squandering of effort because the very foundations of science rest on categorical statements about what cannot be done. For example, thermodynamics shows that perpetual-motion machines are impossible. The principles of biology assert the impossibility of a spontaneous generation of life and of the transmission of acquired characteristics; the uncertainty principle places absolute limits on the precision of certain measurements conducted simultaneously; great mathematical discoveries have revealed the impossibility of solving certain problems.

Absolute as these impossibilities are, they are not absolutely absolute but are so only in certain specific contexts. Progress in science is the generalization of contexts. Thus the conservation of mechanical energy can be circumvented by converting other forms of energy into mechanical energy. The simpler conservation law is violated, but it is re-established in a more general thermodynamic context. In this form it can again be seemingly violated, but it is again re-established in the still broader context of $E = mc^2$. Angles can be mechanically trisected by instruments more complicated than the straightedge and the compass. Life can probably be synthesized, but not in the form of maggots springing from rotting meat; acquired characteristics can probably be genetically transmitted, but not by exercising muscles.

The negative verdicts of science have often been accompanied by positive codicils. The power conferred by science, then, resides in the knowledge of what cannot be done and, by implication, of what can be done and of what it takes to do it.

The knowledge we derive from game theory is of the same kind. Starting with the simplest type of game, for example two-person zero-sum games with saddle points, we learn from game-theory analysis that the outcome of such games is predetermined. This leads to a verdict of impossibility: neither player can do better than his best. Once these bests are discovered, it is useless to play such a game. If war were a two-person zero-sum game with a saddle point, the outcome of each war could conceivably be calculated in advance and the war would not need to be fought. (The conclusion that wars need to be fought be-

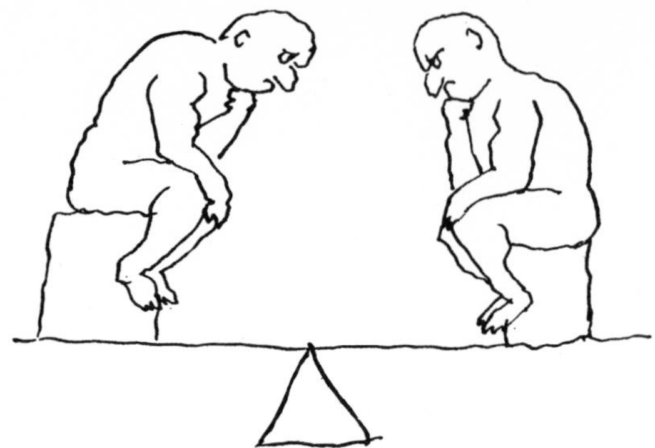

Strategic thinking in a two-person zero-sum situation with a saddle point

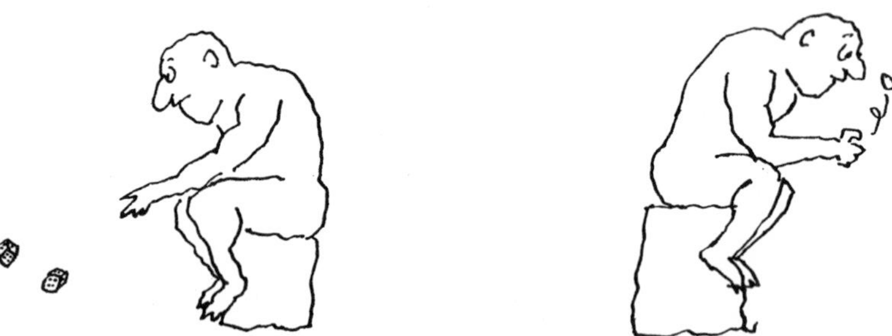

Strategic thinking in a two-person zero-sum situation without a saddle point

Strategic thinking in a two-person nonzero-sum situation

Strategic thinking in a three-person constant-sum situation with a coalition

Communication is a prerequisite for the resolution of conflict

cause they are not two-person zero-sum games with saddle points is not warranted!)

Examining now the two-person zero-sum game without a saddle point, we arrive at another verdict of impossibility: It is impossible to prescribe a best strategy in such a game. It is still possible, however, to prescribe a best mixture of strategies. The meaning of a strategy mixture and the advantage of using it can be understood only in a certain context, namely in the context of an expected gain. This in turn requires that our concept of preference be defined with a certain degree of specificity. To choose the best strategy in a saddle-point game it is necessary only to rank-order the preferences for the possible outcomes. To choose the best strategy mixture an interval scale (like that of temperature) must be assigned to our preferences. Unless this more precise quantification of preferences can be made, rational decisions cannot be made in the context of a game without a saddle point.

I have often wondered to what extent decision makers who have been "sold" on game theory have understood this last verdict of impossibility, which is no less categorical than the verdict on squaring the circle with classical tools. I have seen many research proposals and listened to long discussions of how hot and cold wars can be "gamed." Allowing for the moment that hot and cold wars are zero-sum games (which they are not!), the assignment of "utilities" to outcomes must be made on an interval scale. There is the problem. Of course, this problem can be bypassed, and the utilities can be assigned one way or another, so that we can get on with the gaming, which is the most fun. But of what practical use are results based on arbitrary assumptions?

That is not all. By far the most important conflicts that plague the human race do not fit into the two-person zero-sum category at all. The Tosca-Scarpia game and the Abe-Bob-Charlie game are much more realistic models of human conflicts, namely dramas, in which individuals strive for advantage and come to grief. In these games there are neither pure nor mixed strategies that are best in the sense of guaranteeing the biggest pay-offs under the constraints of the game. No argument addressed individually to Tosca or to Scarpia will convince either that it is better to keep the bargain than to double-cross the other. Only an argument addressed to both at once has this force. Only collective rationality will help them to avoid the trap of the double double cross.

Similarly we can tell nothing to Abe, Bob or Charlie about how to behave to best advantage. We can only tell them collectively to settle the matter in accordance with some pre-existing social norm. (For example, they can take 33 cents apiece and donate one to charity.) This solution is based on an ethical principle and not on strategic considerations.

The role of social norms in games with more than two players was not missed by Von Neumann and Morgenstern. The importance of honesty, social responsibility and kindred virtues has been pointed out by sages since the dawn of history. Game theory, however, gives us another perspective on these matters. It shows how the "hardheaded" analysis of conflicts (with which game theory starts) comes to an impasse, how paradoxical conclusions cannot be avoided unless the situation is reformulated in another context and unless other, extra-game-theory concepts are invoked. Thus acquaintance with these deeper aspects of game theory reveals that the poker game is not the most general or the most sophisticated model of conflict, nor the most relevant in application, as professional strategists often implicitly assume.

Game theory, when it is pursued beyond its elementary paradox-free formulations, teaches us what we must be able to do in order to bring the intellect to bear on a science of human conflict. To analyze a conflict scientifically, we must be able to agree on relative values (to assign utilities). We must learn to be perceptive (evaluate the other's assignment of utilities). Furthermore, in order to engage in a conflict thus formalized, we must be able to communicate (give a credible indication to the other of how we assign utilities to outcomes). At times we must learn the meaning of trust, or else both we and our opponents will invariably lose in games of the Tosca-Scarpia type. At times we must be able to convince the other that he ought to play according to certain rules or even that he ought to play a different game. To convince the other we must get him to listen to us, and this cannot usually be done if we ourselves do not listen. Therefore we must learn to listen in the broadest sense of listening, in the sense of assuming for a while the other's world outlook, because only in this way will we make sense of what he is saying.

All these skills are related not to know-how but to wisdom. It may happen that if we acquire the necessary wisdom, many of the conflicts that the strategy experts in their professional zeal insist on formulating as battles of wits (or, worse, as battles of wills) will be resolved of their own accord.

Another prerequisite is the assignment of utilities to outcomes

15

LINEAR PROGRAMMING

WILLIAM W. COOPER AND ABRAHAM CHARNES • August 1954

Imagine that you are manufacturing a product at a number of factories and must freight it to markets in many different parts of the country. How would you go about calculating the pattern of shipments that would deliver the goods from your many warehouses to the many markets at the lowest possible freight cost?

By common sense and trial and error you might readily work out a reasonable schedule. But even a non-mathematician can see that to find the best solution among the infinite number of possible solutions would be a far more formidable problem.

We shall describe in this article a recently developed technique in applied mathematics which makes it possible to solve such problems in a relatively short time by means of simple computations. The theory of linear programming was developed by John von Neumann, G. B. Dantzig, T. C. Koopmans and a few other mathematicians, statisticians and economists. It was first applied as an operating tool by Marshall Wood and his staff in the Air Force's Project SCOOP (Scientific Computation of Optimum Programs). One of its applications was in the Berlin air lift. As a result of work by the Air Force group and others in linear programming and related developments, such as the theory of games, statistical decision theory and input-output analysis, truly scientific methods of analysis are now being applied to many problems in business and logistics which used to be considered beyond the scope of such analyses. In this article we shall confine ourselves to linear programming and explain the principle with a sample problem.

Linear programming derived its name from the fact that the typical problems with which it deals are stated mathematically in the form of linear equations. (Actually "linear" is too narrow a name for the technique, for it may be applied to nonlinear problems as well.) In essence it is a method for considering a number of variables simultaneously and calculating the best possible solution of a given problem within the stated limitations. Any manufacturer will at once appreciate that this is a precise statement of his own problem. In deciding what particular items to manufacture, and in what quantities, he must take into account a great complex of factors: the capacities of his machines, the cost and salability of the various items, and so on. To make matters worse, each subdivision of his problem has its own complexities; for instance, he may have to choose among several possible processes for making a particular item. And all the factors and decisions may interlock and react upon one another in unexpected ways. In the circumstances, the best that any management can hope to achieve is a reasonably workable compromise. With linear programming, however, it becomes possible to locate definitely the optimum solutions among all the available ones, both in the realm of over-all policy and in departmental detail.

To illustrate the method let us take a highly simplified hypothetical case. We have a factory that can make two products, which for simplicity's sake we shall name "widgets" and "gadgets." The factory has three machines—one "bounder" and two "rounders." The same machines can be used to make widgets or gadgets. Each product must first be roughed out on the bounder and then rounded on one of the rounders. There are two possible processes for making each product: We can use the bounder and rounder No. 1 or the bounder and rounder No. 2 for either a widget or a gadget. Let us name the respective processes for the widget One and Two, and for the gadget Three and Four. The key variables are the times involved. To make a widget by Process One requires .002 of an hour on the bounder and .003 of an hour on rounder 1; by Process Two, .002 of an hour on the bounder and .004 of an hour on rounder 2. A gadget by Process Three takes .005 of an hour on the bounder and .008 of an hour on rounder 1; by Process Four, .005 of an hour on the bounder and .010 of an hour on rounder 2. Finally, we know that the capacities of the machines for the period we are considering (say six months) are 1,000 hours of operation on the bounder, 600 hours on rounder 1 and 800 hours on rounder 2.

All this information is summarized at the top of the opposite page. A production superintendent might call this a flow chart; we can think of it as a model which specifies conditions, or constraints, that will govern any production decision we must make. Now it is readily apparent that we can translate these facts into an algebraic model. If we let x_1 represent the unknown number of widgets to be made by Process One, x_2 the number of widgets by Process Two, and x_3 and x_4 the numbers of gadgets to be made by Processes Three and Four, we can write all the information in an algebraic table [*middle of opposite page*]. The inequality sign before the numbers representing hours of capacity on the machines is the well-known symbol meaning "no more than." What this table means is simply that we can make no more widgets and/or gadgets than the capacities of the respective machines will allow. But with the conditions stated in this form, we are now in a position to consider the variables simultaneously and to calculate solutions which will satisfy the constraints. A solution will be called a linear program; linearity here refers to the fact that the available capacity on each machine is used up *in proportion to* the number of items run through it.

It is important to note here that the unknowns x_1, x_2, x_3 or x_4 may be zero but none of them can be a negative number. Of course it is obvious that we cannot produce a minus number of products. But in mathematics the exclusion of negative values must be carefully noted. In fact, the successful development of the theory of linear programming required extensive study of the effects that this restriction would have on traditional methods of solving and analyzing equations.

Having stated the constraints, we can proceed to find the best production schedule attainable within these limitations. What we mean by "best" will of course depend on what criterion we choose to apply. We might decide to seek the schedule that would produce the largest possible number of items, or the one that would use the greatest possible amount of the machines' available running time. But ordinarily the objective would be the greatest possible profit. Let us assume that the profit on each widget produced by Process One is 85 cents, on each widget by Process Two 70 cents, on each gadget by Process Three $1.60, and on each gadget by Process Four $1.30. We then get this equation: Total Profit $= .85x_1 + .70x_2 + 1.60x_3 + 1.30x_4$.

From this information we could calculate the number of each item we should produce to realize the largest possible total profit within the machines' capacity. (Be it noted that gadgets, though yielding a larger per unit profit, should not necessarily pre-empt the machines, for widgets take less time to produce.)

The problem as so far outlined, however, is much too simple to represent an actual situation. To come closer to a real problem we should at least introduce a sales factor. Let us suppose, therefore, that our factory has orders for 450,000 widgets. Elementary arithmetic will show that our present machine capacity cannot turn them out within the time limit. We have enough capacity on the bounder for 500,000 widgets (1,000 hours divided by .002 of an hour per widget) but our two rounders combined could finish no more than 400,000. We

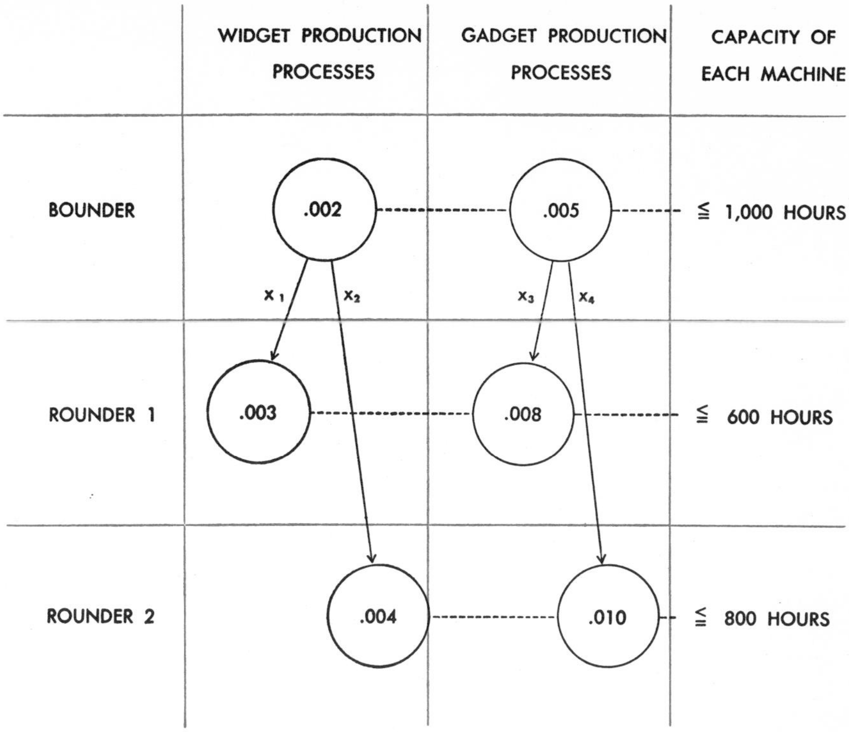

	WIDGET PRODUCTION PROCESSES		GADGET PRODUCTION PROCESSES		CAPACITY OF EACH MACHINE
BOUNDER	.002 (x_1, x_2)		.005 (x_3, x_4)		$\leqq$ 1,000 HOURS
ROUNDER 1	.003 (x_1)		.008 (x_3)		$\leqq$ 600 HOURS
ROUNDER 2		.004 (x_2)		.010 (x_4)	$\leqq$ 800 HOURS

GRAPHIC MODEL depicts the restrictions on production of "widgets" and "gadgets" by three machines: one "bounder" and two "rounders." The numbers in the circles indicate the fraction of an hour required for each machine to perform its function on each part.

BOUNDER	$.002x_1 + .002x_2 + .005x_3 + .005x_4$	$\leqq$ 1,000 HOURS
ROUNDER 1	$.003x_1 + .008x_3$	$\leqq$ 600 HOURS
ROUNDER 2	$.004x_2 + .010x_4$	$\leqq$ 800 HOURS

ALGEBRAIC MODEL of the same conditions represents as x_1, x_2, x_3 and x_4 the numbers of items produced by the processes indicated by arrows in the graphic model. The blank spaces in each column can be disregarded because they represent zero in each case.

BOUNDER	$.002x_1 + .002x_2 + .002x'_1 + .005x_3 + .005x_4 + .005x'_3$	$\leqq$ 1,000 HOURS
ROUNDER 1	$.003x_1 + .008x_3$	$\leqq$ 600 HOURS
ROUNDER 2	$.004x_2 + .010x_4$	$\leqq$ 800 HOURS
ROUNDER 1 (OVERTIME)	$.003x'_1 + .008x'_3$	$\leqq$ 200 HOURS
CONTRACT	$x_1 + x_2 + x'_1$	$\geqq$ 450,000 WIDGETS

COMPLETED MODEL is based on the assumption of additional capacity for one of the machines. This is overtime on rounder 1. Now two new processes are introduced: x'_1 and x'_3. The sign before 450,000 widgets means at least this number must be produced.

must obtain more rounder capacity, and this may be done by authorizing overtime on one or both of the rounders. Suppose, then, we arrange for 200 hours of overtime on the faster of our two rounders (.003 of an hour per widget). Because of higher labor costs for overtime, the profit per widget will be reduced from the usual 85 cents to 60 cents during the overtime period, and if we should use any of the overtime capacity for making gadgets, the unit profit on them will drop from $1.60 to $1.40.

The constraints governing this expansion of the problem are summarized in the algebraic table above (the new symbols x'_1 and x'_3 represent the number of widgets and of gadgets, respectively, to be turned out on rounder 1 during the overtime period). Given the unit profit figures, we are now prepared to calculate the most profitable possible employment of the machines.

The answer can be computed by one of several methods. The most general, devised by Dantzig, is called the simplex method. Certain special methods which are more efficient for the kind of problem being considered here were developed by the authors of this article. These systems, though too involved and lengthy to be explained in detail here, require only simple arithmetical operations which can easily be carried out by clerks or commercially available computers. The simplex method starts from zero use of the machines' capacity, and the computation proceeds by a series of specified steps, each of which advances closer to the ultimate answer.

The answer in this case is that we should produce no gadgets but should make 466,667 widgets, finishing 200,000 on rounder 1 at straight time, another 200,000 on rounder 2 at straight time and the remaining 66,667 at overtime on rounder 1. The total profit will be $350,000. Our system of calculation tells us that it is not possible to devise a production schedule which will yield a larger total profit within our restrictions.

It is possible that there may be other programs which would provide as much (but no more) profit. If there are, the analyst can quickly find them. He can also determine the second best or third best program, and so on. Thus the method is not only powerful but also flexible; it can offer management a range of choices based on different considerations. Furthermore, linear programming methods can be extended to analyze the effects of any change in the restrictions—an improvement in efficiency, an increase or reduction in cost, an increase in capacity. These methods employ a "dual theorem," whereby a maximizing problem (such as the maximization of profits in the case we have been considering) is viewed as the reverse of a related minimizing problem. In this case the minimizing problem is concerned with the worth of the machine capacities. Using the same set of facts and calculations, it is possible to show precisely how much more profitable it is to employ overtime on rounder 1 than on rounder 2. If the overtime on rounder 1 were increased to 300 hours instead of 200 hours, the maximum profit would be $370,000 instead of $350,000. But an increase of overtime from 300 to 301 hours would be worthless, for at that point the possible rounder output would exceed the capacity of the bounder.

In short, linear programming may be applied not only to finding the best program within given restrictions but also to assessing the advisability of changing the restrictions themselves.

The hypothetical problem outlined in this article was simplified to illustrate some of the basic elements of the technique. In any real-life problem the factors at play are both more numerous and more difficult to identify. It is as important to locate the truly pertinent factors as it is to construct the correct mathematical model for dealing with them. The application of linear programming is full of pitfalls. To evaluate the various features of a problem and determine which should be included in the model requires understanding collaboration between the mathematical analyst and the operations people actually working at the job.

The range of problems to which linear programming may be applied is very wide. As we have already indicated, the Air Force has employed it in problems of logistics. In industry the method is solving problems not only in production but even in such matters as devising the most effective salary pattern for executives—a pattern which will not only meet competition for their services from outside but will also avoid inconsistencies within the company.

Through the dual theorem, linear programming has been related to the theory of games; it is thereby enabled to take probabilities as well as known restrictions into account. It also has fundamental, though indirect, connections with statistical decision theory, which the late Abraham Wald related to the theory of games shortly before his recent death in an airplane crash. All three of these disciplines are contributing to one another's progress. Indeed, our own chief interest in linear programming is to develop generalizations which will enlarge the scope of the technique.

It has been highly satisfying to us to see how often research on a particular problem has led to methods of much more general application, sometimes in altogether unexpected fields. For instance, the work we did in adapting linear programming to the problem of the executives' salary schedule opened a new path for studying the field of statistical regression and correlation analysis. Similarly, an investigation of certain problems in economic measurement and management science has paved the way for new approaches in totally unrelated fields of work in engineering and physics, such as plasticity and elasticity.

As research on these new tools of scientific analysis continues, we can expect to find many new uses for them. But what is perhaps most remarkable is the great and continuing revolution that science and technology have wrought in mathematics. As the mathematician and writer Eric Temple Bell has said in his book *The Development of Mathematics*:

"As the sciences . . . became more and more exact, they made constantly increasing demands on mathematical inventiveness, and were mainly responsible for a large part of the enormous expansion of all mathematics since 1637. Again, as industry and invention became increasingly scientific after the industrial revolution of the late 18th and early 19th centuries, they too stimulated mathematical creation. . . . The time curve of mathematical productivity [shoots up] with ever greater rapidity. . . ."

PART FOUR

IMITATIONS OF LIFE

IMITATIONS OF LIFE

INTRODUCTION

Man has always been convinced of and concerned with his position of exalted uniqueness in the known universe. Indeed, a belief in the ultimate distinctiveness, if not divinity, of man has permeated most Western thought for centuries. Man has drawn a clear distinction between the living and nonliving, often imputing a "miraculous" quality to what we call life. He has further distinguished between plants and animals, and, among the animals, man views himself as the crowning achievement of the Universe by virtue of his self-proclaimed soul, his ability to fashion and use tools, his social or political organizations, his ability to use language, or his superior intellect and rationality.

However, man's view of life and particularly of himself is being challenged. The Darwinian revolution of the last century seriously infirmed the belief that man was a creature completely unrelated to lower forms of animal life. Comparative anatomical studies reveal that continuity, rather than discontinuity, is the general rule. Comparative psychologists have shown that many lower animals are capable of reasoning and of at least the rudiments of what might be called creative thought. It is also known that many species develop complex and often permanent social structures and that many animals are capable of imaginative uses of tools.

Man's view of himself and of his key role in the earthly scheme of things is being threatened on yet another flank. This assault is aimed at the traditional distinction between the behavior of living systems and that of nonliving systems. The basic question seems to be, "To what extent are machines capable of performing activities that are typically considered unique to living systems?" It is on this issue that the articles in this section are focused.

Why is this an important issue? Certainly, "yes" or "no" answers to questions like "Can machines think?" or "Is man a machine?" are of little value since the answer depends so critically upon the way we choose to define "think" or "machine." Furthermore, the answers we give to such poorly phrased questions will probably have little impact on the future development of science or society. So why then is this an important issue?

In order to provide even a brief answer to this question it is helpful to distinguish two approaches to the study of the relationship between machine behavior and that of living systems. The first has been called *simulation* and the second, *artificial intelligence.* Although the technique is similar in each, the two differ in intent and use.

The primary goal of artificial intelligence is to create machines whose behavior would be considered to exhibit some measure of intelligence, if the same behavior were performed by a person. However, no claim that the machine behaves in the same manner as the person is made. The machine, in other words, is not intended to be a model of the person. When the machine *is* a model, and its behavior is thus intended to provide an explanation of the behavior of the living organism, it is then a simulation. Of course, one machine can be an example of simulation in one case, if it is to be a means of viewing a behavioral process, and an example of artificial intelligence in another, if it is to be studied solely as an interesting machine.

The development and study of intelligent machines as simulations provides the opportunity for the attainment of new levels of complexity in theories of behavior. Specifically, a theory may be expanded either by elaboration of its detail or by an extension of its breadth, that is, by an increase in the number of variables whose impact on the phenomenon being studied can be assessed simultaneously. Because of the wide range of factors that can influence most behavioral phenomena, the second avenue toward greater complexity is probably the more important of the two.

Twenty-five years ago, many behavioral scientists held the opinion that theories on purposeful or goal-directed activity were necessarily based on mentalistic, subjective, and, hence, unscientific foundations. Early in the history of cybernetics, however, it was shown that simple machines, which exhibited such purposeful behavior, could be built. The key, of course, was in the use of feedback as a control process. Although the demonstration of purposeful behavior in machines did not disprove mentalistic theories of purposeful activity, it did prove that teleological theories did not *have* to be mentalistic. Similar changes have occurred with regard to our conceptions of intelligent behavior, such as problem solving, decision making, and concept learning. Thus, the study of the potentialities of machines has forced a reconsideration and a critical reexamination of our conceptions of the nature of living organisms.

Like simulation, the field of artificial intelligence is destined to be of continually increasing importance in human affairs. Just as machines have taken over much of the physical work that was once done by men, it is becoming more and more apparent that machines are going to assume a sizable part of man's mental labor as well. The harbingers of this change are abundant. Most major industries use computers to handle customer billing and accounting: a simple job to be sure, but one that used to require some mental effort from a large group of employees. Machines that read ZIP codes are replacing postal clerks that read addresses. Computers have successfully replaced the traffic policeman, and now the complete reservations systems of several major airlines are processed solely by machines.

Now that they are proved to be successful at handling these relatively routine tasks, machines are beginning to be used to solve problems for which human judgment was once considered necessary. It is not at all unlikely that computers will have a major function in education. They are already making complex and sophisticated decisions in business and industry. Many governmental and military agencies are highly dependent on the advice and information they receive from their computers. The future will find man becoming more and more dependent on the intelligent machines he has created.

In "Man Viewed as a Machine," John G. Kemeny describes some of the seminal ideas underlying the creation of life-imitating machines. His suggestions and illustrations of the way in which basic processes can be combined to perform complex tasks exemplifies the fact that quite intricate processes may be formed from very simple principles. This point is further emphasized by L. S. Penrose in "Self-reproducing Machines." Continuing the discussion of self-reproducing machines begun by Kemeny, Penrose demonstrates how simple mechanical devices that will create replicas of themselves can be constructed.

Each of the remaining papers in this section deal with some aspect of what is typically considered to be intelligent behavior. In "A Machine That Learns," W. Grey Walter describes his *Machina docilis*, an electromechanical creature that not only displays purposeful, goal-directed activity, but also has a rudimentary learning capacity. Alex Bernstein and Michael de V. Roberts discuss their efforts to create a program that would enable a computer to play a respectable game of chess. Marvin L. Minsky, in "Artificial Intelligence," reviews several recent attempts to create computers capable of such abstract (and human) processes as analogical reasoning and the comprehension and solution of algebra problems stated in English. In "Pattern Recognition by Machine," Oliver G. Selfridge and Ulric Neisser contend with the problem of giving the computer a useful sensory or perceptual system that will enable it to learn to classify inputs into appropriate recognition categories.

16

MAN VIEWED AS A MACHINE

JOHN G. KEMENY • April 1955

Is man no more than a machine? The question is often debated these days, usually with more vigor than precision. More than most arguments, this one tends to bog down in definition troubles. What is a machine? And what do we mean by "no more than"? If we define "machine" broadly enough, everything is a machine; and if by "more than" we mean that we are human, then machines are clearly less than we are.

In this article we shall frame the question more modestly. Let us ask: What could a machine do as well or better than a man, now or in the future? We shall not concern ourselves with whether a machine could write sonnets or fall in love. Nor shall we waste time laboring the obvious fact that when it comes to muscle, machines are far superior to men. What concerns us here is man as a brain-machine. John von Neumann, the mathematician and designer of computers, not long ago made a detailed comparison of human and mechanical brains in a series of lectures at Princeton University. Much of what follows is based on that discussion.

We are often presented with Utopias in which all the hard work is done by machines and we merely push buttons. This may sound like a lazy dream of heaven, but actually man is even lazier than that. He is no sooner presented with this Utopia than he asks: "Couldn't I build a machine to push the buttons for me?" And indeed he began to invent such machines as early as the 18th century. The flyball governor on a steam engine and the thermostat are elementary brain-machines. They control muscle machines, while spending only negligible amounts of energy themselves. Norbert Wiener compared them to the human nervous system.

Consider the progress of the door. Its earliest form must have been a rock rolled in front of a cave entrance. This may have provided excellent protection, but it must also have made the operation of going in and out of the cave quite difficult. Slowly, as man found better means of defending himself, he made lighter and more manageable doors, until today it is literally child's play to open a door. But even this does not satisfy us. To the delight of millions of railroad passengers, the Pennsylvania Railroad installed electric eyes in its New York terminal. Man need only break the invisible signal connecting the two photoelectric "eyes," and immediately the little brain-machine commands the door to open. This control device needs only a negligible amount of energy, is highly efficient and is vastly faster than any doorman.

The central switchboard in an office is another brain-machine, especially if the office has installed the dial system. Messages are carried swiftly and efficiently to hundreds of terminals, at the expense of only a small quantity of electricity. This is one of those brain-machines without which modern life is supposed to be not worth living.

And, finally, there is the example most of us are likely to think of when brain-machines are mentioned: namely, the high-speed computer. Electric eyes and telephone exchanges only relieve us of physical labor, but the calculators can take the place of several human brains.

The Slow Brain

In economy of energy the human brain certainly is still far ahead of all its mechanical rivals. The entire brain with its many billions of cells functions on less than 100 watts. Even with the most efficient present substitute for a brain cell—the transistor—a machine containing as many cells as the brain would need about 100 million watts. We are ahead by a factor of at least a million. But von Neumann has calculated that in theory cells could be 10 billion times more efficient in the use of energy than the brain cells actually are. Thus there seems to be no technical reason why mechanical brains should not become more efficient energy-users than their human cousins. After all, just recently by inventing the transistor, which requires only about a hundredth of a watt, we have improved the efficiency of our machines by a factor of 100; in view of this the factor of a million should not frighten us.

While we are still ahead in the use of energy, we are certainly far behind in speed. Whereas a nerve cannot be used more than 100 times a second, a vacuum tube can easily be turned on and off a million times a second. It could be made to work even faster, but this would not contribute much to speeding

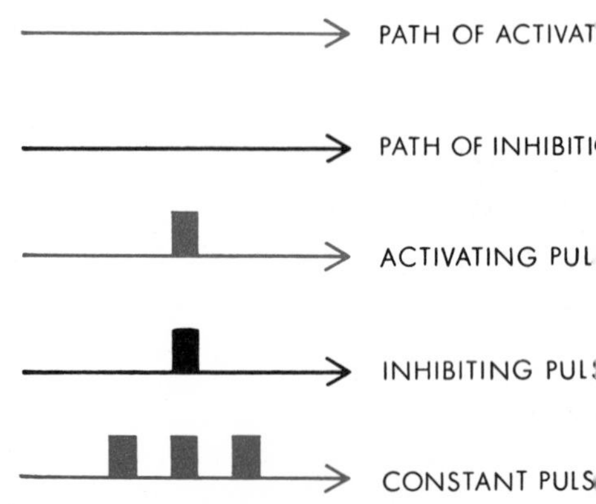

SIMPLE CIRCUITS for a brain machine are dep ed on the next five pages. The activating and inh iting pulses are identical but follow different pa

up the mechanical brain at the moment. No machine is faster than its slowest part, so we must evaluate various components of the machine.

In a calculating machine four different problems confront the designer: the actual computations, the "logical control," the memory and the feeding of information to the machine and getting answers out. Speed of computation, a bottleneck in mechanical computers such as the desk calculator, has been taken care of by the vacuum tube. The next bottleneck was the logical control—the system for telling the machine what to do next after each step. The early IBM punch-card machine took this function out of the hands of a human operator by using a wiring setup on a central board which commanded the sequence of operations. This is perfectly all right as long as the machine has to perform only one type of operation. But if the sequence has to be changed frequently, the wiring of the board becomes very clumsy indeed. To improve speed the machine must be given an internal logical control. Perhaps the greatest step forward on this problem has been accomplished by MANIAC, built at the Institute for Advanced Study in Princeton. This machine can change instructions as quickly as it completes calculations, so that it can operate as fast as its vacuum tubes will allow.

That still leaves the problems of speeding up the memory and the input and output of information. The two problems are closely related. The larger the memory, the less often the operator has to feed the machine information. But the very fact that the machine performs large numbers of computations between instructions clogs its memory and slows it down. This is because an accumulation of rounding errors makes it necessary to carry out all figures in a calculation to a great number of digits. In each computation the machine necessarily rounds off the last digit; in succeeding operations the digit becomes less and less precise. If the computations are continued, the next-to-last digit begins to be affected, and so on. It can be shown that after 100 computations the last digit is worthless; after 10,000 the last two digits; after 1,000,000, the last three. In the large new computers an answer might easily contain four worthless figures. Hence to insure accuracy the machine must carry more digits than are actually significant; it is not uncommon to carry from eight to 12 digits for each number throughout the calculation. When the machine operates on the binary system of numbers, instead of the decimal system, the situation is even worse, for it takes about three times as many digits to express a number in the binary scale.

MANIAC uses up to 40 binary digits to express a number. Due to the necessity for carrying this large number of digits, even MANIAC's celebrated memory can hold no more than about 1,000 numbers. It has an "external memory," in the form of a magnetic tape and magnetic drums, in which it can store more information, but reading from the tape or drums is a much slower operation than doing electrical computations.

In spite of the present limitations, the machines already are ahead of the human brain in speed by a factor of at least 10,000—usually a great deal more than 10,000. They are most impressive on tasks such as arise in astronomy or ballistics. It would be child's play for MANIAC to figure out the position of the planets for the next million years.

Still we are left with the feeling that there are many things we can do that a machine cannot do. The brain has more than 10 billion cells, while a computer has only a few tens of thousands of parts. Even with transistors, which overcome the cost and space problems, the difficulty of construction will hardly allow more than a million parts to a machine. So we can safely say that the human brain for a long time to come will be about 10,000 times more complex than the most complicated machine. And it is well known that an increase of parts by a factor of 10 can bring about differences in kind. For example, if we have a unit that can do addition and multiplication, by combining a few such units with a logical control mechanism we can do subtraction, division, raising to powers, interpolation and many other operations qualitatively different from the original.

The Complex Memory

Part of man's superior complexity is his remarkable memory. How does MANIAC's memory compare with it? For simplicity's sake let us measure the information a memory may hold in "bits" (for binary digits). A vacuum tube can hold one digit of a binary number (the digit is 1 if the tube is on, 0 if it is off). In vacuum-tube language it takes 1,500 bits to express the multiplication table. Now MANIAC's memory holds about 40,000 bits, not in 40,000 separate tubes but as spots on 40 special picture tubes, each of which can hold about 1,000 spots (light or dark). Estimates as to how much the human memory holds vary widely, but we certainly can say conservatively that the brain can remember at least 1,000 items as complex

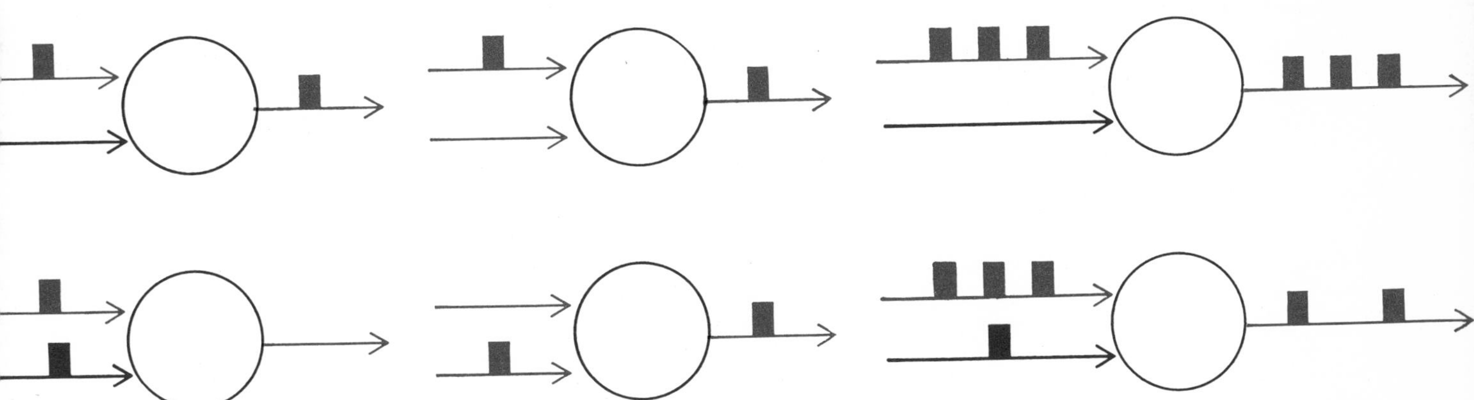

BASIC CELL (*circle*) **will fire when it is activated** (*top*)**. It will not fire, however, if it is inhibited at the same time** (*bottom*)**.**

"OR" CIRCUIT requires two paths of activation. The cell fires if a pulse arrives on one path (*top*) **"or" the other** (*bottom*)**.**

"NOT" CIRCUIT incorporates constant activating pulses. The cell can thus fire constantly (*top*)**. It signals "not" when it is briefly inhibited** (*bottom*)**.**

as the multiplication table (1.5 million bits), and a reasonable guess is that its capacity is closer to 100 million bits—which amounts to acquiring one bit per 20 seconds throughout life. So our memory exceeds that of MANIAC by a factor of 1,000 at least.

Is the difference just a matter of complexity? No, the fact is that machines have not yet imitated the human brain's method of storing and recovering information. For instance, if we tried to increase MANIAC's memory by any considerable amount, we would soon find it almost impossible to extract information. We would have to use a complex system of coding to enable the machine to hunt up a given item of information, and this coding would load down the memory further and make the logical control more complex. Only when we acquire a better understanding of the brain's amazing ability to call forth information will we be able to give a machine anything more than a limited memory.

The Logical Machine

Let us now consider the inevitable question: Can a machine "think"? We start with a simple model of the nervous system such as has been constructed by Walter Pitts and Warren S. McCulloch of the Massachusetts Institute of Technology. Its basic unit is the neuron—a cell that can be made to emit pulses of energy. The firing of one neuron may activate the next or it may inhibit it. The neurons are assumed to work in cycles. This corresponds to our knowledge that after firing a neuron must be inactive for a period. To simplify the model it is assumed that the various neurons' cycles are synchronized, *i.e.*, all the neurons active during a given period fire at the same time. For a given neuron to fire in a given cycle two conditions must be satisfied: in the previous cycle it must have been (1) activated and (2) not inhibited. If, for example, a neuron has two others terminating in it of which one activates and one inhibits, and if the former fires in a given cycle and the latter does not, then the neuron will fire in the following cycle. Otherwise it will be inactive for a cycle.

Out of this basic pattern we can build the most complex logical machine. We can have a combination that will fire if a connected neuron did not fire (representing "not") or one that will fire if at least one of two incoming neurons fired (representing "or") or one that will fire only if both incoming neurons fired (representing "and"). Combining these, we can imitate many logical operations of the brain. The simple arrangement diagrammed on pages 116 and 117 will count up to four, and it is easy to see how to generalize this technique.

We can also construct a very primitive memory: *e.g.*, a system that will "remember" that it has been activated until it is instructed to "forget" it. But if it is to remember anything at all complex, it must have an unthinkably large number of neurons—another illustration of the fact that human memory acts on different principles from a machine.

The Turing Machine

If we were to stop here, we might conclude that practical limitations of memory and complexity must forever restrict the cleverness or versatility of any machine. But we have not yet plumbed the full possibilities. The late A. M. Turing of England showed, by a brilliant analysis, that by combining a certain few simple operations in sufficient number a machine could perform feats of amazing complexity. Turing's machines may be clumsy and slow, but they present the clearest picture of what a machine can do.

A Turing machine can be thought of as a mechanical calculator which literally works with pencil and paper. The paper it uses is a long tape divided into successive squares, and it operates on one square at a time. As it confronts a particular square it can do one of six things: (1) write down the letter X; (2) write down the digit 1; (3) erase either of these marks if it is already in the square; (4) move the tape one square to the left; (5) move the tape one square to the right; (6) stop.

Essentially this machine is a number writer. It writes its numbers in the simplest possible form, as a string of units. This is even simpler than the binary system. In the binary system the number 35, for example, is written 100011. In a Turing machine it is a string of 1's in 35 successive squares. The X's are merely punctuation marks to show where each number starts and ends.

The machine has the following parts: a device that writes or erases, a scanner, a motor to move the tape, a numbered dial with a pointer, and a logical control consisting of neuron-like elements, say vacuum tubes. The logical control operates from a prepared table of commands which specifies what the machine is to do in each given state. The

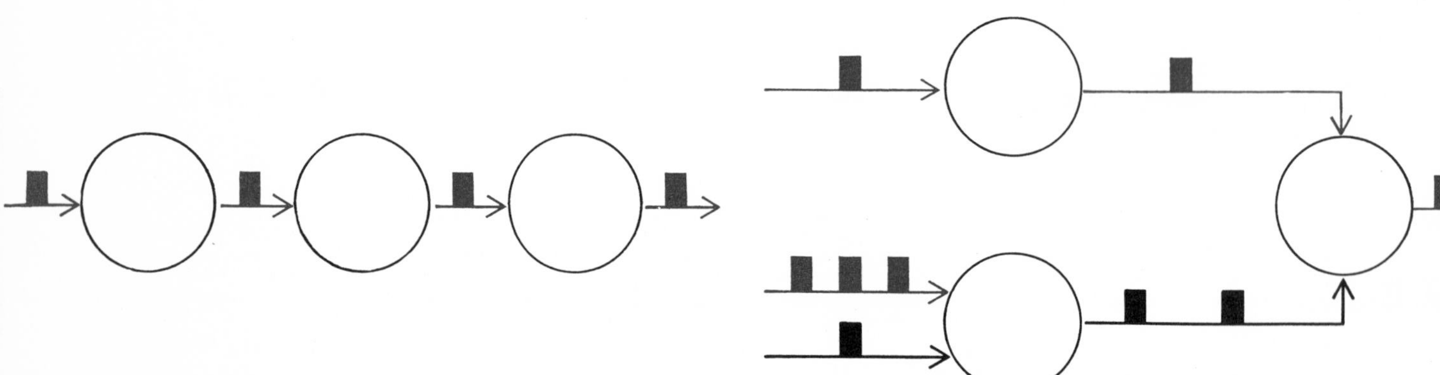

DELAY CIRCUIT is based on the fact that the basic cell receives a pulse in one "cycle" and fires it in the next. In this arrangement of three basic cells the pulse would be delayed three cycles.

"AND" CIRCUIT utilizes three cells. The first (*upper left*) has only an vating input. The second (*lower left*) has a constant activating input an inhibiting input. The third (*right*) is the conventional basic cell. In the

state consists of two elements: what the scanner "sees" in the square before it, and where the pointer is on the dial. For example, the table of instructions may say that whenever the square has an X and the pointer is at the number 1 on the dial, the machine is to erase the X, and move the pointer to the number 2 on the dial. As the machine proceeds from step to step, the logical control gives it such commands, the command in each case depending both on the position of the dial and on what the scanner sees in the square confronting it. Observe that the dial functions as a primitive "memory," in the sense that its position at any stage is a consequence of what the scanner saw and where the pointer stood at the step immediately preceding. It carries over the machine's experience from step to step.

Turing's machine thus consists of a tape with X's and 1's in some of its squares, a dial-memory with a certain number of positions, and a logical control which instructs the machine what to do, according to what it sees and what its memory says. The diagram on pages 118 and 119 shows a very simple version of the machine, with a dial having only six positions. Since the scanner may see one of three things in a square—blank, 1 or X—the machine has 18 possible states, and the logical control has a command for each case [*see table at right of illustration*]. This machine is designed to perform a single task: it can add two numbers—any two numbers. Suppose it is to add 2 and 3. The numbers are written as strings of 1's with X's at the ends. Say we start with the dial at position 1 and the scanner looking at the second digit of the number 3 [*see diagram*]. The instructions in the table say that when it is in this state the machine is to move the tape one square to the right and keep the dial at position 1. This operation brings the square to the left, containing another digit 1, under the scanner. Again the instructions are the same: "Move the tape one square to the right and keep the dial at position 1." Now the scanner sees an X. The instructions, with the dial at position 1, are: "Erase (the X) and move the dial to position 2." The machine now confronts a blank square. The command becomes: "Move the tape one square to the right and keep the dial at position 2." In this manner the machine will eventually write two digit 1's next to the three at the right and end with the answer 5—a row of five digits enclosed by X's. When it finishes, an exclamation point signifies that it is to stop. The reader is advised to try adding two other numbers in the same fashion.

This surely is a cumbersome method of adding. However, the machine becomes more impressive when it is expanded so that it can solve a problem such as the following: "Multiply the number you are looking at by two and take the cube root of the answer if the fifth number to the left is less than 150." By adding positions to the dial and enlarging the table of instructions we can endow such a machine with the ability to carry out the most complex tasks, though each operational step is very simple. The Turing machine in fact resembles a model of the human nervous system, which can be thought of as having a dial with very many positions and combining many simple acts to accomplish the enormous number of tasks a human being is capable of.

Turing gave his machines an infinite memory. Of course the dial can have only a finite number of positions, but he allowed the machine a tape infinite in length, endless in both directions. Actually the tape does not have to be infinite—just long enough for the task. We may provide for all emergencies by allowing the machine to ask for more tape if it needs it. The human memory is infinite in the same sense: we can always make more paper to make notes on.

The Universal Machine

If we allow the unlimited tape, the Turing idea astounds us further with a universal machine. Not only can we build a machine for each task, but we can design a single machine that is versatile enough to accomplish all these tasks! We must try to understand how this is done, because it will give us the key to our whole problem.

The secret of the universal machine is that it can imitate. Suppose we build a highly complex machine for a difficult task. If we then supply the universal machine with a description of the task and of our special machine, it will figure out how to perform the task. It proceeds very simply, deducing from what it knows about our machine just what it would do at each step. Of course this slows the universal machine down considerably. Between any two steps it must carry out a long argument to analyze what our machine would do. But we care only about its ability to succeed, not its speed. There is no doubt about it: anything any logical machine can do can be done by this single mechanism.

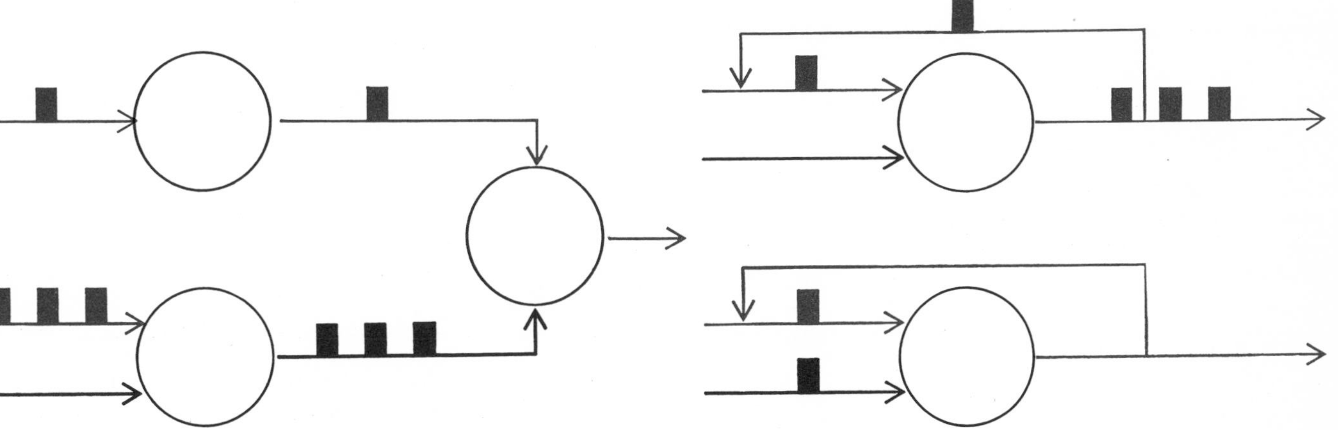

gram the pulse received by the first cell is not fired by the third. The third will fire the pulse only if the activating pulse of the first cell "and" the ibiting pulse of the second are fired on the same cycle (*second diagram*).

MEMORY CIRCUIT feeds the output of a cell back into its input. Thus if the cell is activated, it "remembers" by firing constantly (*top*). If it is inhibited at any time later, it stops firing (*bottom*).

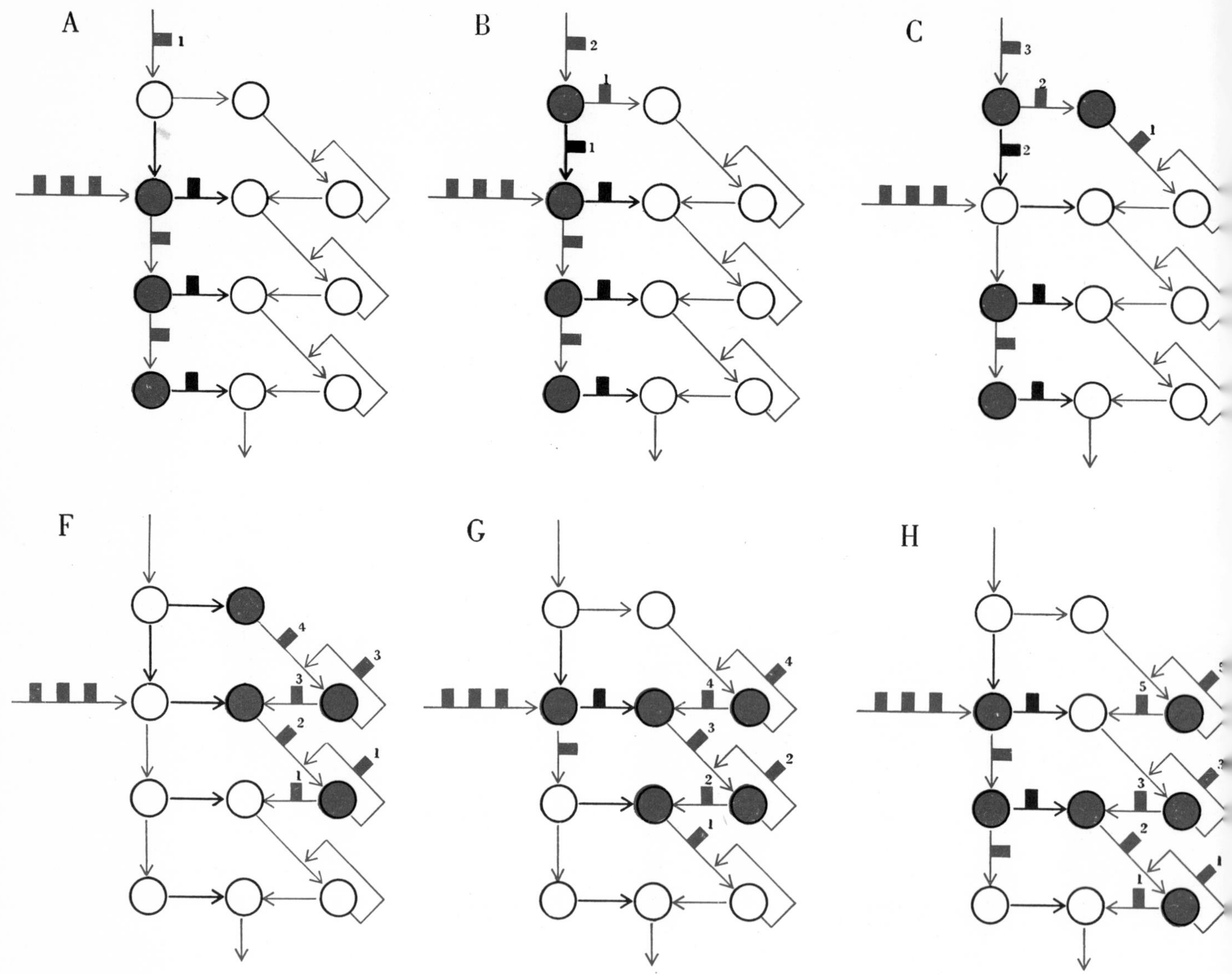

COUNTING CIRCUIT "counts" to four and then fires. The conventions in this series of diagrams are the same as those in the illus trations on the four preceding pages, with two important exceptions. The first is that, where the diagrams on the preceding pages show each circuit during two or more cycles, each of these diagrams shows the circuit during a single cycle. The second exception is that, when a cell fires, it lights up *(brown tone)*. The input of this circuit is the activating pathway at the top. The output of the circuit is the activating pathway at the bottom. In addition one of the cells has a constant activating input *(left)*. The three cells at the right are memory cells *(see diagram at the right on preceding page)*. These cells can activate the three cells to the left of them.

The key question is: How do you describe a complex machine in terms that a relatively simple machine can understand? The answer is that you devise a simple code which can describe any machine (or at least any Turing machine), and that you design the universal machine so that it will be able to understand this code. To understand a Turing machine we need only know its table of commands, so it suffices to have a simple code for tables of commands. We will sketch one possible way of representing each conceivable table of commands by an integer. Of course there are infinitely many such tables, but there are also infinitely many integers—that is why they are so useful in mathematics.

A table of commands consists of P rows. Each row has three commands in it, corresponding to seeing a blank, an X or a 1. The first step is to get rid of the letters in the table [*refer again to page 119*]. This can be done by replacing E, X, D, L, R and S by 1 through 6 respectively. Thus the commands on the first line of the table of our sample machine become 3–6, 1–2, 5–1. Step two: Get rid of the question mark and the exclamation point, say by putting 1 and 2 for them respectively. (Since these occur only in conjunction with an S, there is no danger of confusing them with memory positions 1 and 2.) Thus the second row of our table becomes 5–2, 1–3, 6–1. Step three: Represent each row by a single integer. There is a famous simple way of doing this; namely by treating the numbers as exponents to primes and obtaining a product which completely specifies the series of numbers. As the final step, we epresent the entire table with a single number obtained by the same trick. Our code number for this table will be $2^{2991509440920}$ times 3 raised to the number of the second row. It is an enormous number, but it does identify our table of commands uniquely. And it is a straightforward mechanical task to design the universal machine so that it can

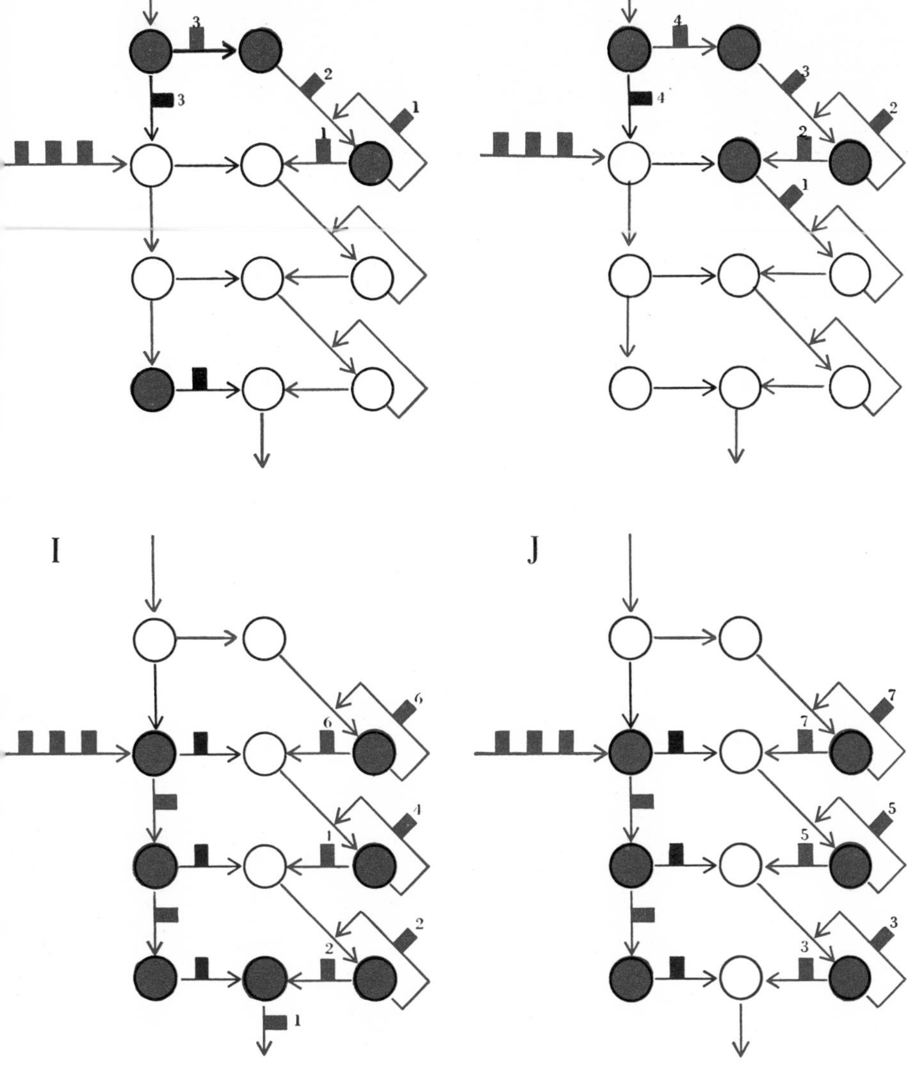

sand entries, it seems to be able to do essentially all the problem-solving tasks that we can. Of course it might take a billion years to do something we can do in an hour. The "outside world" from which it can learn is much more restricted than ours, being limited to Turing machines. But may not all this be just a difference of degree? Are we, as rational beings, basically different from universal Turing machines?

The usual answer is that whatever else machines can do, it still takes a man to build the machine. Who would dare to say that a machine can reproduce itself and make other machines?

Von Neumann would. As a matter of fact, he has blue-printed just such a machine.

The Reproducing Machine

What do we mean by reproduction? If we mean the creation of an object like the original out of nothing, then no machine can reproduce, but neither can a human being. If reproduction is not to violate the conservation of energy principle, building materials must be available. The characteristic feature of the reproduction of life is that the living organism can create a new organism like itself out of inert matter surrounding it.

If we agree that machines are not alive, and if we insist that the creation of life is an essential feature of reproduction, then we have begged the question: A machine cannot reproduce. So we must reformulate the problem in a way that won't make machine reproduction logically impossible. We must omit the word "living." We shall ask that the machine create a new organism like itself out of simple parts contained in the environment.

These three cells can in turn be inhibited by the three cells to the left of them. Now in the first four cycles (A, B, C and D) four pulses are put into the circuit. The position of each pulse in succeeding cycles is indicated by small numbers. In the ninth cycle (I) the circuit, having "counted" the four pulses, fires once. In the 10th cycle (J) the circuit returns to its original state with the exception that pulses are still circulating through the memory cells. A practical counting circuit would be fitted with a device to wipe out these memories.

decode the large number and reproduce the table of commands. With the table of commands written down, the machine then knows what the machine it is copying would do in any given situation.

The universal machine is remarkably human. It starts with very limited abilities, and it learns more and more by imitation and by absorbing information from the outside. We feel that the potentialities of the human brain are inexhaustible. But would this be the case if we were unable to communicate with the world around us? A man robbed of his five senses is comparable to a Turing machine with a fixed tape, but a normal human being is like the universal machine. Given enough time, he can learn to do anything.

But some readers will feel we have given in too soon to Turing's persuasive argument. After all a human being must step in and give the universal machine the code number. If we allow that, why not give the machine the answer in the first place? Turing's reply would have been that the universal machine does not need a man to encode the table; it can be designed to do its own coding, just as it can be designed to decode.

So we grant this amazing machine its universal status. And although its table of logical control has only a few thou-

Human beings find the raw material in the form of food; that is, quite highly organized chemicals. Thus we cannot even say that we produce order out of complete disorder, but rather we transform more simply organized matter into complex matter. We must accordingly assume that the machine is surrounded with pieces of matter, simpler than any part of the machine. The hypothetical parts list would be rolls of tape, pencils, erasers, vacuum tubes, dials, photoelectric cells, motors, shafts, wire, batteries and so on. We must endow the machine with the ability to transform pieces of matter into these parts and to organize them into a new machine.

Von Neumann simplified the problem by making a number of reasonable assumptions. First of all he realized that it is inessential for the machine to be able to move around. Rather, he has the mechanism sending out impulses which organize the surroundings by remote control. Secondly, he asssumed that space is divided into cubical cells, and that each part of the machine and each piece of raw material occupies just one cell. Thirdly, he assumed that the processes are quantized not only in space but in time; that is, we have cycles during which all action takes place. It is not even necessary to have three dimensions: a two-dimensional lattice will serve as well as the network of cubes.

Our space will be a very large (in principle infinite) sheet, divided into squares. A machine occupies a connected area consisting of a large number of squares. Since each square represents a part of the machine, the number of squares occupied is a measure of the complexity of the machine. The machine is surrounded by inert cells, which it has to organize. To make this possible the machine must be a combination of a brain and a brawn machine, since it not only organizes but also transforms matter. Accordingly the von Neumann machine has three kinds of parts. It has neurons similar to those discussed in the model of the nervous system. These provide the logical control. Then it has transmission cells, which carry messages from the control centers. They have an opening through which they can receive impulses, and an output through which the impulse is passed on a cycle later. A string of transmission cells, properly adjoined, forms a channel through which messages can be sent. In addition the machine has muscles. These cells can change the surrounding cells, building them up from less highly organized to more complex cells or breaking them down. They bring about changes analogous to those produced by a combination of muscular and chemical action in the human body. Their primary use is, of course, the changing of an inert cell into a machine part.

As in the nervous system, the operation proceeds by steps: the state of every cell is determined by its state and the state of its neighbors a cycle earlier. The neurons and transmission cells are either quiescent or they can send out an impulse if properly stimulated. The muscle cells receive commands from the neurons through the transmission cells, and react either by "killing" some undesired part (*i.e.*, making it inert) or by transforming some inert cell in the environment to a machine part of a specified kind. So far the machine is similar in structure to a higher animal. Its neurons form the central nervous system; the transmission cells establish contact with various organs; the organs perform their designated tasks upon receiving a command.

The instructions may be very long. Hence they must in a sense be external. Von Neumann's machine has a tail containing the blueprint of what it is to build. This tail is a very long strip containing coded instructions. The basic box performs two types of functions: it follows instructions from its tail, and it is able to copy the tail. Suppose the tail contains a coded description of the basic box. Then the box will, following instructions, build another box like itself. When it is finished, it proceeds to copy its own tail, attaching it to the new box. And so it reproduces itself.

The secret of the machine is that it does not try to copy itself. Von Neumann designed a machine that can build any machine from a description of it, and hence can build one like itself. Then it is an easy matter to copy the large but simple tail containing the instructions and attach it to the offspring. Thereafter the new machine can go on producing more and more machines until all the raw material is used up or until the machines get into conflict with each other—imitating even in this their human designers.

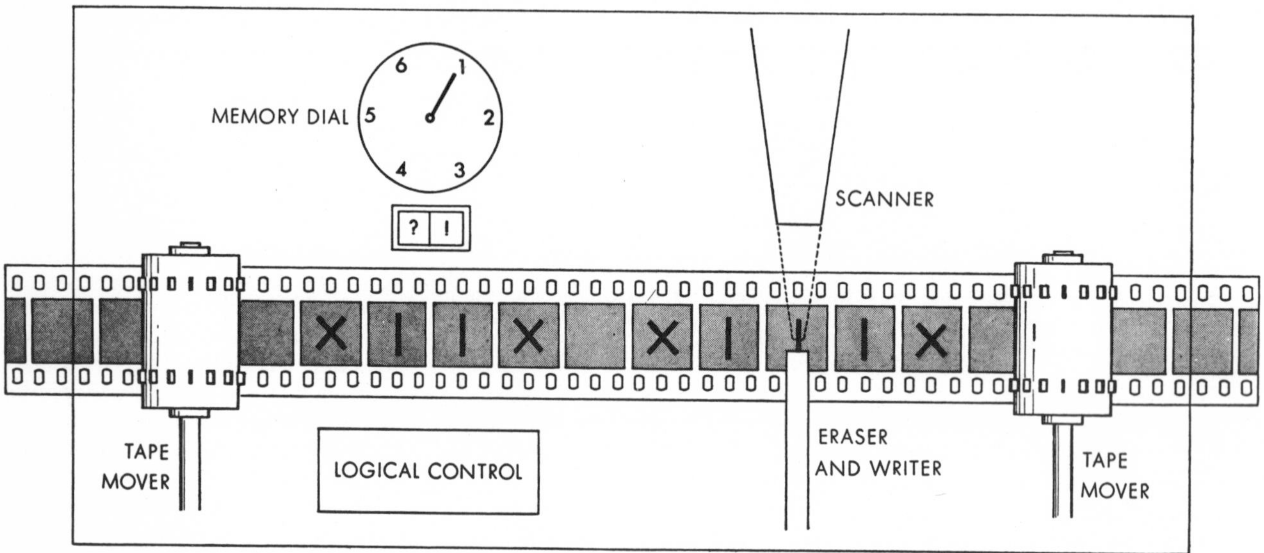

TURING MACHINE designed for simple addition is confronted with the numbers 2 and 3. The numbers are indicated on the tape; each digit is represented by a 1. X is a signal that a number is about to begin or has just ended. The logical control of the machine is depicted in the table on the opposite page. The horizontal rows of the table represent the position of the memory dial (*1, 2, 3, 4, 5 or 6*). The vertical columns represent the symbol on the tape (*blank, X or 1*). The symbols at the intersection of the rows and columns are commands to the machine. E means erase the symbol on the tape; X, write an X on the tape; D, write the digit 1 on the tape; R, move the tape one frame to the right; L, move the tape one frame to the left; S, stop; ?, something is wrong; !, the operation is completed; 1, 2, 3, 4, 5 or 6, turn the memory dial to that position. Thus at the upper left in the table the memory dial is in position 1 and the tape is blank; the command is D6, or write the digit 1 on the tape and turn the memory dial to position 6. Then in the beginning position shown above the machine begins to operate as follows. In the first step the memory dial is in position 1 and the tape shows a 1. The command is R1: move the tape one frame to the right and leave the memory dial in position 1. In the second

It is amazing to see how few parts such a machine needs to have. Von Neumann's blueprints call for a basic box of 80 by 400 squares, plus a tail 150,000 squares long. The basic box has the three kinds of parts described—neurons, transmission cells and muscle cells. The three types of cells differ only as to their state of excitation and the way in which they are connected. The tail is even simpler: it has cells, which are either "on" or "off," holding a code. So we have about 200,000 cells, most of which are of the simplest possible kind, and of which only a negligible fraction is even as complex as the logical control neuron. No matter how we measure complexity, this is vastly simpler than a human being, and yet the machine is self-reproducing.

The Genetic Tail

Pressing the analogy between the machine and the human organism, we might compare the tail to the set of chromosomes. Our machine always copies its tail for the new machine, just as each daughter cell in the body copies the chromosomes of its parent. It is most significant that while the chromosomes take up a minute part of the body, the tail is larger than the entire basic box in the machine. This indicates that the coding of traits by chromosomes is amazingly efficient and compact. But in all fairness we must point out that the chromosomes serve a lesser role than the tail. The tail contains a complete description of the basic box, while the chromosome description is incomplete: the offspring only resembles the parent; it is not an exact duplicate. It would be most interesting to try to continue von Neumann's pioneer work by designing a machine that could take an incomplete description and build a reasonable likeness of itself.

Could such machines go through an evolutionary process? One might design the tails in such a way that in every cycle a small number of random changes occurred (*e.g.*, changing an "on" to an "off" in the code or *vice versa*). These would be like mutations; if the machine could still produce offspring, it would pass the changes on. One could further arrange to limit the supply of raw material, so that the machines would have to compete for *Lebensraum*, even to the extent of killing one another.

Of course none of the machines described in this article has actually been built, so far as I know, but they are all buildable. We have considered systematically what man can do, and how much of this a machine can duplicate. We have found that the brain's superiority rests on the greater complexity of the human nervous system and on the greater efficiency of the human memory. But is this an essential difference, or is it only a matter of degree that can be overcome with the progress of technology? This article attempted to show that there is no conclusive evidence for an essential gap between man and a machine. For every human activity we can conceive of a mechanical counterpart.

Naturally we still have not answered the question whether man is more than a machine. The reader will have to answer that question for himself.

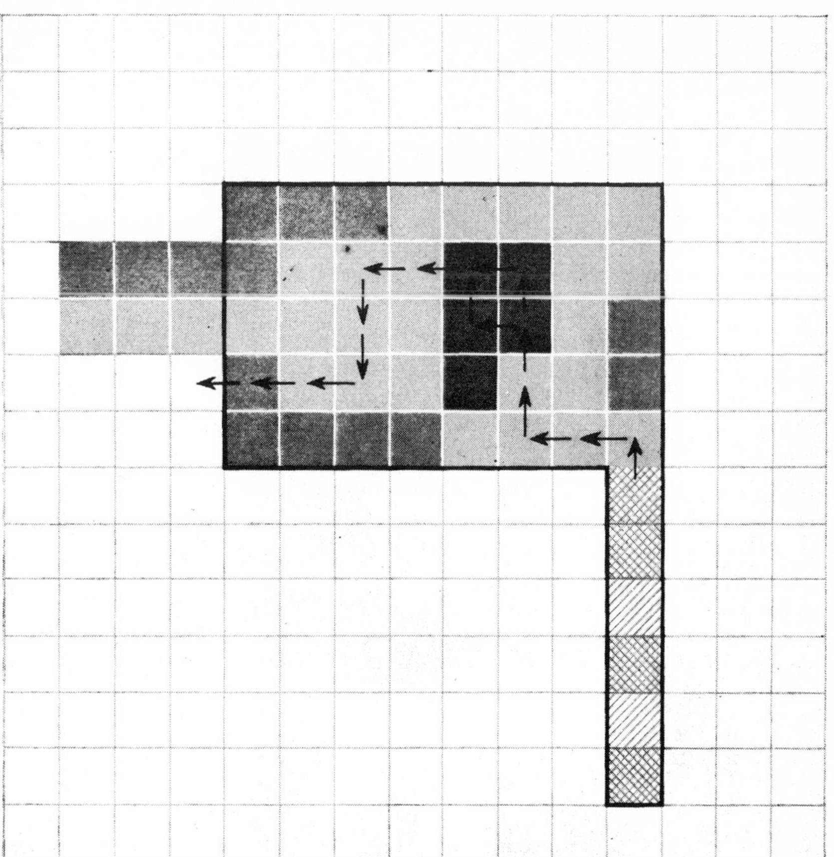

VON NEUMANN MACHINE is theoretically capable of reproducing itself. This is a highly simplified diagram of its conceptual units. The darkest squares are the "nerve cells" of the "brain." The next lightest squares are "muscle cells." The next lightest are transmission cells. The crosshatched squares are the "tail" which bears the instructions of the machine. The double hatching represents an "on" signal; the single hatching, an "off" signal. The empty squares are units of the environment which the machine manipulates. The arrows indicate that instructions are coming from the tail, on the basis of which the brain instructs a muscle cell to act on its surroundings. The machine has sent out a "feeler" to the left.

	☐	X	I
1	D6	E2	R1
2	R2	E3	?2
3	R3	E4	E5
4	L4	?4	R6
5	L5	?5	R1
6	X6	!6	R3

step the situation and the response are the same. In the third step the memory dial is in position 1 and the tape shows an X. The command is E2: erase the X and turn the memory dial to position 2. In this way the machine comes up with the answer 5 on its memory dial in 36 steps. On the 37th step the machine stops and signals with a ! that it is finished. If the reader is skeptical and hardy, he is invited to trace the whole process!

17

SELF-REPRODUCING MACHINES

L. S. PENROSE • June 1959

The mass production of multiple copies of the same object by printing or by assembly of prefabricated parts is an event so commonplace that examples can immediately be called to mind. The reader has one such example at hand in the copy of the book in which he reads these words. The idea of an object reproducing itself, however, is so closely associated with the fundamental processes of biology that it carries with it a suggestion of magic. Indeed, the construction of a machine capable of building itself might be judged to be impossible and to belong to the category of perpetual-motion engines. At the present time, however, advances in genetics are rapidly leading biologists to focus their attention upon the structure and function of self-reproducing molecular chains which, in the nuclei of living cells, preside over all their functional activities. The structure of these chains of nucleic acid is already quite well understood. But the general theory of self-reproduction, in which the replication of nucleic acid would represent a special case, has not been much investigated.

The theory has two aspects, which can be called the logical and the mechanical. The logical part was first investigated by the late John von Neumann of the Institute for Advanced Study in Princeton, N. J. He decided in 1951 that it must be possible to build an engine that would have the property of self-reproduction. The method would be to construct a machine that is capable of building any describable machine. It would follow logically that such a machine would be able to build another machine just like itself. Each machine would carry a sort of tail bearing a code describing how to make the body of the machine and also how to reprint the code. According to von Neumann's associate John G. Kemeny, the body of the machine would be a box containing a minimum of 32,000 constituent parts and the "tail" would comprise 150,000 units of information. On the mechanical side the elementary parts, out of which this object was to be built, were considered to be likely to include rolls of tape, pencils, erasers, vacuum tubes, dials, photoelectric cells, motors, batteries and other devices. The machine would assemble these parts from raw material in its environment, organize them and transform them into a new replica of itself [see "Man Viewed as a Machine," by John G. Kemeny, beginning on page 112 in this volume]. Since the aim of von Neumann's reflections was to resolve the logical conditions of the problem, the stupendous mechanical complexity of the machine was of no consequence.

The mechanical problems involved in constructing such a machine have been investigated by Homer Jacobson of Brooklyn College in New York. In one experiment he built an electrically powered railroad track around which two kinds of trucks, respectively called "head" and "tail," could circulate. Initially these trucks were arranged in a random order. If a head and a tail were first assembled upon a siding, however, they would signal to another head and another tail to connect up on an adjacent siding. So long as there were trucks and sidings available this process could continue, and the head-tail machines would be assembled automatically. The design of the trucks and of the railroad itself involved considerable complexity and a great many different elements such as wires, tubes, batteries, switches, wheels, photoelectric cells and resistances. This intricate apparatus generated only one kind of building operation, but the operation was indeed a kind of self-replication.

SELF-REPRODUCING DESIGN is identical with its own photographic negative, except for checkerboard border surrounding it.

Together with Roger Penrose I have approached the problem in a more radical manner, without the encumbrance of prefabricated units such as wheels and photoelectric cells. Our idea was to design and, if possible, to construct simple units or bricks with such properties that a self-reproducing machine could be built out of them. One everyday example of mechanical self-replication involving simple units is the "zipper" fastener. Here the self-replicating unit is the pair of interlocked hooks; the zipper-slide provides the energy to push each pair of hooks together. As soon as one pair is connected, a whole chain made up of similarly connected pairs can be formed. The example is defective in that only one type of connection is formed in the zipper, and the units are not completely separate before the action takes place. Another simple instance of self-replication is offered by a suitably designed mold, template or photograph. Ordinarily such replication calls first for a negative from which a positive like the original can be recovered. A negative can, however, be combined with the positive in such a way that, by replicating both at the same time, the two steps are reduced to one. Thus in the illustration on the preceding page we have a design whose negative will be identical with the original because of its peculiar symmetry. This suggests that it is convenient, and perhaps necessary, for a self-replicating object to carry its own template or negative.

In the design of the units or bricks for our self-replicating machine we laid down certain arbitrary standards. The units, we decided, must be as simple as possible. They must be of as few different kinds as possible. And they must be capable of forming at least two (preferably an unlimited number) of distinct self-reproducing structures. Finally we decided that the energy necessary to engage these units in the process of self-replication should be supplied in the simplest manner, by merely shaking the units in a confined space but otherwise allowing them as much freedom of movement as possible.

One essential condition was to be that the units would not form self-reproducing machines just because they were moved about. They were to reproduce themselves only when the object to be replicated was introduced as a pattern for copying. The logic of this condition is to be found in William Harvey's maxim: *Omne vivum ex ovo* (in modern form: No life except from life). By definition, self-reproduction requires a "self" to be reproduced.

In fanciful terms, we visualized the process of mechanical self-replication proceeding somewhat as follows: Suppose we have a sack or some other container full of units jostling one another as the sack is shaken and distorted in all manner of ways. In spite of this, the units remain detached from one another. Then we put into the sack a prearranged connected structure made from units exactly similar to those already within the sack. Such a structure might arise, of course, by chance in response to random shaking, but this would be very unlikely indeed, as is the case with the analogous process of mutation in genetics. Now we agitate the sack again in the same random and vigorous manner, with the seed structure jostling about among the neutral units. This time we find that replicas of the seed structure have been assembled from the formerly neutral or "lifeless" material. It follows that each replica is capable of self-reproduction like the original seed, and that reproduction will continue until all the "food" is used up.

The building of actual models in our investigation began with a much simpler experiment in mind. In the inorganic world the most obvious analogy to self-reproduction in living matter is the growth of a crystal. The construction of an artificial crystal that would repeat some prearranged pattern indefinitely seemed to offer a useful starting point. The first machine built on these lines proved most illuminating. It consisted of two pieces of plywood cut to a special shape, each about four inches long and a quarter-inch thick, standing end to end on the inner surface of the long side of a shallow rectangular box resting on its side [*see illustration labeled "a" on these two pages*]. The box can be subjected to side-to-side agitation of a vigorous and irregular character, causing the pieces of plywood to move in one dimension from side to side, each colliding with its nearest neighbors. In the "neutral" position in which the pieces of plywood appear, however, they do not link under the influence of shaking alone. But if a "seed" consisting of two linked pieces is added, this seed will link up with adjacent pieces standing on either side of it on the track. Eventually all the available neutral pieces will become attached to the "crystal." If the seed is inclined in the opposite direction, a complementary aggregate is built.

Certain principles become evident from the study of this machine. Here copying consists in imparting the same tilt to each unit. The seed carries, as it were, a positive pattern at one end and a complementary negative pattern at the other. These patterns influence the neutral units as they come into close contact with the seed, causing them to tilt in the positive or negative manner. Once tilted or "activated," the units are caught and locked to the growing crystal by the complementary notches cut into the profiles of the plywood pieces. These notches enable energy to be trapped and thus convert the energy of motion conveyed by agitation into the potential energy

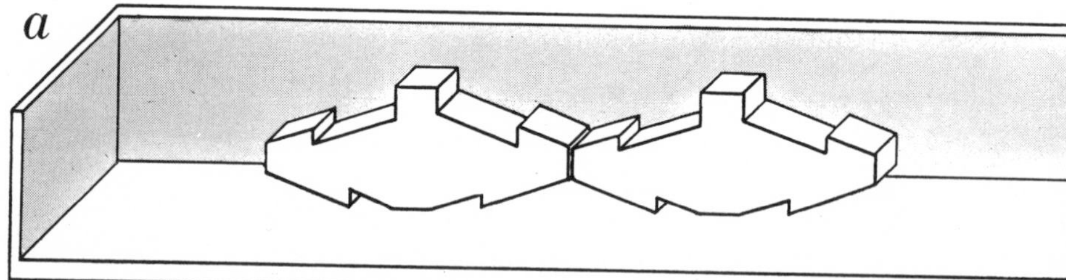

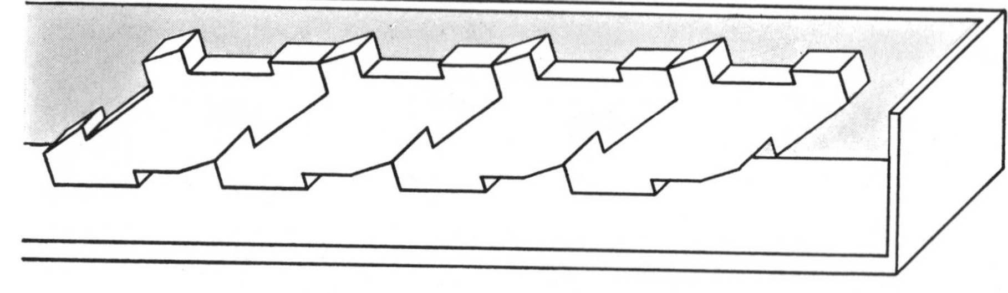

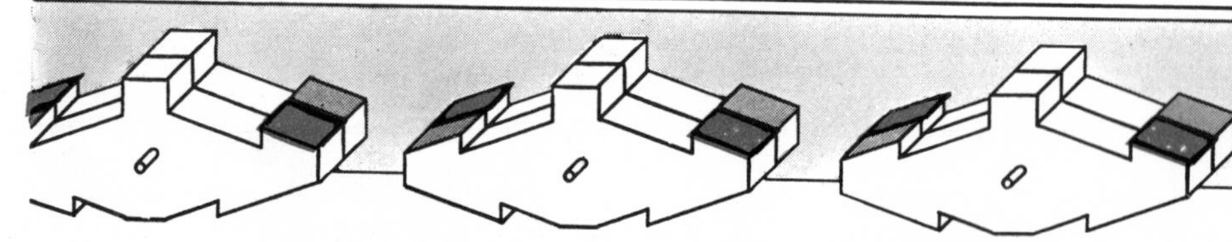

MECHANICAL "CRYSTAL" demonstrates some of the underlying principles of self-reproducing machines. At upper left in *a* appear two identical units at the "neutral" position in which they are unable to link up with one another. Introduction of two linked units

that binds the structure. Energy traps are characteristic of living matter, although they occur also in artificial and natural structures. A pool that retains water after a tide has receded is typical. In chemistry the bonding of an endothermic compound is analogous to a latch. Unless our synthetic structures contained more potential energy than their constituent units separately, it would be difficult to prevent spontaneous aggregation.

The crystallizing or, we might say, the polymerizing machine can be greatly improved by making units out of two plywood elements tied together by an axle so that they can pivot in opposite directions [*see illustration labeled "b" on these two pages*]. As can be seen, there are four ways of arranging the seed, of which two are essentially the same and the other two are mirror images. Besides giving rise to more types of seed in the case where the two parts of each unit are tilted in opposite senses, the double units form much stronger structures than single units.

The problem of reproducing an object the same size as the seed has now to be solved. This is done with surprising facility. It is only necessary to alter the basic units by removing one pair of notches from each of them. In effect the crystal is broken up into discrete bodies, each made of two units [*see top illustration on next page*]. Two stable mirror-image seeds can be constructed, and either may be used as a starter. In a long box or track, populated with neutral units randomly arranged, the presence of a seed causes other structures of its own kind to be built wherever two neutral units are in the appropriate relative positions.

This design provides a simple and convincing demonstration of artificial self-reproduction. Either type of seed may be introduced into the track; since they and their offspring are easily distinguished, it can be seen that each breeds true to type.

A point that emerges here, when the process is critically examined, is that during agitation some units transmit the tilted pattern of the seed although they do not find a partner to link with. These temporarily activated units tend to slide away from one another and from the completed structures, thereby tending to push some of the completed structures apart when agitation has subsided. It is convenient in self-reproduction to arrange that the fresh complexes should repel one another once they have been formed. If they separate widely, they can pick up "food" from different places and they do not interfere with one another's subsequent reproduction. In a restricted one-dimensional track this point is irrelevant. But it becomes significant in the next phase of the discussion, when we consider how we might lift the one-dimensional restriction of the track and make it possible for our self-replicating

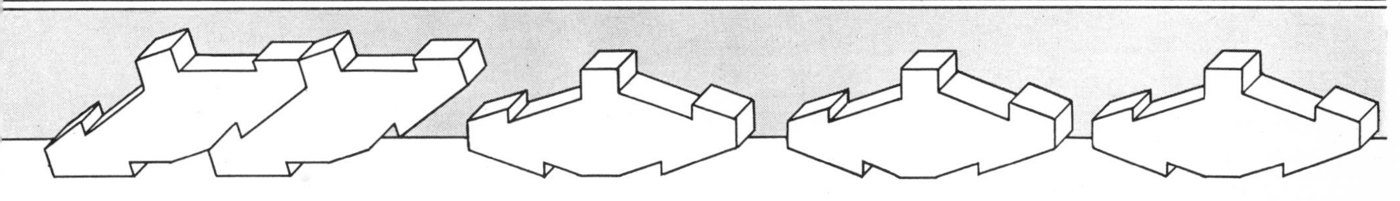

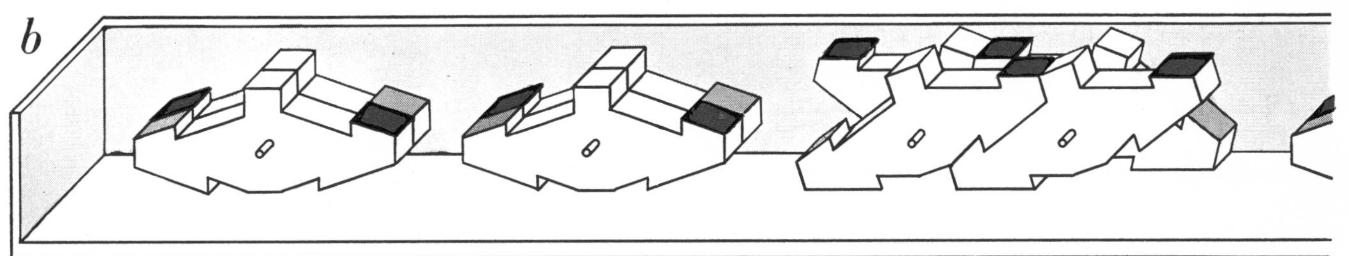

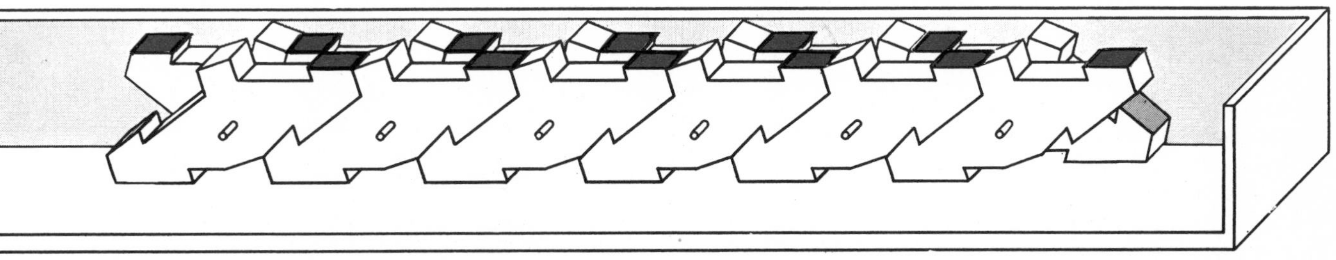

as a "seed" in panel at upper right imparts tilt and makes it possible for entire group of units to link up and form a single structure when subjected to agitation in the horizontal plane. In *b* two doubled units are shown, first in neutral position and then linked up to form a seed. When this seed is agitated with neutral units at lower left, all join to form the crystal structure at lower right.

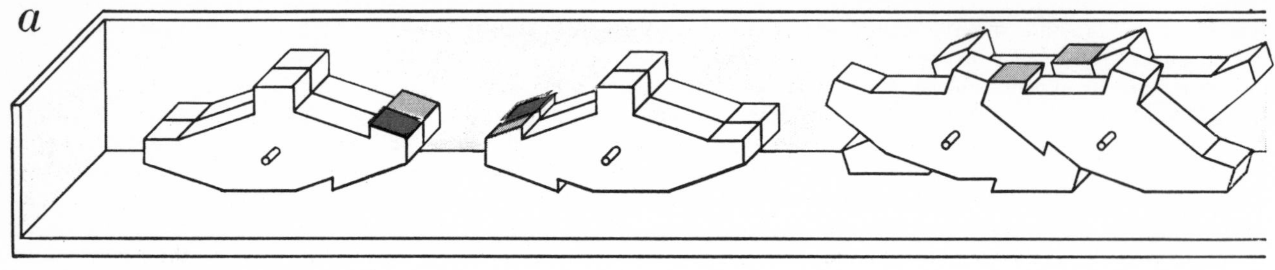

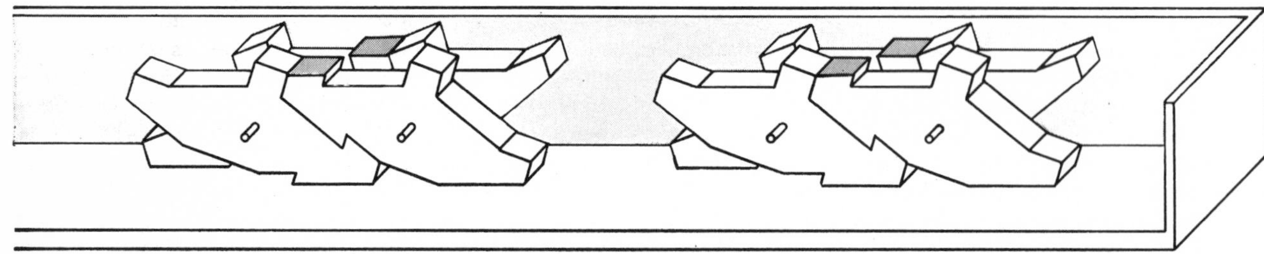

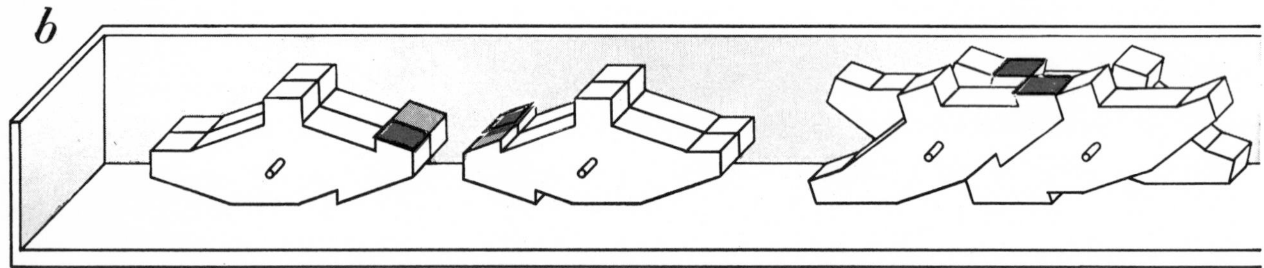

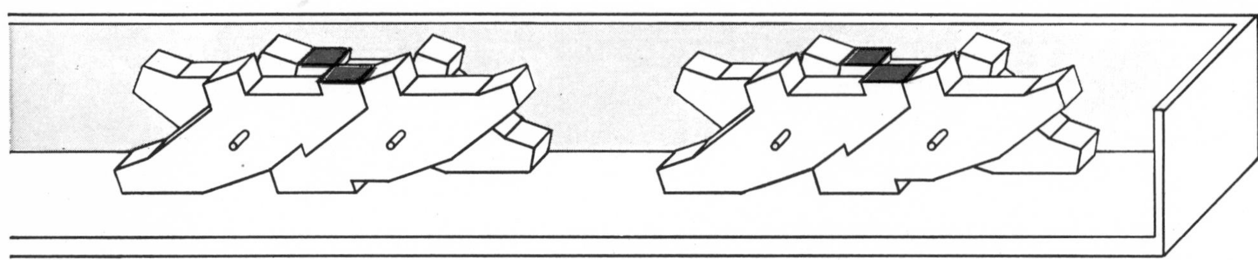

SELF-REPRODUCTION is here demonstrated by units of a simple kind, identical with those that form the "crystal" on the preceding two pages except that the units each lack hooks at one end. In *a* the seed is formed with the gray telltale mark showing at the linkage; in *b* the seed unit is formed with the colored telltale mark showing. When the seed of each kind is agitated in the horizontal plane with neutral units, the appropriate tilt is imparted to the neutral units and they link up to reproduce the structure of their seed.

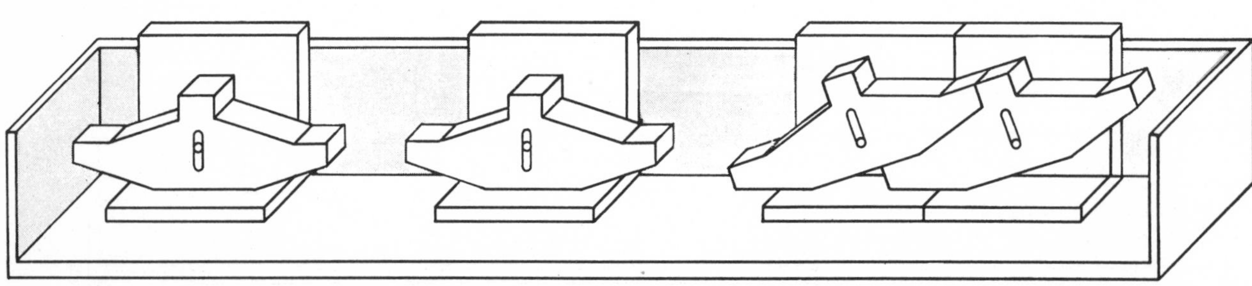

ACTIVATING CAM-LEVER incorporates the simple tilting principle of the self-reproducing machines shown above for use with more complex structures shown on page 127. These cams, held in tilted position by dowel in slot, transmit activation but do not link.

structures to move about freely in two dimensions.

In order to fit the units for self-reproduction into the larger world of two dimensions, it is necessary to complicate their design beyond the rudimentary shapes that have worked thus far. With units moving over a plane surface, without the support of the back wall of the one-dimensional track, a firm base for each must be provided. A simple solution is to mount the plywood element on a horizontal pivot fixed to an upright, which is in turn attached to the base of the unit. The element capable of tilting and transmitting its tilt then becomes a sliding cam-lever. To allow greater variety of interaction between units, the hooking mechanism can now be separated and made independent of the tilting process by transferring it to a different part of the unit [*see bottom illustration on opposite page*].

In the two-dimensional situation the simpler design permitted an activated unit to slide away and lose contact with a "live" group after it had gone part of the way toward building a new replica. This is quite uneconomical from the energy standpoint. We must therefore arrange matters so that a unit may hook on to a two-unit live group temporarily and be released when a fourth unit becomes attached to the group. We are thus led to consider mechanisms for making and releasing links in special circumstances. One such latch depends for its release upon the presence of another unit in close contact. The effect of this, as shown in the illustration at right, is to maintain combinations already built out of new pieces. But this arrangement produces no fresh structures. It would give us a sort of steady state. In order to make a reproducing complex with this device, the system of linkage and release must be doubled as shown in the illustration on the next page. Here each unit contains two releasable hooks facing in opposite directions. Though they are shown one above the other, they would in practice be mounted side by side on the same axle. With such an arrangement of latches the addition of a third unit to a linked pair creates a triple complex that does not separate until a fourth unit is added. When this has taken place, the two similar pairs of units disengage and gently repel each other as their hooks settle down to their lowest possible states of energy.

It must be noted that this system of reproduction is incomplete because two pieces can link without any previous activation, that is, tilting caused by contact with a special seed. An activating element of some kind must be supplied so that neutral units cannot form links except in the presence of a live group that carries the activating principle. For this purpose the sliding cam-lever can be used to preserve a tilt and transmit it to neutral units; only those units that have been thus activated can approach each other close enough to link.

An interesting feature of this system is that it can replicate in two ways. If a live structure made of two units receives two neutral food units, both of them from either its left or right side, it will link them to itself and then release them linked to each other. On the other hand, if the original structure receives two food units, one on either side, it will link them to itself and then come apart in the middle [*see bottom illustration on page 127*]. As in the case of a single-celled organism, the original unit is destroyed in the process of replication. By the addition of special devices to the units it is possible to distinguish between these two kinds of replication; that is, one device will ensure that two units of food will always be taken in on one side, and another device will ensure that the two neutral units are added one on each side. If there is no scarcity of food, it is likely that neutral units will be simultaneously available on both sides. For efficient reproduction, therefore, the second type of replication, that is, addition on either side and division of the seed, should be adopted as the standard.

Another useful adjunct is a counting device. This can take the form shown in the top illustration on page 127. Such an element, which prevents more than four units from coming into close contact with one another, can be attached to each unit. The counter exerts its effect in that phase of reproduction, just before division, when the complex must cease accepting food. Before reproduction can be resumed the accretion of neutral units must stop long enough to enable the enlarged complex to come apart. The self-reproducing machine may also be equipped to make a kind of protective covering for itself out of "skin" units available in the environment. The skin would have to be thrown off in order to repeat self-replication.

The self-reproducing machine now requires one more adjunct to fit it for activity in two-dimensional space. To bring units into proper alignment for interlocking when random motion causes them to collide, their bases must be pro-

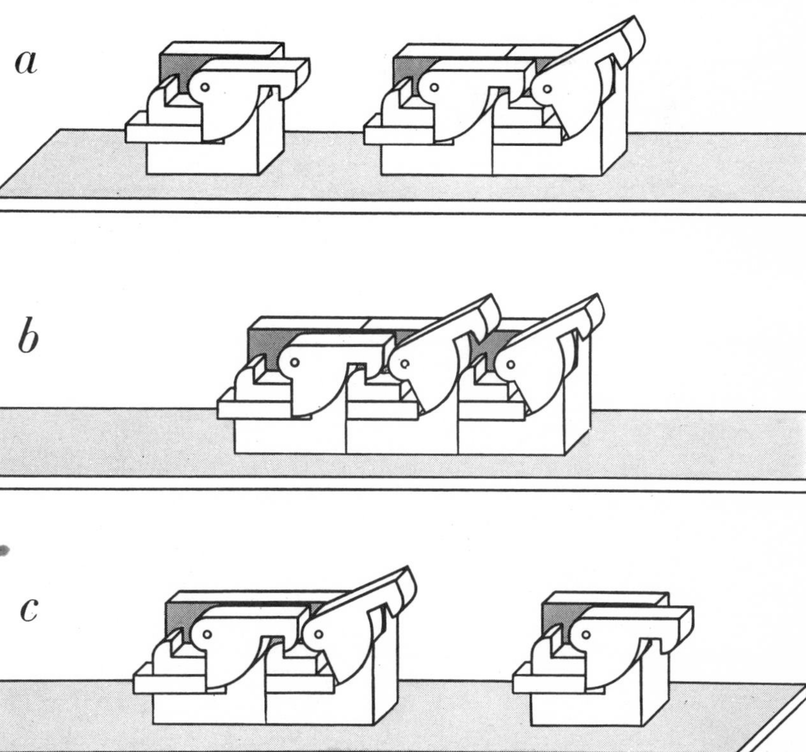

STEADY-STATE SYSTEM of hook and release is demonstrated here. When two units abut one another (*a*), one hooks onto the other, but the one that is hooked is itself set in release position. The addition from the left of a third unit (*b*) causes the first two to unhook (*c*).

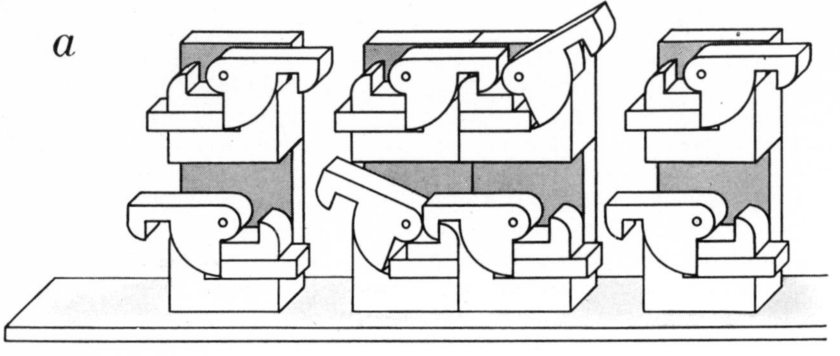

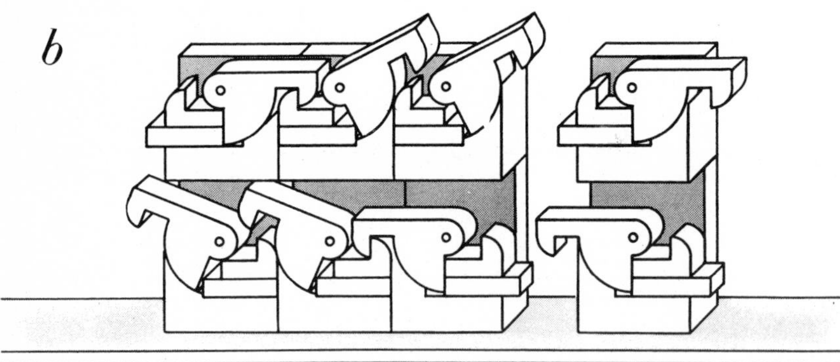

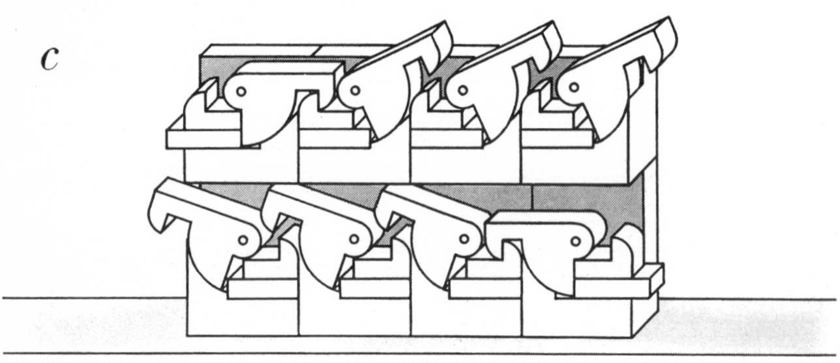

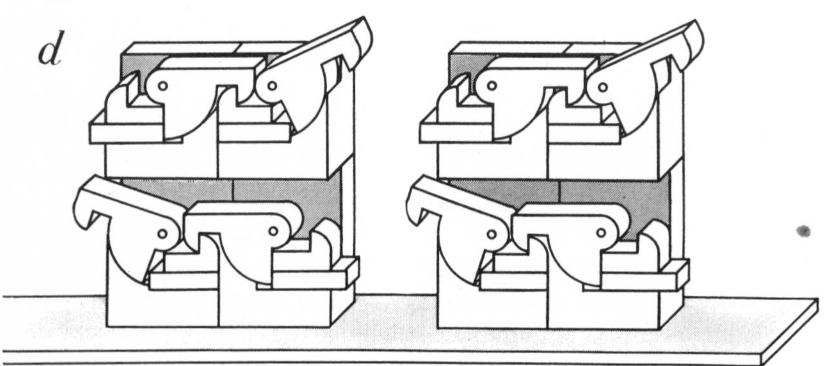

DOUBLE-HOOK UNITS, in contrast to steady-state system, possess capacity for self-reproduction. Cycle begins with linked group and two neutral units (*a*). Addition of neutral unit at left (*b*) causes one of two hooks in linked group to release. Addition of fourth unit (*c*) causes second hook in linked group to release. Linked group parts (*d*) in two replicas.

vided with interdigitating guides. The guides can also serve passively as hooks [*see top illustration on page 128*]. Some of the guides ensure correct apposition of hooks or activating levers and others cause the firm attachment of rows of pieces. With this additional device our units are endowed with a sufficient number of mechanical principles to enable self-reproducing machines of any desired degree of complexity to be built from them. Yet the units are of fairly simple construction and are either all of one kind or of a few different kinds.

The replication scheme of one such machine, made out of a set of units of two kinds, is shown in the bottom illustration on page 128. To ensure that replication proceeds regularly and that attempts at interconnection do not end in a tangle of hooks and guides, an ordering mechanism is included; an asterisk in the diagram indicates positions where the ordering mechanism permits new units to be added. The units each have two levers of the kind which can be activated positively or negatively, that is, tilted up or down; thus four types of activated units or rows of units are possible. The chain of units acting as a seed may be built in any predetermined number of rows and each row can be set with any one of four types of activation. When a fresh unit is added on either side of the double chain, no additional units of the same kind can attach themselves in that row. A different type of unit now forms a nonreplicating protective "skin" chain in response to the activating pattern of the complex. When all the open positions are filled with appropriate units, the self-replicating machine splits in two, sheds its skin, and the process may begin again.

The design of units suitable for forming the protective chains presented peculiar difficulties; in overcoming these I came upon a new method of controlling and sequencing the latching and unlatching which provides an elegant solution of the von Neumann problem. A single string of determinate length, made up of units of a slightly different design, can replicate itself in the manner shown in the illustration on page 129. The addition of each new unit to the daughter chain has the effect of releasing the one behind it from the original chain. The final unit to join the new chain does not attach itself to the old chain at all, although it releases the new one from the old.

Here it should be emphasized that

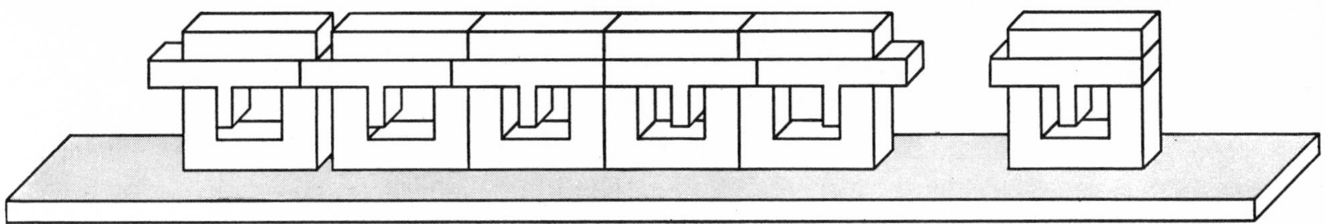

BLOCKING DEVICE prevents more than four units from coming close together. When four units are in close contact, the sliding bar protrudes at either end of the group, keeping other units away. Device keeps groups from growing too large before they divide.

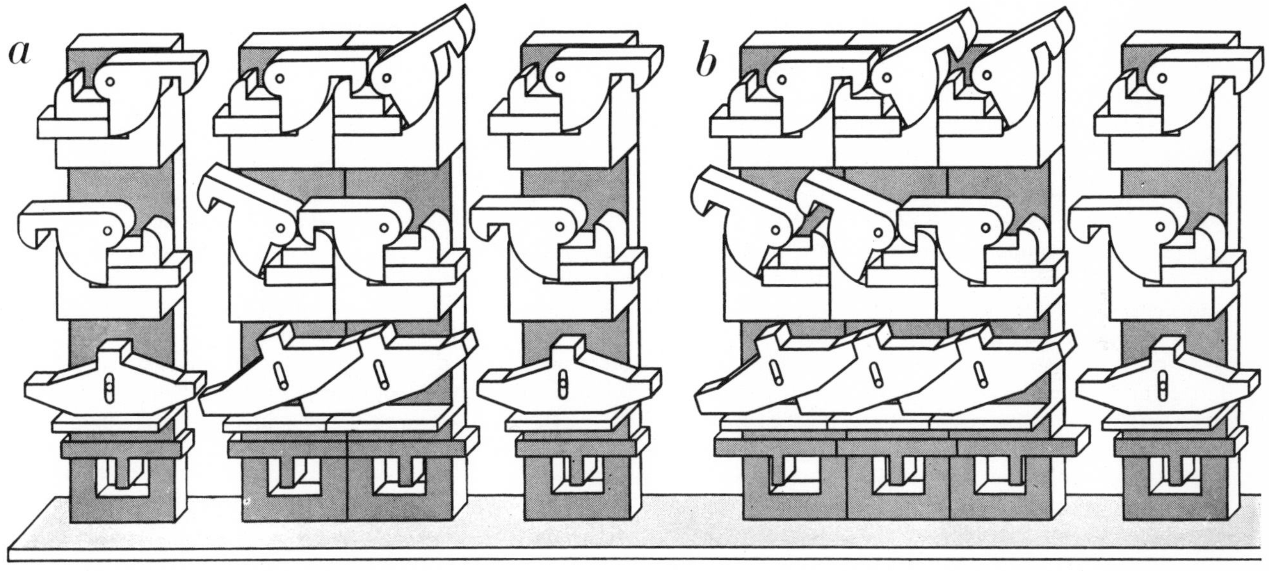

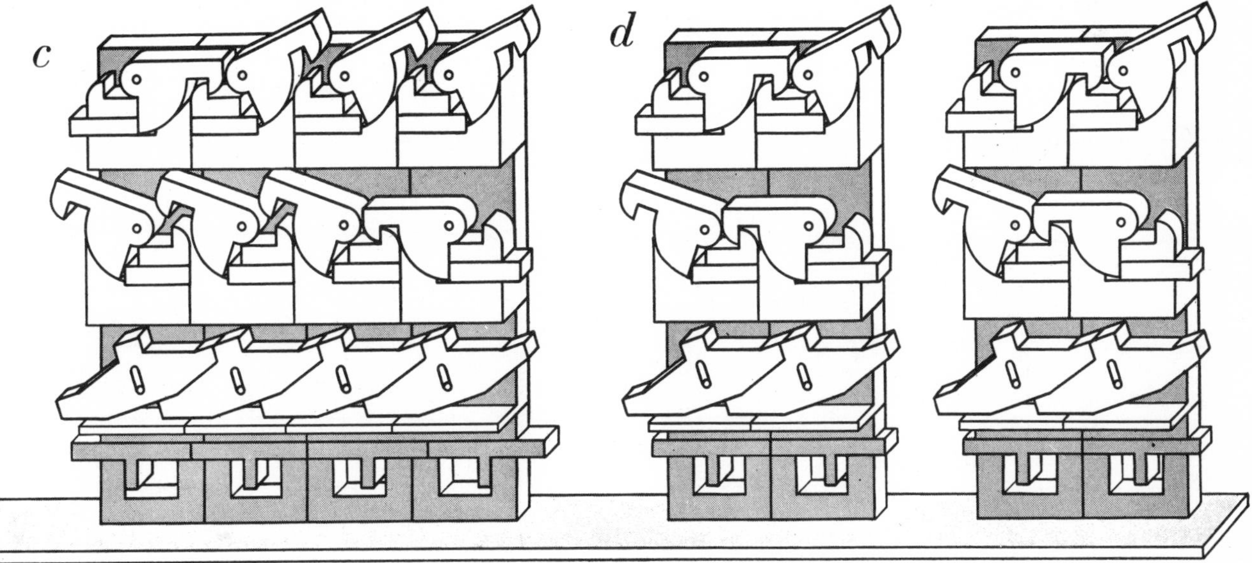

COMPLETE SELF-REPRODUCING MACHINE incorporates the basic elements and principles depicted in the preceding illustrations. The seed (at center in *a*) is linked by double hooks, incorporates the tilted cam-lever activating principle and is protected by the blocking device in its base. When the neutral unit at left joins the seed (*b*), it disengages one of the hooks holding the seed together and sets the blocking mechanism so that only one more neutral unit can be added. When the fourth unit joins the triple group (*c*), it disengages the second hook in the original seed, causing it to come apart in the middle and form two replicas of itself (*d*).

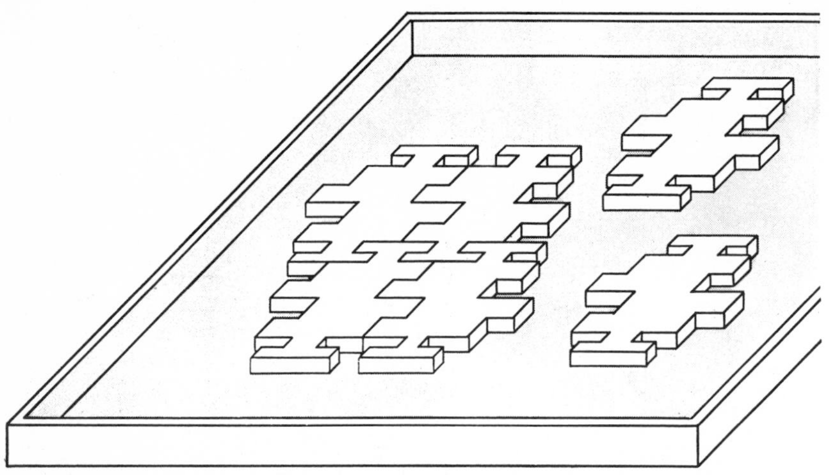

INTERDIGITATING BASES, on which superstructures capable of activation, hooking and release can be mounted, are designed to permit self-reproducing machines to operate in two dimensions and to orient themselves to one another for the purposes of self-reproduction.

each activated unit contains a message, that is, information that it transmits to neutral units. The total quantity of information depends upon the number of tilted levers and sometimes upon other features. The nucleus of a living cell also contains information that enables it to collect and build the substances necessary for its own replication. Natural selection encourages the reproduction of nuclei that have the most efficient information for dealing with their surroundings. In artificial self-reproduction, equivalent programs of information would equip the machine not only to assemble themselves, but to build up their own structures out of their environment, to release energy sources and, in a sense, to provide their own track or table to guide interactions. Such an elaborate scheme is so far unattainable in practice. We have to be content with making a very parasitic organism. It is not, however, much more helpless than a virus. With such an object we can even provide a mechanical demonstration of the role of information in natural selection. To two machines, distinguished by key arrangements of their tilting cam-levers, we present neutral units locked up in a kind of matrix. These food units can be unlocked and brought into circulation by certain arrangements of tilting and not by others. Thus one mechanical creature will be able to unlock a plentiful supply of food while the other will starve and be shown to be relatively unfit in the struggle for self-replication.

Another feature of living things can be incorporated in the self-replicating machine. This is the capacity to change the program of information it transmits to its daughters. Of course change might be introduced by mistakes in reproduction even with well-constructed machines, but this, like genetic mutation in living things, is likely to be unfavorable and must be avoided by an efficient designer. Living organisms, however, exchange parts of their programs in a process known as recombination. In a very elementary form, something like this can be imitated mechanically. Now

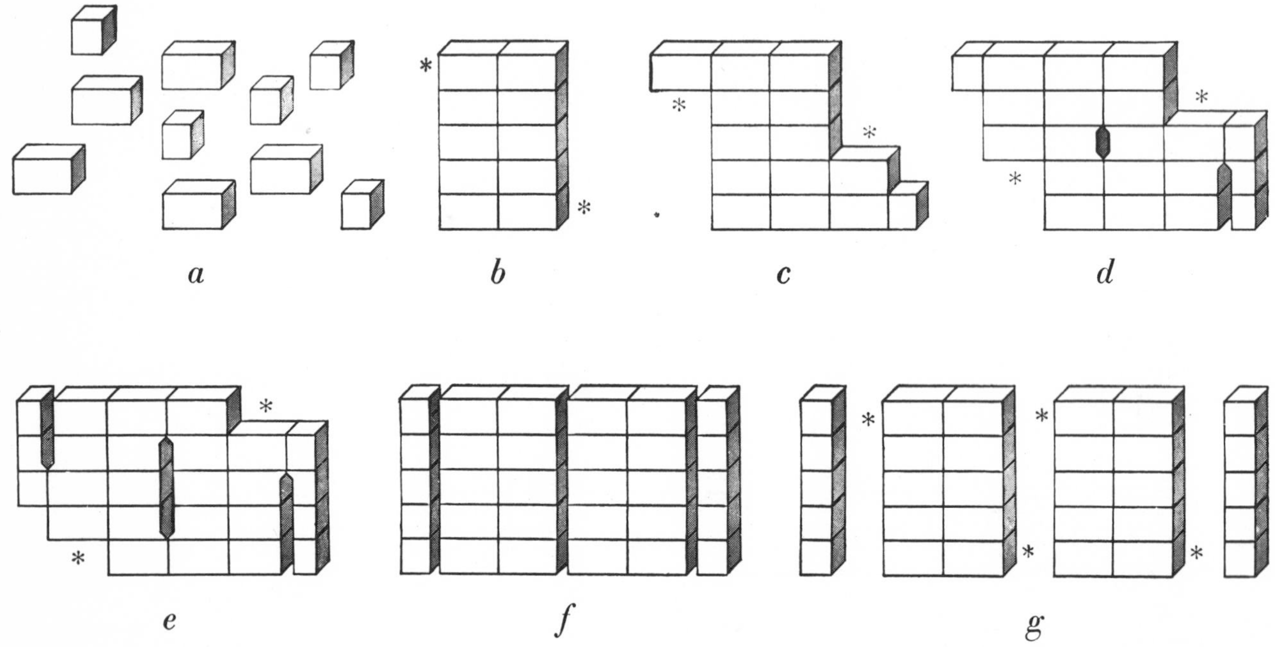

GENERALIZED SYSTEM of self-reproduction is based on units of two kinds (*a*). The larger "body" units (*b*) form a live group; the asterisks indicate activated points at which units of the same kind can be added. The group begins to grow (*c*), with a smaller "skin" unit attaching itself at lower right. When units are attached at corresponding points on both sides (*d*), the body units come apart and the skin units also begin to peel off (*e*). With growth completed, the original group splits, yielding two replicas of itself (*f*). As the skin units come loose (*g*) the two daughter groups become activated and are ready to begin the reproduction cycle again.

if two machines carrying different programs should stand for a moment side by side, new units, approaching in one particular direction, might pick up their program half from one and half from the other. Thus if the program of one parental complex is described as AA and the other as BB, the new complex generated in these circumstances would have the program AB. This is easy to accomplish with a machine consisting of a single pair of units, but for a chain it presents many mechanical difficulties. These complexes would, in the ordinary way, breed true; only on rare occasions would the pieces come into apposition in the manner that is necessary to produce recombination.

It has been said that the fundamental mechanisms of the biological machine may perhaps be elucidated with the aid of theoretical models. The machines discussed here, however, are not models in this sense. They are machines in their own right, conceived for the specific purpose of self-reproduction. In some ways they may resemble living organisms and, insofar as this is so, they may help to explain how some primitive forms of life originated, maintained themselves and eventually developed into more complex and more stable structures.

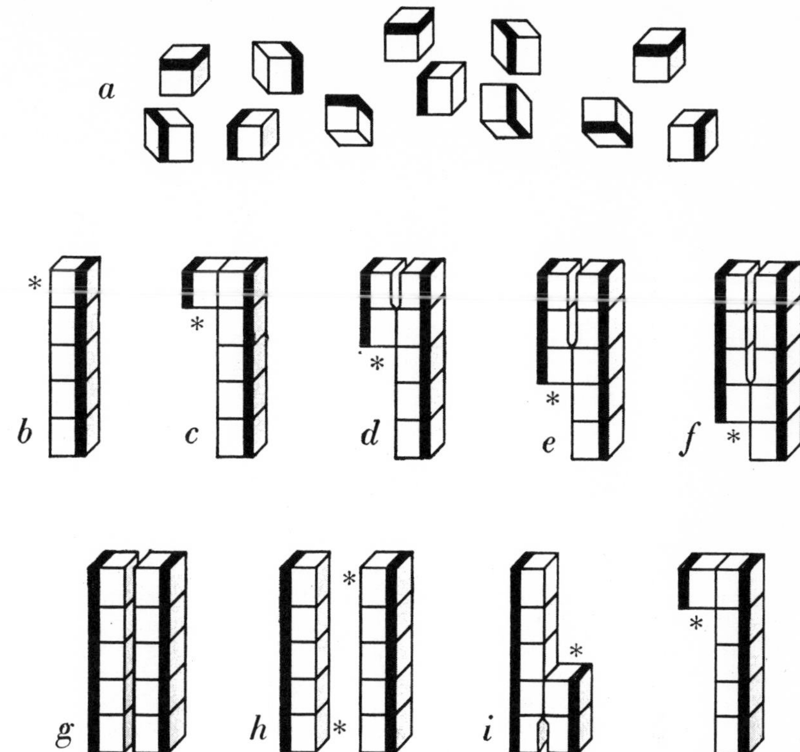

MORE ELEGANT DESIGN for a self-reproducing system is depicted. Identical units (*a*) form a live five-unit group (*b*), activated for growth at the point indicated by asterisk. As growth proceeds (*c*, *d* and *e*) each new unit causes the preceding unit in the new column to become detached from the old. Addition of the last unit (*f*) causes the two groups to come apart (*g*). The activated daughter groups (*h*) now reproduce from neutral units (*i*).

Self-reproductive chains of mechanical units may help to explain the way in which nucleic acids in living cells actually replicate. But they are more likely to assist in the understanding of systems of simpler character, like those that must have preceded the nucleic acids in the evolution of life. These structures may have occurred in molecules composed of polysaccharides, amino acids or phosphates. At least we need not suppose that they were anything like as complex as the nucleic acids. Such organic counterparts of the self-replicating machine are not, perhaps, accessible to our observation today in nature. Charles Darwin suggested in 1871 that the spontaneous appearance of very elementary forms of life might still be occurring. But he also pointed out that if a protein compound ready to undergo complex changes were spontaneously produced in the present day, it "would be instantly devoured or absorbed, which would not have been the case before living creatures were formed."

18

A MACHINE THAT LEARNS

W. GREY WALTER • August 1951

THIS ARTICLE is a sequel to one I published previously that described experiments with a simple little machine designed to mimic certain elementary features of animal behavior ("An Imitation of Life," SCIENTIFIC AMERICAN, May, 1950). Consisting only of two vacuum tubes, two motors, a photoelectric cell and a touch contact, all enclosed in a tortoise-shaped shell, the model was a species of artificial creature which could explore its surroundings and seek out favorable conditions. It was named *Machina speculatrix.* Although it possessed just three simple characteristics—the properties of being attracted to moderate light and repelled by bright light or by material obstacles—*M. speculatrix* displayed complex and unpredictable habits of behavior, resembling in some ways the random variability, or "free will," of an animal's responses to stimuli. But its responses were in no way modified by experience; in other words, it lacked the power to learn.

We have gone on from that early model to the design of a more advanced mechanical creature which does possess the ability to learn. The present report will describe this new creature, named *M. docilis* from the Latin word meaning teachable.

The mechanism of learning is of course one of the most enthralling and baffling mysteries in the field of biology. In its simplest experimental form modification of behavior by experience is often called "conditioning," a term suggested by the Russian physiologist I. P. Pavlov, whose original experiments on "conditioned reflexes" brought the study of higher nervous function into the realm of brain physiology. The basic event in this form of learning is that an unrelated stimulus, when repeatedly coupled with one that evokes a certain response, comes to acquire the meaning of the original stimulus. In the classical experiments on animals the activity used as the basis for conditioning was a simple reflex—the flow of saliva when food enters the mouth, or the withdrawal of a leg when a painful stimulus is given to the foot. The food or the pain is called the unconditioned, or specific, stimulus. The conditioned, or neutral, stimulus to which the animal is trained to respond with the same behavior can be any event to which the animal is sensitive: a light, a sound, a touch—anything at all. If, for example, a bell is rung on 10 or 20 occasions just as food is offered, the flow of saliva, which originally occurred only at the sight of the food, eventually is conditioned to begin as soon as the bell is rung. After about 20 more repetitions the bell alone, without the presence of food, evokes almost as copious a flow of saliva as does the food itself. One may say that the bell comes to "mean" food.

SUCH learning is of course perfectly familiar in ourselves and is the basis of all animal training. Indeed it has been argued that all learning is based on conditioning, for any bodily function can be made the basis of a conditioned reflex, and one conditioned reflex can be built on another. Even quite unconscious changes, such as quickening of the pulse, dilation of the pupils, a rise in blood sugar or a fall in temperature, can be "conditioned" to some previously neutral stimulus by mere repetition. In this way it is possible to obtain control over functions originally quite involuntary. A man can "learn" to slow his pulse, flush, go pale, secrete sugar in his urine and so forth by a process of simple conditioning. This process may be conscious and deliberate, and such training accounts for the feats of Yogi fakirs. It may also be unconscious and even undesired by the subject, sometimes producing "psychosomatic" disorders, in which symptoms of bodily disease are attributable to nervous strain or conflict.

In spite of the vast mass of empirical information collected by Pavlov and his pupils, we still do not understand the process whereby the neutral stimulus acquires the meaning of the original one. But it is clear that one of the principal requirements for this associative learning is a complex mechanism of memory, capable not only of storing the traces of the two series of events but also of providing the information that the coincidence between the two is greater than would be expected by chance. The creation of such a memory mechanism was the problem to which we addressed ourselves in designing *M. docilis.*

Our earlier model, *M. speculatrix,* had a very elementary form of memory. In order to get around an obstacle it encountered, the model had to remember it long enough to get well away from the hindrance before resuming its journey to the attracting light. Even among living creatures such a memory is not universal; the absence or brevity of this memory accounts for the tireless and ineffective buzzing of a fly on a windowpane. *M. speculatrix's* elementary memory works as follows: When the model touches an obstacle, the contact closes a circuit which converts its two-stage amplifier into an oscillator of the type known as a "multivibrator." The oscillations thus generated make the model stop, turn, withdraw, and go forward, and these maneuvers are repeated until the contact is opened by clearance of the obstacle. It is a characteristic of this simple circuit that while it is oscillating it cannot amplify, so the model is blind to the attracting light while circumventing a material difficulty. Furthermore, even after the touch contact is opened, one more oscillatory discharge takes place, and this ensures that the model moves well away from the obstacle before regaining its vision. The after-discharge in the oscillatory circuit is an example of the most elementary form of memory trace, in which the internal effect of a stimulus outlasts its external duration. Such an after-discharge is common in the reflex activity of the spinal cord of animals, and the more complex the reflex, the longer the after-discharge is likely to last. When you step on a tack, your leg is withdrawn by reflex action, but the withdrawal continues after your foot has left the tack, so that when you straighten your leg again it does not come down on the same place.

ON first analysis the problem of transforming *M. speculatrix* into an educable species seemed quite simple.

Its essentials are illustrated by the upper of the two diagrams at the lower left-hand side of the next page. In *M. speculatrix* we had a reflex mechanism with three elements: a specific stimulus Ss (a light or touch), which produced a specific effect Es (the operation of the motor relays) by way of a transmission system T_1 (the two-stage amplifier). To introduce the factor of conditioning, this mechanism must be linked with a second activated by a neutral stimulus which does not initially produce the effect Es. The second arrangement would consist of the neutral stimulus Sn and a transmission system T_2. (It might produce a specific effect of its own, Es_2, but with this we are not at the moment concerned.) T_1 must be linked with T_2 in such a way that the former comes to respond to the neutral stimulus with its normal effect Es, as if Sn were in fact Ss. This means that there must be a "learning box" of some kind between T_1 and T_2. The question is: What are we to put into the learning box (L)?

Obviously it must contain an apparatus which will receive signals from both T_1 and T_2 and combine them in such a manner that after Ss and Sn have occurred together more often than they would by chance, Sn can find its way through the learning box and have the effect Es. We experimented with some simple electronic circuits suggested by these requirements, but the first trials were disappointing. We soon realized that a more detailed analysis of the learning process would be necessary. It was clear that the statistical relation between Ss and Sn would have to be assessed before we could determine how to establish an association between them. That is, circuits must be provided to deal with any particular Ss and Sn in such a way that only a significant degree of coincidence between them would be registered. For example, an animal being trained to expect food when a bell is rung must first decide whether the ringing of the bell is really worth noticing. If bells are rung and food is offered entirely at random, there is no basis for supposing the two to be in any way related.

It took some time to appreciate the number and complexity of the operations involved in establishing a connection between different stimuli to achieve a conditioned response. Eventually it was found that no fewer than seven distinct operations must be performed. They are:

1. The beginning of the specific stimulus must be sharply differentiated from the absence of the stimulus. That is, it is the change that is important, *e.g.*, the transition from no food to food in the case of an animal, rather than the duration of the stimulus.

2. On the other hand, the impact of the neutral stimulus must be extended in time. This is because it may occur some while before the specific stimulus and must therefore be "remembered" long enough for its significance to be noticed.

3. The series of clipped Ss and stretched Sn must be mixed in such a way that their areas of coincidence are appreciated.

4. The coincident areas must all be summated, or integrated, to form a consolidated stimulus.

5. When the sum of all the areas of coincidence reaches a value greater than would ever be obtained by chance, the memory process is activated. This activation is in the nature of a trigger process—a single event, analogous to a flash of insight into a contingency previously ignored.

6. Once the existence of a significant degree of coincidence between Ss and Sn has been registered, it is preserved in the memory for some time and fades away gradually. In the *M. docilis* model the memory takes the form of a damped oscillation, but it could well be any mechanical, chemical or electrical process in which stored energy is slowly released, as in the escapement of a watch. It is

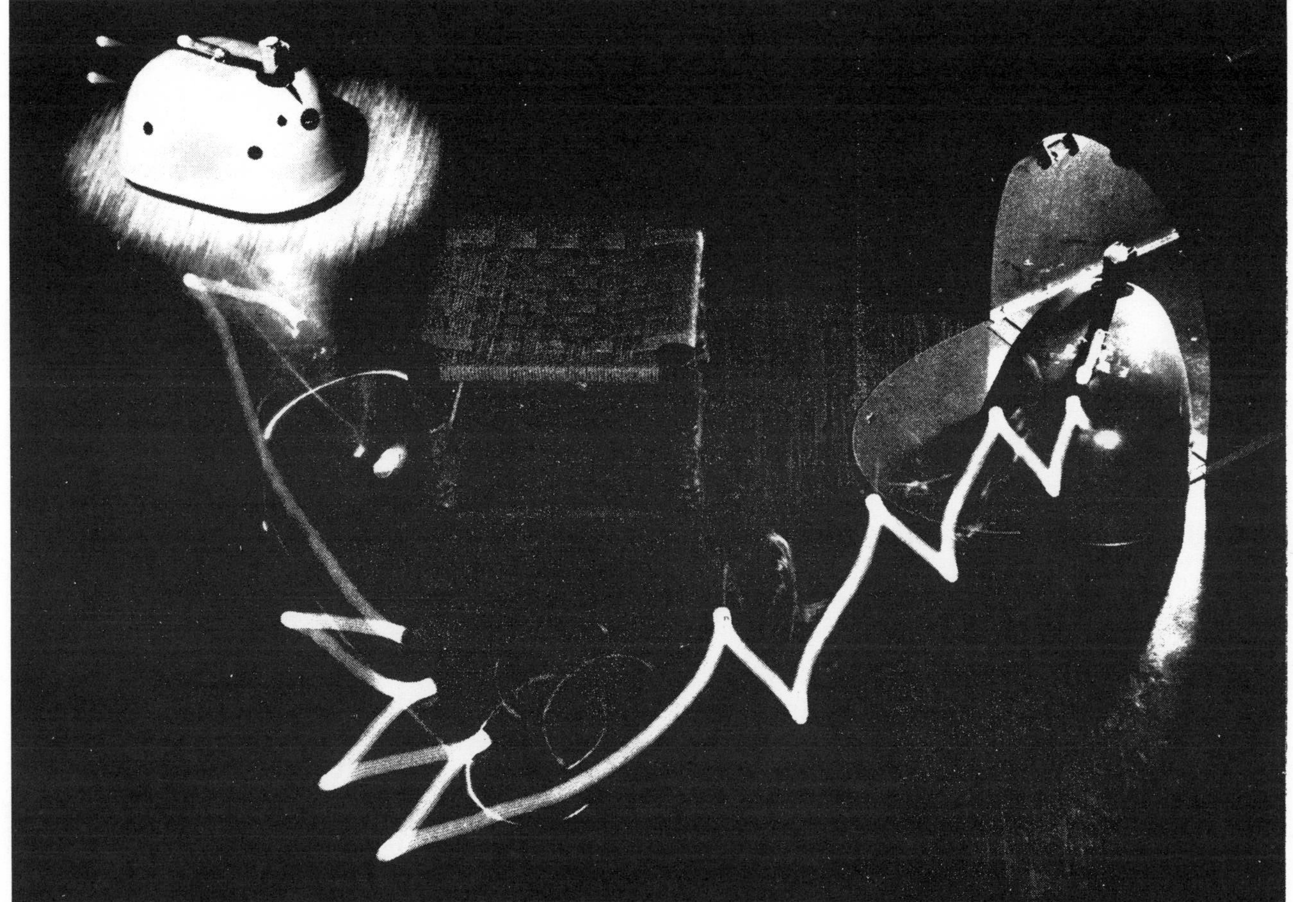

MACHINA SPECULATRIX, photographed by time exposure, is attracted by light in hutch at right. It begins at left, encounters obstacle, backs away, encounters obstacle again, backs away again and enters the hutch.

essential only that the energy should be in such a form that it can be readily available for the final operation.

7. This final phase is the combination of the preserved trace with a fresh Sn to give Es as the new conditioned response. The operation is analogous to the testing by experiment of a hypothesis, the hypothesis here being the likelihood of a correlation between Ss and Sn.

In terms of conditioned reflexes, the acquired response must be reinforced, otherwise it will vanish without trace. Consequently when the fresh Sn is presented in the seventh operation, it must be followed by the confirming Ss. Eventually, after a number of such events, the new response Sn → Es is permanently established and requires no further corroboration.

ALL THIS can be represented in a diagram of a simple nervous system (*see the lower of the two diagrams at the lower left-hand side of this page*). In this drawing there are two series of nerve cells—two reflex arcs—which correspond to the transmission systems T_1 and T_2. Between the two is a network of nerve cells which serve to perform the seven operations detailed above. Branching off from the first reflex arc is a synapse (1) with the property of discharging only at the beginning of the stimulus; this corresponds to the perception of food. In the second reflex arc is a synapse (2) with a long after-discharge: the prolongation of the neutral stimulus. The signals from the two stimuli both reach a neurone at (3), are mixed there and added together at (4). When the summated inputs reach a certain level, they discharge a trigger neurone (5). This introduces a pulse into the quiescent closed circuit at (6) which, by reason of positive feedback, continues to oscillate for a long while. An output from this leads to a mixing neurone at (7), which is also connected directly with the second reflex arc. This neurone can only discharge when it is activated simultaneously by signals from the storage circuit at (6) and a signal from the second reflex arc. When it does receive signals from both, its discharge is conducted to the output of the first reflex and has the specific effect Es. It thus acts as a gate to Es—normally shut to Sn but opened by the memory that Sn has often been followed by Ss.

Once this scheme had been worked out, it became possible to create an electronic circuit to perform the necessary operations (*see diagram at the lower right-hand side of these two pages*). The details are perhaps of interest only to an electrical engineer; the system involves a number of electronic tubes coupled with capacitors, resistors and so on in such a way that the signals are properly amplified, timed and mixed, and the resulting pulses are combined to produce the desired results.

In one arrangement of the working model of *M. docilis* the specific stimulus is a moderate light and the neutral one is the sound of a whistle. The whistle is blown just before the light is seen; after this has been repeated 10 or 20 times the model has "learned" that the sound means light and will come to the whistle as though it were a light. If it is teased by withholding of the light, it soon forgets the lesson and disregards the sound. In another arrangement the specific stimulus is touch, that is, an encounter with an obstacle. In that case the whistle is blown just as the model comes into contact with the obstacle, so that after a while the warning whistle triggers a withdrawal and avoidance reaction. This process may of course be accelerated by formal education: instead of waiting for the creature to hit a natural obstacle the experimenter can blow the whistle and kick the model. After a dozen kicks the model will know that a whistle means trouble, and it can thus be guided away from danger by its master. This last is an example of a negative or defensive conditioned reflex; as in an animal, responses of this type are more easily established and retained than any other. Because the mechanism sets up very large oscillating pulses which keep feeding into the learning circuit, the conditioned reflex, once established, lasts as long as the decay time of the memory and requires little or no reinforcement.

SEVERAL interesting problems arose in the working out of these experiments. For example, the use of sound as a conditioned stimulus was convenient, but the internal noise of the motors and gears was so loud compared with an external sound that the model could not "hear" the signal. It was found necessary to provide a special amplifier with a resistance-capacitance feedback circuit sharply tuned to the note of a whistle—about 3,000 cycles per second. As an alternative we tried arranging a muting

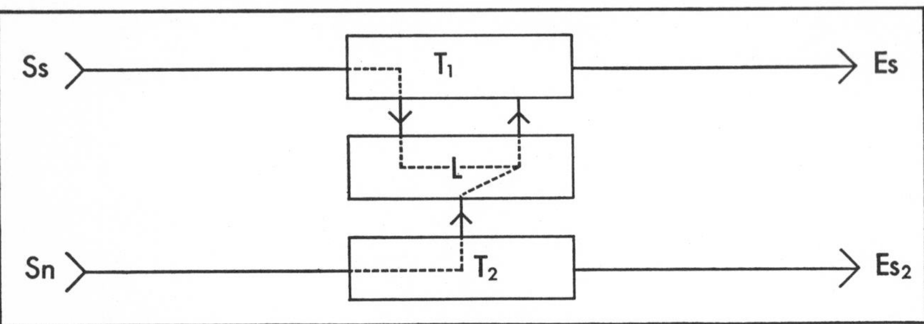

LEARNING links two systems. Ss and Sn are specific and neutral stimuli; Es and Es_2, effects; T_1 and T_2, transmission systems; L, learning box.

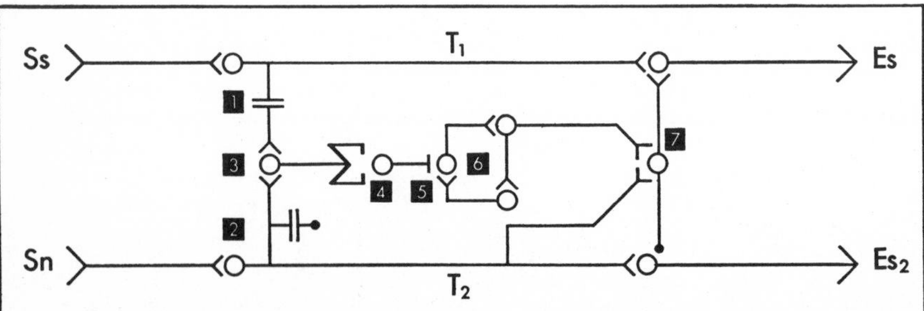

CONDITIONED REFLEX requires this arrangement of nerve cells. Numbers correspond to operations described in text and to diagram at right.

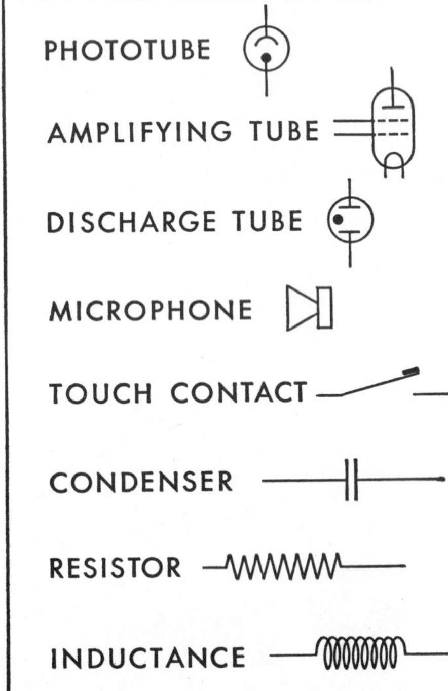

CIRCUIT for Cora, which stands for conditioned reflex analogue, is out-mechanism whereby the motors were turned off periodically and the microphone was simultaneously switched on for a moment to pick up any extraneous sound. This type of gating mechanism emphasizes the importance of the stretching operation applied to the sound signal, for the information the latter conveys is used after the brief listening period, which may occur only once a second for a tenth of a second. The muting-pulse device was not adopted because it seemed more complicated than the sharply tuned amplifier, but the former may be more akin to the physiological mechanisms in living creatures.

Further complications in *M. docilis* arise when the sound amplifier (neutral stimulus) is arranged to produce its own specific effect. For example, it can easily be arranged to make the sound switch off all motors, so that the model "freezes" when it hears the whistle. Such a reaction is very common in animals; many marsupials and rodents "play 'possum" when they hear a strange noise. If now it is intended to teach the model that sound means light, which may mean food, the freezing reaction must be inhibited to permit conditioning of the new response. A separate branch must therefore be taken from the output of the mixing tube at (7) to the output of the sound amplifier, whereby the "instinctive" effect of the latter is suppressed as soon as the positive conditioning has been established.

WE have described so far the simplest possible mechanism, consisting only of a single learning circuit connected to two signal amplifiers. With this arrangement the model is reasonably docile. But if we introduce a second learning circuit, or build in two neutral or specific signals instead of one, it becomes only too easy to establish an experimental neurosis. Thus if the arrangement is such that the sound becomes positively associated both with the attracting light and with the withdrawal from an obstacle, it is possible for both a light and a sound to set up a paradoxical withdrawal. The "instinctive" attraction to a light is abolished and the model can no longer approach its source of nourishment. This state seems remarkably similar to the neurotic behavior produced in human beings by exposure to conflicting influences or inconsistent education. In the model such ineffective and even destructive conditions can be terminated by rest, by switching off or by disconnecting one of the circuits. These treatments seem analogous to the therapeutic devices of the psychiatrist—sleep, shock and psychosurgery.

In *M. docilis* the memory of association is formed by electric oscillations in a feedback circuit. The decay of these oscillations is analogous to forgetting; their evocation, to recall. If several learning pathways are introduced, the creature's oscillatory memory becomes endowed with a very valuable feature: the frequency of each oscillation, or memory, is its identity tag. A latent memory can be detected and identified among others by a process of frequency analysis, and a complex of memories can be represented as a synthesis of oscillations which yields a characteristic wave pattern. Furthermore a "memory" can be evoked by an internal signal at the correct frequency, which resonates with the desired oscillation. The implications of these effects are of considerable interest to those who study the brain, for rhythmic electrical oscillation is the prime feature of brain activity. We may gain new respect for the speculations of the English physician-philosopher David Hartley, who 200 years ago suggested that ideas were represented in the brain as vibrations and "vibratiuncles."

THESE models are of course so simple that any more detailed comparison between them and living creatures would be purely conjectural. Experiments with larger numbers of circuits are perfectly feasible and will certainly be instructive. One weakness of more elaborate systems can be predicted with confidence: extreme plasticity cannot be gained without some loss of stability. In the real world an animal must be prepared to associate almost any event with almost any other; this means that if a nervous system contains N specific receptor-effector pathways, it should also include something of the order of N^2-N learning circuits. In such a system the chances of stability decline rapidly as N increases. It is therefore no wonder that the incidence of neuropsychiatric complaints marches with intellectual attainment and social complexity.

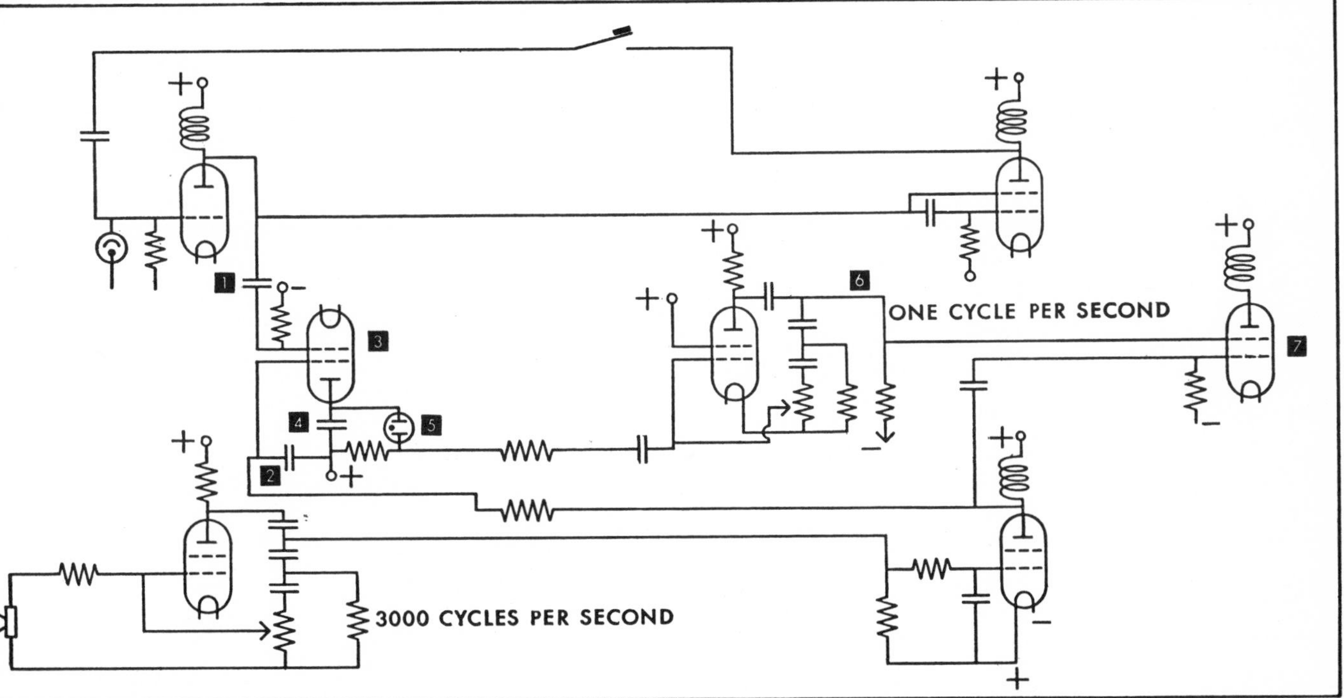

lined by simplified diagram. The circuit element labeled "3,000 cycles per second" is tuned so that Cora responds only to sound of that frequency. The element labeled "one cycle per second" provides machine with memory.

19

COMPUTER v. CHESS-PLAYER

ALEX BERNSTEIN AND MICHAEL DE V. ROBERTS • June 1958

Chess is not only one of the most engaging but also one of the most sophisticated of human activities. The game is so old that we cannot say when or where it was invented; millions of games have been played and thousands of books have been written about it; yet the play is still fresh and forever new. Simple arithmetic tells why. On the average, each move in chess offers a choice of about 30 possibilities, and the average length of a full game is about 40 moves. By this reckoning there are at least 10^{120} possible games. To get some idea of what that number means, let us suppose that we had a superfast computing machine which could play a million games a second (a ridiculous supposition). It would take the machine about 10^{108} years to play all the possible games!

So no conceivable machine could play a perfect game of chess, examining all possible moves. This is what makes the problem of programming a computer to play chess so intriguing. A present-day computing machine, with all its speed of calculation, is about as limited as a human being, on any reasonable time scale, in exploring the likely consequences of a chess move. Since it cannot study all the possibilities, the machine must play the game in human

OPPONENTS IN CHESS GAME depicted here are Alex Bernstein, co-author of this article, and an IBM 704 computer. The game is played on an ordinary chessboard, but information about each move is fed into the machine by controls above the board.

terms—that is, it must detect the strategy and anticipate the judgments of its human opponent. In other words, lacking the omniscience that would enable it to win no matter what its opponent does, it must try to outwit the opponent.

Needless to say, devising a program which would give a machine this property—what amounts to the capacity to think—has proved a very difficult job. The late A. M. Turing, the ingenious British theoretician on thinking machines, was one of the first to try his hand at designing a chess-playing program for a computer, but his machine (MADAM) played a very weak game, made stupid blunders and usually had to resign after a few moves. The problem has interested a number of computer experts in the U. S. [see "A Chess-Playing Machine," by Claude E. Shannon; SCIENTIFIC AMERICAN, February, 1950], and several groups are currently working on chess programs. We want to report here what we believe is the first satisfactory program—one with which the machine plays a game sophisticated enough so that its opponent has to be something more than a novice to beat it. The program was written by four collaborators—the authors of this article, who work for the International Business Machines Corporation, and Timothy Arbuckle and M. A. Belsky of the Service Bureau Corporation. It is designed for the IBM 704, the very rapid digital computer which has performed as many as one billion calculations in a single day in computing the orbit of an artificial satellite.

The program is a set of explicit instructions to the computer on how it must act in each of the specific situations with which it may be confronted. The instructions are given to the machine on a reel of magnetic tape. The operation of the computer is itself fascinating to watch. You sit at the console of the machine with a chessboard in front of you and press the start button. Within four seconds a panel light labeled "Program Stop" lights up on the console, and you now make your choice of black or white: to choose black you flip a switch on the console; if you want white, you simply leave the switch as it is. Suppose you have picked black. To begin the game you press the start button again. The machine now "thinks" about its first move. There is nothing spectacular about this. Some lights flash on the console, but the computer is working so swiftly that it is impossible to say just what these flashes mean. After about eight minutes, the computer

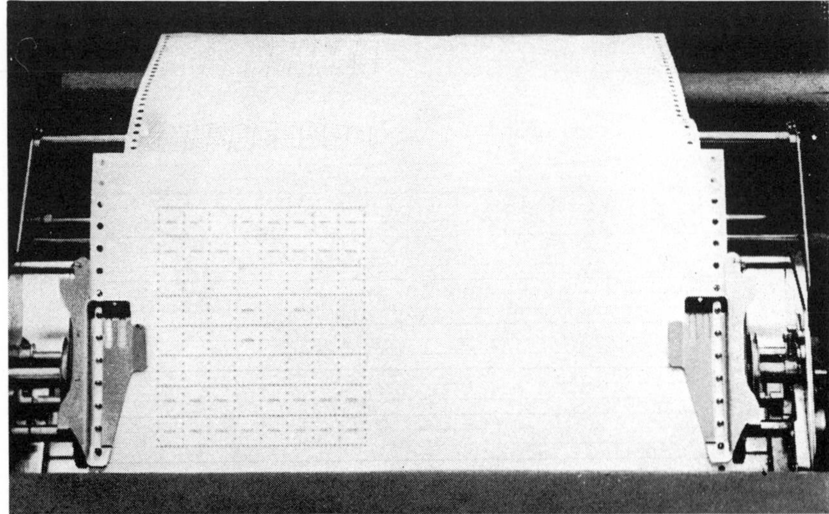

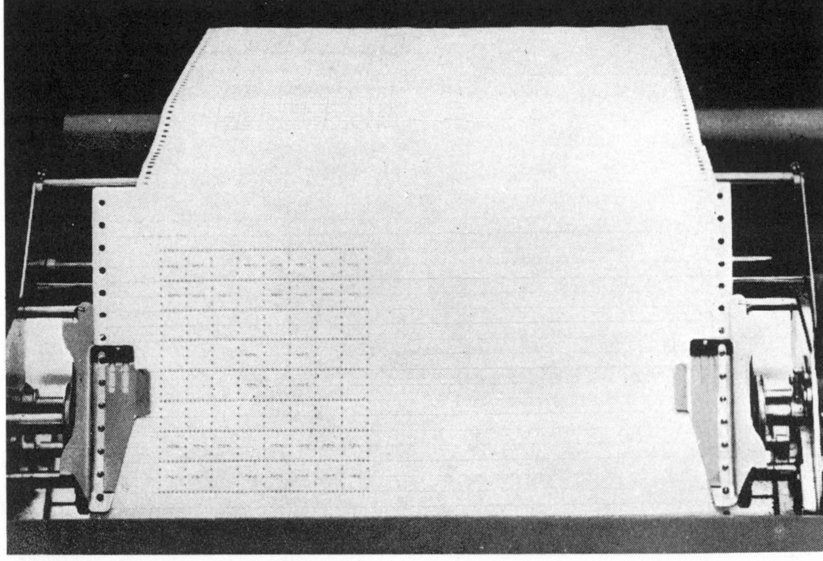

MACHINE TYPES OUT A MOVE in the form of a diagram of the chessboard (*top*). Bernstein makes the move on the board, then makes his own move and communicates it to the machine (*middle*). The machine types this move (*bottom*) before it makes its own.

prints out its move on a sheet of paper.

Let us say the machine's (White's) first move is king's pawn to the king's fourth square. The print-out then is W1 P-K4. The machine proceeds to print the chessboard with the positions of the pieces, designating its own by the letter M and its opponent's by the letter O [*see illustration below*].

Now the "Program Stop" light goes on again and the computer waits for its opponent to reply. You punch your replying move on an IBM card and put this card in a section of the machine which reads it. To signal that it is the machine's turn you press the start button again. The machine prints your move and the new board position and then goes on to calculate its second move. If you have made an illegal move, the computer will refuse to accept it, printing out "PLEASE CHECK LAST MOVE." So the game proceeds. At the end of the game, after a mating move or a resignation, the machine prints the score of the game, and to its opponent. "THANK YOU FOR AN INTERESTING GAME."

In explaining the program of instructions to the machine it will be helpful if we start by contrasting it with an ordinary job performed by a computer—say calculating John Doe's pay check. The machine in the latter case simply takes the data—so many dollars for a 44-hour week, so much for overtime at a certain rate, so much deducted for social security and income tax—and quickly computes what the check has to be. There is one, and only one, correct answer. But in a chess game there are only two questions to which absolutely definite and unavoidable answers can be given: "Is this move legal?" and "Is the game over?" To all other questions there are various possible answers, though some may be more acceptable than others. The problem is to equip the machine with a system of evaluating the merits of the alternatives. This, as

MACHINE

```
*************************************************
*     *     *     *     *     *     *     *     *
* MRK * MNT * MBS * MKG * MQN * MBS * MNT * MRK *
*     *     *     *     *     *     *     *     *
*************************************************
*     *     *     *     *     *     *     *     *
* MPN * MPN * MPN *     * MPN * MPN * MPN * MPN *
*     *     *     *     *     *     *     *     *
*************************************************
*     *     *     *     *     *     *     *     *
*     *     *     *     *     *     *     *     *
*     *     *     *     *     *     *     *     *
*************************************************
*     *     *     *     *     *     *     *     *
*     *     *     * MPN *     *     *     *     *
*     *     *     *     *     *     *     *     *
*************************************************
*     *     *     *     *     *     *     *     *
*     *     *     *     *     *     *     *     *
*     *     *     *     *     *     *     *     *
*************************************************
*     *     *     *     *     *     *     *     *
*     *     *     *     *     *     *     *     *
*     *     *     *     *     *     *     *     *
*************************************************
*     *     *     *     *     *     *     *     *
* OPN * OPN * OPN * OPN * OPN * OPN * OPN * OPN *
*     *     *     *     *     *     *     *     *
*************************************************
*     *     *     *     *     *     *     *     *
* ORK * ONT * OBS * OKG * OQN * OBS * ONT * ORK *
*     *     *     *     *     *     *     *     *
*************************************************
```

OPPONENT

CHESSBOARD TYPED OUT BY MACHINE represents the machine's pieces by M and the opponent's pieces by O. The second and third letters in each of the small squares represent rook (RK), knight (NT), bishop (BS), king (KG), queen (QN) and pawn (PN). In chess terminology the move shown here is P-K4 (pawn to king's column, fourth row).

	MACHINE (WHITE)	OPPONENT (BLACK)
1.	P — K4	P — K4
2.	B — B4	P — QN3
3.	P — Q3	N — KB3
4.	B — KN5	B — N2

Black is preparing for a direct attack on the center, via P — Q4.

5.	B × N	Q × B
6.	N — KB3	P — B3
7.	O — O	P — Q4
8.	P × P	P × P
9.	B — N5 ch	N — B3
10.	P — B4?	P × P

White 10 N × P is better because if black replies Q × N, then R — K1. Since the pawn is defended by the queen, N × P seemingly loses material, and the move is discarded.

11.	B × N ch	Q × B
12.	P × P?	P — K5

White 12 is bad, R — K1 is better.

13.	N — N5	Q — N3
14.	N — KR3	P — K6
15.	P — B3	B — B4
16.	R — K1	O — O
17.	N — B3	

Fiddling while Rome burns.

		P — K7 dis ch
18.	N — B2	B × P
19.	P — KN3	P × Q = Q
20.	N (QB3) × Q	Q — B7
21.	P — N3	R (QR1) — Q1
22.	P — KR4	R × N
23.	Resigns	

ACTUAL GAME between computer and human opponent is described in conventional chess terminology. The comments of the human opponent have been interpolated.

we have remarked, is what makes the task interesting. If cut-and-dried answers to all possible situations could be worked out by a computer, chess would immediately lose its fascination.

Obviously the machine's first job is to size up the board. The instructions therefore direct it to start by examining the state of the squares. The computer painstakingly and single-mindedly considers square by square, giving the same minute attention to squares of little interest as to those of key importance. It asks about each square whether it is occupied, by whose man, whether it is attacked, whether it is defended, whether it can be occupied. The information is summed up in tables compiled by the machine. All this takes about one tenth of a second, which is a long time by computer standards. The computer then proceeds to consider its best move.

Here we reach the most difficult and controversial part of the program, for to find a workable basis for the machine's decisions we must make some hypotheses about how a human being plays chess. To begin with, we have to decide on what basis a human player (or the machine) will select the moves that are to be given serious consideration (full consideration of all possible moves being out of the question). There are two distinct philosophies about this. One is that the player concentrates on the moves that look most plausible in the immediate situation. The other is that the player's approach to the selection is dictated by a grand strategy, and as far as he can he looks for moves which will further his plan. We built our program on the second hypothesis.

Of the various possible moves it might make (usually about 30) the machine selects seven for detailed analysis. It picks these on the basis of eight questions, which it asks in the following order:

1. Am I in check, and if so, can I capture the checking piece, interpose a piece or move away?
2. Are any exchanges possible, and if so, can I gain material by entering upon the exchange, or should I move my man away?
3. If I have not castled, can I do so now?
4. Can I develop a minor piece?
5. Can I occupy an open file?
6. Do I have any men that I can put on the critical squares created by pawn chains?
7. Can I make a pawn move?
8. Can I make a piece move?

Let us take the opening move for illustration. Examining the initial setup of the board, the machine finds that questions 1, 2 and 3 must be answered "No." The answer to question 4 is "Yes"; the machine notes that it can move either knight and has four possible knight moves (N-KR3, N-QR3, N-KB3, N-QB3). To questions 5 and 6 the answer is "No." It is "Yes" to question 7. Any of the eight pawns may be moved, but the instructions tell the machine to give priority to P-K4, P-K3 and P-Q4. These three pawn moves, with the four knight moves, provide the machine with seven moves for study.

It now proceeds to test each of the seven in turn through four moves ahead, considering its opponent's possible replies and its own possible counter-responses in each case. The machine starts with one of the seven moves and asks itself what it might reply were it the opponent. It generates seven possible replies, on the basis of the questions listed above, and now it takes the first of these and considers its own possible responses. After generating seven plausible responses, it again takes the first of these and in turn generates seven plausible replies by the opponent to this move.

The machine has reached the fourth level: initial move, reply, counter-reply and now the opponent's seven potential responses to its counter-reply [*see diagram below*]. It goes on to examine each of these seven moves to see which one would net the highest value for its opponent. The value, or score, is measured by four considerations: (1) gain of material (a pawn counting as one unit,

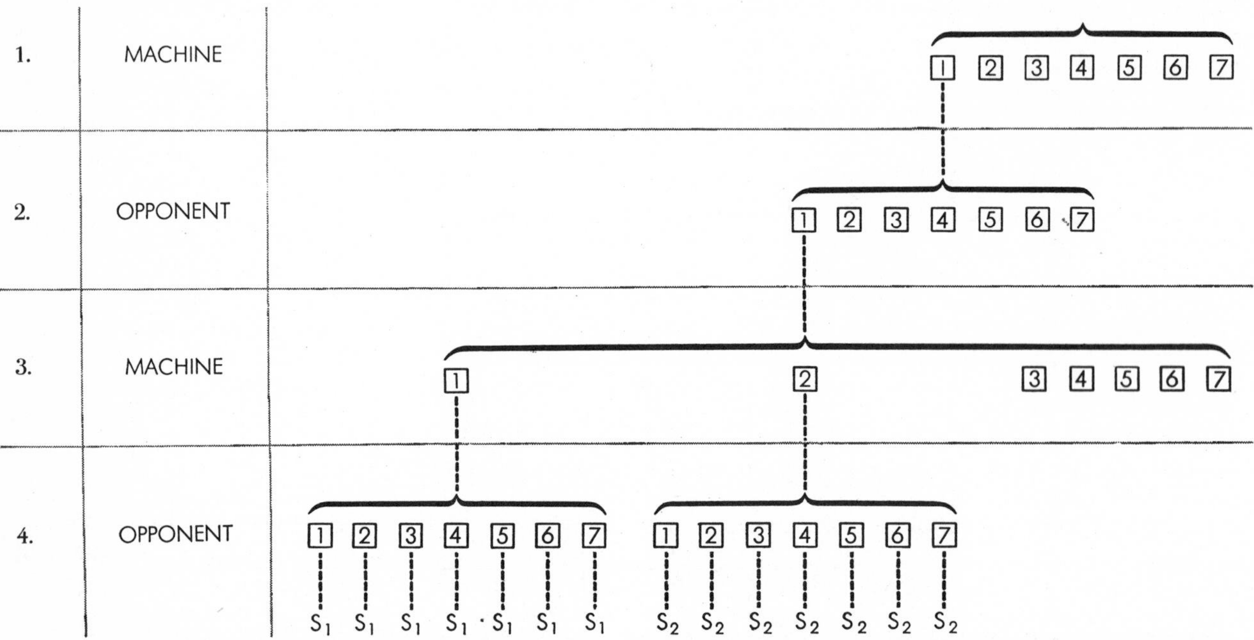

MACHINE MAKES A MOVE by the procedure suggested in this diagram. First, the machine selects, on the basis of eight questions, its seven most logical moves (*row 1*). Second, the machine selects its opponent's seven most logical responses to the first of these seven moves (*row 2*). Third, the machine selects its seven most logical counter-responses to the first of its opponent's responses (*row 3*). Fourth, the machine selects its opponent's seven most logical responses to the first of its seven counter-responses (*row 4*). Fifth, the machine scores its opponent's seven responses to the first of its seven counter-responses (S_1). Sixth, the machine selects its opponent's seven most logical responses to the second of its seven counter-responses. Seventh, the machine scores its opponent's responses to the second of its seven counter-responses (S_2). The machine continues in this manner until it has examined all moves.

a knight or bishop three, a rook five and the queen nine); (2) defense of the king; (3) mobility of the pieces; (4) control of important squares. After the machine has determined the score for the opponent's best move in level 4, it carries this back as the score for its own move 1 in level 3.

In this manner the machine investigates all the possible sequences of plays, taking each of the seven moves at every level of the "tree," and arrives at scores for all the outcomes at the fourth level. In all, it examines 2,800 possible positions. After this examination, the machine then chooses as its first move the one that will lead to the highest score both for itself and for its opponent. It acts, in other words, as if its opponent will make his best possible moves within the limits it is programmed to explore.

These limits—four half-moves ahead with seven choices at each step—are dictated by the time factor. It takes the machine close to eight minutes to decide on each move in most cases. If it had to weigh eight plausible moves instead of seven at each level, it would take about 15 minutes for a move. If it carried the examination through to one more level ahead, a single move would take some six and a half hours. So the present program is considered about the limit for a machine operating at the speed of the IBM 704.

MACHINE

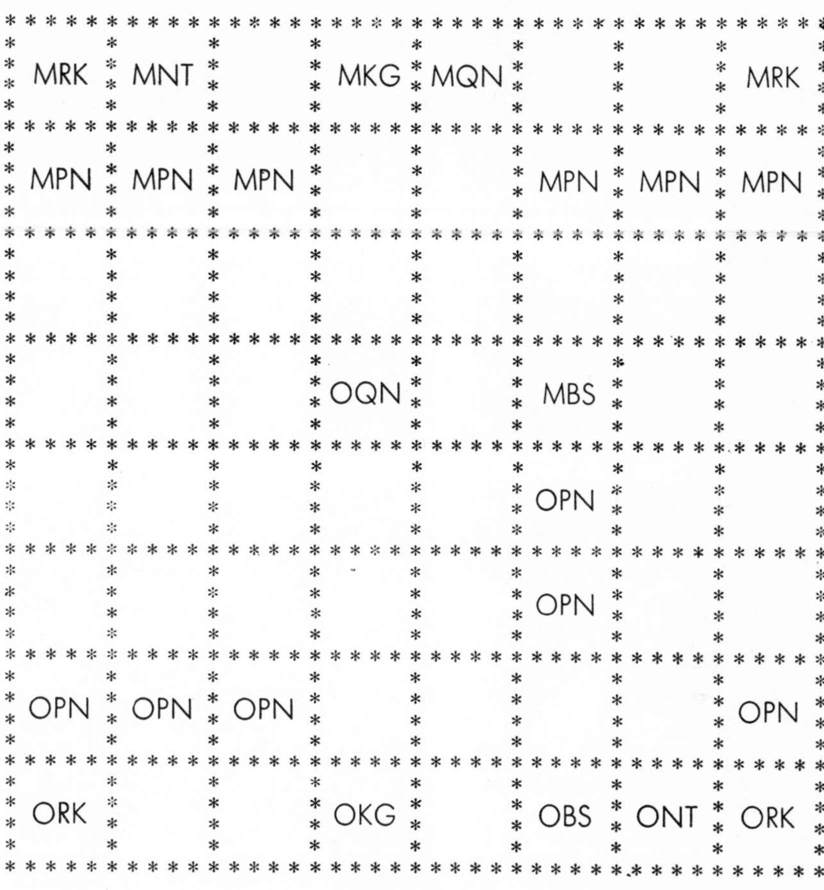

OPPONENT

MASTERLY MOVE was made out of this position by the machine. The move was Q-K2 (queen to king's column, row 2). Experts would consider this the only satisfactory move.

How does the machine make out with this program? In the first place, the machine is never absent-minded. It makes no blatant blunders such as letting a piece be caught *en prise,* as every chess master has done at some time or other. When its opponent is careless enough to expose a piece, the machine takes instant advantage of the opportunity to capture it. Secondly, in its choice of individual moves the machine often plays like a master, making what an expert would consider the only satisfactory move [*see example on this page*]. Thirdly, the machine is certainly not in the master class in the play of a complete game.

A typical game played by the machine against a skillful opponent is shown at the right on page 137. We have deliberately chosen a game which the machine lost, because we want to emphasize the point that a machine is not infallible and also because it is more instructive to watch the computer lose than to watch it win. The machine's opening moves in this game are quite acceptable. But by middle game the machine betrays its chief weakness: namely, a heavy bias toward moving attacked pieces rather than defending them (a weakness which could be corrected only by increasing the time for considering moves). At the tenth move White (the machine) makes a weak move which puts Black in a strong position; by the thirteenth move White's position is clearly hopeless, and 10 moves later, seeing the inevitability of a forced mate, the machine resigns.

Our contests with the machine show that anyone good enough to construct a three-move trap can beat it. Knowing how it selects its moves for consideration, you can often think of moves which you can be confident the machine will not consider. The machine will invariably accept a "sacrifice" (but then, so did the grand master José Capablanca). It will offer a sacrifice only to avoid being mated or if it can see an almost immediate mate of its opponent.

Yet notwithstanding its weaknesses, the IBM 704 plays a respectable and not-too-obvious game of chess—a game about which one can ask such questions as "Why did it make that move?" and "What does it have in mind?" We can even say frequently that "It made an excellent move at this point," or "At this stage it had a good position."

Undoubtedly our chess player is only a prototype for far more skillful players to be built in the future. Probably they will not go much farther in depth of planning: even with much faster computers than any now in existence it will be impracticable to consider more than about six half-moves ahead, investigating eight possible moves at each stage. A more promising line of attack is to program the computer to learn from experience. As things stand now, after losing a game the machine quite happily makes the same moves again and loses again in exactly the same way. But there are some glimmerings of ideas about how to program a machine to avoid repeating its mistakes, and some day—not overnight—we may have machines which will improve their game as they gain experience in play against their human opponents.

1
2
3
4
5
6
7
8
9

20

ARTIFICIAL INTELLIGENCE

MARVIN L. MINSKY • September 1966

At first the idea of an intelligent machine seems implausible. Can a computer really be intelligent? In this article I shall describe some programs that enable a computer to behave in ways that probably everyone would agree seem to show intelligence.

The machine achievements discussed here are remarkable in themselves, but even more interesting and significant than what the programs do accomplish are the methods they involve. They set up goals, make plans, consider hypotheses, recognize analogies and carry out various other intellectual activities. As I shall show by example, a profound change has taken place with the discovery that descriptions of thought processes can be turned into prescriptions for the design of machines or, what is the same thing, the design of programs.

The turning point came sharply in 1943 with the publication of three theoretical papers on what is now called cybernetics. Norbert Wiener, Arturo Rosenblueth and Julian H. Bigelow of the Massachusetts Institute of Technology suggested ways to build goals and purposes into machines; Warren S. McCulloch of the University of Illinois College of Medicine and Walter H. Pitts of M.I.T. showed how machines might use concepts of logic and abstraction, and K. J. W. Craik of the University of Cambridge proposed that machines could use models and analogies to solve problems. With these new foundations the use of psychological language for describing machines became a constructive and powerful tool. Such ideas remained in the realm of theoretical speculation, however, until the mid-1950's. By that time computers had reached a level of capacity and flexibility to permit the programming of processes with the required complexity.

In the summer of 1956 a group of investigators met at Dartmouth College to discuss the possibility of constructing genuinely intelligent machines. Among others, the group included Arthur L. Samuel of the International Business Machines Corporation, who had already written a program that played a good game of checkers and incorporated several techniques to improve its own play. Allen Newell, Clifford Shaw and Herbert A. Simon of the Rand Corporation had constructed a theorem-proving program and were well along in work on a "General Problem Solver," a program that administers a hierarchy of goal-seeking subprograms.

John McCarthy was working on a system to do "commonsense reasoning" and I was working on plans for a program to prove theorems in plane geometry. (I was hoping eventually to have the computer use analogical reasoning on diagrams.) After the conference the workers continued in a number of independent investigations. Newell and Simon built up a research group at the Carnegie Institute of Technology with the goal of developing models of human behavior. McCarthy and I built up a group at M.I.T. to make machines intelligent without particular concern with human behavior. (McCarthy is now at Stanford University.) Although the approaches of the various groups were different, it is significant that their studies have resulted in closely parallel results.

Work in this field of intelligent machines and the number of investigators increased rapidly; by 1963 the bibliography of relevant publications had grown to some 900 papers and books. I shall try to give the reader an impression of the state of the field by presenting some examples of what has been happening recently.

The general approach to creating a program that can solve difficult problems will first be illustrated by considering the game of checkers. This game exemplifies the fact that many problems can in principle be solved by trying all possibilities—in this case exploring all possible moves, all the opponent's possible replies, all the player's possible replies to the opponent's replies and so on. If this could be done, the player could see which move has the best chance of winning. In practice, however, this approach is out of the question, even for a computer; the tracking down of every possible line of play would involve some 10^{40} different board positions. (A similar analysis for the game of chess would call for some 10^{120} positions.) Most interesting problems present far too many possibilities for complete trial-and-error analysis. Hence one must discover rules that will

ABSTRACT REASONING is required to complete a figure on the basis of partial information. A program developed by Lawrence G. Roberts in a doctoral thesis at the Massachusetts Institute of Technology allows a computer to interpret a two-dimensional image and reconstruct the three-dimensional object. As shown on the opposite page, the computer scans a photograph of the object (*1*), displays its local features (*2*) and combines line segments (*3*) to prepare a complete line drawing (*4*). It accounts for the drawing as a compound of three-dimensional shapes (*5–7*) and draws in all the interior lines (*8*). Then it can display the structure from any point of view on request, suppressing lines that would be hidden (*9*).

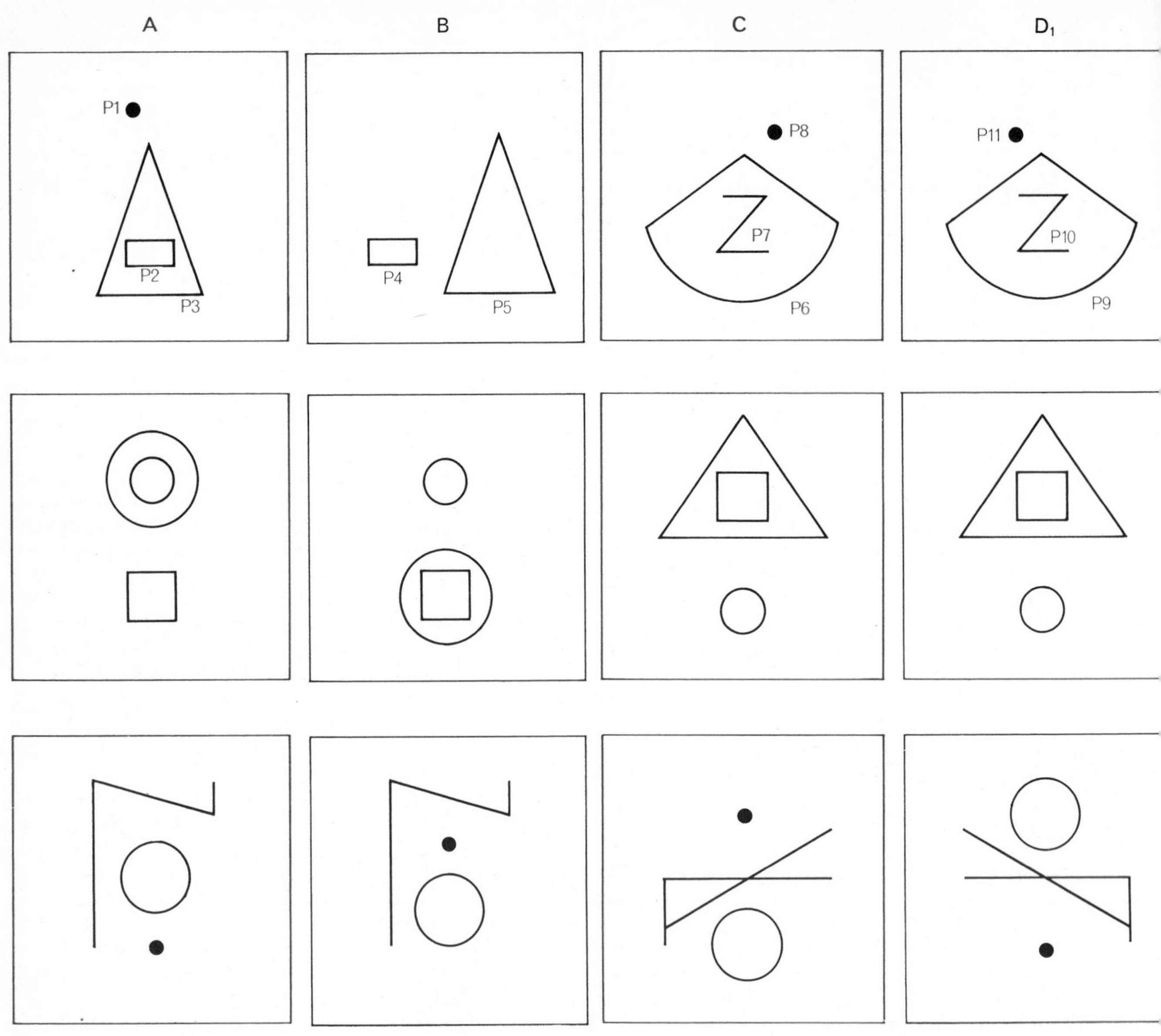

ANALOGICAL REASONING is exhibited in a program developed by Thomas Evans in an M.I.T. doctoral thesis for answering a class of problems frequently included in intelligence tests: "*A* is to *B* as *C* is to (D_1, D_2, D_3, D_4 or D_5?)." Three such problems are illustrated

try the most likely routes to a solution as early as possible.

Samuel's checker-playing program explores thousands of board positions but not millions. Instead of tracking down every possible line of play the program uses a partial analysis (a "static evaluation") of a relatively small number of carefully selected features of a board position—how many men there are on each side, how advanced they are and certain other simple relations. This incomplete analysis is not in itself adequate for choosing the best move for a player in a current position. By combining the partial analysis with a limited search for some of the consequences of the possible moves from the current position, however, the program selects its move as if on the basis of a much deeper analysis. The program contains a collection of rules for deciding when to continue the search and when to stop. When it stops, it assesses the merits of the "terminal" position in terms of the static evaluation. If the computer finds by this search that a given move leads to an advantage for the player in all the likely positions that may occur a few moves later, whatever the opponent does, it can select this move with confidence.

What is interesting and significant about such a program is not simply that it can use trial and error to solve problems. What makes for intelligent behavior is the collection of methods and techniques that select what is to be tried next, that size up the situation and choose a plausible (if not always good) move and use information gained in previous attempts to steer subsequent analysis in better directions. To be sure, the programs described below do use search, but in the examples we present the solutions were found among the first few attempts rather than after millions of attempts.

A program that makes such judgments about what is best to try next is termed heuristic. Our examples of heuristic programs demonstrate some capabilities similar in principle to those of the checkers program, and others that may be even more clearly recognized as ways of "thinking."

In developing a heuristic program one usually begins by programming some methods and techniques that can solve comparatively uncomplicated

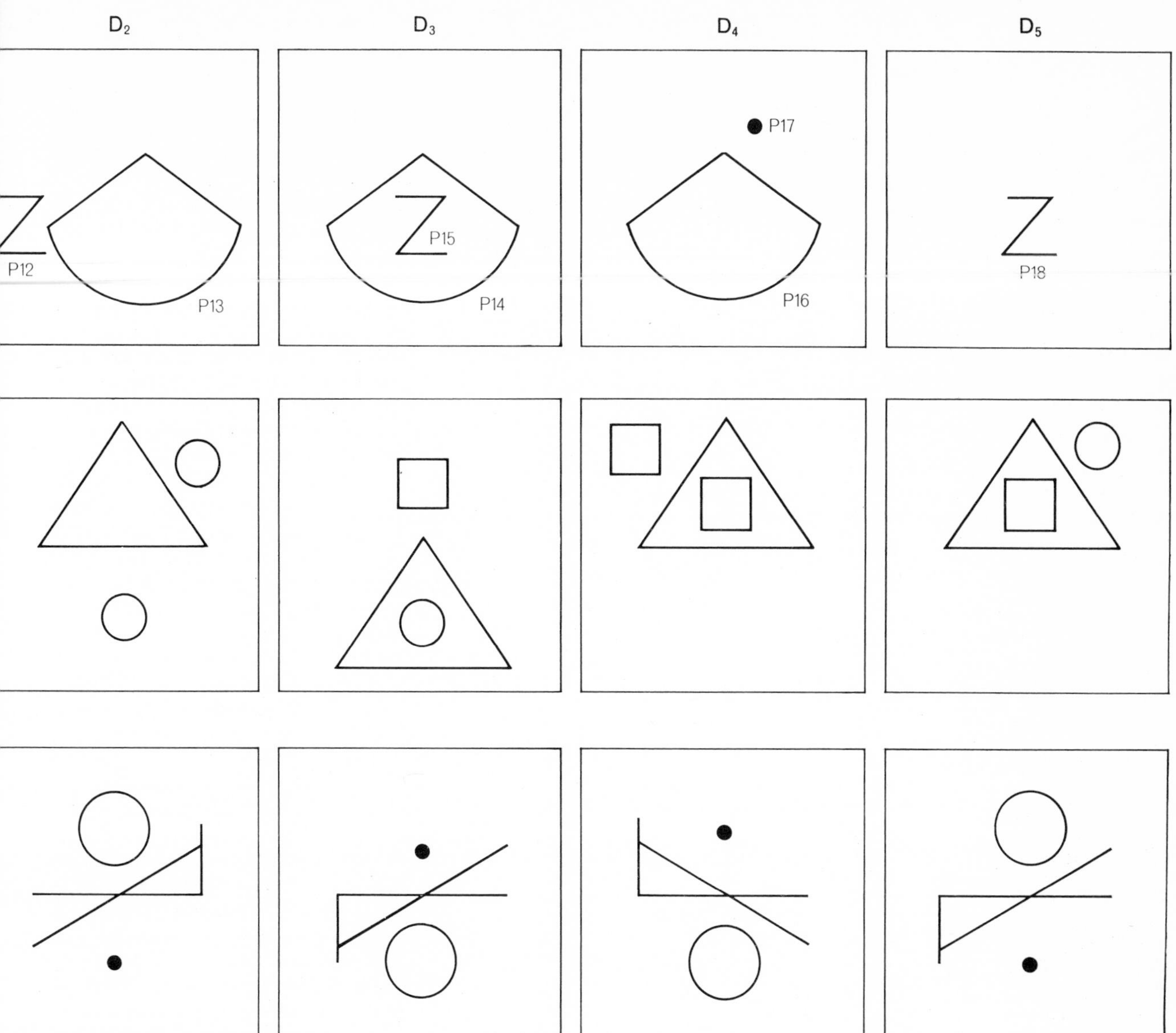

here. A computer selected the "best" answer to the top example and the middle one but missed on the bottom one because the program is weak in assessing relations among more than two objects. A typical solution is demonstrated in the illustrations that follow.

problems. To solve harder problems one might work directly to improve these basic methods, but it is much more profitable to try to extend the problem solver's general ability to bring a harder problem within reach by breaking it down into subproblems. The machine is provided with a program for a three-step process: (1) break down the problems into subproblems, keeping a record of the relations between these parts as part of the total problem, (2) solve the subproblems and (3) combine the results to form a solution to the problem as a whole. If a subproblem is still too hard, apply the procedure again. It has been found that the key to success in such a procedure often lies in finding a form of description for the problem situation (a descriptive "language") that makes it easy to break the problem down in a useful way.

Our next example of a heuristic program illustrates how descriptive languages can be used to enable a computer to employ analogical reasoning. The program was developed by Thomas Evans, a graduate student at M.I.T., as the basis for his doctoral thesis, and is the best example so far both of the use of descriptions and of how to handle analogies in a computer program.

The problem selected was the recognition of analogies between geometric figures. It was taken from a well-known test widely used for college-admission examinations because its level of difficulty is considered to require considerable intelligence. The general format is familiar: Given two figures bearing a certain relation to each other, find a similar relation between a third figure and one of five choices offered. The problem is usually written: "*A* is to *B* as *C* is to (D_1, D_2, D_3, D_4 or D_5?)." The particularly attractive feature of this kind of problem as a test of machine intelligence is that it has no uniquely "correct" answer. Indeed, performance on such tests is not graded by any known rule but is judged on the basis of the selections of highly intelligent people on whom the test is tried.

Now, there is a common superstition that "a computer can solve a problem only when every step in the solution is clearly specified by the programmer." In a superficial sense the statement is true, but it is dangerously misleading if

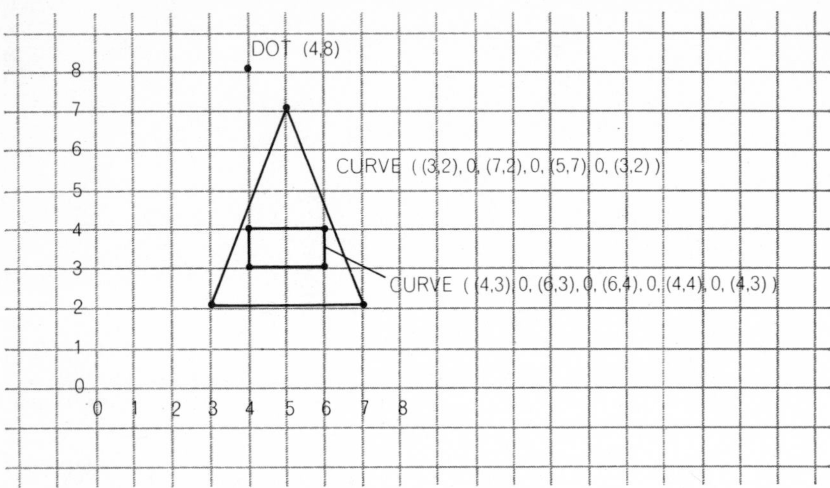

FIRST STEP of the program describes the parts of each figure in terms of a coordinate system, as shown for *A* in the top problem on the preceding two pages. The triangle and rectangle are "curves" whose apexes are connected by lines of zero curvature, indicated by *0*.

	RELATIONS WITHIN
(INSIDE (P_2,P_3), ABOVE (P_1,P_3), ABOVE (P_1,P_2))	A
(LEFT (P_4,P_5))	B
(INSIDE (P_7,P_6), ABOVE (P_8,P_6), ABOVE (P_8,P_7))	C
(INSIDE (P_{10},P_9), ABOVE (P_{11},P_9), ABOVE (P_{11},P_{10}))	D_1
(LEFT (P_{12},P_{13}))	D_2
(INSIDE (P_{15},P_{14}))	D_3
(ABOVE (P_{17},P_{16}))	D_4
(NONE)	D_5

	SIMILARITIES BETWEEN
SIM $(P_2,P_4,0°)$ $(P_2,P_4,180°)$ $(P_3,P_5,0°)$	A AND B
SIM $(P_1,P_8,0°)$	A AND C
NIL	B AND C
SIM $(P_6,P_9,0°)$ $(P_7,P_{10},0°)$ $(P_7,P_{10},180°)$ $(P_8,P_{11},0°)$	C AND D_1
SIM $(P_6,P_{13},0°)$ $(P_7,P_{12},0°)$ $(P_7,P_{12},180°)$	C AND D_2
SIM $(P_6,P_{14},0°)$ $(P_7,P_{15},0°)$ $(P_7,P_{15},180°)$	C AND D_3
SIM $(P_6,P_{16},0°)$ $(P_8,P_{17},0°)$	C AND D_4
SIM $(P_7,P_{18},0°)$ $(P_7,P_{18},180°)$	C AND D_5
SIM $(P_1,P_{11},0°)$ $(P_1,P_{17},0°)$	A AND D_1, A AND D_4

RELATIONS AND SIMILARITIES are discovered by the program. It notes, for example, that the rectangle (P_2) is inside the triangle (P_3), the dot (P_1) above both the triangle and the rectangle, and so on. Then it lists similarities between such elements in different figures and also notes whether or not the similarity persists if an element is rotated 180 degrees.

it is taken literally. Here we understood the basic concepts Evans wrote into the program, but until the program was completed and tested we had no idea of how the machine's level of performance would compare to the test scores of human subjects.

Evans began his work on the problem of comparing geometric figures by proposing a theory of the steps or processes the human brain might use in dealing with such a situation. His theory suggested a program of four steps that can be described in psychological terms. First, in comparing the features of the figures *A* and *B* one must select from various possibilities some way in which a description of *A* can be transformed into a description of *B*. This transformation defines certain relations between *A* and *B*. (For example, in the top series of drawings in the illustration on the preceding two pages a small rectangle is inside the triangle in the figure *A* and outside the triangle in the figure *B*.) There may be several such explanations "plausible" enough to be considered. Second, one looks for items or parts in *C* that correspond to parts in *A*. There may be several such "matches" worthy of consideration. Third, in each of the five figures offering answer choices one searches for features that may relate the figure to *C* in a way similar to the way in which the corresponding features in *B* are related to those in *A*. Wherever the correspondence, if any, is not perfect, one can make it more so by "weakening" the relation, which means accepting a modified, less detailed version of the relation. Fourth and last, one can select as the best answer the figure that required the least modification of relations in order to relate it to *C* as *B* is related to *A*.

This set of hypotheses became the framework of Evans' program. (I feel sure that rules or procedures of the same general character are involved in any kind of analogical reasoning.) His next problem was to translate this rather complex sketch of mental processes into a detailed program for the computer. To do so he had to develop what is certainly one of the most complex programs ever written. The technical device that made the translation possible was the LISP ("list-processor") programming language McCarthy had developed on the basis of earlier work by Newell, Simon and Shaw. This system provides many automatic services for manipulating expressions and complicated data structures. In particular it is a most convenient method of handling descriptions consisting of lists of items. And it makes it easy to write interlocked programs that can, for example, use one another as subprograms.

The input for a specific problem in Evans' program is in the form of lists of vertices, lines and curves describing the geometric figures. A subprogram analyzes this information, identifies the separate parts of the figure and reconstructs them in terms of points on a graph and the connecting lines. The steps and processes in the solution of a problem are given in some detail in the illustrations on these two pages. Briefly, the program takes the following course: After receiving the descriptions of the figures (*A*, *B*, *C* and the five answer choices) it searches out topological and geometric relations between the parts in each picture (such as that one object is inside or to the left of or above another). It then identifies and lists similarities between pairs of pictures (*A* and *B*, *A* and *C*, *C* and D_1 and so on). The program proceeds to discover all the ways in which the parts of *A* and *B* can be matched up, and on the basis of this examination it develops a hypothesis about the relation of *A* to *B* (what was removed, added, moved or otherwise changed to transform one picture into the other). Next it considers correspondences between the parts of *A* and the parts of *C*. It goes on to look for matchings of the *A*-to-*B* kind between the parts in *C* and each of the *D* figures (the answer choices). When it finds something approaching a match that is consistent with its hypothesis of the relation between *A* and *B*, it proceeds to measure the degree of divergence of the *C*-to-*D* relation from the *A*-to-*B* relation by stripping away the details of the *A*-to-*B* transformation one by one until both relations (*A*-to-*B* and *C*-to-*D*) are essentially alike. In this way it eventually identifies the *D* figure that seems to come closest to a relation to *C* analogous to the *A* and *B* relation.

Evans' program is capable of solving problems considerably more complex or subtle than the one we have considered step by step. Among other things, in making decisions about the details of a picture it can take into account deductions from the situation as a whole [*see bottom illustration on this page*]. No one has taken the trouble to make a detailed comparison of the machine's performance with that of human subjects on the same problems, but Evans' evidence suggests that the present program can score at about the 10th-grade level, and with certain improvements of the program that have already been proposed it should do even better. Evans' work on his program had to stop when he reached the limitations of the computer machinery available to him. His program could no longer fit in one piece into the core memory of the computer, and mainly for this reason it took several minutes to run each problem in the machine. With the very large memory just installed at M.I.T.'s Project MAC the program could be run in a few seconds. The new capacity will make possible further research on more sophisticated versions of such programs.

The Evans program is of course a single-minded affair: it can deal only with problems in geometrical analogy. Although its ability in this respect compares favorably with the ability of humans, in no other respect can it pretend to approach the scope or versatility of human intelligence. Yet in its limited way it does display qualities we usually think of as requiring "intuition," "taste" or other subjective operations of the mind. With his analysis of such operations and his clarification of their components in terms precise enough to express them symbolically and make them available for use by a machine, Evans laid a foundation for the further development (with less effort) of programs employing analogical reasoning.

Moreover, it is becoming clear that analogical reasoning itself can be an important tool for expanding artificial

```
(REMOVE A1 ((ABOVE A1 A3) (ABOVE
   A1 A2) (SIM OB3 A1 (((1.0 . 0.0) .
   (N.N)))))))

(MATCH A2 (((INSIDE A2 A3) (ABOVE
   A1 A2) (SIM OB2 A2 (((1.0 . 0.0) .
   (N.N)))))) . ((LEFT A2 A3) (SIM
   OB2 A2 (((1.0 . 0.0) . (N.N)) ((1.0 .
   3.14) . (N.N)))))) (SIMTRAN (((1.0 .
   0.0) . (N.N)) ((1.0 . 3.14) . (N.N)
   ))))))

(MATCH A3 (((INSIDE A2 A3) (ABOVE
   A1 A3) (SIM OB1 A3 (((1.0 . 0.0) .
   (N.N)))))) . ((LEFT A2 A3)  (SIM
   OB1  A3  (((1.0 . 0.0) . (N.N))))
   (SIMTRAN  (((1.0 . 0.0) . (N.N)
   ))))))
```

HYPOTHESIS about how *A* is related to *B* is constructed by the program, which finds ways in which parts of the two figures can be matched up. It lists each element removed, added or matched and also the properties, relations and similarities associated with the element.

```
(REMOVE A1 ((ABOVE A1 A3) (ABOVE
   A1 A2) (SIM OB3 A1 (((1.0 . 0.0) .
   (N.N)))))))

(MATCH A2 (((INSIDE A2 A3) (ABOVE
   A1 A2)) . ((LEFT A2 A3) (SIMTRAN
   (((1.0 . 0.0) . (N.N)) ((1.0 . 3.14)
   (N.N))))))))

(MATCH A3 (((INSIDE A2 A3) (ABOVE
   A1 A3)) . ((LEFT A2 A3) (SIMTRAN
   (((1.0 . 0.0) . (N.N))))))))
```

PROGRAM CONCLUDES, after trying matchings between *C* and each of the five *D* figures, that D_2 is the best answer. It does so by considering *C*-*D* matchings that are consistent with the *A*-*B* hypothesis. By removing details from the *A*-*B* expression until it fits the *C*-*D* matching, the program selects the *C*-*D* match that is least different from the *A*-*B* hypothesis.

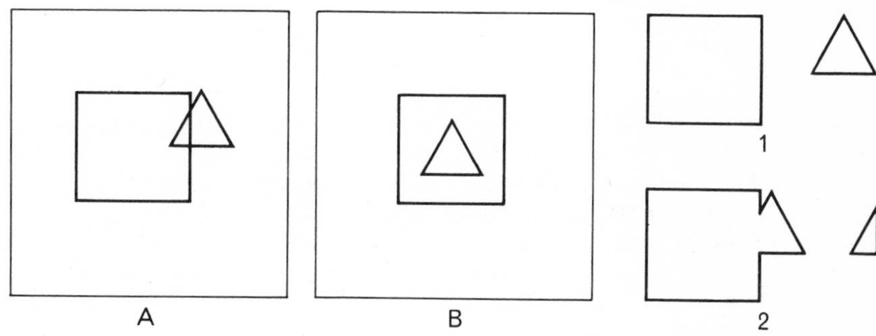

REASONING POWER of the program is illustrated in a different example by its ability to resolve the overlapping objects in *A* into a rectangle and triangle (*1*) rather than the other pieces (*2*). It makes the distinction by observing that the objects at *1* occur in figure *B* whereas the others do not. That is, program can recognize a "global" aspect of the situation.

```
(THE PROBLEM TO BE SOLVED IS)
(MARY IS TWICE AS OLD AS ANN WAS WHEN MARY WAS AS OLD AS ANN
IS NOW . IF MARY IS 24 YEARS OLD , HOW OLD IS ANN Q.)

(WITH MANDATORY SUBSTITUTIONS THE PROBLEM IS)
(MARY IS 2 TIMES AS OLD AS ANN WAS WHEN MARY WAS AS OLD AS
ANN IS NOW . IF MARY IS 24 YEARS OLD , WHAT IS ANN Q.)

(WITH WORDS TAGGED BY FUNCTION THE PROBLEM IS)
((MARY / PERSON) IS 2 (TIMES / OP 1) AS OLD AS (ANN / PERSON)
WAS WHEN (MARY / PERSON) WAS AS OLD AS (ANN / PERSON) IS NOW
(PERIOD / DLM) IF (MARY / PERSON) IS 24 YEARS OLD , (WHAT /
QWORD) IS (ANN / PERSON) (QMARK / DLM))


(THE SIMPLE SENTENCES ARE)

((MARY / PERSON) S AGE IS 2 (TIMES / OP 1) (ANN / PERSON) S
AGE G02521 YEARS AGO (PERIOD / DLM))

(G02521 YEARS AGO (MARY / PERSON) S AGE IS (ANN / PERSON) S
AGE NOW (PERIOD / DLM))

((MARY / PERSON) S AGE IS 24 (PERIOD / DLM))

((WHAT / QWORD) IS (ANN / PERSON) S AGE (QMARK / DLM))


(THE EQUATIONS TO BE SOLVED ARE)

(EQUAL G02522 ((ANN / PERSON) S AGE))

(EQUAL ((MARY / PERSON) S AGE) 24)

(EQUAL (PLUS ((MARY / PERSON) S AGE) (MINUS (G02521))) ((ANN
/ PERSON) S AGE))

(EQUAL ((MARY / PERSON) S AGE) (TIMES 2 (PLUS ((ANN / PERSON)
S AGE) (MINUS (G02521)))))


(ANN S AGE IS  18)
```

"STUDENT," an English-reading program created by Daniel Bobrow, solves algebra problems. As shown here, Student restates a problem, then analyzes the words in terms of its library of definitions and relations, sets up the proper equations and gives the solution. The machine has invented the symbol *G02521* to represent the *X* used in text of the article.

intelligence. I believe it will eventually be possible for programs, by resorting to analogical reasoning, to apply the experience they have gained from solving one kind of problem to the solution of quite different problems. Consider a situation in which a machine is presented with a problem that is too complicated for solution by any method it knows. Ordinarily to cope with such contingencies the computer would be programmed to split the problem into subproblems or subgoals, so that by solving these it can arrive at a solution to the main problem. In a difficult case, however, the machine may be unable to break the problem down or may become lost in a growing maze of irrelevant subgoals. If a machine is to be able to deal, then, with very hard problems, it must have some kind of planning ability—an ability to find a suitable strategy.

What does the rather imprecise word "planning" mean in this context? We can think of a definition in terms of machine operations that might be useful: (1) Replace the given problem by a similar but simpler one; (2) solve this analogous problem and remember the steps in its solution; (3) try to adapt the steps of the solution to solve the original problem. Newell and Simon have actually completed an experiment embodying a simple version of such a program. It seems to me that this area is one of the most important for research on making machine intelligence more versatile.

I should now like to give a third example of a program exhibiting intelligence. This program has to do with the handling of information written in the English language.

Since the beginnings of the volution of modern computers it has been obvious that a computer could be a superb file clerk that would provide instant access to any of its information—provided that the files were totally and neatly organized and that the kinds of questions the computer was called on to answer could be completely programmed. But what if, as in real life, the information is scattered through the files and is expressed in various forms of human discourse? It is widely supposed that the handling of information of this informal character is beyond the capability of any machine.

Daniel Bobrow, for his doctoral research at M.I.T., attacked this problem directly: How could a computer be programmed to understand a limited range of ordinary English? For subject matter he chose statements of problems in high school algebra. The purely mathematical solution of these problems would be child's play for the computer, but Bobrow's main concern was to provide the computer with the ability to read the informal verbal statement of a problem and derive from that language the equations required to solve the problem. (This, and not solution of the equations, is what is hard for students too.)

The basic strategy of the program (which is named "Student") is this: The machine "reads in" the statement of the problem and tries to rewrite it as a number of simple sentences. Then it tries to convert each simple sentence into an equation. Finally it tries to solve the set of equations and present the required answer (converted back to a simple English sentence). Each of these steps in interpreting the meaning is done with the help of a library (stored in the core memory) that includes a dictionary, a variety of factual statements and several special-purpose programs for solving particular kinds of problems. To write the program for the machine Bobrow used the LISP programming language with some new extensions of his own and incorporated techniques that had been developed by Victor H. Yngve in earlier work on language at M.I.T.

The problems the machine has to face in interpreting the English statements are sometimes quite difficult. It may have to figure out the antecedent of a pronoun, recognize that two different phrases have the same meaning or discover that a necessary piece of information is missing. Bobrow's program is a model of informality. Its filing system is so loosely organized (although it is readily accessible) that new information can be added to the dictionary by dumping it in anywhere. Perhaps the program's most interesting technical aspect is the way it cuts across the linguist's formal distinction between syntax and semantics, thus avoiding problems that, it seems to me, have more hindered than helped most studies of language.

The illustrations on page 147 and on this page show three problems as they were solved by Student. The remarkable thing about Student is not so much that it understands English as that it shows a basic capacity for understanding anything at all. When it runs into difficulty, it asks usually pertinent questions. Sometimes it has to ask the person operating the computer, but often it resolves the difficulty by referring to the knowledge in its files. When, for instance, it meets a statement such as "Mary is twice as old as Ann was when Mary was as old as Ann is now," the program knows how to make the meaning of "was when" more precise by rewriting the statement as two simple sentences: "Mary is twice as old as Ann was *X* years ago. *X* years ago Mary was as old as Ann is now."

Bobrow's program can handle only a small part of the grammar of the English language, and its semantic dictionaries are quite limited. Yet even though it can make many kinds of mistakes within its linguistic limitations, it probably surpasses the average person in its ability to handle algebra problems stated verbally. Bobrow believes that, given a larger computer memory, he could make Student understand most of the problems that are presented in high school first-algebra textbooks.

As an example of another kind of intelligence programmed into a machine, a program developed by Lawrence G. Roberts as a doctoral thesis at M.I.T. endows a computer with some ability to analyze three-dimensional objects [*see illustration on page 140*]. In a single two-dimensional photograph of a solid object the program detects a number of the object's geometrical features. It uses these to form a description in terms of lines and then tries to analyze the figure as a composite of simpler building blocks (rectangular forms and prisms). Once the program has performed this analysis it can reconstruct the figure from any requested point of view, drawing in lines that were originally hidden and suppressing lines that should not appear in the new picture. The program employs some rather abstract symbolic reasoning.

The exploration of machine intelligence has hardly begun. There have been about 30 experiments at the general level of those described here. Each investigator has had time to try out a few ideas; each program works only in a narrow problem area. How can we make the programs more versatile? It cannot be done simply by putting together a collection of old programs; they differ so much in their representation of objects and concepts that there could be no effective communication among them.

If we ask, "Why are the programs not more intelligent than they are?" a simple answer is that until recently resources—in people, time and computer capacity—have been quite limited. A number of the more careful and serious attempts have come close to their goal (usually after two or three years of work); others have been limited by core-memory capacity; still others encountered programming difficulties. A few projects have not progressed nearly as much as was hoped, notably projects in language translation and mathematical theorem-proving. Both cases, I think, represent premature attempts to handle complex formalisms without also somehow representing their meaning.

The problem of combining programs is more serious. Partly because of the very brief history of the field there is a shortage of well-developed ideas about systems for the communication of partial results between different programs, and for modifying programs already written to meet new conditions. Until this situation is improved it will remain hard to combine the results of separate research projects. Warren Teitelman of our laboratory has recently developed a programming system that may help in this regard; he has demonstrated it by re-creating in a matter of hours the results of some earlier programs that took weeks to write.

The questions people most often ask are: Can the programs learn through experience and thus improve themselves? Is this not the obvious path to making them intelligent? The answer to each is both yes and no. Even at this early stage the programs use many kinds of processes that might be called learning; they remember and use the methods that solved other problems; they adjust some of their internal characteristics for the best performance; they

```
(THE PROBLEM TO BE SOLVED IS)
(THE GAS CONSUMPTION OF MY CAR IS 15 MILES PER GALLON . THE
DISTANCE BETWEEN BOSTON AND NEW YORK IS 250 MILES . WHAT IS
THE NUMBER OF GALLONS OF GAS USED ON A TRIP BETWEEN NEW YORK
AND BOSTON Q.)

(THE EQUATIONS TO BE SOLVED ARE)

(EQUAL G02556 (NUMBER OF GALLONS OF GAS USED ON TRIP BETWEEN
NEW YORK AND BOSTON))

(EQUAL (DISTANCE BETWEEN BOSTON AND NEW YORK) (TIMES 250 (MILES)))

(EQUAL (GAS CONSUMPTION OF MY CAR) (QUOTIENT (TIMES 15 (MILES))
(TIMES 1 (GALLONS))))

THE EQUATIONS WERE INSUFFICIENT TO FIND A SOLUTION

(USING THE FOLLOWING KNOWN RELATIONSHIPS)
((EQUAL (DISTANCE) (TIMES (SPEED) (TIME))) (EQUAL (DISTANCE)
(TIMES (GAS CONSUMPTION) (NUMBER OF GALLONS OF GAS USED))))

(ASSUMING THAT)
((DISTANCE) IS EQUAL TO (DISTANCE BETWEEN BOSTON AND NEW YORK))

(ASSUMING THAT)
((GAS CONSUMPTION) IS EQUAL TO (GAS CONSUMPTION OF MY CAR))

(ASSUMING THAT)
((NUMBER OF GALLONS OF GAS USED) IS EQUAL TO (NUMBER OF GALLONS
OF GAS USED ON TRIP BETWEEN NEW YORK AND BOSTON))

(THE NUMBER OF GALLONS OF GAS USED ON A TRIP BETWEEN NEW YORK
AND BOSTON IS 16.66 GALLONS)
```

MOMENTARILY STUMPED at finding unknowns for which it has no equations, Student makes a guess that two phrases describe the same thing and goes on to solve the problem.

```
(THE PROBLEM TO BE SOLVED IS)
(THE GROSS WEIGHT OF A SHIP IS 20000 TONS . IF ITS NET WEIGHT
IS 15000 TONS , WHAT IS THE WEIGHT OF THE SHIPS CARGO Q.)

THE EQUATIONS WERE INSUFFICIENT TO FIND A SOLUTION

TRYING POSSIBLE IDIOMS

(DO YOU KNOW ANY MORE RELATIONSHIPS AMONG THESE VARIABLES)

(GROSS WEIGHT OF SHIP)

(TONS)

(ITS NET WEIGHT)

(WEIGHT OF SHIPS CARGO)

yes
TELL ME

(the weight of a ships cargo is the difference between
the gross weight and the net weight)

THE EQUATIONS WERE INSUFFICIENT TO FIND A SOLUTION

(ASSUMING THAT)
((NET WEIGHT) IS EQUAL TO (ITS NET WEIGHT))

(ASSUMING THAT)
((GROSS WEIGHT) IS EQUAL TO (GROSS WEIGHT OF SHIP))

(THE WEIGHT OF THE SHIPS CARGO IS 5000 TONS)
```

LACKING INFORMATION with which to solve a problem, Student asks for help. The operator (typing in lowercase letters) provides the necessary relations but does not use the same words as the problem used, forcing literal-minded Student to make some assumptions.

"associate" symbols that have been correlated in the past. No program today, however, can work any genuinely important change in its own basic structure. (A number of early experiments on "self-organizing" programs failed because of excessive reliance on random trial and error. A somewhat later attempt by the Carnegie Institute group to get their General Problem Solver to improve its descriptive ability was based on much sounder ideas; this project was left unfinished when it encountered difficulties in communication between programs, but it probably could be completed with the programming tools now available.)

In order for a program to improve itself substantially it would have to have at least a rudimentary understanding of its own problem-solving process and some ability to recognize an improvement when it found one. There is no inherent reason why this should be impossible for a machine. Given a model of its own workings, it could use its problem-solving power to work on the problem of self-improvement. The present programs are not quite smart enough for this purpose; they can only deal with the improvement of programs much simpler than themselves.

Once we have devised programs with a genuine capacity for self-improvement a rapid evolutionary process will begin. As the machine improves both itself and its model of itself, we shall begin to see all the phenomena associated with the terms "consciousness," "intuition" and "intelligence" itself. It is hard to say how close we are to this threshold, but once it is crossed the world will not be the same.

It is reasonable, I suppose, to be unconvinced by our examples and to be skeptical about whether machines will ever be intelligent. It is unreasonable, however, to think machines could become *nearly* as intelligent as we are and then stop, or to suppose we will always be able to compete with them in wit or wisdom. Whether or not we could retain some sort of control of the machines, assuming that we would want to, the nature of our activities and aspirations would be changed utterly by the presence on earth of intellectually superior beings.

```
((STUDENT    ($)    (/ (*S ORGPRB 1))                          *)
(*      ($)     (1 (FN TERPRI) (FN TERPRI) (FN TERPRI))        *)
(*      ((*P THE PROBLEM TO BE SOLVED IS))                     *)
(IDIOMS ($)                                                    *)
(*      (HOW OLD)   (WHAT)                                IDIOMS)
(*      (IS EQUAL TO)  (IS)                               IDIOMS)
(*      (YEARS YOUNGER THAN)   (LESS THAN)                IDIOMS)
(*      (YEARS OLDER THAN)   (PLUS)                       IDIOMS)
(*      (PERCENT LESS THAN)   (PERLESS)                   IDIOMS)
(*      (LESS THAN)   (LESSTHAN)                          IDIOMS)
(*      (THESE)   (THE)                                   IDIOMS)
(*      (MORE THAN)   (PLUS)                              IDIOMS)
(*      (FIRST TWO NUMBERS)   (THE FIRST NUMBER AND THE
            SECOND NUMBER)                                IDIOMS)
(*      (THREE NUMBERS)   (THE FIRST NUMBER AND THE SECOND
             NUMBER AND THE THIRD NUMBER)                 IDIOMS)
(*      (ONE HALF)  ( .5000)                              IDIOMS)
(*      (TWICE)   (2 TIMES)                               IDIOMS)
(*      (TWO NUMBERS)                                        SIM)
(*      ((* DOLLAR) $1)   (2 DOLLARS)                     IDIOMS)
(*      (CONSECUTIVE TO)   ((QUOTE 1) PLUS)               IDIOMS)
(*      (LARGER THAN)   (PLUS)                            IDIOMS)
(*      (PER CENT)   (PERCENT)                            IDIOMS)
(*      (HOW MANY)   (HOWM)                               IDIOMS)
(*      (SQUARE OF)   (SQUARE)                            IDIOMS)
(*      (($.1S) MULTIPLIED BY)   (TIMES)                  IDIOMS)
(*      (($.1S) DIVIDED BY)   (DIVBY)                     IDIOMS)
(*      (THE SUM OF)   (SUM)                              IDIOMS)
(*      ($)   (/ (*S NONID 1))                                 *)
(WORDS  ($1)   0   (/ (*Q SHELF (FN GETDCT 1 DICT)))
            WORDS)
(*      ($)   ((*A SHELF))                                     *)
(THE    (THE THE)   (1)                                      THE)
(*      ($)   (/ (*S MARKWD 1))                                *)
(*      (AS OLD AS)                                      AGEPROB)
(*      (AGE)                                            AGEPROB)
(*      (YEARS OLD)                                      AGEPROB)
(*      ($)   (/ (*D RETURN SENTENCE))                   BRACKET)
(SENTENCE   ($)   ((*N PROBLEM))                               *)
(*      ($1)   0   (/ (*S FIND (*E-1)) (*D RETURN SENTENCE
            ))                                            OPFORM)
(QUIET  ($)                                                    *)
(SUBSTITUTIONS  ($)   ((FN TERPRI) (*A NONID))                 *)
(*      ((*P WITH MANDATORY SUBSTITUTIONS THE PROBLEM IS))
              *)
(TAGGING    ($)   ((FN TERPRI) (*A MARKWD))                    *)
(*      ((*P WITH WORDS TAGGED BY FUNCTION THE PROBLEM IS)
            )                                                  *)
```

BOBROW'S PROGRAM is written in a language, METEOR, that he developed from the established programming language LISP. A small part of the program is illustrated here.

```
REMEMBER((
(PEOPLE IS THE PLURAL OF PERSON)
(FEET IS THE PLURAL OF FOOT)
(YARDS IS THE PLURAL OF YARD)
(FATHOMS IS THE PLURAL OF FATHOM)
(INCHES IS THE PLURAL OF INCH)
(SPANS IS THE PLURAL OF SPAN)
(ONE HALF ALWAYS MEANS  0.5  )
(THREE NUMBERS ALWAYS MEANS THE FIRST NUMBER AND THE SECOND
NUMBER AND THE THIRD NUMBER)
(FIRST TWO NUMBERS ALWAYS MEANS
THE FIRST NUMBER AND THE SECOND NUMBER)
(MORE THAN ALWAYS MEANS PLUS)
(THESE ALWAYS MEANS THE)
(TWO NUMBERS SOMETIMES MEANS ONE NUMBER AND THE
    OTHER NUMBER)
(TWO NUMBERS SOMETIMES MEANS ONE OF THE
    NUMBERS AND THE OTHER NUMBER)
(HAS IS A VERB)
(GETS IS A VERB)
(HAVE IS A VERB)
(LESS THAN ALWAYS MEANS LESSTHAN)
(LESSTHAN IS AN OPERATOR OF LEVEL 2)
(PERCENT IS AN OPERATOR OF LEVEL 2)
(PERCENT LESS THAN ALWAYS MEANS PERLESS)
(PERLESS IS AN OPERATOR OF LEVEL 2)
(PLUS IS AN OPERATOR OF LEVEL  2)
(SUM IS AN OPERATOR)
(TIMES IS AN OPERATOR OF LEVEL 1)
(SQUARE IS AN OPERATOR OF LEVEL 1)
(DIVBY IS AN OPERATOR OF LEVEL 1)
(OF IS AN OPERATOR)
(DIFFERENCE IS AN OPERATOR)
(SQUARED IS AN OPERATOR)
(MINUS IS AN OPERATOR OF LEVEL 2)
(PER IS AN OPERATOR)
(SQUARED IS AN OPERATOR)
(YEARS OLDER THAN ALWAYS MEANS PLUS)
(YEARS YOUNGER THAN ALWAYS MEANS LESS THAN)
(IS EQUAL TO ALWAYS MEANS IS)
(PLUSS IS AN OPERATOR)
(MINUSS IS AN OPERATOR)
(HOW OLD ALWAYS MEANS WHAT)
(THE PERIMETER OF $1 RECTANGLE SOMETIMES MEANS
TWICE THE SUM OF THE LENGTH AND  WIDTH OF THE RECTANGLE)
(GALLONS IS THE PLURAL OF GALLON)
(HOURS IS THE PLURAL OF HOUR)
(MARY IS A PERSON)
(ANN IS A PERSON)
(BILL IS A PERSON)
(A FATHER IS A PERSON)
(AN UNCLE IS A PERSON)
(POUNDS IS THE PLURAL OF POUND)
(WEIGHS IS A VERB)
))
REMEMBER ((
(DISTANCE EQUALS SPEED TIMES TIME)
(DISTANCE EQUALS GAS CONSUMPTION TIMES
NUMBER OF GALLONS OF GAS USED)
(1 FOOT EQUALS 12 INCHES)
(1 YARD EQUALS 3 FEET)
))
```

FILING SYSTEM for Student is loosely organized, with different kinds of information listed in an unordered dictionary. This makes it easy to add new information as needed.

21

PATTERN RECOGNITION BY MACHINE

OLIVER G. SELFRIDGE AND ULRIC NEISSER • August 1960

Can a machine think? The answer to this old chestnut is certainly yes: Computers have been made to play chess and checkers, to prove theorems, to solve intricate problems of strategy. Yet the intelligence implied by such activities has an elusive, unnatural quality. It is not based on any orderly development of cognitive skills. In particular, the machines are not well equipped to select from their environment the things, or the relations, they are going to think about.

In this they are sharply distinguished from intelligent living organisms. Every child learns to analyze speech into meaningful patterns long before he can prove any propositions. Computers can find proofs, but they cannot understand the simplest spoken instructions. Even the earliest computers could do arithmetic superbly, but only very recently have they begun to read the written digits that a child recognizes before he learns to add them. Understanding speech and reading print are examples of a basic intellectual skill that can variously be called cognition, abstraction or perception; perhaps the best general term for it is pattern recognition.

Except for their inability to recognize patterns, machines (or, more accurately, the programs that tell machines what to do) have now met most of the classic criteria of intelligence that skeptics have proposed. They *can* outperform their designers: The checker-playing program devised by Arthur L. Samuel of International Business Machines Corporation usually beats him. They *are* original: The "logic theorist," a creation of a group from the Carnegie Institute of Technology and the Rand Corporation (Allen Newell, Herbert Simon and J. C. Shaw) has found proofs for many of the theorems in *Principia Mathematica*, the monumental work in mathematical logic by A. N. Whitehead and Bertrand Russell. At least one proof is more elegant than the Whitehead-Russell version.

Sensible as they are, the machines are not perceptive. The information they receive must be fed to them one "bit" (a contraction of "binary digit," denoting a unit of information) at a time, up to perhaps millions of bits. Computers do not organize or classify the material in any very subtle or generally applicable way. They perform only highly specialized operations on carefully prepared inputs.

In contrast, a man is continuously exposed to a welter of data from his senses, and abstracts from it the patterns relevant to his activity at the moment. His ability to solve problems, prove theorems and generally run his life depends on this type of perception. We suspect that until programs to perceive patterns can be developed, achievements in mechanical problem-solving will remain isolated technical triumphs.

Developing pattern-recognition programs has proved rather difficult. One reason for the difficulty lies in the nature of the task. A man who abstracts a pattern from a complex of stimuli has essentially classified the possible inputs. But very often the basis of classification is unknown, even to himself; it is too complex to be specified explicitly. Asked to define a pattern, the man does so by example; as a logician might say, ostensively. This letter is A, that person is mother, these speech sounds are a request to pass the salt. The important patterns are defined by experience. Every human being acquires his pattern classes by adapting to a social or environmental consensus—in short, by learning.

In company with workers at various institutions our group at the Lincoln Laboratory of the Massachusetts Institute of Technology has been working on mechanical recognition of patterns. Thus far only a few simple cases have been tackled. We shall discuss two examples. The first one is MAUDE (for Morse Automatic Decoder), a program for translating, or rather transliterating, hand-sent Morse code. This program was developed at the Lincoln Laboratory by a group of workers under the direction of Bernard Gold.

If telegraphers sent ideal Morse, recognition would be easy. The keyings, or "marks," for dashes would be exactly three times as long as the marks for dots; spaces separating the marks within a letter or other character (mark spaces) would be as long as dots; spaces between characters (character spaces), three times as long; spaces separating words (word spaces), seven times as long. Unfortunately human operators do not transmit these ideal intervals. A machine that processed a signal on the assumption that they do would perform very poorly indeed. In an actual message the distinction between dots and dashes is far from clear. There is a great deal of variation among the dots and dashes, and also among the three kinds of space. In fact, when a long message sent by a single operator is analyzed, it frequently turns out that some dots are longer than some dashes, and that some mark spaces are longer than some character spaces.

With a little practice in receiving code, the average person has no trouble with these irregularities. The patterns of the letters are defined for him in terms of the continuing consensus of experience, and he adapts to them as he listens. Soon he does not hear dots and dashes at all, but perceives the characters as wholes. Exactly how he does so is still obscure, and the mechanism probably varies widely from one operator to another. In any event transliteration is impossible if each mark and space is considered individually. MAUDE therefore uses contextual information, but far less than is available to a trained operator. The machine program knows all the standard Morse characters and a few compound ones, but no syllables or words. A trained operator, on the other hand, hears the characters themselves embedded in a meaningful context.

Empirically it is easier to distinguish between the two kinds of mark than among the three kinds of space. The main problem for any mechanical Morse translator is to segment the message into its characters by identifying the character spaces. MAUDE begins by assuming that the longest of each six consecutive spaces is a character space (since no Morse character is more than six marks long), and the shortest is a mark space. It is important to note that although the former rule follows logically from the structure of the ideal code, and that the latter seems quite plausible, their effectiveness can be demonstrated only by experiment. In fact the rules fail less than once in 10,000 times.

The decoding process proceeds as follows [*see illustration on page 156*]. The marks and spaces, received by the machine in the form of electrical pulses, are converted into a sequence of numbers measuring their duration. (For technical reasons these numbers are then converted into their logarithms.) The sequence of durations representing spaces

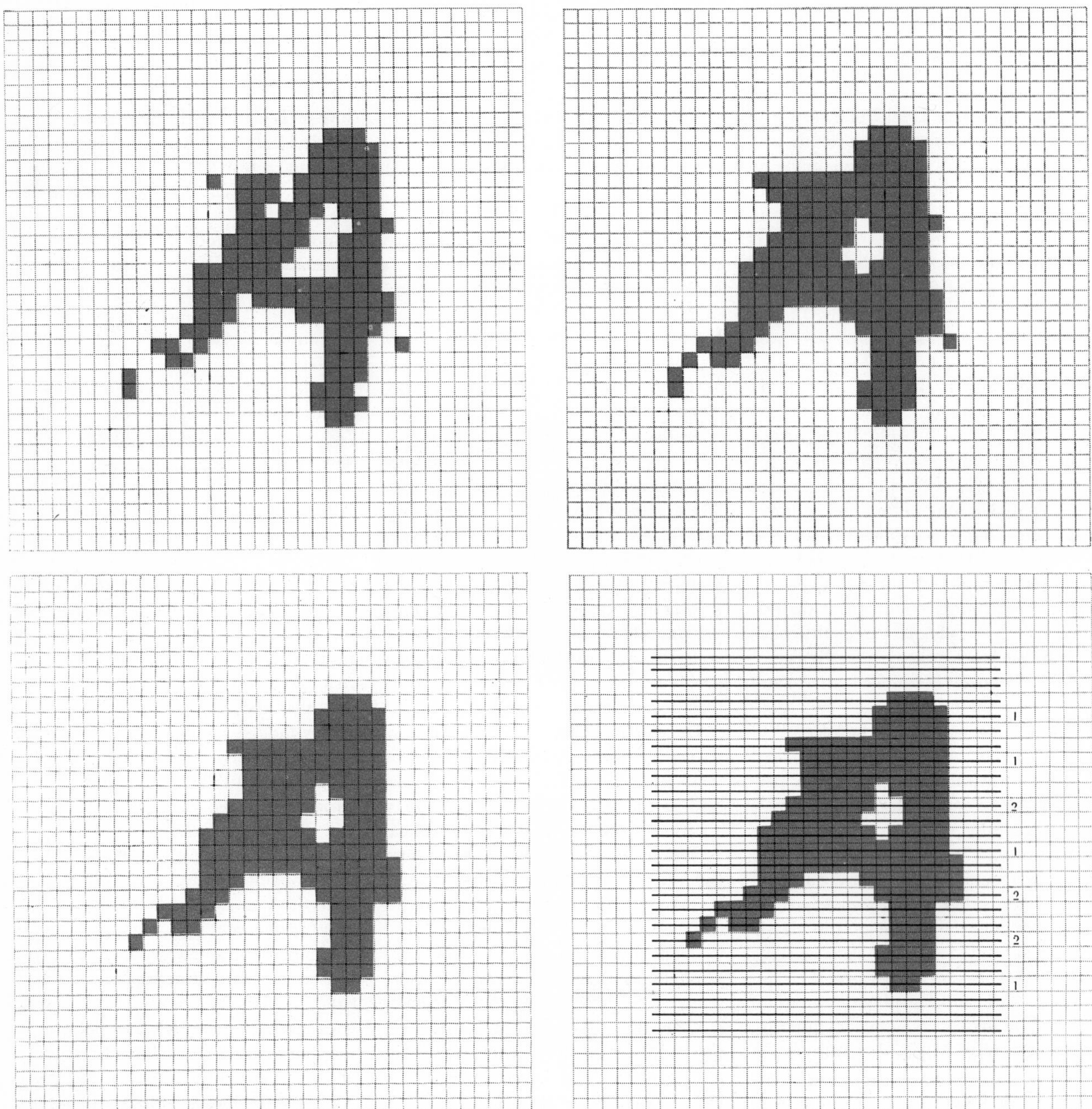

HAND-PRINTED LETTER A is processed for recognition by computer. Original sample is placed on grid and converted to a cellular pattern by completely filling in all squares through which lines pass (*top left*). The computer then cleans up the sample, filling in gaps (*top right*) and eliminating isolated cells (*bottom left*). The program tests the pattern for a variety of features. The test illustrated here (*bottom right*) is for the maximum number of intersections of the sample with all horizontal lines across the grid.

is processed first. The machine examines each group of six (spaces one through six, two through seven, three through eight and so on), recording in each the longest and shortest durations. When this process is complete, about 75 per cent of the character spaces and about 50 per cent of the mark spaces will have been identified.

To classify the remaining spaces a threshold is computed. It is set at the most plausible dividing line between the range of durations in which mark spaces have been found and the range of the identified character spaces. Every unclassified number larger than the threshold is then identified as a character space; every one smaller than the threshold, as a mark space.

Now, by a similar process, the numbers representing marks are identified as dots and dashes. Combining the classified marks and spaces gives a string of tentative segments, separated by character spaces. These are inspected and compared to a set of proper Morse characters stored in the machine. (There are about 50 of these, out of the total of 127 possible sequences of six or fewer marks.) Experience has shown that when one of the tentative segments is not acceptable, it is most likely that one of the supposed mark spaces within the segment should be a character space instead. The program reclassifies the longest space in the segment as a character space and examines the two new characters thus formed. The procedure continues until every segment is an acceptable character, whereupon the message is printed out.

In the course of transmitting a long message, operators usually change speed from time to time. MAUDE adapts to these changes. The computed thresholds are local, moving averages that shift with the general lengthening or shortening of marks and spaces. Thus a mark of a certain duration could be classified as a dot in one part of the message and a dash in another.

MAUDE's error rate is only slightly higher than that of a skilled human operator. Thus it is at least possible for a machine to recognize patterns even where the basis of classification is variable and not fully specified in advance. Moreover, the program illustrates an important general point. Its success depends on the rules by which the continuous message is divided into appropriate segments. Segmentation seems likely to be a primary problem in all mechanical pattern-recognition, particularly in the recognition of speech, since the natural pauses in spoken language do not generally come between words. MAUDE handles the segmentation problems in terms of context, and this will often be appropriate. In other respects MAUDE does not provide an adequate basis for generalizing about pattern recognition. The patterns of Morse code are too easy, and the processing is rather specialized.

Our second example deals with a more challenging problem: the recognition of hand-printed letters of the alphabet. The characters that people print in the ordinary course of filling out forms and questionnaires are surprisingly varied. Gaps abound where continuous lines might be expected; curves and sharp angles appear interchangeably; there is almost every imaginable distortion of slant, shape and size. Even human readers cannot always identify such characters; their error rate is about 3 per cent on randomly selected letters and numbers, seen out of context.

The first step in designing a mechanical reader is to provide it with a means of assimilating the visual data. By nature computers consider information in strings of bits: sequences of zeros and ones recorded in on-off devices. The simplest way to encode a character into such a sequence is to convert it into a sort of half-tone by splitting it into a mesh or matrix of squares as fine as may be necessary. Each square is then either black or white—a binary situation that the machine is designed to handle. Making such half-tones presents no problem. For example, an image of the letter could be projected on a bank of photocells, with the output of each cell controlling a binary device in the computer. In the ex-

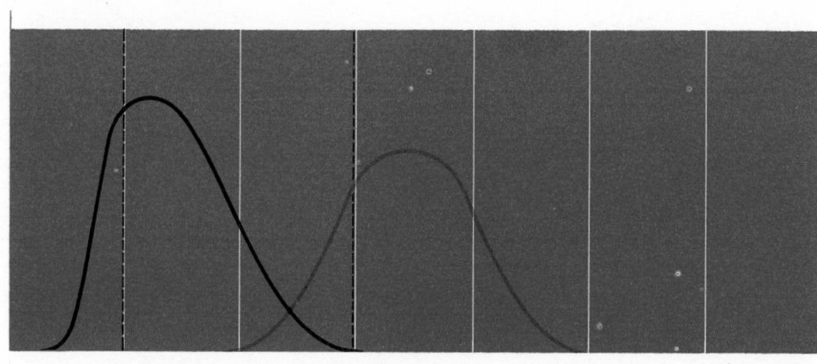

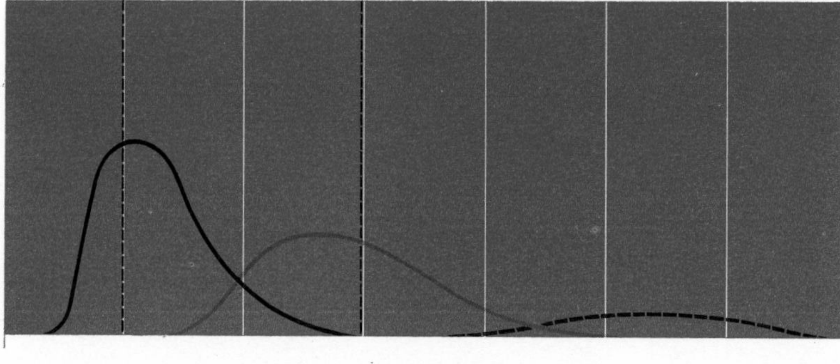

VARIABILITY OF MORSE CODE sent by a human operator is illustrated in these curves. Upper graph shows range of durations for dots (*black curve*) and dashes (*gray curve*) in a message. Lower graph gives the same information for spaces between marks within a character (*solid black curve*), spaces between characters (*gray curve*) and between words (*broken curve*). Ideal durations are shown by brackets at top and vertical broken lines.

periments to be described here the appropriate digital information from the matrix was recorded on punch cards and was fed into the computer in this form.

Once this sequence of bits has been put in, how shall the program proceed to identify it? Perhaps the most obvious approach is a simple matching scheme, which would evaluate the similarity of the unknown to a series of ideal templates of all the letters, previously stored in digital form in the machine. The sequence of zeros and ones representing the unknown letter would be compared to each template sequence, and the number of matching digits recorded in each case. The highest number of matches would identify the letter.

In its primitive form the scheme would clearly fail. Even if the unknown were identical to the template, slight changes in position, orientation or size could destroy the match completely [*see top illustration on page 157*]. This difficulty has long been recognized, and in some character-recognition programs it has been met by inserting a level of information-processing ahead of the template-matching procedure. The sample is shifted, rotated and magnified or reduced in order to put it into a standard, or at least a more tractable, form.

Although obviously an improvement over raw matching, such a procedure is still inadequate. What it does is to compare shapes rather successfully. But letters are a good deal more than mere shapes. Even when a sample has been converted to standard size, position and orientation, it may match a wrong template more closely than it matches the right one [*see bottom illustration on page 157*].

Nevertheless the scheme illustrates what we believe to be an important general principle. The critical change was from a program with a single level of operation to a program with two distinctly different levels. The first level shifts, and the second one matches. Such a hierarchical structure is forced on the recognition system by the nature of the entities to be recognized. The letter A is defined by the set of configurations that people call A, and their selections can be described—or imitated—only by a multilevel program.

We have said that letter patterns cannot be described merely as shapes. It appears that they can be specified only in terms of a preponderance of certain *features*. Thus A tends to be thinner at the top than at the bottom; it is roughly concave at the bottom; it usually has two main strokes more vertical than horizontal, one more horizontal than vertical, and so on. All these features taken together characterize A rather more closely than they characterize any other letter. Singly none of them is sufficient. For example, W is also roughly concave

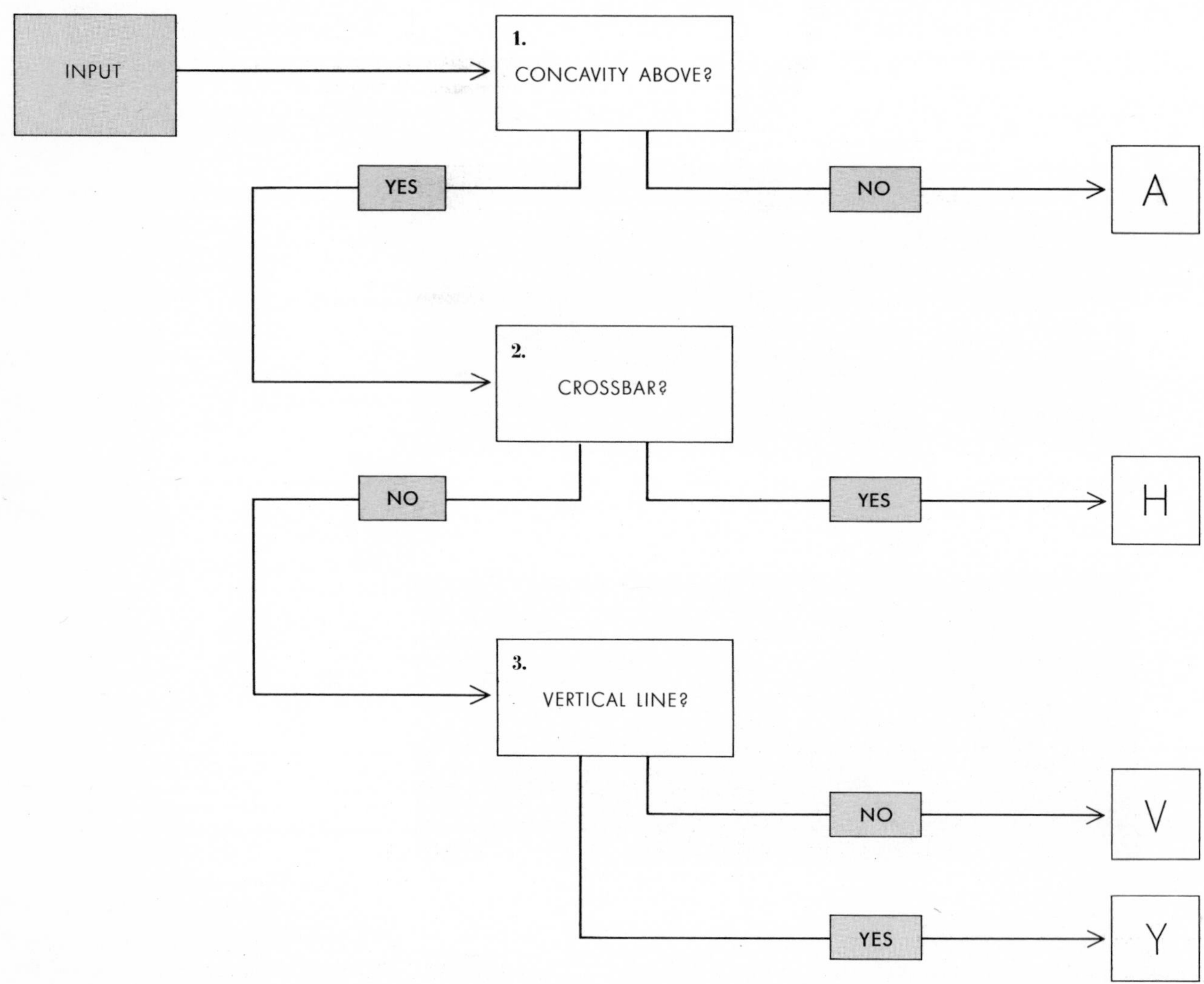

SEQUENTIAL-PROCESSING program for distinguishing four letters, A, H, V and Y employs three test features: presence or absence of a concavity above, a crossbar and a vertical line. The tests are applied in order, with each outcome determining the next step.

at the bottom, and H has a pattern of horizontal and vertical strokes similar to that described for A. Each letter has its own set of probable features, and a successful character recognizer will determine which set is the best fit to an unknown sample.

So far nothing has been said about how the features are to be determined and how the program will use them. The template-matching scheme represents one approach. Its "features," in a sense, are the individual cells of the matrix representing the unknown sample, and its procedure is to match them with corresponding cells in the template. Both features and procedure are determined by the designer. We have seen that this scheme will not succeed. In fact, any system must fail if it tries to specify every detail of a procedure for identifying patterns that are themselves defined only ostensively. A pattern-recognition system must learn. But how much?

At one extreme there have been attempts to make it learn, or generate, everything: the features, the processing, the decision procedure. The initial state of such a system is called a "random net." A large number of on-off computer elements are multiply interconnected in a random way. Each is thus fed by several others. The thresholds of the elements (the number of signals that must be received before the element fires) are then adjusted on the basis of performance. In other words, the system learns by reinforcing some pathways through the net and weakening others.

How far a random net can evolve is controversial. Probably a net can come to act as though it used templates. However, none has yet been shown capable of generating features more sophisticated than those based, like templates, on single matrix-cells. Indeed, we do not believe that this is possible.

At present the only way the machine can get an adequate set of features is from a human programmer. The effectiveness of any particular set can be demonstrated only by experiment. In general there is probably safety in numbers. The designer will do well to include all the features he can think of that might plausibly be useful.

A program that does not develop its own features may nevertheless be capable of modifying some subsequent level of the decision procedure, as we shall see. First however, let us consider that procedure itself. There are two fundamentally different possibilities: sequential and parallel processing. In sequential processing the features are inspected in a predetermined order, the outcome of each test determining the next step. Each letter is represented by a unique sequence of binary decisions. To take a simple example, a program to distinguish the letters A, H, V and Y

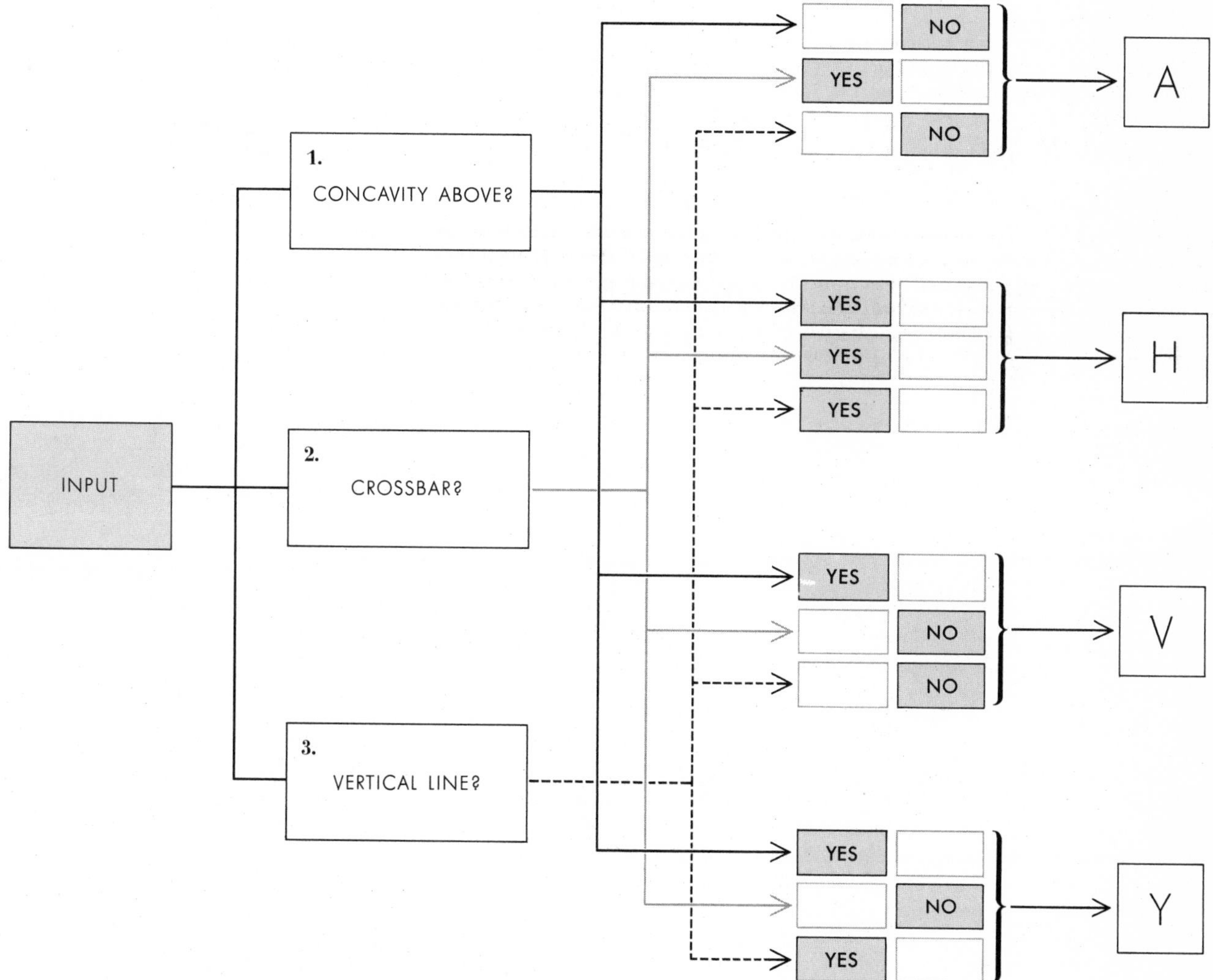

PARALLEL-PROCESSING program uses the same test features as the sequential program on opposite page, but applies all tests simultaneously and makes decision on the basis of the combined outcomes. The input is a sample of one of the letters A, H, V and Y.

LETTER	SAMPLES	OUTCOME			
		1	2	3	4
A	39		33	6	
E	46	6	35	5	
I	25	25			
L	24	7	17		
M	24			18	6
N	28		2	25	1
O	34		27	7	
R	33		28	4	1
S	38	8	30		
T	39	10	22	7	
TOTAL	330	56	194	72	8

"CENSUS" represents information learned by letter-recognition program during training period. This table summarizes the outcomes of the test for maximum number of intersections with a horizontal line, applied to a total of 330 identified samples in the learning process.

might decide among them on the basis of the presence or absence of three features: a concavity at the top, a crossbar and a vertical line. The sequential process would ask first: "Is there a concavity at the top?" If the answer is no, the sample is A. If the answer is yes, the program asks: "Is there a crossbar?" If yes, the letter is H; if no, then: "Is there a vertical line?" If yes, the letter is Y; if no, V [*see illustration on page 152*].

In parallel processing all the questions would be asked at once, and all the answers presented simultaneously to the decision-maker [*see illustration on preceding page*]. Different combinations identify the different letters. One might think of the various features as being inspected by little demons, all of whom then shout the answers in concert to a decision-making demon. From this conceit comes the name "Pandemonium" for parallel processing.

Of the two systems the sequential type is the more natural for a machine. Computer programs are sequences of instructions, in which choices or alternatives are usually introduced as "conditional transfers": Follow one set of instructions if a certain number is negative (say) and another set of instructions if it is not. Programs of this kind can be highly efficient, especially in cases where any given decision is almost certain to be right. But in "noisy" situations sequential programs require elaborate checking and back-tracking procedures to compensate for erroneous decisions. Parallel processing, on the other hand, need make no special allowance for error and uncertainty.

Furthermore, some features are simply not subject to a reasonable dichotomy. An A very surely has a crossbar, an O very surely has not. But what about B? The most we can say is that it has more of a crossbar than O, and less than A. A Pandemonium program can handle the situation by having the demons shout more or less loudly. In other words, the information flowing through the system need not be binary; it can represent the quantitative preponderance of the various features.

Still another advantage of parallel processing lies in the possibility of making small changes in a network for experimental purposes. In typical sequential programs the only possible changes involve replacing a zero with a one, or vice versa. In parallel ones, on the other hand, the weight given to crossbarness in deciding if the unknown is actually B may be changed by as small an amount as desired. Experimental changes of this kind need not be made by the programmer alone. A program can be designed to alter internal weights as a result of experience and to profit from its mistakes. Such learning is much easier to incorporate into a Pandemonium than into a sequential system, where a change at any point has grave consequences for large parts of the system.

Parallel processing seems to be the human way of handling pattern recognition as well. Speech can be understood if all acoustic frequencies above 2,000 cycles per second are eliminated, but it can also be understood if those below 2,000 are eliminated instead. Depth perception is excellent if both eyes are open and the head is held still; it is also excellent if one eye is open and the head is allowed to move.

A Pandemonium system that learns from experience has been tested by Worthie Doyle of the Lincoln Laboratory. At present it is programmed to identify 10 hand-printed characters, and has been tested on samples of A, E, I, L, M, N, O, R, S and T. The program has six levels: (1) input, (2) clean-up, (3) inspection of features, (4) comparison with learned-feature distribution, (5) computation of probabilities and (6) decision. The input is a 1,024-cell matrix, 32 on a side. At the second level the sample character is smoothed by filling in isolated gaps and eliminating isolated patches [*see illustration on page 150*].

Recognition is based on such features as the relative length of different edges and the maximum number of intersections of the sample with a horizontal line. (The computer "draws" the lines by inspecting every horizontal row in the matrix, and recognizes "intersections" as sequences of ones separated by sequences of zeros.) No single feature is essential to recognition, and various numbers of them have been tried. The particular program shown here [*see illustration on opposite page*] uses 28.

Every letter fed into the machine is tested for each of the features. During the learning phase a number of samples

RECOGNITION PROGRAM for hand-printed letters applies the 28 feature tests listed by code name at left. Names represent such features as maximum intersections with horizontal line (HOMSXC), concavity facing south (SOUCAV) and so on. Figures in right-hand section of table are relative probabilities of all letters for each test outcome. The program decides on the letter with the largest total of all probabilities. In the example shown here the decision is for the letter A, with a probability total of 4.579.

TYPE OF TEST AND DESIGNATION		OUTCOME	A	E	I	L	M	N	O	R	S	T
HORIZONTAL AND VERTICAL CROSS-SECTIONS	HOMSXC	3	.083	.070			.250	.347	.097	.056		.097
	VEMSXC	3	.073	.339			.040		.008	.194	.258	.089
	HORUNS	2111111		.500						.500		
	VERUNS	2111111						1.000				
STROKES	HORSTR	1	.182	.006	.125	.125	.125	.146	.016	.057	.016	.203
	VERSTR	2	.178	.007			.170	.207	.229	.207		
EDGE LENGTHS AND RATIOS	SEDGE	1	.267	.007		.014	.158	.115	.007	.165		.266
	WEDGE	1	.083	.071	.024	.024	.035	.012		.047	.318	.389
	NEDGE	2	.259	.024	.153	.024	.106	.106	.071	.059	.189	.012
	EEDGE	4	.232		.161		.214	.286	.107			
	NO:SOU	4	.513				.205	.077		.128		.077
	EA:WES	1	.055	.400		.309	.018	.036		.163		.018
PROFILES	SOUCAV	3	.150				.800	.050				
	WESCAV	2	.047	.094	.023	.012	.023	.035	.035	.059	.412	.259
	NORCAV	1	.133	.177	.100	.092	.004		.133	.108	.116	.137
	EASCAV	1	.155	.005	.115	.095	.105	.130	.170	.010	.050	.165
	SOUBOT	220	.268	.106		.068	.159	.167	.008	.220	.008	
	WESBOT	221	.030	.030	.061						.364	.515
	NORBOT	121	.290	.145					.354	.042	.042	.125
	EASBOT	121	.326				.020	.102	.266	.020	.245	.020
INTERNAL STRUCTURE	SBOTSG	2	.250	.008		.016	.125	.141	.219	.203	.039	
	WBOTSG	1	.161	.076	.090	.099	.108	.121	.063	.081	.045	.157
	NBOTSG	1	.119	.190	.111	.102	.013	.018	.089	.040	.159	.159
	EBOTSG	1	.147	.058	.098	.103	.103	.121	.062	.071	.076	.061
	SOUBEN	20					.333	.167				.500
	WESBEN	10	.198	.143	.011	.022	.121	.132	.011	.099	.022	.241
	NORBEN	10	.169	.180		.135	.079			.146	.247	.045
	EASBEN	10	.211	.012	.012	.118	.176	.106		.176		.188
TOTAL SCORE			4.579	2.648	1.084	1.358	3.490	3.622	1.945	2.851	2.606	3.823

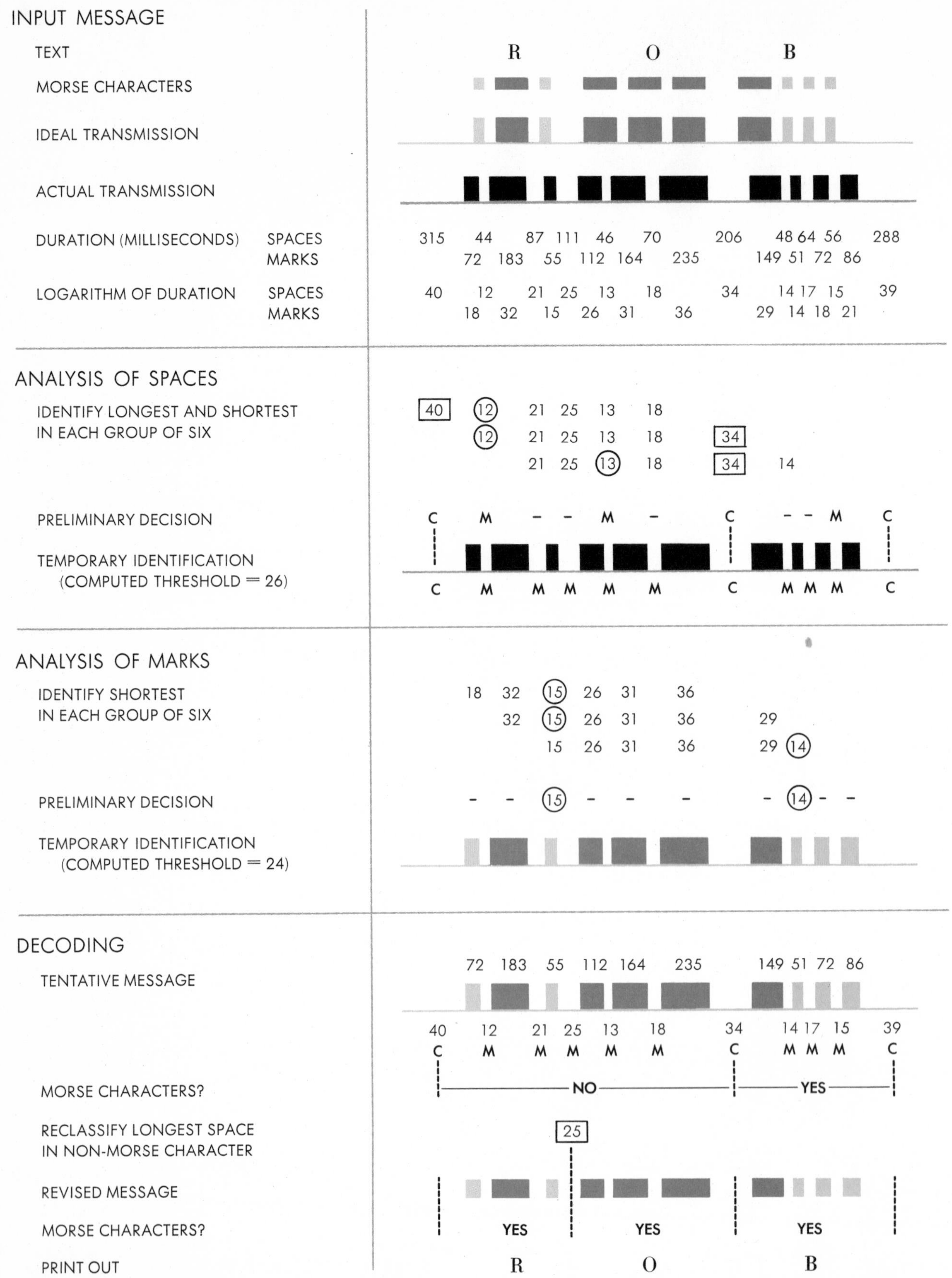

"MAUDE" PROGRAM, described in text, translates Morse code. Marks identified as dots are shown in light color; marks identified as dashes, in dark color. Unidentified marks are in black. Character spaces are denoted by C; mark spaces, by M. A circle around a number indicates that it is the smallest in a group; a rectangle means it is the largest. Analysis of spaces and marks proceeds by an examination of successive groups of six throughout the message. The table shows only the first three such groups in each case.

of each of the 10 letters is presented and identified. For every feature the program compiles a table or "census." It tests each sample and enters the outcome under the appropriate letter. When the learning period is finished, the table shows how many times each outcome occurred for each of the 10 letters. The table on page 154, which refers to maximum intersections with a horizontal line, represents the experience gained from a total of 330 training samples. It shows, for example, that the outcome (three intersections) occurred 72 times distributed among six A's, five E's, 18 M's, 25 N's, seven O's, four R's, seven T's and no other letters. The other possible outcomes are similarly recorded.

TEMPLATE MATCHING cannot succeed when the unknown letter (*color*) has the wrong size, orientation or position. The program must begin by adjusting sample to standard form.

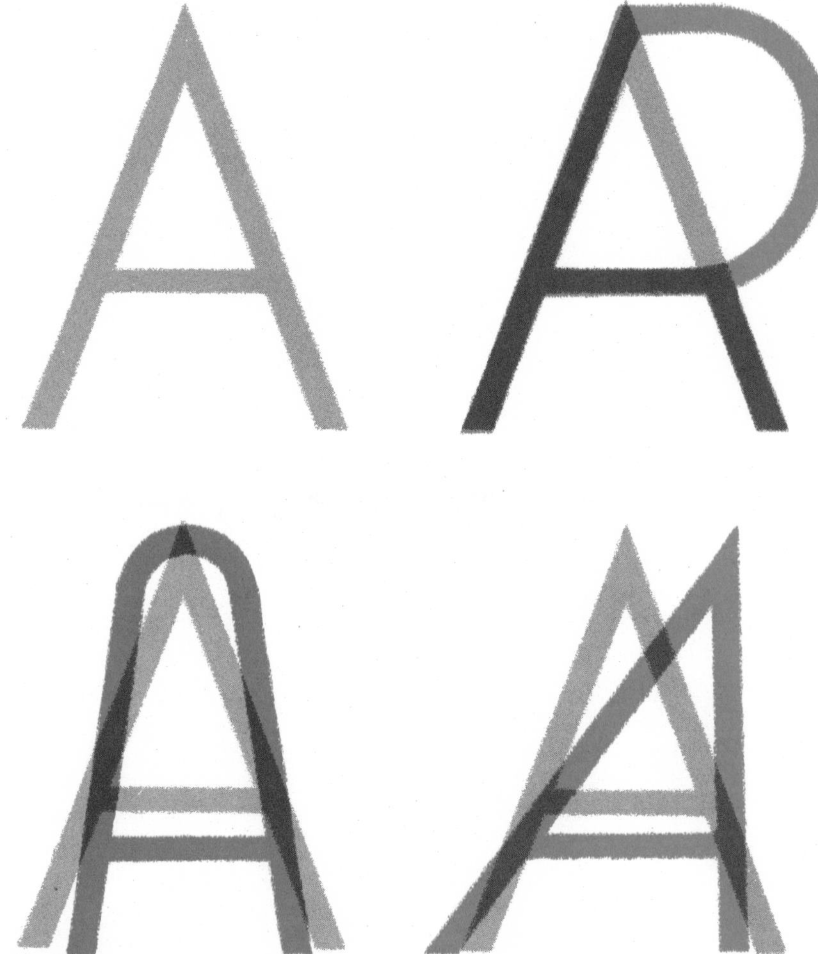

INCORRECT MATCH may result even when sample (*color*) has been converted to standard form. Here R matches A template more closely than do samples of the correct letter.

Next the 28 censuses are converted to tables of estimated probabilities, by dividing each entry by the appropriate total. Thus the outcome—three intersections—comes from an A with a probability of .083 (6/72); an E, with a probability of .070 (5/72), and so on.

Now the system is ready to consider an unknown sample. It carries out the 28 tests and "looks up" each outcome in the corresponding feature census, entering the estimated probabilities in a table. Then the total probabilities are computed for each letter. The final decision is made by choosing the letter with the highest probability.

This program makes only about 10 per cent fewer correct identifications than human readers make—a respectable performance, to be sure. At the same time, the things it cannot do point to the difficulties that still lie ahead. We would emphasize three general problems: segmentation, hierarchical learning and feature generation.

Characters must be fed in one at a time. The program is unable to segment continuous written material. The problem will doubtless be relatively easy to solve for text consisting of separate printed characters, but will be more formidable in the case of cursive script.

The program learns on one level only. The relation between feature presence and character probability is determined by experience; everything else is fixed by the designer. It would certainly be desirable for a character recognizer to use experience for more general improvements: to change its clean-up procedures, alter the way probabilities are combined and refine its decision process. Eventually we look to recognition of words; at that point the program will have to learn a vocabulary so that it can use context in identifying dubious letters. At the moment, however, neither we nor any other designers have any experience with the interaction of several levels of learning.

The most important learning process of all is still untouched: No current program can generate test features of its own. The effectiveness of all of them is forever restricted by the ingenuity or arbitrariness of their programmers. We can barely guess how this restriction might be overcome. Until it is, "artificial intelligence" will remain tainted with artifice.

PART FIVE

RECENT COMPUTER APPLICATIONS

RECENT COMPUTER APPLICATIONS

INTRODUCTION

General assertions that digital computers will revolutionize science, technology, and even society, are by now as hackneyed as they are true. Progress in the physical sciences has been greatly accelerated by these machines, and there is every reason to believe that their impact on the social and behavioral sciences will be at least as great.

Several of the articles in the preceding section dealt with attempts to turn the computer into an intelligent machine. The extent to which these efforts are or will be successful depends upon the ability of scientists to exploit three basic potentialities of the machine—raw computing power, flexibility, and, for want of a better word, sociability. These three characteristics make the digital computer capable of becoming one of the most important tools that has ever been available to the general scientific community and to the behavioral scientist in particular.

The computer's most important characteristic, by far, is its ability to process information rapidly and accurately. Many recently developed machines are capable of performing a thousand numerical operations (additions, subtractions, and so forth) in a second. It is not surprising, consequently, that the earliest, and still most prevalent, use of computers in the behavioral sciences is as an inhumanly fast and reliable statistical clerk. For this kind of task, the computer is simply given a set of numbers (the data) and a set of instructions (the program) that tell the machine what operations to perform on the numbers. From these, the computer is able to organize, summarize, and analyze immense masses of data in a small fraction of the time required by the human with a desk calculator.

The computer's contribution to behavioral sciences in this menial role of glorified clerk should not be undervalued. The availability of such computing power has made feasible numerous developments that would have been prohibitively expensive otherwise. At one time, the scope of empirical studies in the social sciences was limited by the number of man-hours required to tabulate and summarize the data. Statistical techniques for analyzing data had to be kept simple enough that the results of a study could be made available within a decade. The development of more sophisticated and powerful analytic techniques was little more than intellectual amusement, simply because the numerical computations required for use of the techniques could tie up several assistants for as long as a year. Finally, the development of mathematical theories of behavioral phenomena was both thwarted and channeled by the absence of computational power. That the emergence of such formal theories was thwarted can be inferred from the fact that many current mathematical theories are so dependent on computers that their usefulness would be seriously vitiated if computers were unavailable. Those which did emerge were, more often than not, unrealistically simple.

Thus, the sheer calculating power afforded by the computer has removed an obstacle that was seriously impeding the growth of fertile mathematical thinking in the behavioral sciences. Furthermore, the computer's flexibility makes it something quite different from the Ultimate Desk Calculator. A desk calculator can process only numerical information, for example, while a computer is capable of handling words, sentences, pictures, and many other types of information in addition to numbers. Additional flexibility derives from the computer's ability to perform nonnumerical operations, such as "compare," "shift," "erase," and "transfer." Finally, the computer, unlike a desk calculator, can be made to respond differentially to the results of previous operations. When a desk calculator is instructed to multiply two numbers, for example, it does so and stops. It is elementary, however, to give a computer an instruction that might say in effect, "multiply x and y, and if the product is less than z do operation A, but if the product is equal to or greater than z do operation B." The computer's ability to "branch," to react to complex contingencies, is its most important source of flexibility.

The value of the computer to behavioral scientists is enhanced even more by the fact that it can be made sociable. This means simply that the machine can be made to interact in a meaningful and often intimate fashion with people. This potential allows man and the machine to work together in a coordinated and cooperative manner. It allows the individual (in many cases the scientist) to ask questions to which the computer can provide an answer within seconds. In other tasks, particularly in computer-aided instruction, it is the computer that poses the questions and the individual who must come up with the answer. Every effort is being made to improve the technology of sociability to a point at which man-machine interactions will require little more technical knowledge than that required for typical human interaction. Programming languages have been made more and more similar to natural language, and a rich variety of input and output devices which allow for diverse forms of communication between man and machine have been invented. As more of these "interpersonal" skills are developed for computers, men become less constrained to use the computer's language and more able to select a mode of communication that is ideally suited to the problem under investigation.

The articles in this section have one feature in common. Each of them describes the way in which digital computers have contributed to the study and understanding of a behavioral phenomenon. Because the specific natures of the applications discussed in these papers are nearly as varied as the substantive issues themselves, the articles nicely illustrate the range of possibilities for computer applications in research.

In "Computers," Stanislaw M. Ulam, after giving a thumbnail history of computers, describes a number of ways in which such machines have been usefully applied in mathematical research. The next two articles discuss applications that depend primarily on the computer's tremendous computational facility. In "Numerical Taxonomy," Robert R. Sokal describes how the computer is used to process lengthy numerical descriptions of a variety of organisms and to compute indices that measure the relative similarity or dissimilarity among them. Criticisms of traditional taxonomic procedures would have much less weight were it not for the fact that computers have provided the opportunity for the application of the more complex numerical techniques. Bela Julesz devotes his article "Texture and Visual Perception" mainly to a description of human perceptual processes, but he also points out the value of using the computer to generate the visual displays employed in his experiments. Not only can random patterns of dots be easily constructed for use in laboratory experiments, but the statistical nature of the "randomness" and the degree of organization of the pattern can be precisely controlled.

In "The Analysis of Brain Waves," Mary A. B. Brazier describes the invaluable role of the computer in the extraction of reliable biological signals from the deafening noise of the nervous system. She also notes the potentialities for man-machine interaction in the study of the electrical activity of the nervous system. Robert S. Ledley and Frank H. Ruddle, in "Chromosome Analysis by Computer," discuss a computer routine they have developed for the recognition, classification, and analysis of chromosomes. Their work not only represents an important example of a pattern recognition program, but also illustrates the convenience of using an unusual input (photographic film) and of obtaining a variety of outputs. In the final article "The Use of Computers in Education," Patrick Suppes describes several facets of what is now called "computer-assisted instruction." Suppes enumerates some of the advances and problems encountered in several facets of the student-machine interaction he has been studying. The importance of developing highly "social" machines, which can, for example, recognize spoken words, is evident in applications of this type.

22

COMPUTERS

STANISLAW M. ULAM • September 1964

Although to many people the electronic computer has come to symbolize the importance of mathematics in the modern world, few professional mathematicians are closely acquainted with the machine. Some, in fact, seem even to fear that individual scientific efforts will be pushed into the background or replaced by less imaginative, purely mechanical habits of research. I believe such fears to be quite groundless. It is preferable to regard the computer as a handy device for manipulating and displaying symbols. Even the most abstract thinkers agree that the simple act of writing down a few symbols on a piece of paper facilitates concentration. In this respect alone—and it is not a trivial one—the new electronic machines enlarge our effective memory and provide a marvelous extension of the means for experimenting with symbols in science. In this article I shall try to indicate how the computer can be useful in mathematical research.

The idea of using mechanical or semiautomatic means to perform arithmetical calculations is very old. The origin of the abacus is lost in antiquity, and computers of some kind were evidently built by the ancient Greeks. Blaise Pascal in the 17th century constructed a working mechanism to perform arithmetical operations. Gottfried Wilhelm von Leibniz, one of the creators of mathematical logic as well as the coinventor of the infinitesimal calculus, outlined a program for what would now be called automatized thinking. The man who clearly visualized a general-purpose computer, complete with a flexible programming scheme and memory units, was Charles Babbage of England. He described a machine he called the analytical engine in 1833 and spent the rest of his life and much of his fortune trying to build it.

Among the leading contributors to modern computer technology were an electrical engineer, J. Presper Eckert, Jr., a physicist, John W. Mauchly, and one of the leading mathematicians of this century, John von Neumann. In 1944 Eckert and Mauchly were deep in the development of a machine known as ENIAC, which stands for Electronic Numerical Integrator and Computer. Designed to compute artillery firing tables for the Army Ordnance Department, ENIAC was finally completed late in 1945. It was wired to perform a specific sequence of calculations; if a different sequence was needed, it had to be extensively rewired. On hearing of the ENIAC project during a visit to the Aberdeen Proving Ground in the summer of 1944, von Neumann became fascinated by the idea and began developing the logical design of a computer capable of using a flexible stored program: a program that could be changed at will without revising the computer's circuits.

A major stimulus for von Neumann's enthusiasm was the task he faced as consultant to the theoretical group at Los Alamos, which was charged with solving computational problems connected with the atomic-bomb project. After a discussion in which we reviewed one of these problems von Neumann turned to me and said: "Probably in its solution we shall have to perform more elementary arithmetical steps than the total in all the computations performed by the human race heretofore." I reminded him that there were millions of schoolchildren in the world and that the total number of additions, multiplications and divisions they were obliged to perform every day over a period of a few years would certainly exceed that needed in our problem. Unfortunately we could not harness this great reservoir of talent for our purposes, nor could we in 1944 command the services of an electronic computer. The atomic-bomb calculations had to be simplified to the point where they could be solved with paper and pencil and the help of old-fashioned desk calculators.

Down the hall from my present office at the Los Alamos Scientific Laboratory is an electronic computer known as MANIAC II (Mathematical Analyzer, Numerical Integrator and Computer), an advanced version of MANIAC I, which von Neumann and his associates completed at the Institute for Advanced Study in 1952. MANIAC II, which was put in operation in 1957, can add two numbers consisting of 13 decimal digits (43 binary digits) in about six microseconds (six millionths of a second). In a separate building nearby is a still newer computer called STRETCH, built by the International Business Machines Corporation, which can manipulate numbers containing 48 binary digits with about 10 times the overall speed of MANIAC II.

MANIAC II and STRETCH are examples of dozens of custom-designed computers built throughout the world in the past 20 years. The first of the big commercially built computers, UNIVAC I, was delivered to the Bureau of the Census in 1951; three years later the General Electric Company became the first industrial user of a UNIVAC I. In the 13 years since the first UNIVAC more than 16,000 computer systems of various makes and sizes have been put to work by the U.S. Government, industry and universities. Of these about 250 are of the largest type, with speed and power roughly

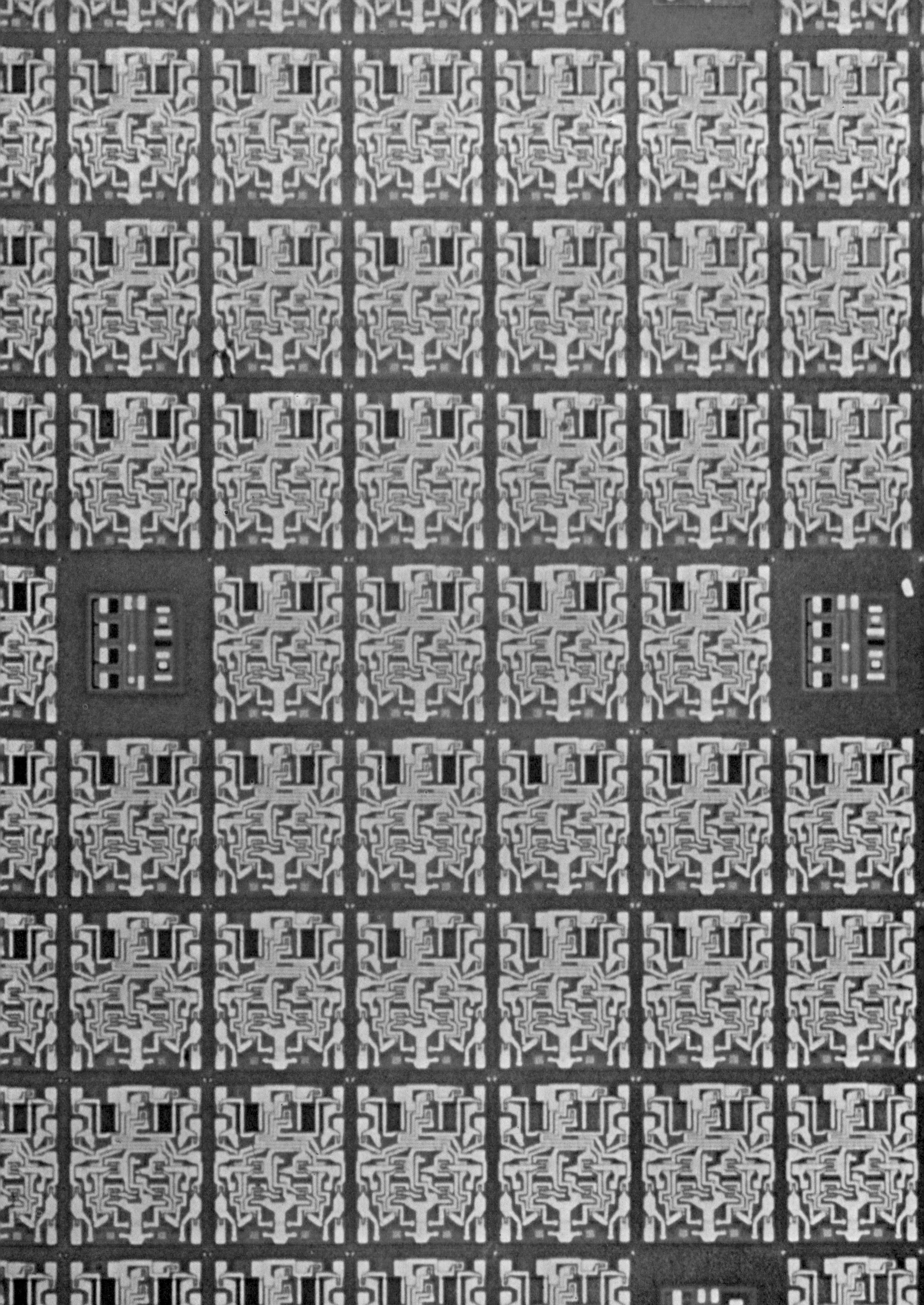

comparable to MANIAC II.

Together with increases in arithmetical speed have come increases in memory capacity and in speed of access to stored numbers and instructions. In the biggest electronic machines the memory capacity is now up to about 100,000 "words," or several million individual binary digits. I am referring here to the "fast" memory, to which the access time can be as short as a microsecond. This time is steadily being reduced; a hundredfold increase in speed seems possible in the near future. A "slow" memory, used as an adjunct to the fast one, normally consists of digits stored on magnetic tape and can be of almost unlimited capacity. The size of memory devices and basic electronic circuits has been steadily reduced, until now even the most elaborate computers can fit into a small room. The next generation of computers, employing microelectronic circuits, will be smaller by a factor of 100 to 1,000.

It is apparent that many problems are so difficult that they would tax the capacity of any machine one can imagine being built in the next decade. For example, the hydrodynamics of compressible fluids can be studied reasonably well on existing machines if the investigation is limited to problems in two dimensions, but it cannot be studied very satisfactorily in three dimensions. In a two-dimensional study one can imagine that the fluid is confined in a "box" that has been divided into, say, 10,000 cells; the cells are expressed in terms of two coordinates, each of which is divided into 100 parts. In each cell are stored several values, such as those for density and velocity, and a new set of values must be computed for each successive chosen unit of time. It is obvious that if this same problem is simply extended to include a third di-

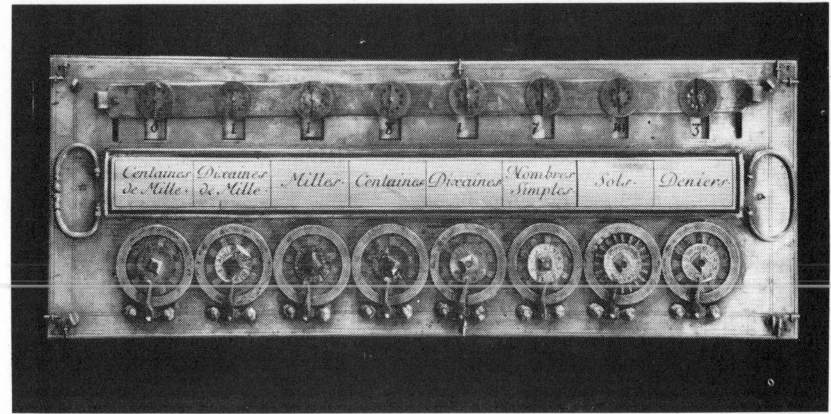

FIRST MECHANICAL COMPUTER was probably this adding machine, designed in 1642 by the French philosopher and mathematician Blaise Pascal. The machine adds when the wheels are turned with a stylus. Gears inside automatically "carry" numbers from one wheel to the next. Similar but somewhat simpler devices, made of plastic, are widely sold.

"DIFFERENCE ENGINE," often called the first modern mathematical machine, was conceived in 1820 by the English mathematician Charles Babbage. He built a small version of it but the larger engine he envisioned was never completed. Parts of it, such as this unit, are now in South Kensington Science Museum. Babbage spent many years trying unsuccessfully to create an "analytical engine" that would do almost everything the modern computer does.

COMPUTER CIRCUITS have become almost microscopic. Although each of the Westinghouse binary integrated circuits (*square units*) on the opposite page is smaller than the head of a pin, it contains six transistors, 12 diodes, 11 resistors and two capacitors. The tiny units are now employed primarily in special computers for military and space applications. More than 100 of them are made at one time on a thin silicon wafer the size of a half-dollar. The four patterns that do not match the others are used for alignment and testing during fabrication. In commercial computers such circuits are expected to provide greater speed and reliability at lower cost than the larger circuits in common use today.

mension, storage must be provided for a million cells, which exceeds the capacity of present machines. One of the studies that is limited in this way is the effort to forecast the weather, for which it would be desirable to use a many-celled three-dimensional model of the atmosphere.

Sometimes when a problem is too complex to be solved in full detail by computer, it is possible to obtain a representative collection of specific solutions by the "Monte Carlo" method. Many years ago I happened to consider ways of calculating what fraction of all games of solitaire could be completed satisfactorily to the last card. When I could not devise a general solution, it occurred to me that the problem could be examined heuristically, that is, in such a way that the examination would at least give an idea of the solution. This would involve actually playing out a number of games, say 100 or 200, and simply recording the results. It was an ideal task for a computer and was at the origin of the Monte Carlo method.

This method is commonly applied to problems of mathematical physics such as those presented by the design of nuclear reactors. In a reactor neutrons are released; they collide, scatter, multiply and are absorbed or escape with various probabilities, depending on the geometry and the composition of the fuel elements and other components. In a complicated geometry no way is known to compute directly the number of neutrons in any given range of energy, direction and velocity. Instead one resorts to a sampling procedure in which the computer traces out a large number of possible histories of individual particles. The computer does not consider all the possible things that might happen to the particle, which would form a very complicated tree of branching eventualities, but selects at each branching point just one of the eventualities with a suitable probability (which is known to the physicist) and examines a large class of such possible chains of events. By gathering statistics on many such chains one can get an idea of the behavior of the system. The class of chains may have to be quite large but it is small compared with the much larger class of all possible branchings. Such sampling procedures, which would be impracticable without the computer, have been applied to many diverse problems.

The variety of work in mathematical physics that has been made possible in recent years through the use of computers is impressive indeed. Astronomy journals, for instance, contain an increasing number of computer results bearing on such matters as the history of stars, the motions of stars in clusters, the complex behavior of stellar atmospheres and the testing of cosmological theories. It has long been recognized that it is mathematically difficult to obtain particular solutions to problems involving the general theory of relativity so that the predictions of alternative formulations can be tested by observation or experiment. The computer is

FIRST ELECTRONIC DIGITAL COMPUTER, the Electronic Numerical Integrator and Computer (ENIAC), was built at the University of Pennsylvania for the Army Ordnance Department. Completed in the fall of 1945, it had 19,000 vacuum tubes, 1,500 relays and hundreds of thousands of resistors, capacitors and inductors. It consumed almost 200 kilowatts of electric power. Power and tube failures and other difficulties plagued its first few years of operation. To change its program it was necessary to rewire thousands of circuits. With constant improvements ENIAC was kept in service at the Ballistic Research Center, Aberdeen, Md., until late 1955.

now making it possible to obtain such predictions in many cases. A similar situation exists in nuclear physics with regard to alternative field theories.

I should now like to discuss some particular examples of how the computer can perform work that is both interesting and useful to a mathematician. The first examples are problems in number theory. This subject deals with properties of ordinary integers and particularly with those properties that concern the two most fundamental operations on them: addition and multiplication.

As in so much of "pure" mathematics the objective is to discover and then prove a theorem containing some general truth about numbers. It is often easy to see a relation that holds true in special cases; the task is to show that it holds true in general.

Karl Friedrich Gauss, called "the prince of mathematicians" by his contemporaries, greatly favored experiments on special cases and diligent work with examples to obtain his inspirations for finding general truths in number theory. Asked how he divined some of the remarkable regularities of numbers, he replied, "*Durch planmässiges tattonieren*" —through systematic trying. Srinivasa Ramanujan, the phenomenal Indian number theorist, was equally addicted to experimentation with examples. One can imagine that in the hands of such men the computer would have stimulated many more discoveries in number theory.

A fascinating area of number theory is that dealing with primes, the class of integers that are divisible only by themselves and by one. The Greeks proved that the number of primes is infinite, but even after centuries of work some of the most elementary questions about primes remain unanswered.

For example, can every even number be represented as the sum of two primes? This is the famous Goldbach conjecture. Thus $100 = 53 + 47$ and $200 = 103 + 97$. It has been shown that all even numbers smaller than 2,000,000 can be represented as the sum of two primes, but there is no proof that this holds true for *all* even integers.

MANIAC II (Mathematical Analyzer, Numerical Integrator and Computer) was built at the Los Alamos Scientific Laboratory in 1957. STRETCH, built by the International Business Machines Corporation and installed at Los Alamos four years later, is about 10 times faster than MANIAC II. Both have been used extensively by the author and his colleagues for experimentation in mathematics.

It is an interesting fact that there are many pairs of primes differing by two, for instance 11 and 13, 17 and 19, 311 and 313. Although it might seem simple to show that there are infinitely many such pairs of "twin primes," no one has been able to do it. These two unsolved problems demonstrate that the inquiring human mind can almost immediately find mathematical statements of great simplicity whose truth or falsehood are inordinately difficult to decide. Such statements present a continual challenge to mathematicians.

The existence of a proof does not always appease the mathematician. Although it is easily proved that there is an infinite number of primes, one would like to have a formula for writing down an arbitrarily large prime. No such formula has been found. No mathematician can now write on demand a prime with, say, 10 million digits, although one surely exists.

One of the largest known primes was found not long ago with the help of an electronic computer in Sweden. It is $2^{3217} - 1$, a number containing 967 digits. A number of this form, $2^n - 1$, is called a Mersenne number. There may be an infinite number of primes of this form. No one knows.

Other special numbers that may or may not yield many primes are Fermat numbers, which have the form $2^{2^n} + 1$. For n's of 0, 1, 2 and 3 the corresponding Fermat numbers are 3, 5, 17 and 257. Even for moderate values of n Fermat numbers become extremely large. It is not known, for instance, if the Fermat number with an n of 13 is a prime (the number is $2^{2^{13}} + 1$, or $2^{8192} + 1$).

It is convenient for computer experimentation that both Mersenne and Fermat numbers have a particularly simple appearance when they are written in binary notation [*see top illustration on next page*]. Fermat numbers start with a 1, are followed by 0's and end with a 1. Mersenne numbers in binary notation consist exclusively of 1's. With computers it is an easy matter to study empirically the appearance of primes written in binary form.

The following statement is most likely true: There exists a number n such that an infinite number of primes can be written in a binary sequence that contains exactly n 1's. (The number of 0's interspersed among the 1's, of course, would be unlimited.) Although this statement cannot be proved with the present means of number theory, I suspect that experimental work with a computer might provide some insight into the behavior of binary sequences containing various numbers of 1's. The following experience may help to explain this feeling.

SHRINKAGE OF COMPONENTS has meant greater reliability and speed plus substantial savings in construction and operation of computer systems. The vacuum-tube assembly at top was used in first generation of computers built by International Business Machines Corporation, starting in 1946. First transistorized computers, built in 1955, used circuits such as that at lower left. At lower right is a card of six microminiaturized circuits, each containing several transistors and diodes, which is going into the newest IBM computers.

A few years ago my colleague Mark B. Wells and I planned a computer program to study some combinatorial properties of the distribution of 0's and 1's in prime numbers when expressed in binary form. One day Wells remarked: "Of course, one cannot expect the primes to have, asymptotically, the same number of ones and zeros in their development, since the numbers divisible by three have an even number of ones." This statement was based on the following argument: One would expect a priori that in a large sample of integers expressed in binary form the number of 1's and 0's ought to be randomly distributed and that this should also be the case for a large sample of primes. On the other hand, if it were true that all numbers divisible by three contain an even number of 1's, then the distribution of 1's and 0's in a large sample of primes should not be random.

Returning to my office, I tried to prove Wells's statement about numbers divisible by three but was unsuccessful. After a while I noticed that the statement is not even true. The first number to disprove it is 21, which has three 1's in its binary representation [*see middle illustration on next page*].

Nevertheless, a great majority of the integers divisible by three seem to have an even number of 1's. Beginning with this observation, Wells managed to prove a general theorem: Among all the integers divisible by three from 1 to 2^n, those that have an even number of 1's always predominate, and the difference between their number and the number of those with an odd number of 1's can be computed exactly: it is

MERSENNE NUMBER $(2^n - 1)$			FERMAT NUMBER $(2^{2^n} + 1)$		
n	DECIMAL	BINARY	n	DECIMAL	BINARY
1	1	1	0	3	11
2	3	11	1	5	101
3	7	111	2	17	10001
4	15	1111	3	257	100000001
5	31	11111	4	65,537	10000000000000001

MERSENNE AND FERMAT NUMBERS have a simple appearance when written in binary notation. Although many Mersenne numbers are not primes (for example 15), there may be an infinite number of primes of this form. There may also be an infinite number of Fermat primes, but even the Fermat number for an *n* as small as 13 has not yet been tested.

3	11	27	11011
6	110	30	11110
9	1001	33	100001
12	1100	36	100100
15	1111	39	100111
18	10010	42	101010
21	10101	45	101101
24	11000	48	110000

INTEGERS DIVISIBLE BY THREE usually contain an even number of 1's when written in binary form. This observation led to the proof of a general theorem, described in the text.

$3^{(n-1)/2}$. Wells developed corresponding proofs for statements on integers divisible by five, seven and certain other numbers, although he found these theorems increasingly harder to prove.

By now quite a few problems in number theory have been studied experimentally on computers. Not all of this work is restricted to tables, special examples and sundry curiosities. D. H. Lehmer of the University of California at Berkeley has made unusually effective use of the computer in number theory. With its help he has recently obtained several general theorems. Essentially what he has done is to reduce general statements to the examination of a large number of special cases. The number of cases was so large that it would have been impracticable, if not impossible, to go through them by hand computation. With the help of the computer, however, Lehmer and his associates were able to determine all exceptions explicitly and thereby discover the theorem that was valid for all other cases. Unfortunately Lehmer's interesting work is at a difficult mathematical level and to describe it would take us far afield.

It must be emphasized that Lehmer's theorems were not proved entirely by machine. The machine was instrumental in enabling him to obtain the proof. This is quite different from having a program that can guide a computer to produce a complete formal proof of a mathematical statement. Such a program, however, is not beyond the realm of possibility. The computer can operate not only with numbers but also with the symbols needed to perform logical operations. Thus it can execute simple orders corresponding to the basic "Boolean" operations. These are essentially the Aristotelian expressions of "and," "or" and "not." Under a set of instructions the computer can follow such orders in a prescribed sequence and explore a labyrinth of possibilities, choosing among the possible alternatives the ones that satisfy, at any moment, the result of previous computations.

With such techniques it has been possible to program a computer to find proofs of elementary theorems in Euclid's geometry. Some of these efforts, particularly those pursued at the International Business Machines Research Center, have been quite successful. Other programs have enabled the computer to find proofs of simple facts of

1,2	1,3	1,4	1,5	1,6	1,7
	2,3	2,4	2,5	2,6	2,7
		3,4	3,5	3,6	3,7
			4,5	4,6	4,7
				5,6	5,7
					6,7

1,2,3	1,3	1,4,5,	1,5	1,6,7	1,7
	2,3	2,4,6	2,5,7	2,6	2,7
		3,4,7	3,5,6	3,6	3,7
			4,5	4,6	4,7
				5,6	5,7
					6,7

STEINER PROBLEM poses this question: Given *n* objects, can they be arranged in a set of triplets so that every pair of objects appears once and only once in every triplet? The problem can be solved only when $n = 6k + 1$ or $6k + 3$, in which k can be any integer. One solution for $k = 1$, in which case $n = 7$, is shown here. The table at left lists all possible pairs of seven objects. The table at right shows seven triplets that contain all pairs only once. The 21 digits in these triplets can be regrouped into other triplets.

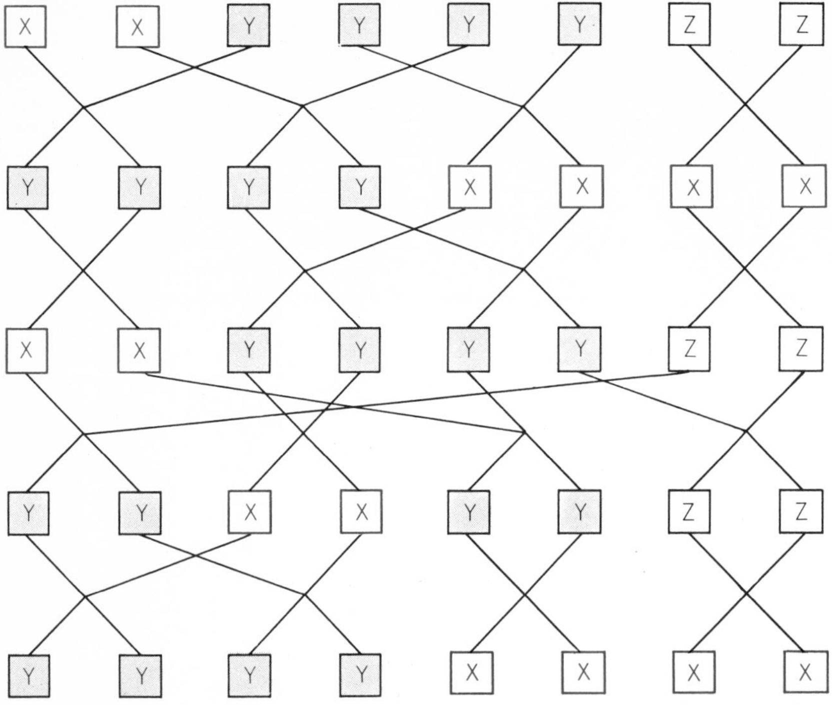

GENEALOGICAL "TREES" raise many interesting combinatorial questions. In the simple case shown here individuals of three different colors mate in pairs. Strictly, x, y and z specify the fraction of each color in each generation, but here they also identify color type. Each mating produces a pair of offspring and the color of the offspring is uniquely determined by the colors of the parents according to a fixed rule. (For example, 2 y's or 2 z's produce 2 x's.) Assuming an initial population containing hundreds of members, one might ask such questions as these: Given an individual in the fifth generation, how many different ancestors does he have in, say, the first generation? What are the proportions of x's, y's and z's among the ancestors of a given individual in the nth generation?

projective geometry. I have no doubt that these efforts mark only the beginnings; the future role of computers in dealing with the "effective" parts of mathematics will be much larger.

I shall now turn from the study of integers to combinatorial analysis and discuss some of the uses of the computer in this field. Very briefly, combinatorial analysis deals with the properties of arrangements and patterns defined by means of a finite class of "points." Familiar examples are the problems on permutations and combinations studied in high school algebra. In a typical case one starts with a finite set of n points and assumes certain given, or prescribed, relations between any two of them or, more generally, among any k of them. One may then wish to enumerate the number of all possible structures that are related in the prescribed way, or one may want to know the number of equivalent structures. In some cases one may consider the finite set of given objects to be transformations of a set on itself. In the broadest sense one could say that combinatorial analysis deals with relations and patterns, their classification and morphology. In this field too electronic computers have proved to be extremely useful. Here are some examples.

Consider the well-known problem of placing eight queens on a chessboard in such a way that no one of them attacks another. For an ordinary 8×8 chessboard there are only 12 fundamentally different solutions. The mathematician would like to know in how many different ways the problem can be solved for n queens on an $n \times n$ board. Such enumeration problems are in general difficult but computer studies can assist in their solution.

The following problem was first proposed in the 19th century by the Swiss mathematician Jakob Steiner: Given n objects, can one arrange them in a set of triplets in such a way that every pair of objects appears once and only once in a triplet? If n is five, for example, there are 10 possible pairs of five objects, but a little experimentation will show that there is no way to put them all in triplets without repeating some of the pairs. The problem can be solved only when $n = 6k + 1$ or $6k + 3$, in which k is any integer. The solution for $k = 1$ (in which case $n = 7$) is shown at the bottom of page 169. The number of triplets in the solution is seven. In how many ways can the problem be solved? Again, the computer is very useful when k is a large number.

The shortest-route problem, often called the traveling-salesman problem, is another familiar one in combinatorics. Given are the positions of n points, either in a plane or in space. The problem is to connect all the points so that the total route between them is as short as possible. Another version of this problem is to find the route through a network of points (without necessarily touching all the points) that would take the minimum time to traverse [see "Control Theory," page 74]. These problems differ from the two preceding ones in that they necessitate finding a method, or recipe, for constructing the minimum route. Strictly speaking, therefore, they are problems in "meta-combinatorics." This term signifies that a precise formulation of the problem requires a definition of what one means by a recipe for construction. Such a definition is possible, and precise formulations can be made. When the n points are distributed in a multidimensional space, the problem can hardly be tackled without a computer.

A final example of combinatorics can be expressed as a problem in genealogy. Assume, for the sake of simplicity, that a population consists of many individuals who combine at random, and that each pair produces, after a certain time, another pair. Let the process continue through many generations and assume that the production of offspring takes place at the same time for all parents in each generation. Many interesting questions of combinatorial character arise immediately.

For instance, given an individual in the 15th generation of this process, how many different ancestors does he have in, say, the ninth generation? Since this is six generations back it is obvious that the maximum number of different ancestors is 2^6, but this assumes no kinship between any of the ancestors. As in human genealogy there is a certain probability that kinship exists and that the actual number is smaller than 2^6 What is the probability of finding various smaller numbers?

Suppose the original population consists of two classes (that is, each individual has one or the other of two characteristics); how are these classes mixed in the course of many generations? In other words, considering any individual in the nth generation, one would like to know the proportion of the two characteristics among all his ancestors.

Let us now make a slightly more realistic assumption. Consider the process as before but with the restriction removed that all offspring appear at the same time from parents of the same age. Assume instead that the production of the new generation is spread over a finite period of time according to a specific probability distribution. After this process has continued for some time the individuals of the most recent generation will be, so to speak, of different generations. A process of this kind actually occurs in human populations because mothers tend to be younger, on the average, than fathers. Therefore going back, say, 10 generations through the chain of mothers yields a smaller number of total years than going back through the chain of 10 fathers. It becomes a complex combinatorial problem to calculate the average number of generations represented in the genealogical history of each individual after many years have elapsed from time zero. This and many similar questions are difficult to treat analytically. By imitating the process on a computer, however, it is easy to obtain data that throw some light on the matter.

The last mathematical area I should like to discuss in connection with computers is the rather broad but little-explored one of nonlinearity. A linear function of one variable has the form $x' = ax + b$, where a and b are constants. Functions and transformations of this form are the simplest ones mathematically, and they occur extensively in the natural sciences and in technology. For example, quantum theory employs linear mathematics, although there are now indications that future understanding of nuclear and subnuclear phenomena will require nonlinear theories. In many physical theories, such as hydrodynamics, the equations are nonlinear from the outset.

The simplest nonlinear functions are quadratic; for one variable such functions have the form $y = ax^2 + bx + c$, where a, b and c are constants. It may surprise nonmathematical readers how little is known about the properties of such nonlinear functions and transformations. Some of the simplest questions concerning their properties remain unanswered.

As an example, mathematicians would like to learn more about the behavior of nonlinear functions when subjected to the process known as iteration. This simply means repeated application of the function (or transformation) to some starting value. For instance, if the point described by a function is the square root of x, the iteration would be the square root of the square root of x; each succeeding iteration would consist of again taking the square root.

A transformation given by two functions containing two variables each defines a point on a plane; its iteration gives rise to successive points, or "images" [*see illustration below*]. Finding the properties of the sequence of iterated images of a single point, when described by a nonlinear function, is in general difficult. Present techniques of analysis are inadequate to unravel the behavior of these quite simply defined transformations.

Here again empirical work with the

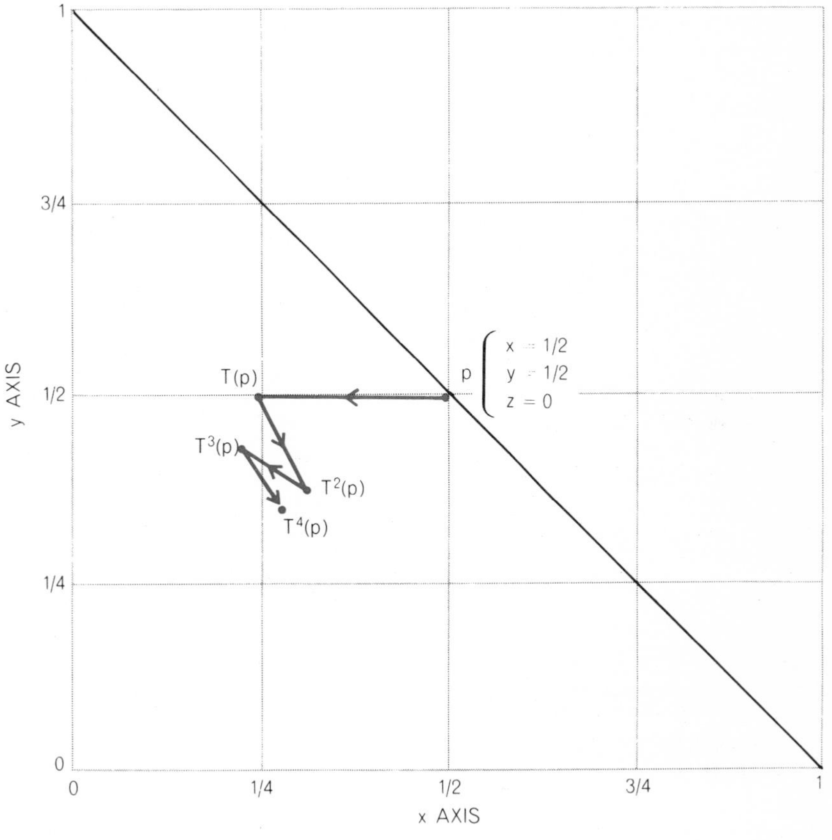

$x' = y^2 + z^2 \quad y' = 2xy + 2xz \quad z' = x^2 + 2yz$

INITIAL POINT p	FIRST ITERATION T(p)	SECOND ITERATION $T^2(p)$	THIRD ITERATION $T^3(p)$	FOURTH ITERATION $T^4(p)$
$x = 1/2$	$x' = 1/4$	$x'' = 5/16$	$x''' = 61/256 = .238$	$x'''' = .295$
$y = 1/2$	$y' = 2/4$	$y'' = 6/16$	$y''' = 110/256 = .430$	$y'''' = .363$
$z = 0$	$z' = 1/4$	$z'' = 5/16$	$z''' = 85/256 = .332$	$z'''' = .342$
SUM 1	1	1	1 = 1.000	1.000

PROCESS OF ITERATION involves repeated application of a function (or transformation) to an initial value or a point. Here three equations containing three variables define a point in a plane. Iteration gives rise to successive points, or "images." Because the three variables always add up to 1, only two variables (say x and y) need be plotted. The first iteration, $T(p)$, is obtained by inserting the initial values of x, y and z (½, ½, 0) in the three equations. The new values, x', y', z' (¼, ½, ¼), are then inserted to produce the second iteration, $T^2(p)$, and so on. Computers can quickly compute and display thousands of iterations of a point so that their behavior can be studied (*see examples on next page*).

computer can be of great help, particularly if the computer is equipped to display visually the location of many iterated points on the face of an oscilloscope. MANIAC II at Los Alamos has been equipped in this way and enables us to see at a glance the results of hundreds of iterations.

In examining such displays the mathematician is curious to learn whether or not the succession of iterated images converge to a single location, or "fixed point." Frequently the images do not converge but jump around in what appears to be a haphazard fashion—when they are viewed one by one. But if hundreds of images are examined, it may be seen that they converge to curves that are often most unexpected and peculiar, as illustrated in the four oscilloscope traces below. Such empirical work has led my associates and me to some general conjectures and to the finding of some new properties of nonlinear transformations.

What are the obvious desiderata that would make the electronic computer an even more valuable tool than it is today? One important need is the ability to handle a broader range of logical operations. As I have noted, the simplest operations of logic, the Boolean operations, have been incorporated in electronic computers from the outset. In order to encompass more of contemporary mathematics the computer needs a "universal quantifier" and an "existential quantifier." The universal quantifier is required to express the statement one sees so frequently in mathematical papers: "*For all x* such and such holds." The existential quantifier is needed to express another common statement: "*There exists* an *x* so that such and such is true." If one could add these two quantifiers to the Boolean operations, one could formulate for computer examination most of traditional and much of modern mathematics. Unfortunately there is no good computer program that will manipulate the concepts "for all" and "there exists."

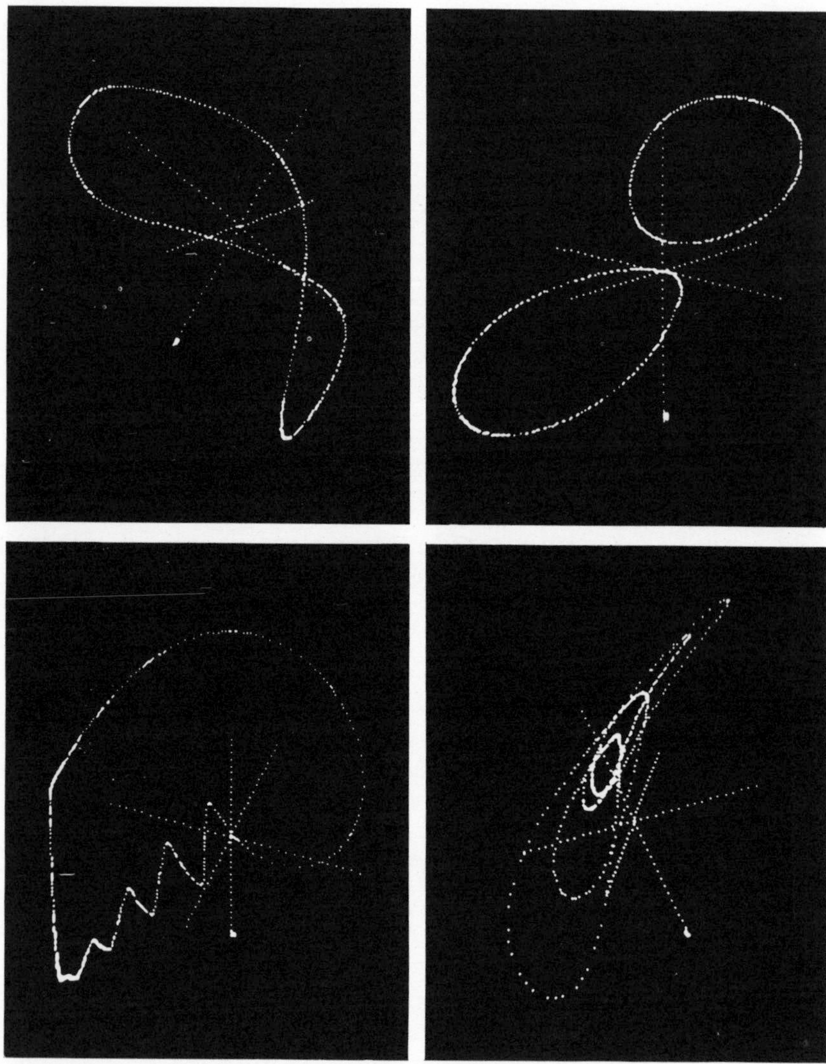

ITERATIONS OF NONLINEAR TRANSFORMATIONS performed by high-speed Los Alamos computers are displayed on the face of an oscilloscope. The objective of this study by P. R. Stein and the author was to examine the asymptotic properties, or "limit sets," of iterates of certain nonlinear transformations of relatively simple form. These iterations are for sets of four functions containing four variables and therefore must be plotted in three dimensions; the straight dotted lines indicate the coordinate axes (*see two-dimensional plotting on preceding page*). The figure at top left is a twisted space curve. That at top right consists of two plane curves. The two bottom figures are more complicated.

One can take for granted that there will be continued increases in processing speed and in memory capacity. There will be more fundamental developments too. Present computers operate in a linear sequence: they do one thing at a time. It is a challenge to design a machine more on the model of the animal nervous system, which can carry out many operations simultaneously. Indeed, plans exist for machines in which arithmetical operations would proceed simultaneously in different locations.

A multitrack machine would be of great value in the Monte Carlo method. The task of the machine is to compute individual histories of fictitious particles, and in many problems the fates of the particles are independent of one another. This means that they could be computed in parallel rather than in series. Moreover, it is not necessary that the computations be carried out to the many decimal places provided by present high-speed machines; an accuracy of four or five digits would often be enough. Thus it would be valuable to have a machine that could compute hundreds of histories simultaneously with only moderate accuracy. There are many other cases where a machine of such design would be efficient.

Further development is also desirable in facilitating the ease of transaction between the computer and its operator. At present it is difficult to change the course of a calculation as partial results become available. If access to the machine were more flexible and if the problem could be studied visually during the course of its development, many mathematicians would find experimentation on the computer more congenial than they do today.

One can imagine new methods of calculation specifically adapted to the automatic computer. Thanks to the speed of the machine one will be able to explore, almost palpably, so to say, geometrical configurations in spaces of more than three dimensions and one will be able to obtain, through practice, new intuitions. These will stimulate the mathematician working in topology and in the combinatorics of new mathematical objects. These objects may be ordinary integers, but integers far exceeding in size and number any now used for experimentation. One should also be able to develop mathematical expressions with many more existential quantifiers than are now employed in formal mathematical definitions. New games will be played on future machines; new objects and their motions will be considered in spaces now hard to visualize with our present experience, which is essentially limited to three dimensions.

The old philosophical question remains: Is mathematics largely a free creation of the human brain, or has the choice of definitions, axioms and problems been suggested largely by the external physical world? (I would include as part of the physical world the anatomy of the brain itself.) It is likely that work with electronic machines, in the course of the next decade or so, will shed some light on this question. Further insight may come from the study of similarities between the workings of the human nervous system and the organization of computers. There will be novel applications of mathematics in the biological sciences, and new problems in mathematics will be suggested by the study of living matter.

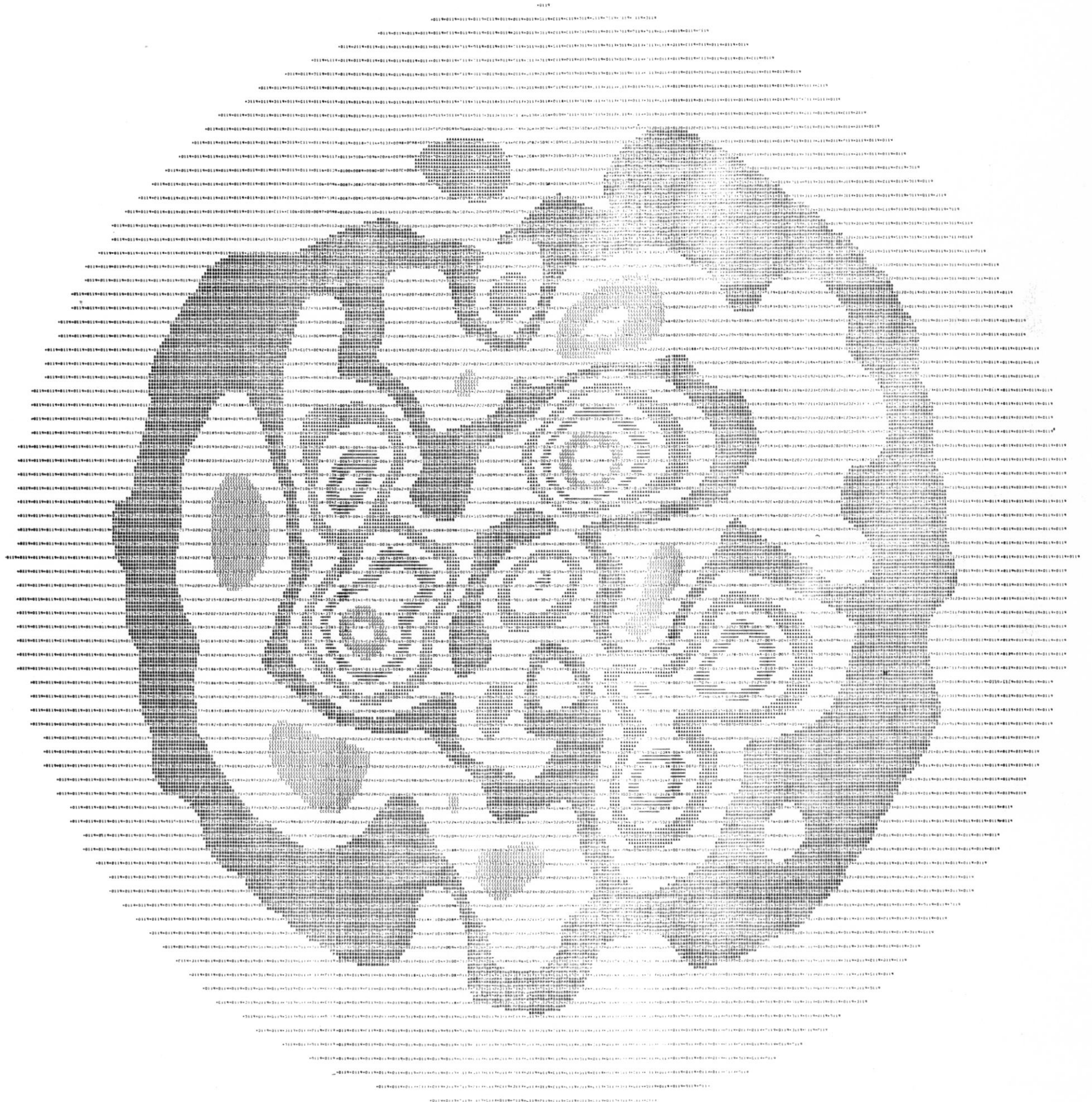

SIMULATED WEATHER PATTERN for the entire Northern Hemisphere was produced by the STRETCH computer at the General Circulation Research Laboratory of the U.S. Weather Bureau. In an effort to develop and test new theories of atmospheric behavior, investigators program the computer with equations that attempt to account for atmospheric phenomena. Data from real observations are then fed in, from which the computer produces changing model weather patterns for days and weeks. These are compared with actual observations over the period. The shaded "contours" on this map show simulated sea-level atmospheric pressure during one of these studies. The pattern is built up entirely of densely packed numbers and letters printed out directly by the computer itself.

23

NUMERICAL TAXONOMY

ROBERT R. SOKAL • December 1966

Classification is one of the fundamental concerns of science. Facts and objects must be arranged in an orderly fashion before their unifying principles can be discovered and used as the basis for prediction. Many phenomena occur in such variety and profusion that unless some system is created among them they would be unlikely to provide any useful information. Chemical compounds (particularly organic ones), groups of stars and the two million or so species of living organisms that inhabit the earth are examples of such phenomena.

The development of high-speed electronic computers has had a profound impact on the methods of classification in many scientific fields. The rapidity of the computer's operation has made it possible for the first time to consider large numbers of characteristics in classifying many phenomena. The writing of computer programs for such work has led to a renewed interest in the principles of classification, reviving such old questions as: What makes one classification better than another? What is a "natural" classification? What is similarity, and can it be quantified? The inquiry has progressed furthest in the field of taxonomy, or biological classification. The methods of numerical taxonomy (as this new field has come to be called), the conceptual revolution it has wrought, the nature of the controversy surrounding it, some future prospects for the field and its relevance to problems of classification in other sciences will be discussed in this article.

Many of the new procedures of numerical taxonomy and their theoretical justification have been the subject of intense disagreement between numerical taxonomists and supporters of traditional taxonomic practices and principles. Controversy, of course, is nothing new in science. Time and again the introduction of a new concept or the development of a new technique has aroused the passions of scientists representing conflicting points of view. Although debate about numerical taxonomy has not been as acrimonious as some debates in the history of science, it has certainly been spirited and continues undiminished. At recent biological conferences the symposiums on numerical taxonomy have been unusually well attended, often by people only remotely interested in the field who have heard that "a

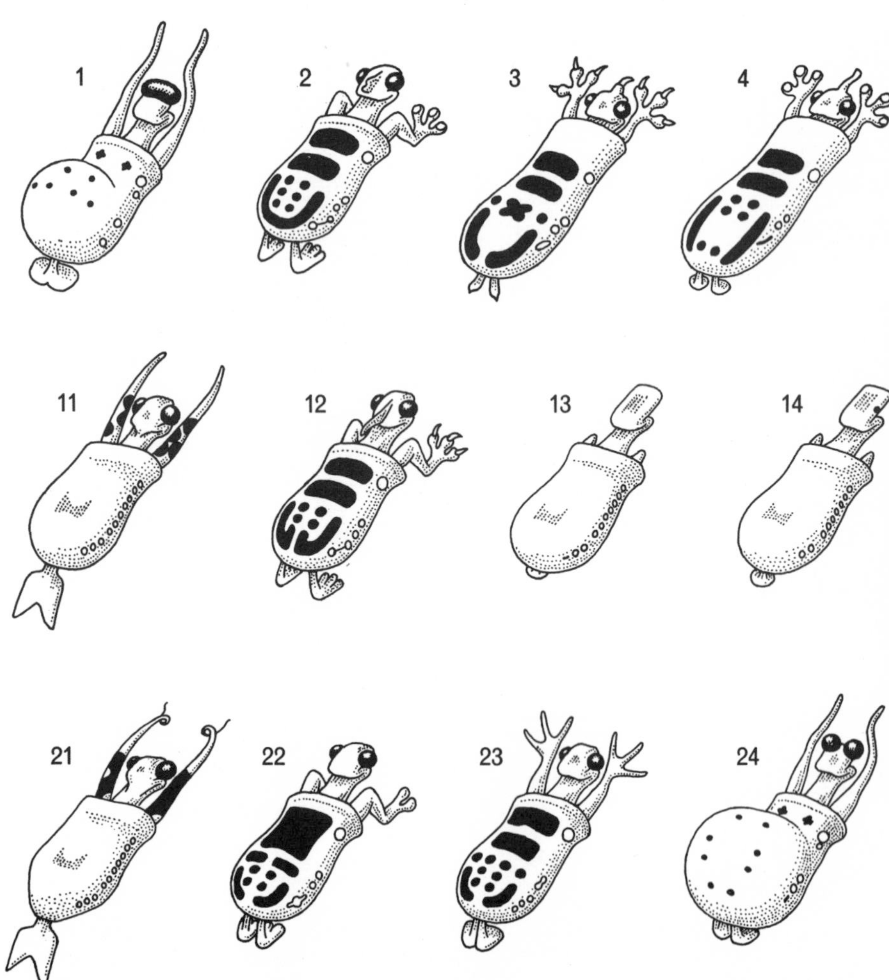

IMAGINARY ANIMALS, called Caminalcules after their creator, Joseph H. Camin of the University of Kansas, are used in experiments on the principles and practices of tax-

good fight" was about to take place in that session. What is all the shooting about?

In the early days of modern science, and for special purposes even today, classifications were based on a single property or characteristic, the choice of which might be quite arbitrary. Metals are divided into conductors and nonconductors, other substances into those that are soluble in water and those that are not; organisms are divided into unicellular ones and multicellular ones. Some of these classifications are arbitrary in the sense that there is a continuum of properties—as in the case of solubility, for which the line between soluble substances and insoluble ones is not distinct. In contrast one can almost always say whether an organism is unicellular or multicellular, so that with properties such as these the decisions can be quite clear-cut. Classifications based on one or only a few characters are generally called "monothetic," which means that all the objects allocated to one class must share the character or characters under consideration. Thus the members of the class of "soluble substances" must in fact be soluble.

Classifications based on many characters, on the other hand, are called "polythetic." They do not require any one character or property to be universal for a class. Thus there are birds that lack wings, vertebrates that lack red blood and mammals that do not bear their young. In such cases a given "taxon," or class, is established because it contains a substantial portion of the characters employed in the classification. Assignment to the taxon is not on the basis of a single property but on the aggregate of properties, and any pair of members of the class will not necessarily share every character.

It is obviously much more complicated to establish classifications based on many characters than it is to establish classifications based on only one character. The human mind finds it difficult to tabulate and process large numbers of characters without favoring one aspect or another. The comparative subjectivity of traditional approaches and the inability of taxonomists to communicate to one another the nature of their procedures have contributed to making taxonomy more of an art than a science.

The arrival of the computer has reversed this trend, and a new field with many possibilities for objective and explicit classification has opened up. Computer techniques have indeed been a principal force behind the gradual adoption of an operational approach in taxonomy; in order to use such techniques, classificatory procedures must be outlined in such a form that any scientist or a properly programmed computer can carry out the indicated operations and, given the same input data, arrive at the same results. This would preclude the often arbitrary decisions of conventional taxonomists, epitomized by the statement that "a species is whatever a competent taxonomist decides to call a species."

Before proceeding further I should remove a possible source of confusion.

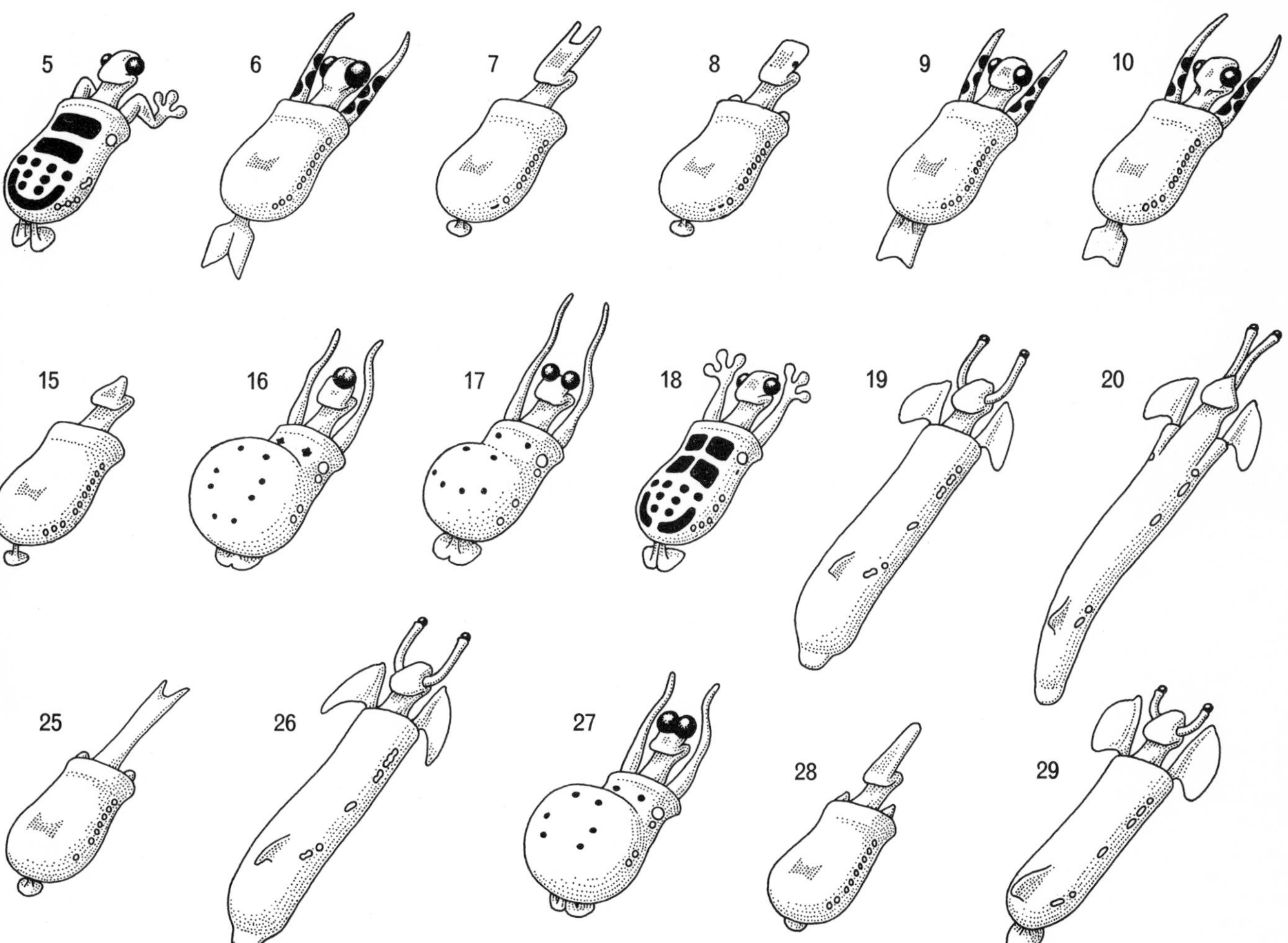

onomy, or biological classification. The 29 "recent" species of the organisms, depicted on these two pages, were generated by Camin according to rules known so far only to him. The drawings are based on Camin's originals, with slight modifications in perspective.

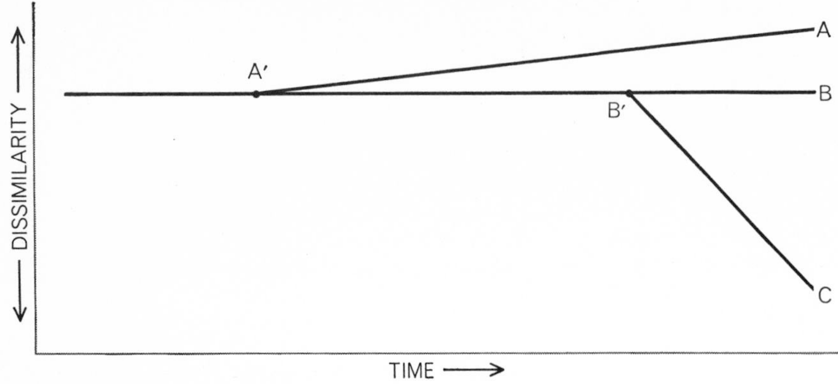

TAXONOMIC RELATIONSHIPS can be viewed from three distinct aspects. "Phenetically" (based on overall similarity among the objects to be classified) organism *B* is more closely related to organism *A* than it is to organism *C*, even though *C* evolved much later than *A* as a branch of stem *B*. "Cladistically" (based on common lines of descent) organisms *B* and *C* are closer to each other than either is to *A*, since they have an ancestor (*B′*) in common before either has a common ancestor (*A′*) with *A*. "Chronistically" (based on time) *A*, *B* and *C* are closer to one another than any of them is to *B′*, since they occupy same time horizon.

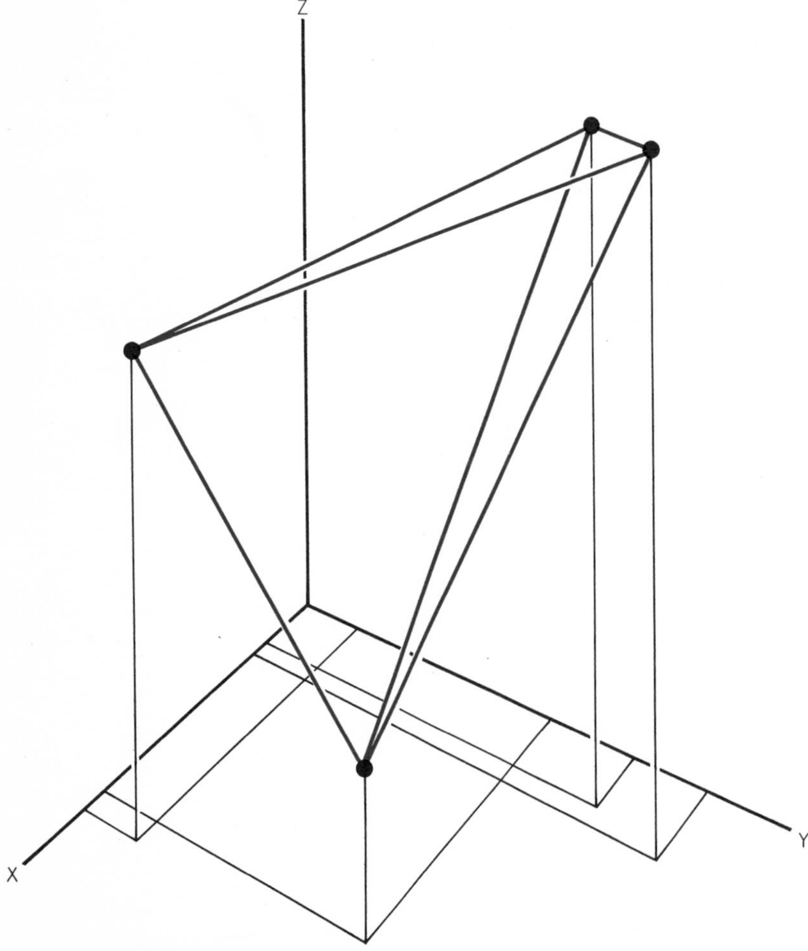

SIMILARITY CAN BE REPRESENTED as the distance between the objects to be classified (called operational taxonomic units, or OTU's for short) in a multidimensional space. In this example the similarity between all possible pairs taken from four objects is estimated on the basis of three characters, which are represented by the three coordinates axes *X*, *Y* and *Z*. The OTU's (*black balls*) are then plotted into this three-dimensional space according to their state, or value, for the three characters. Similar objects are plotted much closer to one another than dissimilar ones. In any real case there will, of course, be more than three characters and a multidimensional space—called a "hyperspace"—would be necessary.

This is the difference between the terms "classification" and "identification." When a set of unordered objects has been grouped on the basis of like properties, biologists call this "classification." Once a classification has been established the allocation of additional unidentified objects to the correct class is generally known as "identification." Thus a person using a key to the known wild flowers of Yellowstone National Park "identifies" a given specimen as a goldenrod. Some mathematicians and philosophers would also call this second process classification, but I shall strictly distinguish between the two. Here I am principally concerned with classification in the biologist's sense.

The purpose of taxonomy is to group the objects to be classified into "natural" taxa. Naturalness has been variously defined, but underlying the several definitions is the common idea that members of a natural taxon are mutually more highly related to one another than they are to nonmembers. This leads us to try to define what we mean by "taxonomic relationship." Conventional taxonomists wish to equate taxonomic relationships with evolutionary relationships, but numerical taxonomists have pointed out that taxonomic relations are actually of three kinds. "Phenetic" relationships are those based on overall similarity among the objects to be classified. "Cladistic" relationships are based on common lines of descent. Although close cladistic relationship generally implies close phenetic similarity, it is not always the case. Differences in evolutionary rates may give rise to lineages that diverged long ago but appear more similar than a subsequently diverged pair of stems, one or both of which has undergone rapid evolution [*see top illustration at left*]. The third kind of taxonomic relationship is the "chronistic," or temporal, relation among various evolutionary branches. Cladistic relationships for most organisms are known scantily, if at all, and are generally inferred from phenetic evidence. The "phylogenetic" classifications of conventional taxonomy are usually based on an undefined mixture of phenetic and cladistic relationships, and often merely represent an overall similarity among the classified organisms disguised in evolutionary terminology.

In view of these considerations numerical taxonomists propose to base classifications entirely on resemblance, defining natural classifications as those yielding taxa whose members are in some sense more similar to one another than they are to members of other taxa. It follows from this concept of naturalness, which is based on the ideas of J. S. L. Gilmour, a botanist at the University of Cambridge, that a natural taxon will be most predictive. If a classification is based on many correlated characters, predictions about the states of other characters in various groupings of the classification should be more successful than if the taxonomy were based on few characters. Furthermore, it is likely that a classification based on a great variety of characters will be of general utility to biology as a whole, whereas a classification resting on only a few characters is less likely to be generally useful, except for the special purposes relevant to the chosen characters. Thus a classification of animals into "swamp dwellers" and "animals not living in swamps" may be very useful for a study of the ecology of swamps but not for general zoology.

Overall phenetic similarity is based on all available characters without any differential weighting of some characters over others. A substantial part of the controversy about numerical taxonomy has centered on this point. Conventional taxonomists usually employ only a few characters in classification and weight these in terms of their presumed evolutionary importance. Numerical taxonomists contend that evolutionary importance is undefinable and generally unknown and that no consistent scheme for weighting characters before undertaking a classification has yet been proposed. To weight characters on the basis of their ability to distinguish groups in a classification, as is frequently advocated, is a logical fallacy. Since the purpose of employing the characters is to establish a classification, one cannot first assume what these classes are and then use them to measure the diagnostic weight of a character.

The nature of similarity is, of course, a fundamental problem of taxonomy, whatever one's theoretical approach. This ancient philosophical problem has recently become acute in a variety of fields because of the introduction of automata for classification and identification. What is the meaning of the statement "*A* is similar to *B*"? Only when qualified to the effect that "*A* is similar to *B* in such and such a respect" has this statement any meaning. It is one of the underlying assumptions

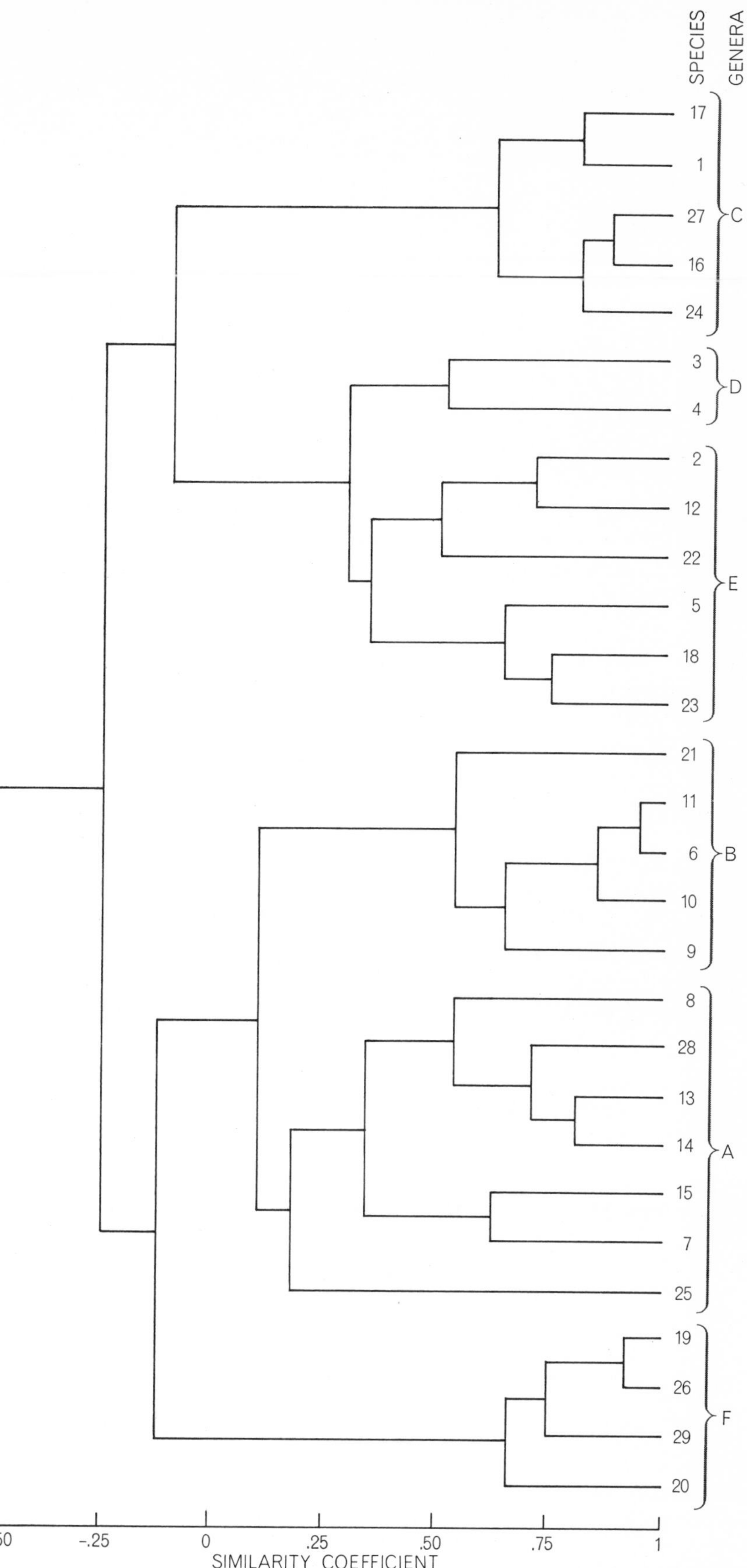

PHENOGRAM is a convenient two-dimensional representation of the results of a numerical classification, in this case the results of classifying the 29 recent species of Caminalcules depicted on pages 174 and 175. The various species are indicated by the numbers at the tips of the branches. Phenograms tend to distort the original multidimensional relationships.

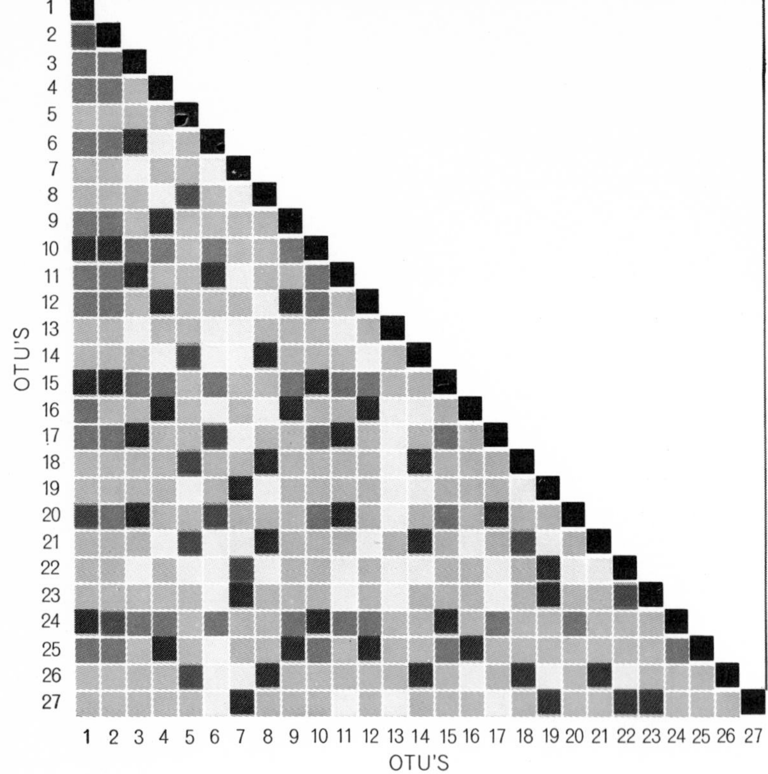

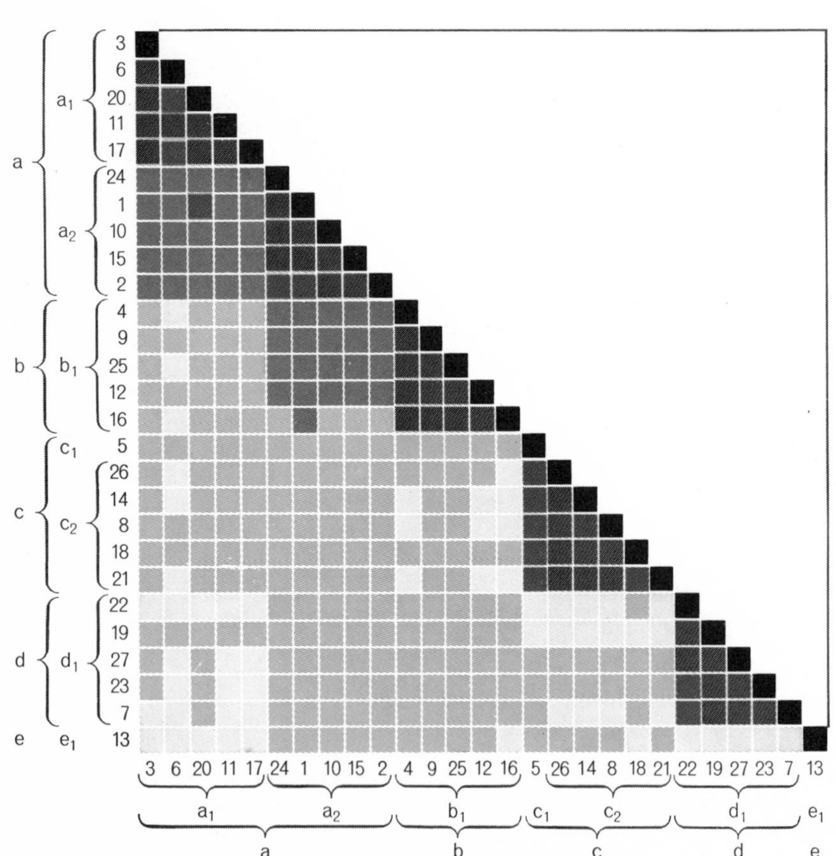

of numerical taxonomy that quantification of degrees of similarity is possible. The establishment of comparative similarities—for example "*A* is more similar to *B* than it is to *C*"—is fundamental to any attempt at clustering objects into homogeneous groups.

Similarity can be established only on the basis of homologous, or corresponding, characters. Hence it is not possible to compare the forelimbs of vertebrates without prior agreement on what to call a forelimb in each of the vertebrates to be compared, and on the correspondences between constituent parts of the appendages. Homology, as interpreted by numerical taxonomists, is the existing overall similarity in structure rather than similarity due to common ancestry, although this may often be the underlying cause. To describe such essential similarity one needs to base it on numerous "unit characters" of the structures to be compared. Numerical taxonomists regard unit characters as those that cannot be subdivided into logically or empirically independent characters. This is a complex subject, however, since the same set of biological characters can be described in innumerable slightly varying ways. One would not wish to use all these descriptions, yet how can one avoid redundancy by choosing the best ones?

Another problem is how many characters to choose for describing phenetic similarities. Is there an asymptotic similarity among organisms that is approached as more and more characters are measured, or will each additional set of characters contribute a new dimension to similarity, making the taxonomic structure of a group inherently unstable? All the evidence on this complicated question is not yet in. It might be assumed that if one knew the genetic fine structure of organisms, one could then develop an overall measure of similarity among organisms based on similarity of genetic structure.

SIMILARITY MATRIXES have been shaded to show the degree of similarity between pairs of 27 OTU's (in this case individuals from seven species of nematode worms). The darker the squares, the greater the similarity. The matrix at top has the OTU's arranged according to an arbitrary sequence of code numbers. The matrix at bottom has been rearranged to yield clusters of similar OTU's. The dark triangles along the diagonal indicate species; larger, less dark triangles represent genera. OTU 13 is not closely related to any of the other OTU's (*see illustration on opposite page*).

Yet even this would present complications, since the genetic code as it is now understood is in the nature of a program, certain portions of which come into play at different times during the development of an organism. Similarity in the programs might not reflect similarity in the products, and it is by no means certain whether genes or their effects should form the basis of a classification.

Moreover, since we do not as yet have measures of similarity between different genetic codes (except for certain limited instances), we are forced to resort to the morphological and physiological characters employed in conventional taxonomy. Recently we have found that although different types of characters in a taxonomic study may be correlated, this correlation is not sufficiently strong for a classification based on one set of characters (for example external characters) to agree fully with a classification based on a second set (for example internal characters). Thus a taxonomy of males may differ somewhat from one of females, and a classification of skeletal parts may not agree entirely with one based on soft parts. This is a necessary consequence of phenetic classification, and in order to obtain valid measures of overall similarity one has to use as many and as varied sets of characters as possible.

If classifications are to be established on overall similarity, numerical taxonomy is required to put the procedures on an operational and quantitative basis. Some of the procedures of numerical taxonomy were developed as early as the beginning of this century, but before the introduction of digital computers they never caught on, presumably because of the insuperable computational difficulties. The philosophical origins of the present development in taxonomy derive from the work of Michel Adanson, an 18th-century French botanist, who first rejected a priori assumptions on the importance of different characters and proposed basing natural taxa on his essentially phenetic concept of "affinity."

The recent development of numerical taxonomy starts with the almost simultaneous publication in 1957 of papers advocating this method by Peter H. A. Sneath, a British microbiologist, and by Charles D. Michener and myself, both entomologists at the University of Kansas. Two further independent studies by workers at the University of Ox-

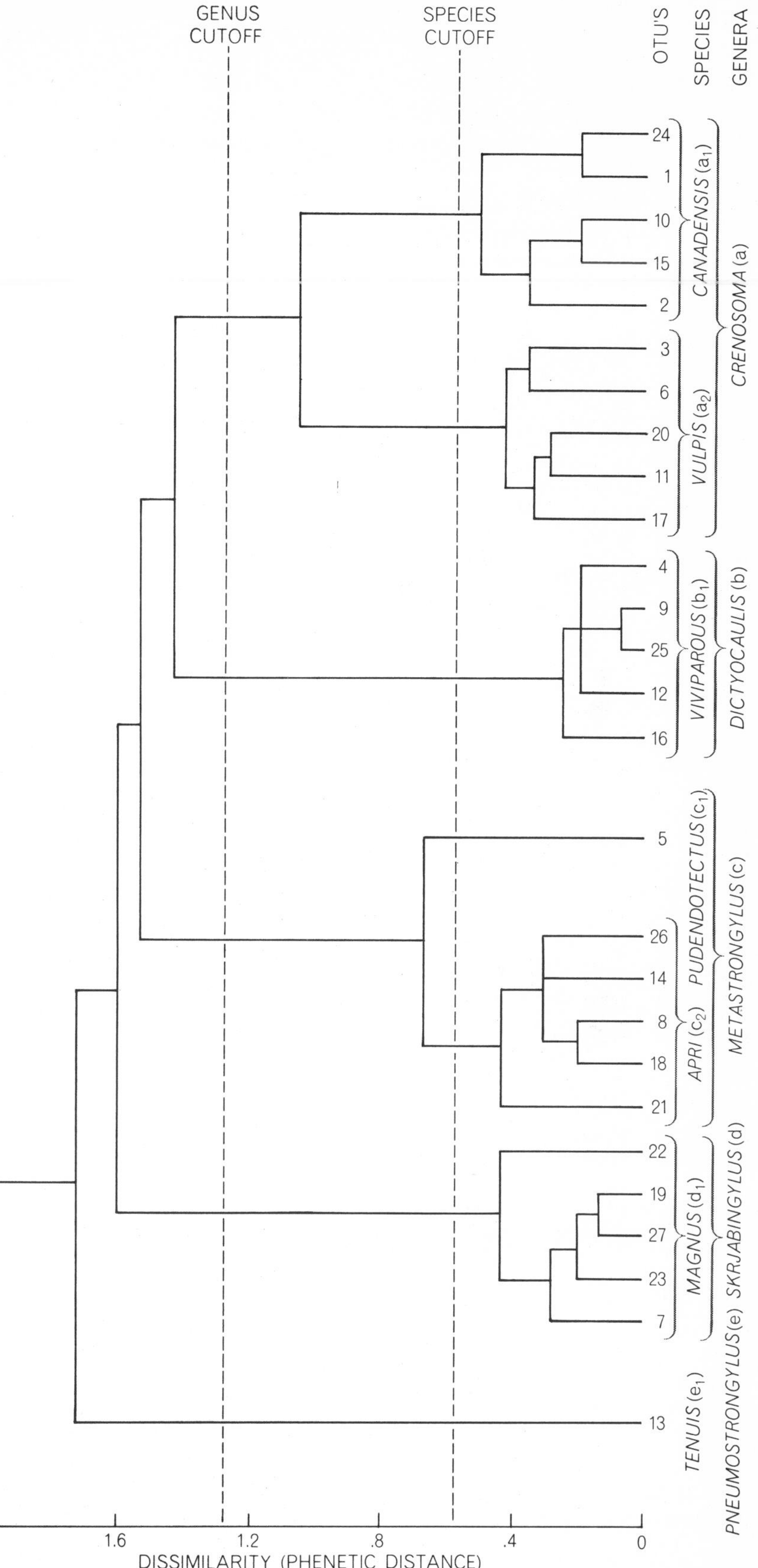

NEMATODE PHENOGRAM is based on the similarity matrix at bottom of opposite page. The brackets and lettering correspond to similar brackets and lettering in the similarity matrix. Broken vertical lines are "cutoff lines" for recognizing species and genera, which are indicated by their full names at right. Code numbers for OTU's are at tips of branches. Rearrangement of first two species has no effect on the taxonomic relationship illustrated.

ford and at the New York Botanical Garden followed in 1958 and 1960 respectively. Since that time the literature and the number of workers in the field have grown rapidly. At last count there were at least 200 published papers on numerical taxonomy, with more than 60 papers applying numerical taxonomy to diverse groups of organisms.

How does one produce a classification by numerical taxonomy? The objects to be classified are called "operational taxonomic units," or OTU's for short. They may be individuals as such, individuals representing species or higher-ranking taxa such as genera or families of plants or animals, or statistical abstractions of the higher-ranking taxonomic groups.

Classifications by numerical taxonomy are based on many numerically

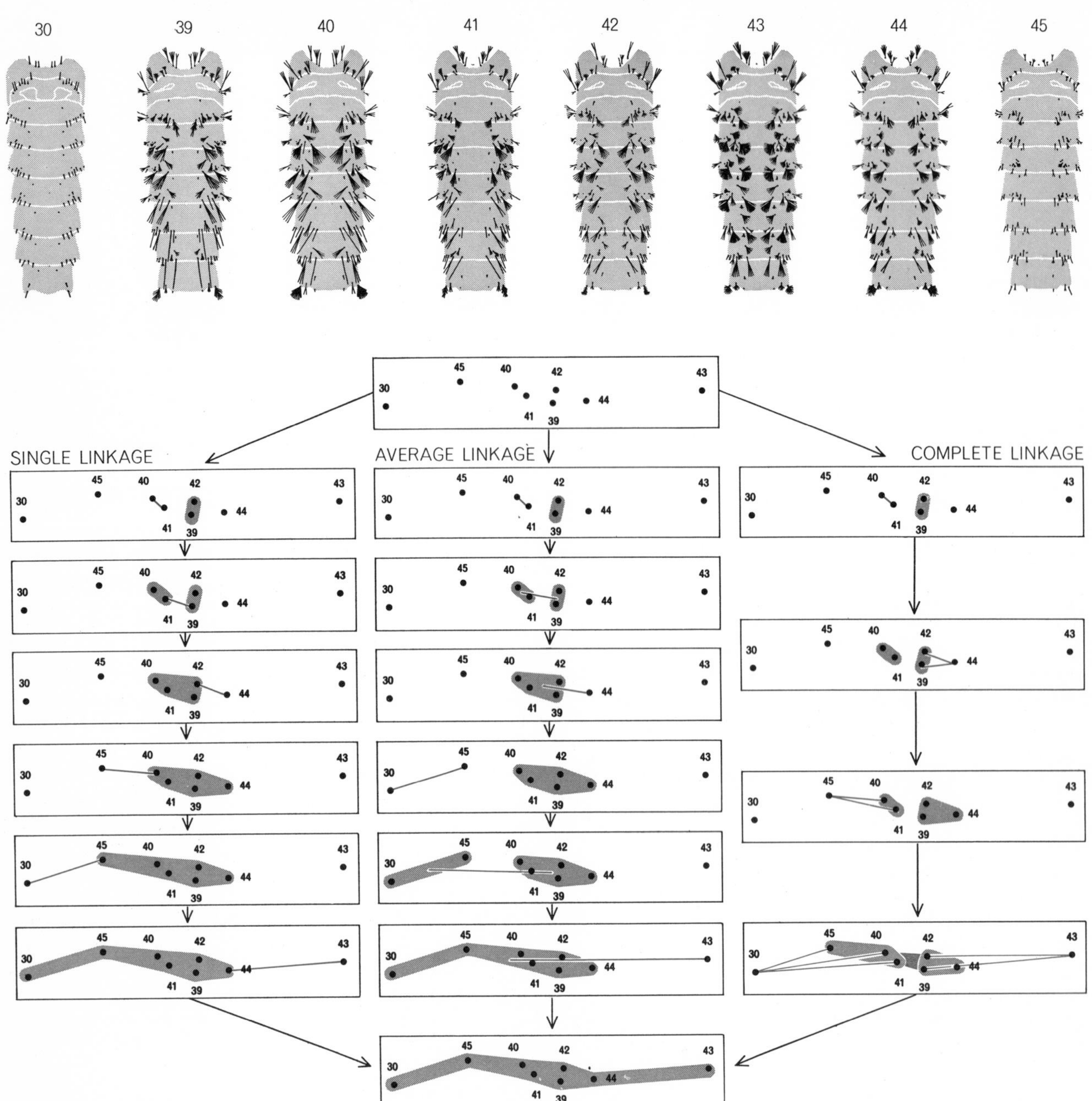

DIFFERENT CLUSTERING TECHNIQUES yield different classifications of the same taxonomic units. The numbered black dots represent eight species of mosquitoes described by pupal characteristics only (*drawings at top*). Species 30 belongs to the genus *Mansonia;* the others are species of *Anopheles.* For convenience of representation, distances among OTU's are shown in two-dimensional space only. Linkages between OTU's and clusters and between pairs of clusters are shown by solid-colored lines, previously established clusters by light-colored shading of the area occupied by the clustered OTU's. As clustering proceeds step by step the criteria for joining become less stringent; in other words, the distances between prospective joiners and established clusters increase. The single-linkage method (*left*) starts with the shortest distance between any pair of OTU's and takes up the other distances in order of magnitude. In average linkage (*center*) an OTU will join a cluster if the average distance between it and the "center of gravity" of the cluster is less than for any other such distance in the study. In complete linkage (*right*) joining takes place only when the relationships between a candidate for joining and established members of the clusters are all at the minimum criterion for a given clustering cycle. Although the initial clustering step is the same for all three methods and the final cluster, including all the OTU's, must necessarily also be the same, the intermediate clustering steps are obviously quite different at roughly equivalent stages. The results depicted here will not necessarily agree with comparable studies that include additional closely related OTU's.

recorded characters. These may be measurements that are appropriately represented numerically, or they may be coded in such a way that the differences between them are proportional to their dissimilarity. For example, a character called "hairiness of leaf" might be coded as follows: hairless, 0; sparsely haired, 1; regularly haired, 2; densely haired, 3. By this coding system we imply that the dissimilarity between densely haired and hairless is approximately three times the dissimilarity between sparsely haired and hairless. In some fields, such as microbiology, characters are almost always expressed by only two states corresponding to the presence (1) or the absence (0) of a given character, for example an enzyme.

All the characters and the taxonomic units to be classified are arranged in a data matrix, and the similarities between all possible pairs of OTU's are then computed based on all the characters. We shall not concern ourselves here with the variety of mathematical coefficients that have been devised to represent similarity between objects. One way of representing similarity (actually dissimilarity) is the distance between OTU's in a multidimensional space. Suppose the similarity between all possible pairs taken from four objects is to be estimated on the basis of three characters. We can visualize these characters as representing three coordinate axes [*see bottom illustration on page 176*]. Each OTU is then plotted into this three-dimensional space according to its state, or value, for the three characters. Those objects that are very similar will be plotted close to each other; dissimilar ones will be considerably farther apart. The computation of such straight-line distances is quite simple. In any real case there will, of course, be more than three characters and a multidimensional space would be necessary. Although it is not possible to represent such a "hyperspace" pictorially, the computation of distances within it is still quite simple. Thus we can view the objects to be classified as clusters of points in multidimensional space.

The similarities between pairs of OTU's are evaluated by a computer and printed out in a "similarity matrix," which shows the similarity value of each OTU with respect to every other one. Rather than give such a numerical table here, I have illustrated it graphically on page 178, indicating the magnitude of the similarity coefficient by depth of shading. Unless the OTU's to be classified have been ordered previously, the pattern of shading in the similarity matrix is likely to be complex. We can attempt, however, to alter the arrangement of the OTU's in such a way that the dark-shaded areas (high-similarity values) will condense in triangular groups along the diagonal of the table. This procedure will yield a rough classification of these OTU's into groups.

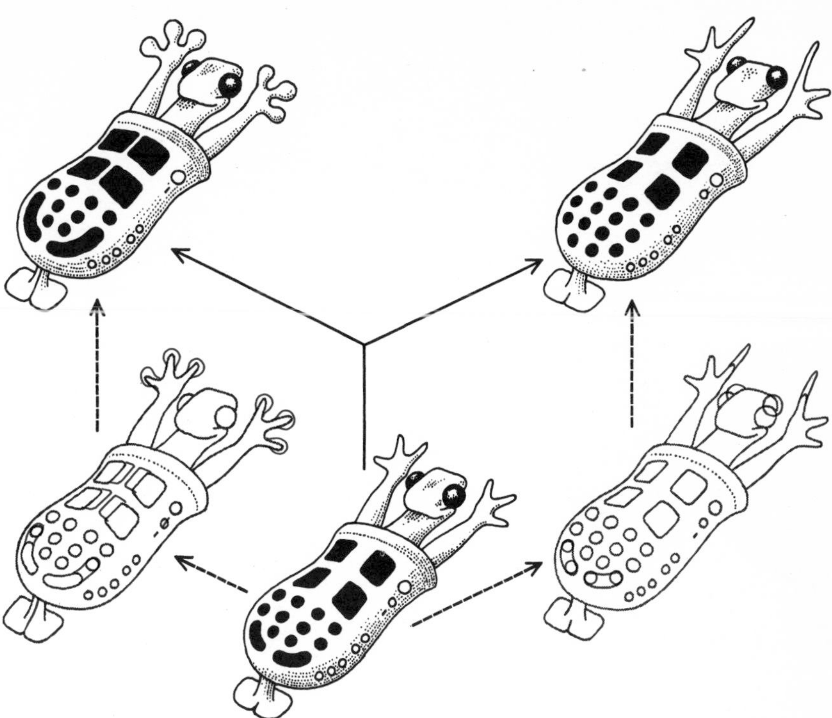

GENETIC CONTINUITY was accomplished in the generation of the Caminalcules by tracing the drawing of the primitive species (*bottom*) from sheet to sheet, making possible the preservation of all characters except for the desired morphological modifications (*color*).

For more precise classifications a variety of numerical clustering procedures have been developed, and these procedures are routinely carried out on the computer after the similarity matrix has been calculated. There is no generally accepted clustering method. Different methods will yield different results, depending on the underlying "similarity structure" of the objects to be clustered [*see illustration on opposite page*]. Attempts are being made currently to define an "optimal" classification mathematically so that the results of a numerical classification can be evaluated by this criterion.

The results of a numerical classification are usually represented by means of a "phenogram." These treelike diagrams indicate the similarity between OTU's or stems bearing more than one OTU along one axis. Because phenograms collapse multidimensional relationships into two dimensions, there is appreciable distortion of the original relationships as shown in the similarity matrix. Estimates of the degree of distortion in a given phenogram are made routinely in numerical taxonomic studies as a precaution. Representing phenetic relationships by three-dimensional models of OTU's avoids some of the distortions encountered in phenograms. Since such models cannot be circulated widely, the possibility of publishing computer-produced "stereograms"—two-dimensional projections of three-dimensional models—is currently being investigated.

Describing the similarities among organisms is only one aim of taxonomy. Another is to trace the evolutionary lineages that gave rise to the diversity of organic life that exists today. To reconstruct the taxonomic relationships and evolutionary trends among a group of organisms one would need to describe their phenetic relationships through all points in time. One would also have to describe the group's "cladistics," the branching sequences in the evolutionary trees. Finally, one must furnish a correct time scale to the evolutionary reconstruction. At the moment there is no known way—short of a multidimensional reconstruction, which is impossible of practical achievement—to incorporate these elements into a unified system without large distortion of the phenetic relationships.

Some substantial recent advances in

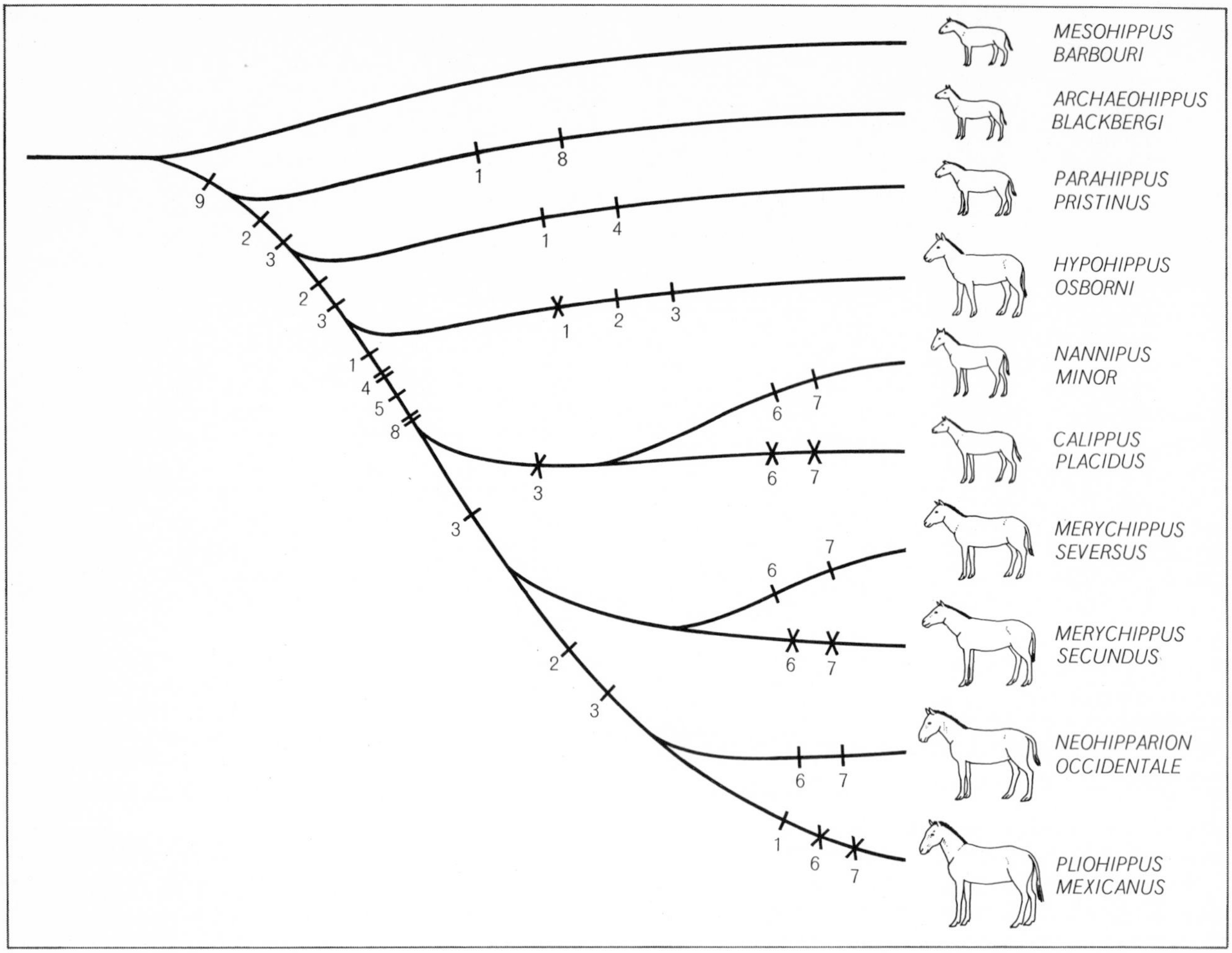

MESOHIPPUS BARBOURI
ARCHAEOHIPPUS BLACKBERGI
PARAHIPPUS PRISTINUS
HYPOHIPPUS OSBORNI
NANNIPUS MINOR
CALIPPUS PLACIDUS
MERYCHIPPUS SEVERSUS
MERYCHIPPUS SECUNDUS
NEOHIPPARION OCCIDENTALE
PLIOHIPPUS MEXICANUS

MESOHIPPUS BARBOURI
HYPOHIPPUS OSBORNI
ARCHAEOHIPPUS BLACKBERGI
PARAHIPPUS PRISTINUS
MERYCHIPPUS SEVERSUS
NANNIPUS MINOR
NEOHIPPARION OCCIDENTALE
CALIPPUS PLACIDUS
MERYCHIPPUS SECUNDUS
PLIOHIPPUS MEXICANUS

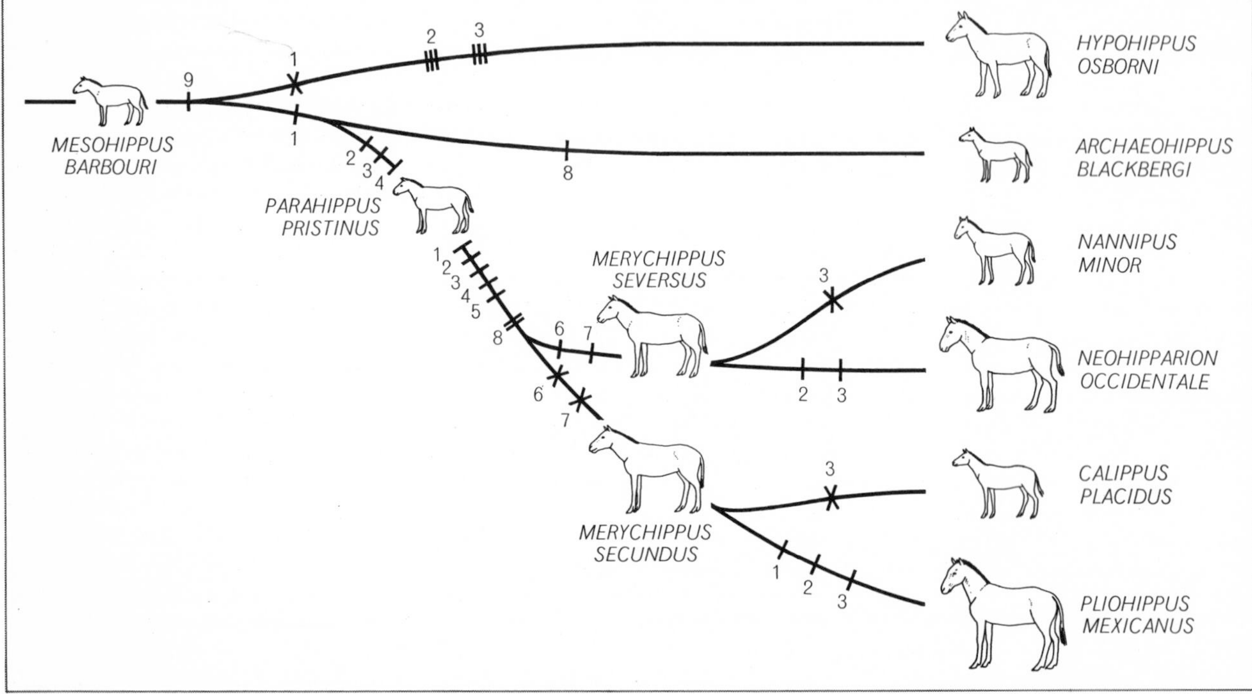

CLADOGRAMS, diagrams that delineate the branching sequences in an evolutionary tree, are shown here for a group of fossil horses. A computer program developed by Camin and the author constructs cladograms with the fewest number of evolutionary steps. The cladogram at top shows an early stage in the procedure; the one at bottom shows the most parsimonious solution, in which the 35 steps at top have been reduced to 31 steps. The cladogram at bottom corresponds to evolutionary branching sequence generally accepted by paleontologists. The evolutionary steps for various numbered skeletal and dental characters are marked on the branches. In the bidirectional evolution of a character one direction is shown by lines across branches, the other by *X* marks.

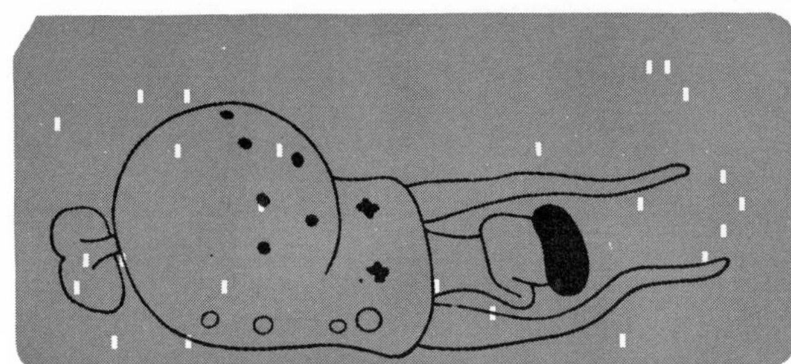

AUTOMATIC SCANNING of organisms for the purpose of establishing phenetic classifications was proved to be feasible in a recent experiment performed by F. James Rohlf and the author in which they successively placed 25 punch cards, each perforated with 25 randomly chosen holes, over drawings of a group of Caminalcules. One of the punch cards is shown at left superposed over a drawing of a Caminalcule belonging to species 1. In making the composite at right each of the 625 holes was scored 1 when a black line appeared through it and 0 when no black showed. (Actually fewer than 625 holes are visible here, since many holes on different cards coincided.) The illustrations of the organisms were compared on the basis of matching scores for corresponding masks and holes.

techniques for reconstructing cladistic sequences grew out of an experiment on the principles and practices of taxonomy carried out by a group of graduate students and faculty members at the University of Kansas. The study was based on a group of imaginary animals generated by Joseph H. Camin according to rules known so far only to him but believed to be consistent with what is generally known of evolutionary principles. Genetic continuity was accomplished by tracing the drawings of the animals from sheet to sheet, permitting the preservation of all characters except for the modifications that were desired. All 29 "recent" species of these "organisms," irreverently named Caminalcules by the graduate students, are shown on pages 174 and 175. Detailed studies of the assemblage of hypothetical animals by orthodox phylogenetic methodology by various team members resulted in differing, but internally consistent, cladistic schemes, the choice among which was not easily apparent. Comparison by Camin of these various schemes with the "truth" led him to the observation that those trees that most closely resembled the true cladistic sequence invariably required for their construction the fewest number of postulated evolutionary steps for the characters studied.

Our experiments were based on three working assumptions: first, that character states could be numerically coded according to their presumed evolutionary trends; second, that evolution is irreversible, so that when a character evolves to state 2, it will not revert to state 1; third, that nature is fundamentally parsimonious, so that the diversity in character states within a given group was achieved at or close to the minimum number of evolutionary steps. From these assumptions Camin and I developed a computational technique that constructs the most parsimonious cladistic tree, or cladogram, from an original data matrix. A computer program carries out these computations. The cladograms on the opposite page illustrate the type of change that is routinely carried out by the computer program. The cladograms estimate the branching sequences that occurred in the evolutionary history of a group of fossil horses. These methods have also given apparently meaningful results in studies of bees, vipers, certain plants, fossil protozoa and the structural rearrangements of chromosomes in blackflies and drosophila.

The computer program also evaluates the compatibility of each characteristic with all the other characters and weights it in terms of this criterion. It points out inconsistencies and has repeatedly discovered errors in coding, transcription or interpretation of the data.

A major impetus for the development and application of numerical taxonomy is the current introduction of automatic sensing and data-recording devices: The development of such instruments has proceeded very rapidly in recent years. Most prominent among the devices likely to be useful in taxonomy are optical scanners, which digitize drawings, photographs, microscope preparations and results of biochemical analysis. The veritable flood of information that will flow from these automatic sensors will require computer-based processing and classification, since the human mind is not able to digest these data by traditional means.

Recently F. James Rohlf and I have shown that data of this kind, collected in a quite unsophisticated manner, can be used to form adequate phenetic classifications. We employed the straightforward approach of recording agreement in visible structures over randomly selected minute areas of the images of pairs of organisms. Such a procedure would be feasible by means of optical scanners. Random masks, made from 25 punch cards each perforated with 25 randomly chosen holes, were placed over black-and-white drawings of two groups of "organisms." One group consisted of the 29 recent species of the Caminalcules; the second comprised published illustrations of the pupae of 32 species of mosquitoes. Each illustration was overlaid with all the masks, and each of the 625 holes was scored 1 when a black line appeared through it and 0 when no black showed [*see illustration above*]. Illustrations were compared on the basis of matching scores for corresponding masks and holes. A numerical classification of the images was surprisingly similar to studies by conventional taxonomy or by numerical taxonomy based on the detailed description of characters. Whenever phenetic taxonomies are acceptable, automatic scanning and classification may provide a rapid and reliable approach. Problems of the size and orientation of the organisms remain to be worked out, but they should not present insuperable technical difficulties. The implications of the success of this method are that experience and insight into the presumed biological and phylogenetic significance of characters may be less important for obtaining satisfactory classifications than had been generally supposed.

Thus there is every reason to believe that classifications from automatically obtained characters are possible. This finding will, of course, lead not only to automatic classification but also to automatic identification, which should be one of the more exciting prospects for research workers faced with routine identification problems.

Numerical taxonomists working in biological taxonomy are continually surprised and impressed by the applicability of their principles in numerous sciences and other fields of human activity. They marvel at the rapidity with which this knowledge is spreading throughout the biological, medical, geological and social sciences, as well as the humanities. Numerical taxonomy has been employed to classify soils and diseases, politicians and plant communities, archaeological artifacts and oil-bearing strata, socioeconomic neighborhoods and psychological types, languages and television programs—to name just some of the applications. Sneath has even used it to solve a jigsaw puzzle. This broad spectrum of applications for numerical taxonomy should not surprise us. After all, the precise categorization of human experience is one of the foundations for a scientific understanding of the universe. We should not, however, be overly impressed by the similarities in approach in these various sciences. There are appreciable differences in the principles of classification in diverse fields, and it is necessary to know when the problems of one discipline part company with those of another. Nonetheless, the common fund of basic ideas on similarity and classification is great enough to serve as the basis for a general science of taxonomy.

Biological taxonomy will be affected by the computer in many ways besides numerical taxonomy. Automatic data processing will revolutionize the storage and retrieval of taxonomic information for museums and catalogues. The approaches of numerical taxonomy have already done much to de-emphasize the often legalistic and sterile aspects of naming organisms. It is likely that developments in automatic data processing will rapidly relegate problems of nomenclature to the position of relative unimportance they merit. Some of the birth pangs of automation will be felt in taxonomy as in other fields, and traditionally-minded workers will presumably resist the changes. The controversy about numerical taxonomy will doubtless continue for some time to come until a new "synthetic" theory of taxonomy, accepting what is soundest from various schools, becomes established. The revolution the computer has wrought in taxonomy has only just begun.

TEXTURE AND VISUAL PERCEPTION

BELA JULESZ • February 1965

Because we are surrounded every waking minute by objects of different sizes, shapes, colors and textures we are scarcely surprised that we can tell them apart. There are so many visual clues to the distinctiveness of objects that we hardly ever make the mistake of believing that two different objects are one object unless we have been deliberately tricked.

Four years ago I became interested in studying the extent to which one can perceive differences in visual patterns when all familiar cues are removed. In this way I hoped to dissociate the primitive mechanisms of perception from the more complex ones that depend on lifelong learned habits of recognition. To obtain suitable patterns for this investigation a computer was used to generate displays that had subtly controlled statistical, topological or other properties but entirely lacked familiar features.

This method is basically different from those employed earlier by workers interested in visual perception. One method that has been widely used is to impoverish or degrade the images presented to the subject. This can be done by adding visual "noise," by presenting the stimuli for a limited time or by otherwise impairing the normal conditions of viewing. Another approach is to study human subjects whose perceptual mechanisms are known to be deficient (for example people who are colorblind) or animals whose perceptual mechanisms have been altered by surgical operations. I hoped that my approach of "familiarity deprivation" might be a useful addition to these other methods.

In a broad sense I was interested in the same kind of problem that has long concerned psychologists of the *Gestalt* school. One such problem has been to explain why it is that under certain conditions an outline drawing is seen as a unified whole—as a *Gestalt*—and under other conditions is seen as having two or more parts. I undertook to reduce this problem to how one discriminated between the parts (or did not discriminate between them). In my investigations, which have been conducted at the Bell Telephone Laboratories, I have been concerned with two specific questions. First, can two unfamiliar objects connected in space be discriminated solely by differences in their surface texture? Second, can two unfamiliar objects with identical surface texture be discriminated solely on the basis of their separation in space?

To make these questions less abstract let me give examples that could arise in real life. The first question would be involved if you wanted to replace a section of wallpaper and discovered that the original pattern was no longer available. If the pattern happened to be nonrepresentational and irregular, you might be able to find a new pattern that could not easily be discriminated from the old one when the two were placed side by side. Yet if you studied the two patterns closely, you might find that they differed substantially in detail. You would conclude that the matching must be attributable to the similarity of certain critical features in the two patterns.

The second question has its counterpart in aerial reconnaissance to detect objects that have been camouflaged. Flying at a height of several thousand feet, an observer can easily be deceived by the camouflage because normal binocular depth perception is inoperative beyond 100 feet or so. But if he photographs the ground from two points several hundred feet apart and views the resulting pictures stereoscopically, he will usually discover that even a camouflaged object will stand out vividly in three dimensions.

Of course neither of these examples provides an adequate test of the discrimination problems I hoped to examine with artificial displays. The weakness in the wallpaper analogy is that most wallpaper patterns, including irregular ones, have repetitive features and even forms that suggest familiar objects. The aerial reconnaissance example has the important defect that most camouflaged objects have contours that can be recognized monocularly as shapes of some sort; they are not, in other words, random patterns.

These and other difficulties are quite easily circumvented by using a computer to generate random-dot patterns in which all familiar cues and other unwanted factors are eliminated. For the purpose of studying the first problem—the role of texture in discrimination—random-dot patterns with different properties were generated side by side. The objective was to determine those pattern properties that make it possible to discriminate between the adjacent visual displays. I was concerned primarily with the discrimination that can be achieved immediately. Such discrimination can be regarded as a spontaneous process and thus can be ascribed to a primitive perceptual mechanism.

An example of spontaneous discrimination is given by the illustration at bottom left on page 188. Both fields of the pattern contain black, gray and white dots with equal first-order, or overall, probability; therefore if the pattern is viewed from a distance, both fields appear uniformly gray. When the two fields are viewed at close range, however, they exhibit a different second-order, or detailed, probability. This shows up immediately as a difference in granularity.

The illustration at bottom right on page 188 represents a case in which there

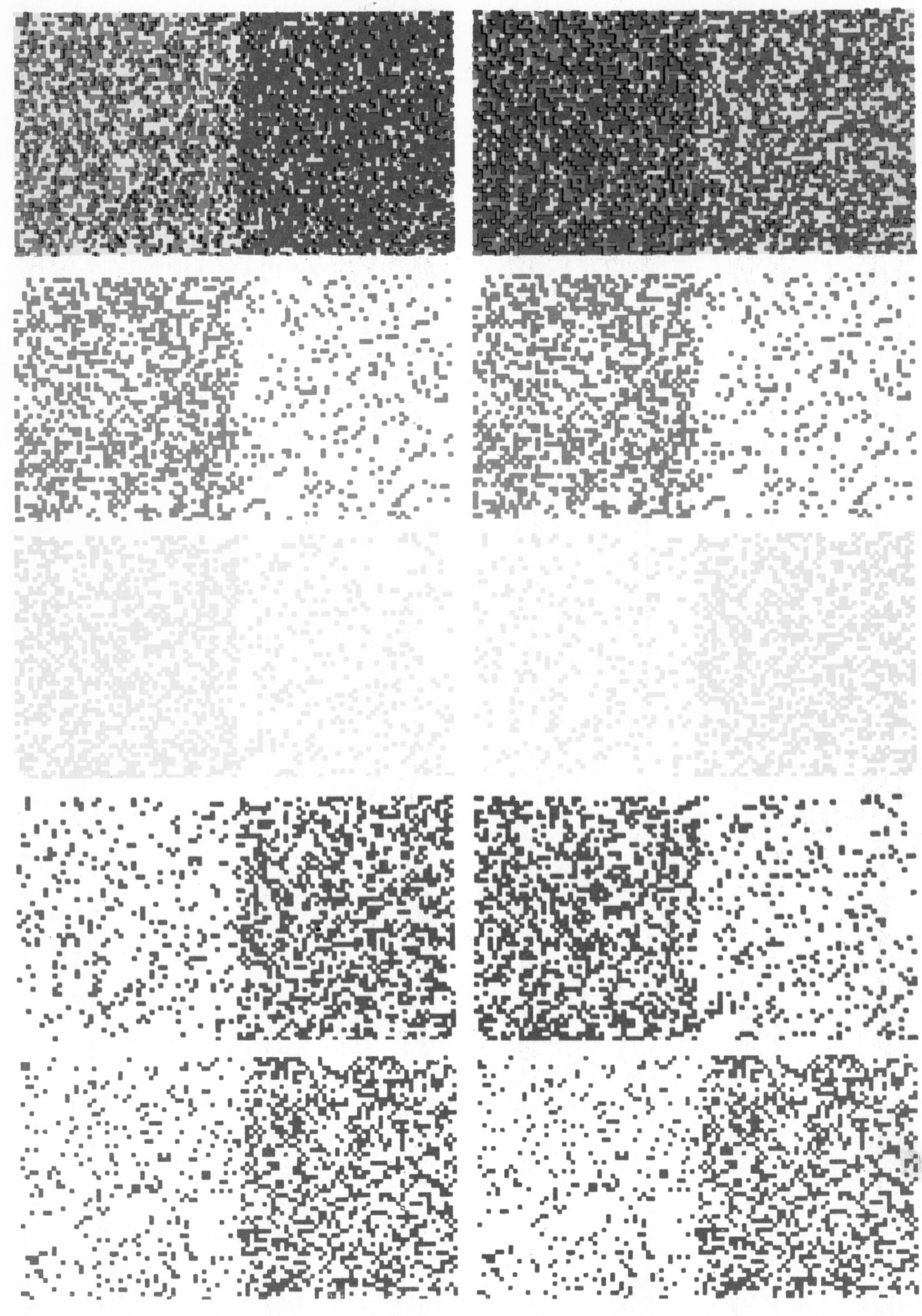

can be no spontaneous discrimination between two fields. In this case discrimination can be achieved only by someone who knows the difference between English words and random sequences of letters. Here discrimination requires a sophisticated kind of pattern recognition. This article is concerned only with discrimination of the spontaneous type.

In the case of random-dot patterns one might expect that discrimination of visual texture is fundamentally governed by variations in the statistical properties of the patterns. That is true in the most general sense, because any two different patterns must differ in some such property. It turns out, however, that simple statistical measurements of brightness distribution are not adequate to describe perceptual performance.

This is demonstrated in the illustration at upper left on this page, which consists of two patterns made up of black, gray and white dots. In one quadrant the dots are distributed with equal probability and completely at random. The surrounding area matches the quadrant in overall brightness, but it also contains small triangular units composed of black, white and gray dots in various arrangements. Although these triangular units occur with equal probability, the only ones observed are those made up entirely of black dots; the others pass unnoticed.

This indicates that discrimination of visual texture is not based on complex statistical analysis of brightness distribution but involves a kind of preprocessing. Evidently the preprocessing extracts neighboring points that have similar brightness values, which are perceived as forming clusters or lines. This process, which should not be confused with the actual spatial connection of objects, might be called connectivity detection. It is on the relatively simple statistics of these clusters and some simple description of them, such as spatial extent, that texture discrimination is really based.

The lower pair of illustrations above shows this connectivity detection even more clearly. In the left member of the pair two textures are easily discriminated; in the right member discrimination is difficult, if not impossible. In the pattern at the left every fifth horizontal and vertical row is gray; in the pattern at the right, which is otherwise identical, every fifth row is randomly peppered black and white. The "noise" added to the pattern at the right has only a minor effect on the statistics of the two subpatterns to be discriminated, yet it breaks up the connectivity of the subpatterns enough for them to merge into one field. The black and white "S" shapes that appear so clearly in the pattern at the left are completely destroyed in the pattern at the right. If the disrupted pattern is viewed at a sharp angle, however, the line clusters reappear and discrimination is facilitated.

The importance of proximity and similarity was emphasized early in the

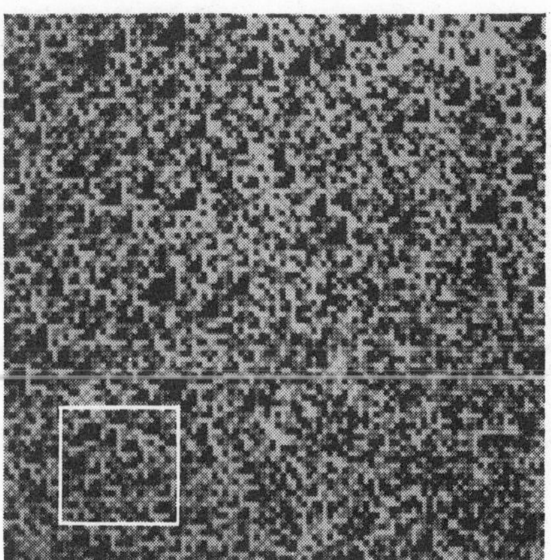

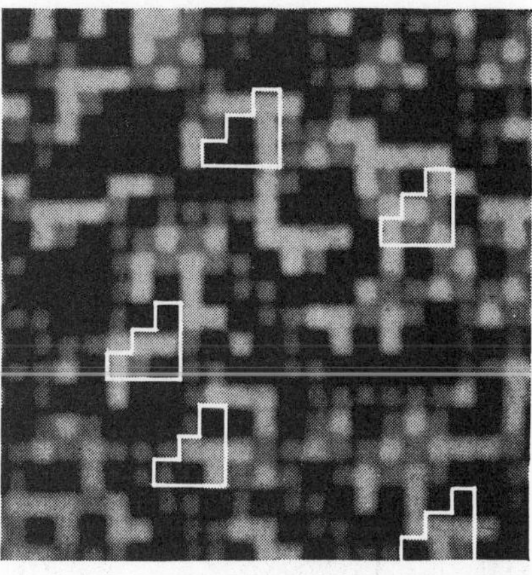

CLUSTER IDENTIFICATION in the pattern at left extends only to triangular shapes made up entirely of black dots. Other equally probable triangles containing dots of mixed brightness do not form clusters. These are marked in the enlargement at right.

EFFECT OF "NOISE" is demonstrated in these two patterns. In the pattern at left the two subpatterns containing either black or white "S" shapes are easily discriminated. Moreover, every fifth horizontal and vertical row is gray. The pattern at right is identical except that the dots in the gray rows have been made black or white at random. By breaking up the connectivity of the pattern in this way the subpatterns are almost obliterated.

TEXTURE DISCRIMINATION in random fields of colored dots is highly dependent on the way the component colors are paired. The two patterns at the top of the opposite page do not adequately reproduce the author's laboratory demonstration, in which patterns were created by colored lights of equal subjective brightness. This condition could be simulated by reducing the brightness of the yellow picture elements by a fine-mesh overlay of black dots. Use of such an overlay, however, would have the disadvantage of making the yellow areas look greenish. In the illustration on the opposite page the black-dot overlay has not been used, with the result that the yellow elements are much too bright. The purpose of the illustration is to show that a texture composed chiefly of red and yellow dots is readily discriminated from a texture composed chiefly of blue and green dots whereas a texture composed chiefly of red and green dots is not so readily discriminated from one composed chiefly of blue and yellow dots. These paired textures—one easily discriminable, the other less so—are respectively repeated at top left and right on the opposite page. The makeup of each top panel is shown in the four panels below it. The only difference is in the transposition of yellow and green.

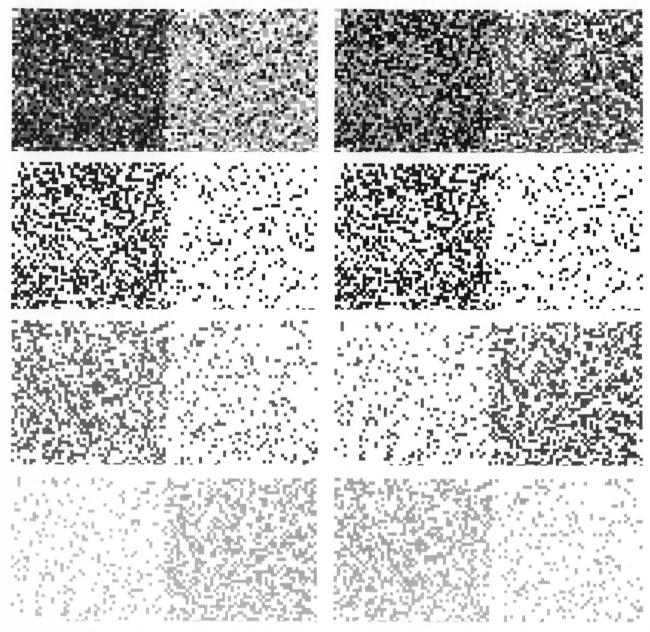

EASE OF DISCRIMINATION in random patterns of various brightness levels seems to depend on whether or not adjacent dots of different values form clusters. The pattern at top left forms two easily discriminated areas because the half field on the left contains mostly black and dark gray dots, which form dark clusters, whereas the half field on the right contains mostly light gray and white dots, which form light clusters. When the dark gray and light gray components are reversed (*top right*), the clustering does not take place and the half fields are not so readily discriminated. The composition of each top pattern is shown in the three panels below it.

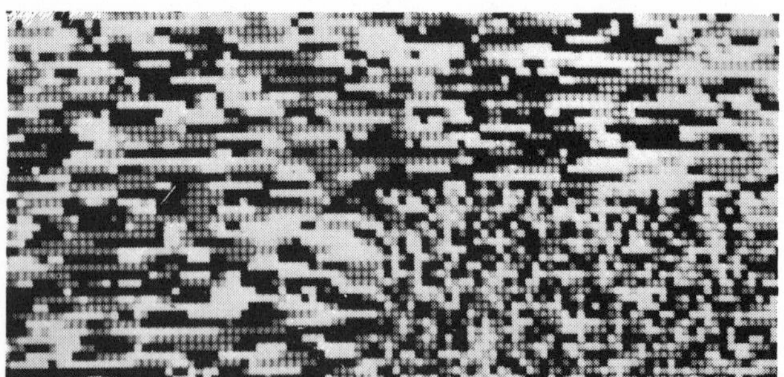

SPONTANEOUS DISCRIMINATION occurs even though the smaller field has the same average tonal quality as the larger field because the granularity of the two fields is different. At a distance the granularity is less noticeable and discrimination more difficult.

```
SCIENCE SPECIFY PRECISE SUBJECT MERCURY GOVERNS ECNEICS YFICEPS ESICERP TCEJBUS YRUCREM SNREVOG
METHODS RECORDS OXIDIZE COLUMNS CERTAIN QUICKLY SDOHTEM SDROCER EZIDIXO SNMULOC NIATREC YLKCIUQ
DEPICTS ENGLISH CERTAIN RECORDS EXAMPLE SCIENCE STCIPED HSILGNE NIATREC SDROCER ELPMAXE ECNEICS
SUBJECT PUNCHED GOVERNS MERCURY SPECIFY PRECISE TCEJBUS DEHCNUP SNREVOG YRUCREM YFICEPS ESICERP
EXAMPLE QUICKLY SPECIFY METHODS COLUMNS MERCURY ELPMAXE YLKCIUQ YFICEPS SDOHTEM SNMULOC YRUCREM
SCIENCE PRECISE EXAMPLE CERTAIN DEPICTS ENGLISH ECNEICS ESICERP ELPMAXE NIATREC STCIPED HSILGNE
SPECIFY MERCURY PUNCHED QUICKLY METHODS EXAMPLE YFICEPS YRUCREM DEHCNUP YLKCIUQ SDOHTEM ELPMAXE
EXAMPLE GOVERNS OXIDIZE ENGLISH SUBJECT RECORDS ELPMAXE SNREVOG EZIDIXO HSILGNE TCEJBUS SDROCER
COLUMNS SUBJECT PRECISE MERCURY PUNCHED CERTAIN SNMULOC TCEJBUS ESICERP YRUCREM DEHCNUP NIATREC
ENGLISH RECORDS EXAMPLE SUBJECT OXIDIZE GOVERNS HSILGNE SDROCER ELPMAXE TCEJBUS EZIDIXO SNREVOG
CERTAIN PRECISE PUNCHED METHODS ENGLISH COLUMNS NIATREC ESICERP DEHCNUP SDOHTEM HSILGNE SNMULOC
OXIDIZE QUICKLY SCIENCE DEPICTS SPECIFY PRECISE EZIDIXO YLKCIUQ ECNEICS STCIPED YFICEPS ESICERP
DEPICTS EXAMPLE ENGLISH CERTAIN RECORDS SCIENCE STCIPED ELPMAXE HSILGNE NIATREC SDROCER ECNEICS
SPECIFY MERCURY GOVERNS PRECISE QUICKLY METHODS YFICEPS YRUCREM SNREVOG ESICERP YLKCIUQ SKOHTEM
```

NONSPONTANEOUS DISCRIMINATION is represented by two half fields that have the same apparent texture and granularity. The left half field, however, contains familiar English words, whereas the right half field contains only random sequences of seven letters.

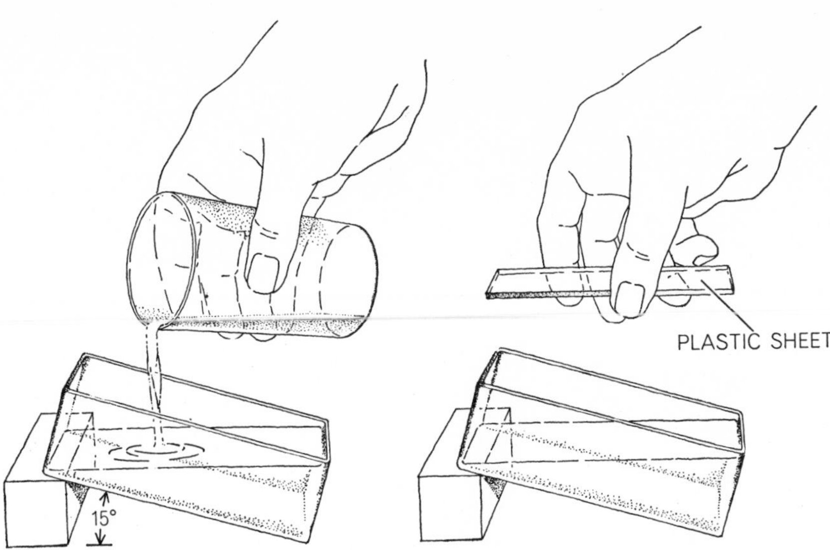

GELATIN PRISM provides a simple stereoscopic viewer. A clear plastic box for holding the gelatin can be obtained at a five-and-ten-cent store. Use five parts of very hot water to one part of household gelatin and mix thoroughly. Tilt the box about 15 degrees and pour in the gelatin solution. In about 30 minutes, when the solution has gelled, dampen the surface and press a rectangular sheet of clear plastic (or glass) against it. The prism will ordinarily work without this top sheet, but images may appear fuzzy.

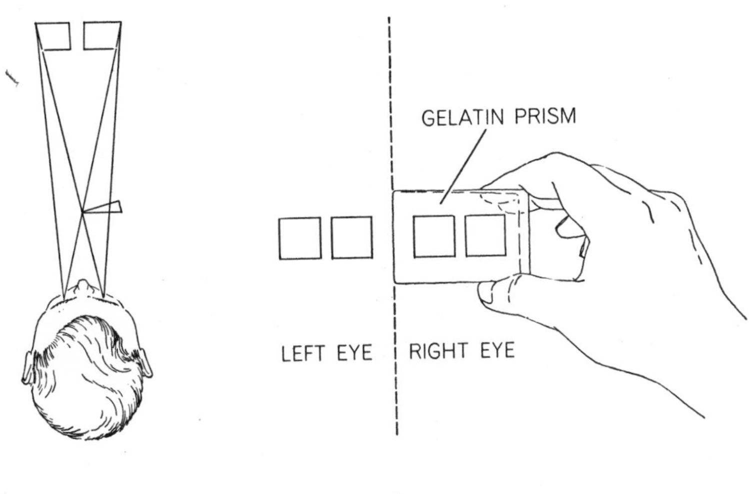

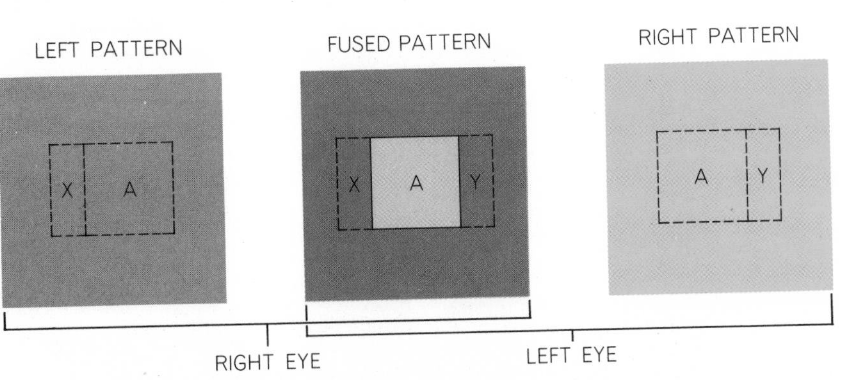

TO USE PRISM hold it about six inches in front of the right eye, thin edge toward the nose. Adjust the prism so that both stereoscopic images can be seen through it. Both images should also be visible to the left eye, as shown in the upper two diagrams. With little difficulty the images should rearrange themselves so that there appear to be only three images, of which the center one is the fused stereoscopic image. Once binocular fusion has occurred the image can be made sharper by moving the prism closer to the right eye.

work of the *Gestalt* psychologists, particularly that of Kurt Koffka and Max Wertheimer. Now, with the help of the random-dot-pattern technique one can give a more precise meaning to these notions. For example, the last experiment, in which the disrupted pattern is viewed at an angle, shows that neighboring points need not touch each other to appear connected. This notion comes as no surprise. On the other hand, when one observes that neighboring points of similar brightness are perceived as clusters, the meaning of "similar brightness" requires further clarification. How dissimilar in brightness can adjacent points be and still be perceived as clusters? In order to examine this question two computer patterns were generated.

In one pattern, shown at top left on page 188, the field at the left is composed chiefly of black and dark gray random dots; the field at the right contains mostly white and light gray dots. As a result the field at the left forms a large dark cluster and the field at the right forms a light cluster, with a fairly sharp boundary between them. In the adjacent pattern the light gray and dark gray dots are transposed so that the field at the left contains chiefly black and light gray dots and the field at the right contains chiefly white and dark gray dots. Here discrimination between the two fields is more difficult. These and similar results suggest that the visual system incorporates a slicer mechanism that separates adjacent brightness levels into two broad categories: dark and light. The level of slicing can be adjusted up and down, but it is impossible to form clusters by shifting our attention to dots that are not adjacent in brightness.

One might argue that the eye could hardly respond otherwise when brightness levels are involved. It can be shown, however, that the same connectivity rules hold for patterns that are composed of dots of different colors adjusted to have the same subjective brightness. This is the demonstration that is shown on page 186. Since these patterns are made up of colored inks that do not reflect light with equal intensity, they do not fully simulate the laboratory demonstration, in which the dots are projected on a screen in such a way that their subjective brightness can be carefully balanced. Nonetheless, the printed demonstration that is illustrated on page 186 is reasonably effective. In the top row of the illustration what one observes is that the lefthand pattern is immediately discriminated into a red-yellow field on the left and a blue green field on the right, whereas the righthand pattern seems more or less uniform in texture across its entire width. This uniformity in texture is achieved simply by transposing the yellow and green random elements so that the field at the left is composed mostly of red and green dots and the field at the right is composed mostly of blue and yellow dots. The first demonstration shows that red and yellow dots form clusters that are easily discriminated from the clusters formed by blue and green dots. The second demonstration shows that dots of nonadjacent hue, such as red and green or blue and yellow, do not form clusters.

Evidently this clustering, whether it is of adjacent brightness levels or of adjacent hues, represents a preprocessing mechanism of great importance in the visual system. Instead of performing complex statistical analyses when presented with complex patterns, the visual system wherever possible detects clusters and evaluates only a few of their relatively simple properties. One now

STEREOSCOPIC IMAGES investigated by the author consist of random-dot patterns generated by a computer. When these two images are viewed with a stereoscope or with a prism held in front of one eye, a center panel should be seen floating above the background, as illustrated at the far right. The principle employed in making such stereoscopic images is explained below.

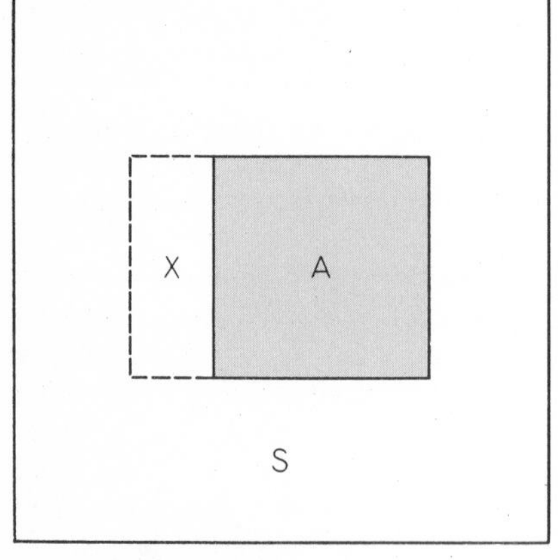

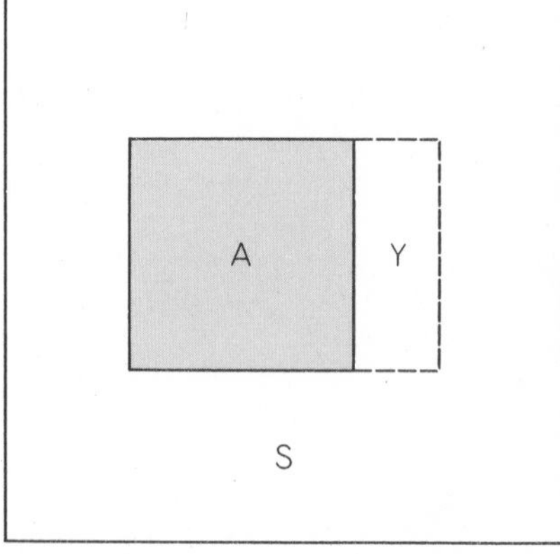

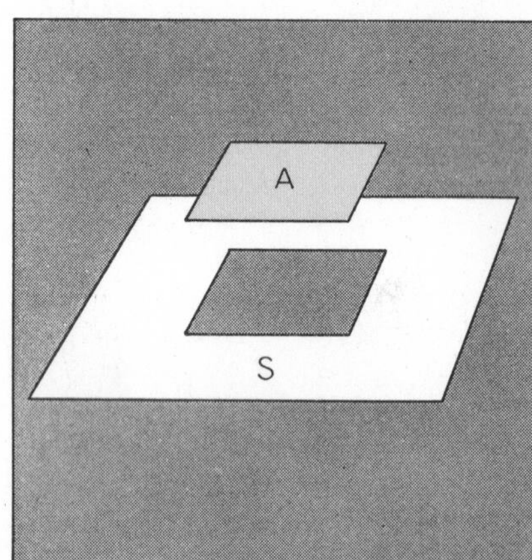

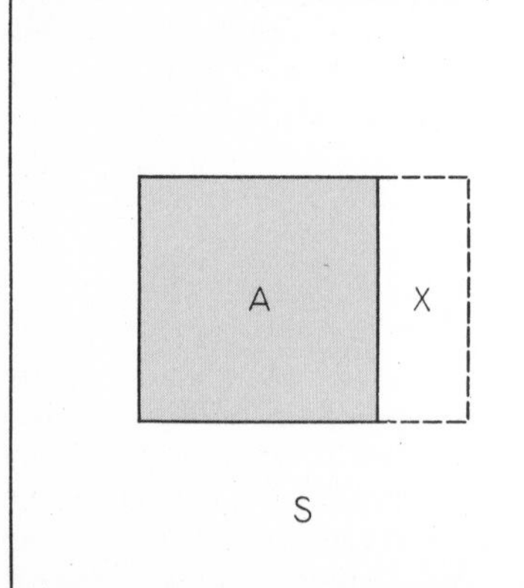

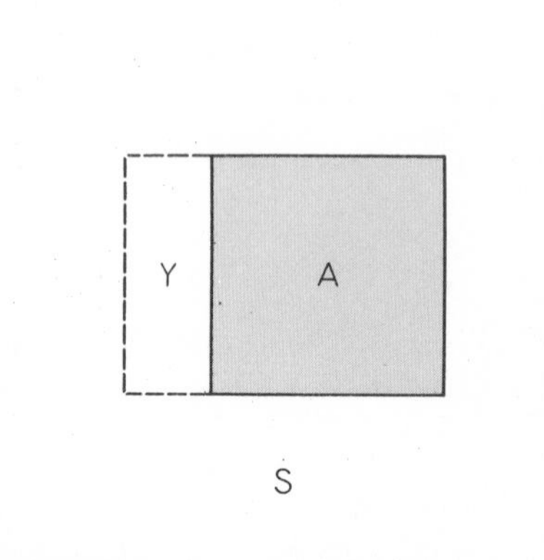

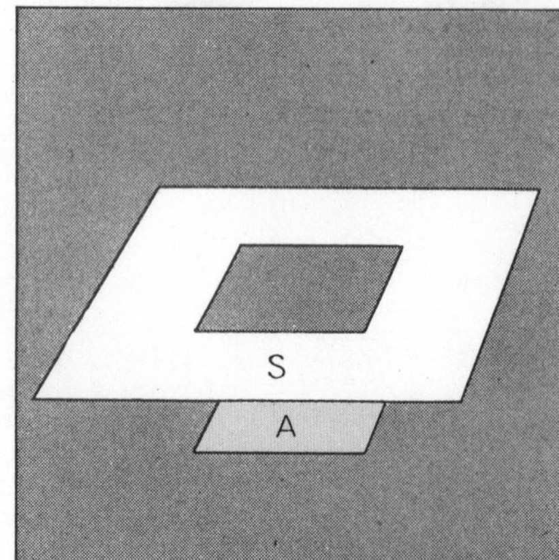

STEREOSCOPIC PRINCIPLE is simply that identical areas that appear in both fields must be shifted horizontally with respect to each other. Because these areas are themselves random-dot patterns they cannot be seen monocularly against a random-dot surround. In these diagrams *A* identifies the area common to both fields. In the upper pair of fields *A* is shifted inward, leaving two areas, *X* and *Y*, that are filled in with different random-dot patterns. When viewed stereoscopically, *A* seems to float above the surround. When *A* is shifted outward as shown in the two lower fields, *A* seems to lie behind the surround.

has a formula for matching wallpaper patterns. As long as the brightness value, the spatial extent, the orientation and the density of clusters are kept similar in two patterns, they will be perceived as one. Even for familiar patterns with recognizable and different forms discrimination can be made very difficult or impossible if the simple rules that govern clustering are observed. Thus a wallpaper pattern made up of seven-letter English words arranged in columns, as in the illustration at bottom right on page 188, would appear to be matched by a similar pattern containing nonsense sequences. The seven-letter nonwords would form clusters that could not be discriminated spontaneously from English words.

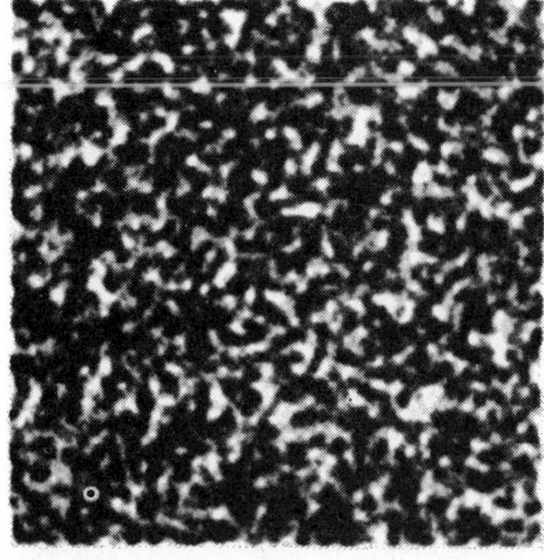
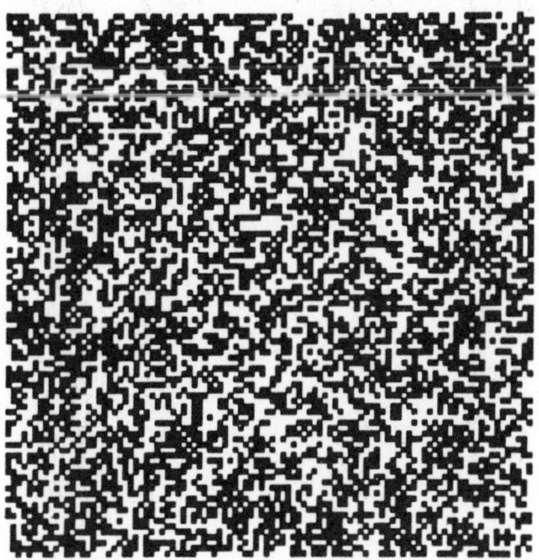

BLURRED IMAGE was produced by defocusing the field at left in the random-dot stereoscopic patterns on the preceding page. The field at right is unchanged. In spite of the blurring the two fields will fuse into a stereoscopic image; moreover, the image looks sharp.

REDUCED IMAGE also does not interfere seriously with the ability to obtain a good stereoscopic image. The two random-dot patterns are again those shown on the preceding page. The stereoscopic field at left, however, has been reduced about 10 percent in size.

NOISY IMAGE (*left*) is produced by breaking up triplets of black dots along one diagonal and white triplets along the other diagonal wherever they occur in the left field on the preceding page. Nevertheless, the two fields will still fuse stereoscopically.

These findings answer in the affirmative the first question raised at the beginning. Objects can indeed be discriminated by differences in their surface texture alone even if they are spatially connected and cannot be recognized. The basis of this texture discrimination depends on simple properties of clusters, which are detected according to simple rules. Cluster detection seems to be a quite primitive and general process. Recent neurophysiological studies of frogs and cats have disclosed that their visual systems extract certain basic features of a scene prior to more complex processing [see "Vision in Frogs," by W. R. A. Muntz, SCIENTIFIC AMERICAN Offprint #179 and "The Visual Cortex of the Brain," by David H. Hubel, SCIENTIFIC AMERICAN Offprint #168]. The "bug" detector in the frog's visual system and the slit detector in the cat's visual system are special cases of connectivity detection. It will be interesting to see if neurophysiologists can find evidence for cluster detectors of the type suggested by these perception experiments.

We are now ready to consider the second question: Can two unfamiliar objects of identical texture be discriminated solely on the basis of their spatial separation? To study this question it was necessary to create patterns that were unfamiliar, that had the same surface texture and that could be perceived in depth. Again the problem was solved with the help of random-dot patterns generated by a computer. This time the computer was used to generate pairs of patterns that were identical except for a central area that was displaced in various ways. I had hoped that one would obtain a sensation of depth when the two patterns were viewed stereoscopically, and I was delighted when that turned out to be the case. This proved that one can perceive a camouflaged object in depth even when the camouflage is perfect and the hidden object cannot be discerned monocularly. In short, the answer to the second question is also yes.

A pair of these random-dot stereoscopic patterns is shown in the upper illustration on the preceding page. The two patterns are identical except for a center square that is shifted horizontally to the left by six dots in the pattern at the right. By virtue of this shift the

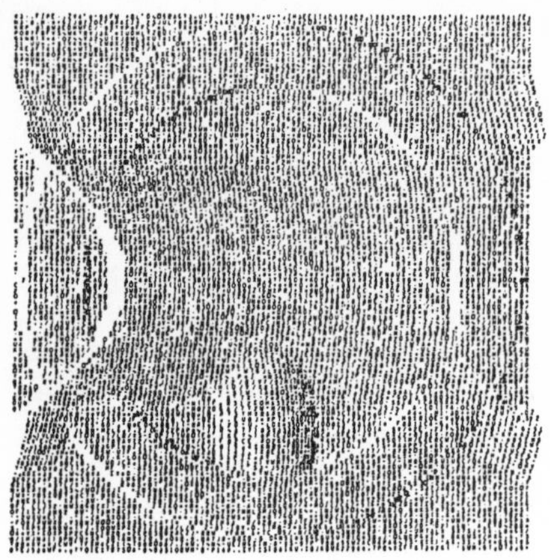

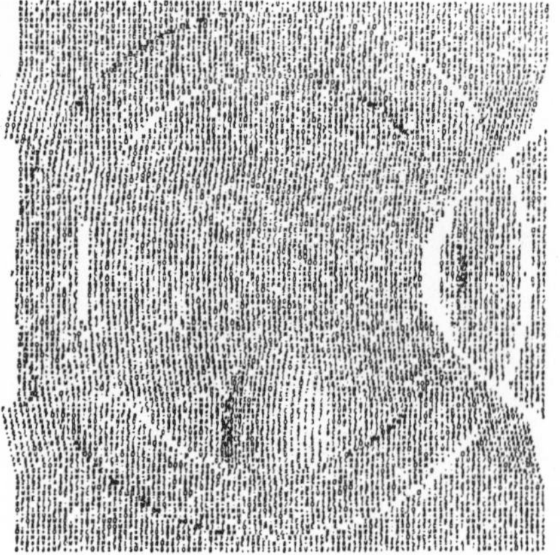

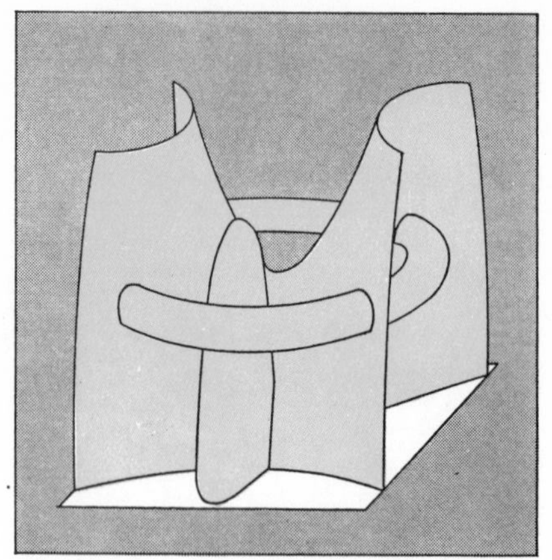

SADDLE-SHAPED FIGURE (*far right*) was transformed into left and right stereoscopic fields by a computer program devised by the author. The picture elements consist of 64 standard characters randomly selected but paired in the left and right fields.

square seems to float above the background when it is viewed stereoscopically. If the reader does not have an old-fashioned stereoscopic viewer at hand, by following the instructions on page 189 he can easily make a prism of gelatin that will serve the same purpose.

The phenomenon demonstrated by the binocular fusion of such random-dot patterns has a number of surprising implications. First of all, as the original statement of the problem requires, the stereoscopic picture is completely devoid of all familiarity and depth cues. Although the area selected for stereoscopic displacement in the first example is a simple square, it could be of any shape and it could also give the illusion of having more than one level [*see illustration above*]. The fact that the center square and its surround are horizontally shifted by different amounts in the fields at left and right corresponds to the different depth levels that are perceived. Thus spatial disconnectivity alone is enough for the center square and its surround to be perceived as two distinct objects.

The demonstration also demolishes a long-standing hypothesis of stereopsis, or binocular depth perception, in which it is assumed that the slightly different images that are simultaneously projected on the retinas of the two eyes are first monocularly recognized and then matched. The process was thought to be somewhat analogous to the operation of an optical range finder, in which the corresponding separate images are first recognized and then brought into alignment. This last step corresponds to measuring the amount of displacement between patterns and determining the amount of depth by simple trigonometry (which the range finder performs automatically).

Research in stereopsis has traditionally been devoted to the problem of relating the displacement, or disparity, of images and the perception of depth. It has become increasingly apparent that depth perception involves many cues and cannot be described by trigonometry alone. Little or no attention was paid to the more fundamental problem of how the visual system is able to identify the same object in the separate two-dimensional images formed on each retina. The studies with random-dot patterns have now shown that monocular recognition of shapes is unnecessary for depth perception.

The method of producing random-dot stereoscopic images is shown in the lower illustration on page 190. The surround (S) is composed of randomly selected but identical dot patterns in the fields at left and right. The center panel (*A*) is also identical in the two fields but is shifted in one field with respect to the other as if it were a solid sheet. If the shift is inward (toward the nose of the observer), the center panel seems to float in front of the surround. If the shift is in the opposite direction, the panel seems to lie behind the surround. The greater the parallax shift, the greater the perceived depth.

If one simply cut a panel out of a random-dot pattern and shifted it, say, to the left, an empty space would be exposed along the right edge of the panel. The empty region (labeled *Y* in the middle diagram on page 190) is simply filled in with more random dots. A similar region (labeled *X*) must be filled when the panel is shifted to the right. Each region is projected onto only one retina (*X* onto the left retina and *Y* onto the right) and therefore exhibits no displacement. It is curious that these regions are always perceived as being the continuation of the adjacent area that seems to be farthest away.

By further manipulation of the random-dot patterns, it is possible to produce panels whose apparent location in space is ambiguous. If the *X* and *Y* regions described above are filled in with the same random-dot pattern, which we will label *B*, then when the two fields are viewed stereoscopically the center panel *A* may seem to be raised above the surround or area *B* may seem to lie below the surround. The diagram on page *10* illustrates the reason for this ambiguity. If the center panel is to be wider than the parallax shift (that is, wider than *B*), it must contain repeating vertical stripes of *ABAB* and so on in one field and stripes of *BABA* and so on in the other. An ambiguous panel created in this way is shown in the lower pair of stereoscopic images on page 194.

All these depth phenomena can be perceived in a very short interval, provided that the two fields are presented to the observer in reasonable alignment. The presentation time is so short (a few milliseconds) that there is no time for the eye to move and thus no time for a range-finder mechanism to operate. One must therefore conclude that depth perception occurs at some point in the central nervous system after the images projected onto the left and right retinas have been fed into a common neural pathway. This was actually demonstrated as long ago as 1841 by Heinrich Wilhelm Dove of Germany, who used brief electric sparks to illuminate stereoscopic images only three years after Charles Wheatstone of England had first shown how the young art of photography could be used to produce them. Evidently the convergence movements of the eye serve mainly to bring the images on the left and right retinas into approximate register. This does not mean, however, that convergence motions do not influence the perception of depth when the presentation time is of long duration.

The processing in the nervous system that gives rise to depth perception is now more of a mystery than ever. The German physiologist Ewald Hering believed that this processing involves the crossing or uncrossing of images that are initially perceived as double because they lie either in front of or behind the eyes' point of convergence. The extent to which this cue is utilized could not previously be determined because double images were inherent in stereoscopic presentation. The random-dot stereoscopic images, on the other hand, do not contain recognizable images prior to their actual perception in depth; thus it is impossible to perceive double images either before or after fusion.

It could still be argued that although random-dot stereoscopic pairs do not contain recognizable shapes, some similar patterns can be perceived in the two fields and these might serve as the basis for fusion. This possibility can be tested in several ways. In the top stereoscopic pair on page 191 the field at the left has been blurred by being printed out of focus. Even when the patterns are almost obliterated in this way, stereopsis is easily obtained. What is more surprising is that the perceived image resembles the sharp one. The blurred image serves only to convey the required disparity information and is then suppressed.

The bottom stereoscopic pair on page 191 carries the disruption of patterns still further. This is achieved by breaking the diagonal connectivity in the field at the left. Along one diagonal whenever three adjacent dots were black, the middle dot was changed to white, and along the other diagonal whenever three adjacent dots were white, the middle one was changed to black. In the field at the right diagonally adjacent groups of three black or white dots were left unchanged. This procedure changes 20 percent of the picture elements in the field at the left and so removes them from the fusion process. The fact that the two fields look so different when viewed monocularly and yet can be perceived in depth when viewed stereoscopically provides additional evidence that no monocular pattern recognition is necessary and that the ultimate three-dimensional pattern emerges only after fusion has taken place.

Although the random-dot stereoscopic images lack monocular depth cues, which normally augment depth perception, they are actually easier to perceive in depth than stereoscopic images of real objects. The explanation is that each black or white dot in a random pattern contributes depth information, whereas in actual objects there are large homogeneous areas that carry no depth information. Thus random-dot stereoscope fields that differ in size by 10 percent or more can easily be perceived in depth [*see middle illustration on page 191*].

It is probably obvious that these find-

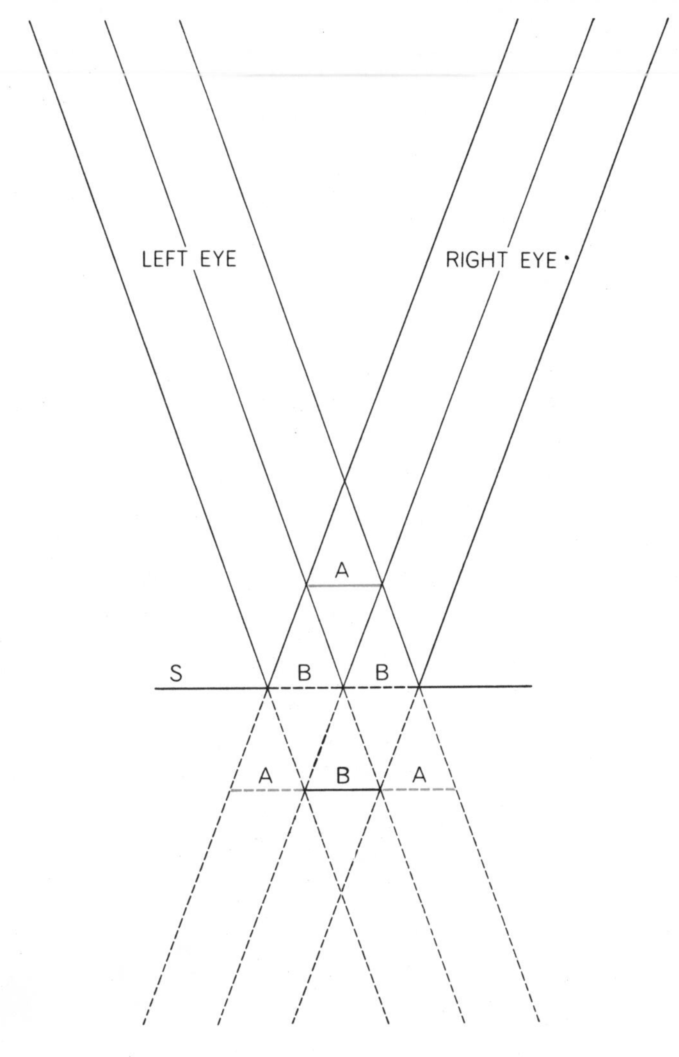

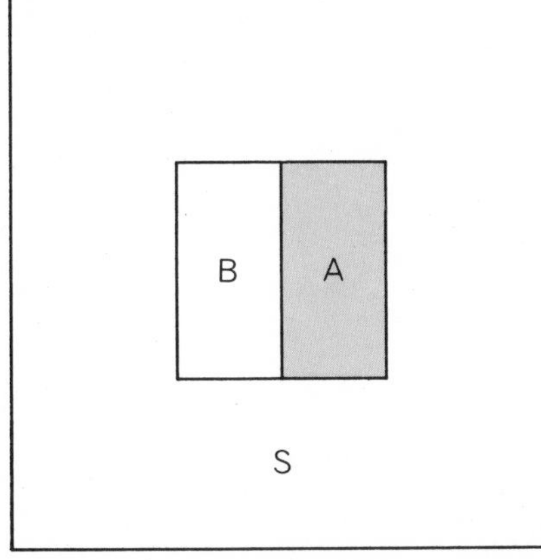

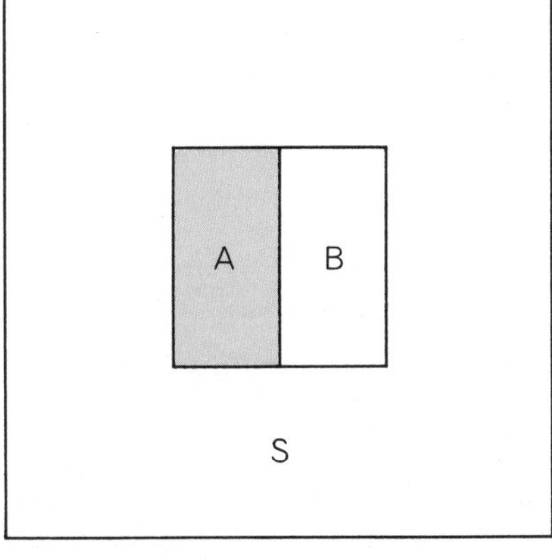

AMBIGUOUS DEPTH EFFECT can be obtained by transposing the *A* and *B* fields in the random-dot patterns. When viewed stereoscopically (*top diagram*), area *A* may seem to be raised above the surround or area *B* may seem to lie below it. In either case the nonfused area seems to be a continuation of the field that looks farthest away.

ings have important implications for *Gestalt* psychology. According to this school stereoptic perception is not a result of disparity in the images projected on the two retinas; rather each eye works up its complex of stimuli into a *Gestalt* and it is the difference between the two *Gestalten* that gives rise to the impression of depth. The fact that stereopsis can be obtained in random-dot images without any monocular cues decisively settles this question, since no *Gestalten* can be worked up.

It might still be argued that *Gestalt* factors may operate after the binocular fusion of the two fields. In this connection it is interesting to look closely at the vertical boundaries of the raised panel formed by the top stereoscopic pair on page 190. The boundaries are fuzzy. The reason is that the black-and-white picture elements along the boundary have an equal probability of being perceived as belonging either to the raised panel or to the surround. Because a square has a "good *Gestalt*" one might expect to perceive these points as forming a straight line. That they do not suggests that perception is governed by simple considerations of probability.

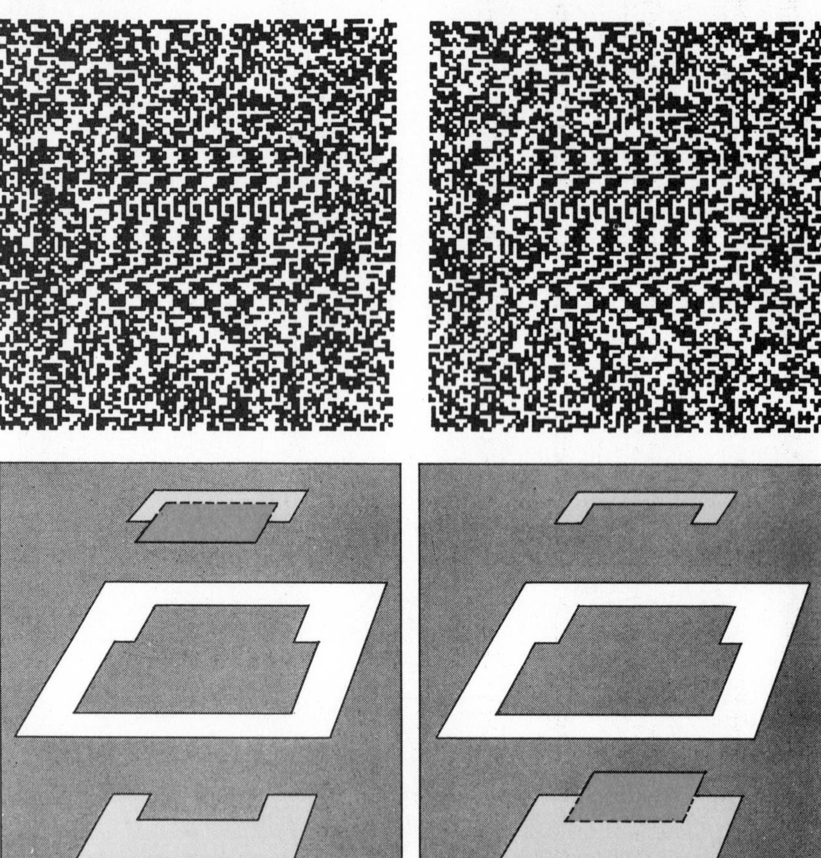

AREA OF AMBIGUOUS DEPTH appears in the middle of this periodically striped stereoscopic pattern. Sometimes it will seem to be a continuation of an elevated panel (*lower left*); at other times it will seem to be part of a depressed panel (*lower right*).

In presenting random-dot stereoscopic pairs for very brief intervals I have found evidence for a restricted but unmistakable kind of subliminal perception. This term refers, of course, to the idea that an individual can be influenced by a stimulus he does not consciously perceive. Efforts to demonstrate this phenomenon by other techniques have been inconclusive and controversial.

The finding was made while I was trying to measure the minimum time needed to perceive stereopsis in random-dot images. The time cannot be measured simply by presenting the images for briefer and briefer periods, for the reason that an afterimage remains on the retina for an indeterminate time. I found that it was possible to "erase" these afterimages by a new technique in which a second stereoscopic pair of random-dot images is flashed onto a screen almost immediately after the first pair.

In these short-interval experiments the first stereoscopic pair flashed onto a screen has a panel that is unmistakably either in front of the surround or behind it. This pair is followed quickly by another in which the location of the panel is ambiguous; under more leisurely viewing conditions it will seem to lie either in front of or behind the surround. Not only were the subjects unaware that the second pair was ambiguous but if the interval between the two presentations was made short enough they were also unaware that they were seeing anything but the second pair. The second pair erased all conscious knowledge of the first. The real presentation time of the first pair could therefore be established because it was governed by the time allowed to elapse before presentation of the second pair.

The main result was that the first stereoscopic pair, although not consciously perceived, can influence the way in which the second pair—the ambiguous pair—is perceived. When the presentation time of the first pair was long enough, the ambiguous panel in the second pair consistently seemed to be at the same depth as the panel in the first pair. A presentation time adequate to produce this result was about 40 milliseconds; it can be regarded as the "minimum perception time" for stereopsis. When the first pair is presented for a shorter time, or when the second pair is delayed by more than a certain interval, which I have called the "attention time," the second pair is removed from the subliminal influence of the first and is perceived ambiguously. These experiments suggest that the first pair serves as a "depth marker" and determines which of the two possible depth organizations in the second pair should be favored. All this processing must take place in the central nervous system because the times are too short for any eye motion to be initiated.

The various studies described in this article indicate that visual texture discrimination and binocular depth perception operate under simpler conditions than has been thought, since they do not require the recognition of form. This finding makes it attractive to try to design a machine that will automatically produce contour maps according to information contained in aerial stereoscopic photographs. As long as it seemed that such a task could only be done by a machine that could recognize complex and virtually unpredictable shapes, the job seemed all but hopeless. On the basis of the new findings I have helped to devise a computer program (called Automap-1) that can be used to compile a three-dimensional contour map from high-resolution stereoscopic images [*see illustration on page 195*]. This computer program not only should be useful for reducing the tedium of pro-

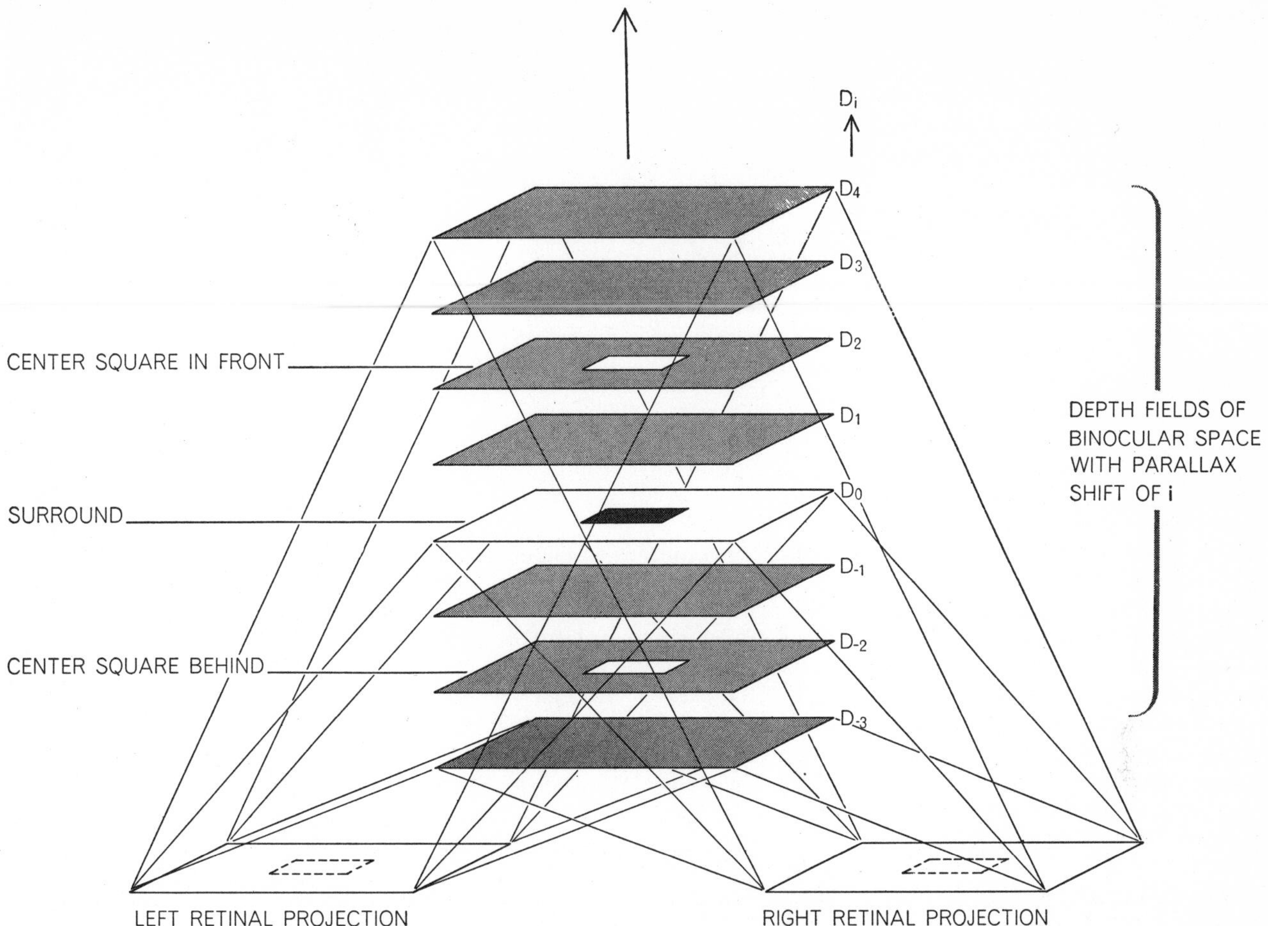

AUTOMAP-1 is a computer program that compiles a three-dimensional contour map from two-dimensional stereoscopic images. The program compares left and right fields point by point and subtracts the brightness of each point from its counterpart. Where the two fields match, the difference is zero, shown above as a white area. Thus the surround (D_0) is white except where there is a shifted center panel. The program repeats the point-by-point comparison after shifting one field horizontally (both left and right) by one unit, two units and so on. This provides an ordered set of depth planes (D_i). When a shift such as D_2 or D_{-2} brings a shifted panel into alignment, the points in the panel cancel and show up as zero (white). Form recognition is not needed.

ducing such maps but since it is based on psychologically observed phenomena it is also a crude model of part of the visual system.

This article has described methods for studying visual texture discrimination and depth perception in their purest form. The methods have shown that connectivity detection is basic to both visual tasks and that it is a more primitive process than form recognition. It remains to be seen if on the psychological level a simpler "explanation" can be given. I hope that the next findings in this area will come from neurophysiologists.

25

THE ANALYSIS OF BRAIN WAVES

MARY A. B. BRAZIER • January 1962

The electrical activity that can be recorded from the surface of the human head is probably the most baffling cryptogram to be found in nature. It is therefore not surprising that electrophysiologists have turned to electronic computers for help. First observed in animals by the English physiologist Richard Caton in 1875, the surface waves reflect the rich and constantly changing electrical activity of the brain. The first recordings from the human brain were made in 1924 by Hans Berger, a German psychiatrist who, because of his oddly secretive nature, withheld publication of his "electroencephalograms" until 1929. The reception was at first skeptical, but the electroencephalogram, or EEG, soon demonstrated its value in the diagnosis of epilepsy and other brain damage. Now, within the past 20 years, physiologists have made a start at decoding the EEG and have begun to show how it is related to the functioning of the nervous system.

For analyzing the electrical activity of the brain the electronic computer has emerged as an instrument of great power and versatility. One of the principal uses of the computer is to extract meaningful signals from the background electrical noise generated by the brain, which normally makes any single recording undecipherable. Although analyses of this sort are usually performed with magnetic-tape records of the brain's activity, the computer becomes even more useful when it is designed to make its analyses in "real" time, while the subject is still connected to the recording apparatus and while the investigator is still able to manipulate the experimental variables. Employed in this way, the computer becomes a subtle new tool for the studies of neurophysiology.

In man the fluctuating potential difference between leads on the unshaved scalp is commonly between 50 and 100 millionths of a volt, or about a tenth the magnitude of electrocardiographic potentials. These waves are most prominent at the back of the head over the visual-association areas of the brain; waves recorded there are called alpha waves. The alpha rhythm, which has a frequency of between eight and 13 per second in adult subjects, is most conspicuous when the eyes are closed. The alpha waves disappear momentarily when the eyes are opened.

Because of the regularity of the alpha rhythm, its frequency characteristics received most of the attention in the early days of electroencephalography. Physi-

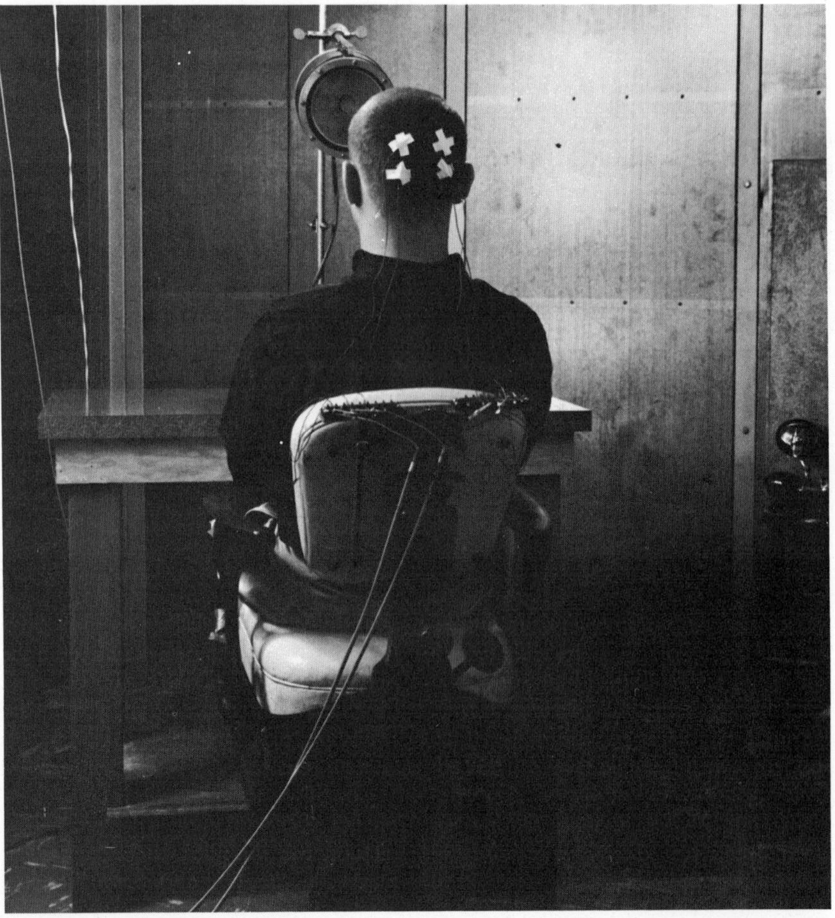

ELECTRODES ON SCALP detect brain waves. This subject, in an isolated room, is viewing brief flashes of light at regular intervals. A special computer simultaneously analyzes the brain waves from the visual region in back of head, producing the record seen in illustration on page 204. The photograph was made at the Massachusetts Institute of Technology.

ologists reasoned that if these waves were analyzed mathematically, using the technique known as Fourier analysis, components might be uncovered that were hidden to the unaided eye. The principle behind Fourier analysis is that any periodic wave form, however complex, can be resolved into elementary sine-wave components. Unfortunately the brain emits so many irregular and nonperiodic potential changes that the usefulness of this well-known principle is open to challenge.

During World War II W. Grey Walter of the Burden Neurological Institute in England spearheaded the development of the first practical instrument for making an automatic frequency analysis of consecutive short segments—each arbitrarily limited to 10 seconds—of an EEG trace. The Walter analyzer reports the mean relative amplitude at each frequency over the whole period being integrated but cannot indicate the time sequence in which the frequencies occur. A short wave train of high amplitude has the same effect on the integrating device as a long train of low amplitude. Also lost is all information about phase relations between trains of waves.

This type of analysis proved especially valuable when coupled with the finding that the frequency characteristics of the human EEG can often be controlled by having the subject look at a flashing light; the technique, called photic driving, was discovered in the early 1940's. Subsequently it was found that flashes of specific frequency will induce epileptic seizures in some epileptic patients. This is an example of a physiological finding reaching over into medicine to become a clinical diagnostic test. The Walter analyzer, which can be regarded as an early form of computer, still provides the simplest and most practical method for obtaining the average frequency spectrum of an EEG trace.

The rapid development of high-speed general-purpose and special-purpose computers in the past decade has opened up many new ways of analyzing the brain's electrical activity. At the same time techniques have been perfected for recording from electrodes implanted within the unanesthetized brain and left in place for weeks or months. Although used primarily with animals, the technique has been extended to man for diagnostic and therapeutic purposes.

It is therefore now possible to study the relation of the brain's electrical activity to behavioral performance and, in the case of man, to subjective experience. After a long period of concentrating on the rhythm observable when the subject was at rest with the eyes closed, electroencephalographers began to divert their attention from "the engine when idling" to the "engine at work," thereby examining how the brain responds to various stimuli.

Many types of stimulation can be used —sounds, odors, flashes of light, touch and so on—and their effect can be traced in brain recordings made both at the surface and deep within the brain. When such studies were first attempted in unanesthetized animals and man, it was soon discovered that the specific responses were largely masked, in the unanalyzed trace, by the ongoing EEG activity of the normal brain, activity that

AVERAGE RESPONSE COMPUTER (ARC) was designed by W. A. Clark, Jr., of the Lincoln Laboratory of M.I.T. It samples the brain waves for a prescribed interval after each stimulus, adding and averaging the samples. Oscilloscope face on computer *(left)* displays trace of average as the experiment proceeds. Reels of magnetic tape *(center, rear)* permanently record all the raw data. In the foreground, beside the laboratory technician, is an "X-Y plotter," which makes pen tracings of the averaged data.

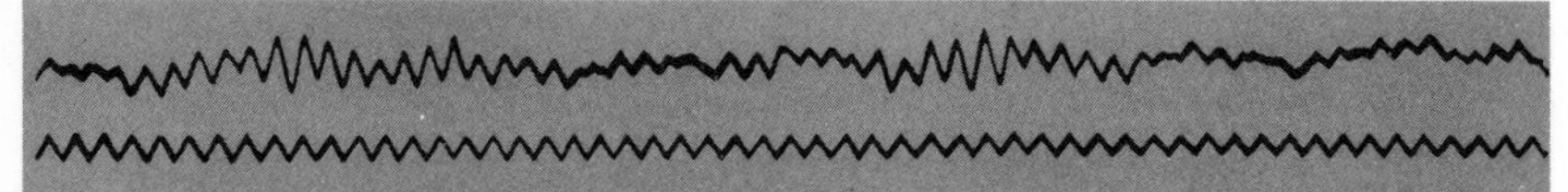

FIRST PUBLISHED ELECTROENCEPHALOGRAM (EEG) of man appeared in 1929. The recording was made by the German psychiatrist Hans Berger from the scalp of his young son. Upper channel is the EEG, lower one an artificial sine wave used as a marker.

had been conveniently depressed by the anesthetic agents in the earlier studies. Since the electrodes used must be small enough to discriminate between neuronal structures less than a millimeter apart, appropriate computer techniques are essential for detecting the faint signals that are all but lost in the roar of biological noise that is the normal milieu of the active brain.

The principal means for increasing the signal-to-noise ratio is simply to have the computer add up a large number of responses—anywhere from a few dozen to a few hundred—and calculate an average response. One can then regard this average response, or certain features of it, as the characteristic "signal" elicited by a given stimulus. In applying this technique the neurophysiologist must necessarily make certain assumptions about the character of the biological phenomena he regards as signal and that which he chooses to call noise.

In the usual averaging procedure the brain's potential changes, as picked up by several electrodes, are recorded on multichannel magnetic tape, in which one channel carries a pulse coincident with delivery of the stimulus. Since the stimulus may be presented at irregular intervals, a pulse is needed as a time marker from which the responses are "lined up" for averaging. In the averaging process only those potential changes that occur with a constant time relation to the pulse are preserved and emphasized. Those unrelated in time cancel out in the averaging process, even though in any single record they may be of higher amplitude. In this way responses never before detectable at the surface of the human skull not only can be found but also can be correlated with the subject's report of his sensations.

For example, the lightest of taps on the back of the hand is found to evoke a clear-cut response in one special area on the opposite side of the head [*see illustrations on page 202*]. Other computer analyses show that a click in the ear gives a decipherable response in another location on the scalp. A flash of light not only evokes an immediate sharp response in the visual area at the back of the head but also gives rise to a long-lasting train of waves, all time-locked to the flash [*see illustration on page 204*]. It has been shown, moreover, that clinical patients who report a disturbance in their subjective sensation of touch, hearing or sight produce EEG traces that reveal distortions when analyzed by computer.

The long-lasting train of waves evoked by a flash of light raises a number of questions. Is this the electrical sign of further processing of the initial message received by the eye? Is it the sign that the experience is being passed into storage, initiating in its passage the cellular changes that underlie memory? There is already evidence that under conditions that retain the initial sharp response but obliterate the subsequent wave train all memory of the experience is expunged. Two such conditions, which support this suggestion in human experiments, are anesthesia and hypnotically induced blindness.

Valuable though computers can be for averaging taped EEG records, they still leave the investigator feeling somewhat frustrated. Hours, and sometimes days, may elapse between the experiment and the completed analysis of the recordings. When he sees the results, the investigator often wishes he could have changed the experimental conditions slightly, perhaps to accentuate a trend of some sort that seemed to be developing, but it is too late. The experimental material of the biologist, and particularly of the electrophysiologist studying the brain, is living, changing material from which he must seize the opportunity to extract all possible information before the passage of time introduces new variables. The computers familiar to business and industry have not been designed with this problem in mind.

To meet the needs of the neurophysiologist a few computers have now been built that process brain recordings virtually as fast as data is fed in from the electrodes. The investigator can observe the results of his manipulations on the face of a cathode-ray tube or other display device and can modify his experiment at will. One of the first machines built to operate in this way is the Average Response Computer (ARC), designed by W. A. Clark, Jr., of the Lincoln Laboratory of the Massachusetts Institute of Technology [*see illustration on preceding page*]. ARC is a simple-to-operate, special-purpose digital computer that requires no programmer as a middleman between the biologist and the machine.

When searching for an evoked response, Clark's computer samples the EEG at a prescribed interval after the stimulus, converts it into a seven-digit binary number proportional to the amplitude and sends the number into one of the many memory registers. This particular register receives and adds all further numbers obtained at the same interval after each stimulus. ARC is equipped to sample the EEG at 254 different time intervals and to store thousands of samples at each interval. Only rarely, however, is the full capacity of the register required. The cumulative sums in each register are displayed on an oscilloscope after each stimulus [*see illustration on page 200*]. The investigator watches the cumulative display and stops the stimulation when he sees that he has enough signal-to-noise discrimination to satisfy the needs of the experiment. He can then photograph the face of the oscilloscope or have the cumulative wave form printed out graphically by a plotter.

What might one see if one were to watch the build-up of summed re-

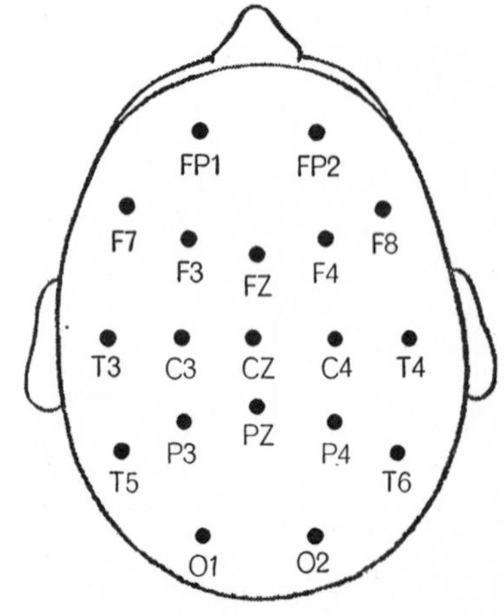

TYPICAL MODERN EEG shows that different regions of cortex give rhythms that differ widely. Berger thought the whole brain

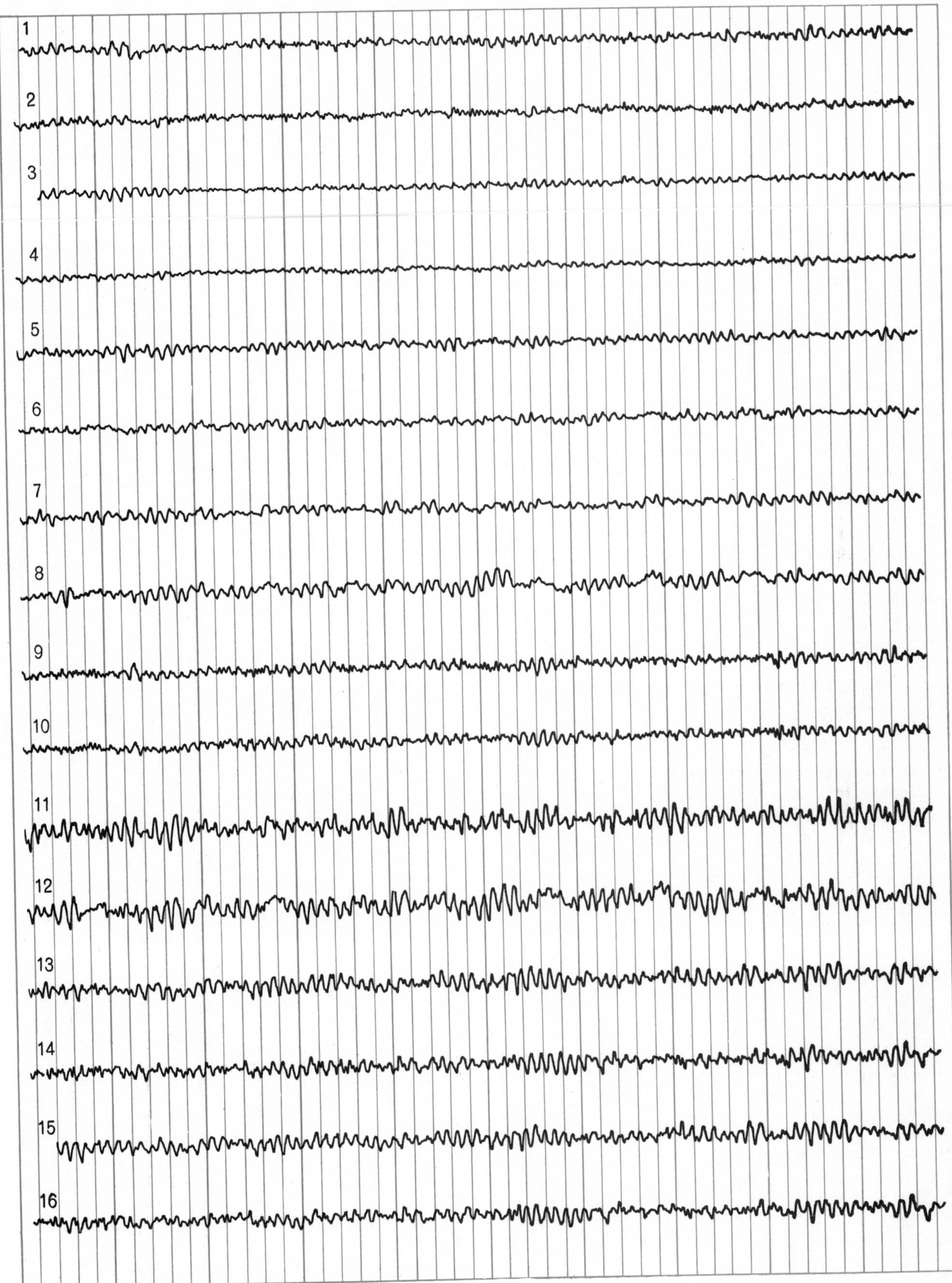

emitted only one rhythm. Today as many as 16, 24 and even 32 channels can be used. The great complexity obviously makes computer analysis desirable. Each EEG trace records changes in electric potential between two electrodes. Thus line 1 came from electrodes FP1 and F7 on head as diagramed at left, while line 10 came from FP2 and C4. This data has not been processed by a computer.

sponses? If the man or animal being studied were anesthetized, the response would be markedly stereotyped; the averaged sum of 100 responses would look very much like the average of 50 responses. This is not so if the subject is unanesthetized. Responses to a series of clicks or flashes of light may show great variation, both in wave shape and in amplitude, and may require many samples before the characteristic signal emerges clearly from the background noise.

Operating in another of its modes, ARC can give an amplitude histogram, or profile, at any chosen interval after the stimulus. Such histograms indicate the degree of fluctuation of the response and its complexity. They supply the investigator with important clues to the behavioral state of the subject, to his level of wakefulness, to the degree of attention he is paying to the stimulus and to the feelings the stimulus arouses.

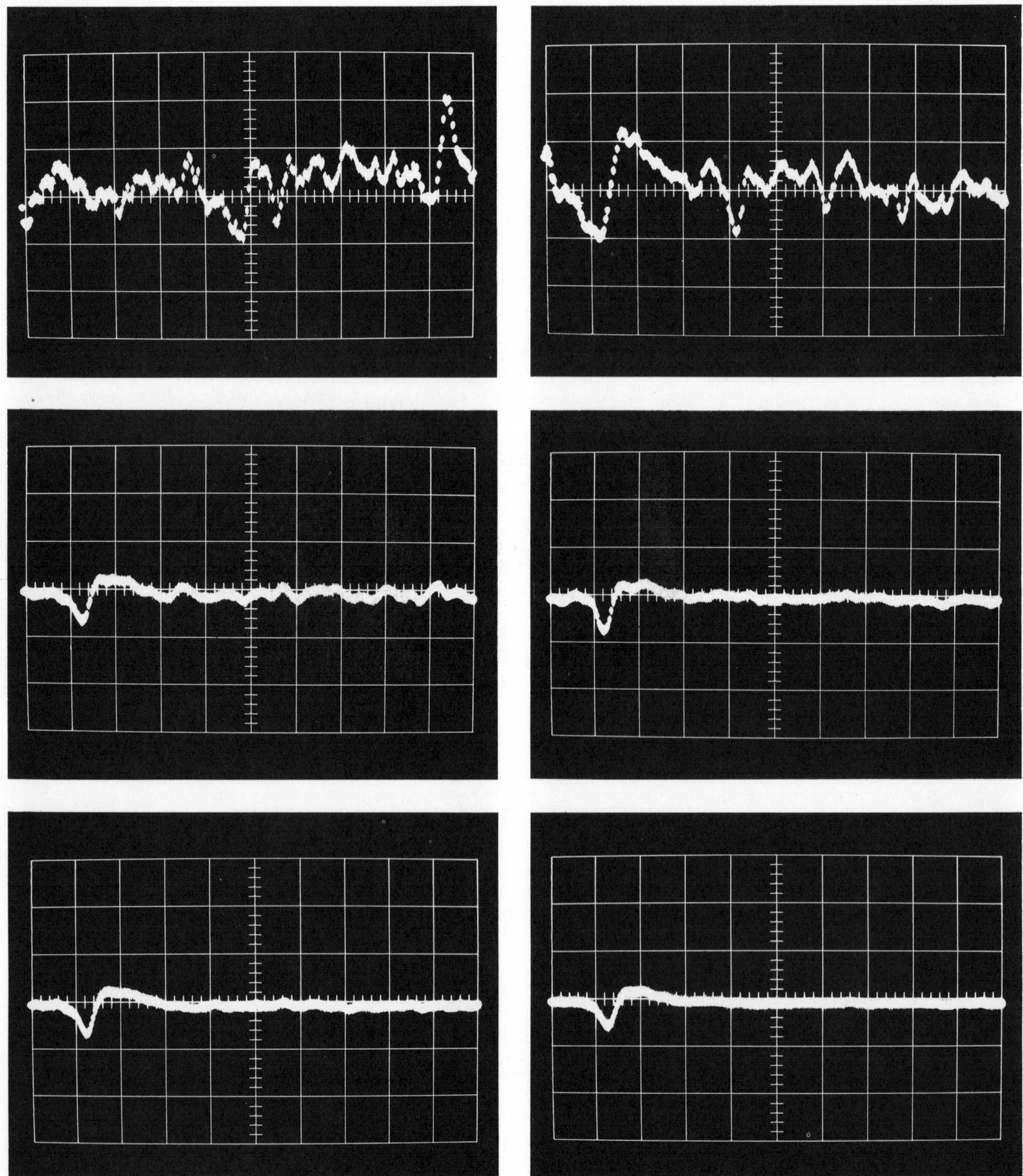

OSCILLOSCOPE TRACES of responses as averaged by computer appear while experiment is in progress, enabling experimenter to observe in "real time." As a result he can change conditions and stop when he has enough data. The traces (*left to right, top to bottom*) are averages of 1, 2, 32, 64, 128 and 512 responses. These traces appeared during an experiment by Nelson Kiang of the Eaton-Peabody Laboratory of the Massachusetts Eye and Ear Infirmary in Boston. The subject was responding to a long series of clicks.

When ARC is operated in the histogram mode, the memory registers are set to count the number of times the amplitude, or voltage, of the EEG falls within a certain preset range. Each register is set for a different range and the results are finally written out as a histogram for the chosen interval [*see top illustration on this page*]. By analyzing other intervals similarly one can put together a composite survey.

The study of such records may reveal little dispersion of amplitude at some particular interval after the stimulus and a much greater dispersion at some other interval. This may be a clue that the neuronal message in the first case has traveled over a nerve pathway containing few synapses, or relays, and thus has been subject to little dispersion, whereas in the second case the message has reached the recording site after traveling through multiple paths that finally converge. The complex wave train evoked by a single flash of light is susceptible to this interpretation. The initial deflection is caused by impulses that have traveled through a few synapses only and by means of the large, rapidly conducting fibers of the specific visual system. The subsequent shallower waves—so clearly revealed by the computer—reach the cortex through the more slowly conducting, indirect, nonspecific system with its many relay stations. The histogram of the earlier event, being more stereotyped, shows less dispersion around the median than does the histogram of the later events. Still more elaborate processing of histograms can show whether the amplitudes follow a normal, bell-shaped distribution pattern or are skewed in some manner.

If a physicist were to analyze the results of a series of complex experiments in his field, he would normally expect to find the results to be invariant. The biologist, working with an unanesthetized animal or man, can search in vain for an invariant response. It is precisely this subtlety of variation that electrophysiologists have recently identified as the concomitant of behavioral change. One such change is known as habituation. Early workers in electrophysiology could perceive, in their unanalyzed records, subtle changes in the shape of an EEG trace when the subject had been repeatedly exposed to the same stimulus. Computer analyses have now revealed clearly that under such conditions significant changes take place not only in the EEG as recorded outside the skull but even more markedly in recordings made deep within the brain.

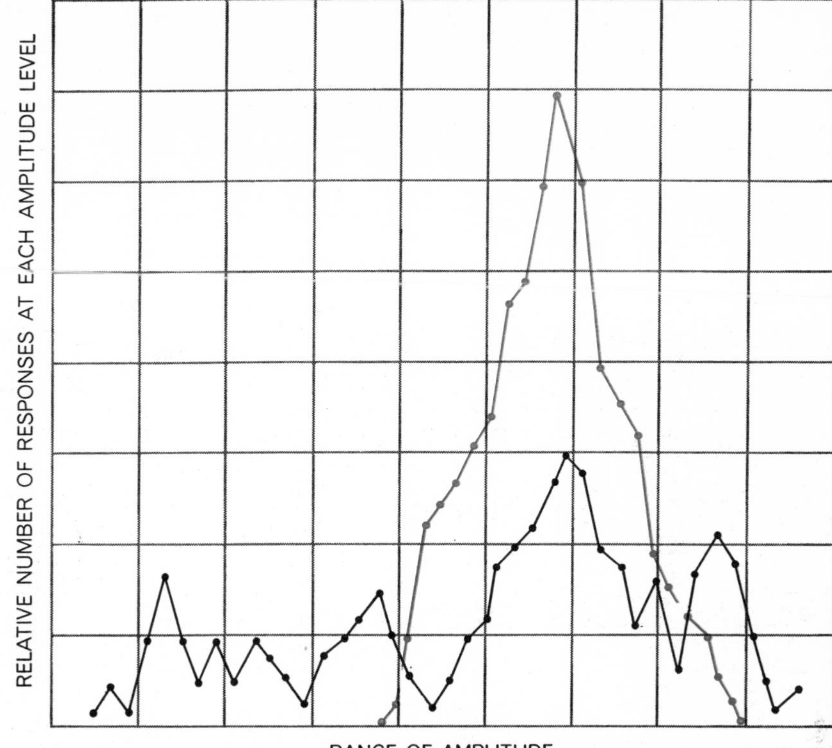

STEREOTYPED RESPONSE of brain of anesthetized animal to flash of light (*colored curve*) shows plainly when computer is programed to give information on amplitude variation. Unanesthetized animal gives widely fluctuating response (*black curve*). In each case the computer analyzed point in time at which response reached its maximum amplitude.

For example, the Average Response Computer has been used to analyze the electrical activity recorded from a particular relay station in a nucleus located deep in the mid-line region of an animal's brain. The nucleus, in turn, lies within the portion of the brain called the thalamus. Until a dozen years ago little except its anatomy was known about this mid-line region of the thalamus and its inflow from the portion of the brain stem called the reticular formation. The thalamic region and the reticular formation together constitute the nonspecific sensory system mentioned earlier.

In 1949 H. W. Magoun (now at the

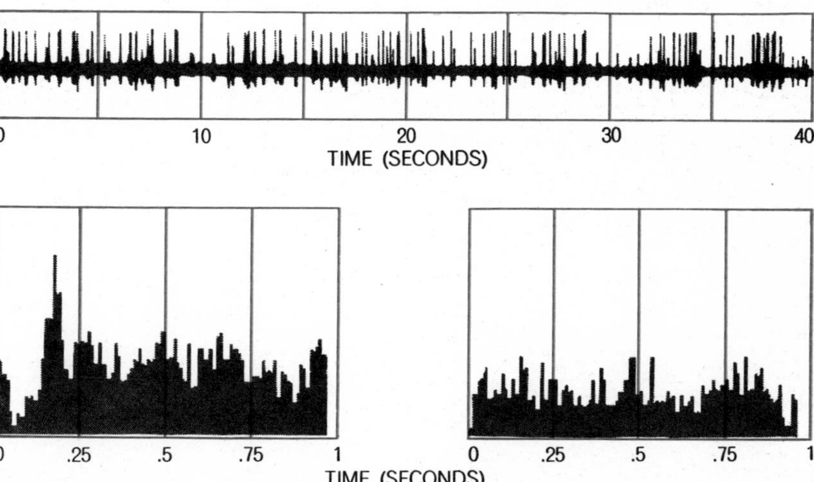

HISTOGRAMS showing distribution of cell discharges relative to stimulus were made by George L. Gerstein at M.I.T. Upper line shows a short section of raw data consisting of cell discharges in the auditory part of a cat's brain in response to one-per-second clicks. The histogram at left shows number of cell discharges at fractional-second intervals after clicks. The histogram at right shows same analysis of cell discharges when no click occurred.

University of California in Los Angeles) and G. Moruzzi (now at the University of Pisa) jointly discovered that the reticular system is crucially concerned with the organism's state of alertness and with the behavioral nuances that lie in the continuum between vigilant attention and the oblivion of sleep. Later work has revealed further nuances that can be discerned in the electrical record only with the fine-grained analyses that a computer can provide.

Computer analyses of records from one of the mid-line nuclei of this nonspecific sensory system in an unanesthetized animal have detected many unsuspected details. For example, when a light, flashing at a constant rate, is directed into the animal's eye, the ARC oscilloscope reveals that the averaged response is not at all simple but contains

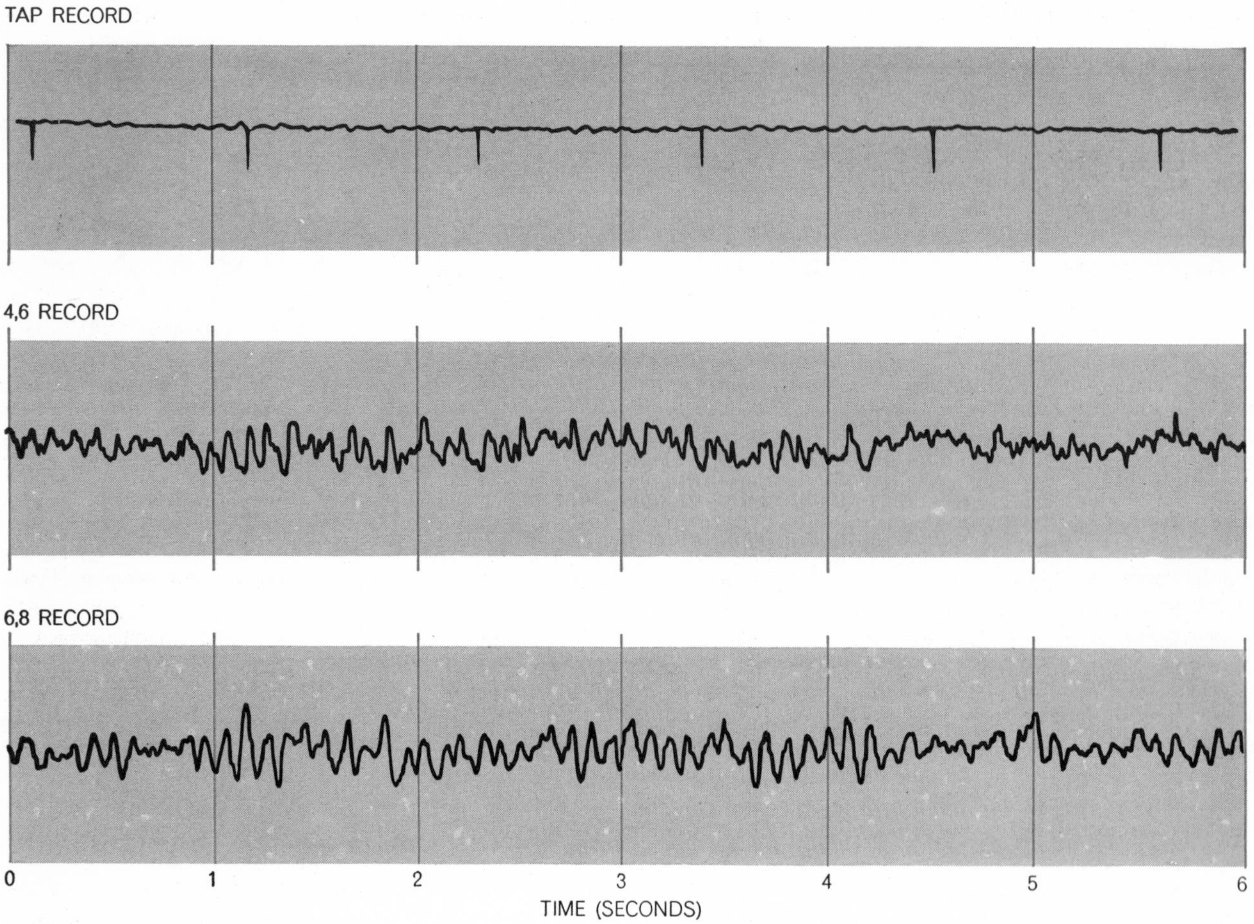

4,6 RECORD

6,8 RECORD

0 1 2 3 4 5 6

TIME (SECONDS)

REGULAR TAPS ON LEFT HAND, indicated by top trace, do not show up in standard EEG (*next two traces*). Ongoing activity of brain drowns signal even though electrode 4 (*see diagram of head on opposite page*) is over area that receives nerve inflow from hand.

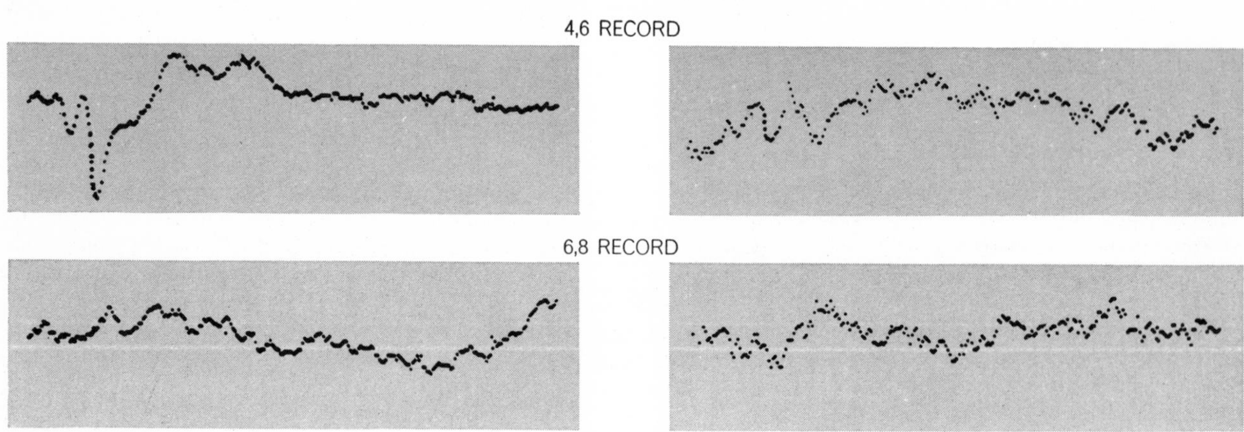

AVERAGED RESPONSE after 90 taps, however, tells a different story. Upper trace at left, from electrodes 4 and 6, shows that the brain definitely reacts to the taps. The computer also detects a faint response when the right hand, which is on the same side of the body as the electrodes, is tapped. (Nerves on the left side of the body are connected with the right side of the brain and vice versa.)

three distinct components and that, as time passes, one of these components gradually fades out. If the computer's mode of operation is then changed so as to produce amplitude histograms, the third component is found to have a greater dispersion than the other two and a skewed distribution.

A hypothesis suggests itself. One of the relatively constant components may pass on to the visual cortex, thereby signifying to the animal that the stimulus is visual and not, say, olfactory or auditory. Perhaps the second component indicates that the stimulus is a recurrent one. The third and waning component may be signaling "unexpectedness" and, by dropping out, may carry the message that the stimulus is simply repeating over and over without change. It may be saying, in effect, that the stimulus is devoid of novelty (or information) and can be safely ignored.

The experimenter, still watching the computer's oscilloscope, can then proceed to test this hypothesis by introducing novelty into the stimulus. For example, he can change the strength of the flash, its wavelength or its repetition rate, and watch for the reappearance of the third component. In this way the three-way interlocution between investigator, subject and machine proceeds.

The questions the investigator asks are not exhausted by those outlined above. He may want to know what the individual cells of the brain are doing. It has been known for many years that the frequency of action "spikes" in a nerve fiber is related to the intensity of the stimulus. As a rule the more intense the stimulus, the higher the firing rate. But how wasteful of "channel capacity" (to use the language of information theory) it would be if the only information conveyed by the action spikes were limited to stimulus intensity.

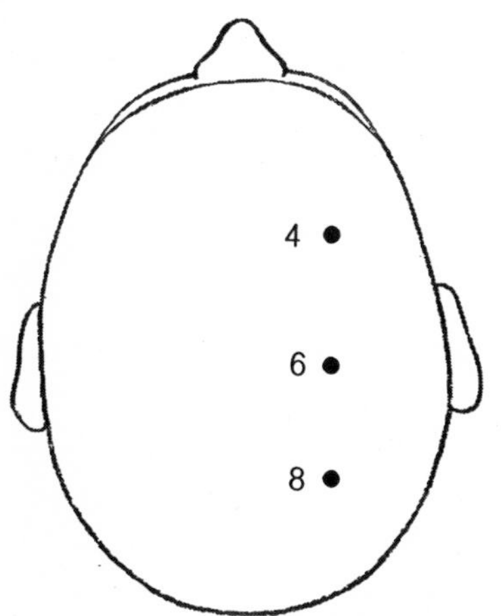

The averaged record from electrodes 6 and 8, which are not over the "hand area" of the brain, shows no response to the taps.

This has led investigators to consider the fluctuations in the groupings of these unit discharges. The unanalyzed record is bewildering, because different kinds of cell give different patterns of response to a given stimulus. Some that were busily active stop firing when the stimulus is given; others wake from idleness and burst into activity; still others signal their response by a change in the pattern of discharge.

Computers are invaluable for this type of analysis. The Average Response Computer, as one example, has a special mode of operation that helps to clarify this patterning of activity in individual brain cells. It does this by giving a histogram of the time intervals between successive cell discharges. Each of its memory registers is allotted a different interspike interval. Whenever a cell fires, the interval since the last firing is established and a digit is added to the appropriate register. On command, the digits accumulated in the different registers are written out as a histogram [*see bottom illustration on page 201*]. Analyses of this kind, pioneered by George L. Gerstein with the TX-O computer at the Massachusetts Institute of Technology, have revealed a differentiation of response mechanisms among cortical cells that indicates a far greater degree of discriminatory capability than the old frequency-intensity rule would suggest.

Among other computer techniques under development are those for identification of temporal patterns in the EEG. These techniques should relieve the electroencephalographer of the tedium of searching many yards of records for meaningful changes. For example, Belmont Farley of the Lincoln Laboratory of M.I.T. has worked out programs for analyzing the trains of alpha rhythm that come and go in the EEG of man and provide clues to his level of consciousness and to the normality of his brain.

Farley's program specifies the range of amplitude, frequency and duration of the pattern known as an alpha burst. The program allows the investigator to make a statistical examination of the EEG of the same individual, as recorded under different experimental circumstances. The investigator may be interested in the effect of drugs or the changes brought about by conditioning of behavior. The degree of variation in the EEG can be accurately and objectively assessed, removing the hazards of subjective judgment. It is obvious that such objective methods of appraisal can be of great value in the clinical use of the EEG.

The rhythmicity of the EEG, as exemplified in the alpha rhythm, continues to be a mystery. It was first thought that brain waves were merely the envelopes of the spike discharges of the underlying neurons. But this view had to be abandoned when microelectrodes, reporting from inside the brain, showed the hypothesis untenable. It is now thought that the EEG waves reflect the waxing and waning of excitability in what are called the dendritic layers of the cortex. (Dendrites are hairlike processes that extend from the body of a nerve cell.) Quite unlike the explosive discharge of the nerve cell itself, the finely graded changes in dendritic activity seem to modulate cortical excitability.

In the common laboratory animals, with their comparatively small association cortexes, the simple, almost sinusoidal oscillation of the alpha rhythm is hard to find, if it exists at all. It is therefore tempting to relate rhythmic waves to the large volume of association cortex possessed by man. These rhythmic waves usually signify that the brain is not under bombardment by stimuli, and their stability may reflect the homeostatic, or self-stabilizing, processes of the association cortex when undisturbed by the processing of transmitted messages.

In the course of evolution homeostatic processes throughout the body, largely under the control of the brain stem, have provided the higher animals with a remarkably constant internal environment. The constancy of this *milieu intérieur*, as the French physiologist Claude Bernard pointed out, is "la condition de la vie libre." Conceivably it is the stabilizing effect of the brain stem that frees the cortex of man for its highest achievements.

Whatever the case, it has been discovered by the statistical method of autocorrelation analysis that EEG recordings from man often show a long-persisting phase constancy that has not been found in lower animals. There are also individual differences. In some people phase-locking of oscillations is, for long periods, nearly as predictable as a clock. In others (a minority) there is little, if any, stability of phase. Are the people who lack a stable phase-locked oscillation unable to clear their association cortex of interfering activity? Have they not yet attained the "free life" of Claude Bernard?

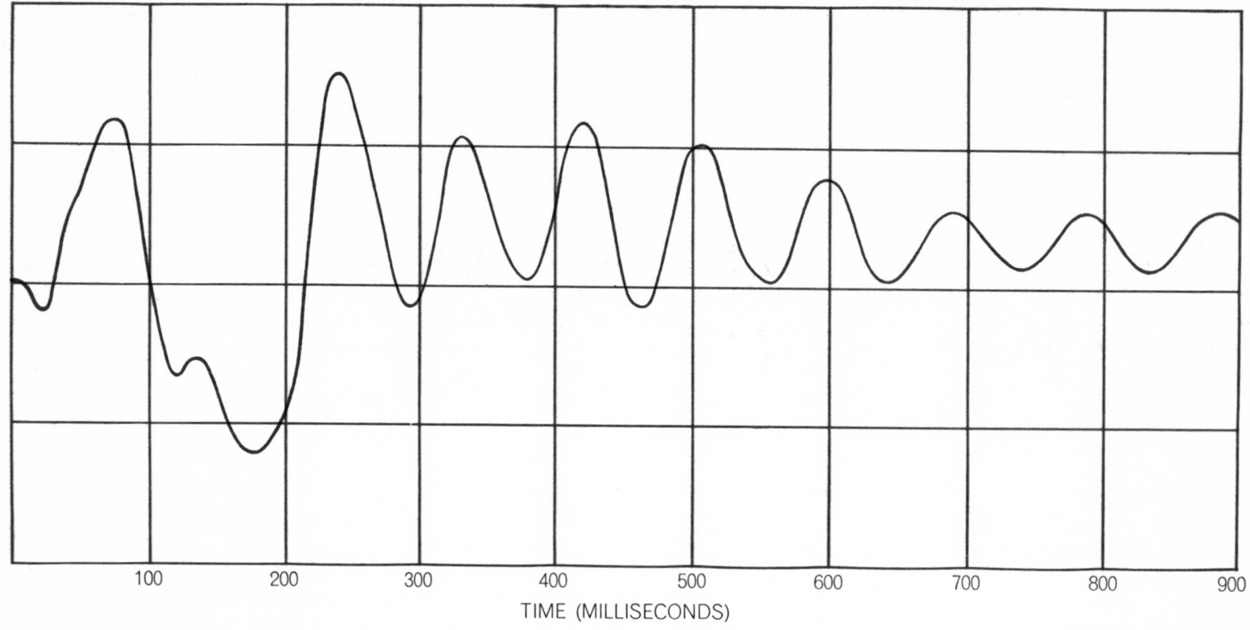

LONG-LASTING TRAIN OF WAVES can be recorded from scalp following flash of light. This, of course, is an averaged record of many responses to many flashes. It emphasizes only the changes in electric potential time-locked to the flash and washes out the "noisy" background activity, which is actually of much higher amplitude. The flashes were all synchronized with beginning of trace.

One of the earliest workers to encourage electroencephalographers to explore this approach was the M.I.T. mathematician Norbert Wiener. His strong influence lies behind much of the computer work in this area, and especially that which has come from the laboratory of Walter A. Rosenblith of M.I.T.'s Research Laboratory for Electronics.

No account of the electroencephalographer's use of computers should omit their recent use in seeking information about the correlations between deep and superficial activity in various parts of the brain. What is the correlation between the waves recorded from the outside of man's skull and activity in the depths? With what confidence can one say that an EEG is "normal" when only scalp recordings can be made?

The first answers to these and many other questions are just emerging as computer analyses of electrical potentials from inside man's head are being correlated with those simultaneously recorded from his scalp. As more and more clinical investigators adopt computer techniques it should be possible to build up for the electroencephalographer, who can record only from the surface of the unopened scalp, a reference library of correlations to use in assessing the probability of events in the hidden depths of the brain.

Nearly all the applications of the computer described here have involved averaging. This is not only because the average is an empirically useful statistic but also because many brain investigators suspect that the brain may work on a probabilistic basis rather than a deterministic one. To analyze the myriad complexities of the brain's function by nonstatistical description is too gigantic a task to be conceived, but exploration in terms of probability theory is both practical and rational. In characterizing nervous activity one would not therefore attempt the precise definition that arithmetic demands but would seek the statistical characteristics of the phenomena that appear to be relevant.

The margin of safety that the brain has for acting appropriately on a probabilistic basis would be much greater than that which would be imposed by a deterministic, arithmetically precise operation. Chaos would result from the least slip-up of the latter, whereas only a major divergence from the mean would disturb a system working on a probability basis. The rigidity of arithmetic is not for the brain, and a search for a deterministic code based on arithmetical precision is surely doomed to disappointment.

One can speculate how a brain might work on statistical principles. Incoming sensory messages would be compared with the statistical distribution of nerve cell characteristics that have developed as functions of the past activities of these cells. Significance of the message would then be evaluated and, according to the odds, its message could be appropriately acted on or ignored. The brain, with its wealth of interconnections, has an enormous capacity for storage, and one can observe the development of appropriate responses by watching the limited capacity of the child grow to the superior capacity of the man.

One might ask why it is the brain investigator, among biological scientists, who has reached out most eagerly to the computer for help. A likely answer is that within man's skull—a not very large, rigidly limited space—a greater number of transactions are taking place simultaneously than in any other known system of its size. The multiplicity of signals that these transactions emit and the truly formidable complexity of codes that they may use have proved beyond the capabilities of analysis by the methods of an earlier age.

The neurophysiologist cannot hope to study a single variable in isolation. The living brain will not still its busy activity so that the investigator can control whatever he wishes; neither will it forget its past. Every stimulus, however "constant" the experimenter may succeed in making it, enters a nervous system that is in an ever changing state. The "stimulus-response" experiment of an earlier day is no longer adequate. Experiment has to enter a phase of greater sophistication that may well prove out of reach without the help of the computer.

26

CHROMOSOME ANALYSIS BY COMPUTER

ROBERT S. LEDLEY AND FRANK H. RUDDLE • April 1966

In recent years a number of human disorders have been found to be related to abnormalities in the chromosomes, the bodies in the living cell that contain the genetic material. Accordingly many medical institutions have undertaken programs of examining in the microscope the chromosomes of samples of tissue taken from numerous patients. Such programs have been limited by the fact that the examination of chromosomes takes time and calls for individuals who have been trained in recognizing chromosomal abnormalities. An obvious way to circumvent this limitation is to devise some kind of machine that can examine the chromosomes automatically, although of course it is less obvious how the machine would work. Such a machine, the central component of which is an electronic computer, has now been assembled and successfully operated.

Human somatic cells (as distinguished from sperm or egg cells) normally contain 46 chromosomes. The chromosomes can most conveniently be examined in the white cells of the blood, which are readily available in a blood sample. (Mature red blood cells contain no chromosomes.) After the white cells have been segregated, however, they must be kept alive in tissue culture and induced to undergo mitosis, or to divide; it is only during mitosis that chromosomes and their abnormalities are clearly visible. Treating the cells with the drug colchicine halts mitosis exactly at metaphase—the stage of somatic-cell division in which each chromosome has divided into two mirror-image halves lying side by side and connected at one point called the centromere. The cell preparation is now treated with a dilute salt solution, which causes the cells to swell and the chromosomes to move apart. Finally the cells are fixed and stained, so that the chromosomes can be observed and photographed through the microscope [*see upper illustration on page 206*].

For purposes of analysis a photomicrograph must be made and enlarged; then the chromosome images are cut out and arranged on a white card in what is called an idiogram. The chromosomes are matched into 22 pairs of homologous, or related, chromosomes, plus the two sex chromosomes. (One member of each pair and one sex chromosome is descended from each parent at the fertilization of the egg.) The pairs are arranged in a standardized order based on size, shape and the ratio of the length of the "arms" on each side of the centromere [*see lower illustration on page 206*]. Only when the cells are thus arranged can abnormalities be readily identified. Even when the abnormality is as gross as the presence of extra chromosomes the idiogram is needed to detect with which normal pair the extra chromosome is associated. Some of the disorders that have been linked with chromosomal abnormalities are Down's syndrome (mongolism), chronic myeloid leukemia, Klinefelter's syndrome (a congenital disorder of males involving infertility) and Turner's syndrome (a congenital disorder of females involving infertility). Also detectable by such analysis is chromosome damage caused by certain substances or by ionizing radiation; accordingly chromosome analysis can play an important role in the screening of foods and drugs and in the evaluation of radiation hazards.

The construction and examination of the idiogram—both of which are time-consuming and somewhat subjective procedures—are eliminated by the automatic regime we shall describe. This means of analysis still requires the collection of blood samples, of course, and the preparation of cells for photomicrography, but the photomicrographs need not be enlarged and the manual analysis need not be made. Instead a series of photomicrographs on a roll of film are "read" directly into the memory unit of a computer by a scanning device called FIDAC (Film Input to Digital Automatic Computer). The computer is programmed to recognize and classify the objects under consideration by doing the same things an investigator would: counting the total number of chromosomes and measuring their lengths, areas and other morphological features. The FIDAC procedure reduces the time required to study the human complement of 46 chromosomes to about 20 seconds; this is some 500 times faster than analysis by visual means.

When a roll of photographic film is ready for examination, it is placed in the film-transport unit of the FIDAC instrument and the "Start" button of the computer is pushed. The computer system—FIDACSYS, a combination of several basic programs for recognizing and analyzing patterns—signals FIDAC to consider the first frame. The instrument scans the photomicrograph and within .3 second transmits a digital image of it into the magnetic-core memory unit of the computer. In this digitalized image the photomicrograph is represented by a rectangular grid of numbers that correspond to the densities of points in a similar grid on the photomicrograph. The numbers on this "gray scale" run from 0 to 6; the number 7 is reserved to denote boundaries during processing. If at this stage the contents of the memory are printed out, they form a rudimentary image of the objects in the photomicrograph [*see illustration on opposite page*].

No significant information is lost in translating the pictorial data into numerical data. The resolution of a good optical microscope at a magnification of 1,000 is .2 micron, that is, .2 micron is the narrowest spacing that can be distinguished between two lines. The FIDAC instrument can sample three picture points within a span of .2 micron on the specimen; in other words, its resolution is comparable to that of the microscope. The instrument has another feature worth mentioning: because it transmits directly ("on line") into the computer's memory, information that would ordinarily be rerecorded onto intermediate magnetic storage tapes can remain instead on the original roll of photomicrographic film for reprocessing whenever it is desired. A 100-foot roll of this 16-millimeter film, containing 4,000 photomicrographs, can fit into a can smaller than four inches in diameter. Recording that much information on magnetic tapes would require more than 50 reels, making a stack more than four feet high.

When the processing of a frame has been completed, the computer program signals FIDAC to advance the film and consider the next frame. If any frame is blank—that is, either 98 percent black or 98 percent white—the program signals FIDAC to move to the next frame. In this way blank frames or leader can be skipped automatically. If the frame is not blank, the computer program establishes a value on the gray scale as a cutoff level between those values that represent points inside the chromosomes and those that represent the background. The task of recognizing patterns in the frames as chromosomes is accomplished by first sweeping a programmable "bug," or detecting pointer, in a horizontal raster pattern to find points with a gray value greater than the cutoff level. The bug then traces around the boundary of each object, and every number in the original digital representation of the boundary that has a value just above the cutoff level is replaced by 7. The silhouette that is formed is now automatically examined to determine if it has the most obvious feature of a chromosome: arms originating at a centromere. If the silhouette does not meet this criterion, it is eliminated from further analysis.

When all the chromosomes in a frame have been silhouetted, the bug will have reached the lower right-hand corner of the frame. At this point the machine evaluates the contents of the frame. The chromosomes are counted and their total length is computed, so that the length of individual chromosomes can be considered as a fraction of the total

PHOTOMICROGRAPH OF CHROMOSOMES from the white blood cell of a man reveals an abnormal total of 47 (one too many). It is impossible to determine which one is in excess until the chromosomes are reassembled into a standard classification called an idiogram.

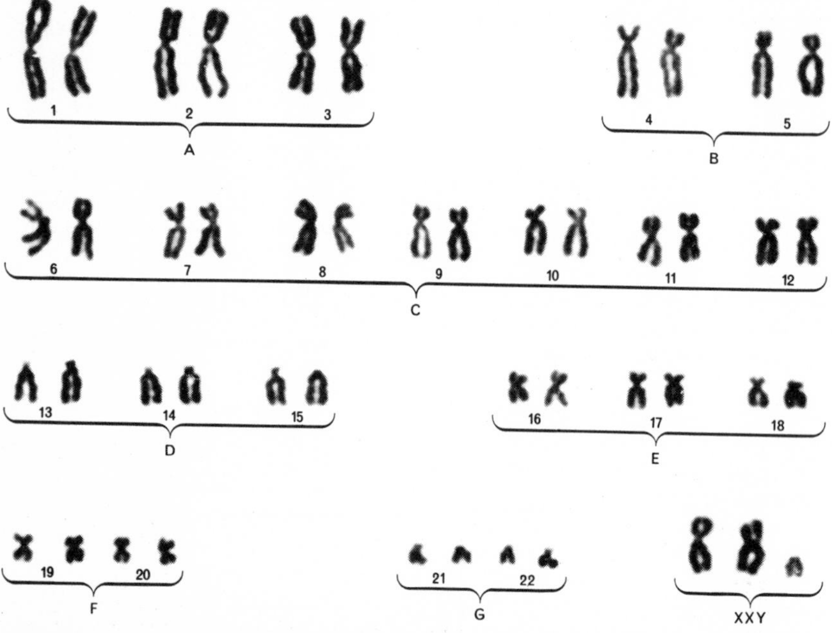

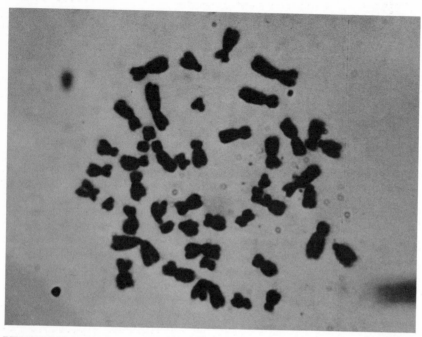

IDIOGRAM of a complement of human chromosomes reveals an abnormality. Chromosomes matched according to size, area and ratio of the lengths of the "arms" on each side of the centromere were put into sequence by Herbert A. Lubs, Jr., of Yale University. The three sex chromosomes at right of bottom row (normal men have one *X* and one *Y* sex chromosome) provide evidence of Klinefelter's syndrome, a disorder of males involving infertility.

IMAGES OF CHROMOSOMES appear as grid of numerals in computer print-out that provides a rudimentary picture of a photomicrograph. Details of the micrograph were conveyed to memory unit of the computer by a scanning device called FIDAC. Numerals from 0 to 6 on a gray scale describe the darkness of corresponding points on micrograph, made during phase of cell division at which a chromosome consists of two strands (chromatids) connected in one area (the centromere). Dots correspond to the background.

COMPUTER AND SCANNING DEVICE used by the authors are located at the Goddard Space Flight Center outside Washington, D.C. The IBM 7094 computer (*foreground*) receives descriptions of photomicrographs of chromosomes from the FIDAC scanner (*background*), on the basis of which it counts, analyzes and collates data on the chromosomes.

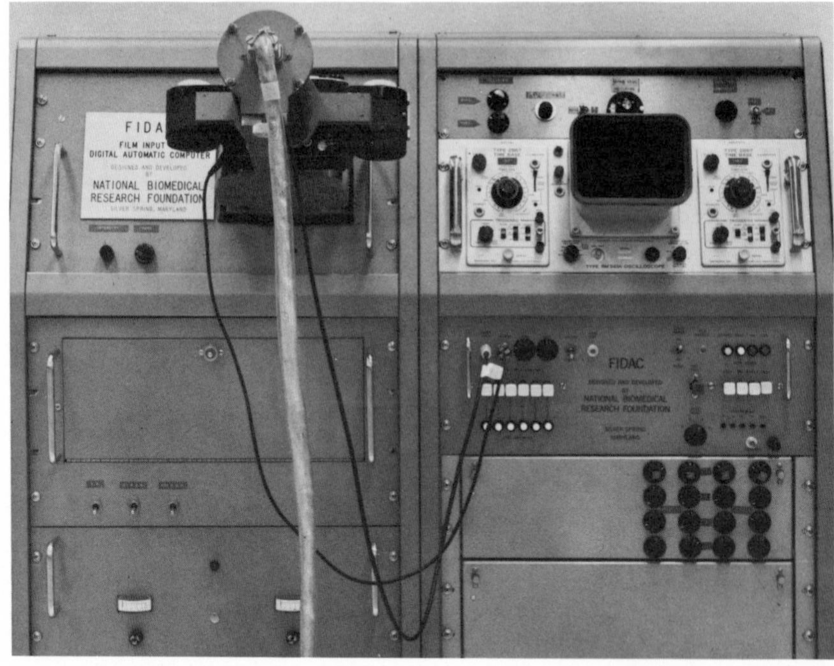

FIDAC INSTRUMENT is named for its function: "Film Input to Digital Automatic Computer." A roll of film containing a great many photomicrographs of chromosomes is put into the film transport unit at top left (*behind the cylindrical photomultiplier*). A detailed description of each micrograph is transmitted by FIDAC to the memory unit of the computer. A video amplifier displays the micrograph being scanned on the small screen at top right.

length of the chromosomes in the frame. Homologous chromosomes are matched according to area, length and arm-length ratio, and the pairs are classified according to the standardized sequence of the idiogram. When the analysis of a frame is finished, the FIDAC instrument is instructed to move to the next frame and the process is repeated. After a predetermined number of frames have been processed the statistics of all the photomicrographs on the roll of film are automatically collated and analyzed.

Let us consider more closely the essential step in this procedure: the recognition and analysis of individual chromosomes. The location of anything encountered by the bug—the boundary of an object, for example—can be given in a Cartesian-coordinate system mapping the entire frame. Thus when the bug first meets an object, its point of contact can be located on a grid in terms of horizontal and vertical positions denoted by X and Y coordinates. The bug now proceeds along the boundary of the object in a clockwise direction, and points on the boundary are delineated in the same notation. When a certain number of boundary points have been traversed, they are said to constitute a segment. The bug continues to mark boundary points and segments until it returns to the original point of contact; it is now ready to search for a "next object."

The computer program characterizes the individual segments in terms of their direction and curvature. This involves several measurements. First the center point of a segment is ascertained. The arc of the segment reached by moving clockwise from the center point is called the leading half; the arc reached by moving counterclockwise, the trailing half. A vector arrow is drawn in each half; the length of the segment is chosen as a distance short enough so that the angle between the leading and the trailing vector will be an approximation of the segment's curvature. The arrow that is the vector sum of the leading and trailing vectors is approximately the tangent to the segment at its center point and so provides a measure of the direction of the segment.

In determining the curvature of the segments the FIDAC system uses a small vocabulary of 13 terms to describe degrees of curvature. For purposes of explanation let us consider a vocabulary of four terms: a fairly straight segment is called Type O; a clockwise curve, Type E; a slight counterclockwise curve, Type V, and a pronounced counterclockwise curve, Type Y. By combining such terms the complete outline of a chromosome can be described.

The program by which the computer "builds up" the shape of a chromosome from combinations of curve types is relatively simple in conception. One arm of a chromosome, for example, might have Type O curves on its sides and a Type E curve at its end; between this arm and another on the same chromosome there would be a Type Y curve. The programmer's role is to set forth, *a*

START → SET p = 1

READ IN FRAME p

DO SPECTRUM

IS PICTURE BLANK? (NO / YES)

PROCESS FRAME p

IS THERE ANOTHER FRAME? (YES / NO)

p → p+1

SIGNAL **FIDAC** TO MOVE TO NEXT FRAME

DO STATISTICAL ANALYSIS ON RESULTS → END

b

SET i = 1

SEARCH FOR NEXT OBJECT i

IS THERE A NEXT OBJECT? (NO / YES)

PROCESS OBJECT i

i → i+1

EVALUATE RESULTS OF MEASUREMENTS ON OBJECTS OF THIS FRAME p

c

CHARACTERIZE THE BOUNDARY OF OBJECT i

ERASE OBJECT i AND FIND AND CHARACTERIZE ANY HOLES

DETERMINE BASIC PARTS

RECOGNIZE DERIVED PARTS OF THE OBJECT BY SYNTAX-DIRECTED PATTERN RECOGNITION

IS THE OBJECT A CHROMOSOME? (NO / YES)

PERFORM MEASUREMENTS OF THE CHROMOSOME

d

RECORD POINT OF ENTRY TO BOUNDARY

SET k = 1

DETERMINE CENTER OF SEGMENT k

DETERMINE LEADING AND TRAILING ARROWS OF SEGMENT k

HAS ENTRY BOUNDARY POINT BEEN REACHED? (NO / YES)

k → k+1

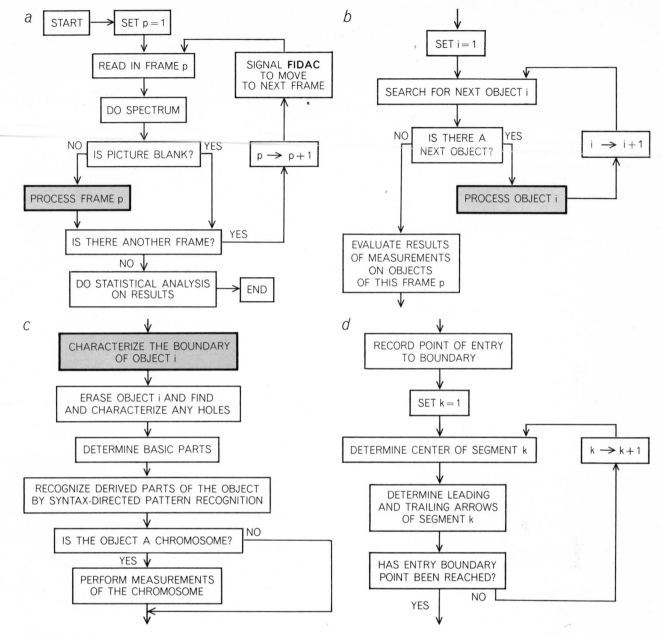

STEPS PERFORMED BY COMPUTER in examining photomicrographs of chromosomes are presented on four levels of detail. The overall procedure (*a*) entails advancing the roll of photomicrographic film, instructing FIDAC to "read" the image of a frame into the computer's memory unit, computing the spectrum of the image, processing the frame if it is not blank, again advancing the film and finally, when the roll is finished, collating data pertaining to all the photomicrographs that have been inspected. The key step in the sequence is the processing of a frame (*b*), which involves a search for individual objects. The boundary of each object is considered (*c*) in terms of the segments that comprise it. The curvature and directionality of each segment are analyzed (*d*) and the segments are defined as "curve types." Certain sequences of curve types are recognized by the program as arms or other parts of chromosomes. (This is called "syntax-directed pattern recognition.") An object composed of such parts is thus identified as a chromosome.

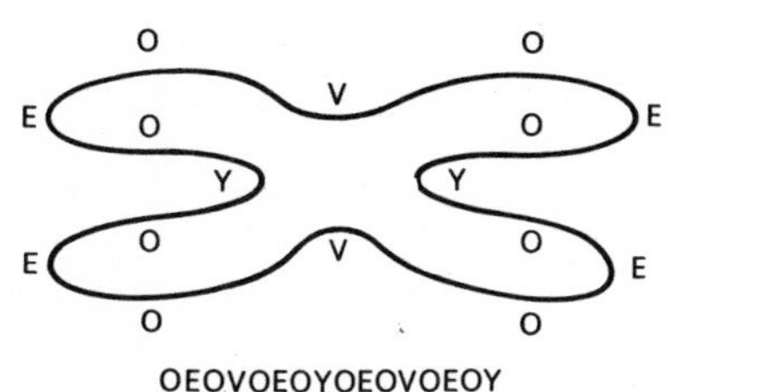

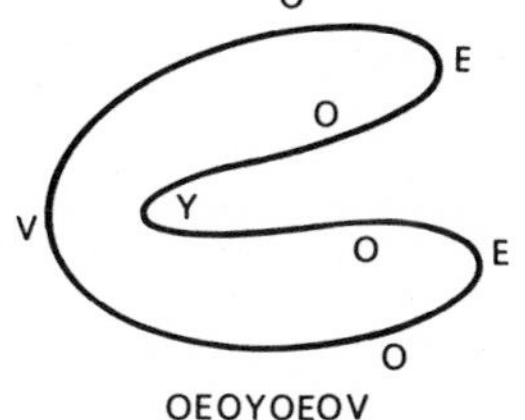

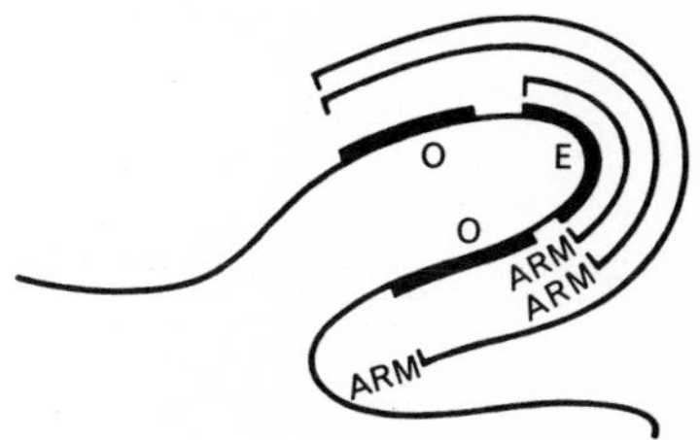

SEGMENTS on boundary of a chromosome are defined as types of curve. *O* is a fairly straight segment; *E*, a clockwise curve; *V*, a slight counterclockwise curve; *Y*, a sharp counterclockwise curve. Different sequences of curve types represent a four-armed submedian chromosome (*left*) and a teleocentric chromosome (*right*) in the computer program.

ARM IS IDENTIFIED in stages by program. Type *E* curve is tentatively called an arm (*notation outside brackets*). Scan showing it between *O* types confirms this fact.

in the notation of symbolic logic, a recursive definition (one that can be used repetitively in the program) by which a "derived part" such as an arm can be recognized from its component curves [*see bottom illustrations on preceding page*]. The process is then taken up by an element of FIDACSYS called the mobilizer, which is analogous to the translator program for a computer language. The mobilizer operates on a list of terms describing the parts of a particular object; by using a general syntactical description of various kinds of chromosome it determines whether or not an object is a chromosome and, if so, what type of chromosome it is. This technique, called syntax-directed pattern recognition, was developed by one of the authors (Ledley) at the National Biomedical Research Foundation in Silver Spring, Md.

The results of each step in the analytic process can be printed out by the computer. First come data describing the coordinates of the chromosome's center of gravity, its area and its perimeter. The lengths of the arms are given and the arm-length ratio is computed by comparing the average length of the two long arms to the overall length of the chromosome [*see illustration at right*]. Next come the coordinates locating the centers of the boundary segments and designations describing the curvature of these "basic parts." FIDACSYS then prints out the derived parts, giving coordinates for the positions of the arms and the centromere. In the print-outs the code letter *E* is placed at points representing the ends of the arms, and the letter *C* at the points marking the centromere. On the basis of all these data an automatic plotting device makes a tracing of all the chromosomes in the original photomicrograph. The plotter also numbers the chromosomes and draws a line to indicate their centromeres [*see illustration on next page*].

There is still another way in which a computer programmed by FIDACSYS translates numerical data back into graphic form: the final print-out consists of a schematic idiogram of the complement of chromosomes under inspection. To evaluate the accuracy of chromosome analysis by computer we must ask: How does the automatic idiogram compare with one based on visual observation and measurement? Assessments made by the authors indicate that the figures for areas and arm lengths worked out by computer are sufficiently precise. There is reason to

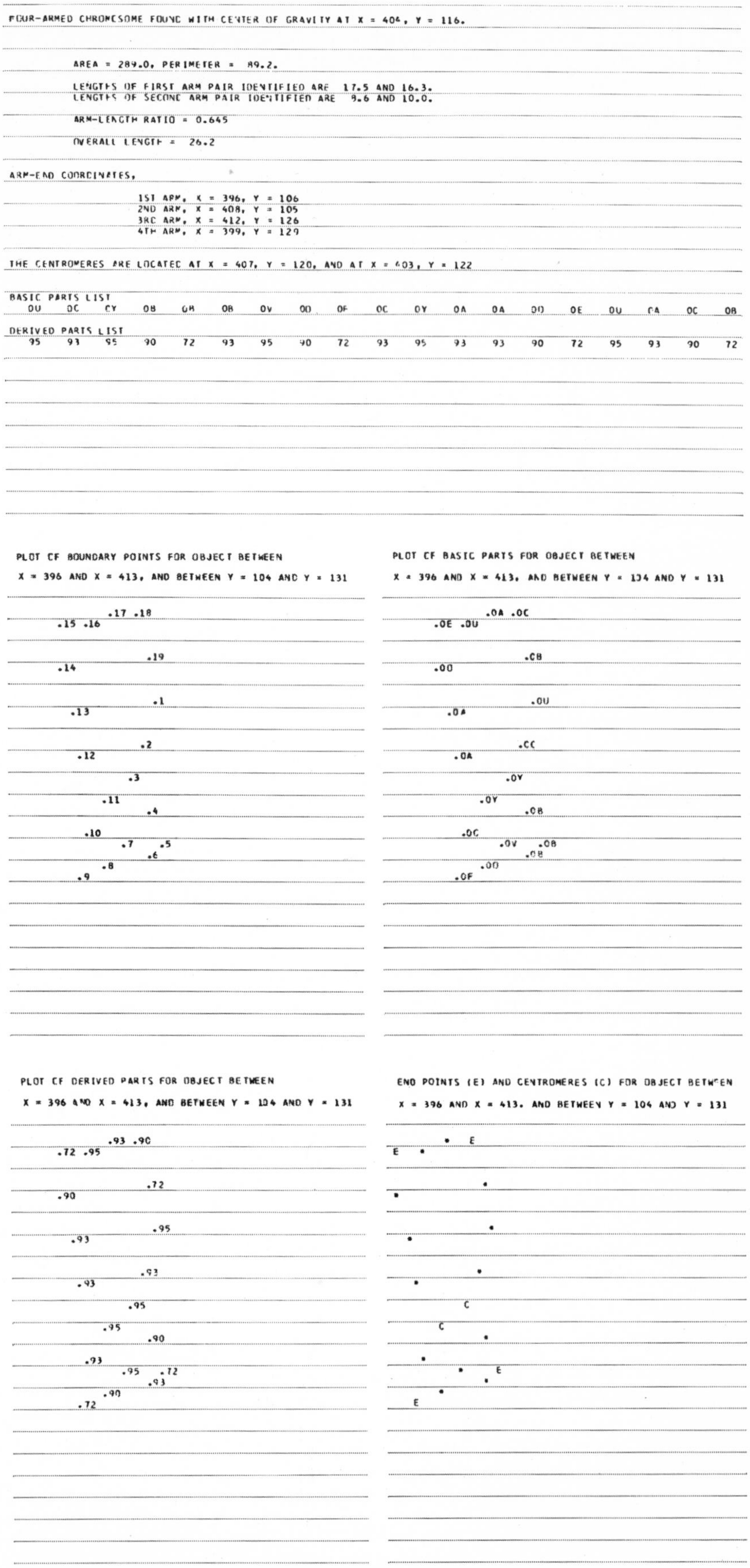

```
FOUR-ARMED CHROMOSOME FOUND WITH CENTER OF GRAVITY AT X = 404, Y = 116.

          AREA = 289.0, PERIMETER =  89.2.

          LENGTHS OF FIRST ARM PAIR IDENTIFIED ARE  17.5 AND 16.3.
          LENGTHS OF SECOND ARM PAIR IDENTIFIED ARE  9.6 AND 10.0.

          ARM-LENGTH RATIO = 0.645

          OVERALL LENGTH =  26.2

ARM-END COORDINATES,

                    1ST ARM, X = 396, Y = 106
                    2ND ARM, X = 408, Y = 105
                    3RD ARM, X = 412, Y = 126
                    4TH ARM, X = 399, Y = 129

THE CENTROMERES ARE LOCATED AT X = 407, Y = 120, AND AT X = 403, Y = 122

BASIC PARTS LIST
   OU   OC   CY   OB   OB   OB   OV   OD   OF   OC   OY   OA   OA   OD   OE   OU   CA   OC   OB
DERIVED PARTS LIST
   95   93   95   90   72   93   95   90   72   93   95   93   93   90   72   95   93   90   72
```

```
PLOT OF BOUNDARY POINTS FOR OBJECT BETWEEN
X = 396 AND X = 413, AND BETWEEN Y = 104 AND Y = 131

            .17 .18
     .15 .16

                 .19
     .14

                  .1
       .13

                .2
        .12
              .3
           .11
                 .4
        .10
              .7   .5
                 .6
           .8
        .9
```

```
PLOT OF BASIC PARTS FOR OBJECT BETWEEN
X = 396 AND X = 413, AND BETWEEN Y = 104 AND Y = 131

            .OA .OC
     .OE .OU

                 .CB
     .OO

                  .OU
       .OA

                .CC
        .OA
              .OV
           .OY
                 .OB
        .OC
              .OV   .OB
                 .OB
           .OD
        .OF
```

```
PLOT OF DERIVED PARTS FOR OBJECT BETWEEN
X = 396 AND X = 413, AND BETWEEN Y = 104 AND Y = 131

            .93 .90
     .72 .95

                 .72
     .90

                  .95
       .93

                .93
        .93
              .95
           .95
                 .90
        .93
              .95   .72
                 .93
           .90
        .72
```

```
END POINTS (E) AND CENTROMERES (C) FOR OBJECT BETWEEN
X = 396 AND X = 413. AND BETWEEN Y = 104 AND Y = 131

          .   E
E    .

              .
.

               .
  .

             .
   .
            C
        C
              .
    .
          .   E
              .
        .
   E
```

INTERMEDIATE PRINT-OUTS from computer examining chromosomes by syntax-directed pattern recognition are assembled. At top are data giving location and size of chromosome and its arm-length ratio; in middle, plots of boundary points and segments ("Basic parts"); at bottom, plots with labels for ends of arms and centromere ("Derived parts").

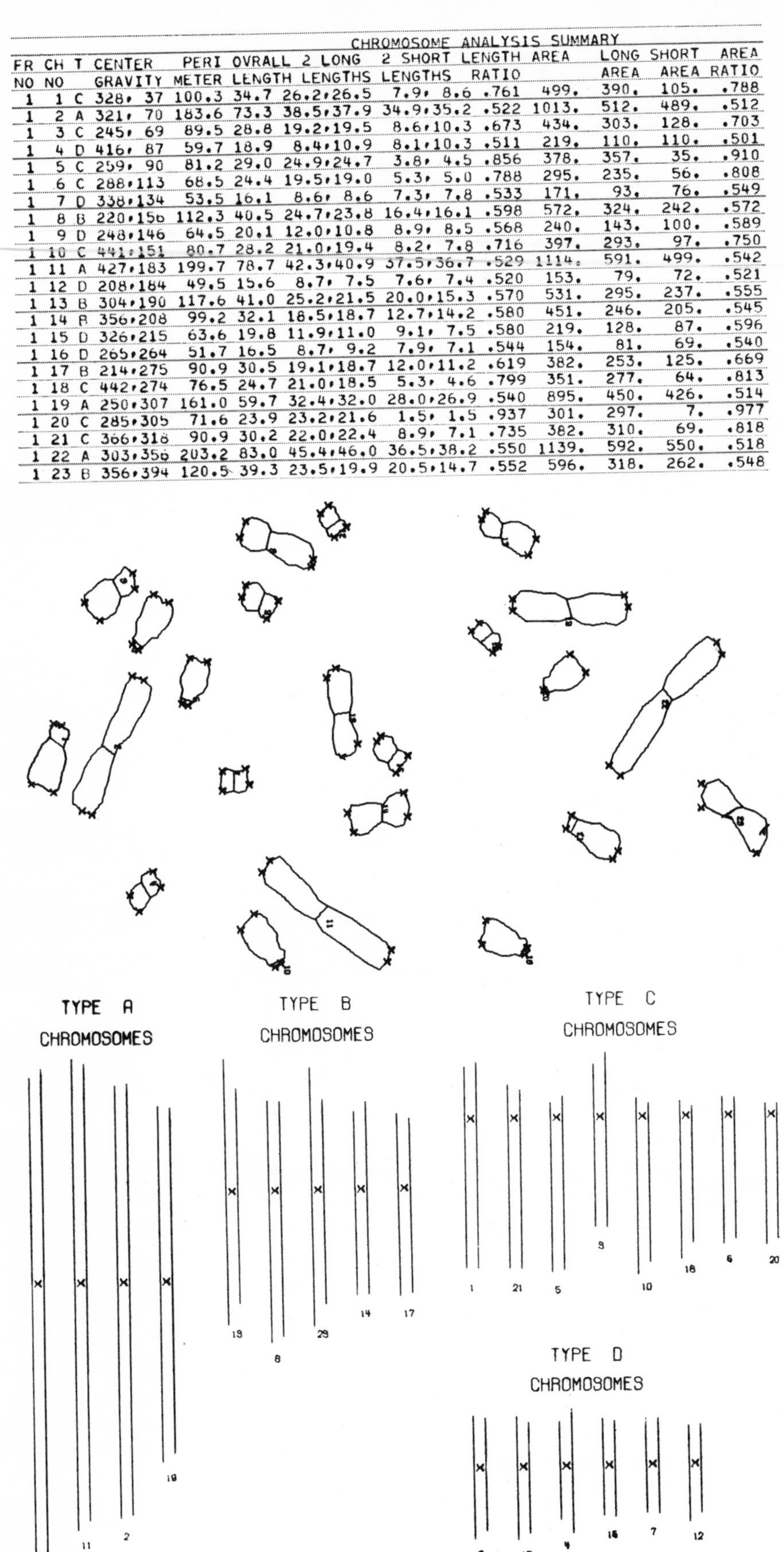

CHROMOSOME ANALYSIS SUMMARY

FR NO	CH NO	T	CENTER GRAVITY	PERI METER	OVRALL LENGTH	2 LONG LENGTHS	2 SHORT LENGTHS	LENGTH RATIO	AREA	LONG AREA	SHORT AREA	AREA RATIO
1	1	C	328, 37	100.3	34.7	26.2,26.5	7.9, 8.6	.761	499.	390.	105.	.788
1	2	A	321, 70	183.6	73.3	38.5,37.9	34.9,35.2	.522	1013.	512.	489.	.512
1	3	C	245, 69	89.5	28.8	19.2,19.5	8.6,10.3	.673	434.	303.	128.	.703
1	4	D	416, 87	59.7	18.9	8.4,10.9	8.1,10.3	.511	219.	110.	110.	.501
1	5	C	259, 90	81.2	29.0	24.9,24.7	3.8, 4.5	.856	378.	357.	35.	.910
1	6	C	288,113	68.5	24.4	19.5,19.0	5.3, 5.0	.788	295.	235.	56.	.808
1	7	D	338,134	53.5	16.1	8.6, 8.6	7.3, 7.8	.533	171.	93.	76.	.549
1	8	B	220,156	112.3	40.5	24.7,23.8	16.4,16.1	.598	572.	324.	242.	.572
1	9	D	248,146	64.5	20.1	12.0,10.8	8.9, 8.5	.568	240.	143.	100.	.589
1	10	C	441,151	80.7	28.2	21.0,19.4	8.2, 7.8	.716	397.	293.	97.	.750
1	11	A	427,183	199.7	78.7	42.3,40.9	37.5,36.7	.529	1114.	591.	499.	.542
1	12	D	208,184	49.5	15.6	8.7, 7.5	7.6, 7.4	.520	153.	79.	72.	.521
1	13	B	304,190	117.6	41.0	25.2,21.5	20.0,15.3	.570	531.	295.	237.	.555
1	14	A	356,208	99.2	32.1	18.5,18.7	12.7,14.2	.580	451.	246.	205.	.545
1	15	D	326,215	63.6	19.8	11.9,11.0	9.1, 7.5	.580	219.	128.	87.	.596
1	16	D	265,264	51.7	16.5	8.7, 9.2	7.9, 7.1	.544	154.	81.	69.	.540
1	17	B	214,275	90.9	30.5	19.1,18.7	12.0,11.2	.619	382.	253.	125.	.669
1	18	C	442,274	76.5	24.7	21.0,18.5	5.3, 4.6	.799	351.	277.	64.	.813
1	19	A	250,307	161.0	59.7	32.4,32.0	28.0,26.9	.540	895.	450.	426.	.514
1	20	C	285,305	71.6	23.9	23.2,21.6	1.5, 1.5	.937	301.	297.	7.	.977
1	21	C	366,318	90.9	30.2	22.0,22.4	8.9, 7.1	.735	382.	310.	69.	.818
1	22	A	303,356	203.2	83.0	45.4,46.0	36.5,38.2	.550	1139.	592.	550.	.518
1	23	B	356,394	120.5	39.3	23.5,19.9	20.5,14.7	.552	596.	318.	262.	.548

THREE DESCRIPTIONS of the complement of chromosomes of a Chinese hamster were printed by machine. At top are data describing the morphology of each of the animal's 23 chromosomes. In middle is a tracing of the chromosomes, made by an automatic plotting device in which chromosomes are numbered, ends of arms marked and centromeres represented by a line. At bottom is an idiogram of the chromosomes arranged by computer.

hope that analysis by computer will eventually uncover small but important chromosomal abnormalities that have not been discerned by eye. It is known, for example, that one of the chromosomes in the cells of individuals with chronic myeloid leukemia lacks only a small portion of one arm; it is quite likely that other small deletions or additions have been overlooked by investigators and will be revealed by means of the computer.

It can be said with some assurance that the procedure we have described will soon be sufficiently refined and tested for clinical use by physicians who want to examine the chromosomes of a significant number of people. The method will also be available for screening new drugs and biologicals (such as vaccines) for possible chromosomal effects. Moreover, it will now be possible to conduct large-scale studies in such matters as the effects of radiation and aging on chromosomes. The main limitations of the procedure—limits on the speed of the scan and on the number of points that are sampled per picture—are imposed not by the FIDAC device or the basic technique of syntax-directed pattern recognition but by the cycle time and capacity of the memory of the International Business Machines 7094 computer we have been using in our investigations. Newer machines, such as the IBM 360-series computers, will have a larger memory and greater speed, allowing an even faster and more accurate procedure.

It is also safe to predict that methods of automatic analysis closely akin to those described in this article will be employed by biologists and research physicians for tasks other than the study of human chromosomes. There are many branches of biology in which pictorial data have been collected in quantities so large that systematic analysis has heretofore seemed impractical. Examples of such material are sequences of pictures made through the microscope that show the myriad dendritic extensions of nerve cells; electron micrographs of muscle fibers or virus particles; autoradiographs showing the uptake of a tracer element, and X-ray pictures of bone revealing the distribution of calcium. Pictures from these and other categories of material, which describe the structural characteristics of cells in terms of lengths, areas, volumes and densities, can be translated into numerical information. Like photomicrographs of chromosomes, they readily lend themselves to study by computer.

27

THE USES OF COMPUTERS IN EDUCATION

PATRICK SUPPES • September 1966

As other articles in this volume make abundantly clear, both the processing and the uses of information are undergoing an unprecedented technological revolution. Not only are machines now able to deal with many kinds of information at high speed and in large quantities but also it is possible to manipulate these quantities of information so as to benefit from them in entirely novel ways. This is perhaps nowhere truer than in the field of education. One can predict that in a few more years millions of schoolchildren will have access to what Philip of Macedon's son Alexander enjoyed as a royal prerogative: the personal services of a tutor as well-informed and responsive as Aristotle.

The basis for this seemingly extravagant prediction is not apparent in many examinations of the computer's role in education today. In themselves, however, such examinations provide impressive evidence of the importance of computers on the educational scene. As an example, a recent report of the National Academy of Sciences states that by mid-1965 more than 800 computers were in service on the campuses of various American universities and that these institutions spent $175 million for computers that year. The report goes on to forecast that by 1968 the universities' annual budget for computer operations will reach $300 million and that their total investment in computing facilities will pass $500 million.

A similar example is represented by the fact that most colleges of engineering and even many high schools now use computers to train students in computer programming. Perhaps just as important as the imposition of formal course requirements at the college level is the increasingly widespread attitude among college students that a knowledge of computers is a "must" if their engineering or scientific training is to be up to date. Undergraduates of my generation who majored in engineering, for instance, considered a slide rule the symbol of their developing technical prowess. Today being able to program a computer in a standard language such as FORTRAN or ALGOL is much more likely to be the appropriate symbol.

At the graduate level students in the social sciences and in business administration are already making use of computers in a variety of ways, ranging from the large-scale analysis of data to the simulation of an industry. The time is rapidly approaching when a high percentage of all university graduates will have had some systematic training in the use of computers; a significant percentage of them will have had quite sophisticated training. An indication of the growth of student interest in computers is the increase in student units of computer-science instruction we have had at Stanford University over the past four years. Although total enrollment at Stanford increased only slightly during that period, the number of student units rose from 2,572 in 1962–1963 to 5,642 in 1965–1966.

That time-sharing programs are rapidly becoming operational in many university computation centers justifies the forecast of another increase in the impact of computers on the universities [see "Time-sharing on Computers," by Fano and Corbató, SCIENTIFIC AMERICAN, September, 1966]. Under time-sharing regimes a much larger number of students can be given direct "on line" experience, which in itself is psychologically attractive and, from the practical viewpoint, facilitates deeper study of the use of computers. There is still another far from trivial way in which the computer serves the interests of education: The large school system that does not depend on computers for many administrative and service functions is today the exception rather than the rule.

The truly revolutionary function of computers in education, however, lies in the novel area of computer-assisted instruction. This role of the computer is scarcely implemented as yet but, assuming the continuation of the present pace of technological development, it cannot fail to have profound effects in the near future. In this article I shall describe some experiments in computer-assisted instruction that are currently being conducted at levels ranging from the comparatively simple to the quite complex and then examine some unsuspected problems that these experiments have revealed. First, however, the reader deserves an explanation of why computer-assisted instruction is considered desirable at all.

The single most powerful argument

COMPUTER-ASSISTED INSTRUCTION in elementary arithmetic is illustrated in the photographs on the opposite page. A first-grade pupil, receiving "readiness" work preparatory to instruction in addition, is shown two possible answers to a question implicit in the symbols occupying the top line of a cathode-ray-tube display. As he watches (*top photograph*), his earphones carry a verbal message asking him to select from the symbolic statements of union shown in the second and third lines of the display the one that is identical with the equation shown in the top line. The pupil signals his choice (*bottom photograph*) by pointing to the statement he prefers with machine's light pen; the computer then records the answer.

for computer-assisted instruction is an old one in education. It concerns the advantages, partly demonstrated and partly conjectured, of individualized instruction. The concept of individualized instruction became the core of an explicit body of doctrine at the end of the 19th century, although in practice it was known some 2,000 years earlier in ancient Greece. For many centuries the education of the aristocracy was primarily tutorial. At the university level individualized tutorial instruction has been one of the glories of Oxford and Cambridge. Modern criticisms of the method are not directed at its intrinsic merit but rather at its economic inefficiency. It is widely agreed that the more an educational curriculum can adapt in a unique fashion to individual learners—each of whom has his own characteristic initial ability, rate and even "style" of learning—the better the chance is of providing the student with a successful learning experience.

The computer makes the individualization of instruction easier because it can be programmed to follow each student's history of learning successes and failures and to use his past performance as a basis for selecting the new problems and new concepts to which he should be exposed next. With modern information-storage devices it is possible to store both a large body of curriculum material and the past histories of many students working in the curriculum. Such storage is well within the capacity of current technology, whether the subject is primary school mathematics, secondary school French or elementary statistics at the college level. In fact, the principal obstacles to computer-assisted instruction are not technological but pedagogical: how to devise ways of individualizing instruction and of designing a curriculum that are suited to individuals instead of groups. Certain obvious steps that take account of different rates of learning can be made with little difficulty; these are the main things that have been done so far. We have still, however, cut only a narrow path into a rich jungle of possibilities. We do not have any really clear scientific idea of the extent to which instruction can be individualized. It will probably be some time before a discipline of such matters begins to operate at anything like an appropriately deep conceptual level.

A second important aspect of computers in education is closer in character to such familiar administrative functions as routine record-keeping. Before the advent of computers it was extremely difficult to collect systematic data on how children succeed in the process of learning a given subject. Evaluative tests of achievement at the end of learning have (and will undoubtedly continue to have) a place both in the process of classifying students and in the process of comparing different curriculum approaches to the same subject. Nonetheless, such tests remain blunt and insensitive instruments, particularly with respect to detailed problems of instruction and curriculum revision. It is not possible on the basis of poor results in a test of children's mastery of subtraction or of irregular verbs in French to draw clear inferences about ways to improve the curriculum. A computer, on the other hand, can provide daily information about how students are performing on each part of the curriculum as it is presented, making it possible to evaluate not only individual pages but also individual exercises. This use of computers will have important consequences for all students in the immediate future. Even if students are not themselves receiving computer-assisted instruction, the results of such instruction will certainly be used to revise and improve ordinary texts and workbooks.

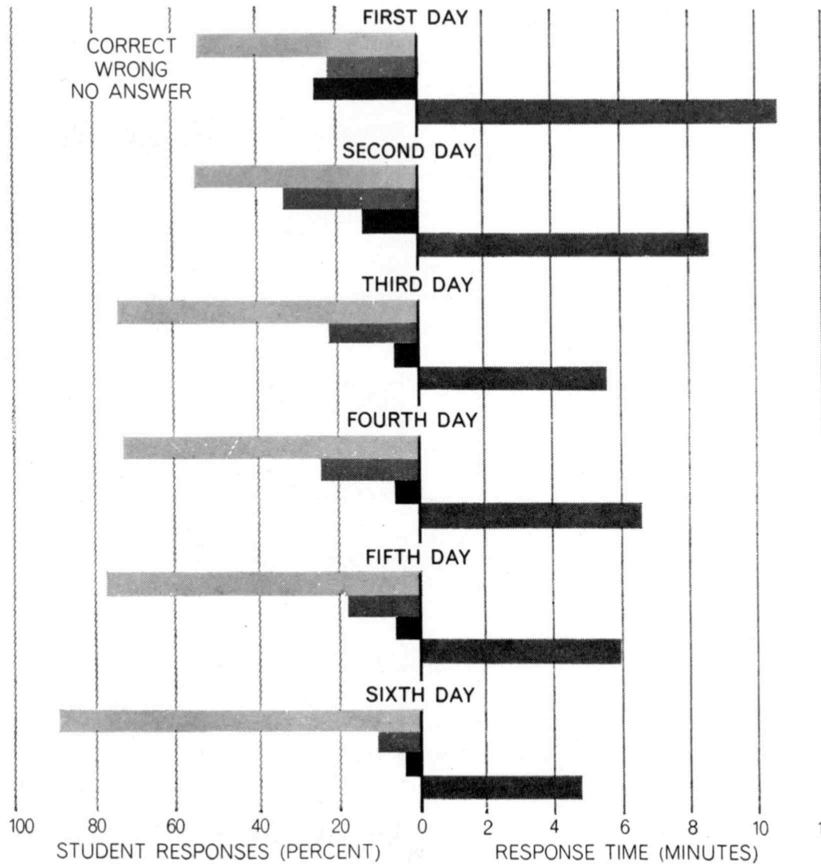

IMPROVEMENT IN LEARNING is one evident result of drill and practice. The graph summarizes the results of a six-day drill on the commutative, associative and distributive laws of arithmetic. The computer program covered 48 concepts; each day's session presented 24 problems. Two days' drill therefore reviewed all 48 concepts, although no identical problems were presented during the six days. By the last day student responses were more than 90 percent correct and the speed of reply was twice what it was at the start.

Let me now take up some of the work in computer-assisted instruction we have been doing at Stanford. It should be emphasized that similar work is in progress at other centers, including the University of Illinois, Pennsylvania State University, the University of Pittsburgh, the University of Michigan, the University of Texas, Florida State University and the University of California at Santa Barbara, and within such companies as the International Business Machines Corporation, the Systems Development Corporation and Bolt, Beranek and Newman. This list is by no means exhaustive. The work at these various places runs from a primary emphasis on the development of computer hardware to the construction of short courses in subjects ranging from physics to typing. Although all these efforts, including ours at Stanford, are still in the developmental stage, the instruction of large numbers of students at computer terminals will soon (if academic and industrial soothsayers are right) be one of the most important fields of application for computers.

At Stanford our students are mainly at the elementary school level; the terminals they use, however, are also suitable for secondary school and university students. At each terminal there is a visual device on which the student may view displays brought up from the computer memory as part of the instruction program. A device that is coming into wide use for this purpose is the cathode ray tube; messages can be generated directly by the computer on the face of the tube, which resembles a television screen. Mounted with the cathode ray tube is a typewriter keyboard the student can use to respond to problems shown on the screen. At some additional cost the student can also have a light pen that enables him to respond directly by touching the pen to the screen instead of typing on the keyboard. Such a device is particularly useful for students in the lowest elementary grades, although when only single-digit numerical responses or single-character alphabetical ones are required, the use of a keyboard is quite easy even for kindergarten children to learn.

After the display screen and the keyboard the next most important element at a terminal is the appropriate sound device. Presenting spoken messages to students is desirable at all educational levels, but it is particularly needed for younger children. It would be hard to overemphasize the importance of such spoken messages, programmed to be properly sensitive to points at which the student may encounter difficulty in learning. Such

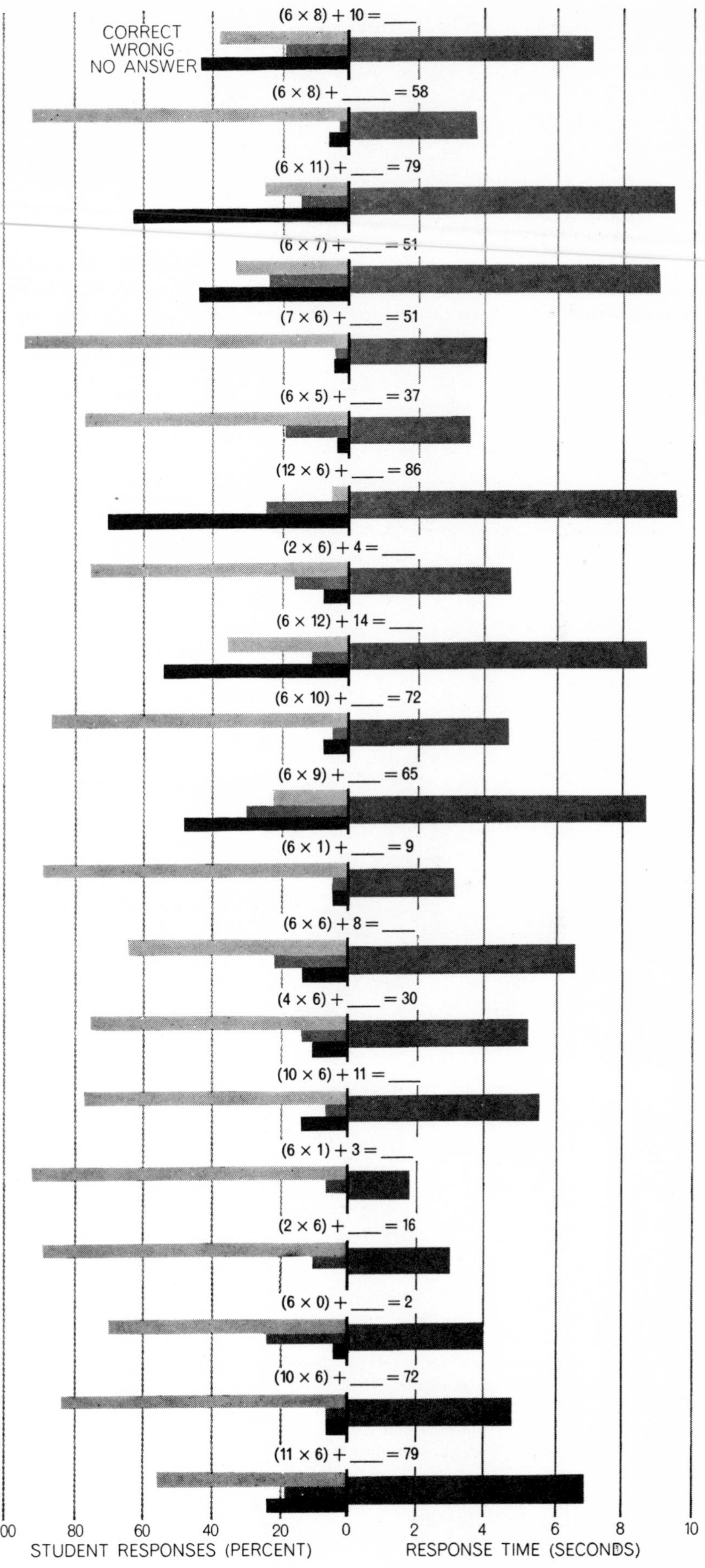

COMPUTER SUMMARY of drill results makes possible the analysis essential for assessment and revision of various study curriculums. The results of 37 children's replies to 20 questions designed to test elementary arithmetic skills are summarized graphically in this illustration. The most troublesome question proved to be No. 7; not only did it take the most time to answer but also 26 students failed to answer it at all and only two answered it correctly. Although question No. 9 is the exact reverse of question No. 7, it received 13 correct answers. Evidently obtaining an unknown quantity by subtraction is harder than obtaining one by addition, and the students found it harder to multiply 12 by 6 than to multiply 6 by 12.

messages are the main help a good tutor gives his pupil; they are the crucial missing element in noncomputerized teaching machines. All of us have observed that children, especially the younger ones, learn at least as much by ear as they do by eye. The effectiveness of the spoken word is probably stronger than any visual stimulus, not only for children but also most of the time for adults. It is particularly significant that elementary school children, whose reading skills are comparatively undeveloped, comprehend rather complicated spoken messages.

A cathode ray tube, a keyboard and a loudspeaker or earphones therefore constitute the essential devices for computer-assisted instruction. Additional visual displays such as motion pictures or line drawings can also be useful at almost all levels of instruction. Ordinary film projectors under computer control can provide such displays.

So far three levels of interaction between the student and the computer program have received experimental attention. At the most superficial level (and accordingly the most economical

GLOSSARY

α MOIST AIR RISES

β MOIST AIR COOLS OR WILL COOL

γ CLOUDS WILL FORM

→ FORMAL IMPLICATION

¬ NOT

RULES OF INFERENCE

TRI TRANSIVITY OF IMPLICATION (FROM X→Y AND Y→Z, DERIVE X→Z)

IF MODUS PONENS (FROM X→Y AND X, DERIVE Y)

CP CONTRAPOSITIVE (FROM X→Y, DERIVE ¬Y→¬X)

DNEG DOUBLE NEGATION (FROM ¬¬X, DERIVE X)

RED CONTRADICTION OF CONSEQUENT (FROM Y AND X→¬Y, DERIVE ¬X)

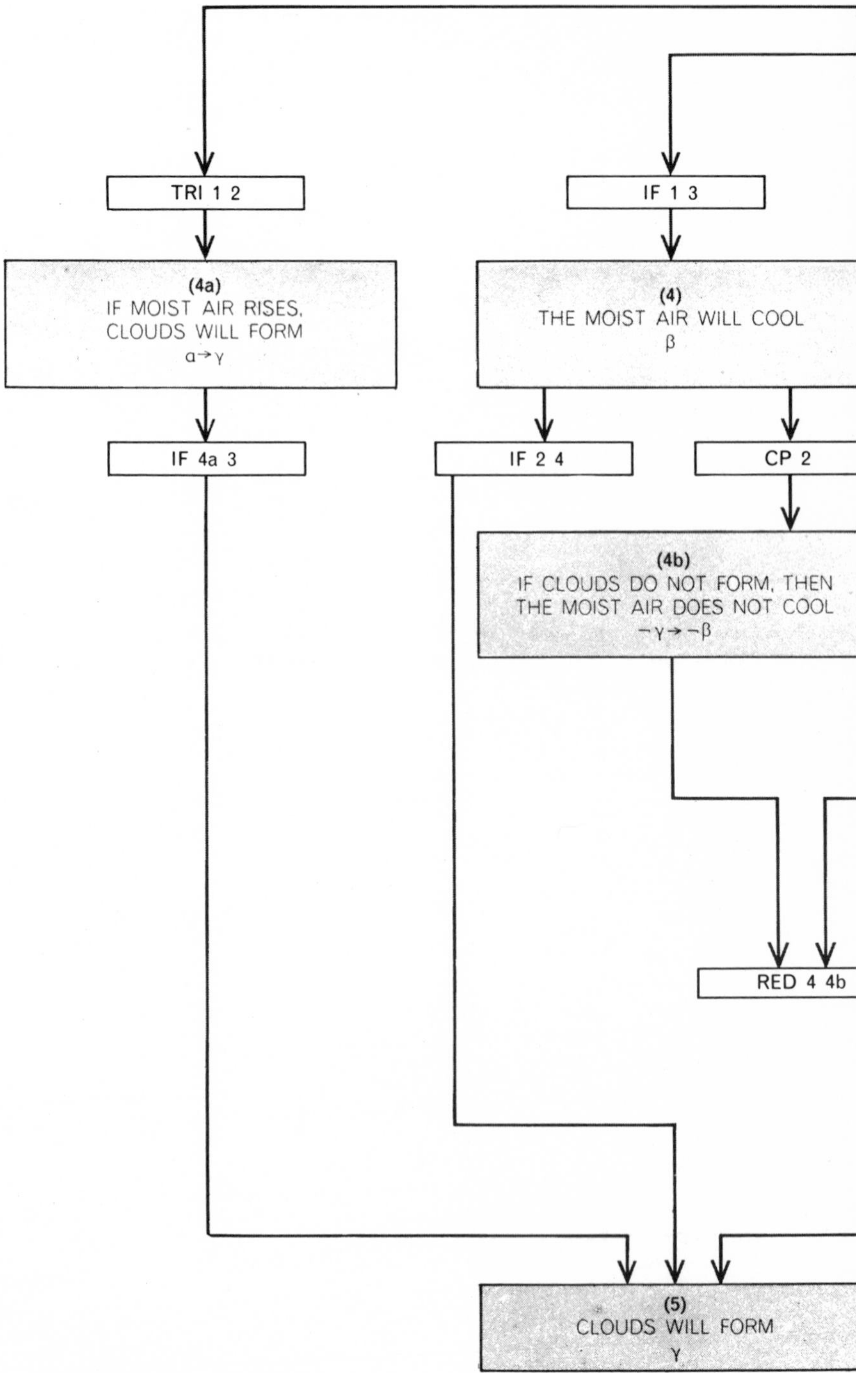

TUTORIAL EXERCISE in mathematical logic is an example of a more complex variety of computer-assisted instruction. The student may proceed from a set of given hypotheses (*top*) to a given conclusion (*bottom*) by any one of several routes. Each of the illustrated downward paths represents a legitimate logical attack on the problem and each constitutes a unique sequence of inferences (*see legend and statements in logical notation below each of the numbered verbal statements*). Ideally a tutorial computer program will show no preference for one path over another but will check the soundness of each step along any path and tell the student if he makes any mistakes in logic.

one) are "drill and practice" systems. Instruction programs that fall under this heading are merely supplements to a regular curriculum taught by a teacher. At Stanford we have experimented a great deal with elementary school mathematics at the drill-and-practice level, and I shall draw on our experience for examples of what can be accomplished with this kind of supplementation of a regular curriculum by computer methods.

Over the past 40 years both pedagogical and psychological studies have provided abundant evidence that students need a great deal of practice in order to master the algorithms, or basic procedures, of arithmetic. Tests have shown that the same situation obtains for students learning the "new math." There seems to be no way to avoid a good deal of practice in learning to execute the basic algorithms with speed and accuracy. At the elementary level the most important way in which computer-assisted instruction differs from traditional methods of providing practice is that we are in no sense committed to giving each child the same set of problems, as would be the case if textbooks or other written materials were used. Once a number

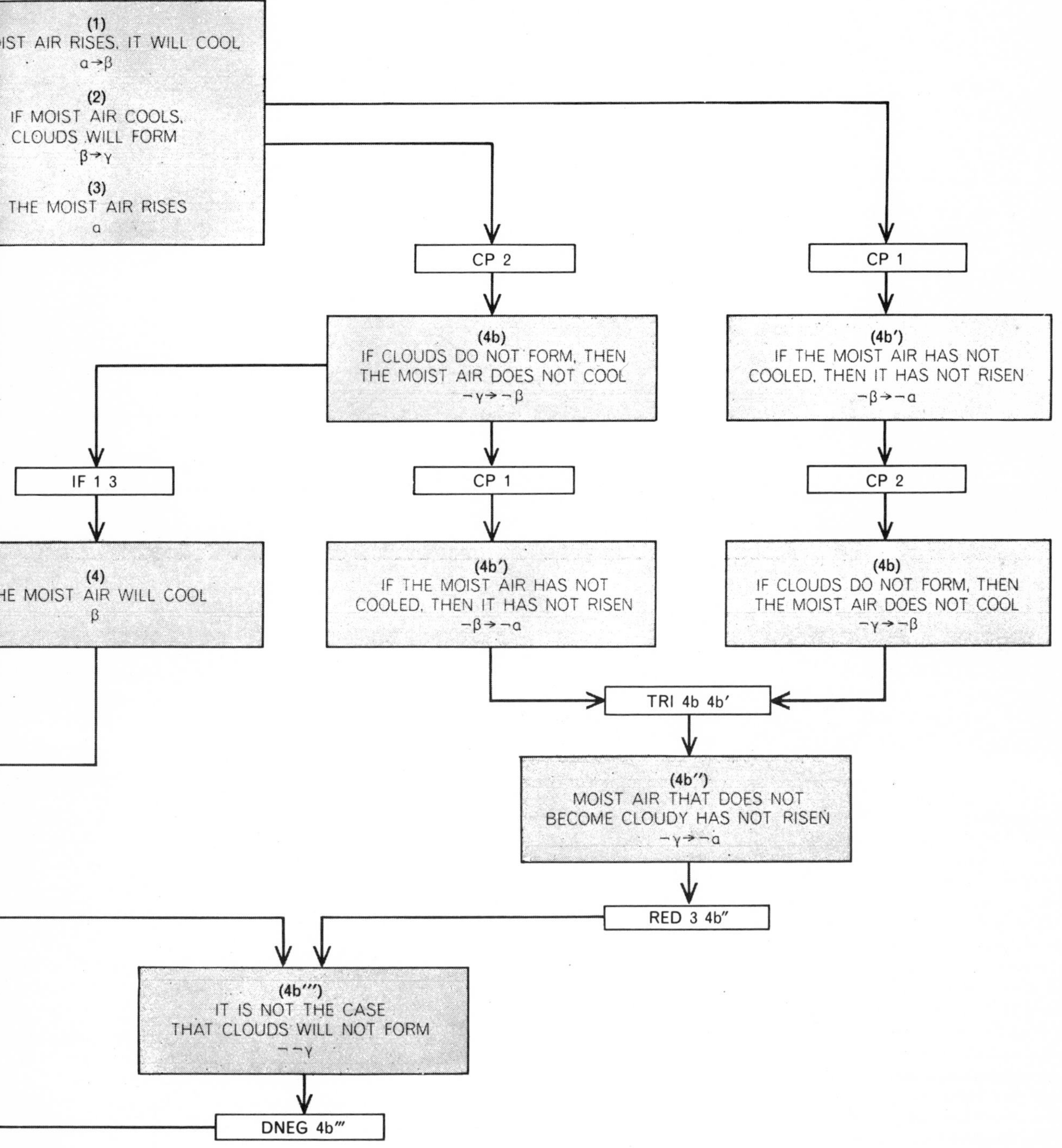

```
PLEASE TYPE YOUR NAME

ROBERT VALENTINE

DRILL NUMBER 604032

L.C.M.  MEANS  LEAST COMMON MULTIPLE

___ IS THE L.C.M. OF  4 AND  9

TIME IS UP

_36 IS THE L.C.M. OF  4 AND  9

_23 IS THE L.C.M. OF 12 AND  8

WRONG

_24 IS THE L.C.M. OF 12 AND  8

_1_ IS THE L.C.M. OF 15 AND 10

WRONG

___ IS THE L.C.M. OF 15 AND 10

TIME IS UP, ANSWER IS 30

_30 IS THE L.C.M. OF 15 AND 10

_60 IS THE L.C.M. OF 12 AND 30

_12 IS THE L.C.M. OF  2,  4, AND  6
```

```
_40 IS THE L.C.M. OF  8, 10, AND  5

S. FOR SUMMARY S.

              NUMBER    PERCENT
CORRECT         14        70
WRONG            5        25
TIMEOUT          1         5
70% CORRECT IN BLOCK, 70% OVERALL TO DATE
GOOD BYE, O FEARLESS DRILL TESTER.
TEAR OFF ON DOTTED LINE

...............................................
```

DRILL-AND-PRACTICE EXERCISE, shown in abbreviated form, is typical of a simple computer-assisted instruction program that is designed to be responsive to the needs of individual students. The illustrated exercise is one of five that differ in their degree of difficulty; when the student types his name (*color*), the exercise best suited to him on the basis of computer-memory records of his previous performance is selected automatically. The first three questions and answers exemplify the ways in which the computer is programmed to deal with various shortcomings. The student fails to answer the first question within the allotted 10-second time limit; the computer therefore prints TIME IS UP and repeats the question, which the student then answers correctly (*color*). A wrong answer to the next question causes the computer to announce the error and repeat the question automatically; a second chance again elicits a correct answer. A wrong answer to the third question is compounded by failure to respond to the reiterated question within the time limit. Because this question has now drawn two unsatisfactory responses the automatic TIME IS UP statement is followed by a printing of the correct answer. The question is now repeated for a third and last time. Whether or not the student elects to copy the correct answer (he does so in this instance), the computer automatically produces the next question. Only six of the 20 questions that compose the drill are shown in the example. After the student's last answer the computer proceeds to print a summary of the student's score for the drill as well as his combined average for this and earlier drills in the same series. The drill-and-practice exercise then concludes with a cheery farewell to the student and an instruction to tear off the teletype tape.

of study "tracks," representing various levels of difficulty, have been prepared as a curriculum, it is only a matter of computer programming to offer students exercises of varying degrees of difficulty and to select the appropriate level of difficulty for each student according to his past performance.

In the program we ran in elementary grades at schools near Stanford during the academic year 1965–1966 five levels of difficulty were programmed for each grade level. A typical three-day block of problems on the addition of fractions, for example, would vary in the following way. Students at the lowest level (Level 1) received problems involving only fractions that had the same denominator in common. On the first two days levels 2 and 3 also received only problems in which the denominators were the same. On the third day the fraction problems for levels 2 and 3 had denominators that differed by a factor of 2. At Level 4 the problems had denominators that differed by a factor of 2 on the first day. At Level 5 the denominators differed by a factor of 3, 4, 5 or 6 on the first day. Under the program the student moved up and down within the five levels of difficulty on the basis of his performance on the previous day. If more than 80 percent of his exercises were done correctly, he moved up a level. If fewer than 60 percent of the exercises were done correctly, he moved down a level. The selection of five levels and of 80 and 60 percent has no specific theoretical basis; they are founded on practical and pedagogical intuition. As data are accumulated we expect to modify the structure of the curriculum.

Our key effort in drill-and-practice systems is being conducted in an elementary school (grades three through six) a few miles from Stanford. The terminals used there are ordinary teletype machines, each connected to our computer at Stanford by means of individual telephone lines. There are eight teletypes in all, one for each school classroom. The students take turns using the teletype in a fixed order; each student uses the machine once a day for five to 10 minutes. During this period he receives a number of exercises (usually 20), most of which are devoted to a single concept in the elementary school mathematics curriculum. The concept reviewed on any given day can range from ordinary two-digit addition to intuitive logical inference. In every case the teacher has already presented the concept and the pupil has had some classroom practice; the computer-assisted drill-and-practice work therefore supplements the teacher's instruction.

The machine's first instruction—PLEASE TYPE YOUR NAME—is already on the teletype paper when the student begins his drill. The number of characters required to respond to this instruction is by far the longest message the elementary student ever has to type on the keyboard, and it is our experience that every child greatly enjoys learning how to type his own name. When the name has been typed, the pupil's record is looked up in the master file at the computer and the set of exercises he is to receive is determined on the basis of his performance the previous day. The teletype now writes, for example, DRILL 604032. The first digit (6) refers to the grade level, the next two digits (04) to the number of the concept in the sequence of concepts being reviewed during the year, the next two digits (03) to the day in terms of days devoted to that concept (in this case the third day devoted to the fourth concept) and the final digit (2) to the level of difficulty on a scale ranging from one to five.

The real work now begins. The computer types out the first exercise [*see illustration on opposite page*]. The carriage returns to a position at which the pupil should type in his answer. At this point one of three things can happen. If the pupil types the correct answer, the computer immediately types the second exercise. If the pupil types a wrong answer, the computer types WRONG and repeats the exercise without telling the pupil the correct answer. If the pupil does not answer within a fixed time (in most cases 10 seconds), the computer types TIME IS UP and repeats the exercise. This second presentation of the exercise follows the same procedure regardless of whether the pupil was wrong or ran out of time on the first presentation. If his answer is not correct at the second presentation, however, the correct answer is given and the exercise is typed a third time. The pupil is now expected to type the correct answer, but whether he does or not the program goes on to the next exercise. As soon as the exercises are finished the computer prints a summary for the student showing the number of problems correct, the number wrong, the number in which time ran out and the corresponding percentages. The pupil is also shown his cumulative record up to that point, including the amount of time he has spent at the terminal.

A much more extensive summary of student results is available to the teacher. By typing in a simple code the teacher can receive a summary of the work by the class on a given day, of the class's work on a given concept, of the work of any pupil and of a number of other descriptive statistics I shall not specify here. Indeed, there are so many questions about performance that can be asked and that the computer can answer that teachers, administrators and supervisors are in danger of being swamped by more summary information than they can possibly digest. We are only in the process of learning what summaries are most useful from the pedagogical standpoint.

A question that is often asked about drill-and-practice systems is whether we have evidence that learning is improved by this kind of teaching. We do not have all the answers to this complex question, but preliminary analysis of improvement in skills and concepts looks impressive when compared with the records of control classes that have not received computer-assisted instruction. Even though the analysis is still under way, I should like to cite one example that suggests the kind of improvement that can result from continued practice, even when no explicit instructions are given either by the teacher or by the computer program.

During the academic year 1964–1965 we noticed that some fourth-grade pupils seemed to have difficulty changing rapidly from one type of problem format to another within a given set of exercises. We decided to test whether or not this aspect of performance would improve with comparatively prolonged practice. Because we were also dissatisfied with the level of performance on problems involving the fundamental commutative, associative and distributive laws of arithmetic, we selected 48 cases from this domain.

For a six-day period the pupils were cycled through each of these 48 types of exercise every two days, 24 exercises being given each day [*see illustration on page 214*]. No specific problem was repeated; instead the same problem types were encountered every two days on a random basis. The initial performance was poor, with an average probability of success of .53, but over the six-day period the advance in performance was marked. The proportion of correct answers increased and the total time taken to complete the exercises showed much improvement (diminishing from an average of 630 seconds to 279 seconds). Analysis of the individual data showed that every pupil in the class had advanced both in the proportion of correct responses and in the reduction of the time required to respond.

The next level of interaction of the pupil and the computer program is made up of "tutorial" systems, which are more complex than drill-and-practice systems. In tutorial systems the aim is to take over from the classroom teacher the main responsibility for instruction. As an example, many children who enter the first grade cannot properly use the words "top" and "bottom," "first" and "last" and so forth, yet it is highly desirable that the first-grader have a clear understanding of these words so that he can respond in unequivocal fashion to instructions containing them. Here is a typical tutorial sequence we designed to establish these concepts: 1. The child uses his light pen to point to the picture of a familiar object displayed on the cathode-ray-tube screen. 2. The child puts the tip of his light pen in a small square box displayed next to the picture. (This is the first step in preparing the student to make a standard response to a multiple-choice exercise.) 3. The words FIRST and LAST are introduced. (The instruction here is spoken rather than written; FIRST and LAST refer mainly to the order in which elements are introduced on the screen from left to right.) 4. The words TOP and BOTTOM are introduced. (An instruction to familiarize the child with the use of these words might be: PUT YOUR LIGHT PEN ON THE TOY TRUCK SHOWN AT THE TOP.) 5. The two concepts are combined in order to select one of several things. (The instruction might be: PUT YOUR LIGHT PEN ON THE FIRST ANIMAL SHOWN AT THE TOP.)

With such a tutorial system we can individualize instruction for a child entering the first grade. The bright child of middle-class background who has gone to kindergarten and nursery school for three years before entering the first grade and has a large speaking vocabulary could easily finish work on the concepts I have listed in a single 30-minute session. A culturally deprived child who has not attended kindergarten may need as many as four or five sessions to acquire these concepts. It is important to keep the deprived child from developing a sense of failure or defeat at the start of his schooling. Tutorial "branches" must be provided that move downward to very simple presentations, just as a good tutor will use an increasingly simplified approach when he realizes that his pupil is failing to understand what is being said. It is equally important that a tutorial program have enough flexibility to avoid boring a bright child with repetitive exercises he already understands. We have found it best that each pupil progress from one concept in the curriculum to another only after he meets a reasonably stiff criterion of performance. The rate at which the brightest children advance may be five to 10 times faster than that of the slowest children.

In discussing curriculum materials one commonly distinguishes between "multiple-choice responses" and "constructed responses." Multiple-choice exercises usually limit the student to three, four or five choices. A constructed response is one that can be selected by the student from a fairly large set of possibilities. There are two kinds of constructed response: the one that is uniquely determined by the exercise and the one that is not. Although a good part of our first-grade arithmetic program allows constructed responses, almost all the responses are unique. For example, when we ask for the sum of 2 plus 3, we expect 5 as the unique response. We have, however, developed a program in mathematical logic that allows constructed responses that are not unique. The student can make any one of several inferences; the main function of the computer is to evaluate the validity of the inference he makes. Whether or not the approach taken by the student is a wise one is not indicated until he has taken at least one step in an attempt to find a correct derivation of the required conclusion. No two students need find the same proof; the tutorial program is designed to accept any proof that is valid [*see illustration on pages 216 and 217*]. When the student makes a mistake, the program tells him what is wrong with his response; when he is unable to take another step, the program gives him a hint.

It will be evident from these examples that well-structured subjects such as reading and mathematics can easily be handled by tutorial systems. At present they are the subjects we best understand how to teach, and we should be able to use computer-controlled tutorial systems to carry the main load of teaching such subjects. It should be empha-

ESSENTIAL COMPONENTS that allow interaction of computer and student are grouped at this terminal console. The cathode ray tube (*right*) replaces the earlier teletypewriter roll as a more flexible means of displaying computer instructions and questions. Earphones or a loudspeaker reproduce spoken words that are particularly important in primary school instruction. Students may respond to instructions by use of the terminal's keyboard or by use of a light pen (*extreme right*); programs that will enable the computer to receive and respond to the student's spoken words are under study. Supplemental displays are shown on the screen at left.

sized, however, that no tutorial program designed in the near future will be able to handle every kind of problem that arises in student learning. It will remain the teacher's responsibility to attempt the challenging task of helping students who are not proceeding successfully with the tutorial program and who need special attention.

Thus a dual objective may be achieved. Not only will the tutorial program itself be aimed at individualized instruction but also it will free the teacher from many classroom responsibilities so that he will have time to individualize his own instructional efforts. At Stanford we program into our tutorial sessions an instruction to the computer that we have named TEACHER CALL. When a student has run through all branches of a concept and has not yet met the required criterion of performance, the computer sends a teacher call to the proctor station. The teacher at the proctor station then goes to the student and gives him as much individualized instruction as he needs.

At the third and deepest level of student-computer interaction are systems that allow a genuine dialogue between the student and the program. "Dialogue systems" exist only as elementary prototypes; the successful implementation of such systems will require the solving of two central problems. The first may be described as follows: Suppose in a program on economic theory at the college level the student types the question: WHY ARE DEMAND CURVES ALWAYS CONVEX WITH RESPECT TO THE ORIGIN? It is difficult to write programs that will recognize and provide answers to questions that are so broad and complex, yet the situation is not hopeless. In curriculum areas that have been stable for a long time and that deal with a clearly bounded area of subject matter, it is possible to analyze the kinds of questions students ask; on the basis of such an analysis one can make considerable progress toward the recognition of the questions by the computer. Nonetheless, the central intellectual problem cannot be dodged. It is not enough to provide information that will give an answer; what is needed is an ability on the part of the computer program to recognize precisely what question has been asked. This is no less than asking the computer program to understand the meaning of a sentence.

The second problem of the dialogue system is one that is particularly critical with respect to the teaching of elementary school children. Here it is essential that the computer program be able to recognize the child's spoken words. A child in the first grade will probably not be able to type even a simple question, but he can voice quite complex ones. The problem of recognizing speech adds another dimension to the problem of recognizing the meaning of sentences.

In giving an example of the kind of dialogue system we are currently developing at Stanford I must emphasize that the program I am describing (which represents an extension of our work in mathematical logic) is not yet wholly operational. Our objective is to introduce students to simple proofs using the associative and commutative laws and also the definitions of natural numbers as successors of the next smallest number (for example, $2 = 1 + 1$, $3 = 2 + 1$ and $4 = 3 + 1$). Our aim is to enable the student to construct proofs of simple identities; the following would be typical instances: $5 = 2 + 3$ and $8 = (4 + 2) + 2$. We want the student to be able to tell the computer by oral command what steps to take in constructing the proof, using such expressions as REPLACE 2 BY 1 + 1 or USE THE ASSOCIATIVE LAW ON LINE 3. This program is perfectly practical with our present computer system as long as the commands are transmitted by typing a few characters on the keyboard. A major effort to substitute voice for the keyboard is planned for the coming year; our preliminary work in this direction seems promising.

But these are essentially technological problems. In summarizing some other problems that face us in the task of realizing the rich potential of computer-assisted individual instruction, I should prefer to emphasize the behavioral rather than the technological ones. The central technological problem must be mentioned, however; it has to do with reliability. Computer systems in education must work with a much higher degree of reliability than is expected in computer centers where the users are sophisticated scientists, or even in factory-control systems where the users are experienced engineers. If in the school setting young people are put at computer terminals for sustained periods and the program and machines do not perform as they should, the result is chaos. Reliability is as important in schools as it is in airplanes and space vehicles; when failure occurs, the disasters are of different kinds, but they are equally conclusive.

The primary behavioral problem involves the organization of a curriculum. For example, in what order should the ideas in elementary mathematics be presented to students? In the elementary teaching of a foreign language, to what extent should pattern drill precede expansion of vocabulary? What mixture of phonics and look-and-say is appropriate for the beginning stages of reading? These are perplexing questions. They inevitably arise in the practical context of preparing curriculum materials; unfortunately we are far from having detailed answers to any of them. Individualized instruction, whether under the supervision of a computer or a human tutor, must for some time proceed on the basis of practical judgment and rough-and-ready pedagogical intuition. The magnitude of the problem of evolving curriculum sequences is difficult to overestimate: the number of possible sequences of concepts and subject matter in elementary school mathematics alone is in excess of 10^{100}, a number larger than even generous estimates of the total number of elementary particles in the universe.

One of the few hopes for emerging from this combinatorial jungle lies in the development of an adequate body of fundamental theory about the learning and retention capacity of students. It is to be hoped that, as systematic bodies of data become available from computer systems of instruction, we shall be able to think about these problems in a more scientific fashion and thereby learn to develop a more adequate fundamental theory than we now possess.

Another problem arises from the fact that it is not yet clear how critical various kinds of responses may be. I have mentioned the problem of interpreting sentences freely presented by the student, either by the written or by the spoken word. How essential complex constructed responses to such questions may be in the process of learning most elementary subjects is not fully known. A problem at least as difficult as this one is how computer programs can be organized to take advantage of unanticipated student responses in an insightful and informative way. For the immediate future perhaps the best we can do with unanticipated responses is to record them and have them available for subsequent analysis by those responsible for improving the curriculum.

The possible types of psychological "reinforcement" also present problems. The evidence is conflicting, for instance, whether students should be immediately informed each time they make a mistake. It is not clear to what extent students should be forced to seek the right answer, and indeed whether this search should take place primarily in what is called either the discovery mode or the inductive mode, as opposed to more traditional methods wherein a rule is given and followed by examples and then by exercises or problems that exemplify the rule. Another central weakness of traditional psychological theories of reinforcement is that too much of the theory has been tested by experiments in which the information transmitted in the reinforcement procedure is essentially very simple; as a result the information content of reinforcement has not been sufficiently emphasized in theoretical discussions. A further question is whether or not different kinds of reinforcement and different reinforcement schedules should be given to children of different basic personality types. As far as I know, variables of this kind have not been built into any large-scale curriculum effort now under way in this country.

Another pressing problem involves the effective use of information about the student's past performance. In standard classroom teaching it is impossible to use such records in a sensitive way; we actually have little experience in the theory or practice of the use of such information. A gifted tutor will store in his own memory many facts about the past performance of his pupil and take advantage of these facts in his tutorial course of study, but scientific studies of how this should be done are in their infancy. Practical decisions about the amount of review work needed by the individual, the time needed for the introduction of new concepts and so forth will be mandatory in order to develop the educational computer systems of the future. Those of us who are faced with making these decisions are aware of the inadequacy of our knowledge. The power of the computer to assemble and provide data as a basis for such decisions will be perhaps the most powerful impetus to the development of education theory yet to appear. It is likely that a different breed of education research worker will be needed to feel at home with these vast masses of data. The millions of observational records that computers now process in the field of nuclear physics will be rivaled in quantity and complexity by the information generated by computers in the field of instruction.

When students are put to work on an individualized basis, the problem of keeping records of their successes and failures is enormous, particularly when those records are intended for use in making decisions about the next stage of instruction. In planning ways to process the records of several thousand students at Stanford each day, we found that one of the most difficult decisions is that of selecting the small amount of total information it is possible to record permanently. It is not at all difficult to have the data output run to 1,000 pages a day when 5,000 students use the terminals. An output of this magnitude is simply more than any human being can digest on a regular basis. The problem is to reduce the data from 1,000 pages to something like 25 or 30. As with the other problems I have mentioned, one difficulty is that we do not yet have the well-defined theoretical ideas that could provide the guidelines for making such a reduction. At present our decisions are based primarily on pedagogical intuition and the traditions of data analysis in the field of experimental psychology. Neither of these guidelines is very effective.

A body of evidence exists that attempts to show that children have different cognitive styles. For example, they may be either impulsive or reflective in their basic approach to learning. The central difficulty in research on cognitive styles, as it bears on the construction of the curriculum, is that the research is primarily at an empirical level. It is not at all clear how evidence for the existence of different cognitive styles can be used to guide the design and organization of individualized curriculum materials adapted to these different styles. Indeed, what we face is a fundamental question of educational philosophy: To what extent does society want to commit itself to accentuating differences in cognitive style by individualized techniques of teaching that cater to these differences? The introduction of computers in education raises this question in a new and pressing way. The present economics of education is such that, whatever we may think about the desirability of having a diverse curriculum for children of different cognitive styles, such diversity is not possible because of the expense. But as computers become widely used to offer instruction in the ways I have described here, it will indeed be possible to offer a highly diversified body of curriculum material. When this occurs, we shall for the first time be faced with the practical problem of deciding how much diversity we want to have. That is the challenge for which we should be prepared.

BIOGRAPHICAL NOTES AND BIBLIOGRAPHIES

PART ONE • THE ANALYSIS OF UNCERTAINTY: PROBABILITY

1. Chance

The Author

A. J. AYER is Wykeham Professor of Logic at the University of Oxford. He has held that position since 1959; for 13 years before going to Oxford he was Grote Professor of the Philosophy of Mind and Logic at the University of London. A graduate of Eton and Oxford, Ayer began his teaching career in 1932 as a lecturer in philosophy at Christ Church College of the University of Oxford. During World War II he enlisted in the Welsh Guards, receiving an officer's commission the same year. Among the books that Ayer has written are *Language, Truth and Logic, The Foundations of Empirical Knowledge, The Problem of Knowledge* and *The Concept of a Person.*

Bibliography

LOGICAL FOUNDATIONS OF PROBABILITY. Rudolf Carnap. The University of Chicago Press, 1962.

PRINCIPLES OF THE THEORY OF PROBABILITY. Ernest Nagel. The University of Chicago Press, 1939.

A TREATISE OF PROBABILITY. John Maynard Keynes. Harper & Row Publishers, 1962.

2. What is Probability?

The Author

RUDOLF CARNAP is professor of philosophy at the University of California at Los Angeles. He was born in Germany in 1891 and educated at the University of Jena, receiving his Ph.D. there in 1921. Carnap taught at the University of Vienna and at the German University of Prague until 1935, when he came to the U.S. to accept a post at Chicago. He received an honorary doctorate of science from Harvard in 1936. A leader of the logical empiricist school of philosophy, he has pioneered in applying semantics and the methods of symbolic logic to the theory of knowledge and reasoning.

Bibliography

A TREATISE ON PROBABILITY. John Maynard Keynes. Macmillan and Company, Ltd., 1921.

THE NATURE AND APPLICATION OF INDUCTIVE LOGIC. Rudolf Carnap. The University of Chicago Press, 1951.

PROBABILITY, STATISTICS, AND TRUTH. Richard von Mises. W. Hodge and Company, Ltd., 1939.

3. Subjective Probability

The Author

JOHN COHEN is a mathematically-minded professor of psychology in the University of Manchester. He received his training at University College, London, where from 1933 to 1940 he did research under Cyril Burt on the application of factor analysis to human intelligence, physique and temperament. A resourceful experimentalist, Cohen has interests in psychology which are anything but narrowly technical. He collaborated with R. M. W. Travers and R. B. Cattell on works called *Human Affairs* and *Educating for Democracy.* World War II and its aftermath provided Cohen with many opportunities to apply statistical methods to social questions. For UNESCO he studied the tensions arising at international congresses, and for the British Government he reported on the usefulness of psychologists and psychiatrists in the services and the proper allocation of nurses. Later, studying the distribution of personnel in various professions, he discovered that Britain's seventh largest industry is gambling, employing more than 300,000 persons with 10 million customers. Cohen since then has delved deeply into man's gaming instinct, and with C. E. M. Hansel he wrote a book entitled *Risk and Gambling.*

Bibliography

DECISION PROCESSES. Edited by R. M. Thrall, C. H. Coombs and R. L. Davis. John Wiley & Sons, Inc., 1954.

LA GENÈSE DE L'IDÉE DE HASARD CHEZ L'ENFANT. Jean Piaget. Presses Universitaires de France, 1951.

RISK AND GAMBLING: THE STUDY OF SUBJECTIVE PROBABILITY. John Cohen and C. E. M. Hansel. Philosophical Library Inc., 1956.

4. Probability

The Author

MARK KAC is professor of mathematics at the Rockfeller Institute. Kac was born in Krzemieniec, Poland, in 1914 and educated at John Casimir University in Lwow, where he received a Ph.D. in 1937. He came to the U.S. in 1938 as a Parnas Foundation Fellow at Johns Hopkins University and a year later joined the faculty at Cornell University. During the academic year 1951–1952 he was a member of the Institute for Advanced Study in Princeton, N.J. He left Cornell in 1961 to take up his present post. Kac was awarded the Chauvenet Prize of the Mathematics Association of America in 1950 for his paper "Random Walk and the Theory of Brownian Motion." His main scientific activity for the past few years has been in the field of statistical mechanics; he is particularly interested in the study of mathematical models of changes of phase.

Bibliography

CHOICE AND CHANCE: WITH ONE THOUSAND EXERCISES. William Allen Whitworth. Hafner Publishing Co., 1951.

A HISTORY OF THE MATHEMATICAL THEORY OF PROBABILITY FROM THE TIME OF PASCAL TO THAT OF LAPLACE. I. Todhunter. Chelsea Publishing Company, 1949.

AN INTRODUCTION TO PROBABILITY THEORY AND ITS APPLICATIONS. William Feller. John Wiley & Sons, Inc., 1957.

LADY LUCK. Warren Weaver. Doubleday & Company, Inc., 1963.

PROBABILITY, STATISTICS AND TRUTH. Richard von Mises. The Macmillan Company, 1957.

5. The Monte Carlo Method

The Author

DANIEL D. MCCRACKEN is a numerical analyst in the aircraft gas turbine division of the General Electric Company at Cincinnati. He joined General Electric in 1951 after graduating from the Central Washington College of Education with degrees in chemistry and mathematics. Most of his work has been in the field of electronic computing, and he is now on the staff that operates G.E.'s IBM 701 at Cincinnati. He is an amateur musician and, on vacations in the Northwest, a mountain climber.

Bibliography

NUMERICAL SOLUTION OF DIFFERENTIAL EQUATIONS. William Edmund Milne. John Wiley & Sons, Inc., 1953.

PRINCIPLES OF NUMERICAL ANALYSIS. Alston S. Householder. McGraw-Hill Book Company, Inc., 1953.

RANDOM SAMPLING (MONTE CARLO) TECHNIQUES IN NEUTRON ATTENUATION PROBLEMS. Herman Kahn in *Nucleonics*, Vol. 6, No. 5, pages 27–33, 37; May, 1950. Vol. 6, No. 6, pages 60–65; June, 1950.

PART TWO • COMMUNICATION AND CONTROL

6. Cybernetics

The Author

NORBERT WIENER was emeritus professor of mathematics at the Massachusetts Institute of Technology before his death in 1964. Wiener joined the staff at M.I.T. in 1919, interrupting his teaching there in 1926–27, when he was awarded a Guggenheim fellowship, and again in 1935–36, when he went to Tsing Hua University in China as a visiting professor.

Bibliography

A MATHEMATICAL THEORY OF COMMUNICATION. C. E. Shannon in *The Bell System Technical Journal*, Vol. 27, No. 3, pages 379–423; July, 1948.

CYBERNETICS. Norbert Wiener. John Wiley, 1948.

7. The Mathematics of Communication

The Author

WARREN WEAVER was vice president of the Alfred P. Sloan Foundation until 1964. He is still associated with the Foundation as a trustee and consultant on scientific affairs. Weaver was professor of mathematics at the University of Wisconsin and for four years was chairman of the department. After he left the University of Wisconsin in 1932, he was director of natural sciences at the Rockefeller Foundation and vice president of natural and medical sciences at the Sloan-Kettering Institute. He joined the Sloan Foundation as its director of natural sciences in 1959.

Bibliography

A MATHEMATICAL THEORY OF COMMUNICATION. C. E. Shannon in *Bell System Technical Journal*, Vol. 27, pages 379–423; July, 1948. Pages 623–656; October, 1948.

8. Error-correcting Codes

The Author

W. WESLEY PETERSON received an A.B. in mathematics from the University of Michigan in 1948, a master's degree in electrical engineering in 1950 and a Ph.D. in electrical engineering in 1954. Peterson began to study error-correcting codes in 1955, while working at the IBM Engineering Laboratories. He joined the faculty of the University of Florida in 1956 and in 1959 spent a year at the Massachusetts Institute of Technology, where he worked with Robert M. Fano and John McReynolds Wozencraft on error-correcting codes. He has been professor of electrical engineering at the University of Hawaii since 1964.

Bibliography

CYCLIC CODES FOR ERROR DETECTION. W. W. Peterson and D. T. Brown in *Proceedings of the IRE*, Vol. 49, No. 1, pages 228–235; January, 1961.

ERROR-CORRECTING CODES. W. Wesley Peterson. John Wiley & Sons, Inc., and The M.I.T. Press, 1961.

ERROR DETECTING AND ERROR CORRECTING CODES. R. W. Hamming in *Bell System Technical Journal*, Vol. 29, No. 2, pages 147–160; April 26, 1950.

INFORMATION. Gilbert W. King in *Scientific American*, Vol. 187, No. 3, pages 132–148; September, 1952.

THE INFORMATION THEORY. Francis Bello in *Fortune*, Vol. 48, No. 6, pages 136–158; December, 1953.

9. Redundancy in Computers

The Author

WILLIAM H. PIERCE is assistant professor of electrical engineering at the Carnegie Institute of Technology. He is also senior engineer at the Westinghouse Research Laboratory in Pittsburgh. Pierce obtained an A.B. in physics from Harvard College in 1955, and a Ph.D. in electrical engineering from Stanford University in 1961. He has been at the Carnegie Institute since 1961. Among his current research interests are the function of error-correction in the human brain and the role of redundancy in human memory.

Bibliography

INTERWOVEN REDUNDANT LOGIC. William H. Pierce in *The Journal of the Franklin Institute,* Vol. 277, No. 1, pages 55–85; January, 1964.

PROBABILISTIC LOGICS AND THE SYNTHESIS OF RELIABLE ORGANISMS FROM UNRELIABLE COMPONENTS. John von Neumann in *Automata Studies.* Edited by C. E. Shannon and J. McCarthy. Princeton University Press, 1956.

REDUNDANCY TECHNIQUES FOR COMPUTING SYSTEMS. Edited by Richard H. Wilcox and William C. Mann. Spartan Books, 1962.

10. Feedback

The Author

ARNOLD TUSTIN was, until his retirement, professor of electrical engineering at Imperial College of Science and Technology, University of London. Previously, he was on the staff at Birmingham University. He is the author of *DC Machines for Control Systems,* published in 1952, and *The Mechanisms of Economic Systems,* published in 1955.

Bibliography

CYBERNETICS. Norbert Wiener in *Scientific American,* Vol. 179, No. 5, pages 14–19; November, 1948.

FUNDAMENTALS OF AUTOMATIC CONTROL. G. H. Farrington. John Wiley & Sons, Inc., 1951.

AN INTRODUCTION TO THE THEORY OF CONTROL IN MECHANICAL ENGINEERING. R. H. Macmillan. Cambridge University Press, 1951.

SERVOMECHANISM FUNDAMENTALS. Henri Lauer, Robert Lesnick and Leslie E. Matson. McGraw-Hill Book Company, Inc., 1947.

FUNDAMENTAL THEORY OF SERVOMECHANISMS. LeRoy A. MacColl. D. Van Nostrand Company, Inc., 1945.

THEORY OF SERVOMECHANISMS. H. M. James, N. B. Nichols and R. S. Phillips. McGraw-Hill Book Company, Inc., 1947.

AUTOMATIC FEEDBACK CONTROL. W. R. Ahrendt and J. F. Taplin. McGraw-Hill Book Company, Inc., 1951.

11. Control Theory

The Author

RICHARD BELLMAN is professor of mathematics, engineering, and medicine at the University of Southern California. A graduate of Brooklyn College, Bellman received a Ph.D. in mathematics from Princeton University in 1946. During World War II he taught radar in the Air Force, worked on sonar for the Navy and served the Army as a member of the Special Engineering Division working at Los Alamos on the atomic bomb. After the war he taught for two years at Princeton before joining the faculty of Stanford University in 1948. He left Stanford in 1951 to work on thermonuclear weapons at Princeton as a member of Project Matterhorn. He worked at the RAND Corporation from 1952 to 1965. Bellman is the author of more than 17 books and more than 375 published research papers on a wide range of mathematical topics.

Bibliography

ADAPTIVE CONTROL PROCESSES: A GUIDED TOUR. Richard Bellman. Princeton University Press, 1961.

DYNAMIC PROGRAMMING IN CHEMICAL ENGINEERING AND PROCESS CONTROL. Sanford M. Roberts. Academic Press, 1964.

SELECTED PAPERS ON MATHEMATICAL TRENDS IN CONTROL THEORY. Edited by Richard Bellman and Robert Kalaba. Dover Publications, Inc., 1964.

PART THREE • GAMES AND DECISIONS

12. The Theory of Games

The Author

OSKAR MORGENSTERN, a native of Gorlitz, Germany, is professor of political economy and director of the econometric research program at Princeton University. From 1925 to 1928 he was a Rockefeller Foundation fellow at Harvard and the Universities of London, Paris, and Rome. After teaching at the University of Vienna for ten years he returned to the United States in 1938 as a Carnegie visiting professor and joined the staff at Princeton the same year. Morgenstern has also served as a consultant for the Rand Corporation and as a member of the Atomic Energy Commission.

Bibliography

THE THEORY OF GAMES AND ECONOMIC BEHAVIOR. John von Neumann and Oskar Morgenstern. Princeton University Press, 1947.

13. Game Theory and Decisions

The Author

LEONID HURWICZ is a professor of economics and mathematics at the University of Minnesota. Born in Moscow of a Polish family, he took a degree in law at the University of Warsaw in 1938. He came to the U.S. in 1940 and has been associated with the Cowles Commission for Research in Economics, off and on, since 1941. In 1945–46 he held a Guggenheim fellowship. In 1948 Hurwicz assisted the Economic Commission for Europe, which surveyed the postwar economic prospects of the Continent for the United Nations. He has worked on economic applications of the new theory of games, which, he believes, has already made itself useful by giving economists mathematical models for problems of resource allocation.

Bibliography

THEORY OF GAMES AND STATISTICAL DECISIONS. D. H. Blackwell

and M. A. Girshick. John Wiley & Sons, Inc., 1954.

FOUNDATIONS OF STATISTICS. L. J. Savage. John Wiley & Sons, Inc., 1954.

THEORY OF GAMES AND ECONOMIC BEHAVIOR. John von Neumann and Oskar Morgenstern. Princeton University Press, rev. ed., 1955.

THE STRATEGY OF CONFLICT. Thomas C. Schelling. Harvard University Press, 1960.

THEORY OF GAMES AND STATISTICAL DECISIONS. David Blackwell and M. A. Girshick. John Wiley & Sons, Inc., 1954.

THEORY OF GAMES AS A TOOL FOR THE MORAL PHILOSOPHER. R. B. Braithwaite. Cambridge University Press, 1955.

14. The Use and Misuse of Game Theory

The Author

ANATOL RAPOPORT is professor and senior research mathematician at the Mental Health Research Institute of the University of Michigan. Rapoport was born in Russia, educated in Chicago's public schools and trained in music at the Vienna State Academy of Music, which gave him degrees in composition, piano and conducting. For the next four years he gave concerts in Europe, the U.S. and Mexico. In 1937 (at the age of 26) he enrolled as a freshman at the University of Chicago, and in 1941 he received his Ph.D. in mathematics. Following service in the Air Force as a liaison officer with the Soviet Air Force in Alaska during World War II, Rapoport taught mathematics for a year at the Illinois Institute of Technology, was research associate and later assistant professor of mathematical biophysics at the University of Chicago from 1947 to 1954, and spent a year at the Center for Advanced Study in the Behavioral Sciences. He went to Michigan in 1955.

Bibliography

THE COMPLEAT STRATEGYST: BEING A PRIMER ON THE THEORY OF GAMES OF STRATEGY. J. D. Williams. McGraw-Hill Book Co., Inc., 1954.

INTRODUCTION TO THE THEORY OF GAMES. J. C. C. McKinsey. The Rand Corporation. McGraw-Hill Book Co., Inc. 1952.

STRATEGY AND MARKET STRUCTURE: COMPETITION, OLIGOPOLY AND THE THEORY OF GAMES. Martin Shubik. John Wiley & Sons, Inc., 1959.

15. Linear Programming

The Authors

WILLIAM W. COOPER and ABRAHAM CHARNES were, at the time they collaborated on this article, both at the graduate school of Industrial Administration of the Carnegie Institute of Technology, where they combined both economics and mathematics in their teaching and research. Cooper is currently professor of economics at Carnegie. In 1954, he was president of the Institute of Management Sciences, which is concerned with applying scientific analysis in business. Charnes is professor of applied mathematics and economics at Northwestern University. After he left Carnegie Institute of Technology he was professor of mathematics and director of the research department at Purdue for two years before he joined the staff at Northwestern in 1957. Like Cooper, he has been active in the Institute of Management Sciences and was its president in 1960.

Bibliography

AN INTRODUCTION TO LINEAR PROGRAMMING. A. Charnes, W. W. Cooper and A. Henderson. John Wiley & Sons, Inc., 1953.

ACTIVITY ANALYSIS OF PRODUCTION AND ALLOCATION. Edited by T. C. Koopmans. John Wiley & Sons, Inc., 1951.

BLENDING AVIATION GASOLINES: A STUDY IN PROGRAMMING INTERDEPENDENT ACTIVITIES IN AN INTEGRATED OIL COMPANY. A. Charnes, W. W. Cooper and B. Mellon in *Econometrica*, Vol. 20, No. 2; April, 1952.

PART FOUR • IMITATIONS OF LIFE

16. Man Viewed as a Machine

The Author

JOHN G. KEMENY is professor of mathematics and chairman of the department at Dartmouth College. Born in Budapest, Hungary, he came to the U.S. at the age of 13 and attended George Washington High School in New York City, graduating first in his class. He then entered Princeton University, but was interrupted by the U.S. Army, which put him to work on calculating machines at Los Alamos. He returned to Princeton, graduated first in his class and went on to take a Ph.D. in mathematics. He spent his last year of graduate study as Albert Einstein's assistant at the Institute for Advanced Study. Most of his own research has been in symbolic logic.

Bibliography

SOLVABLE AND UNSOLVABLE PROBLEMS. A. M. Turing in *Science News*, No. 31, pages 7–23. Penguin Books, 1954.

17. Self-reproducing Machines

The Author

LIONEL S. PENROSE is Galton Professor of Eugenics at University College London. He pursued his undergraduate studies at St. John's College in the University of Cambridge, then studied medicine at St. Thomas's Hospital in London. In 1928 he became a member of the Royal College of Surgeons and a licentiate of the Royal College of Physicians (the licensing bodies for physicians for England and for London, respectively). Two years later he obtained at Cambridge the degree of M.D. (in British practice an advanced research degree). During the 1930s Penrose was research medical officer of the Royal Eastern Counties' Institution of Colchester. From 1939 to 1945 he directed psychiatric research for the Canadian province of Ontario.

Bibliography

ARTIFICIAL LIVING PLANTS. Edward F. Moore in *Scientific*

American, Vol. 195, No. 4, pages 118–127; October, 1956.

COMPUTABILITY AND λ-DEFINABILITY. A. M. Turing in *The Journal of Symbolic Logic,* Vol. II, No. 4, pages 153–163; December, 1937.

THE GENERAL AND LOGICAL THEORY OF AUTOMATA. John von Neumann in *Cerebral Mechanisms in Behavior,* edited by Lloyd A. Jeffress, pages 1–41; John Wiley & Sons, Inc., 1951.

MAN VIEWED AS A MACHINE. John G. Kemeny in *Scientific American,* Vol. 192, No. 4, pages 58–67; April, 1955.

THE ORIGINS OF LIFE. J. B. S. Haldane in *New Biology,* No. 16, pages 12–27; April, 1954.

18. A Machine That Learns

The Author

W. GREY WALTER is director of the physiological department at the Burden Neurological Institute in Bristol, England. He is the author of *The Living Brain,* published in 1953, *Further Outlook,* published in 1956, and *The Curve of the Snowflake,* published in 1956.

Bibliography

AN IMITATION OF LIFE. W. Grey Walter in *Scientific American,* Vol. 182, No. 5, pages 42–45; May, 1950.

19. Computer v. Chess-Player

The Authors

ALEX BERNSTEIN and MICHAEL DEV. ROBERTS are respectively a mathematician and computer programming expert in the International Business Machines Corporation. Bernstein was born in Italy, graduated from the College of the City of New York, and studied medieval literature and industrial engineering at Columbia University. Roberts was born in England, graduated from the University of Manchester and acquired a doctorate in chemistry from the University of Cambridge. While he was at C.C.N.Y. Bernstein was U.S. intercollegiate chess champion.

Bibliography

THE CHESS MACHINE: AN EXAMPLE OF DEALING WITH A COMPLEX TASK BY ADAPTATION. Allen Newell in *Proceedings of the Western Joint Computer Conference,* pages 101–111; 1955.

A CHESS-PLAYING MACHINE. Claude E. Shannon in *Scientific American,* Vol. 182, No. 2, pages 48–51; February, 1950.

EXPERIMENTS IN CHESS. J. Kister, P. Stein, S. Ulam, W. Walden and M. Wells in *Journal of the Association for Computing Machinery,* Vol. 4, No. 2, pages 174–177; April, 1957.

20. Artificial Intelligence

The Author

MARVIN L. MINSKY is professor of electrical engineering at the Massachusetts Institute of Technology. He is also director of the artificial-intelligence group there. Minsky was graduated from Harvard College in 1950 and received a doctorate in mathematics at Princeton University in 1954. For the next three years he was a member of the Society of Fellows at Harvard, working on neural theories of learning and on optical microscopy. He joined the mathematics department at M.I.T. in 1958 and transferred to the electrical engineering department in 1962.

Bibliography

COMPUTERS AND THOUGHT. Edited by Edward A. Feigenbaum and Julian Feldman. McGraw-Hill Book Company, Inc., 1963.

MATTER, MIND AND MODELS. M. L. Minsky in *Proceedings of IFIPS Congress, 65: Vol. I,* edited by W. A. Kalenich. Spartan Books, 1965.

SOME STUDIES IN MACHINE LEARNING USING THE GAME OF CHECKERS. A. L. Samuel in *IBM Journal of Research and Development,* Vol. 3, No. 3, pages 210–229; July, 1959.

21. Pattern Recognition by Machine

The Authors

OLIVER G. SELFRIDGE and ULRIC NEISSER are, respectively, a member of the staff at the Lincoln Laboratory of the Massachusetts Institute of Technology, and professor of psychology at Cornell University. Selfridge was born in London in 1926, and he acquired his bachelor's degree in mathematics at M.I.T. in 1945. He pursued graduate work in mathematics there from 1947 to 1950, studied electronic countermeasures at Fort Monmouth in New Jersey for two years and then joined Lincoln Laboratory, where, he says, "my interests in communications techniques and information theory were soon supplemented by an interest in pattern recognition and other aspects of artificial intelligence." Neisser, born in Germany in 1928, took his B.A. in psychology at Harvard University in 1950, his M.A. at Swarthmore College in 1952 and his Ph.D. at Harvard in 1956. He held a post-doctoral fellowship from the National Science Foundation from 1955 to 1957, and then joined the faculty of Brandeis. He was a member of the summer research staff at Lincoln Laboratory in 1958 and 1959. He is the author of the recent book, *Cognitive Psychology.*

Bibliography

DISCUSSION OF PROBLEMS IN PATTERN RECOGNITION. W. W. Bledsoe, J. S. Bomba, I. Browning, R. J. Evey, R. A. Kirsch, R. L. Mattson, M. Minsky, U. Neisser, O. G. Selfridge in *Proceedings of the Eastern Joint Computer Conference,* pages 233–237; 1959.

HOW WE KNOW UNIVERSALS: THE PERCEPTION OF AUDITORY AND VISUAL FORMS. Walter Pitts and Warren S. McCulloch in *The Bulletin of Mathematical Biophysics,* Vol. 9, No. 3, pages 127–147; 1947.

MACHINE RECOGNITION OF HAND-SENT MORSE CODE. Bernard Gold in *IRE Transactions of the Professional Group on Information Theory,* Vol. IT-5, No. 1, pages 17-24; March, 1959.

THE ORGANIZATION OF BEHAVIOR. D. O. Hebb. John Wiley & Sons, Inc., 1949.

PART FIVE • RECENT COMPUTER APPLICATIONS

22. Computers

The Author

STANISLAW ULAM is a research adviser at the Los Alamos Scientific Laboratory of the University of California. A native of Lwow, Poland, Ulam received an M.A. and a D.Sc. in mathematics from the Polytechnic Institute at Lwow in 1932 and 1933 respectively. He lectured at various institutions in Poland, England and France before coming to the U.S. in 1936 as a visiting member of the Institute for Advanced Study in Princeton, N.J. Shortly thereafter he became a fellow of the Harvard University Society of Fellows. He left Harvard in 1940 to join the faculty of the University of Wisconsin. Since going to Los Alamos in 1943 to work on the atomic bomb as a member of the Manhattan Engineer District, Ulam has taught for short terms at the University of Southern California, Harvard, the Massachusetts Institute of Technology, the University of Colorado and the University of California at San Diego. At Los Alamos, Ulam collaborated with Edward Teller on the development of the hydrogen bomb. He also invented the so-called Monte Carlo method, a procedure for finding solutions to mathematical and physical problems by random sampling. This technique, made practical by the development of high-speed computers, permits the solution of problems not amenable to more orthodox methods of analysis. Ulam is the author of *Problems in Modern Mathematics*, published in 1964.

Bibliography

AUTOMATIC DIGITAL COMPUTERS. M. V. Wilkes. John Wiley & Sons, Inc., 1956.

A COLLECTION OF MATHEMATICAL PROBLEMS. Stanislaw Ulam. John Wiley & Sons, Inc., 1960.

THE COMPUTER AND THE BRAIN. John von Neumann. Yale University Press, 1958.

SELF-ORGANIZING SYSTEMS: PROCEEDINGS OF AN INTERDISCIPLINARY CONFERENCE. Edited by Marshall C. Yovits and Scott Cameron. Pergamon Press, 1960.

TEACHING COMBINATORIAL TRICKS TO A COMPUTER. D. H. Lehmer in *Combinatorial Analysis: Proceedings of Symposia in Applied Mathematics*, Vol. 10, American Mathematical Society, 1960.

23. Numerical Taxonomy

The Author

ROBERT R. SOKAL is professor of statistical biology at the University of Kansas. Sokal was born in Vienna in 1926 but moved with his family to China at the beginning of World War II and received his high school and undergraduate education in Shanghai, where he obtained a B.S. in biology from St. John's University. He came to the U.S. in 1947 and acquired a Ph.D. in zoology at the University of Chicago in 1952. He has been a member of the Kansas faculty since 1951. Sokal is a National Institutes of Health career investigator. During 1959–1960 he was a National Science Foundation Senior Postdoctoral Fellow at University College London, and during 1963–1964 he was a Fulbright visiting professor at Hebrew University and Tel Aviv University in Israel. He is coauthor, with Peter H. A. Sneath, of *The Principles of Numerical Taxonomy*. Sokal wishes to acknowledge the assistance and constructive criticisms of Sneath, Joseph H. Camin, Charles D. Michener and F. James Rohlf in the preparation of this article.

Bibliography

A METHOD FOR DEDUCING BRANCHING SEQUENCES IN PHYLOGENY. Joseph H. Camin and Robert R. Sokal in *Evolution*, Vol. 19, No. 3, pages 311–326; September, 1965.

NUMERICAL PHENETICS AND TAXONOMIC THEORY. Ernst Mayr in *Systematic Zoology*, Vol. 14, No. 3, pages 237–243; September, 1965.

PRINCIPLES OF NUMERICAL TAXONOMY. Robert R. Sokal and Peter H. A. Sneath. W. H. Freeman and Company, 1963.

THE TWO TAXONOMIES: AREAS OF AGREEMENT AND OF CONFLICT. Robert R. Sokal and Joseph H. Camin in *Systematic Zoology*, Vol. 14, No. 3, pages 176–195; September, 1965.

24. Texture and Visual Perception

The Author

BELA JULESZ is head of the Sensory and Perceptual Processes Department at the Bell Telephone Laboratories. A native of Hungary, he was graduated from the Technical University of Budapest and the Hungarian Academy of Sciences. He taught and did research in communications systems in Budapest until 1956, when he joined Bell Laboratories. At Bell he was first engaged in studies of systems for reducing television bandwidth and of digital methods for processing pictorial information. Since 1959 he has devoted full time to visual research, particularly in depth perception and pattern recognition.

Bibliography

BINOCULAR DEPTH PERCEPTION WITHOUT FAMILIARITY CUES. Bela Julesz in *Science*, Vol. 145, No. 3630, pages 356–362; July, 1964.

THE OPTICAL SPACE SENSE. Kenneth N. Ogle in *The Eye, Vol. IV: Visual Optics and the Optical Space Sense*, edited by Hugh Davson. Academic Press, 1962.

STEREOPSIS AND BINOCULAR RIVALRY OF CONTOURS. B. Julesz in *Bell Telephone System Technical Publications Monograph 4609*, 1963.

TOWARDS THE AUTOMATION OF BINOCULAR DEPTH PERCEPTION. B. Julesz in *Information Processing 1962: Proceedings of IFIP Congress 62*. North-Holland Publishing Company, 1962.

25. The Analysis of Brain Waves

The Author

MARY A. B. BRAZIER is a neurophysiologist who holds a National Institutes of Health Career Professorship at the University of California at Los Angeles. Although her primary field of interest has been electroencephalography, she has also been interested in the application of computer techniques to the biological and medical sciences. A native of England, she received a Ph.D. in biochemistry and a D.Sc. in neurophysiology from the University of London. She was on the staff of Maudsley Hospital in London from 1930 to 1940, when she came to the U.S. as research associate in neurology at Harvard University and neurophysiologist at the Massachusetts General Hospital. The investigation reported in her article was supported by the National Institutes of Health and the Office of Naval Research.

Bibliography

COMPUTER TECHNIQUES IN EEG ANALYSIS. Edited by Mary A. B. Brazier. *Electroencephalography and Clinical Neurophysiology,* Suppl. 20; 1961.

THE ELECTRICAL ACTIVITY OF THE NERVOUS SYSTEM. Mary A. B. Brazier. The Macmillan Co., 1960.

PROCESSING NEUROELECTRIC DATA. Communications Biophysics Group of Research Laboratory of Electronics and William M. Siebert. The Technology Press of the Massachusetts Institute of Technology, 1959.

SOME USES OF COMPUTERS IN EXPERIMENTAL NEUROLOGY. Mary A. B. Brazier in *Experimental Neurology,* Vol. 2, No. 2, pages 123–143; April, 1960.

THE WAKING BRAIN. H. W. Magoun. Charles C Thomas, Publisher, 1958.

26. Chromosome Analysis by Computer

The Authors

ROBERT S. LEDLEY and FRANK H. RUDDLE are respectively president of the National Biomedical Research Foundation and assistant professor of biology at Yale University. Ledley arrived at his position by an unusual route. At Columbia University he specialized in physics and mathematics, but since "in those days a mathematician or a physicist could not make too much of a living, my parents decided to make a dentist of me." As a dentist Ledley was sent by the Army to do dental research at the National Bureau of Standards. There he had occasion to use a computer, and since he was "not happy using an instrument without knowing how it worked," he became a digital-computer engineer and served for a time as associate professor of electrical engineering at George Washington University. In 1960 he organized the National Biomedical Research Foundation to "apply computers in biomedical research on a full-time basis." Ruddle, who met Ledley during a seminar at Yale, received bachelor's and master's degrees at Wayne State University and a Ph.D. at the University of California at Berkeley.

Bibliography

THE IDENTIFICATION OF INDIVIDUAL CHROMOSOMES, ESPECIALLY IN MAN. Klaus Patau in *The American Journal of Human Genetics,* Vol. 12, No. 3, pages 250–276; September, 1960.

USE OF COMPUTERS IN BIOLOGY AND MEDICINE. Robert Steven Ledley. McGraw-Hill Book Company, 1965.

27. The Use of Computers in Education

The Author

PATRICK SUPPES is professor of philosophy and of statistics at Stanford University and also chairman of the department of philosophy and director of the Institute for Mathematical Studies in the Social Sciences at the university. Suppes went to Stanford as an instructor in 1950, the year he obtained a Ph.D. at Columbia University. He did his undergraduate work at the University of Chicago, from which he was graduated in 1943. His extensive writings include two books, *Introduction to Logic* and *Axiomatic Set Theory;* three other books of which he is a coauthor; and several mathematics books for use in elementary schools. His particular interests are mathematical methods in the social sciences and the philosophy of science.

Bibliography

AUTOMATED EDUCATION HANDBOOK. Edited by E. Goodman. Automated Education Center, 1965.

THE COMPUTER IN AMERICAN EDUCATION. Edited by Donald D. Bushnell and Dwight W. Allen. John Wiley & Sons, Inc., in press.

PROGRAMMED LEARNING AND COMPUTER-BASED INSTRUCTION. Edited by John E. Coulson. John Wiley & Sons, Inc., 1962.

INDEX